AMERICA'S BEST VALUE COLLEGES

The Princeton Review

AMERICA'S BEST VALUE COLLEGES

ERIC OWENS, TOM MELTZER,
AND THE STAFF OF THE PRINCETON REVIEW

Random House, Inc.
New York
PrincetonReview.com

The Princeton Review Inc.
2315 Broadway
New York, NY 10024
Email: bookeditor@review.com

ISBN 978-0-375-76601-5

Editorial Director: Robert Franek
Editor: Adam O. Davis
Production Manager and Designer: Scott Harris
Production Editor: Christine LaRubio
Contributing Authors: Alex Altman, Kerry Dexter, Adam Dressler, Landon Hall, Tom
    Haushalter, Hayley Heaton, Andrea Kornstein, Chris Meier, Lisa Marie Rovito, Maya
    Payne Smart

Printed in the United States of America.

9 8 7 6 5 4 3 2

2007 Edition

ACKNOWLEDGMENTS

It would be impossible to individually thank everyone who either directly contributed to the book or helped me in some indirect way to get it done.

I would like, however, to name a few names.

Rachel Brown for supporting me in so many ways for so many years.

John Katzman for creating The Princeton Review and in the process giving me—and so many other young people—a chance to do work they love and believe in.

Erik Olson for his advice and ideas for this and other books.

Robert Franek for his publishing savvy.

Thanks also to the data collection team at The Princeton Review, headed by Ben Zelevansky and David Soto. Without them there wouldn't be any college data in the book. Come to think of it, there wouldn't be any book at all.

Finally, there is no way you would be holding this book right now if it were not for the extraordinary help of numerous media relations folks and institutional researchers at all of the 165 colleges profiled within its pages. Although I can't name them all here, I owe each one many thanks.

Eric Owens

January 2007

CONTENTS

INTRODUCTION

WHY THESE SCHOOLS?

This book was originally inspired by a ranking of the Top 20 Best Academic Bang for Your Buck schools, which used to appear in our annual guide to the *361 Best Colleges* (an excellent resource, by the way). To produce that ranking, we examined several different aspects of each school in the *Best Colleges*. Specifically, we looked at how each school stacks up against all the others using three measures: the Academic Rating, Financial Aid Rating and Tuition, and GPA. We recalculated all three measures annually based on loads of data we collect both from the schools themselves and from the students who currently attend them.

America's Best Value Colleges has gone through a lot of changes over the years in our bid to make the most comprehensive and informative college guide out there. Two years ago, in addition to the Tuition GPA and Academic and Financial Aid Ratings, we took two other factors into consideration: The percentage of graduating seniors who borrowed from any loan programs, and the average dollar amount of debt those students had at graduation. We used these two additional factors as part of the calculation to select schools, as we have continued to do in this year's selection process.

Then last year, we separated our previous Top Ten Best Value Colleges ranking list into two top ten rankings, one for private colleges, and the other for public institutions. We felt that providing a broader range of schools better served the interests of our student readers. In that edition we also expanded the pool of contenders. In fact, we've done the same this year, thoroughly researching students' academic and financial experiences at more than 650 schools nationwide to arrive at 165 featured Best Value Colleges. Why more colleges, you ask? Well, it's simple: The mounting success and accompanying media interest in this book told us that best value colleges was indeed an area in which students and their families were hungry for information. Knowing there are scores of great schools that offer terrific values, we decided to include not only the schools that appear in our *Best 361 Colleges* book but also those that have been included in each of the region-specific editions of the *Best Colleges*. Ultimately, our gain is their gain is your gain.

Although this expanded research has resulted in some new content for this book, other factors have also produced the changes that are new to this edition. Increasing tuition costs across the board and the manner in which each college responds to those increases has caused—and will continue to cause—some schools to drop off the list and others to make it for the first time.

Does all this mean that last year's list of Best Value Colleges is invalid? Of course not. It simply means that this year's list of Best Value Colleges—Public and Private are even better, and that any colleges that have made the list this year as they did last (and even the year before that!) continue to offer students and their families great academic bang for their buck.

In addition to the criteria we just mentioned, the schools that appear in this book are based on the following measures:

Academic Rating

We combine students' opinions about the education they receive with a bunch of admissions and other statistics reported to us by each school to create this rating. The admissions stats basically tell us how hard it is to get into the school. The vast amount of student opinion data that we collect from current students at every college tells us everything else. Are students known to pick up a book now and again? Can the professors teach, or do they manage to suck every crumb of life from the materials? Are professors accessible outside of class? Do students spend most of their class time in auditoriums with 500 strangers listening to a guy with a microphone, or in small classrooms with a dozen or so of their new best friends?

Financial Aid Rating

This rating is also based on a combination of school-reported data and student opinion. We ask schools about the amount of need-based aid they give students. We ask students who receive financial aid how happy they are with their award packages. Very few students, it seems, are ever totally elated about their financial aid packages and the service (or lack thereof) that offices of financial aid provide. Nevertheless, students at some schools are a lot happier than students at other schools.

FEES

Fees are important to note because some schools do not nominally charge tuition but do have required "educational" or "registration" fees. The schools of the University of California system, for example, don't charge tuition to in-state students, but they do have pretty sizable fees that everyone must pay, regardless of residency.

Tuition GPA (or the Real Cost of College)

We start with the sticker price of each college's tuition, required fees, and room and board, and subtract the average gift aid

(scholarships and grants) awarded to students. We don't subtract work-study or student loans, since those are costs that students ultimately have to bear.

We take all of this data and stir it up in an algorithm based on the idea that bang for your buck means excellent academics, great financial aid, and/or low tuition. It means value.

Of the more than 650 schools on which we performed this computation, the 165 schools in this book stood out as the very best academic values. A school really shows off its value in two different ways: by offering a very affordable tuition sticker price right off the bat — some schools even do the seemingly impossible: charge $0 for tuition, though there still may be some required fees to take care of— while also delivering a quality education, or by making a higher tuition cost affordable to anyone who is invited to attend. A school does the latter by distributing generous amounts of financial aid in the form of scholarships and grants, possibly combined, to a lesser degree, with work-study and loans. The schools we present here make measurable efforts to keep out-of-pocket costs reasonable and within reach while delivering an amazing college experience that's worth every penny.

Upon determining this year's list of Best Value Colleges, we went ahead and did some digging to find out exactly how these institutions are able to provide such a fabulous education at such a modest price. This book lets us tell you how they did it.

The Importance of Cost in the Overall Scheme of Things

If you haven't checked lately (and, if you're reading this book, we're guessing you have), four years of college can be painfully expensive. In fact, at some places, just *one* year of college can be painfully expensive.

Generally, a school's cost is a pretty good indicator of the quality of the academics it offers. Otherwise, why would perfectly reasonable people shell out so much cash to go to one school over another that charges significantly less? But there are definitely exceptions to that rule. Some schools are simply overpriced. Other schools—like the 165 in this book, for instance—are, for one reason or another, exceptionally good deals. There's a really good chance that you will find happiness *and* a great education at one of these schools.

You should also keep in mind that many factors will probably influence your decision about which colleges you apply to, and where you ultimately decide to go. In addition to cost, there's location, size, and your intended major. Intangible qualities are important, too. What's the school's reputation? Does the campus look like a little slice of paradise or a cross between Legoland and the seventh ring of Hell? Will you learn anything? Will you have anything remotely resembling a good time during your four years?

In a nutshell, our advice about how you should choose the best college for you is to take the best deal you can get at a school where you think you'll get a great education while having a great time. Attending a school just because it is affordable makes no sense if you are going to be miserable for (at least) four years. College should be fun. On the other hand, it makes no sense to pay out the nose at some swanky private school if you can go to a school that's cheaper, just as good, and able to provide equally bright prospects for your future.

Nonmonetary Factors to Consider When Choosing a College

Ultimately, every school in this book offers a fabulous education. Only a few schools, however, offer world-renowned cooperative education programs, student housing on the beach, a broad core curriculum, the opportunity to be a fighter pilot, or classes in that obscure language that you have set your sights on learning.

Here are some things to consider as you embark upon your college search.

Shady Statistics

Just because a school publishes fancy-sounding statistics doesn't mean those numbers are important. While some figures can shed light on what you may find once you hit campus, other figures that merely look impressive can be misleading. Don't be fooled into focusing on the following statistics.

Student/Faculty Ratio

Don't use the student/faculty ratio to assess average class size; it's not the same thing. At almost every college, the average class size—*particularly for first- and second-year students*—is larger than its student/faculty ratio appears to indicate, and it's even larger at many big universities. Ignore this statistic. What matters most is whether students at a

> ### PUBLIC SCHOOLS
> ### VS.
> ### PRIVATE SCHOOLS
> Nearly 40 percent of the respondents to The Chronicle of Higher Education's *recent Survey of Public Opinion on Higher Education said that, in their opinion, on the whole, public school education and private school education are pretty much the same. Of course, a little over 40 percent of the respondents in the same survey said that private colleges and universities are better. Meanwhile, 13 percent said public universities are better. Who's right? Who knows?*

school actually *like* their teachers and their classes. Visit the school instead and ask the students how happy they are with their courses and whether they think their professors are accessible. Better yet, sit in on a few core curriculum courses or general education courses (both basically mean "required") for first-year students to see firsthand how you're likely to be spending much of your freshman year. As a side note, many students actually cite their lecture classes as some of their favorites.

The School's Acceptance Rate

Knowing the percentage of applicants who are admitted each year is helpful, but it can be deceiving. Why? Because many schools have self-selecting applicant pools. Brigham Young University, for instance, has a very high acceptance rate, but don't even try waltzing in there with a B average and middle-range ACT scores. Despite its relatively high acceptance rate, BYU remains

> College graduates earn an average of $16,000 to $30,000 more per year than high school graduates.

exceptionally difficult to get into because virtually every applicant belongs to the Church of Jesus Christ of Latter-day Saints *and* has very strong academic credentials. Another obvious example is state schools. You will face a notably more selective evaluation as a nonresident (out-of-state) applicant than applicants to the same school who are state residents.

Percentage of Students Who Go on to Graduate or Professional School

Never allow yourself to be overly impressed by this one. High percentages mean either that the college is an intellectual enclave of incubating professors or that it is a bastion of future lawyers and doctors. Low percentages mean graduates are going out and getting real jobs. These outcomes are neither good nor bad.

Medical School Acceptance Rates

Virtually every college in the country can boast of high acceptance rates to medical school for its graduates because premed programs are designed to weed out those who will not be strong candidates before they even get to apply. If you're thinking about medical school, ask colleges *how many* of their students apply to medical school each year.

THE FLUTIE FACTOR

In 1984, on live national television, Boston College quarterback Doug Flutie threw arguably the most amazing "Hail Mary" touchdown pass in football history to beat Miami, the defending national champion. Over the next two years, applications to Boston College rose over 25 percent. Coincidence? We don't think so (though there's a pretty fierce debate in stuffy academic circles). Recently, the number of applications to Gonzaga, a little Jesuit school in Spokane, Washington, rose over 70 percent of the usual applications after the Zags' basketball team made a few impressive runs in the NCAA Men's Basketball Tournament.

SAT AND ACT AVERAGES

Speaking of lies and statistics, it's important to remember that *average* does not mean the same thing as *minimum*. Some students look at colleges in college guides like this one and eliminate schools where the average SAT or ACT score is higher than their own. Don't do this. *An average is not a cutoff.* If a college's average verbal SAT (for the new SAT) is 2050, it can only mean that approximately half of its students scored *below* 2050. Also, many colleges artificially inflate their average by excluding certain groups (like athletes or legacies) who generally score lower. Don't exclude schools with combined SAT averages 150 points over—or under—your own.

Understand that schools will find a way to look beyond your test scores if you belong to a traditionally underrepresented group (for example, if you are an ethnic minority or if you grew up on a turnip farm out in the sticks); if you can throw a baseball, swim laps, or hurl a discus better than most people in your town; or if your dad is the president of the school—or the country.

LOCATION, LOCATION, LOCATION

Hopping urban nightlife or rural serenity? Weekends at the beach, or strapping on your snowshoes? Close to home, or in a galaxy far, far away? Remember that you're selecting not only a school but also a place to live. If you just can't decide between Bates College in Maine and California State University in Long Beach, don't scrutinize their academics. Think about the weather!

There's also a really good chance that many of the employers who recruit on campus will be from the area. And, speaking of work, a big city (or a big-time college town) will offer more employment opportunities if you're going to have to work your way through school. It will be easier to find jobs that won't bring you into constant contact with your schoolmates, too, if the prospect of them seeing you waiting tables in a shirt and silly bowtie bothers you.

BIG SCHOOL OR SMALL SCHOOL?

Big schools have more diverse student populations, a ton of extracurricular activities, and gargantuan libraries. Though classes are often huge and impersonal, there are a lot more of them to choose from. Oftentimes big schools are full of annoying red tape, but life is not as overwhelming as you might think because the university is divided into smaller colleges. Big schools are often located in big cities or college towns, where a wealth of cultural and social activities are constantly available. There will probably be a 24-hour grocery store within walking distance of where you live. Sporting events are exhilarating, nationally televised, and larger than life.

Small schools, by contrast, have smaller classes—and fewer of them. Students are taught by real professors (not by inexperienced graduate students, as you often find at large schools) in intimate classroom settings. If you want to ask a question in class, you can do so without feeling foolish. You'll meet most of the people in your class and much of the administration. You are likely to develop more friendships at a smaller school, but you'll have to choose your friends, your boyfriends, your girlfriends, and your enemies all from the same small group of people. If you're a good athlete but not all-state, you'll get the chance to play intercollegiate sports at a smaller school. And if you are into theater but not plotting a gilded path to Broadway, you'll still land parts in your school's productions. There will be fewer extracurricular activities overall, but more opportunities to be deeply involved in a particular pursuit and to secure leadership roles.

SOCIAL LIFE

Some schools are party schools. Other schools are filled with eggheads who study all the time. Most schools are a mix of both—much of it depending on which crowd you choose to hang with. Do you picture the base camp of your social life to be on campus or off campus? Does a huge fraternity scene excite or alarm you? Do you want a school where the football (or lacrosse, or basketball) team is the main focus of social life? These are just some of the things you want to consider.

FELLOW STUDENTS

At some schools, every student does his or her own thing, and many different ethnicities, nationalities, religions, and cultures are represented. At other schools, everybody looks and acts pretty much the same. Some schools settle in between these two extremes. Make sure you choose a school where you'll be able to get along and feel comfortable with your peers for (at least) four years.

WHAT COLLEGES SAY IN VIEWBOOKS, VIDEOS, BROCHURES, AND CATALOGS

If you are a junior or senior in high school and you've taken the PSAT, you've probably received your fair share of material. While cool to look at, don't kid yourself: No college that spends half a million dollars on glossy marketing materials is going to be objective when designing and writing them. In the best of this material, you can get a decent idea of the academic offerings and the basic admissions requirements. You will see some of the best-looking students and the most appealing architecture on campus, and you won't hear about anything that is remotely unpleasant (whether it's the way-too-spread-out campus, the antiquated registration system , or the baked ziti in the cafeteria that seems to look older each time it's served). Look this stuff over, but don't make any decisions based solely, or even primarily, on what you read or see in these shiny, happy materials.

WHAT YOUR FRIENDS SAY

No one knows colleges and universities better than the students who currently attend them. Seek out any and all personal friends, sons and daughters of family friends, and recent graduates of your high school who attend college, especially those who attend colleges that you are considering. Call them. Drop them an e-mail. Stop by their houses. (They'd love to see you.) Arrange to stay with them when you visit their colleges. Pick their brains about everything they know. You simply won't find any information more direct and honest.

WHAT YOUR PARENTS THINK

You're probably going to need your parents' help in financing your education. So it's not a good idea to alienate them by telling them that you don't care what they think. (This is true even if you actually don't care.) Involve them in the process, and don't be afraid to talk about things like finances and the school's location. Going off to school with their blessing and support makes the process so much less stressful for everyone.

WHAT YOUR GUIDANCE COUNSELOR THINKS

SCHOLARSHIPS

They're out there! Your local library and guidance counselor's office are a good place to start your search. Then cheak out our Scholarships & Aid Center on www.PrincetonReview.com. You can search through more than 10,000 scholarships and find those for which you qualify.

Most counselors are knowledgeable and want to see you end up at a school that's right for you. Listen to what they have to say. Never anger them, if only because many schools want a recommendation from them. Once you've developed some ideas about your personal inventory and college options, schedule a meeting with your counselor. The more research you've done before you get together, the more help you're likely to get. Good advice comes out of thoughtful discussion, not from the expectation that your counselor will do your work for you.

WHAT ONLINE RESOURCES SAY

There's a lot out there. And frankly some of it is not to be trusted. Of course you should check out the school websites first, since that is where you'll get the most updated information about tuition costs and academic offerings. Just keep in mind that their websites are not going to readily give you negative information about themselves, so using those sites as your only source isn't a good idea. It's also important to find out how other websites obtain their information and who they are getting it from. As you begin to map out your list of potential colleges, we recommend using our website as a primary source of unbiased information. Because we're in the business of admissions information, we make sure to go to both the schools and the students who attend them—this way, you get information that covers all of your needs in searching for a school. The Counselor-O-Matic tool on our site can help you narrow down your list of colleges based on a very broad range of different criteria—from academics and extracurriculars, to geographic and social attributes. This will help you plunge into the process of coming up with your final list of schools. Check it out at PrincetonReview.com.

Naturally, we're pretty sure that our tools are the most useful and best designed, but we're not the only game in town. Look around and compare your findings against one another.

VISITS AND INTERVIEWS

If at all financially possible, visit *all* the schools to which you are seriously considering applying. Try to arrange through the Admissions Office to stay on campus with a current student who can show you the real ins and outs of the school.

GETTING IN

MATCHMAKING

If you simply keep matchmaking at the forefront of your mind when choosing a school and filling out applications, you will have a lot more control over where you wind up going, and you will be a happier, more successful student as a result.

Obviously, you want to find a college that has the educational and social environment you're looking for, and where you will be well suited to flourish as a full-blown college student. You should begin with a thorough self-examination or personal inventory. Once you identify the things that are most important to you, make a chart. When you visit a school or as you navigate through its website, note how well the school fits your chart. The best colleges for you will gradually begin to stand out.

YOUR CHART

Divide the far left column of your chart into the following two sections:

Biographical

The first section is biographical and includes your high school course selection, GPA, SAT or ACT scores, class rank, and other personal information, such as favorite extracurricular activities, especially the ones you plan to continue in college.

College Characteristics

The second section should be a listing of the characteristics you need or want in the college you'll ultimately attend. This list should include anything and everything you consider important such as cost, location, size of the student body, availability of scholarships, dormitory options, clubs, activities, party scene (or lack thereof), quality of the library and computer labs, fitness and recreational facilities, and anything else you can think of. Be flexible. Be organic. (We honestly knew a girl who thought it was fate that one of her top colleges used her favorite color—*purple*—on all of their school paraphernalia.) This part of your inventory will change as you become more aware of what is truly important to you.

List each college you are considering as the rest of your column headers. Filling in your chart is easy. As you sort through information about different colleges, check off each item from your personal inventory that a particular college satisfies. In the biographical section, make a general assessment of how you compare academically to each college's freshman profile.

AN EXAMPLE OF WHAT YOUR COLLEGE CHART MIGHT LOOK LIKE

Biographical	Grinnell College	Occidental College	Amherst College
GPA 3.02	3.53	???	???
SAT 1410 (720V, 690M)	1352 (682V, 670M)	1260 (630V, 630M)	1417 (710V, 707M)
Cross Country	yes (team is good)	yes (team is very good)	yes (team is good)
Radio station	yes (KDIC)	yes (KOXY)	yes (WAMH)
College Characteristics			
Tuition and fees	$25,082/year	$29,120/year	$29,728/year
Dorms	85% live on campus	70% live on campus	98% live on campus
Location	small Iowa town	metropolitan LA	college town
Student Population	about 1,500	about 1,800	about 1,600
Party scene	small but hopping/ no frats	small Greek scene lots to do in LA	good small parties
Religious Affiliation	none	none	none
Mascot	Pioneers	Tigers	Lord Jeffs

WAITING UNTIL THE LAST MINUTE IS NO GOOD

Once you've narrowed down your options and decided where to apply, obtain application materials immediately and fill them out. When you receive a hard copy of the application or open an online application packet, immediately remove/print the recommendation forms (if they are required) and give them to the carefully selected teachers and counselors (or anyone else) who you've kindly asked to complete them. They'll have a better opportunity to write a thorough and supportive recommendation if you give them more than one night to complete them; so don't give them the materials just before they are due! This is also the time to request official transcripts. It takes time to do all these things, so plan ahead.

WHAT COLLEGES WANT

When colleges describe their ideal candidate, they all describe more or less the same person. This ideal candidate has top-notch grades, high standardized test scores, exemplary extracurricular activities (e.g. editor of the newspaper, captain of the swim team), a fascinating after-school job (e.g. teaching English to immigrant children), terrific hobbies (e.g. managing the local canned food drive, playing medieval instruments), and a shelf filled with awards.

Real college applicants sometimes become depressed or feel they are meager candidates when they compare this ideal applicant to themselves. They should take heart because there is *no* ideal candidate. Mostly everybody who goes to college is ordinary. Even extremely selective schools have to dip into the general run of humanity to fill their first-year classes. Don't discount your chances simply because you feel you don't measure up to the ideal.

Additionally, even those students who come frighteningly close to the ideal picture we've painted don't always get in to the school of their dreams. There are lots of good people out there, but even schools who have an eye out for the ideal have their other eye out for something else: diversity. It takes all kinds to make an interesting group of people on campus.

No matter who you are, nobody's application is "perfect." Yours can be a little closer to the ideal, however, if you follow our advice. Here's some food for thought.

YOUR TRANSCRIPT: READING BETWEEN THE LINES

College Admissions Officers really want to know that if they admit you, you won't flunk out. In a nutshell, that's why they care so much about your transcript. And that's why you ought to pay attention to the courses you take and to how you do in them.

All A's Are *Not* Created Equal

That A you earned in media studies or archery is not going to shine as brightly as the A you earned in AP chemistry. Anybody can inflate their grade point average by taking a lot of easy electives that don't require much thought or academic muscle. Take as many challenging English, foreign language, math, history, and science classes as you can while still consistently making A's and perhaps a few B's.

Is a B in a Hard Course Better Than an A in an Easy Course?

Yes, big time. If you can handle the work in honors, AP, or other accelerated courses, you should be taking at least a few of them. If it is obvious from your transcript that you are taking a lighter load than you can handle, Admissions Officers at selective colleges are going to wonder about your motivation. Again, take as many hard classes as you feel you can handle while still getting good grades.

Does Class Rank Matter?

You betcha. Many colleges say that class rank is more revealing than grade point average. (Though most are interested in both.) This isn't rocket science; students who end up near the bottom of their high school classes tend to end up near the bottom of their college classes. So, start getting higher grades if you want to move up in the world.

Never Take a Real Academic Course Pass/Fail

Admissions Officers don't know what to make of a "pass" on your transcript. They may even count your pass as a C or D when they calculate your grade point average, and they will certainly decide that you were coasting when you took that course. Drivers' education and typing are different; they're not what we're talking about.

COLLEGE ADVICE

Not sure who to ask about life at college? The articles and advice on www.PrincetonReview.com range from how to settle on a school and what to do when you're waitlisted to how to choose a major, get good grades, find the right dorm, manage college stress, and afford to study abroad.

Junior and Senior Year Grades Matter More than Freshman and Sophomore Grades

This is not an excuse to slack off your first two years of high school, however, because your overall GPA for four years of high school inhabits a very prominent position in every college application. But if you are reading this book at the beginning of your junior year and your grades are only mediocre, all hope is definitely not lost. Students who show steady improvement in their grades the closer they get to graduation—and in harder classes—prove they are maturing and developing their potential.

Don't Take It Easy During Your Senior Year!

If steady improvement in your grades as you progress through school conveys maturation to an Admissions Officer, a senior year decline conveys the opposite. It may also indicate laziness, and that is even worse. In a nutshell, colleges really do care about your senior grades. It would be nice to coast, but don't. Colleges routinely request senior-year grades, and they expect you to take challenging academic courses and keep your grades up throughout your high school career.

> ### SOME IMPRESSIVE EXTRACURRICULAR ACTIVITIES
>
> * Student newspaper
> * Student government
> * Choir, orchestra, jazz band, marching band
> * Varsity sports
> * Community service activities
> * All-state anything

EXTRACURRICULAR ACTIVITIES

They're important. They aren't nearly as important as grades and test scores, but admissions committees want to know how you fill up your time when you aren't studying. (And you shouldn't be studying *all* the time.) Extracurricular activities aren't limited to sports and leadership roles. Community service, part-time employment, forensics, band, and Boy Scouts and Girl Scouts—to name only a few—all tell Admissions Officers what you can be expected to share with your fellow classmates during the next four years.

> ### SOME UNIMPRESSIVE EXTRACURRICULAR ACTIVITIES
>
> * Science Fiction Club
> * You're really good at Dungeons & Dragons
> * Any radical political organization (if in doubt, don't mention it)
> * Any impressive-sounding activity that you don't really have any interest in
> * Any organization that might be considered a cult

Our biggest advice is to avoid a laundry list. Nobody can really dedicate themselves to twenty three organizations. Colleges want to see that you stuck with a few activities that mattered to you, and that you excelled at them, even assuming a leadership role in them.

PAYING FOR COLLEGE 101

While the future cost of college can be intimidating, studies by the American Council on Education have shown that most Americans actually overestimate the cost and mistakenly think they need to save the full amount. But unless you are completely loaded or get a full-tuition scholarship somewhere, you will end up paying for college through some combination of your income, your parents' income, savings, partial scholarships, grants, and loans.

IDEAL SCENARIOS

Your parents began saving for college when you were very small, first in small increments, then gradually increasing the amounts as you and your siblings got older and their earning power grew; therefore, the cost of college isn't incredibly daunting. Or, you live in a mansion on a piece of property large enough to be called an "estate," you have access to a yacht, there is a fleet of European touring sedans in your many garages, and a fellow named Jeeves dutifully takes orders from you all day long; therefore, paying for college is no problem.

A MORE LIKELY SCENARIO

If you're like most of us, you probably began thinking seriously about college just a few years ago. Your parents have not been able to put aside large amounts of money because other things like the mortgage and food kept coming up.

Don't despair. Keep in mind that while college is costly, few people pay the actual sticker price. The whole point of financial aid is to bridge the gap between what you can afford to pay for school and what the school charges. Families who understand the process will come out ahead and avoid a lot of the stress. You have to have your finances in order before you can get the most financial aid possible.

FEDERAL METHODOLOGY EXPLAINED

There's a set of fairly Byzantine laws that govern the way most financial aid is distributed in the United States. You don't need to read the laws. Nevertheless, it's a good idea to have a basic understanding of the principles involved and the process in general.

> There are way too many college financing strategies—both long- and short-term—for us to include them all in this book. That's why we have a book entirely devoted to them called, Paying for College Without Going Broke, by Kalman A. Chany. If you or your child will be going to college in the next couple of years and you have no idea how you're going to pay for it, pick up the most recent edition of this book. No matter what your financial situation (and we mean that), you will be surprised to find how much aid you are eligible to receive.

Forms! Forms! Forms!

If you want any type of federally-funded financial aid, you must complete the Free Application for Federal Student Aid (FAFSA). You may also be asked to fill out the CSS/PROFILE form. A few schools also require forms specific to their institutions. The good news is that you only have to fill out one FAFSA and one CSS/PROFILE form each year no matter how many schools to which you apply, because you send your forms to a need analysis company, which then sends reports out to you and to the colleges you designate.

So, while you fill out your admissions applications, your parents should be gathering their financial records. January 1 of your senior year in high school is the earliest date you can file the FAFSA, but the closer you file these forms to the priority deadline for financial aid (which often falls in early to mid-February), the better. By no means should you miss the priority filing deadline at any of the colleges to which you're applying. Forms are assessed by the colleges in batches, beginning with the first batch that comes in before the priority filing deadline. If you miss that date, your forms could be sitting there until the office decides to process another batch—by which time there will be significantly less aid to go around.

Use common sense when mailing your completed forms; if the instructions tell you that the form has to be postmarked by a certain date, then don't leave the post office until the postal worker puts the postmark on the envelope and shows it to you. If it has to be received by a certain date, allow two weeks for delivery with the U.S. Postal Service's Express Mail Service. You must use the U.S. Postal Service (and not Federal Express, Airborne Express, or UPS) because all mail goes to a PO box. Use registered mail and get a return receipt.

- You can find the FAFSA on the Web at www.fafsa.ed.gov.

- You can find the CSS PROFILE on the Web at http://profileonline.collegeboard.com.

Your guidance counselor will have the financial aid forms you'll need. You can also download these forms from websites (see above). Check with your individual colleges to make sure that you are filling out the forms required by those colleges.

Basically, the person who looks at the information you provide in your FAFSA and in other forms is trying to determine four things:

- Your parents' available income

- Your parents' available assets (savings and stuff they own, like houses and farms)

- Your available income

- Your available assets (savings and stuff you own, like houses and farms)

Your Family's Need

The total cost of a year at college includes the following:

- Tuition and fees

- Room and board

- Personal expenses

- Books and supplies

- Travel expenses

Missing a financial aid deadline is worse than missing a mortgage payment. Your bank will probably give you a second chance. Colleges won't. They process their financial aid candidates in batches. Financial aid applications are collected in a pile up until the priority filing deadline and then assessed in a big batch. If you send in your application three weeks before the priority filing deadline, you will not be better off than someone who just makes the deadline. However, if your application arrives a day late, it will waste away in a pile of late applications until applicants in the first batch have received aid. You'll get the leftovers, if any are still available.

After you've been accepted to a college, the people in the Financial Aid Office will apply a formula (called the federal methodology) to the information you provided in the FAFSA to decide what portion of your income and assets you can afford to part with to pay for college your first year.

The amount they determine you can afford to pay is called your Expected Family Contribution (EFC). It will most likely be more than you think you can afford. Each college's Office of Financial Aid will then put together a package of grants, need-based scholarships, work-study, and loans that will make up the difference between your EFC and what the school actually costs.

In theory, your EFC will be approximately the same at every school. The idea is that you and your parents will be expected to pay for your college education *to the extent you are able.* Let's say, for example, your EFC is calculated

Make sure you use the most up-to-date version of all forms. Don't laugh. We've seen plenty of parents and students fill out the prior year's form.

to be $8,300. The total cost of a year at State U. is $15,000. In this scenario, if State U. guarantees to meet 100 percent of your financial need, you would pay about $8,300 and the school would make up the difference—in this case, $6,700—with an aid package. Now, say that the total cost of a year at Private U. is $31,000. If Private U. guarantees to meet 100 percent of your financial need, you would still pay about $8,300, and the school would make up the difference with an aid package worth approximately $22,700.

Sticker price is very misleading. At expensive private schools, the average student pays out-of-pocket only about half of the list price.

The concept of EFC means that your contribution may be the same (or less!) at more expensive schools compared to less expensive ones. This is one of the best things about paying for college.

The EFC index number, in conjunction with the Cost of Attendance (COA), determines the types of financial aid for which you are eligible. The COA includes tuition and fees, books, supplies, room and board, transportation, and personal expenses. It's based on in-state or out-of-state residency; housing status (living on campus, with parents or relatives, or off campus); and enrollment hours (attending full-time, three-quarter time, half-time, or less-than-half time). Your financial need is defined as the school's Cost of Attendance (COA) minus your Expected Family Contribution (EFC).

$$COA - EFC = Need$$

WHAT COMES IN AID PACKAGES?

Grants

These are usually based on financial need and don't have to be paid back. Essentially, a grant is free money. Some grant money comes from the federal government, some from state governments, and some from the schools themselves. The good news is that grant money is almost always tax-free.

Your state government may have a grant program established to assist financially needy students, usually to attend schools within the state. Every state's program is a little different. Georgia's and Florida's are notably awesome.

Federal Work-Study

The federal government subsidizes this nationwide program, which provides part-time, on-campus jobs to students with financial need. You get paid just like you would at any job, and you can spend the money however you like. Take care of tuition, books, and food first.

Student Loans

Loans are not free money. You have to repay your student loans, and then some. You usually take student loans out directly, not through your parents (although your parents can borrow additional money, too). Student loans are often subsidized by state or the federal government, meaning the interest your loans accrue while you are in school *could* be taken care of by Big Brother. No repayment is required until you have graduated or otherwise left college.

These days, some students burden themselves with very high levels of student loan debt. And many would say student loan debt is becoming a serious problem. The average cumulative debt of student loan borrowers at public colleges is well over $16,000 (according to *The Chronicle of Higher Education*). Students attending private colleges are borrowing even more.

Legislators across the country are considering increasing student loan limits, which are currently capped at certain amounts depending on how many years of college you have completed and whether you are a dependent or independent undergraduate. Allowing students to take on more loans is a solution, but not necessarily the best one. So think twice before you sign your way into thousands of dollars in debt. If you graduate with an English degree and $25,000 in debt—even at low interest rates—your employment options are limited. You're not likely to land a high-paying job right off the bat (although one may well come along). Colleges and universities that really care about your financial future will try to limit the amount of loan debt you have to take on in order to attend.

It's generally advised by personal financial experts that your monthly student loan repayment shouldn't exceed 8 percent of your monthly income. If you have a pretty good idea of either how much your monthly student loan payment will be or how much you'll make annually once you graduate, you can figure out what a safe figure is for the other amount. For example, if your student loan monthly payment will be $256, you should be making at least $38,400 a year (a). Similarly, if you'll be making $35,000 a year, your monthly loan payment probably shouldn't exceed $233 (b).

(a) $256 (monthly payment) ÷ 0.08 (8 percent) = $3,200 (minimum monthly income)

$3,200 × 12 (months in a year) = $38,400 (minimum annual income to comfortably meet student loan payments)

(b) $35,000 (annual income) ÷ 12 (months in a year) = $2917 (average monthly income)

$2917 × 0.08 (8 percent) = $233

Scholarships

Scholarships are also free money, although there may be some strings attached. Scholarships can be based on anything—grades, standardized test scores, athletic prowess, ability to carry a tune, religious affiliation, ethnicity, and/or your last name. As already mentioned, scholarships may also be based on need, which means that if your financial circumstances change while you are in college, the amount of your need-based scholarship can change too.

A Word on Outside Scholarships

Obviously, it's great if you can get one or more scholarships from sources besides the school you will attend. Don't overestimate these outside scholarships. Don't underestimate them either. The thing is that schools treat them differently. If you get an outside scholarship, some schools (like Bates College) will give you the same amount of scholarship and grant aid they would have given you anyway. Other schools aren't so generous; they may count your scholarship against what they were going to give you and still saddle you with the same amount of student loans. Policies differ by school and are subject to change. *Be sure to find out how each school treats outside scholarships.*

> *Your parents' employers, churches, rotary clubs, labor unions, and any number of other organizations are would-be sources of merit-based, need-based, or simply existence-based scholarships. Look into them.*

Qualified State Tuition Programs

All fifty states and the District of Columbia currently or will soon offer or will soon offer special programs that are designed to help families plan ahead for college costs. These programs, which are sometimes called Section 529 plans (after the relevant section of the Internal Revenue Code), come in two basic forms: tuition pre-payment plans and tuition savings accounts. Most states offer one type of the other, but a number of states offer or will soon offer both. As of 2004, individual colleges and universities and large consortiums of colleges and universities also offer pre-paid tuition plans. Plans and options differ widely by state. Many pre-paid tuition plans guarantee that you will be able to pay future tuition (at in-state public colleges) at today's prices. College savings plans are more flexible in terms of where you can go to school but don't offer guarantees against price increases.

Some Section 529 plans have state residency requirements. Others (like California) will allow anyone from anywhere in the United States to participate. While some states limit who can contribute funds to the plan (usually parents and grandparents), other states have no such restrictions. Any benefactor will do. With some plans, the contributor can name himself or herself as the beneficiary as well.

> No discussion of outside scholarships would be complete without a warning about scams. Here's a good rule of thumb: don't pay a fee to apply for a scholarship. Scholarships are money for you, not for the provider of the scholarship.

Most plans allow you to make payments in a lump sum, and others let you pay in installments; some even have the option of deducting the payment right from your bank account. With some states, the buildup in value is partially or entirely free of state income taxes for state residents. For example, New York's College Savings program gives its residents up to a $5,000 deduction (up to $10,000 for joint filers) on the state income tax return for amounts contributed during a particular tax year; spouses filing jointly can deduct up to $10,000 per year in contributions.

We know what you are thinking; you heard these pre-paid plans were a rotten deal. Yeah, they were. But now, these state-sponsored plans have become flexible, letting you take money out-of-state or to a private university in your own state. Also, it didn't really make any sense to put your money in one of these programs when you could reap the windfalls on the stock and bond market. These days, with the stock market contraction that started in 2000 and reminded everyone that it is not a sure thing, qualified tuition programs are much more appealing. A major benefit of these prepayment plans is the peace of mind that comes from knowing that no matter how much tuition inflation there is, you've already paid for a certain number of course credits at the time of purchase. Plus, given the recent declines in the stock market and the reduced rates of return on CDs and bonds, prepaid plans are looking mighty attractive. So while many investment advisors may still tell families they are better off avoiding these pre-paid plans and funding the college nest egg using other investment vehicles that are likely to earn a higher rate of return, the pre-paid plans are something to consider—particularly if you or someone in your family will start college in the next few years.

Negotiating Financial Aid

Financial Aid Offices have a lot of latitude when it comes to doling out their schools' financial aid money. After looking at your financial information, they might decide your

EFC should be lower or higher than the number calculated by using the basic federal methodology. More importantly, the packages that Financial Aid officers put together reflect how badly admissions offices want individual students.

Your award also reflects the general financial health of the college. Some schools like Rice and Amherst have massive endowments and can afford to be generous. If a school is truly anxious to get you to attend, it may sweeten the deal by offering a grant or scholarship not based on need, which would very likely reduce your expected family contribution.

Almost 60 percent of all financial aid comes in the form of loans. This is up from approximately 40 percent in the 1980s.

Other schools are financially strapped—or they may not really want you that badly—and may therefore offer you only the minimum.

Unmet Need

In some cases, the college may tell you that you have *unmet need*. This is a nice way of saying that the school is unable or unwilling to supply the full difference between the Cost of Attendance and your Expected Family Contribution. Hence, if you really want to attend this college, you will have to pony up even *more* money than the college's need analysis determined that you could pay.

We hate to shatter any dreamy optimism you might have, but financial aid award packages containing federal, state, or institutional assistance cannot exceed the Cost of Attendance at a given school. (Every school publishes its Cost of Attendance annually. Look around for it on their websites.) You can't make money with scholarships and grants. Having someone else pay for tuition, books, room and board, and transportation expenses is the best it's going to get; but that certainly isn't bad.

This means that if you decide to attend, you will probably need to take on additional debt. Sometimes, the college will be willing to lend you the money. If not, you'll need to look at the other attractive, low-cost options out there. Federal Parent Loans for Undergraduate Students (PLUS) offer good rates, and, with capped rates kept fairly low, this option might work for you. If your parents own a home or some other valuable property, a home equity loan might do the trick (and it's also tax deductible). Other loan products have sprung up to help with educational expenses as well. There will always be institutions that stand ready to lend you money—for a price.

Sifting Through the Offers

Acceptance and award letter season can be tough, especially as you deal with the economic realities presented by the different schools' offers. Just as it is important to select an academic safety school, it is also important to select a financial safety school— a school that is cheap enough to afford if the more expensive schools do not meet your full financial need. Incidentally, your admissions safety and financial safety schools are often one in the same because if you are a desirable academic candidate, you are likely to get a good financial aid package.

You should also consider what sort of financial aid the schools have recently been awarding to students at the schools to which you are applying, as well as each school's economic health. (You can find lots of this information on our website. Just type the name of the school in the "Search by School Name" box. You can also request an annual report directly from a school.) What we mean by economic health is that you've looked at the size of the endowments a school has relative to the size and price of the school; the alumni giving rate; the annual operating budget, and so on. While these may seem like minor factors in the scheme of finding the right school, an institution suffering from poor economic health may signal sharp tuition increases in the near future.

Let the college pick up the tab for phone calls whenever possible. Many schools have free telephone numbers that they don't like to publish in books like this one. If the number we have listed for a particular college or university is not an 800 number, it doesn't necessarily mean that you have to pay every time you call the school. Check out the school's website, or ask for the 800 number when the first time you call.

When schools are struggling on a fiscal level, the burden is often pushed off on the students so they can help cover the costs. In particular, state schools are at the mercy of the state legislature. If the state government cuts an institution's costs on a whim, the school is forced to cut seats, facilities, staff, or amenities, *and* boost their rates. A school may have a reasonable tuition rate when you apply, but that could all change by the time you're registering for your sophomore-year courses. Even if a school guarantees you a $5,000 scholarship for all four years, that $5,000 is going to be worth less and less if their tuition continues to skyrocket. A best value school for you and your family means that it will remain a best value for all four years.

That being said, it is also vital to make sure the school expects that the aid package will be available to you for all of your four years. How high do your grades have to be to keep the package intact? Are any of the grants or scholarships one-time-only (awarded only for your freshman year) or are they renewable? Do juniors and seniors at this school mysteriously receive lower aid packages than freshmen and sophomores? The federal loan limits (the amount of money a student can legally borrow) are higher for juniors and seniors, which means your need-based gift aid (grants and scholarships) could (and probably will) be reduced and your loan amounts increase as you progress through college. This is *a lot* more common than it ought to be, by the way. Once you've received an offer, these are questions to ask the Financial Aid Office, as well as anyone else you think might know.

If you are offered a package that does not meet your financial requirements, you may still be able to negotiate a better deal. Over the past few years, we have noticed that initial aid offers at some of the more selective schools seem to have become subject to negotiation. The key in these negotiations is to ask for more financial aid in a very friendly, yet firm, way. When you call, know what you want to say and be ready to provide any documentation. Be prepared to explain why you need or deserve more money. You've also got to be in a position to say "Thanks, but no thanks" in a perfectly cordial way if necessary. If Amherst is your dream school and happens to be the only school of nationally spectacular caliber to accept you, then you don't have much bargaining power; you probably shouldn't waste the Financial Aid Staff's precious time (honestly). However, if you also have been accepted to Brown, and you would be reasonably happy going there, negotiating for a better deal at Amherst would be worthwhile for you. In some cases, the school may magically find some more money for you. If not, you've done yourself no harm in asking. You certainly won't be denied admittance, nor will your aid package suddenly become lower.

Same Time Next Year

The financial aid package you accept will last one year. If it takes you four years to finish college, you will have to go through the financial aid process four separate times. You'll fill out a new FAFSA and a bunch of other forms every year. If your financial situation stays exactly the same, the following year's aid package will probably be similar to the one you received your first year.

FINANCIAL AID Q & A

Q: Am I eligible for financial aid?
A: Most people are, so you probably are too. In fact, more than 70 percent of students today receive some form of financial aid.

Q: When should I apply?
A: After January 1 of your senior year of high school, you will submit the Free Application for Federal Student Aid (FAFSA) and possibly the CSS/PROFILE form to start the financial aid process. You'll also get additional forms to complete from each university to which you apply. You need both your and your parents'

completed tax returns to complete these forms. File them well before the priority filing deadline set by each school where you have applied.

Q: *What is the process once I've applied for aid?*

A: The FAFSA is used to determine your Expected Family Contribution (EFC), which is the amount that your family will be expected to contribute toward your first year of college. Based on the information you provide in your FAFSA, every school that admits you will put together a package of grants, scholarships, and/or loans that will likely make up the difference between the cost of attending and your EFC.

Q: *What if the package isn't enough?*

A: There may be some room for negotiation, particularly if your family's financial situation has changed since you submitted the FAFSA. Be sure to discuss alternative funding sources with every school's Financial Aid Office. You can also look into unsubsidized student loans, home equity loans, and other loans that are not dependent on financial need. You can definitely find somebody to lend you enough money, just don't bite off more loan than you can chew.

Q: *When will I get aid for which I am approved?*

A: Typically, aid is disbursed once in the fall and once in the winter. Tuition tends to get paid directly to the school, while living expenses may get paid directly to you or wired into your bank account. Your financial aid office can give you more details.

Q: *How often do I need to apply?*

A: You will need to complete the FAFSA and other forms *every year* that you are in school. Be aware that many scholarships and grants may be granted *only for your first year*. Try to plan accordingly. Reapplying will especially help if you have brothers or sisters who start college while you are still in school because your family's situation will have changed significantly. Changes in federal law may have an impact on the financial aid you receive as well.

Q: *Will financial aid cover study abroad?*

A: As a rule, yes.

Q: What is the difference between subsidized and unsubsidized student loans?

A: With subsidized student loans, the government pays the interest on your loan as long as you are a student (and for a rather short grace period after your graduate). Unsubsidized loans accrue interest that you have to pay, starting on the day you get the money. (You can defer paying the in-school interest until after you have graduated, but it will still accrue and be added to your payment amount once you leave school.)

Q: What happens to my student loan if I take a semester off?

A: Find out ahead of time whether you will be able to continue deferring repayment. Ask your loan servicer or someone in-the-know in your school's Office of Financial Aid.

Q: What is a Stafford Loan?

A: You can obtain a Stafford Loan if you attend an accredited institution of higher education at least half-time. The loan is insured by a state or national guarantee agency and reinsured by the federal government. If you're a dependent student but your parents are denied a PLUS loan, you may borrow up to the amount that an independent student could borrow. If you can demonstrate financial need, the government will pay your interest while you attend school. This is a great benefit. While you are in school, you are getting an interest-free loan! If you can't demonstrate financial need, you can still get a loan but interest on the loan will accrue while you're in school.

Q: What are the interest rates on Stafford Loans?

A: For 2006–2007 interest rates on unsubsidized Stafford Loans are calculated at the 91-day T-bill rate plus 6.543 percent while you're in school (or during a grace period or deferment). During repayment, the rate for both unsubsidized and subsidized Stafford Loans is the 91-day T-bill plus 7.143 percent, with a capped rate of 8.25 percent. After July 1, 2006, the rate for unsubsidized loans while in school, grace, or deferment, has a fixed interest rate of 6.8 percent, while the rate during repayment is the same.

Q: What are PLUS Loans?

A: PLUS loans are made to parents, stepparents, or legal guardians for dependent students who are enrolled in school at least half-time. Parents may borrow an amount equal to the cost of the education, less any money received from grants and any other financial aid. There are no loan limits for PLUS loans and parents do not have to demonstrate financial need to apply—though they are subject to a mandatory credit check. Parents with a very poor credit history may not be approved for PLUS loans. Repayment of PLUS loans begins 60 days after you receive the money and the period for repayment may extend up to 10 years.

Q: What are the interest rates on PLUS Loans?

A: Interest on the PLUS loan is one of the lowest-cost credit-based loans that parents can get. PLUS loans have a fixed annual rate of 8.5.

Q: Are all student loans alike?

A: No. Look for lenders that provide loans that are cheaper or easier to repay and that offer benefits for on-time payment, no pre-payment penalties, and strong customer service.

We obviously can't anticipate or answer all of your questions here, but we come awfully close to doing so in *Paying for College Without Going Broke.* No matter what your financial situation, if you're planning to go to college or to send one of your children in the very near future, you should own this book. It will pay for itself many times over, and you will be amazed by all the options available to you. Really.

WHAT CAN STUDENTS DO?

Getting a job would be the most obvious idea. Earning too much, however, will decrease the financial aid that you can receive faster than the earnings can be deposited in your bank account. Of course, if your family isn't eligible for aid, get out there and earn as much as possible. But if your family stands a chance of qualifying for aid, your time would be better spent by making the most of educational opportunities.

Study Like Crazy

Good grades make you desirable to good colleges. They also translate directly into dollars and cents. The single most productive way you can invest in your future is by doing as well as possible during high school. Every tenth of a point you raise your high school GPA can save you thousands of dollars in student loans. Get good grades; get free money.

Take an SAT or ACT Course

Nothing can change your fortune faster than a big score increase on a standardized test. Look at it this way: It takes four years to accumulate your grades from high school. It takes six weeks to take a preparatory course. Students who take preparatory courses improve their scores by leaps and bounds, and those increases make them more desirable in the eyes of the

Financial Aid Officers, thus increasing the size of aid packages. If money is a consideration, you should know that some test preparatory companies offer financial aid. The Princeton Review certainly does. Give us a call at 800-2-REVIEW.

Take Advance Placement Courses

Many high schools offer AP courses or other accelerated academic programs that prepare you for AP exams. By passing an AP test at the end of the year, you can earn college credits without paying college tuition. Not all colleges accept AP credits, but many do; this enables you to save your family literally thousands of dollars. Some students are able to skip their entire freshman year in this way, thus cutting the entire cost of their college education by one quarter. Consult with the colleges to see if they accept AP credits and with your high school to see which AP courses are offered and how to sign up.

Condense Your College Education

Motivated students can complete a four-year education in three years, though it could be argued that you would have to be a little crazy to try it. Your family may not see big savings on the tuition itself (since some schools charge by the credit) but they will save on room and board, and you'll be able to get out into the work force sooner. A more reasonable goal might be to reduce your time in college by a semester, which you can do by attending summer school (which is often less expensive than the regular terms). Be careful, though. Even at half a year, this strategy may take its toll. Academics are only one part of the college experience, and by accelerating the process, you may lose out on some of the opportunities and friendships that make your college years meaningful.

> *On average, college graduates earn over 75 percent more than people who only graduate from high school. Over the course of your life after college, you will probably earn more than $1 million more than you would have if you didn't get a college degree.*

Defer Admission

Many schools allow students to defer admission for a year. If your family is financially strapped, use this year to earn money. You should always remember that earning above a certain dollar amount reduces aid eligibility. Thus, this strategy could backfire. However, if the college you really want to attend decides you aren't eligible for aid and your family cannot shoulder the entire cost of college, this might be the only way to make up the difference. Be extremely careful in making a decision like this. If there is no reasonable plan for how you can meet the entire four years' worth of college bills, you should consider other options.

Become a Soldier

If you are willing to commit some of your time to Uncle Sam before, during, or after college, it can be lucrative. The Montgomery GI Bill provides money for college if you'll serve a couple of years in the military first. The Reserves and National Guard have programs, too. Many schools offer Reserve Officers' Training Corps (ROTC) Programs, which provide scholarships of various sizes. Scholarship recipients participate in training while in college, at the very least. Upon graduation they are guaranteed—and committed to—a job within the military service. You should also note military financial aid is not based on need.

Stay in Your State

Many states give substantial financial incentives to residents who attend in-state schools. Georgia, with its HOPE Scholarship Program, is our favorite, but pretty much every state gives some cash to its academically talented and cash-strapped students who attend an in-state public (and sometimes private) school.

Go to School Part-time

Some schools allow students to attend college part-time so they can earn money while in school. If you choose this route, make sure you stay in school half-time. If you don't, you'll have to start paying back any student loans you take out. Also, the financial aid options available for part-time students are fewer.

Go to a School with a Great Co-op Program

Cooperative education combines traditional academics with real paying off-campus jobs related to what you are studying. You make righteous cash while gaining practical work experience. We're thinking Georgia Tech or the University of Missouri—Rolla in particular, but there are others. Many of them are engineering-focused schools.

Transfer in Later: Option 1

If your family is on a very tight budget, a good way to finance a four-year college education is to start with a two-year college education. Two-year community colleges or junior colleges, where the average annual tuition in 2005–2006 was just $2,191, represent an outstanding way to save money. A student with a good academic record at a community college (perhaps earned while still living at home) can then transfer to a slightly more expensive state college for two more years to earn a BA. The total cost would be only a fraction of the cost of a private college, and still thousands of dollars less than that of a four-year program at the state college. If this is your plan, you'll want to check with the state colleges you are considering to make sure credits will transfer and how to begin that process.

Transfer in Later: Option 2

If you really have your heart set on a particular private college but your family cannot afford it, there is another option. Go to a public college for the first two years and then transfer into the private school. You will get the private college degree at a much more affordable price. Obviously, you would have to get accepted by the private school as a transfer student, and this can be quite difficult. Outstanding college grades are a must. You'll need to choose a public college that will make you happy all four years in the event that you don't make it in to the private college after all.

Transfer in Later: Option 3 (or Generic College, Designer Graduate School)

Extending the previous strategy, you could attend a good public university during all four of your undergraduate years, and then go to a top-of-the-line private graduate school. The undergraduate savings would be huge, but again, whether you attend a private or a public undergraduate college, a compelling academic record is enormously important to ensure acceptance to a prestigious graduate school.

A WORD ON STATE RESIDENCY

With some planning and foresight, you shouldn't have to pay out-of-state tuition for more than one year at a public school in a state that's different from where you or your child went to high school.

Becoming a resident is harder in some states and easier in others. You usually have to wait a year. The key is to do things that show that you have the *intent* to stay in that state and that you aren't planning to leave at any time in the foreseeable future. You want to accumulate evidence of your intent. Get a state driver's license. Get in-state license plates. Register to vote. Get a job so you can pay state income taxes. If you live off campus or in a fraternity house, do everything you can to show that you have actually resided in the state for a year (even if you have spent some time as a guest in your parents' house over the holidays and during the summer). The sooner you can establish yourself as someone who lives in the new state, the sooner you can start paying in-state tuition.

"Knowledge is good."

– Emil Faber

THE INCREDIBLE
SOARING TUITION

In addition to death and taxes, the inevitable includes perpetually escalating college tuition. Some years, college prices skyrocket. Other years, they creep up so slightly that you hardly even notice. Partly in response to increased demand and partly because state budgets have been slashed, the rate of tuition increase at state schools has risen dramatically—especially for out-of-state students. Will these trends continue? Almost certainly.

THE COST OF A PRIVATE COLLEGE

According to a study by The College Board, during 2006 and 2007 the total cost of a year's tuition, fees, and room and board at a four-year private college averaged at approximately $30,738. Of course, at the most prestigious private schools, the costs were even higher. For example, the total cost for a year at Brown for 2005–2006 rings in at $41,770, and it will be more next year. Many experts predict an increase in tuition at private schools of 5 percent a year for the foreseeable future. That means that in 15 years, the *average* annual cost to attend a private college will be more than $55,000.

THE COST OF A PUBLIC COLLEGE

Public colleges are cheaper than private colleges because they are subsidized by state taxpayers. But costs perpetually increase at public universities, too—sometimes quite drastically. The same College Board study found that during 2006 and 2007, these costs went up by 6.3 percent. According to the study, the total cost of a year's tuition, fees, and room and board at a public university is over $12,800. That means that in 15 years, at a 5 percent increase every year, the *average* annual cost to attend a public college will be just over $22,400. The cost of the "public ivies"—the Universities of Michigan, Virginia, Berkeley—will be higher.

WHAT THE #$&! IS GOING ON?

Why do most schools, public and private, continue to increase tuition, even when there isn't a fiscal crisis like the ones the states faced during 2002 and 2003? When did this trend start? What's the average rate of increase? How does that rate stack up against inflation? How can schools get away with it?

The Permanent Tuition Increase

Throughout the 1970s, college tuition stayed basically stagnant. In the 1980s, prices at all colleges increased much more rapidly than prices for everything else. Costs at public colleges and universities alone shot up more than 140 percent during the 1980s (that averages out to 14 percent per year), more than double the overall inflation rate. In other words, college tuition costs have increased far more than the cost of housing, food, health care, and cars. In the 1990s, after adjusting for inflation, costs at both public and private four-year colleges and universities continued to rise, albeit more gradually than they did in the 1980s. The reasons for nationwide college tuition increases are, as they say, complex and numerous.

The Economics of the Higher Education Industry

It's a little unusual to think of higher education as an industry, like the meatpacking or construction industry. But colleges do indeed form an industry, one that provides a valuable service to its consumers.

Let's compare Swankbury College to Fred's Car Wash. Both Swankbury and Fred's have a few fixed (or basically fixed) costs. In a nutshell, Swankbury has teachers' and administrators' salaries, the physical plant (e.g., buildings, landscaping, maintenance), and supplies. Fred's has the salaries of the guys who dry the cars and all other employees, its own physical plant, and soap, water, high-pressure hoses, wax, etc. Both Swankbury and Fred's also have a few basic revenue streams. Swankbury has tuition and fees, state and federal money (tons of it if Swankbury is public), corporate and alumni gifts, and interest earned on its endowment. Fred's receives money every time someone comes in for a car wash or buys a can of Turtle Wax.

Both Swankbury College and Fred's Car Wash are ambitious, competitive, and driven to be successful. Swankbury wants to be the best college around. Fred's wants to be the best car wash around.

There are some differences, though. Swankbury considers itself above the fray of ordinary economics. Fred's does not.

For example, let's say Fred's introduces a new automated jet-dry service, but nobody buys it. In all likelihood, Fred's will simply drop the service. Similarly, let's say Fred's has offered a wax-while-you-wait option for years. It was really popular in the 1970s, but these days nobody ever buys it. Again, Fred's will probably stop offering waxing.

Swankbury is altogether different. If Swankbury introduces a new academic program, that program is very likely to be around for a long, long time to come, even if it isn't popular or useful. To understand why, consider what might happen if Swankbury tried to drop the Acadian language program, which has graduated only three students since 1983. Alumni would come out of the woodwork (the three graduates and a few linguists, at least) and make a big stink; students would protest; and the Acadian program would very likely continue its existence.

There's another difference. Fred's is happy being the best car wash. Colleges and universities often feel self-inflicted pressure to be everything to everybody—to offer every major, to have the best jazz band, to be the most ethnically diversified, to win the most national championships, to have the poshest dorms, and to have most up-to-date high-speed Internet connectivity.

We're not saying that Fred's is any better than Swankbury. In fact, we think that higher education is far more important than clean cars in the overall scheme of things. Nevertheless, Swankbury College is spending a lot more money (on things that their customers aren't interested in buying) than Fred's Car Wash, and in all probability it continues to increase its costs as the years go by. At the very least, its costs remain constant even as its state and federal subsidies, endowed interest, and alumni donations go down. That missing money has got to come from somewhere. And tuition hikes is where it comes from.

Supply and Demand

It's no coincidence that tuition skyrocketed in the 1980s. That's when more and more high school graduates decided that college would be a good idea. The supply of college education was essentially fixed. It's not as if a bunch of new colleges and universities sprouted up (though a few certainly did). Meanwhile, demand was rising rapidly.

Think about it. In any unregulated market, an increase in demand when supply is more or less fixed is a recipe for pushing the price upward. If Fred's were the only car wash in town and the number of cars in the area suddenly increased significantly, Fred could and would charge more for each car wash. It's the same with Swankbury College.

Another really important thing happened in the 1980s—this was when the current structure of financial aid programs in the United States really began to take shape. In previous decades, grant- and loan-based financial aid was only available to financially disadvantaged students or to people who served in the military (or not available at all). The framework for the current financial aid system evolved in the 1960s and 1970s thanks to federal legislation aimed at helping more people to go to college by way of grants and loans. Things really mushroomed in 1978 with the Middle Income Student Assistance Act, which broadened federal student assistance programs to include many more middle-income students.

Thus, today undergraduate education in the United States is very heavily subsidized. One reason that college tuition continues to rise at the rate it does is precisely because it is so subsidized. When you subsidize the cost of something, the natural and rational response of suppliers of that something is to raise prices. They can, so they do. If the government were to start giving people money to get their cars washed, Fred would very likely raise his prices. Since the government is giving so many people money to go college, Swankbury raises its prices.

Though not an unorthodox view, it doesn't sit well with some people because it doesn't account for some evil underlying cause. It also makes subsidies look bad when in reality they are a perfectly acceptable solution to the problem of creating an educated, skilled populace. Without such subsidies a lot of people could never go to college. Perpetually rising tuition is just the unavoidable social cost of trying to make a product available and affordable to more people.

OTHER REASONS WHY COLLEGE COSTS ARE RISING

The Research Monster

At public universities, state legislatures have acquiesced to a significantly increased emphasis on research because it can bring big-time prestige for the school and the state. Research also has the potential to bring truckloads of patent royalty money and corporate cash to a college. However, research is itself an expensive undertaking. That 43,000 square-foot nuclear magnetic resonance lab on the outskirts of campus where nobody is allowed to go wasn't built for free, you know, and it's not exactly cheap to maintain.

More research has also caused class sizes to soar. Professors who are in the lab cannot be bothered with mundane responsibilities such as teaching classes (and heaven forbid that tenured professors would have to teach *introductory* classes). Time spent researching, writing books and articles, attending posh conferences at fancy hotels, and doing every-thing tangentially related to education *except* teaching has diminished the amount of time that professors can spend with students. Research (about research, strangely enough) has shown that professors' salaries are inversely related to the number of hours they actually teach. Fewer hours in the classroom and more time in the lab means a bigger paycheck. Many professors at mammoth research universities teach few (if any) classes. If we may get on our soapbox for a second, we can't begin to tell you how wrong we think it is to shift focus from classroom teaching to academic research. College is for teaching and learning.

Regardless of what we believe, however, until the incentives for professors to focus on students outweigh the incentives to conduct research, many professors will continue to pay closer attention to their own projects instead of their students' needs.

Increased Government Regulation

Government regulation means that colleges have to do things to comply with government rules. Colleges have to keep crime statistics and graduation rates. They have to make sure all the males at the school are signed up for the selective service. They have to keep close tabs on the foreign nationals studying on their campuses. Doing these things costs money and requires a substantially larger number of administrative employees.

Bloated Administrations

Just as tuition is growing uncontrollably, so are administrative costs. This is very disconcerting because, as a rule, students *love* their professors and *can't stand* the administration. In the late 1980s, according to the *Washington Post*, almost 50 cents of every tuition dollar went toward administrative costs. In 1950, it was 27 cents. In 1930, it was 19 cents. Similarly, college and university administrations have grown by 60 percent in recent years. Full-time faculties have grown by just over 5 percent.

Increases in Institution-Based Financial Aid

Our moms always told us that money doesn't grow on trees. It's the same way at colleges. If schools want to provide more financial aid to certain students, they've got to get the money from somewhere. Very often, that somewhere is a tuition increase imposed on all students.

Slashed Government Funding

In most states, tax dollars reserved for state colleges and universities is considered discretionary spending, so when these states' legislatures decide to cut costs by decreasing the amount of money flowing to these state institutions, the schools have to make up the difference somehow. Tuition increases are usually the preferred solution.

A Modest Proposal?

It's funny. College tuition increases—even severe ones—are pretty run-of-the-mill. When money problems arise at colleges and universities, you almost never see the kind of fiscal responsibility and budget-cutting that you would see during a budget crunch at your house, for example.

At the time of this book's writing, there are some key people in our government who want to see this situation changed. U.S. Representatives Buck McKeon (R-CA) and John

Boehner (R-OH), for starters, are among those who have been advocating for ways to make sure colleges put the brakes on the rising costs they plan to pass on to families.

By introducing and supporting bills such as the Financial Aid Simplification Act and the Affordability in Higher Education Act, these two men have already seen a number of major colleges and universities take voluntary steps to curb tuition growth for students and parents. One major higher education organization—the American Association of State Colleges and Universities—has also come forward and expressed a willingness to work with Congress to address the college cost crisis. Encouraged by this, Buck McKeon then offered to remove a highly publicized provision in the Affordability in Higher Education Act in exchange for continued commitment on the part of institutions to avoid excessive tuition hikes. McKeon sees these voluntary actions as a victory for low- and middle-income students and hopes to see a continuation of this trend on the part of schools to actively fight the ever-growing costs of an education. If he doesn't, McKeon vows to put the provision back in the bill and press on. The provision, which sparked a national debate, would allow federally funded institutions to lose a portion of their federal aid if they repeatedly engage in excessive tuition hikes.

In May 2004, Boehner and McKeon introduced the College Access & Opportunity Act, which would further simplify the financial aid process for low- and middle-income students and families. In addition to increasing loan limits and decreasing loan fees, the bill would allow dependent students to earn more money without negatively impacting their eligibility to receive federal student aid. It also aims to ensure that those who have been awarded aid receive it quickly.

This dynamic Boehner-McKeon duo—crusaders of truth, justice, and education for all—along with others, are the voices that strive to speak on behalf of thousands of college-bound students across the country. So while students and parents will always face the burdens college costs, strides are being made to lessen those burdens and to make certain they won't be facing them alone.

How to Use This Book

It's pretty self-explanatory.

The first part—you are reading it now—is a primer on choosing and getting admitted to selective colleges, as well as paying the tab once you enroll. There's a lot of really good information about how scholarships, grants, loans, and the financial aid process as a whole work.

The second part is the real meat and potatoes of *America's Best Value Colleges*: profiles of the 150 best bargains among competitive colleges and universities in the United States. Each profile contains the same basic information and follows the same format. The Princeton Review collects all of the data you see in all the sidebars of each school. As is customary with college guides, our numbers usually reflect the figures for the academic year prior to publication. (That is usually the most recent year for which colleges have completed data.)* Since college offerings and demographics significantly vary from one institution to another, and some colleges report data more thoroughly than others, some entries will not include all of the individual data described below.

Please know that we take our data collection process seriously. We reach out to schools numerous times throughout the process to ensure we can present you with the most accurate and up-to-date facts, figures, and deadlines. Each profile in this book goes through a series of checkpoints to ensure accuracy of the information. Even so, a book is dated from the moment it hits the printing press. If a school changes its policies, procedures, requirements, or application deadline once our book is already on the shelves, it's too late for us to change it. Be sure to double-check with any schools to which you plan to apply to make sure you are able to get them everything they need in order to meet their deadline.

WHAT'S IN THE PROFILES

The Text

There are seven sections of text in each profile.

About

This very aptly named section is primarily full of information about the academic character of the school. You'll also find a succinct description of student life and what the student population is like.

*See Nota Bene at the end of this chapter.

Bang for Your Buck

In this section, we try to convey exactly what makes each school such a great bargain. Is it free, like the United States Military Academy or the Franklin W. Olin College of Engineering? Is tuition simply really low, like at Grove City College? How and why are grants, scholarships, and other financial aid awards disbursed? How big of a factor is financial need in the financial aid process? How big of a factor are grades, test scores, and other merit-based factors?

Getting In

Many of the schools in this book—like Amherst, for instance—are very difficult to get into. Others, like Emporia State, are not. Basically, this section covers the credentials you need to get admitted to the school. What are the most important components of each school's application and what is unique about its application process? What test scores do you need? What grade point average do you need? What high school classes do you need on your transcript? When feasible, we've also tried to note those schools that have separate admissions criteria for different major programs and undergraduate colleges within the larger university.

What Do Graduates Do?

We cover the percentage of graduates that heads directly (or more or less directly) to graduate and professional schools. We also try to convey a sense of the major industries in which graduates work and the big-name companies that recruit on campus and hire newly minted graduates year in and year out. In lieu of the above, we included information about some notable alumni and what they do (or did, if they are deceased).

The Bottom Line

Our personal favorite. How much real cash do average students and their families have to part with over the course of an academic year for tuition, room and board, books, and living expenses? This number should give you a decent indicator of the actual cost of the college (which is often significantly less than the sticker price). Obviously, if you are wealthier than the average person, you'll probably pay more out-of-pocket. If you are poorer than the average person, you'll ideally pay *less* out-of-pocket because you will receive more need-based financial aid.

Fun Facts

This is just what it says. We list neat and interesting information about the school.

Students Say

We pored over the thousands and thousands of student surveys we collect every year to find representative quotes from real students about what they believe makes their schools great values. If you happen to be a current college student, you can give us *your* opinion about your school at http://survey.review.com.

The Data

Not all of the data categories will be listed for every school. If a school fails to report their numbers for a certain category, that category is not included in their profile.

The Heading

The first thing you will see for each profile is (obviously) the school's name. Just below the name, you'll find the snail mail address, telephone numbers (regular and toll free), fax number, and e-mail address of the school's Admissions Office. Since this is a book so closely concerned with costs, you'll also find the Financial Aid Office's phone number. Call them. Get to know the people behind the inner workings of your financial aid award letter.

Religious Affiliation

This lets you know any religious order with which the school is affiliated.

Calendar

This is the school's schedule of academic terms. A semester schedule has two long terms, usually starting in September and January. A trimester schedule has three terms, one usually beginning before Christmas and two after. A quarterly schedule has four terms, which go by very quickly: the entire term, including exams usually lasts only nine or ten weeks. A 4-1-4 schedule is like a semester schedule, but with a month-long term in between the fall and spring semesters. (Similarly, a 4-4-1 has a short term following two longer semesters.) When a school's academic calendar doesn't match any of these traditional schedules, we note that with *other*. It is best to call the admissions office for details about schools that list *other* as their calendar.

Students

Total Undergraduate Enrollment

This lists the total number of full-time undergraduates.

% Male/Female Through % International

These list the demographic breakdown of the full-time undergraduate student body.

% from Out of State

This lists the percentage of undergraduate students who aren't residents of the state in which the school is located. We trust that you can figure out the percentage of students from the school's home state.

Retention Rate

This lists the percentage of the previous year's freshmen who were still enrolled as students at the institution during the most recent year for which data was available. This is a statistic you should pay attention to because it's a relatively good predictor of how happy students are. If the schools retention rate is lower than most of its peer institutions, you should reconsider your application.

% of Students Living on Campus

This statistic is often a very good indicator of whether the college or university is residential (most students live on campus and social life revolves around school) or commuter (most students live off campus and students do their own thing). And the percentage of students not who are not living on campus, obviously are living off campus.

% in Fraternities and % in Sororities

This lists the percentage of undergraduate male students who join fraternities and the percentage of undergraduate female students who join sororities. Some students want to attend a school where Greek organizations dominate the student social life, while others want the complete opposite. A quick glance at these statistics should give you a sense of how much—if at all—student life revolves around the Greeks.

Admissions

of Applicants

This is the total number of students that applied for acceptance into the most recent freshman class.

% Accepted

This lists the percentage of the total number of applicants to whom the school offered admission.

% Enrolled

This lists the percentage of accepted students who enrolled at the school. This statistic is also called "yield" by admissions cognoscenti.

of Early Decision Applicants

The total number of students that applied for acceptance into the most recent freshman class through the school's early decision plan. Early decision plans allow students to apply to one school for early notification of admissions. Early decision plans are binding on the student. That is, if a student is accepted under a specific school's early decision plan, that student must promise to enroll at the school. Early *action* plans allow students to receive early notification of acceptance but are not binding.

% Accepted Early Decision

This lists the percentage of the total number of early decision applicants to whom the school offered admission. By the very nature of early decision, the vast majority of students accepted under it enroll at the school.

Transfer Applicants

This lists the total number of students who applied as transfer students.

% Transfer Applicants Accepted

Self-explanatory.

High School Units Required

If a college requires high school course work in specific subjects, the subjects will be listed, with the number of units next to them. One unit equals one year of study.

High School Units Recommended

This is the same as high school units required, except you don't *have* to have studied these subjects for however many years listed to be considered for admission. It just works in your favor if you have.

Academic and Non-academic Factors Considered for Admission

These are the things that each school told us it considers either important or very important when it evaluates applicants. Academic factors may include the student's secondary school record, class rank, recommendations, standardized test scores, and essays. Non-academic factors may include the student's interview with an Admissions Officer, extracurricular activities, talents/abilities, character/personal qualities, alumni/ae relations, geographical residence, state residency, religious affiliation/ commitment, minority status, volunteer work, and work experience.

Average High School GPA

Unless a school reports this some other way (like on a 0–100 scale), this is on a scale of 0–4. Your GPA is unquestionably one of the key factors in college admissions. Keep it up until you graduate from high school; don't get lazy the second semester of your senior year. Even if you have already received acceptance letters from a college, your grades will still be important in the consideration of scholarships.

Range SAT Verbal*, Range SAT Math, Range ACT Composite

This lists the middle 50 percent of test scores of entering freshmen. If your scores are lower than the smaller number in each scale, don't lose hope; that smaller number represents the 25th percentile of entering freshmen's scores, which means that a quarter of the entering class had scores lower than that.

*In March 2005, the College Board added a writing section to the SAT exam. This addition has affected each prospective college-bound student considering admission since Fall 2006. The Range SAT Verbal score presented in this book is taken from the most recent information made available to us by each school. While we strive to provide the most current statistics possible, we recommend that you double-check these figures with each institution for information on the Range SAT Critical Reading and Writing scores.

Minimum TOEFL

This lists the minimum test score necessary for entering freshmen who are required to take the TOEFL (Test of English as a Foreign Language). Most schools will require all international students or non-native English speakers to take the TOEFL in order to be considered for admission.

Application Deadlines

This lists the deadlines for submission of early decision/action and regular decision applications. Both early decision and early action deadlines will be denoted by *early decision.*

Note: Do check with the school before you apply to ensure that their deadline has not changed since this book went to press.

Academics

Student/Faculty Ratio

This lists the ratio of full-time undergraduate students to full-time teaching faculty. This is a sneaky figure, so don't make any decisions based on it. What it does *not* represent is the average number of students in any given class.

% of Faculty Teaching Undergraduates

This lists the percentage of the full-time faculty who teach at least one undergraduate course each year. This percentage obviously excludes any faculty who only do research for the school.

% of Classes Taught by Graduate Students

This is pretty self-explanatory, too. Graduate students are often very accessible, sometimes more so than full-time faculty. On the minus side, they often have little to no teaching experience and lack the big picture understanding of a subject that professors (really should) have.

Most Popular Majors

This lists the three most popular undergraduate majors.

Education Requirements

Some colleges have core curricula (a set of specific classes all students must take), while others have distribution requirements (requirements that students take a certain number of classes in certain subjects or faculties). Some colleges have no curricular requirements at all. If the college requires course work in any subject, you'll see the subject named here. The possibilities are the following: arts/fine arts, computer literacy, English (including composition), foreign languages, history, humanities, mathematics, philosophy, science (biological or physical), social science, and other. This last catch-all category includes things like theology/religious studies and cross-disciplinary or school-specific courses. When feasible, we've listed what these other requirements are.

Financial Info

Tuition

The average cost of tuition for an academic year. For public schools, we list in-state and out-of-state tuition.

Please note that in cases in which tuition is listed as $0 for a school, there could still be some comprehensive fees that would apply to students who choose to attend. These fees may be covered by the school through grants, scholarships, work-study, or a student may need to pay them out of pocket. Be sure to check with the schools that interest you about any and all hidden costs and fees that are passed on to incoming students.

Room and Board

This is the school's estimate of what it costs to buy meals and to pay for a dorm room for the academic year.

Average Book Expense

Indicates how much students can expect to shell out for textbooks during the academic year.

Required Fees

In addition to tuition, room and board, and the cost of books, colleges and universities generally hit students up for additional fees to pay for use of the campus sports and recreation center, participation in school-sponsored clubs and activities, school ID cards, etc. Note: Schools in the University of California system call everything fees.

Average Need-Based Grant

The average annual gift aid award (money that doesn't have to be paid back) the college gave to undergraduates who applied for financial aid and were determined to have financial need by the Financial Aid Office.

Average Need-Based Loan

The average annual loan (money that has to be paid back) disbursed by the college to undergraduates who applied for financial aid and were determined to have financial need by the Financial Aid Office.

% Graduating Who Borrowed

The percentage of the previous year's graduating class who borrowed money through any loan program while enrolled. The vast majority of students who borrow money during college do not pay off their loans before graduating.

Average Indebtedness

The average student loan debt of graduating seniors who borrowed any money while they were in college.

Required Forms

The forms the college requires students who are applying for student financial aid to complete and submit. They may include FAFSA (Free Application for Federal Student Aid), Institutional (the institution's own financial aid form), PROFILE (The College Scholarship Search PROFILE form), State (the state's aid form), Parent's Statement (the Noncustodial Parent's Statement), and the Business/Farm Supplement. If the school requires any other forms, *other* will appear. It's advised that you contact the college's Financial Aid Office directly to find out about that *other* form.

Application Deadline

This lists the priority and final deadlines for submitting applications for financial aid. These usually do not coincide with the application for admission.

Postgrads

% Going to Graduate School Through % Going to Medical School

These list the percentages of graduates who went on to graduate school (in the arts and sciences), business school, law school, or medical school.

Career Services

These are the services offered by the campus career center to undergraduates. They may include an alumni network (directories), alumni services, career/job search classes, career assessment, internships (listings), and regional alumni (directories).

Off-campus Employment

The college's rating of off-campus part-time employment opportunities for undergraduates.

Nota Bene

The data reported in this book, unless otherwise noted, was collected from the included colleges from the fall of 2005 through the summer of 2006. Some colleges opted to include 2006–2007 figures. Because enrollment and financial statistics, as well as deadlines, fluctuate from one year to the next, please contact the colleges directly for the most accurate figures and dates.

TOP TEN
BEST VALUE
COLLEGES

Top Ten Best Value—Public Colleges

1. New College of Florida
2. Truman State University
3. The University of North Carolina at Asheville
4. University of Virginia
5. University of California—Berkeley
6. University of California—San Diego
7. University of California—Santa Cruz
8. University of Minnesota—Morris
9. University of Wisconsin—Madison
10. St. Mary's College of Maryland

Top Ten Best Value—Private Colleges

1. Rice University
2. Williams College
3. Grinnell College
4. Swarthmore College
5. Thomas Aquinas College
6. Wabash College
7. Whitman College
8. Amherst College
9. Scripps College
10. Harvard College

We chose the schools that appear on our Top Ten Best Value Public and Private Colleges lists based on institutional data and student opinion surveys collected from colleges and universities from the fall of 2005 through the summer of 2006. Broadly speaking, the factors we weighed covered undergraduate academics, costs, and financial aid.

More specifically, academic factors included the quality of students the schools attract, as measured by admissions credentials, as well as how students rated their academic experiences.

Cost considerations were tuition, room and board, and required fees.

Financial aid factors included the average gift aid (grants and scholarships, or free money) awarded to students, the average percentage of financial need met for students who demonstrated need, the percentage of students with financial need whose need was fully met by the school, the percentage of graduating students who took out loans to pay for school, and the average debt of those students. We also took into consideration how satisfied students were with the financial aid packages they received.

In a nutshell, the Top Ten Best Value Colleges—Public and Private lists names schools that we believe offer solid academics and enroll good students who are happy with the education they are receiving, and, additionally—and more importantly—do not have to mortgage their futures because their school is charging them way too much.

The schools appear in rank order, with #1 positions being the overall Best Value College—Public and Private.

THE SCHOOLS

AGNES SCOTT COLLEGE

141 East College Avenue, Atlanta/Decatur, GA 30030-3797
www.AgnesScott.edu • Admissions: 404-471-6285
Fax: 404-471-6414 • E-mail: admission@agnesscott.edu • Financial Aid: 404-471-6395

STUDENTS

Religious affiliation
                         Presbyterian
Academic year
   calendar   semester
Undergrad
   enrollment   875
% male/female   0/100
% Asian   5
% Black, non-Latino   19
% Latino   3
% international   7
% from out of state   54
% freshmen return for
sophomore year   84
% freshmen graduate
   within 4 years   60

STUDENT LIFE

% of students living
   on campus   92

ADMISSIONS

of applicants   1,526
% accepted   53
% enrolled   28
# of early decision/action
   applicants   78
% accepted early
   decision/action   17

HIGH SCHOOL UNITS RECOMMENDED

4 English, 3 math, 2 science
(2 science lab), 2 foreign
language, 2 social studies

ABOUT AGNES SCOTT COLLEGE

Founded in 1889, this liberal arts college for women has a small (100-acre) but exceptionally beautiful campus in Decatur, Georgia. Although it touts its academic achievements in the traditionally male-dominated fields of economics, mathematics, and hard sciences, the school has plenty to offer in the fields of English, foreign languages, psychology, religion, social sciences, visual and performing arts, and, of course, gender studies. Student satisfaction runs high here; the vast majority praises professors for their ability to make topics accessible and interesting, and for offering generous support during office hours while still managing to remember every student's name.

The student population, which is racially, religiously, and politically diverse, features every type from Old South–style debutantes to militant hippies to computer-game junkies. And while some groups may be more vocal than others, the atmosphere is one of general acceptance—a very good thing, as the average enrollment comes to about 1,000 per year and most students live in campus housing.

Outside of class, the vibe is bustling. The students are very self-motivated, and when they're not burning the midnight oil in McCain Library or comparing notes in group study sessions, they're out participating in a variety of extracurricular activities, from theater to charity work to a wide array of athletics (basketball, cross-country, soccer, tennis, swimming, and so on). What about partying, you ask? With the administration's strict rules regarding alcohol and after-hours decibel levels, there isn't much of it on campus. But those able to catch a ride (which isn't difficult—over 40 percent of students own a car) will find themselves mere minutes away from a little town called Atlanta, where the partying hasn't stopped since William Tecumseh Sherman's departure on November 15, 1864. Just don't forget the designated driver.

BANG FOR YOUR BUCK

Despite the widespread rise in the cost of higher education, Agnes Scott has managed to keep its tuition low. More importantly, the school is committed to finding every way possible to provide both need-based and merit-based financial support to its students. Over 50 percent of students receive hefty financial aid packages, and if you need an extra year of school, it's on the house (provided you've fulfilled your degree requirements and have a specific goal for another year of study). That's right—the fifth year's tuition is free.

Students Say

"Agnes Scott is not a college—it is a community of academics. That's how I knew it was for me!"

While merit-based scholarships take into account academic performance and in-school achievements, they also recognize involvement in community service and leadership activities. Merit-based financial aid packages weigh in at a hefty $13,000 on average. Prestigious scholarships include the renewable Presidential Scholarships (which completely cover tuition, room, and board), the Dean's Scholarships, Frances Winship Scholarships, and Agnes Scott Scholarships (which carry annual awards of $20,000, $10,000, and $5,000, respectively). They also offer several special-consideration scholarships, such as the Goizueta Foundation Scholarships, which give strong preference to Hispanic/Latina women and cover the full cost of tuition, room, and board, and the Agnes Scott Presbyterian Scholarships, which carry an award of $10,000 per year.

GETTING IN

On average, over half of all applicants are accepted. Admissions officers look for students who have taken four years of English, three of math, and at least two of science, foreign languages, and social studies. As with most schools, close attention is paid to grades, difficulty of high school classes, standardized test scores, the essay, recommendations, as well as demonstrated talents and personal qualities; secondary consideration is given to extracurricular activities, volunteer work, and work experience. Applicants must submit either SAT or ACT scores (for the latter a Writing Component is highly recommended, but not required). The average incoming freshman scores a composite 1220 on the former (Math and Critical Reading only) and a 26 on the latter. The average high school GPA is a 3.72.

WHAT DO GRADUATES DO?

Agnes Scott provides many resources to help students get a head start on their careers with numerous career fairs, resume workshops, and networking opportunities. The school also offers a variety of "externships"—a 40-hour week working on an assigned project in one's field of interest. Participating organizations include Amnesty International, BellSouth Communications, the High Museum of Art, and many more.

VERY IMPORTANT ADMISSION FACTORS

Academic GPA, application essay, character/personal qualities, class rank, recommendation(s), rigor of secondary school record, standardized test scores, talent/ability

IMPORTANT ADMISSION FACTORS

Extracurricular activities, volunteer work, work experience

Average HS GPA	3.72
Range SAT Verbal	570–685
Range SAT Math	540–650
Range ACT	24–29
Minimum TOEFL (paper/computer)	577/250

APPLICATION DEADLINES

Early decision	11/15
Early decision notification	12/15
# of transfer applicants	156
% of transfer applicants accepted	15

ACADEMICS

Student/faculty ratio	10:1
% faculty teaching undergraduates	98
% of classes taught by graduate students	0

MOST POPULAR MAJORS

- Biology/biological sciences
- English language and literature
- Psychology

Arts/fine arts, English (including composition), foreign languages, history, humanities, math, philosophy, sciences (biological or physical), social science

FINANCIAL INFO

Tuition	$25,100
Room & board	$8,990
Average book expense	$700
Required fees	$685
Average freshman need-based grant	$17,390
Average freshman need-based loan	$2,606
% of graduates who borrowed	71.1
Average indebtedness	$22,081

FINANCIAL AID FORMS

Students must submit FAFSA, provide previous year's tax return.

Financial Aid filing deadline	5/1

POSTGRAD

% going to graduate school	35
% going to law school	4
% going to business school	1
% going to medical school	2

CAREER SERVICES

Alumni network, alumni services, career assessment, career/job search classes, internships, on-campus job interviews.

In addition, the school welcomes recruiters for many high-powered businesses and graduate schools onto campus. Past recruiters have included, among others, Harvard Divinity School, IBM, the Bryn Mawr School of Social Work, the Savannah School of Art and Design, the FBI, the John Marshall Law School, and—always keeping an eye out for fresh talent—Anheuser-Busch. Those graduates who elect not to pursue higher degrees tend to land jobs in the medical and financial fields, publishing, art, and education. Seniors who receive their first job offer or acceptance to a graduate school are invited to ring their own bells—literally—Fridays at noon in the bell tower.

THE BOTTOM LINE

The school meets over 96 percent of the financial needs of those students who are awarded need-based aid, with over 74 percent of it coming from scholarships and grants, leaving these students, on average, with a trim $1,805 annual out-of-pocket expense. Those who cannot demonstrate financial need receive significant help as well, leaving them with $7,710 to pay per year. Students can expect to pay an additional $685 for required fees and $8,990 for room and board, and a combined $2,500 or so for books and supplies, transportation, and miscellaneous expenses.

FUN FACTS

You might say the campus is so beautiful it's scary—*Scream II*, among other movies, was filmed there.

The school is home to the Blackfriars, the oldest continuously operating theater group in or around Atlanta. Until 1930, when men were first allowed to participate, women played the male roles.

Robert Frost regularly visited the school for nearly 30 years. A statue of him stands in the Alumnae Garden and McCain Library houses one of the finest collections of his works.

Ever since 1936, students have been tossing their newly engaged classmates into the Alumnae Garden pond.

Black Cat, a tradition begun in 1915, is a week filled with assorted zany activities, from dressing up as the school mascot (yes, the aforementioned black cat) to bell-ringing to pranks to a field day to bonfires (sorry, all you pyromaniacs—this is a safely contained conflagration).

ALBION COLLEGE

611 East Porter, Albion, MI 49224
www.Albion.edu • Admissions: 517-629-0321
Fax: 517-629-0569 • E-mail: admissions@albion.edu • Financial Aid: 517-629-0440

STUDENTS

Religious affiliation
Methodist
Academic year
calendar   semester
Undergrad
enrollment   1,953
% male/female   44/56
% Asian   2
% Black, non-Latino   4
% Latino   1
% Native American   1
% international   1
% from out of state   10
% freshmen return for
sophomore year   86
% freshmen graduate
within 4 years   67

STUDENT LIFE

% of students living
on campus   99
% in fraternities   32
% in sororities   32

ADMISSIONS

of applicants   1,946
% accepted   82
% enrolled   36

HIGH SCHOOL UNITS REQUIRED

4 English, 3 math, 3
science (1 science lab), 3
social studies, 3 history

HIGH SCHOOL UNITS RECOMMENDED

4 English, 3 math, 3
science, 3 foreign language,
3 social studies, 3 history

ABOUT ALBION COLLEGE

A welcoming campus, approachable professors, and an active student body greet newcomers at Michigan's Albion College. The small liberal arts school with Methodist ties is a veritable training ground for tomorrow's doctors, dentists, politicians, and businesspeople. And many of the 131 professors who teach them are almost as likely to be seen at sports games, arts shows, and other campus events as in the classroom. You could say they take the lead from Albion's highly visible president who makes a habit of mingling with students.

With a student/faculty ratio of thirteen to one and the most frequent class size between ten and nineteen students, it's hard to get lost in the crowd. Economics and psychology are the most popular majors and Albion's commitment to academic excellence is obvious in classrooms where professors prove themselves a dedicated bunch. Simply put: You'll never struggle through a course here with an inept graduate assistant at the helm.

While it's no party school, students love Albion's vibrant campus, which offers plenty of opportunities to meet new people, serve the community, get in shape, and develop leadership skills. More than 40 percent of the college's 1,900 students participate in varsity athletics. And Greek life is strong with almost a third of the campus bonding, volunteering, and keg-standing with a dozen fraternities and sororities. Gatherings large and small keep things interesting despite a shortage of things to do off campus beyond trips to the local movie theater. Plus, there are more than 100 campus organizations—from the canoe club to the Student Volunteer Bureau—to keep students busy.

BANG FOR YOUR BUCK

Albion College prides itself on working hand in hand with students and parents to develop the best financial aid package for each individual. Communication concerning the lengthy investigation of each candidate's financial need and external scholarships and awards comes early and often. Moreover, the college aims for a stress-free discovery process that uncovers all academic information, notable achievements, financial need, and other factors required to calculate aid or qualify for academic and talent-based scholarships.

"The greatest strength of Albion is that it is a clean, safe, and friendly place. I honestly feel like the faculty and staff want you to be happy here, and that they will go beyond the normal call of duty to see that you are enjoying yourself and preparing yourself for the future."

VERY IMPORTANT ADMISSION FACTORS

Academic GPA, character/personal qualities, interview, recommendation(s), rigor of secondary school record, volunteer work

IMPORTANT ADMISSION FACTORS

Application essay, extracurricular activities, standardized test scores, talent/ability

Average HS GPA   3.55
Range SAT Verbal 520–645
Range SAT Math   540–670
Range ACT   22–27
Minimum TOEFL
  (paper/computer) 550/270

APPLICATION DEADLINES

Regular admission   3/1
Regular notification   rolling
# of transfer applicants   93
% of transfer applicants
  accepted   52

ACADEMICS

Student/faculty ratio   13:1
% faculty teaching
  undergraduates   100
% of classes taught by
  graduate students   0

MOST POPULAR MAJORS

• Biology/biological sciences
      • Economics
      • Psychology

Ultimately, Albion helps students fund their private educations with a generous helping of scholarships and financial aid. The school gave nearly $20 million in scholarship and grant dollars for the 2005–2006 school year. Sixty percent of Albion undergraduates receive some form of need-based aid, and Albion fully met the needs of 60 percent of that population without loans. On average, the school met 94 percent of need for students who were awarded need-based aid. Albion students filled the narrow gap with low interest loans, work-study jobs, and alternative payment plans. The college also offers several academic scholarships that range from $10,000 to full tuition and are awarded without regard to need.

GETTING IN

Excellent high school achievement is a major factor for admissions at this college. The average GPA for Albion's 2005 class was 3.54. But it's not enough to do well in less-than-rigorous classes because the admissions office looks for students who have challenged themselves with advanced-placement and honors-level courses. Admissions staff also considers how students spend their time outside of the classroom, be it participating in sports, delving into the arts, or giving a helping hand to those in need. And don't discount the power of a well-written personal essay—Albion values them highly for additional insight into what motivates and inspires admission candidates. Other important factors include, not surprisingly, an interest in Albion. If possible, visit the campus, meet with faculty, and talk with admissions counselors.

What do Graduates Do?

Albion's career development office strives to help students "put your liberal arts education to work." And many alumni who turned to the department for help in picking a major, finding an internship, preparing for graduate school, and getting a job were not disappointed. Albion graduates have wound up working in cost analysis, intelligence, foreign trade analysis, and urban planning for government agencies. They have also headed into the corporate world as analysts and consultants with market research firms, consumer goods companies, and consulting firms. Others found positions in human resources, hospitality, sales, and health care management while some opted to take jobs in counseling, advocacy, case management, community relations, and mental health services after graduation.

The Bottom Line

The estimated cost of attending Albion College for the 2005–2006 school year was $35,018, including tuition of $25,668. Room and board ran about $7,496 in addition to required fees of $454, books and supplies of $700 and transportation and personal expenses of $700. The average out-of-pocket cost for need-based financial aid recipients in 2005–2006 was approximately $8,404.

Fun Facts

Albion graduates have made significant strides in the arts and entertainment, medicine, business and government. Notable alumni include Richard Smith, chairman and editor-in-chief of *Newsweek;* Michael David, Broadway producer; Dr. James Wilson, director of the Human Gene Therapy Institute; and David Camp, member of the U.S. House of Representatives.

EDUCATION REQUIREMENTS

Arts/fine arts, humanities, sciences (biological or physical), social science; students complete courses in 5 modes of inquiry and 4 categories of learning(see catalog).

FINANCIAL INFO

Tuition	$25,668
Room & board	$7,496
Average book expense	$700
Required fees	$454
Average freshman need-based grant	$17,560
Average freshman need-based loan	$3,373
% of graduates who borrowed	63
Average indebtedness	$23,010

FINANCIAL AID FORMS

Students must submit FAFSA.

Financial Aid filing deadline	3/1

POSTGRAD

% going to graduate school	38
% going to law school	6
% going to business school	1
% going to medical school	15

AMHERST COLLEGE

Campus Box 2231, PO Box 5000, Amherst, MA 01002
www.Amherst.edu • Admissions: 413-542-2328
Fax: 413-542-2040 • E-mail: admission@amherst.edu • Financial Aid: 413-542-2296

STUDENTS

Religious affiliation
                 No Affiliation
Academic year
  calendar   semester
Undergrad
  enrollment   1,612
% male/female   52/48
% Asian   13
% Black, non-Latino   9
% Latino   6
% international   7
% from out of state   87
% freshmen return for
sophomore year   97
% freshmen graduate
  within 4 years   89

STUDENT LIFE

% of students living
  on campus   97

ADMISSIONS

of applicants   6,284
% accepted   19
% enrolled   37
# of early decision/action
  applicants   364
% accepted early
  decision/action   35

HIGH SCHOOL UNITS RECOMMENDED

4 English, 4 math, 3 science
(1 science lab), 4 foreign
language, 2 social studies, 2
history

ABOUT AMHERST COLLEGE

Amherst College, a lush 1,000-acre campus bordering Amherst, Massachusetts (population: 35,000), has long distinguished itself among the best liberal arts colleges in the nation. Students love the intellectual atmosphere fostered by friendly and supportive faculty members. The school is also surprisingly diverse; minorities make up 37 percent (as of Fall 2006) of the student body. Amherst students come from nearly every state and over forty countries, meaning that the world is literally at its doorstep.

The school has institutionalized the exploratory vibe with a virtually requirement-free curriculum that gives students unprecedented academic freedom. The school offers a bachelor's of arts degree in thirty-three areas of study—from chemistry to classics—and doesn't make any particular courses mandatory. What's more, it encourages students to invent a major that suits their individual interests. One in four Amherst students creates an interdisciplinary major like third world development or comparative literature. They can even attend courses at neighboring colleges: Smith, Mount Holyoke, Hampshire, and University of Massachusetts—Amherst.

Whether in a classroom, coffee shop, or sports arena, you'll find students engaged in lively (and sometimes heated) discussions concerning politics, environmental issues, ethics, and philosophy. Debate is a part of the Amherst culture, and ambitious students are eager to share their perspectives and hear those of others. Approximately 43 percent of Amherst students also pack their bags during their junior year to explore other cultures in Africa, Asia, Europe, the Middle East, and elsewhere in study abroad programs. For those who remain campus-bound, Amherst's student government funds 100 student-run clubs, activities, and associations from a cappella groups to the snowboarding team that serve every interest. A word to the toga-inclined: Greek life is nonexistent at Amherst, as social life is varied, and students find it easier to fit in. The fact that Amherst has just one dining hall also brings students together.

Bang for Your Buck

Amherst College backs its commitment to diversity with a need-blind admissions process that ensures that the best students, regardless of their financial circumstances, can attend the school. Amherst guarantees financial aid equal to financial need, making college accessible to many who thought they couldn't afford higher education. Income from the school's hefty endowment and donor gifts subsidize an Amherst education for everyone. The college estimates that the true cost per student exceeds $75,000. The school gave $23.6 million in grants and scholarships for the 2005–2006 academic year with 48 percent of undergraduates receiving some form of aid.

Getting In

Amherst makes no secret of its pursuit of a multidimensional student body. The school looks for intellectually gifted candidates from a variety of ethnic groups, races, and social classes. The admissions staff reviews each application thoroughly, paying the most attention to prospective students' high school transcripts. They consider standardized test scores, letters of recommendation, and essays, but believe that the difficulty of high school courses and student performance in them is most informative. Admissions counselors view International Baccalaureate, advanced placement, and college course work taken in high school favorably. Interviews are not offered for prospective students, but campus visits are encouraged.

What do Graduates Do?

The school's extraordinary alumni donations illustrate graduates' satisfaction with their Amherst experiences—nearly 70 percent of graduates give back to the school annually. That impressive alumni network is also a godsend for students in the hunt for internship and job opportunities. Many students say alums helped them get great gigs in stellar locations. Most Amherst alumni eventually move on to advanced study through graduate or professional schools before fully launching careers in law, medicine, business, and education.

VERY IMPORTANT ADMISSION FACTORS

Academic GPA, application essay, character/personal qualities, extracurricular activities, first generation, recommendation(s), rigor of secondary school record, standardized test scores, talent/ability

IMPORTANT ADMISSION FACTORS

Alumni/ae relation, class rank, volunteer work

Average HS GPA	
Range SAT Verbal	670–780
Range SAT Math	680–780
Range ACT	29–33
Minimum TOEFL (paper/computer)	600/250

APPLICATION DEADLINES

Early decision	11/15
Early decision notification	12/15
Regular admission	1/1
Regular notification	4/5
# of transfer applicants	168
% of transfer applicants accepted	15

ACADEMICS

Student/faculty ratio	8:1
% faculty teaching undergraduates	100
% of classes taught by graduate students	0

MOST POPULAR MAJORS

- Economics
- English language and
literature
- Political science and
government

EDUCATION REQUIREMENTS

Amherst offers an open
curriculum with no core or
distribution requirements.

FINANCIAL INFO

Tuition	$34,280
Room & board	$9,080
Average book	
expense	$1,000
Required fees	$636
Average freshman	
need-based grant	$29,373
Average freshman	
need-based loan	$1,620
% of graduates	
who borrowed	47
Average	
indebtedness	$12,109

FINANCIAL AID FORMS

Students must submit
FAFSA, CSS/financial aid
profile, noncustodial (divorced/
separated) parent's statement,
business/farm supplement,
income documentation (tax
forms, W-2's).

POSTGRAD

% going to	
graduate school	33
% going to	
law school	9
% going to	
medical school	10

CAREER SERVICES

Alumni network, alumni
services, career/job search
classes, career assessment,
internships, regional
alumni, on-campus job
interviews. Off-campus job
opportunities are good.

THE BOTTOM LINE

The estimated cost of attending Amherst College for the 2005–2006 school
year was $47,296. The breakdown is as follows: $34,280 for tuition, room
and board at about $9,080, required fees of $636, $1000 for books and sup-
plies, and transportation and personal expenses estimated at $2,300. For
the 48 percent of Amherst students who received financial aid, a flawless
100 percent of need was met.

FUN FACTS

Amherst doesn't let its small size determine its global influence. The liberal arts
powerhouse has produced a U.S. Supreme Court chief justice, Harlan Fiske Stone;
a U.S. president, Calvin Coolidge; and several Nobel laureates and Pulitzer Prize
winners. Amherst has even educated a president of another country—1981 graduate Francisco Flores led El Salvador from 1999 to 2004.

The college has fostered the development of noteworthy writers as well. Screen-
play writer Susannah Grant penned *Erin Brockovich* and *Pocahontas*, and author
Dan Brown caused a book-selling and -burning fury with *The Da Vinci Code*.

APPALACHIAN STATE UNIVERSITY

Office of Admissions, PO Box 32004, Boone, NC 28608-2004
www.AppState.edu • Admissions: 828-262-2120
Fax: 828-262-3296 • E-mail: admissions@appstate.edu • Financial Aid: 828-262-2190

STUDENTS

Religious affiliation
No Affiliation
Academic year
calendar   semester
Undergrad
enrollment   13,447
% male/female   50/50
% Asian   1
% Black, non-Latino   3
% Latino   2
% from out of state   9
% freshmen return for
sophomore year   86
% freshmen graduate
within 4 years   37

STUDENT LIFE

% of students living
on campus   38
% in fraternities   8
% in sororities   9

ADMISSIONS

of applicants   10,419
% accepted   69
% enrolled   38

HIGH SCHOOL UNITS REQUIRED

4 English, 4 math, 3 science
(1 science lab), 2 foreign
language, 1 social studies, 1
history

VERY IMPORTANT ADMISSION FACTORS

Academic GPA, class rank,
rigor of secondary school
record, standardized test
scores

ABOUT APPALACHIAN STATE UNIVERSITY

Appalachian State University is the mountain retreat home of 12,936 outdoor-loving, environmentally conscious undergraduates who enjoy hiking, fishing, hunting, and a bit of white-water rafting. Students agree that watching the sun rise above the mountaintops is the perfect way to start the day in Boone, North Carolina. Challenging courses, accessible faculty, and welcoming administrators are among its other treasures—not to mention more than 170 degree programs available through the College of Arts & Sciences, College of Fine and Applied Arts, Hayes School of Music, Reich College of Education, and Walker College of Business. The student/faculty ratio is 19:1, and professors take their roles as educators beyond the classroom to serve as mentors and advisors within a cohesive community. Students have 1,500 courses to choose from during their time at Appalachian, where the average class has fewer than 25 students. In addition, the school offers programs in New York, Washington, Paris, and London.

Though lacking somewhat in diversity (the majority of its students are white and hail from North Carolina), Appalachian charges itself with bringing the best and brightest entertainers to Boone, such as Dave Matthews, Bob Dylan, and Wynton Marsalis, all of whom recently put on shows at the school. The school also boasts an impressive array of 300 student activities from the Appalachian Popular Programming Society—which allows students to plan and market campus films and concerts—to student-run art galleries and rock-climbing clubs. Sororities and fraternities also add to the social mix: About 9 percent of students take part in Greek life. Blue Ridge Parkway (only 10 minutes away) and several ski slopes (an easy half-hour's drive) are popular day-trip destinations. And for those who want to spend some time in the big city, the school offers programs in New York and Washington, DC.

Average HS GPA   3.74
Range SAT Verbal   510–600
Range SAT Math   530–620
Range ACT   20–25
Minimum TOEFL
  (paper/computer) 500/173

APPLICATION DEADLINES

Regular notification   9/1
# of transfer
  applicants   1,504
% of transfer applicants
  accepted   88

ACADEMICS

Student/faculty ratio   17:1
% faculty teaching
  undergraduates   98
% of classes taught by
  graduate students   1

MOST POPULAR MAJORS

• Business
• Education
• Communications/journalism
• Psychology

EDUCATION REQUIREMENTS

Arts/fine arts, computer literacy, English (including composition), history, humanities, math, sciences (biological or physical), social science, physical activity/wellness

BANG FOR YOUR BUCK

North Carolinians benefit from bargain-basement tuition as a result of the state's constitution that guarantees reasonably priced college education to residents. Out-of-state students can't take advantage of the government-mandated, in-state student tuition steal, but their tuition is still more than competitive by national standards.

Appalachian awarded $17.6 million in scholarships and grants for the 2005–2006 school year in its quest to eliminate financial barriers to education. Its admissions counselors guided thousands of students toward a mix of scholarships, financial aid, and student work to cover their education costs. About 30 percent of students receive need-based aid and 40 percent of those students have their need fully met. The school also awards more than $2 million of merit-based scholarships to particularly motivated and talented students. Lastly, about 7 percent of Appalachian students were awarded non-need-based scholarship or grant money.

GETTING IN

Strong high school performance is a prerequisite for entrance at Appalachian. The average high school grade-point average for Appalachian's 2005 class was 3.73. Class rank and standardized test scores are also given careful consideration by the admissions staff. The average SAT score was 1101 and the average ACT score was 25. Recommendations from school counselors and teachers, student essays, and extracurricular activities are reviewed, but given less emphasis. Interviews are not considered.

What do Graduates Do?

Many Appalachian students become teachers. More education majors graduate from the Reich College of Education than from any other North Carolina campus, and about 16 percent of the state's new teachers are trained in Boone. Others choose to enter the corporate world in sales, marketing, and management positions. Companies including Ameriprise Financial, BB&T Corporation, Bobcats Sports and Entertainment, Crown Plaza Resort, Duke Energy, Eaton Corporation, and Progressive Insurance all recruit Appalachian students during events hosted by the career development center. Still others head down entrepreneurial paths, like the two 2006 graduates who sold their e-commerce idea to an Atlanta interactive marketing firm, fetching a more than tidy sum of half a million dollars.

The Bottom Line

Appalachian State University is a real bargain for in-state students who paid about $12,636 for the 2005–2006 academic year. Tuition cost them $2,221. Out-of-staters didn't fare so badly, either, with costs totaling approximately $22,378. Their estimated tuition costs were $11,963, while room and board averaged about $5,760. Students can also expect to spend $1,966 on required fees, $436 on books and supplies, and $2,253 on transportation and personal expenses. Upon graduating, the average Appalachian student has accumulated about $15,574 in undergraduate debt.

Fun Facts

Each year, the school hosts the Appalachian Summer Festival, a celebration of regional artists and a multitude of artistic media. The event, which has run for more than 20 seasons, strives to introduce new audiences to fine art. The picturesque mountains provide a memorable backdrop for this award-winning event that attracts around 25,000 people annually.

Appalachian's student-led Outdoor Programs organizes dozens of adventurous excursions throughout the year, such as kayak touring, rock climbing, backpacking, hiking, and rafting.

FINANCIAL INFO

In-state tuition	$2,221
Out-of-state tuition	$11,963
Room & board	$5,760
Average book expense	$436
Required fees	$1,966
Average freshman need-based grant	$5,040
Average freshman need-based loan	$2,489
% of graduates who borrowed	52
Average indebtedness	$15,574

FINANCIAL AID FORMS

Students must submit FAFSA.

ARIZONA STATE UNIVERSITY— TEMPE, POLYTECHNIC, AND WEST

Box 870112, Tempe, AZ 85287-0112
www.ASU.edu • Admissions: 480-965-7788
Fax: 480-965-3610 • E-mail: ugradinq@asu.edu • Financial Aid: 480-965-3355

STUDENTS

Religious affiliation
                    No Affiliation
Academic year
   calendar   semester
Undergrad
   enrollment   39,649
% male/female   49/51
% Asian   5
% Black, non-Latino   4
% Latino   13
% Native American   2
% international   3
% from out of state   24
% freshmen return for
sophomore year   79
% freshmen graduate within
4 years   27

STUDENT LIFE

% of students living
   on campus   14
% in fraternities   6
% in sororities   6

ADMISSIONS

of applicants   19,914
% accepted   91
% enrolled   43

HIGH SCHOOL UNITS REQUIRED

4 English, 4 math, 3 science
(3 science lab), 2 foreign
language, 1 social studies, 1
history, 1 fine arts

ABOUT ARIZONA STATE UNIVERSITY— TEMPE, POLYTECHNIC, AND WEST

Established on a Tempe cow pasture back in 1885, and originally intended as an institution for the training of public school teachers, Arizona State University has seen almost unimaginable growth and change in its 120-year history. Enrolling over 60,000 undergraduate, graduate, and professional students on three campuses across the state, ASU has become a leading research institution that now trumpets itself as a pioneering prototype of the "New American University."

Despite its forward-looking philosophy, Arizona State certainly offers plenty of access to traditional big-college experiences. Its enormously popular Division I sports teams are often Pac 10 powerhouses, and the centerpieces of a very active campus social scene of academic clubs, social clubs, and fraternities and sororities. The apparent dichotomy doesn't bother students—most list it as a plus, adding that most undergrads find the perfect balance between fun and school. Bars, clubs, and parties are available for the festive minded, while a superior education (including a well-regarded Honors College) is just as accessible for the more serious student. Generally, most students buckle down after their first couple years of fun and hit the books just as hard as they hit the party scene as underclassmen.

ASU students are as image-conscious as the administration. While the campus and facilities are superb and cutting edge—as befits a top research institution—working out and looking good are student priorities on this image-conscious campus. And with warm, desert sunshine nearly every day of the year, why shouldn't it be so?

BANG FOR YOUR BUCK

Arizona State University is affordable—it's the law. We're actually not joking: According to state law, ASU's resident tuition must remain among the lowest third in the nation. With the law on your side, it's not hard to find a good deal. And the administration is not content to sit on its laurels, either—university aid grants have increased 157 percent in the last two years alone. In addition, ASU has just launched ASU Advantage, a new program for Arizona's low-income families. This program provides financial aid to cover a student's direct cost of attendance (tuition and fees, books, and room and board) and does not need to be repaid.

"Many students pay more attention to the college lifestyle and partying more so than studying, at least for the first year or two. As they get older, they take their studies more seriously and seek internships and professional development."

ASU is also serious about using its purse strings to lure top-notch students to Tempe. National Merit, National Hispanic, and National Achievement Scholars are offered generous scholarship packages ($12,500 annually for in-staters, $21,500 annually for out-of-staters.) Top students from Arizona and from all over the country are eligible for merit-based scholarships ranging from $2,000–$9,000 per year.

GETTING IN

With 76 percent of its students from Arizona, there is no mistaking it: Arizona State is first and foremost a state school, and residency definitely helps your chances of admission. That being said, ASU does make an effort to enroll top out-of-state students as well. Aside from where you live, admissions officers are particularly interested in your high school transcript and class rank, with standardized test performance also playing an important role. Outstanding students can apply to the Barrett Honors College within ASU, a small, selective undergraduate college in its own separate community that is modeled after British university systems. Students that enter Barrett average 1310 on their SATs, compared to the 1106 average found in the regular undergraduate program.

WHAT DO GRADUATES DO?

This past year, more than 600 companies recruited ASU students for jobs in fields ranging from financial services and accounting to the aerospace and computer industries. Major employers include Wells Fargo, Honeywell, Intel, and Motorola.

VERY IMPORTANT ADMISSION FACTORS

Academic GPA, class rank, standardized test scores

IMPORTANT ADMISSION FACTORS

State residency

Average HS GPA	3.3
Range SAT Verbal	490–610
Range SAT Math	500–620
Range ACT	20–26
Minimum TOEFL (paper/computer)	500/173

APPLICATION DEADLINES

# of transfer applicants	12,298
% of transfer applicants accepted	65

ACADEMICS

Student/faculty ratio	22:1
% faculty teaching undergraduates	NA

MOST POPULAR MAJORS

- Business administration and management
- Journalism
- Psychology

EDUCATION REQUIREMENTS

Arts/fine arts, computer literacy, English (including composition), foreign languages, history, humanities, math, sciences (biological or physical), social science

FINANCIAL INFO

In-state tuition $4,591
Out-of-state tuition $15,750
Room & board $6,900
Average book
  expense $950
Required fees $97
Average freshman
  need-based grant $6,727
Average freshman
  need-based loan $2,489
% of graduates
  who borrowed   53
Average
  indebtedness $17,358

FINANCIAL AID FORMS
Students must submit
FAFSA.

POSTGRAD

CAREER SERVICES
Alumni services, career/job
search classes, career
assessment, internships,
on-campus job interviews.
Off-campus job opportuni-
ties are excellent.

THE BOTTOM LINE

Arizona State provides financial aid on both a need and merit basis, with 51 percent of the student body receiving some sort of financial aid. Grants, loans, scholarships, and student employment combine to meet student financial needs (in-staters currently pay $4,591
for tuition, while out-of-staters pay $15,750. Room and board is an
additional $6,900). In addition to federal grants, ASU offers two uni-
versity-funded grants (the University and ASU grants),which can total
an additional $3,000. The school has increased the funding for these
grants 157 percent over the past two years.

FUN FACTS

Sparky the Sun Devil, the university mascot, was created by the late Berk
Anthony, an artist for Walt Disney.

The original campus for Arizona State was a 20-acre cow pasture donated
by the leading citizens of Tempe. Now, the university possesses three campuses, with a fourth currently being created in downtown Phoenix.

BATES COLLEGE

23 Campus Avenue, Lindholm House, Lewiston, ME 04240
www.Bates.edu • Admissions: 207-786-6000
Fax: 207-786-6025 • E-mail: • Financial Aid: 207-786-6096

STUDENTS

Religious affiliation
                        No Affiliation
Academic year
  calendar   other
Undergrad
  enrollment   1,684
% male/female   49/51
% Asian   4
% Black, non-Latino   3
% Latino   2
% international   5
% from out of state   89
% freshmen return for
sophomore year   94
% freshmen graduate
  within 4 years   84

STUDENT LIFE

% of students living
  on campus   93

ADMISSIONS

of applicants   4,356
% accepted   29
% enrolled   39
# of early decision/action
  applicants   466
% accepted early
  decision/action   44

HIGH SCHOOL UNITS REQUIRED

4 English, 3 math, 3 science
(2 science lab), 2 foreign
language, 3 social studies/
history

HIGH SCHOOL UNITS RECOMMENDED

4 English, 4 math, 4 science
(3 science lab), 4 foreign
language, 4 social studies/
history

ABOUT BATES COLLEGE

Bates College is a small school that offers the happy, tight-knit, academically challenging atmosphere that every liberal arts school wants you to think it offers. A nifty 4-4-1 calendar—two conventional semesters in the fall and spring and a short, single-class term in May—keeps a brisk academic pace. The short term provides students with opportunities to study less traditional topics or to intern or study off-campus in cool and exotic locales. The Administration at Bates, while far from universally praised, goes out of its way to include students in almost every single administrative committee, including search committees for new professors.

Bates draws many students from New England. In addition to normal kids who receive oodles of financial aid, there are large contingents of granola types, trustifarians, and excessively rich preppies. Everybody is very academically driven, and left-wing politics run rampant (although a sizable and effective Republican organization drew an election-year thank you visit from the Bush twins). Bates has never had a Greek system, leaving the students to mingle in a friendly and inclusive atmosphere. The campus is beautiful, especially during fall. Winter is good for snowball fights, or anything else that involves large quantities of snow. Bates also has good food and an abundance of extracurricular activities, including lectures, seminars, performances, and lots of clubs. Intercollegiate and intramural sports are also popular. The hometown of Lewiston doesn't offer many fun activities for the college crowd (unless your idea of fun is shopping at Patagonia, J.Crew, and L.L. Bean outlets, in which case—welcome to a little slice of heaven). On weekends, Bates students participate in many outdoor activities and throw their fair share of parties.

BANG FOR YOUR BUCK

Financial aid awarded at Bates is need-based, and the school does a laudable job meeting the full financial need of its students. In addition, Bates keeps student loans affordable, aiming for no more than $3,500 per year for each individual student. Perhaps most importantly, Bates has an outside scholarship policy you are going to love; students who are awarded non-Bates scholarships are not penalized. In most cases, financial aid grants are not reduced because of outside awards you receive. Bates also provides institutional aid to students for study abroad programs so that everybody—not just the rich kids—enjoys the same opportunities overseas, especially during the short term. Bates provides financial aid for the short term over and above the regular financial aid package, which shows how much the school values it.

Students Say

"The small school atmosphere makes it feel very homey, the campus is beautiful, and the academic opportunities are incredible."

VERY IMPORTANT ADMISSION FACTORS

Academic GPA, application essay, character/personal qualities, class rank, extracurricular activities, interview, level of applicant's interest, recommendation(s), rigor of secondary school record, talent/ability

Range SAT Verbal 640–710
Range SAT Math 640–700
Minimum TOEFL
(paper/computer) 637/270

APPLICATION DEADLINES

Early decision   11/15
Early decision
  notification   12/20
Regular admission   1/1
Regular notification   3/31
# of transfer applicants 149
% of transfer applicants
  accepted   28

ACADEMICS

Student/faculty ratio   10:1
% faculty teaching
  undergraduates   100
% of classes taught by
  graduate students   0

MOST POPULAR MAJORS

• Economics
• Political science and government
• Psychology

EDUCATION REQUIREMENTS

Humanities, math, sciences (biological or physical), social science

Research grants and other awards outside of the regular financial-aid program also are available. The Arthur Crafts Service Awards (for students who design a service internship with a social service organization or undertake an academic research project dealing with community issues) are especially worth checking. Bates Summer Research Apprenticeships provide stipends and room and board for students in all majors who work directly with Bates faculty members on intensive research projects during the summer.

GETTING IN

The average SAT score of first-year students at Bates College is a little under 1,350, although Bates is one of only a few schools of its caliber that does not require applicants to submit test scores. Average grades are also really good. Therefore, you face some pretty stiff competition for the 400 or so spots in each first-year class. The application includes a counselor evaluation, two teacher evaluations, a personal statement, and biographical information concerning extracurricular interests. You'll also notice that additional writing samples, other evidence of creative ability, and information about your athletic accomplishments are encouraged. If you have the opportunity at this point in your academic career, start enrolling in AP courses with abandon, and do very well in them if you want to get admitted to a school like Bates.

WHAT DO GRADUATES DO?

Over two-thirds of Bates graduates eventually attend law school, medical school, or graduate school and earn an advanced degree. In keeping with the true tradition of a liberal arts education, Bates graduates work in a wide variety of fields with no one field taking center stage. Trust us: A degree from Bates is a credential that will open many doors for you down the road. A few companies that hire Bates graduates include American Express, Fleet Boston Financial, Liberty Mutual, Pfizer, and—the largest single employer, with more than 50 Bates hires in the last three years—IBM.

The Bottom Line

The average yearly grant package is $24,369 and about 650 students receive them. In addition to grants, a typical financial aid package includes a loan ranging from $2,500 to $3,500 and work-study ranging between $1,600 and $1,800. If your family's annual income is $16,000 per year, your contribution would be about $3,000. If your family's annual income is $130,000 per year, your contribution increases to about $21,000. Graduates who borrow money accumulate an average loan debt of approximately $13,636.

Fun Facts

During the short term, students take just one course for five weeks. Typical offerings have included studying geology while sea kayaking along the Maine coast, studying food from ancient Greece and Rome (a course that ends with a Roman banquet), and investigating issues of economic growth and environmental protection in China.

WRBC, Bates's radio station, is beloved by students and very experimental. Among other things, it has aired a first-of-its-kind radio version of *King Lear* that was produced by the student theater group.

On Jazz Nights, physics professor John Smedley organizes late-night jazz jam sessions.

A hallowed, bone-chilling tradition called the Puddle Jump began in 1975 when several Bates students cut a hole in the ice on Lake Andrews, donned bathing suits, and took a bracing dip on St. Patrick's Day. The ritual now includes a Dip Master—the annually-appointed grand pooh-bah of the polar plunge—who cuts the hole in the ice with the same ax used for the original puddle jump. Just before midnight, participants gather in the basement of a nearby dorm to hear the Dip Master read from the "Dip Book," which contains a letter from the ritual founders as well as the names of Dip Masters past. We are *not* making this up.

FINANCIAL INFO

Average book
  expense $1,150
Average freshman
  need-based grant $24,369
Average freshman
  need-based loan $3,282
% of graduates
  who borrowed   46
Average
  indebtedness $13,636

FINANCIAL AID FORMS

Students must submit FAFSA, CSS/financial aid profile, noncustodial (divorced/separated) parent's statement, business/farm supplement.
Financial Aid
  filing deadline   2/1

BELOIT COLLEGE

700 College Street, Beloit, WI 53511
www.Beloit.edu • Admissions: 608-363-2500
Fax: 608-363-2075 • E-mail: admiss@beloit.edu • Financial Aid: 608-363-2500

STUDENTS

Religious affiliation
                 No Affiliation
Academic year
  calendar   semester
Undergrad
  enrollment   1,328
% male/female   41/59
% Asian   3
% Black, non-Latino   3
% Latino   2
% Native American   1
% international   5
% from out of state   82
% freshmen return for
sophomore year   89
% freshmen graduate
within 4 years   62

STUDENT LIFE

% of students living
  on campus   93
% in fraternities   15
% in sororities   5

ADMISSIONS

of applicants   2,054
% accepted   64
% enrolled   25

HIGH SCHOOL UNITS RECOMMENDED

4 English, 4 math, 3
science, 2 foreign language,
4 social studies, 4 history

VERY IMPORTANT ADMISSION FACTORS

Application essay,
recommendation(s), rigor of
secondary school record

ABOUT BELOIT COLLEGE

The student body at Beloit College includes many liberal, politically active, independent thinkers who don't aim to fit in. Voting drives and petition campaigns are par for the course here. The curriculum supports students' independent streaks and encourages them to explore their own interests and even create interdisciplinary majors to delve further into them. Diversity is a part of the Beloit mix: Minorities and international students make up about 14 percent of the student body and 82 percent of students are from outside of Wisconsin. In addition, roughly half of all students study abroad for a semester or longer to learn more about other cultures.

The vast majority of students live on campus and this helps foster relationships with faculty members. Plus, the student/faculty ratio is 11:1 and the average class size is 15 students. Beloit students maintain good relationships with engaging professors who are eager to challenge students to a higher level of excellence.

Six fraternities and sororities throw parties nearly every weekend. But Greek life is far from predominant. Only 15 percent of students are in fraternities; 5 percent are in sororities. There are about 100 other registered organizations and social outlets at Beloit, including a full range of Division III athletics. Students attend guest lectures, produce theater, and catch live bands at the Coughy Haus, a popular campus haunt. Those looking for a low-key evening are often found at the Java Joint, where chess, board games, and puzzles keep students occupied for hours. And those in need of a little concrete and neon are always happy to find Madison, Milwaukee, and Chicago only a few hours away.

BANG FOR YOUR BUCK

For the 2005–2006 school year, Beloit forked out more than $17 million in scholarships and grants to fulfill its pledge to meet every admitted student's full financial need. The college gives no consideration to finances during the admissions process, and the average need-based financial aid package totals $15,676. Nearly 80 percent of freshmen and 77 percent of undergraduates receive need-based financial aid. The average freshman takes out loans totaling $3,364 for the first year of college. Beloit also awards more than $13 million annually in merit-based scholarships for stellar academic performance, leadership potential, music or theater talent, and minority status.

"There is no typical Beloit student. The minute you think you can make a Beloit stereotype—*Bam!*—someone will break the mold. The only stereotype that may apply is [that] the majority of Beloit students are very accepting and unphased by even the most atypical of students. We get all types here, and magically, we'll all get along and even like each other!"

Getting In

The Beloit admissions staff zigzags across the country to find potential students with the right mix of intellectual curiosity and personality. In 2006, admissions interviews were held in locations as widespread as Phoenix, Philadelphia, Boston, and Iowa City. High school academic performance, letters of recommendation from teachers and school counselors, and personal essays rank highly on the list of factors admissions counselors take into account. Standardized test scores are also considered. The average SAT score is 1260, and the average ACT score is 27. The majority of students who apply to Beloit are accepted—about 64 percent. Of those, one in four enrolls in the independent residential college.

What do Graduates Do?

The school takes student/alumni networking seriously and hosts a popular networking fair that brings them together in a relaxed career-exploration setting. Plus, its Annual Alumni Economics Reunion (called "Econ Day" for short) brings economics students to Chicago to meet with alumni and faculty members who may help connect students with postgraduation gigs. About a third of Beloit students go on to graduate school after college and another 7 percent of those attend law, medical, or business schools. Beloit also has a reputation for preparing students to take leadership roles in diplomacy and international service and for training scientists.

Important Admission Factors

Class rank, interview, standardized test scores
Average HS GPA   3.52
Range SAT Verbal 580–700
Range SAT Math   560–660
Range ACT   25–29
Minimum TOEFL
  (paper/computer) 525/197

Application Deadlines

Regular notification   rolling
# of transfer applicants 100
% of transfer applicants
  accepted   46

ACADEMICS

Student/faculty ratio   11:1
% faculty teaching
  undergraduates   100
% of classes taught by
  graduate students   0

Most Popular Majors

- Anthropology
- Creative writing
- Psychology

Education Requirements

English (including composition), humanities, sciences (biological or physical), social science. Graduates must complete 2 units of social sciences, humanities, and sciences (1 unit must be lab science). Graduates are also expected to include international, "experiential" (hands-on), and interdisciplinary credit in their course work.

FINANCIAL INFO

Tuition	$28,130
Room & board	$6,162
Average book expense	$500
Required fees	$220
Average freshman need-based grant	$15,676
Average freshman need-based loan	$4,420
% of graduates who borrowed	61.8
Average indebtedness	$14,781

FINANCIAL AID FORMS

Students must submit FAFSA, institution's own financial aid form, state aid form.

Financial Aid filing deadline	3/1

POSTGRAD

% going to graduate school	30
% going to law school	2
% going to business school	2
% going to medical school	3

CAREER SERVICES

Alumni network, alumni services, career/job search classes, career assessment, internships, regional alumni, on-campus job interviews. Off-campus job opportunities are fair.

THE BOTTOM LINE

All told, Beloit costs a pretty penny to attend—about $35,912. Tuition is approximately $28,130. Required fees of $220, $6,162 for room and board, $500 for books and supplies, and $900 for other expenses can put a strain on many students' respective wallets. Thankfully though, the exemplary financial aid and scholarship options the school offers give shelter to many a piggy bank. On average, students graduate with $14,781 of debt.

FUN FACTS

Beloit College was founded in 1846—two years before Wisconsin became a state. Its mission was to serve society by encouraging learning for its own sake.

Paul Campbell, a Beloit mathematics and computer science professor, teaches a course inspired by the Friday night television show "Numb3rs." Students are required to watch each episode and further investigate the mathematical concepts it explores. Campbell hopes to use the popular show to spark students' interest in advanced mathematics.

A surprising number of Beloit graduates have gone on to clown school, according to a recent issue of Beloit College Magazine. They've eschewed more traditional careers in anthropology or law for life on the road with acrobats, trapeze artists, and bearded women.

In April 2006, 30 Beloit alumni and students persevered through freezing cold, exhaustion, hunger, and failing lights in an effort to break the world record for longest-running ultimate Frisbee game. In true Beloit spirit, the players threw the Frisbee in shifts for 72 hours, 10 minutes, and 5 seconds "just because." With or without a world record, that's an impressive performance.

BIRMINGHAM-SOUTHERN COLLEGE

900 Arkadelphia Road, Birmingham, AL 35254
www.BSC.edu • Admissions: 205-226-4696
Fax: 205-226-3074 • E-mail: admission@bsc.edu • Financial Aid: 205-226-4688

STUDENTS

Religious affiliation
Methodist

Academic year calendar	4-1-4
Undergrad enrollment	1,356
% male/female	42/58
% Asian	3
% Black, non-Latino	6
% Latino	1
% from out of state	26
% freshmen return for sophomore year	86
% freshmen graduate within 4 years	67

STUDENT LIFE

% of students living on campus	79
% in fraternities	48
% in sororities	65

ADMISSIONS

# of applicants	1,157
% accepted	83
% enrolled	37

HIGH SCHOOL UNITS REQUIRED

4 English

HIGH SCHOOL UNITS RECOMMENDED

4 Math, 4 science, 2 foreign language, 2 social studies, 2 history, 10 academic electives

ABOUT BIRMINGHAM-SOUTHERN COLLEGE

Idyllic Birmingham-Southern College is a small, academically intense bastion of the liberal arts. It's particularly fabulous if you think you'll try to get into graduate, law, or medical school one day. Once you navigate the strenuous and very impressive core curriculum requirements, you can choose from more than 50 majors and interdisciplinary programs. BSC students tell us that classes are challenging and intimate, and that professors take the time to get to know students personally. Birmingham-Southern also boasts a unique January interim term. For four weeks between semesters, students participate in a single course or project, sometimes on campus but very often off campus. If you want to complete an independent project—taking photos across the American West, just for example, or documenting homelessness through an oral history—you can work under a contract that you make with a faculty member. Small groups of students also jet off to study various topics in Australia, Ireland, Italy, and Mozambique.

Birmingham-Southern is a conservative, traditionally Southern school. Most students live on campus, and the student government keeps things reasonably hopping. There are free concerts, cookouts, and movies in the dorm quad. BSC also has an enormous Greek population, and fraternities and sororities dominate many aspects of student life. You'll find there's something to do on fraternity row at least three nights a week. Further afield, Alabama's largest city (the Pittsburgh of the South) offers a commendable array of culture and nightlife. The Five Points area is a particular favorite among students for its restaurants, bars, and superb local flavor.

BANG FOR YOUR BUCK

At Birmingham-Southern College, 98 percent of all students receive some sort of financial aid. That's just about everybody. And we aren't talking nickel-and-dime aid, either. Students receive over $22 million in aid annually. The average financial aid package for all entering first-year students, excluding athletes, is currently $14,542.

VERY IMPORTANT ADMISSION FACTORS

Application essay, recommendation(s), rigor of secondary school record, standardized test scores

IMPORTANT ADMISSION FACTORS

Character/personal qualities

Average HS GPA   3.38
Range SAT Verbal 550–670
Range SAT Math   540–640
Range ACT   24–29
Minimum TOEFL
  (paper/computer) 500/173

APPLICATION DEADLINES

Regular notification rolling
# of transfer applicants   84
% of transfer applicants
  accepted   74

ACADEMICS

Student/faculty ratio   12:1
% faculty teaching
  undergraduates   100
% of classes taught by
  graduate students   0

MOST POPULAR MAJORS

• Business administration/
  management
• health/medical preparatory
  programs

The honors scholarships at BSC provide full-ride tuition for a few lucky (and very academically successful) students. To be competitive, you need an ACT composite score of at least 29 or a combined SAT Verbal and Math of at least 1300. You need to take college-prep courses and graduate in the top 10 percent of your high school class, too. Many other academic, art, and fine art–related scholarships are available as well. If you don't walk on water academically, don't worry: BSC offers a substantial amount of need-based financial aid to its student body. There is also a school-funded work-study program that is manifestly *not* operated on the basis of need. If you drive a BMW but you want a campus job, you can get one. Students in this program usually work at the request of faculty members in positions such as teaching assistants, science lab assistants, and lifeguards. Wages are $6 an hour.

GETTING IN

Admissions numbers are solid at Birmingham-Southern. Despite a great deal of national recognition in recent years, this little liberal arts gem is still not as well known as it really ought to be. The average SAT Verbal score for first-year students here is just a hair above 600; their average SAT Math score is just a hair under 600. New students average 27 or so on the ACT. The average high school grade point average is approximately 3.6. Note also that impressing the Admissions Office means completing a solid college-preparatory program. Birmingham-Southern does not have an applicant pool anywhere near the size of, say, Auburn. Consequently, the admissions staff will look very closely at what you have to say in your essay, in addition to the other aspects of your application.

WHAT DO GRADUATES DO?

Each year, a very considerable chunk of newly-minted (and very recent) Birmingham-Southern graduates enroll in graduate and professional schools. In fact, year in and year out, BSC ranks among the nation's best (and virtually always in the state of Alabama) in percentage of all graduates accepted to dental, health, and medical-related career programs. Birmingham-Southern also sends a multitude of its alumni to law school, business school, and graduate school. Graduates who get jobs immediately after school end up at places such as Ernst and Young and HealthSouth.

THE BOTTOM LINE

Birmingham-Southern estimates that the tab for a year for tuition, fees, room and board, and books here will run you about $29,310. The average financial aid package for all incoming first-year students (including scholarships, grants, loans, and work-study awards) is nearly $19,627. Hence, the average out-of-pocket cost for students here floats around $10,043 per year.

FUN FACTS

Birmingham-Southern is home to 14 NCAA Division I sports teams, including a women's air rifle team that was nationally ranked in 2005.

Professors traditionally dress up in the full colors of old-school academic regalia several times throughout each academic year, including for Commencement ceremonies, Honors Day, and the Opening of School Convocation.

Birmingham-Southern College was once two colleges: Southern University and Birmingham College. These two institutions merged on May 30, 1918, under its current name.

The city of Birmingham was recently ranked fourth in the United States in investments from European nations, with almost $274 million being invested here.

Notable people from Birmingham, Alabama, include Secretary of State Condoleezza Rice; Courteney Cox of *Friends*; Colin Powell's wife, Alma; and NBA Hall of Famer Charles Barkley.

EDUCATION REQUIREMENTS

Arts/fine arts, computer literacy, English (including composition), foreign languages, history, humanities, math, philosophy, sciences (biological or physical), social science, foundations curriculum

FINANCIAL INFO

Tuition	$22,260
Room & board	$7,740
Average book expense	$800
Required fees	$780
Average freshman need-based grant	$12,057
Average freshman need-based loan	$3,499
% of graduates who borrowed	40
Average indebtedness	$13,170

FINANCIAL AID FORMS

Students must submit state aid form.

Financial Aid filing deadline	5/1

POSTGRAD

% going to graduate school	65
% going to law school	7
% going to business school	2
% going to medical school	10

BOWDOIN COLLEGE

5000 College Station, Bowdoin College, Brunswick, ME 04011-8441
www.Bowdoin.edu • Admissions: 207-725-3100
Fax: 207-725-3101 • E-mail: admissions@bowdoin.edu • Financial Aid: 207-725-3273

STUDENTS

Religious affiliation
                 No Affiliation
Academic year
  calendar   semester
Undergrad
  enrollment   1,660
% male/female   50/50
% Asian   12
% Black, non-Latino   6
% Latino   7
% Native American   1
% international   3
% from out of state 87
% freshmen return for
sophomore year   97
% freshmen graduate within
4 years   90

STUDENT LIFE

% of students living
  on campus   95

ADMISSIONS

of applicants   5,026
% accepted   25
% enrolled   39
# of early decision/action
  applicants   621
% accepted early
  decision/action   29

HIGH SCHOOL UNITS RECOMMENDED

4 English, 4 math, 4 science
(3 science lab), 4 foreign
language, 4 social studies

ABOUT BOWDOIN COLLEGE

Bowdoin College attracts a steady stream of high school overachievers who held leadership roles, played sports, ran student government, organized the yearbook, and of course, managed to get phenomenal grades too. Though the intelligent and ambitious bunch veer toward preppy and don a disproportionate amount of J. Crew and Abercrombie & Fitch, there is a surprising amount of diversity among them. About 55 percent of students come from public high schools and 87 percent come from out of state. Minority and international students make up about 29 percent of the student body.

The learning environment is warm and encouraging, but also very challenging. Economics, English, history, and political science are the most popular majors, and 95 percent of students live on campus. Topnotch professors spend a good deal of time with students outside of the classroom when they host study groups and meet with students individually. The average class size is between 10 and 19 students, and the student/faculty ratio is 10:1. Students believe the teachers and administrators are cheering them on to success, and faculty members—not teaching assistants—are always at the helm of classrooms. They also rave about the school's internship and study abroad programs, which have high student participation rates.

Even the most studious students need a break from time to time and Bowdoin provides them with many outlets: varsity and intramural athletics, special events, lectures, parties, and more than 100 student groups. Bowdoin also is home to social houses, which students describe as like fraternities and sororities without the pledge paddles and member dues. As such, there is no Greek life at Bowdoin. Off campus, students enjoy downtown Brunswick's cobblestone streets, quaint shops, dining options, and movie theaters.

BANG FOR YOUR BUCK

Bowdoin is committed to making college education accessible to as many qualified students as possible and gives generously toward this end. The school has had a need-blind admissions process for a decade and budgets enough grant aid to fully meet the need of admitted students for their entire Bowdoin careers. The school awarded an estimated $18.8 million in grants and scholarships for the 2005–2006 school year and 39 percent of freshmen received need-based aid. The average need-based financial aid package for freshmen was $28,305 and Bowdoin met 100 percent of need for students who were awarded any need-based aid. The school also awards merit-based scholarships for students who excel academically or in leadership roles.

GETTING IN

The Bowdoin admissions staff believes that past performance is a major predictor of future success. It takes secondary school records, class rank, extracurricular involvement, and letters of recommendation from teachers and school counselors very seriously. It gives a lot of weight to admissions essays. For those who take time, standardized test scores also play a role. The average SAT score for admitted freshmen is 1400 and 78 percent of students were in the top 10 percent of their high school classes. About one in four applicants are accepted to Bowdoin and 39 percent of those enroll.

WHAT DO GRADUATES DO?

Bowdoin has a reputation for strong science programs and many students go on to careers in education, government, and business. Each year, approximately 80 private-sector and nonprofit employers visit campus to recruit students. In addition, another 60 employers interview candidates in Boston and New York City. About 14 percent of Bowdoin grads head off to graduate school and another 8 percent attend law, medical, or business school next.

THE BOTTOM LINE

For the 2005–2006 academic year, Bowdoin's cost was approximately $46,300, all told. The New England school's tuition was $34,280. Room and board was $4,300 and required fees totaled $360. On top of that, students paid another $800 for books and $1,200 for personal expenses. Transportation averages around $350 for the year. At graduation, students owed an average of $15,300 in loans.

VERY IMPORTANT ADMISSION FACTORS

Academic GPA, application essay, character/personal qualities, class rank, extracurricular activities, recommendation(s), rigor of secondary school record, talent/ability

IMPORTANT ADMISSION FACTORS

Alumni/ae relation, first generation, geographical residence, racial/ethnic status, volunteer work, work experience

Range SAT Verbal 660–740
Range SAT Math   660–730
Minimum TOEFL
  (paper/computer) 600/250

APPLICATION DEADLINES

Early decision   11/15
Early decision
  notification   12/31
Regular admission   1/1
Regular notification   4/5
# of transfer applicants 113
% of transfer applicants
  accepted   12

ACADEMICS

Student/faculty ratio   10:1
% faculty teaching
  undergraduates   100
% of classes taught by
  graduate students   0

MOST POPULAR MAJORS

- Economics
- History
- Political science and government
- English

EDUCATION REQUIREMENTS

Arts/fine arts, humanities, math, sciences (biological or physical), social science, non-Eurocentric studies

FINANCIAL INFO

Tuition	$34,280
Room & board	$9,310
Average book expense	$800
Required fees	$360
Average freshman need-based grant	$28,305
Average freshman need-based loan	$2,719
% of graduates who borrowed	54
Average indebtedness	$15,300

FINANCIAL AID FORMS

Students must submit FAFSA, institution's own financial aid form, CSS/financial aid profile, noncustodial (divorced/separated) parent's statement, business/farm supplement.

Financial Aid filing deadline	2/15

POSTGRAD

% going to graduate school	14
% going to law school	4
% going to business school	1
% going to medical school	3

CAREER SERVICES

Alumni network, alumni services, career/job search classes, career assessment, internships, regional alumni, on-campus job interviews. Off-campus job opportunities are good.

FUN FACTS

A U.S. president and major literary figures have all called Bowdoin home. Nathaniel Hawthorne, Henry Wadsworth Longfellow, and Franklin Pierce attended the New England school.

Bowdoin's mascot, the polar bear, was chosen to honor exploration of the polar region by numerous faculty, students, and alumni including Robert Perry. The sun on the Bowdoin college seal is alleged to represent the school's status as the easternmost college in the United States.

Unlike many institutions, Bowdoin never brings in a celebrity speaker for its commencement exercises. Instead, two graduates give speeches and honorary degree recipients briefly address the crowd. A local marching band leads the procession around Bowdoin's Quad as it has done for more than 100 years.

BRIGHAM YOUNG UNIVERSITY (UT)

A-153 ASB, Provo, UT 84602-1110
www.BYU.edu • Admissions: 801-422-2507
Fax: 801-422-0005 • E-mail: admissions@byu.edu • Financial Aid: 801-378-4104

STUDENTS

Religious affiliation
   Church of Jesus Christ of
       Latter-day Saints
Academic year
   calendar   semester
Undergrad
   enrollment   30,798
% male/female   51/49
% Asian   3
% Latino   3
% Native American   1
% international   2
% from out of state   72
% freshmen return for
sophomore year   95

STUDENT LIFE

% of students living
   on campus   20

ADMISSIONS

of applicants   8,696
% accepted   78
% enrolled   79

HIGH SCHOOL UNITS RECOMMENDED

4 English, 4 math, 3 science
(3 science lab), 4 foreign
language

VERY IMPORTANT ADMISSION FACTORS

Academic GPA, character/
personal qualities, interview,
religious affiliation/commit-
ment, rigor of secondary
school record, standardized
test scores

ABOUT BRIGHAM YOUNG UNIVERSITY (UT)

Brigham Young University in Provo, Utah (about 45 minutes south of Salt Lake City), is home to upstanding, respectful, and extremely affable students. BYU is a big school with more than 30,000 undergraduates, and has—not surprisingly—a very friendly atmosphere. It's also a very religious school: It is the educational crown jewel of The Church of Jesus Christ of Latter-day Saints, and secular knowledge is constantly and irrevocably fused with the school's sponsoring faith. For America's (and the world's) Mormon community, BYU provides a comfortable environment where students receive a world-class education at an extraordinarily affordable price. The curriculum includes strong doses of religion. The professors are excellent, and the administration is efficient and fair. Class sizes can be on the large side, but then again, BYU is a large school.

Life at BYU is a lot different from life at a typical university. You will find very little—if any—drunken Bacchanalia. A stringent honor code, initiated by students in 1949, regulates not only academic behavior but also dress, hair length, and diet. Students at BYU agree to abstain from smoking, drinking, and premarital sex as part of their commitment to the university's honor code, which emphasizes honesty, chaste and clean living, and other values encompassed in the doctrines of The Church of Jesus Christ. For fun, students attend dances, watch movies, play games, go hiking, and throw substance-free parties. They also spend a lot of time looking for that special someone to marry.

BANG FOR YOUR BUCK

Financial aid is significantly different at BYU. The theory is that the primary responsibility for financing an education rests with students and their families. Success in educational pursuits is achieved through hard work, wise planning, sacrifice, and the avoidance of unnecessary debt. To that end, BYU has developed a financial planning program that helps students define comprehensive and individualized financial strategies. The Financial Path to Graduation program requires that students who choose to take out loans submit, via an interactive Internet program, a plan for financing their education. The program also helps students forecast future expenses in order to ascertain future borrowing needs and plan for the future. Students are able to test different scenarios. For example, you can find out what impact part-time employment, increasing the number of credit hours per semester, or working full-time for a semester will have on your financial situation. The program also attempts to help students appreciate the benefits of financial frugality and restraint during their in-school experience.

"BYU has a good academic reputation and doesn't charge high tuition. The value of the education you can receive here is incredible."

IMPORTANT ADMISSION FACTORS

Application essay, extracurricular activities, racial/ethnic status, recommendation(s), volunteer work

Average HS GPA	3.73
Range SAT Verbal	550–660
Range SAT Math	570–670
Range ACT	22–36
Minimum TOEFL (paper/computer)	500/173

APPLICATION DEADLINES

Regular admission	2/1
# of transfer applicants	2,259
% of transfer applicants accepted	49

ACADEMICS

Student/faculty ratio 21:1

MOST POPULAR MAJORS

- English language and literature
- Political science and government
- Psychology

EDUCATION REQUIREMENTS

Arts/fine arts, English (including composition), foreign languages, history, math, sciences (biological or physical), social science, religious education, health and wellness

Tuition at BYU is cheaper for members of The Church of Jesus Christ because members of the Church from around the world provide considerable financial support to the university through tithes. If you aren't a Mormon, you'll pay more to attend BYU. Some financial aid at BYU is need-based, but most of it is merit-based. About one-third of all first-year students receive Federal Pell Grants and some form of institutional tuition assistance. BYU also boasts an impressive student-employment program that provides part-time positions for more than 13,000 students at compensation levels well above the federal minimum wage. Additionally, students get paid to help professors with state-of-the-art research projects.

GETTING IN

A high school grade point average of 3.6 or higher and an ACT score of 27 or higher make you a competitive candidate for admission to BYU, though the average high school GPA is 3.74. The school bases its decision on whether to admit you on your grade point average, your standardized test scores, and other subjective factors brought out in the application. It does not take your intended major into consideration when making its decision; however, once you are on campus you may find that certain majors have limited enrollment. All applicants must also receive an endorsement from an ecclesiastical leader, or they will not be admitted even if they have the academic credentials. Of all students admitted to BYU, 96 percent have historically taken four years of Church-related instruction as high school students. Obviously, there is a lot of ground to cover if you want to attend. But don't despair: BYU has a very self-selecting applicant pool (you know who you are). Many colleges and universities of BYU's academic caliber typically admit about 30 percent of all applicants. BYU admits between 70 and 80 percent.

WHAT DO GRADUATES DO?

What companies recruit BYU graduates? Perhaps a better question is: What companies *don't* recruit BYU graduates? You'll find Bain & Company, Deloitte Touche Tohmatsu, Ernst & Young, Ford Motor Company, Hewlett-Packard, IBM, Intel, KPMG, Microsoft, Pfizer (and other large pharmaceutical corporations), PricewaterhouseCoopers, and many more holding annual on-campus interviews. Many students go directly on to graduate or professional school upon graduating. At some point before, during, or after attending BYU, a large percentage of students complete a two-year mission on behalf of the church.

THE BOTTOM LINE

In 2005–2006, the last year this information was available, the average annual out-of-pocket cost for tuition, books, room and board, spending money, and other expenses at BYU is about $13,980 for students who are members of The Church of Jesus Christ. For nonmembers, it's approximately $17,000 per year. Undergraduates who borrow money accrue upon graduation an average student loan debt of less than $13,000. This average figure is far lower than the average at other colleges and universities of BYU's academic caliber.

FUN FACTS

According to a recent NCLEX report, BYU's College of Nursing graduates are consistently among the top 10 percent in the country when it comes to passing the National Council Licensure Examination to become registered nurses.

Brigham Young has one of the largest intramural sports programs in the United States. Some 22,500 students participate in 33 sports, including basketball, ultimate Frisbee, racquetball, volleyball, and water polo.

More than 75 percent of all students at BYU speak a second language. In all, more than 100 languages are spoken on campus. There are more students enrolled in Russian-language classes at BYU than at any other university in the country. BYU was also recently selected by the United States Department of Education as the headquarters of the National Middle East Language Resource Center, which is a consortium of Middle Eastern languages experts.

FINANCIAL INFO

Tuition	$3,620
Room & board	$5,640
Average book expense	$1,380
Average freshman need-based grant	$1,756
Average freshman need-based loan	$837
% of graduates who borrowed	35
Average indebtedness	$12,955

FINANCIAL AID FORMS

Students must submit FAFSA.

CALIFORNIA INSTITUTE OF TECHNOLOGY

1200 East California Boulevard, Mail Code 1-94, Pasadena, CA 91125
www.CalTech.edu • Admissions: 626-395-6341
Fax: 626-683-3026 • E-mail: ugadmissions@caltech.edu • Financial Aid: 626-395-6280

STUDENTS

Religious affiliation
                        No Affiliation
Academic year
  calendar   quarter
Undergrad
  enrollment   869
% male/female
% Asian   37
% Black, non-Latino   1
% Latino   6
% international   8
% from out of state   69
% freshmen return for
sophomore year   97
% freshmen graduate
within 4 years   80

STUDENT LIFE

% of students living
  on campus   92

ADMISSIONS

of applicants   3,330
% accepted   17
% enrolled   37

HIGH SCHOOL UNITS REQUIRED

3 English, 4 math, 2
science (1 science lab), 1
social studies, 1 history

HIGH SCHOOL UNITS RECOMMENDED

4 English, 4 science

VERY IMPORTANT ADMISSION FACTORS

Rigor of secondary school
record

ABOUT CALIFORNIA INSTITUTE OF TECHNOLOGY

Students arrive at Caltech knowing what to expect—namely, a grueling academic experience—and few leave disappointed. As if the extremely demanding curriculum weren't enough, Caltech adds insult to injury with a fast-moving quarter system, under which midterms arrive barely after students have settled in. Fortunately, Caltech attracts a student body that's not only up to the challenge but anxious for it. The undergrads are as ambitious as they are brilliant. The school helps students ease into the grind by making the first two freshman quarters pass/fail. Also helpful is a supportive atmosphere, one in which students work in groups to help each other master the endless stream of complex material.

All the work required means that there's not a whole lot of time for extracurricular fun at Caltech. Students socialize while they work, often at one of the seven theme-based houses in which they live. They occasionally take time out to indulge in pranking, too, a longtime school tradition. Most are harmless and rather whimsical. Students have built a giant jungle gym on the lawn of the faculty club building, for example. Just off campus is Pasadena's shopping district, known as "Old Pas," and students like to hang there when they can find the time, if only to get away from school for a bit. Tech students aren't as monolithically tech-geeky as you might expect. Yes, they're all into technology and they're all really, really smart. But most have plenty of other interests as well, whether they're into the arts, history, literature, music, or politics. The male/female ratio is nearly 70:30, a situation that presents an interesting dating challenge.

BANG FOR YOUR BUCK

Nearly two-thirds of Caltech undergraduates receive some form of financial assistance through the school, either in the form of need-based grants or academic scholarships. The school administers nearly $11 million in institutional need-based grants and scholarships annually.

Caltech provides need-based assistance to 100 percent of all aid-applicants who demonstrate need, and 100 percent of need-based aid packages include some form of need-based grant or scholarship. Get this: on average, the school meets 100 percent of aid recipients' demonstrated need, and meets 100 percent of demonstrated need for every one of its aid recipients. To simplify matters, Caltech guarantees that its aid package will meet all demonstrated need.

Incoming freshmen are eligible for President's Scholarships and Axline Awards, both merit-based. Continuing students are eligible for Upperclass Merit Awards ranging in value from $19,002 to $33,348, along with various departmental awards.

GETTING IN

Caltech is probably among the half-dozen most selective schools in the country. Many of the nation's top math and technology students apply here. The Admissions Committee takes time to consider the entire application package, including high school transcript, standardized test scores, application essays, recommendations, and evidence of extracurricular activities, special talents, and unique personal qualities. It should go without saying that the application should demonstrate a profound interest in mathematics, science, or engineering. Each application is appraised by three readers (two admissions officers and a faculty member) and then submitted to the Admissions Committee for discussion and a final decision. Good luck!

WHAT DO GRADUATES DO?

For the graduating class of 2003 (the last class for which complete figures are available), approximately 55 percent of the graduating class subsequently entered a graduate program. About three-quarters entered PhD or MS/PhD programs. MIT was the most popular destination institution, followed by Stanford. About 18 percent found employment in engineering and applied science, electrical engineering, biology, and other assorted science and technology related fields. The average starting salary for grads was just over $54,000.

IMPORTANT ADMISSION FACTORS

Academic GPA, application essay, character/personal qualities, class rank, extracurricular activities, recommendation(s), standardized test scores

Range SAT Verbal 690–770
Range SAT Math   780–800

APPLICATION DEADLINES

Regular admission   1/1
Regular notification   4/1
# of transfer applicants 119
% of transfer applicants
   accepted   1

ACADEMICS

Student/faculty ratio   3:1
% faculty teaching
   undergraduates
% of classes taught by
   graduate students

MOST POPULAR MAJORS

• Mechanical engineering
   • Physics

EDUCATION REQUIREMENTS

Humanities, math, sciences (biological or physical), social science, physical education (3 terms)

FINANCIAL INFO

Tuition	$28,515
Room & board	$9,102
Average book expense	$1,077
Required fees	$2,901
Average freshman need-based grant	$26,303
Average freshman need-based loan	$1,503
% of graduates who borrowed	45
Average indebtedness	$5,395

FINANCIAL AID FORMS

Students must submit FAFSA, CSS/financial aid profile, state aid form, noncustodial (divorced/separated) parent's statement, business/farm supplement. Noncustodial Parent's Statement and Business/Farm Supplement forms are required only when applicable.

Financial Aid filing deadline	1/15

POSTGRAD

% going to graduate school	53
% going to law school	1
% going to medical school	3

THE BOTTOM LINE

In 2006–2007, tuition and fees at Caltech totaled $28,515. Room and board totaled an additional $9,102. Students should expect to spend $1,077 on books and supplies; $1,926 on additional meals (board covers only 10 meals per week); and approximately $2,907 in personal expenses. Thus, the total cost of attending Caltech was $43,527, not including travel expenses. More than half of all students receive some form of need-based financial aid. The average financial aid package totals $28,508, with $27,325 of that in grants and scholarships.

FUN FACTS

Thirty-one people associated with Caltech, including seventeen alumni, have won Nobel Prizes. Linus Pauling, who received his PhD from Caltech and also taught here, won two Nobels, one in chemistry and one in peace.

Sixty-seven of the Caltech faculty are or have been members of the National Academy of Sciences.

Anti-matter and quarks were discovered at Caltech, as was the nature of the chemical bond. The science of molecular biology also got its start at Caltech, as did modern seismology.

CALIFORNIA POLYTECHNIC STATE UNIVERSITY—SAN LUIS OBISPO

Admissions Office, Cal Poly, San Luis Obispo, CA 93407
www.CalPoly.edu • Admissions: 805-756-2311
Fax: 805-756-5400 • E-mail: admissions@calpoly.edu • Financial Aid: 805-756-2927

STUDENTS

Religious affiliation

No Affiliation

Academic year
calendar   quarter
Undergrad
enrollment   17,488
% male/female   57/43
% Asian   11
% Black, non-Latino 1
% Latino   10
% Native American 1
% from out of state 6
% freshmen return for
sophomore year   91
% freshmen graduate
within 4 years   21

STUDENT LIFE

% of students living
on campus   19

ADMISSIONS

of applicants   23,691
% accepted   45
% enrolled   32
# of early decision/action
applicants   2077
% accepted early
decision/action   36

HIGH SCHOOL UNITS REQUIRED

4 English, 3 math, 3 science
(1 science lab), 2 foreign
language, 2 social studies, 1
history, 1 academic
electives, 1 visual and
performing arts

ABOUT CALIFORNIA POLYTECHNIC STATE UNIVERSITY—SAN LUIS OBISPO

Learning by doing is a major emphasis of California Polytechnic State University—San Luis Obispo, one of 23 campuses in the California State University system. Business, psychology, and architecture are popular majors, but unique programs like graphic communications have won a number of fans and are just as hands-on. The most frequent class size has between 20 and 29 students, and the student/faculty ratio is 20:1. Less than 20 percent of students live on campus.

Students say the school has a disproportionate number of conservatives for a public university with over 17,000 students. The vast majority of students who attend the school, located halfway between Los Angeles and San Francisco, are Californians. In fact, 32 percent of students are from the San Francisco Bay Area and 18 percent come from the Los Angeles area. Hispanic students make up 10 percent of the student body, with Asians making up 11 percent and African American and Native American students make up just 1 percent apiece.

Although San Luis Obispo's small but popular downtown area is lively and has some nice restaurants, big city kids may miss the hustle and bustle of their respective metropolises. Fortunately, the campus has 23 fraternities, 10 sororities, and 375 registered student organizations to keep things interesting. The school also has Division I intercollegiate sports and near-immediate access to California's Central Coast beaches where fun is mandatory and surf boards optional.

BANG FOR YOUR BUCK

Cal Poly's financial aid office offers students a variety of aid including grants, scholarships, loans, and work-study programs and typically meets about 85 percent of need for students who received need-based assistance. The school gave more than $46 million in need- and merit-based scholarships and grants for the 2005–2006 school year. Nearly a third of freshmen received need-based aid, and the average freshman need-based award was $1,459. The average freshman loan was $6,643. Beyond the typical array of federal and state grants that have no student work or repayment obligations, the school offers alumni-sponsored and other scholarships to qualifying students.

Students Say

"Cal Poly goes by a 'learn by doing' mantra, and really seems to reflect that belief in the way it does things. Classes are generally taught in a hands-on, practical way, and students are encouraged to get involved in the school and community."

VERY IMPORTANT ADMISSION FACTORS

Academic GPA, rigor of secondary school record, standardized test scores

Average HS GPA	3.73
Range SAT Verbal	540–630
Range SAT Math	570–670
Range ACT	23–28
Minimum TOEFL (paper/computer)	550/213

APPLICATION DEADLINES

Early decision	10/31
Early decision notification	12/15
Regular admission	11/30
Regular notification	rolling
# of transfer applicants	3,993
% of transfer applicants accepted	44

ACADEMICS

Student/faculty ratio   20:1

MOST POPULAR MAJORS

- Agricultural business
- Architecture
- Business administration
- Engineering

EDUCATION REQUIREMENTS

Arts/fine arts, English (including composition), history, humanities, math, philosophy, sciences (biological or physical), social science, technology

GETTING IN

High school academic performance and standardized test scores are the two big admissions factors at Cal Poly. The school doesn't even consider class rank, letters of recommendation, essays, and interviews. The average SAT score for California Polytechnic students is 1203 and the average ACT score is 26. The entering class had an average GPA of 3.73, and 37 percent were ranked in the top 10 percent of their class. Just under half of all applicants were accepted to the school and nearly a third of those accepted enrolled.

WHAT DO GRADUATES DO?

About 94 percent of Cal Poly's 2005 graduates are employed full time or enrolled in graduate school. In fact, nearly 20 percent of students go on to graduate school. College of Engineering grads won the best salaries with an average of $55,000 after graduation. They took jobs in aerospace, civil, computer, electrical, environmental, industrial, mechanical, and even software engineering. College of Business graduates were a distant second, pulling in $45,000 on average. The school also reports that nearly a third of graduates obtained their positions through personal referrals, so networking is a big part of the job hunt. About 10 percent of graduates accepted job offers earned through on-campus interviews, and 60 percent obtained employment before graduation. The vast majority of career services department survey respondents found work that related to their undergraduate study.

THE BOTTOM LINE

A Cal Poly education cost students around $26,529 for the 2005–2006 academic year. Tuition was a respectable $13,002. Required fees were about $2,832, and room and board were $7,212. Books and supplies cost a whopping $1,260 and personal expenses required another $2,223 on average.

Fun Facts

A 50-foot-long and 35-foot-wide "P" rests on a Poly Hill, marking the school's territory. The iconic landmark first appeared in 1919 as a representation of the school to those traveling on the newly constructed Highway 101 or flying by airplane. Originally constructed of whitewashed stones, the "P" has been rebuilt over the years with more durable materials.

Cal Poly's distinguished alums include George Ramos, a Pulitzer Prize–winning reporter; "Weird Al" Yankovic, the Grammy-winning accordionist and parodist; Ozzie Smith, a Baseball Hall of Fame member; and the founders of Jamba Juice.

The university hosts an annual Culture Fest to celebrate the diverse backgrounds that make the school so vibrant. The free event takes place rain or shine and includes cultural arts, crafts, food, music, and entertainment.

Whether they're a Granny Smith or Red Fuji fan, students can enjoy hand-picking their produce at the school's two-acre organic apple orchard, Swanton Pacific Ranch.

Cal Poly holds 9,768 acres of land (second only to University of California—Berkeley in the state) and uses all of it to support student education and exploration.

FINANCIAL INFO

In-state tuition	$0
Out-of-state tuition	$10,170
Room & board	$8,453
Average book expense	$1,305
Required fees	$4,350
Average freshman need-based grant	$1,459
Average freshman need-based loan	$2,731
% of graduates who borrowed	35
Average indebtedness	$13,788

FINANCIAL AID FORMS

Students must submit FAFSA, institution's own financial aid form.

Financial Aid filing deadline	6/30

POSTGRAD

% going to graduate school	19

CALIFORNIA STATE UNIVERSITY— LONG BEACH

1250 Bellflower Boulevard, Long Beach, CA 90840
www.CSULB.edu • Admissions: 562-985-5471
Fax: 562-985-4973 • E-mail: eslb@csulb.edu • Financial Aid: 562-985-8403

STUDENTS

Religious affiliation	No Affiliation
Academic year calendar	semester
Undergrad enrollment	28,514
% male/female	40/60
% Asian	22
% Black, non-Latino	6
% Latino	25
% Native American	1
% international	5
% from out of state	1
% freshmen return for sophomore year	85
% freshmen graduate within 4 years	11

STUDENT LIFE

% of students living on campus	7
% in fraternities	4
% in sororities	4

ADMISSIONS

# of applicants	38,579
% accepted	55
% enrolled	21

HIGH SCHOOL UNITS RECOMMENDED

4 English, 3 math, 2 science (2 science lab), 2 foreign language, 1 social studies, 1 history, 1 academic electives, 1 fine arts

ABOUT CAL STATE UNIVERSITY—LONG BEACH

A diverse and accepting student body, lots of excellent academic options, and a great location are the reasons you'll see so many students on campus wearing "Go Beach" gear (having such a cool slogan also doesn't hurt, either). Cal State University—Long Beach is predominantly a commuter school situated just 30 minutes from LA to the north and Newport Beach to the south. Its diverse and tolerant student body reflects California—people from all groups who coexist happily. Students are friendly, but the commuter nature of the school makes it difficult to meet people outside your department. The administration certainly does its part—the campus is beautiful and is bursting with activities. It's just difficult to get students back to campus to take advantage of them—and with so many beaches nearby, it's no wonder why. One thing that does draw students is Long Beach's Division I sports programs, which all students can attend free. Volleyball and baseball are particularly outstanding.

Cal State—Long Beach is a large school, and its students must face the headaches that come with an institution of its size. This includes, for one thing, crowding. Many majors are impacted (more students than available space), making it hard to get your classes. Fortunately, an excellent online services system helps students cut through some of the administrative red tape. Students also enjoy a wealth of big-school opportunities, like exposure to famous guest speakers and a host of career, research, and volunteer prospects.

BANG FOR YOUR BUCK

This is the least expensive of the schools in California's CSU system, pricing in at about $2,740 less than their peer institutions for California state residents. But even out-of-staters benefit from Long Beach's good deals: For one academic year at "the Beach," nonresidents will be saving about $2,200 when compared to peer schools.

Aid generally comes in the form of need-based assistance, but is complemented by merit-based programs, with fully half the student body receiving some financial aid. Serious students are encouraged to check out the President's Scholars Program. This four-year scholarship, available to California high school valedictorians as well as National Merit finalists and semifinalists, includes full payment of tuition and general student fees, priority registration, paid on-campus housing, personalized academic advising, opportunity for study abroad, an annual book allowance, and even special parking privileges.

Long Beach works to ensure that as much aid as possible is given in the form of grants or scholarships. This philosophy, considering grants as the first and best option, has resulted in 50 percent of all aid coming in forms that do not need to be repaid. For students who decide not to take out loans, this can mean saving an additional $6,000 over the course of four years.

GETTING IN

CSULB makes a decided effort to attract California's best and brightest. A significant portion of their students list the school as their first choice, whether for academic quality, access to professors rather than graduate assistants at the undergraduate level, the location and safety of our campus, or the cost savings. Applicants must meet the requirements of the California State University eligibility index, with the most critical admissions factors being grade point average, performance on standardized tests, and meeting the subject requirements for your grade. Transfer students who apply to particularly crowded majors may have to meet additional requirements—possibly including a higher required GPA than the school minimum.

WHAT DO GRADUATES DO?

Graduates of CSULB go on to work in a wide variety of fields that reflect the school's diverse areas of expertise. Accounting, engineering, education, government, health care, and law enforcement are all fields that are commonly pursued by CSULB graduates. These graduates are in high demand regionally, with employers such as Boeing, the City and County of Los Angeles, Ernst and Young, Raytheon, and the Los Angeles Unified School District all actively recruiting on campus. The university also has an excellent online job listing system.

VERY IMPORTANT ADMISSION FACTORS

Rigor of secondary school record, standardized test scores

Average HS GPA	3.34
Range SAT Verbal	450–560
Range SAT Math	470–580
Range ACT	17–23
Minimum TOEFL (paper)	525

APPLICATION DEADLINES

Regular admission	11/30
Regular notification	rolling
# of transfer applicants	11,282
% of transfer applicants accepted	54

ACADEMICS

Student/faculty ratio	20:1
% faculty teaching undergraduates	100
% of classes taught by graduate students	8

MOST POPULAR MAJORS

- Corrections and criminal justice
- Management information systems
- Psychology

EDUCATION REQUIREMENTS

Arts/fine arts, English (including composition), history, humanities, math, sciences (biological or physical), social science

FINANCIAL INFO

In-state tuition	$0
Out-of-state tuition	$10,170
Room & board	$6,648
Average book expense	$1,314
Required fees	$2,864
Average freshman need-based grant	$3,550
Average freshman need-based loan	$2,258
% of graduates who borrowed	31
Average indebtedness	$10,842

FINANCIAL AID FORMS
Students must submit FAFSA.

POSTGRAD

CAREER SERVICES
Alumni services, career assessment, internships, on-campus job interviews. Off-campus job opportunities are good.

THE BOTTOM LINE

For state residents, the bottom line at Long Beach is about as good as it gets—tuition is free. They pay only $2,864 in fees. Room and board is an additional $6,648, but many, indeed most, students live off campus anyway. Out-of-state tuition is $10,170. Factor in financial aid and a typical low-income family with an income below $30,000 will have zero out-of-pocket expenses. Grant aid will cover books and living expenses. A middle-income family (income of $52,000) can also look forward to zero out-of-pocket expenses. Loans are available for books and living expenses. A higher-income family (say, with an income of $80,000) will be responsible for about $250 out-of-pocket plus the cost of books and living expenses.

FUN FACTS

Steven Spielberg was a graduate of the Class of 2002, earning his BA in Film and Electronic Arts with an option in Film/Video Production.

Alumna Misty May won the gold medal in women's beach volleyball in the 2004 Olympics in Athens with her teammate, Kerri Walsh.

The Walter Pyramid at CSULB is one of the largest space-frame structures in the United States. The giant blue pyramid located on the campus serves as the university's sports arena and also houses a conference center, fitness center, and the Ukleja Sports Hall of Honor.

CSULB's American Indian Studies Program is the oldest one of its kind west of the Mississippi.

CSULB's College of Liberal Arts is the only college nationally to exclusively offer a bachelor's degree in Spanish Translation and Interpretation focusing on both the medical and judicial fields.

CALIFORNIA STATE UNIVERSITY— STANISLAUS

801 West Monte Vista Avenue, Turlock, CA 95382
www.CSUStan.edu • Admissions: 209-667-3070
Fax: 209-667-3788 • E-mail: outreach_help_desk@csustan.edu • Financial Aid: 209-667-6588

STUDENTS

Religious affiliation
　　　　　　No Affiliation
Academic year
　calendar　　　　4-1-4
Undergrad
　enrollment　　　6,430
% male/female　　34/66
% Asian　　　　　12
% Black, non-Latino　4
% Latino　　　　　28
% Native American　1
% international　　1
% from out of state　1
% freshmen return for
sophomore year　　82
% freshmen graduate within
4 years　　　　　21

STUDENT LIFE

% of students living
　on campus　　　10
% in fraternities　　3
% in sororities　　3

ADMISSIONS

of applicants　　3,016
% accepted　　　　92
% enrolled　　　　31

HIGH SCHOOL UNITS REQUIRED

4 English, 3 math, 2 science
(2 science lab), 2 foreign
language, 1 social studies, 1
history, 1 academic
electives, 1 visual and
performing arts

ABOUT CALIFORNIA STATE UNIVERSITY—STANISLAUS

California State University—Stanislaus is largely a commuter campus that serves the state's northern valley. Business, psychology, social work, criminal justice and biology are popular majors at this relatively small state school with enrollment of 6,430. The average class size has between two and nine students(!) and the student/faculty ratio is 18:1.

Diversity is strong at CSUS: Hispanic students make up 28 percent of the student body, Asians 12 percent, African Americans 4 percent, and international and Native American students 1 percent apiece. The campus is nearly 70 percent female, and about 93 percent of students graduated from public high schools. Many are older returning students who work during the day and have many responsibilities outside of school. It is also worth mentioning that CSUS has one of the highest retention rates among the 23 California State University campuses. Student success is aided by a dense network of on-campus resources that recognize that much of the student body consists of first-generation college students. Consistent advising, frequent contact with professors, and supportive administrators all help the cause.

Though far from a party school, CSUS does have a steady stream of student clubs for everything from rock climbing to crafts, along with many activities organized by residence hall assistants. It goes without saying that commuter students find it more difficult than residential students to tap into the social side of CSUS, though all it takes is a bit of effort. Modesto and San Francisco are popular day-trip destinations. Five fraternities and seven sororities are present on campus, but with just 6 percent of students participating, Greek life isn't pervasive.

Students Say

"The professors have been very accessible and willing to help students, the campus is quite enjoyable, and there is a healthy social network of groups and clubs that provide activities, food, and music throughout the semester. I feel like I am learning what I came here to learn and much, much more, and I've met many wonderful people in the process!"

VERY IMPORTANT ADMISSION FACTORS

Academic GPA, rigor of secondary school record, standardized test scores

IMPORTANT ADMISSION FACTORS

Class rank

Average HS GPA	3.2
Range SAT Verbal	410–540
Range SAT Math	420–540
Range ACT	17–22
Minimum TOEFL (paper/computer)	500/173

APPLICATION DEADLINES

Regular admission	7/1
Regular notification	rolling
# of transfer applicants	2,210
% of transfer applicants accepted	62

ACADEMICS

Student/faculty ratio	18:1
% faculty teaching undergraduates	93

MOST POPULAR MAJORS

• Business administration/ management
• Liberal arts and sciences/ liberal studies
• Psychology

BANG FOR YOUR BUCK

CSUS awarded $15.7 million in merit- and need-based grants and scholarships for the 2005–2006 school year. More than 60 percent of freshmen received need-based aid and the average gift aid for the group was $4,361. The average freshman loan was $4,046. The school also offers merit-based scholarships for students with demonstrated academic excellence. The scholarships range from $100 to $5,000 per school year, averaging at $1,000.

GETTING IN

Secondary school records and standardized test scores are at the top of the admissions staff's priority list when evaluating prospective students. Class rank is also important, but letters of recommendation, essays, interviews, and extracurricular activities don't factor in at all. The average SAT score of freshman was 948, the average ACT score was 19, and most students maintained a B-average in high school. Approximately 92 percent of applicants are accepted at CSUS, and approximately a third of them enroll.

WHAT DO GRADUATES DO?

California government agencies, hospitals and medical centers, banks, and school districts are among the top employers that recruit CSUS students on campus at career fairs. In 2006, AT&T, Frito Lay, Macy's Target, Hertz Corporation, Wells Fargo Financial, and other companies also made appearances on campus. At the annual fall Accounting Night, employers and alumni mingle with accounting and finance students. CSUS also has a strong nursing program that has prepared 700 students for the in-demand field. Many graduates work in hospital nursing, public health nursing, armed services nursing and education.

THE BOTTOM LINE

CSUS students paid about $24,459 for the 2005–2006 school year. Tuition is $10,710. Students also pay around $3,043 in required fees, $7,178 for room and board, and $1,314 for books and supplies. Personal expenses are about $2,214. By graduation, students have accumulated an average of $15,000 in student debt.

FUN FACTS

Part of the school's high retention record may be due to the emphasis it places on welcoming students to campus each year. Village Welcome Week offers a lively series of activities to greet residential students from day one. Activities include rafting trips, comedy nights, sports contests, dances, and movie nights. The very next week brings Campus Welcome Week, which celebrates the arrival of all students with a free lunch and other activities.

Warrior Day and Homecoming are two major campus traditions. A parade, royalty competition, and talent show are all a part of the good cheer brought to campus during Homecoming. In the spring, Warrior Day brings a similarly celebratory mood to campus with food, fun, and live tunes.

The university's art gallery, which opened with the school in 1965, gives students hands-on experience with contemporary art, exposure to other cultures, and opportunities for artistic leadership.

EDUCATION REQUIREMENTS

Arts/fine arts, computer literacy, English (including composition), foreign languages, history, humanities, math, philosophy, sciences (biological or physical), social science, public speaking, Upper Division Writing

FINANCIAL INFO

Out-of-state tuition	$10,170
Room & board	$7,178
Average book expense	$1,314
Required fees	$3,043
Average freshman need-based grant	$4,361
Average freshman need-based loan	$2,654
% of graduates who borrowed	18
Average indebtedness	$15,500

FINANCIAL AID FORMS

Students must submit FAFSA.

POSTGRAD

CAREER SERVICES

Alumni services, career/job search classes, career assessment, internships, regional alumni, on-campus job interviews. Off-campus job opportunities are good.

CENTRE COLLEGE

600 West Walnut Street, Danville, KY 40422
www.Centre.edu • Admissions: 859-238-5350
Fax: 859-238-5373 • E-mail: admission@centre.edu • Financial Aid: 859-238-5365

STUDENTS

Religious affiliation
Presbyterian
Academic year
calendar   4-1-4
Undergrad
enrollment   1,122
% male/female   49/51
% Asian   2
% Black, non-Latino 2
% Latino   1
% international   2
% from out of state 33
% freshmen return for
sophomore year   92
% freshmen graduate
within 4 years   77

STUDENT LIFE

% of students living
on campus   92
% in fraternities   37
% in sororities   38

ADMISSIONS

of applicants   1,989
% accepted   63
% enrolled   25

HIGH SCHOOL UNITS REQUIRED

4 English, 4 math, 2 science
(2 science lab), 2 foreign
language, 2 history

HIGH SCHOOL UNITS RECOMMENDED

3 Science (3 science lab)

VERY IMPORTANT ADMISSION FACTORS

Academic GPA, rigor of
secondary school record

ABOUT CENTRE COLLEGE

An intense academic atmosphere and personal interaction between students and their impressively dedicated professors are highlights at Centre College, a haven of liberal arts in a small Kentucky town. Students here are cultured, but not snobby; Southern hospitality reigns supreme. Centre's rigorous core curriculum ensures that you don't leave without the ability to think critically, speak publicly, and write thoughtfully. If you choose to come here, expect to write plenty of papers, give your fair share of in-class presentations, and get peppered with lots of questions in small, intimate classes. The 4-1-4 academic calendar here involves two regular terms in the spring and fall plus one course during a three-week January term. Creative course offerings have included "Stem Cells, Cloning, and You" and "In Search of Utopia." You can also do an internship, study theater in England, examine marine resources in the Bahamas, or tour the islands of the South Pacific. On-campus diversity is not yet a strong point, however.

Life outside the classroom at Centre is definitely influenced by Greek Row; fraternities and sororities play a significant role in setting the social agenda. Frat parties are open to anybody who wants to attend them, so the gulf between the Greeks and everybody else isn't as pronounced as it is at other schools. The surrounding town of Danville (population: 18,000) is a nice place to spend four years; it's been touted as one of the nation's outstanding small towns by *Time* magazine. When students feel the occasional urge to get away, they head to Lexington or Louisville, both within easy driving distance.

BANG FOR YOUR BUCK

Centre alumni are extraordinarily loyal (perhaps because they're also extraordinarily successful). Year after year, the percentage of alumni who find it in their hearts to contribute to the old alma mater is among the highest of all undergraduate institution in the United States. All of this support from past graduates allows Centre to offer generous scholarships and financial aid, and to keep tuition and other charges reasonably low in the first place. The amount of need-based financial aid and the number of merit scholarships easily make Centre one of the most generous national liberal arts colleges around. Centre provides over $10 million in financial aid. Each year, more than 85 percent of all incoming students receive some form of financial assistance. More than 60 percent of Centre students receive need-based financial aid. There's also the Centre Commitment, which guarantees every student a study abroad opportunity, an internship, and graduation in four years, or they get up to an additional year of study

Students Say

"Centre is challenging. The academics are tough, the atmosphere forces you to grow as a person, and, after the week is over, there is something for everyone to do to relax and have fun."

tuition-free. A whopping 97 percent of Centre's graduates complete their degrees in four years.

Specific programs include Presidential Scholarships, which cover full tuition for four years. The Centre Fellows Program provides a minimum scholarship of $6,000 per year for four years. (To be eligible, you need to graduate in the top 5 percent of your high school class, take a strong college prep curriculum, demonstrate extracurricular dedication, and have a minimum SAT score of 1250 or an ACT score of 28.) If you're from South Carolina, Florida, Georgia, Louisiana, or Tennessee listen up: Centre will match 100 percent of your state's public university scholarship programs. So, essentially, your Bright Futures Scholarships, your HOPE Scholarships, and your TOPS Scholarships are good at Centre College.

GETTING IN

If you want to get into Centre, your best bet is to take and do well in a serious college prep curriculum. Stay as close to the top of your class as humanly possible. Standardized test scores are important at Centre. The range of SAT scores here is roughly from 1160 to 1370. The ACT range is 25 to 30. Also, and this goes for any small school where the admissions staff will have the time to pore over your application—your essay, extracurricular record, and teacher recommendations are significant. By the way, it's worth noting that if you apply online to Centre, it won't cost you a dime.

WHAT DO GRADUATES DO?

More than 95 percent of all graduates are either gainfully employed or pursuing graduate and professional degrees within nine months of donning their caps and gowns. Centre students often take on internships and, naturally, those internships often lead to real jobs after graduation. Finance and insurance firms are popular destinations. Employers of recent Centre grads include ACNielsen BASES, AFLAC, Colgate Palmolive, the Department of Homeland Security, JPMorgan Chase Bank, Humana, National City Bank, Northwestern Mutual, Naval Intelligence Sprint, Toyota, and pharmaceutical companies such as Merck.

IMPORTANT ADMISSION FACTORS

Application essay, standardized test scores

Average HS GPA	3.7
Range SAT Verbal	580–678
Range SAT Math	600–670
Range ACT	25–29
Minimum TOEFL (paper)	580

APPLICATION DEADLINES

Regular admission	2/1
Regular notification	3/15
# of transfer applicants	70
% of transfer applicants accepted	43

ACADEMICS

Student/faculty ratio	11:1
% faculty teaching undergraduates	100
% of classes taught by graduate students	0

MOST POPULAR MAJORS

- Economics
- English language and literature
- History

EDUCATION REQUIREMENTS

Foreign language, history, humanities, math, philosophy, sciences (biological or physical), social science, religion

FINANCIAL INFO

Tuition	$23,110
Room & board	$7,700
Average book expense	$890
Average freshman need-based grant	$17,281
Average freshman need-based loan	$2,716
% of graduates who borrowed	58
Average indebtedness	$13,700

FINANCIAL AID FORMS

Students must submit FAFSA, institution's own financial aid form.

Financial Aid filing deadline	3/1

POSTGRAD

% going to graduate school	41
% going to law school	21
% going to business school	3
% going to medical school	13

CAREER SERVICES

Alumni services, career/job search classes, career assessment, internships, on-campus job interviews. Off-campus job opportunities are fair.

THE BOTTOM LINE

The tab for tuition, fees, and room and board at Centre is $30,210 per academic year. Living expenses will add to that total, of course, but Danville is considerably less expensive than, say, New York City. You could probably get by on $900 per year if you could be even reasonably thrifty. The average first-year student here receives $18,526 in financial aid, leaving an out-pocket-cost of $12,284.

FUN FACTS

More than 75 percent of Centre's students study abroad through Centre's faculty-led programs around the world.

In the last 50 years, Centre has produced two-thirds of Kentucky's Rhodes Scholars. It has produced twenty-two Fulbright winners over the last 10 years.

In 1921, Harvard was the nation's number-one football power, unbeaten in five years. Harvard invited tiny Centre College up north for a "warm-up" before facing Princeton the next week. On October 29th, before 45,000 stunned fans in Cambridge, Centre defeated mighty Harvard 6–0 in "the sports upset of the century." Back in Danville, jubilant students painted the "special chemical formula" C6-H0 on anything and everything, including a few unlucky cows. Centre's team went undefeated in regular season play, besting other national powerhouses. On the 75th anniversary of C6-H0, Centre challenged Harvard to a rematch. Harvard declined. A script is in the works for a major motion picture.

Centre alumnus Fred Vinson died in 1953 and hasn't missed a home football game since. Vinson was a three-sport athlete and a pretty good student at Centre. (For you legal buffs, this is the same Fred Vinson who served as Chief Justice of the U.S. Supreme Court for seven years.) Vinson maintained close contact with Centre—as alumni tend to do here—and always attended football games with his fraternity brothers when he returned to campus. Just after his death, some members of his fraternity decided there was no reason that Justice Vinson couldn't continue to attend the football games he so enjoyed. They began taking his portrait (affectionately known as Dead Fred) to the games and have been taking it ever since. Sometimes, Dead Fred travels to away games when Centre faces a particularly tough opponent. When Centre hosted the Vice-Presidential Debate in 2000, Dead Fred was there.

Another Centre College grad named John Marshall Harlan sat on the Supreme Court. He wrote one of the best dissents in the annals of law, period. On May 18, 1896, in a 7–1 ruling, the United States Supreme Court made "separate but equal" the law of the land when it agreed that Homer Plessy, a Louisianan who was one-eighth Black, could not use the 14th Amendment's prohibition of racial discrimination to claim a seat in the "white" car of a train. Harlan was the lone dissenter. He wrote: "Our Constitution is color-blind, and neither knows nor tolerates classes among citizens. . . . The destinies of the two races, in this country, are indissolubly linked together, and the interests of both require that the common government of all shall not permit the seeds of race hate to be planted under the sanction of law."

CITY UNIVERSITY OF NEW YORK— BARUCH COLLEGE

Undergraduate Admissions, One Bernard Baruch Way Box H-0720, New York, NY 10010
www.Baruch.edu • Admissions: 646-312-1400
Fax: 646-312-1361 • E-mail: admissions@baruch.cuny.edu • Financial Aid: 646-312-1360

STUDENTS

Religious affiliation
No Affiliation
Academic year
calendar semester
Undergrad
enrollment 12,844
% male/female 45/55
% Asian 28
% Black, non-Latino 13
% Latino 17
% international 11
% from out of state 2
% freshmen return for
sophomore year 88
% freshmen graduate
within 4 years 33

STUDENT LIFE

% of students living
on campus 0
% in fraternities 10
% in sororities 10

ADMISSIONS

of applicants 14,917
% accepted 33
% enrolled 33

HIGH SCHOOL UNITS REQUIRED

4 English, 3 math, 2 science
(2 science lab), 2 foreign
language, 4 social studies

HIGH SCHOOL UNITS RECOMMENDED

4 Math, 3 foreign language, 1
academic electives

CITY UNIVERSITY OF NEW YORK—BARUCH COLLEGE

The American Dream is alive and kicking at the City University of New York's Baruch College, home to a mega-diverse group of 12,000 talented and motivated undergrads. You can major in philosophy or history if you want, but the business of Baruch College is unquestionably the biggest. Many Baruch students are the first in their family to attend college. Many students also work while they go to school. Believe us, they are not messing around. These are serious people with serious career aspirations who have come to Baruch to obtain an outstanding, professional education.

Baruch College consists of three schools: the Weissman School of Arts and Sciences, the School of Public Affairs, and the Zicklin School of Business. All undergrads must complete a 60-credit core curriculum of mandatory courses. Flexible class schedules suit both full- and part-time students. Baruch's School of Business—housed in a brand-new state-of-the-art facility—is home to one of the best public schools for accounting in the world. Baruch even has its very own equity trading floor.

With no residence halls, Baruch is a commuter school. Many students commute for hours from the nether reaches of Long Island; they come strictly for class. When students do socialize, they usually go to bars or clubs after class. While a traditional sense of community may be lacking, a sense of excitement is not. Baruch's Gramercy Park neighborhood location puts students in the middle of Manhattan's shopping, dining, and culture. The location also offers endless opportunities for networking possibilities and internships.

BANG FOR YOUR BUCK

The overwhelming majority of students at Baruch receive some kind of financial aid. There are roughly 250 scholarships available specifically to Baruch College students each year, with awards ranging from small stipends to full-ride scholarships. Admission to the Honors College is probably the sweetest deal available at Baruch. These honors students receive a full waiver of tuition and fees, a book allowance of $670 each academic year, access to an educational account of $7,500 (over four years), and a shiny, new laptop computer. If you are a resident of New York City and you graduated from any New York City high school with an academic average of 80 or higher, you are eligible to apply for a Vallone Scholarship (also called a New York City Council Scholarship). It's worth $1,450 yearly. To keep it, you need to maintain at least a 3.0 grade-point average throughout your

VERY IMPORTANT ADMISSION FACTORS

Rigor of secondary school record, standardized test scores

IMPORTANT ADMISSION FACTORS

Application essay, recommendation(s)

Average HS GPA   3.0
Range SAT Verbal   460–570
Range SAT Math   530–630
Minimum TOEFL
   (paper/computer) 620/260

APPLICATION DEADLINES

Early decision   12/13
Early decision
   notification   1/7
Regular admission   2/1
Regular notification   rolling
# of transfer
   applicants   5,705
% of transfer applicants
   accepted   35

ACADEMICS

Student/faculty ratio   19:1
% faculty teaching
   undergraduates   95
% of classes taught by
   graduate students   1

MOST POPULAR MAJORS

• Accounting
• Finance and investments
• Finance
• Marketing

undergrad career. Baruch also has its own in-house work-study program.

Need-based financial aid is ample here as well. Empire State residents who are enrolled full time and on their way toward graduating can participate in New York State's Tuition Assistance Program. To qualify, your parents must have an income of $50,000 or less if they are still claiming you as a dependent. If you are independent and no one can claim you, your income must be less than $10,000.

GETTING IN

If you want to get admitted and succeed, you should take college-preparatory courses exclusively in high school. Beyond that, a combined Verbal and Math SAT score of 1100 and a B average in high school should do the trick.

WHAT DO GRADUATES DO?

The Career Development Center is very active, generating thousands of interviews each year for Baruch students. Career Development coordinates on-campus and off-campus recruiting, hosts career days and internship fairs, and generally does an excellent job at keeping Baruch connected to the world of business. In a given year, over 500 employers interview Baruch students both on and off campus. Nearly all of the top 25 accounting firms cited in *Crain's New York Business* interview students on campus. Baruch alumni are supportive and active as well; they like to hire Baruch graduates. Consequently, interviews and internships are plentiful. Baruch graduates perennially end up climbing the corporate ladder at places you have heard of, including Citigroup, Goldman Sachs, HSBC, Ernst & Young, MetLife, and JP Morgan Chase. Salaries for recent graduates range between $25,000 and $62,000 per year.

The Bottom Line

Tuition for residents of New York State is $4,000 a year for full-time students and $170 per credit hour for part-time students. For non-resident and international students, it's $360 per credit hour. This is a very good deal, any way you slice it—even if you can't get a dime of financial aid. The average financial aid package for students is about $5,000. Students incur an average debt of about $10,000 upon graduation. Ten grand ain't small potatoes, but for what it could have been, we aint complaining.

Fun Facts

In 1999, Baruch tied Harvard University with an equal number of graduates with bachelor's degrees in *Accounting Today*'s "100 most influential people in accounting" list.

According to *Standard & Poor's*, more senior executives hold degrees from the City University of New York than any other university system in the nation.

Nearby Gramercy Park is a small, fenced-in private park in the Gramercy neighborhood of the borough of Manhattan in New York City. The only people who have access to it are residents of certain townhouses in the area who have keys. It is the only remaining private park in the city. If you ever get in, you'll find a statue of one of the neighborhood's most famous residents, Shakespearean actor Edwin Booth (the brother of John Wilkes Booth, the assassin of Abraham Lincoln).

The Lawrence N. Field Center for Entrepreneurship and Small Business offers one-on-one consulting help with Baruch faculty for business owners and potential entrepreneurs. The center assists about 3,900 clients every year with their small and start up businesses.

Education Requirements

Arts/fine arts, computer literacy, English (including composition), foreign languages, history, humanities, math, philosophy, sciences (biological or physical), social science, speech communications

FINANCIAL INFO

In-state tuition	$4,000
Out-of-state tuition	$8,640
Required fees	$320
Average freshman need-based grant	$4,800
Average freshman need-based loan	$2,300
% of graduates who borrowed	19
Average indebtedness	$10,800

Financial Aid Forms

Students must submit FAFSA, state aid form. Financial Aid filing deadline   4/30

Career Services

Career assessment, internships, on-campus job interviews.

CITY UNIVERSITY OF NEW YORK— BROOKLYN COLLEGE

2900 Bedford Avenue, Brooklyn, NY 11210-2889
www.Brooklyn.cuny.edu • Admissions: 718-951-5001
Fax: 718-951-4506 • E-mail: adminqry@brooklyn.cuny.edu • Financial Aid: 718-951-5051

STUDENTS

Religious affiliation
                 No Affiliation
Academic year
  calendar   semester
Undergrad
  enrollment   11,068
% male/female   40/60
% Asian   11
% Black, non-Latino   28
% Latino   12
% international   7
% from out of state   2
% freshmen return for
sophomore year   76
% freshmen graduate
  within 4 years   17

STUDENT LIFE
% of students living
  on campus   0
% in fraternities   2
% in sororities   2

ADMISSIONS
of applicants   13,494
% accepted   46
% enrolled   23

HIGH SCHOOL UNITS RECOMMENDED

4 English, 3 math, 3
science, 3 foreign language,
4 social studies, 4 academic
electives

ABOUT CITY UNIVERSITY OF NEW YORK—BROOKLYN COLLEGE

On the gorgeous campus of Brooklyn College, you'll find a very serious and admirably diverse undergraduate population. Students from virtually every imaginable ethnic origin and age group take advantage of more than 120 majors. Accounting, business, computer science, education, film and television, and speech pathology are among the most popular. A unique aspect of Brooklyn College's curriculum is its rigorous 10-course core requirement, which obliges students to study a broad range of disciplines. You will be exposed to most of the liberal arts and sciences no matter what major you choose.

The area surrounding Brooklyn College is as urban as you can get. It has no dormitories and relatively few of the social components usually found at more traditional undergraduate schools. Most students don't even live near campus. Nevertheless, social activities are readily available. The campus hosts jazz concerts, festivals, plays, and lectures by well-known scholars. Academic clubs, student organizations, and the Greek system also sponsor many social activities. Not into any of those things? Off campus is the Big Apple, where every conceivable distraction can be found. Thanks to mass transit, it's easy to get around the five boroughs and suburban areas. A subway ride from campus to midtown Manhattan takes about thirty minutes.

BANG FOR YOUR BUCK

Tuition for nonresidents is affordable, and tuition for residents is *ridiculously* affordable. As if bargain-basement tuition weren't enough, Brooklyn College also offers a wealth of merit-scholarship programs and meets the financial aid needs of its students through a generous combination of grants, scholarships, and loans.

Students Say

"We have Pulitzer Prize winners, world-famous researchers, internationally-known artists and composers. They're here on this campus, sharing their knowledge with the students."

The Brooklyn College Foundation Presidential Scholarship offers full-tuition four-year scholarships to incoming first-year students with a minimum SAT score of 1200 and at least a B-plus grade point average. To remain eligible, you must maintain continuous full-time enrollment and a 3.0 grade point average. The Minority Access to Research Careers (MARC) Program is an honors program funded by the National Institutes of Health that supports exceptional students interested in biomedical research. The CUNY Honors Scholars Program, which offers full-tuition four-year scholarships *plus* a New York Arts Pass, and the Lorraine Foner Memorial Scholarship, which is for women enrolled in the Special Baccalaureate Degree Program for Adults in the Women's Studies Program, is also worth checking out. Brooklyn College offers an abundance of internships. The Kauffman Entrepreneurial Internship, for example, offers the opportunity to work in paid positions in start-up businesses and innovative nonprofits. The Jewish Foundation for Education of Women Summer Internship Program gives stipends to ten female students each year. The Everett Public Service Internship provides opportunities for students to work for ten weeks during the summer in public service in New York City and Washington, DC.

GETTING IN

As one of the colleges of the City University of New York, Brooklyn College participates in centralized application procedures. The components of an application to Brooklyn College are straightforward and include a completed application form, an official high school transcript, and SAT scores. Grades are most important, followed by types of courses taken and SAT scores. The honors programs—including a combined BA–MD degree, CUNY Honors College, and Brooklyn College Scholars Program—require additional letters of recommendation and personal essays. If you are a B-plus student taking college-preparatory classes and scored above 1000 on your SAT, you'll probably be accepted.

VERY IMPORTANT ADMISSION FACTORS

Academic GPA, rigor of secondary school record, standardized test scores

Average HS GPA   2.8
Range SAT Verbal 450–570
Range SAT Math   490–590
Minimum TOEFL
   (paper/computer) 500/173

APPLICATION DEADLINES
Regular notification rolling

ACADEMICS
Student/faculty ratio   15:1
% faculty teaching
   undergraduates   80
% of classes taught by
   graduate students   2

MOST POPULAR MAJORS

- Business administration/ management
- Education
- Psychology

EDUCATION REQUIREMENTS

Arts/fine arts, computer literacy, English (including composition), foreign languages, history, humanities, math, philosophy, sciences (biological or physical), social science. Most of these areas are part of the core curriculum.

FINANCIAL INFO

In-state tuition	$4,000
Out-of-state tuition	$10,800
Average book expense	$850
Required fees	$377
Average freshman need-based grant	$3,300
Average freshman need-based loan	$2,050
% of graduates who borrowed	30
Average indebtedness	$14,000

FINANCIAL AID FORMS

Students must submit FAFSA, state aid form.

POSTGRAD

% going to graduate school	40
% going to law school	5
% going to business school	12
% going to medical school	2

CAREER SERVICES

Alumni network, alumni services, career/job search classes, career assessment, internships, regional alumni, on-campus job interviews.

WHAT DO GRADUATES DO?

Brooklyn College graduates commonly pursue the fields of business, computer and information science, and finance. Companies like Alliance Capital Management, Bear Stearns, Bloomberg, Met Life, and New York's Franchise Tax Board recruit and employ Brooklyn College graduates.

THE BOTTOM LINE

Tuition for full-time students who are New York State residents is $4,000 a year, and tuition for part-time students who are New York State residents is $170 per credit hour. Full-time and part-time students who are either nonresidents or international students pay $360 per credit hour. The average out-of-pocket cost for tuition, books, transportation, and spending money is a little over $5,600. While student loans are available, the average student borrows a small amount, compared to the national average, over four years. Less than one-third of the students apply for any type of loan.

FUN FACTS

Brooklyn College's campus was used as a training ground for the Barnum & Bailey Circus at the turn of the century. These days, the school is home to hundreds of bright green monk parakeets that build their nests around campus and can be found chirping in just about every tree.

Notable Brooklyn College alumni include United States Senator Barbara Boxer (1962), attorney and Harvard University professor of law Alan Dershowitz (1959), and actor Jimmy Smits (1980).

Brooklyn College's motto is *Nil sine magno labore:* "Nothing without great effort."

Several renowned professors have recently joined the Brooklyn College ranks, including Pulitzer Prize–winning author Michael Cunningham, whose novel *The Hours* was adapted into a motion picture that was nominated for nine Academy Awards.

CITY UNIVERSITY OF NEW YORK— HUNTER COLLEGE

695 Park Avenue, New York, NY 10021
www.Hunter.CUNY.edu • Admissions: 212-772-4490
Fax: 212-650-3336 • E-mail: admissions@hunter.cuny.edu • Financial Aid: 212-772-4820

STUDENTS

Religious affiliation
                    No Affiliation
Academic year
  calendar   semester
Undergrad
  enrollment   15,805
% male/female   32/68
% Asian   17
% Black, non-Latino   14
% Latino   19
% international   9
% from out of state   4
% freshmen return for
sophomore year   82
% freshmen graduate
  within 4 years   12

STUDENT LIFE

% of students living
  on campus   4
% in fraternities   1
% in sororities   1

ADMISSIONS

of applicants   21,830
% accepted   37
% enrolled   25

HIGH SCHOOL UNITS REQUIRED

2 English, 2 math, 1 science
(1 science lab)

HIGH SCHOOL UNITS RECOMMENDED

4 English, 3 math, 2 science
(2 science lab), 2 foreign
language, 4 social studies, 1
visual or performing arts

ABOUT HUNTER COLLEGE

For many New Yorkers seeking a college degree, Hunter College within the CUNY system offers the best, most affordable option available. It is the first choice among many applicants. In many ways, a Hunter education is a no-frills experience: Classes can be overcrowded, bureaucratic tasks can be maddeningly complicated, and facilities are often subpar. Even so, Hunter has a lot to offer beyond its miniscule tuition. The school's faculty is a huge asset, for one. Students agree that professors are expert and that they work hard to accommodate undergraduates. Location is another major plus, as New York City is a virtually limitless source of valuable internship opportunities. For the best possible Hunter experience, apply to the Honors College, where smaller classes create something closer to a conventional undergraduate experience.

Hunter inhabits one the nation's most diverse cities, and its student body reflects this diversity. Many are first-generation college students, first-generation Americans, or both. The population is peppered with lots of nontraditional students as well. Like its home city, Hunter is more hospitable to left-leaning students than to conservatives. For most students, campus life begins and ends with classes and study groups. The Hunter campus consists of three buildings on New York's East Side, the facilities are spartan, and extracurricular activities are relatively rare. Fortunately, there's plenty to do in the immediate area. Those with a few hours to kill between classes can walk to Central Park, the Metropolitan Museum of Art, the Frick Collection, or window-shop the high-end retailers along Fifth Avenue.

BANG FOR YOUR BUCK

An extraordinarily low tuition rate keeps Hunter relatively affordable for all. A combination of work-study jobs, prestigious external grants and scholarships, a diverse group of need-based scholarships, and credit-bearing internships further helps students fund their educations. Each year, Hunter administers over $30 million in federal, state, and institutional need-based aid to undergraduates.

Students Say

"Hunter offers an excellent education without the ridiculous and uncalled-for elitism or cost."

VERY IMPORTANT ADMISSION FACTORS

Academic GPA, rigor of secondary school record, standardized test scores

Average HS GPA   3.0
Range SAT Verbal 490–580
Range SAT Math   500–600
Minimum TOEFL
  (paper/computer) 500/173

APPLICATION DEADLINES

Regular admission   3/15
Regular notification rolling
# of transfer
  applicants   4,259
% of transfer applicants
  accepted   53

ACADEMICS

Student/faculty ratio   16:1
% faculty teaching
  undergraduates   96

MOST POPULAR MAJORS

• Accounting
• English language and
  literature
• Psychology

EDUCATION REQUIREMENTS

Arts/fine arts, English (including composition), foreign languages, history, humanities, math, sciences (biological or physical), social science; students must fulfill a pluralism and diversity requirement.

Hunter provides need-based assistance to 90 percent of all aid applicants who demonstrate need, and 95 percent of the school's need-based aid packages include some form of need-based grant or scholarship. On average, the school meets 80 percent of aid recipients' demonstrated need.

Hunter College offers a variety of scholarship programs for entering freshman who have maintained a high level of academic achievement while in high school and who demonstrate potential for superior scholarship at the college level. The most prestigious award is the Dormitory Scholars Award, which consists of full in-state tuition plus free housing for four years at the Hunter College Residence Hall. Other awards offered are the Scholars Award, which consists of $4,000 a year for four years, and the Athena Award, a $5,000 a year for a four-year scholarship. The Athena Award is based on academic achievement as well as economic qualifications.

GETTING IN

Achievement on the SAT/ACT and a student's GPA in college-prep classes are the two most important components of an application to Hunter. The Admissions Office also takes into consideration the total and type of academic credits, such as AP courses. All undergraduates are admitted to the college of Arts and Sciences as undeclared majors. Only after completing core requirements can students apply for admission to specific programs and schools (e.g., education or nursing). Admissions standards to these programs vary; check the school's website for details.

WHAT DO GRADUATES DO?

Hunter alumni career paths are as varied as New York City itself. Hunter students prepare for their future careers by obtaining internships in all fields. Extensive internship opportunities include but are not limited to the following: broadcast journalism, education, government regulatory agencies, international relations, investment brokerages, museums, nonprofit organizations, nursing, professional athletic teams, publishing, social work, the arts, and urban planning. Many internships help pave the path for a related career, some even resulting in post-graduation job offers.

The Bottom Line

In 2006–2007, full-time undergraduates from New York paid $4,000 in tuition and another $329 in required fees. Most students here commute; those who live in the residence hall pay $3,250 per academic year. There is no meal plan at the residence hall, but there is a café and each floor has its own kitchen. Students should anticipate spending at least $832 per year on books, plus various personal expenses. Hunter evaluates all aid applications individually to compile a package of grant and scholarship aid that will minimize the amount of loans.

Fun Facts

Notable Hunter alums include actors Rhea Perlman (*Cheers*) and Ruby Dee (*Do the Right Thing*), former member of Congress Bella Abzug, and Nobel Laureates Gertrude Elion and Roslyn Yalow.

Hunter students come from 150 countries and speak more than 100 different languages.

Since 1990, Hunter Athletics has amassed 99 City of New York Athletic Conference (CUNYAC) championships, more than any other member in the Conference.

FINANCIAL INFO

In-state tuition	$4,000
Room	$3,250
Average book expense	$832
Required fees	$329
Average freshman need-based grant	$5,321
Average freshman need-based loan	$2,345
% of graduates who borrowed	38
Average indebtedness	$8,780

FINANCIAL AID FORMS

Students must submit a FAFSA, and the Tuition Assistance Application (TAP.

POSTGRAD

CAREER SERVICES

Alumni network, alumni services, career/job search classes, career assessment, internships, on-campus job interviews.

CITY UNIVERSITY OF NEW YORK— QUEENS COLLEGE

65-30 Kissena Boulevard, Flushing, NY 11367
www.qc.cuny.edu • Admissions: 718-997-5600
Fax: 718-997-5617 • E-mail: admissions@qc.edu • Financial Aid: 718-997-5101

STUDENTS

Religious affiliation
                No Affiliation
Academic year
  calendar   semester
Undergrad
  enrollment   12,320
% male/female   39/61
% Asian   18
% Black, non-Latino   9
% Latino   17
% international   8
% from out of state   1
% freshmen return for
sophomore year   86
% freshmen graduate
  within 4 years   23

STUDENT LIFE

% of students living
  on campus   0
% in fraternities   1
% in sororities   1

ADMISSIONS

of applicants   12,023
% accepted   43
% enrolled   29

HIGH SCHOOL UNITS REQUIRED

4 English, 3 math, 2 science, (2 science lab), 3 foreign language, 4 social studies

HIGH SCHOOL UNITS RECOMMENDED

4 English, 3 math, 3 science, (3 science lab), 3 foreign language, 4 social studies

ABOUT CITY UNIVERSITY OF NEW YORK—QUEENS COLLEGE

With the best reputation of all the CUNY undergraduate institutions, Queens College provides a top-rate education at a bargain-basement price, especially if you can score the incredibly low rate for in-state tuition. Academic requirements here emphasize the liberal arts. The excellence of the school's offerings in pre-professional areas is evidenced by the great numbers of undergrads studying accounting, computer science, and pre-medicine. Those who seek out help from professors and teaching assistants find that help is available. The average class size here is below that of the other large CUNY colleges. Students find the course work here interesting and satisfying; many take more than four years to graduate simply because so many of them are working or have other responsibilities that require them to enroll in classes at their own pace. Overall, Queens College is an excellent and affordable education.

Queens College is a commuter school that no longer suffers from a lack of campus activity thanks to the recent hire of a new Vice President of Student Affairs. Where once students would ditch campus after class, they are now sticking around for the bevy of events held at the Student Union, library, and LeFrak Concert Hall. The school has also seen an increased interest in the 120 or so student clubs, which run the gamut from ethnic and cultural to academic, special interest, religious, and honor societies. The campus itself is quite attractive, and, as an added bonus, boasts a tremendous view of the midtown Manhattan skyline. The borough of Queens is home to the most diverse population in the United States, and a tour of its neighborhoods (with their wonderful ethnic restaurants) bears this assertion out. The student body, like the borough that it calls home, is also extremely diverse.

BANG FOR YOUR BUCK

Even for the rare out-of-state student, tuition at Queens College is low. The vast majority of Queens undergrads, though, pay the much lower in-state rate. Meeting tuition and fees is still tough for many students. New York isn't cheap, after all, and the school serves many students at the lower end of the economic spectrum—and for them the school provides grants, institutional scholarships, loans, and work-study opportunities. All told, more than half of Queens undergrads receive need-based financial aid.

Students Say

"Queens College has a very diverse student body that reflects the global population and the population of the great city that it is located in [New York]."

Outstanding merit-based opportunities include participation in the Honors College, a highly competitive program that waives tuition fees (a $4,000 per year savings) and gives students an academic grant of $7,500 for specific purposes (such as study abroad and the National Student Exchange), a free laptop computer, and a New York City Cultural Passport that grants free or discounted admission to theater, music, dance, and other cultural events in the Big Apple. Outstanding students are also eligible for the Queens College Scholar's Scholarship, which provides $4,000 a year for four years, and the Queens Foundation Scholarship, which provides students $2,000 a year for four years. Scholarships earmarked for specific departments are available too, as are some dedicated to helping those in continuing education. Qualified students can also get free tuition and a $10,000 stipend through the MARC program, which is designed to increase the number of underrepresented minorities in the biomedical sciences.

The cost of living is extremely high in New York City, but at least Queens is cheaper than Manhattan. Students deal with the expense in a number of ways. Many live at home with their parents; others double or triple up in apartments; others still work long hours at paying jobs in addition to attending school. All appreciate that there are few cheaper opportunities to receive a first-rate education in New York City. (Cooper Union, which is free, is probably the only better deal available.)

GETTING IN

General admission to Queens College is based primarily on standardized test scores, high school curriculum, and GPA. Only applicants for the CUNY Honors College and scholarship applicants must submit letters of recommendation and essays. Economically and educationally disadvantaged students may apply for freshman entry through the SEEK (Search for Education, Elevation, and Knowledge) Program. Admissions requirements are less stringent than those for general admission; program participants must attend a summer immersion program prior to beginning undergraduate study.

VERY IMPORTANT ADMISSION FACTORS

Academic GPA, rigor of secondary school record, standardized test scores

Average HS GPA   3.2
Range SAT Verbal 440–550
Range SAT Math   490–580
Minimum TOEFL
  (paper/computer) 500/173

APPLICATION DEADLINES
Regular notification rolling
# of transfer
  applicants   4,664
% of transfer applicants
  accepted   59

ACADEMICS
Student/faculty ratio   16:1
% faculty teaching
  undergraduates   90
% of classes taught by
  graduate students   1

MOST POPULAR MAJORS

- Accounting
- Psychology
- Sociology

EDUCATION REQUIREMENTS

Arts/fine arts, English (including composition), foreign languages, humanities, sciences (biological or physical), social science, pre-industrial and/or non-Western civilizations

FINANCIAL INFO

In-state tuition $4,000
Out-of-state tuition $10,800
Required fees $377
Average freshman
need-based grant $3,500
Average freshman
need-based loan $2,625
% of graduates
who borrowed 40
Average
indebtedness $12,000

FINANCIAL AID FORMS

Students must submit
FAFSA, institution's own
financial aid form, state aid
form.

POSTGRAD

% going to
graduate school 25
% going to
law school 3
% going to
business school 1
% going to
medical school 1

CAREER SERVICES

Alumni network, alumni
services, career/job search
classes, career assessment,
internships, on-campus job
interviews. Off-campus job
opportunities are good.

WHAT DO GRADUATES DO?

Accounting, communications, education, financial services, and government and nonprofit are the most popular post-graduate fields for Queens college grads. Notable on-campus recruiters include CBS, Deloitte & Touche, Ernst & Young, Goldman, Sachs and Co., Federal Reserve Bank, J.P. Morgan, Met Life, NBC, PricewaterhouseCoopers, Metropolitan Life, UBS Financial Services, U.S. Securities and Exchange Commission, Con Edison, Bear Stearns, Geico, KPMG, Young Adult Institute, Library of Congress, Grand Thornton, and Memorial Sloan Kettering.

THE BOTTOM LINE

Full-time tuition and fees for Queens undergraduates totals $4,376.70 per year. Students should count on another $879 per semester to cover textbooks and supplies. Most either suck it up and cover the cost out of their own savings, family savings, and earnings, or finance their educations through a combination of federal grants, state grants, work-study, and loans.

FUN FACTS

Jerry Seinfeld is a Queens College graduate. Ray Romano attended Queens College for six years—he studied accounting—but did not graduate, which is why he's not quite as funny as Seinfeld. Some top female comedians graduated from Queens College, too, including Joy Behar and Fran Capo, who holds the record as the "world's fastest talking woman."

Another alumnus, Warren Phillips, went on to become the publisher of *The Wall Street Journal*. Phillips cut his journalistic teeth working on the school yearbook.

Queens College was built on the site previously used as a home for delinquent boys. Some of the original Mediterranean-style buildings from that time are still in use. Under the Quad is a now off-limits network of tunnels connecting the buildings.

Workers discovered a 13-ton boulder on campus during the 1982 excavation for the new science building. Once part of an enormous mountain system on the East Coast of North America, the boulder had lain more than 16 miles beneath the earth's surface. Erosion exposed it and, about 16,000 years ago, glaciers carried it from the highlands northwest of New York City to its location in Queens. Here it remains, appropriately, in a gully behind the science building.

Seminal poet Walt Whitman taught in a one-room schoolhouse on the present site of the college's Student Union. In 2005, the college created a commemorative garden there in his honor to mark the 150th anniversary of the publication of his *Leaves of Grass*.

CLARKE COLLEGE

1550 Clarke Drive, Dubuque, IA 52001-3198
www.Clarke.edu • Admissions: 563-588-6316
Fax: 563-588-6789 • E-mail: admissions@clarke.edu • Financial Aid: 563-588-6327

STUDENTS

Religious affiliation
Roman Catholic
Academic year
  calendar   semester
Undergrad
  enrollment   982
% male/female   29/71
% Asian   1
% Black, non-Latino   3
% Latino   3
% international   1
% from out of state   35
% freshmen return for
sophomore year   79
% freshmen graduate
  within 4 years   45

STUDENT LIFE

% of students living
  on campus   37

ADMISSIONS

of applicants   784
% accepted   61
% enrolled   33

HIGH SCHOOL UNITS REQUIRED

4 English, 3 math, 3 science
(2 science lab), 2 foreign
language, 2 social studies, 4
academic electives

HIGH SCHOOL UNITS RECOMMENDED

4 Math, 4 science

VERY IMPORTANT ADMISSION FACTORS

Academic GPA, rigor of
secondary school record,
standardized test scores

ABOUT CLARKE COLLEGE

Clarke College, a tiny school nestled in Dubuque, Iowa, is over-whelmingly female even though it began admitting male students in 1979. The friendly campus is fairly conservative and draws many students from the surrounding small towns. The university's website describes it as "grounded in the Catholic faith and in the heritage of the Sisters of Charity of the Blessed Virgin Mary." More liberal-leaning and less religious students may sometimes feel out of place; however, the school's small size helps to ensure that people get to know each other for the content of their characters.

Strong bonds are fostered between students, faculty, and administrators within the close-knit Clarke community. Students say flexible office hours, approachable instructors, and small class sizes create a user-friendly college experience. It's not uncommon for students to receive a call or e-mail from a professor if they miss class, not to chastise them (in most cases), but to inquire about their health and well-being. Of its 40 majors, nursing, education, physical therapy, and fine arts are the most popular.

Although Dubuque offers the typical chain stores and restaurants common to the Midwest, it also has some exotic dining options, live music venues, and coffee shops to break up the monotony. Nature lovers find it nearly impossible to resist the area's trails and parks, not the mention the "big river" itself—the mighty Mississippi.

BANG FOR YOUR BUCK

The admissions staff works hard to ensure that students who are accepted to Clarke can afford to attend. The school gave nearly $9 million in need- and merit-based aid for the 2005–2006 school year. About 85 percent of undergraduates receive some form of need-based financial aid, and the average freshman receives $16,125—and takes out $2,918—in loans.

Merit-based scholarships for full-time undergraduates range from $500 to full tuition. The presidential scholarships for students who enter with at least a 3.0 grade point average in high school are the most generous. The renewable awards begin at $3,000 for students at the lower end of the GPA spectrum and top out at $8,500 for students with both a 4.0 GPA and ACT scores around 28. The Mary Frances Clarke Scholarships, named for the school's founder, award full tuition for four years to top students in the incoming class. The college also awards six Trustee Scholarships equal to 75 percent of tuition.

"Never before have I met professors more encouraging of my academics or more receptive to my inquiries either during or after class. I've had the opportunity to develop outside-of-class relationships with every professor I've had thus far, and [I've] nearly graduated! That cannot be said about every school."

IMPORTANT ADMISSION FACTORS

Class rank

Average HS GPA	3.3
Range SAT Verbal	473–628
Range SAT Math	473–643
Range ACT	20–25
Minimum TOEFL (paper)	525

APPLICATION DEADLINES

Regular notification	rolling
# of transfer applicants	252
% of transfer applicants accepted	63

ACADEMICS

Student/faculty ratio	11:1
% faculty teaching undergraduates	100
% of classes taught by graduate students	0

MOST POPULAR MAJORS

- Business administration/ management
- Nursing—registered nurse training (RN, ASN, BSN, MSN)
- Psychology

EDUCATION REQUIREMENTS

Arts/fine arts, computer literacy, English (including composition), foreign languages, history, humanities, math, philosophy, sciences (biological or physical), social science, two sections of Cornerstone and Capstone

GETTING IN

Less-than-flattering letters of recommendation won't affect a prospective student's chances of being admitted to Clarke, as the school doesn't consider recommendations or essays. Instead, the admissions staff focuses on high school grades and standardized test scores. Would-be Clarke students must also make a good impression at interviews. Extracurricular activities, volunteer work, and talents are factors as well. Roughly 60 percent of Clarke applicants are accepted, and a third of them enroll.

WHAT DO GRADUATES DO?

Clarke College boasts a number of pre-professional programs from pre-chiropractic to pre-law. Graduates of these courses of study enjoy fruitful careers as doctors, dentists, lawyers, pharmacists, veterinarians, and physical therapists. Nursing students head straight for health care positions in hospitals, clinics, outpatient facilities, and community health agencies, while others in line with the college's liberal arts focus, become teachers, counselors, and social workers.

THE BOTTOM LINE

Clarke tuition for the 2005–2006 school year was around $18,360. Required fees totaled $585, room and board was $6,445, and books and supplies cost students $700. Personal expenses and transportation pushed annual costs up another $900. All told, Clarke students paid $26,990 for higher education last year, with the average amount of debt after graduation totaling about $18,000.

FUN FACTS

Clarke College's spirit rose from the ashes of a devastating fire in 1984 that destroyed 4 of 11 historic campus buildings. Once the flames were under control, students hung banners proclaiming "Clarke Lives" as a symbol of their perseverance and commitment to the small college.

The college hosts an annual golf fundraiser that has attracted more than 2,500 golfers and generated nearly $1 million for incoming freshman scholarships. The award recipients are selected based on their church involvement, academic performance, and community activities. Attendees receive 18 holes of golf, lunch, a gourmet dinner, and a photograph with the year's celebrity. Chi Chi Rodriquez, Lou Holtz, and Mike Vrabel were past celebrity golfers.

In 2003, a bunch of Clarke volunteers completely renovated a down-and-out lounge in Mary Benedict Hall, transforming it into the "Bean Scene." The space is now home to monthly concerts and craft nights and weekly open-mic nights—and serves cookies, muffins, smoothies, and more.

FINANCIAL INFO

Tuition	$18,360
Room & board	$6,445
Average book expense	$700
Required fees	$585
Average freshman need-based grant	$16,125
Average freshman need-based loan	$2,779
% of graduates who borrowed	75
Average indebtedness	$18,000

FINANCIAL AID FORMS

Students must submit FAFSA.

POSTGRAD

% going to graduate school	25
% going to business school	2

CAREER SERVICES

Alumni services, career/job search classes, career assessment, internships, on-campus job interviews. Off-campus job opportunities are excellent.

COLGATE UNIVERSITY

13 Oak Drive, Hamilton, NY 13346
www.Colgate.edu • Admissions: 315-228-7401
Fax: 315-228-7544 • E-mail: admission@mail.colgate.edu • Financial Aid: 315-228-7431

STUDENTS

Religious affiliation
                 No Affiliation
Academic year
   calendar   semester
Undergrad
   enrollment   2,740
% male/female   49/51
% Asian   6
% Black, non-Latino   4
% Latino   4
% Native American   1
% international   5
% from out of state   69
% freshmen return for
   sophomore year   92
% freshmen graduate
   within 4 years   88

STUDENT LIFE

% of students living
   on campus   89
% in fraternities   33
% in sororities   29

ADMISSIONS

of applicants   8,008
% accepted   27
% enrolled   34
# of early decision/action
   applicants   638
% accepted early
   decision/action   49

HIGH SCHOOL UNITS REQUIRED

4 English, 3 math, 3 science
(2 science lab), 3 foreign
language, 2 social studies, 1
history

ABOUT COLGATE UNIVERSITY

The winters in Colgate University's upstate New York neighborhood are long and cold, but that's one of the very few potential drawbacks at this outstanding private university. Colgate caters to a go-getter student body attracted by superb, state-of-the-art facilities, attentive professors, a demanding curriculum, and, most of all, the prestige conferred by a Colgate diploma. A rigorous battery of core courses, commencing with the First-year Seminar Program, ensure that students leave here with a well-rounded education. So do the numerous opportunities for students to take flight and study abroad. Independent study options are available to anyone willing to take them. Strong offerings in biology, chemistry, and psychology help send many Colgate grads on to medical school.

Gone are the days when the typical Colgate student was preppy, well-to-do, and Caucasian, hailing from the Northeast or Mid-Atlantic regions. Increasingly, Colgate recruits aggressively outside this demographic, with strong results. California is currently the sixth most represented state in the student body. The school was once renowned for its wild, weekend-party atmosphere, but the party scene has subsided in recent years, to be replaced by a slew of concerts, theatrical productions, guest speakers, and other events. Many students immerse themselves in community service, exercise, and athletic competition to stave off the winter blues. Hometown Hamilton, a tiny, good-looking burgh, continually strives to please the college crowd, with the recent additions of new restaurants, happenings around town, and an upgraded movie theater. Hamilton is also extremely accommodating to those whose ideal extracurricular activities include hiking, fly fishing, and skiing. Cooperstown (home to the Baseball Hall of Fame) and Syracuse are only an hour away.

BANG FOR YOUR BUCK

Colgate's financial aid policy is simple; with the exception of a few athletic scholarships, all aid is awarded on the basis of financial need. The school promises to meet the demonstrated financial need of all accepted students and, according to its catalog and website, strives to practice need-blind admissions, but concedes that the process is not 100 percent need-blind.

"Colgate is about studying hard and playing hard. For the difficulty of the classes and the amount of readings we have, the weekends don't come soon enough."

Most financial aid awards here consist of grants, federal loans, and campus jobs. For students who receive outside scholarships, Colgate reduces the student's loan amount or employment eligibility, but not the amount of the Colgate-sponsored grant. The school does reduce its grants, on a dollar-for-dollar basis, for students who receive state- and federally funded entitlements or tuition subsidies as a result of a parent's employment.

After freshman year, most students see their required work hours increase slightly. Loan amounts also increase based on eligibility. Otherwise, aid packages remain the same throughout a student's tenure at Colgate.

GETTING IN

Offering a prestigious degree and substantial financial aid, Colgate can afford to be picky about whom it admits, and it is. Athletes, legacies, and underrepresented minorities have the leg up, but no one gets in here without accomplishing some pretty impressive things in high school. Colgate admissions officers review all applicants' high school records, teacher comments, essays, and extracurricular resumes for evidence of a curious mind and ambitious attitude. Applicants interested in the music or art programs are encouraged to include an audition tape or portfolio with their applications.

WHAT DO GRADUATES DO?

Journalism, finance, law, and public service are just some of the areas into which Colgate graduates move and succeed. On-campus recruiters include Bank of America, CBS, the Chubb Group, the Congressional Budget Office, D'Arcy Advertising, the Ernest & Julio Gallo Winery, ESPN, GE Capital, Independent Educational Services, Johnson & Johnson, Liberty Mutual, Lockheed Martin, the Manhattan District Attorney's Office, the National Football League, NBC, the Peace Corps, Teach For America, the U.S. Department of Justice, and Ziff Davis Media, Inc.

HIGH SCHOOL UNITS RECOMMENDED

4 English, 4 math, 4 science (3 science lab), 4 foreign language, 2 social studies, 3 history

VERY IMPORTANT ADMISSION FACTORS

Academic GPA, class rank, rigor of secondary school record

IMPORTANT ADMISSION FACTORS

Application essay, character/personal qualities, extracurricular activities, recommendation(s), standardized test scores, talent/ability

Average HS GPA   3.6
Range SAT Verbal 630–710
Range SAT Math   650–720
Range ACT   29–32
Minimum TOEFL
 (paper/computer) 600/250

APPLICATION DEADLINES

Early decision   11/15
Early decision
 notification   12/15
Regular admission   1/15
Regular notification   4/1
# of transfer applicants 199
% of transfer applicants
 accepted   16

ACADEMICS

Student/faculty ratio   10:1
% faculty teaching
 undergraduates   100
% of classes taught by
 graduate students   0

- Economics
- English language and literature
- History

Education Requirements

Humanities, sciences, social science. Competency in foreign language must be shown. All students must complete 4 classes in the core curriculum.

FINANCIAL INFO

Tuition	$34,795
Room & board	$8,530
Average book expense	$1,840
Required fees	$814
Average freshman need-based grant	$27,326
Average freshman need-based loan	$2,571
% of graduates who borrowed	38
Average indebtedness	$13,452

Financial Aid Forms

Students must submit FAFSA, CSS/financial aid profile, noncustodial (divorced/separated) parent's statement, business/farm supplement. Financial Aid filing deadline 1/15

POSTGRAD

% going to graduate school	19
% going to law school	6
% going to business school	1
% going to medical school	3

Career Services

Alumni network, alumni services, career assessment, internships, on-campus job interviews.

The Bottom Line

In 2006–2007, the total cost of attending Colgate was almost $45,979; that included $34,795 in tuition, $4,120 for room, $4,410 for board, $814 for the student activities fee, and $1,840 in estimated personal expenses and books. Students not covered by a family health plan must pay an additional $481 per year for health insurance.

Now for the good news: For the same period, the average Colgate grant was for $25,396; the average campus job netted another $2,000; and loans covered another $4,350. The school reports meeting 100 percent of demonstrated need for all incoming students receiving aid; those students constituted approximately 40 percent of the incoming class. Thus, the average aid recipient was left with out-of-pocket expenses amounting to $14,233 for the school year.

Fun Facts

A list of notable Colgate graduates could fill a small telephone book. Their ranks include macabre cartoonist Charles Addams; Gloria Borger, chief political analyst for CBS Television News and *U.S. News* columnist; Howard Fineman, senior editor at *Newsweek*; Adonal Foyle, Center of Golden State Warriors and founder of Democracy Matters; Charles Evans Hughes, Supreme Court Chief Justice from 1930 to 1941; John Marks, creator of "Rudolph the Red-Nosed Reindeer"; Andy Rooney, professional curmudgeon; Ed Werner and John Haney ('72), inventors of *Trivial Pursuit*; Francesca Zambello, international opera star; and Jim Manzi, founder of Lotus software.

Colgate is home to an 80-million-year-old dinosaur egg, one of the first ever discovered.

Tour guides give potential students a Byrne Dairy cookiewich at the end of their admissions tour of the campus. In 2003–2004, Colgate handed out 10,416 of these tasty ice-cream treats.

Colgate's library is in the midst of a $45 million renovation that will transform the existing building into a state-of-the-art technology center.

COLLEGE OF THE ATLANTIC

105 Eden Street, Admission Office, Bar Harbor, ME 04609
www.CoA.edu • Admissions: 800-528-0025
Fax: 207-288-4126 • E-mail: inquiry@coa.edu • Financial Aid: 207-288-5015

STUDENTS

Religious affiliation
No Affiliation
Academic year
calendar   trimester
Undergrad
enrollment   295
% male/female   35/65
% Latino   1
% international   17
% from out of state   63
% freshmen return for
sophomore year   87
% freshmen graduate
within 4 years   45

STUDENT LIFE

% of students living
on campus   35

ADMISSIONS

of applicants   306
% accepted   64
% enrolled   42
# of early decision/action
applicants   32
% accepted early
decision/action   81

HIGH SCHOOL UNITS REQUIRED

4 English, 3 math, 2 science
(2 science lab), 2 social
studies

HIGH SCHOOL UNITS RECOMMENDED

4 math, 3 science, 2 foreign
language, 2 history, 1
academic elective

ABOUT COLLEGE OF THE ATLANTIC

The common theme among students at tiny College of the Atlantic on the oceanside nether reaches of eastern Maine is that everybody is doing their own thing—in their own ecologically sound way. If you are a left-liberal who dreams of going to school with budding novelists, vegans, philosophy geeks, committed social organizers, and performance artists: welcome to Nirvana. Students work to fight being stereotyped solely as hippies, but then again they'll show up to graduation barefoot with flowers in their hair. COA was founded on Bar Harbor's Mount Desert Island back in 1969. Its mission: to provide a practical, ecological education that emphasizes the interrelationships between humans and their culture and surroundings. You'll find a real sense of trust and community here as well as the freedom to design your own program of courses taught by an enthusiastic faculty who are often found in the college's dining hall deep in discussion with students. Every senior is required to create a comprehensive project and present it to the entire community. You can earn exactly one undergraduate degree here, a Bachelor of Arts in Human Ecology—which suits the few hundred students just fine, especially since they can choose to focus on one of several areas in which the college has considerable depth, including arts and design, education, field ecology and conservation biology, literature and writing, marine studies, public policy, and politics. Restless? The school participates in the Ecoleague, a consortium of six schools (Alaska Pacific University, Antioch College, College of the Atlantic, Green Mountain College, Northland College, and Prescott College) that allows you to study for up to a year at any of the others. Those with more international tastes should note that 60 percent of COA students participate in the study abroad program.

Beyond academics, COA's food is organic, healthy, and tasty. The surrounding town of Bar Harbor is famous for its long, bracing, snowy winters, which, on the bright side, are good for skating, cross-country skiing, and snowshoeing. The social scene here is low-key. People cook, play pool, hang out at the pizza-serving movie theater, and spend as much time outdoors as possible. Weather permitting, students can hike and study in the spectacular Acadia National Park, which is right in their own backyard.

BANG FOR YOUR BUCK

Within the school's budgetary constraints, COA offers additional grant money for students with substantial financial need. Some students here with financial need see much of that need covered. Though most aid tends to be need-based, there are a handful of merit-based scholarships as well. These include the Presidential Scholarships that range between $3,000 and

Students Say

"This place is heaven—a close-knit community of conscientious people who are open-minded and love what they do."

VERY IMPORTANT ADMISSION FACTORS

Application essay, recommendation(s)

IMPORTANT ADMISSION FACTORS

Academic GPA, character/personal qualities, extracurricular activities, interview, rigor of secondary school record, talent/ability, volunteer work, work experience

Average HS GPA	3.58
Range SAT Verbal	560–670
Range SAT Math	530–630
Range ACT	23–28
Minimum TOEFL (paper/computer)	567/227

APPLICATION DEADLINES

Early decision	12/1
Early decision notification	12/15
Regular admission	2/15
Regular notification	4/1
# of transfer applicants	44
% of transfer applicants accepted	77

ACADEMICS

Student/faculty ratio	10:1
% faculty teaching undergraduates	100
% of classes taught by graduate students	0

MOST POPULAR MAJORS

- Human ecology

$12,000 per year and are renewable for all four years, as long as you maintain a good-looking academic record. There is no special application for the Presidential Scholarship. The admissions staff selects recipients by reviewing the applications for admission.

More than 90 percent of the students here receive financial aid from the college itself. Typical financial aid packages are comprised of a combination of COA institutional grants, student loans, and work-study awards. In 2005, COA began offering health insurance to all students. One of the biggest values this school offers is an active education in a place that feels completely comfortable for many who may not feel they fit the traditional college student mold.

GETTING IN

On the surface, COA doesn't appear crazy-hard to get into, but that's because the applicant pool is one of the most self-selecting in the country. If you apply here, you'll be competing against some very smart and environmentally dedicated people. Your academic record, essays, and your interview are most important to the admissions staff here. The interview is optional, but we strongly recommend that you make your way to Bar Harbor to see COA for yourself. It's also vital to show a real and lengthy commitment to making a difference, intellectual curiosity, and a sincere desire to be part of a small college with a human ecology focus. Standardized test scores are optional (which is the way it should be everywhere, if you ask us). For admitted applicants who submit scores, SAT scores hover between 1120 and 1310. ACT scores range from 25 to 29. This is an atypical school experience that often opts to admit atypical—and always exceptional—candidates.

WHAT DO GRADUATES DO?

The school's signature academic program is designed to give each student an ecological perspective and arm them with the pre-professional skills appropriate to the fields of the arts, business, design, health, journalism, law, and science. The Education Studies Program works with local public schools to offer an innovative, state-certified teaching program. Graduates go on to teach grades K–8, as well as the sciences, social studies, and English at the secondary level. Students may choose instead to take a museum education path within the program. Internships are part of the COA experience and run the gamut from working on farms and at nonprofit organizations, to health institutes and laboratories—sometimes leading to postgraduation job offers. Sixty percent of COA's alumni have pursued graduate or professional education at some of the country's leading institutions.

The Bottom Line

Tuition and fees for 2006–2007 at this school are $27,705. Room and board adds another $7,710. Kick in another $525 for books and supplies, $560 for personal expenses, and you've got a total estimated Cost of Attendance for 2006–2007 of $36,500. The average freshman gift aid is $23,369, including about $4,303 in loans. Add in an average work-study grant of $2,000, and that leaves the total out-of-pocket expense for COA at about $6,828 per year. The school makes no cost distinctions between students who live in home state Maine and those who do not.

Fun Facts

The Green Business Program at COA provides students with the tools to start, manage, or work within environmentally sound businesses, nonprofits, and community organizations. Sustainability is the central concept. These developing programs incorporate ideas from green technology and design, green and fair trade marketing, organic and community agriculture, socially responsible business, grassroots activism, and old-fashioned management.

COA's mascot is the pesky Black Fly, and Cricket is a popular weekend sport.

Two alumni donated Beech Hill Farm to College of the Atlantic in May, 1999. Today, the farm is a hands-on educational resource for students, farmers, and community members. It includes approximately five acres of diversified, certified organic farmland, several acres of heirloom apple trees (some dating to the Civil War), 65 acres of forest, a barn, farmhouse, outbuildings, and five hoop greenhouses.

Allied Whale, COA's marine mammal research group, conducts research for the conservation of marine mammal populations and their habitats and trains students to enter careers related to marine mammal conservation. While research is primarily based in the Gulf of Maine, efforts extend from Canada to the British Isles, all the way down to South America and Antarctica.

COA's intensive 14-week Yucatán Program includes course work, homestays in Mérida, Mexico with local families, field work, and final independent research projects.

COA is the proud owner of two islands. Mount Desert Rock and Great Duck Island lighthouses were given to COA in 1998 and are used as field stations for the study of, among other things, over 115 different land bird species and 25 species of seabirds. Mount Desert Rock is a great place to study seals, dolphins, porpoises, and whales. Great Duck Island supports a number of rare plant species and a large population of herring gulls and great black-backed gulls. The island field stations are used to train students in the techniques of field ecology, marine ecology, marine mammology, marine ornithology, and all aspects of flora and fauna investigations.

Tuesday night is party night—the college hosts few classes on Wednesdays.

Each September the entire college turns out for the Bar Island swim. The brave and the crazy swim from the College's shores to the island a third of a mile across the bay, while the timid and the sane cheer from kayaks and dry land.

EDUCATION REQUIREMENTS

Arts/fine arts, English (including composition), history, humanities, math, sciences (biological or physical); human ecology core course required of all entering first-year students with less than 9 credits. Math and English competency required, or course completion.

FINANCIAL INFO

Tuition	$27,705
Room & board	$7,710
Average book expense	$525
Required fees	$435
Average freshman need-based grant	$20,016
Average freshman need-based loan	$3,026
% of graduates who borrowed	57
Average indebtedness	$16,705

FINANCIAL AID FORMS

Students must submit FAFSA, institution's own financial aid form, noncustodial (divorced/separated) parent's statement, business/farm supplement. Financial Aid filing deadline 2/15

POSTGRAD

% going to graduate school	25
% going to law school	1
% going to business school	1
% going to medical school	1

CAREER SERVICES

Off-campus job opportunities are fair.

COLLEGE OF CHARLESTON

66 George Street, Charleston, SC 29424
www.CofC.edu • Admissions: 843-953-5670
Fax: 843-953-6322 • E-mail: admissions@cofc.edu • Financial Aid: 843-953-5540

STUDENTS

Religious affiliation
                    No Affiliation
Academic year
  calendar   semester
Undergrad
  enrollment   9,501
% male/female   36/64
% Asian   2
% Black, non-Latino 7
% Latino   2
% international   2
% from out of state 35
% freshmen return for
sophomore year   83
% freshmen graduate
  within 4 years   41

STUDENT LIFE

% of students living
  on campus   30
% in fraternities   13
% in sororities   16

ADMISSIONS

of applicants   8,217
% accepted   66
% enrolled   37

HIGH SCHOOL UNITS REQUIRED

4 English, 3 math, 3 science
(3 science lab), 2 foreign
language, 3 social studies, 4
academic electives

HIGH SCHOOL UNITS RECOMMENDED

4 Math, 4 science, 3 foreign
language, 2 history

ABOUT COLLEGE OF CHARLESTON

Founded in 1770, the College of Charleston is a public liberal arts and sciences university committed to providing its 10,000 students with a intimate liberal arts experience at a public-school price. And though the majority of the student body currently consists of Caucasian southerners, mostly from South Carolina, C of C is attracting a growing number of out-of-staters drawn by the school's liberal arts reputation, small classes, and personalized attention unavailable at most public universities. Additional perks are the warm and sunny climate, proximity to the beach, and the laid-back Southern attitude. The Southern flavor of the school is readily apparent, however, with some northerners feeling out of place, at least initially. (Add to that a 2:1 ratio of women to men and you're looking at a sizable population of classic Southern belles.)

The College of Charleston has a reputation as a party school, and most students won't deny that they deserve the reputation. The campus is overflowing with fraternity- and school-sponsored events, and downtown Charleston's vibrant nightlife and culture is only a block or two from campus, offering everything from bars and clubs to art galleries and an aquarium. Students usually find a balance between work and play, and C of C also offers community service opportunities aplenty. The university's very successful Division I basketball team is also wildly popular.

Academically, students boast that their Charleston experience is anything but the public university stereotype, with six specialized colleges to choose from and lots of student-professor interaction. What's more, programs like the Honors College offer especially gifted students extra discussion classes and perks like priority registration.

BANG FOR YOUR BUCK

Of the 13 four-year public universities in South Carolina, the College of Charleston is the sixth most affordable, and an even better bargain when you factor in the small classes and emphasis on quality undergraduate education over research. Students are required to complete the admissions process by January 15 in order to be eligible for scholarships. Exceptional students should consider applying for the Presidential Scholarship, awarded to the top students in each entering freshman class. The scholarship is not handed out to just anyone; students should have an SAT score of 1300 or ACT score of 30, rank in the top 10 percent of their graduating class, and have a high school GPA of 3.8 or higher scale to be competitive.

Other than scholarships, need-based financial aid is awarded annually based on the results of the Free Application for Federal Student Aid (FAFSA). Need-based aid at C of C is available primarily to residents of South Carolina.

GETTING IN

Admission at College of Charleston is competitive, with high school grade point average and SAT/ACT scores ranking as the most important factors for applicants. Class rank and high school curriculum are also important, and preference is given to South Carolina residents. Your admissions essay, recommendations, skills, and activities can also play a role, albeit a lesser one. Last year's admitted applicants had an average GPA of 3.77, with 96 percent boasting a 3.0 or higher.

WHAT DO GRADUATES DO?

College of Charleston graduates go on to graduate school or to work in fields across the employment spectrum, with many employers actively recruiting and interviewing on campus. Students are able to use C of C's Career Center, and alumni are permitted to interview on campus up to one full semester after their graduation. (May graduates may interview on campus through the following fall semester.)

VERY IMPORTANT ADMISSION FACTORS

Academic GPA, standardized test scores, state residency

IMPORTANT ADMISSION FACTORS

Character/personal qualities, class rank, first generation, rigor of secondary school record, talent/ability

Average HS GPA	3.77
Range SAT Verbal	570–650
Range SAT Math	570–640
Range ACT	22–25
Minimum TOEFL (paper/computer)	550/213

APPLICATION DEADLINES

Regular admission	4/1
# of transfer applicants	1,870
% of transfer applicants accepted	71

ACADEMICS

Student/faculty ratio	14:1
% faculty teaching undergraduates	94
% of classes taught by graduate students	2

MOST POPULAR MAJORS

- Biology/biological sciences
- Business administration/ management
- Communications studies/ speech communication and rhetoric

EDUCATION REQUIREMENTS

English (including composition), foreign languages, history, humanities, math, sciences (biological or physical), social science

FINANCIAL INFO

In-state tuition	$7,234
Out-of-state tuition	$16,800
Room & board	$4,182–$7,182
Average book expense	$966
Average freshman need-based grant	$3,204
Average freshman need-based loan	$2,333
% of graduates who borrowed	45.5
Average indebtedness	$16,143

FINANCIAL AID FORMS

Students must submit FAFSA.

POSTGRAD

% going to graduate school	25
% going to law school	12
% going to business school	12
% going to medical school	26

CAREER SERVICES

Alumni services, career/job search classes, internships, on-campus job interviews. Off-campus job opportunities are excellent.

BOTTOM LINE

State residents are responsible for $7,234 in tuition costs. For nonresidents, this number rises to $16,800. Many students live off campus, but dormitory rooms range from $4,182–$7,182, depending upon the residence hall and whether the room is a single or double occupancy. The average freshman receives $8,192 in need-based gifts and an additional $3,204. Scholarships are available for athletes and exceptional students from out-of-state, but need-based financial aid is available for state residents only.

FUN FACTS

In the spring of 2000, the Student Alumni Associates (SAA) launched an annual event called Oozeball. Oozeball is the nation's largest mud-volleyball tournament, and this year nearly 100 teams competed. In addition to volleyball, the event also features a mud-wrestling tournament, free food, and prizes. Proceeds from the event go to the SAA Leadership Scholarship fund.

Founded in 1770 and chartered in 1785, the College of Charleston is the oldest institution of higher education in the state of South Carolina and the thirteenth oldest in the United States.

The Cougars, C of C's basketball team, has won at least 21 games in each of the last 9 seasons.

COLLEGE OF THE OZARKS

Office of Admissions, Point Lookout, MO 65726
www.CofO.edu • Admissions: 417-334-6411
Fax: 417-335-2618 • E-mail: admiss4@cofo.edu • Financial Aid: 417-334-6411

STUDENTS

Religious affiliation
Presbyterian
Academic year
calendar   semester
Undergrad
enrollment   1,333
% male/female   45/55
% Asian   1
% Black, non-Latino   1
% Latino   1
% Native American   1
% international   2
% from out of state   33
% freshmen return for
sophomore year   86

STUDENT LIFE

% of students living
on campus   84

ADMISSIONS

of applicants   2,666
% accepted   11
% enrolled   85

HIGH SCHOOL UNITS REQUIRED

1 Visual/performing arts

HIGH SCHOOL UNITS RECOMMENDED

4 English, 3 math, 2 science
(1 science lab), 2 foreign
language, 3 social studies

VERY IMPORTANT ADMISSION FACTORS

Character/personal qualities,
class rank, interview, rigor of
secondary school record

ABOUT COLLEGE OF THE OZARKS

College of the Ozarks—near Branson, Missouri—is a small school that offers a very affordable and notably Christian education. College of the Ozarks is called "Hard Work U." with good reason. Full-time students must devote fifteen hours per week (during the school year) and two 40-hour weeks (during breaks) of service in one of 85 areas, including agriculture, construction, lodge and restaurant operations, and fruitcake- and jelly-making. Along with scholarships and grants, earnings from campus jobs cover tuition costs, although room and board, books, and personal expenses are a separate charge for which students are responsible. There are more than 30 academic offerings covering agriculturally-oriented programs, education, hotel management, most of the liberal arts, nursing, and performing arts.

The conservative, friendly, and helpful students at College of the Ozarks mainly come from rural America. Academics and work commitments keep students busy. Many students also work at a second job off campus—specifically in the mega-tourist haven of Branson—to pay for room and board and other expenses. Students can work (and play) at local tourist attractions, including music shows, theme parks, water parks, and an IMAX theater. Campus gates close at 1:00 A.M. every night; opposite sexes are allowed in each other's campus dorms for only three hours on two nights per semester; smoking is allowed only in designated areas; and if you are caught with alcohol by a school official *anywhere* (even if you are over twenty-one), you'll be suspended from school. On-campus activities are wholesome, and the administration works diligently to create a socially and spiritually clean atmosphere.

BANG FOR YOUR BUCK

College of the Ozarks strives to serve "especially those found worthy but who are without sufficient means to procure" a college education. Hence, College of the Ozarks has been dedicated to providing a superior education since 1906 to qualified students who have financial need. Each year, 90 percent of the incoming first-year class is purposefully limited to students who come from families that would have a difficult time financing a traditional college education. The remaining 10 percent of available positions in each first-year class are filled with children of alumni or employees, scholarship recipients, and a few international students.

"The education that you get at College of the Ozarks is not only an education or a qualification for a degree; it is an education for life."

—Lady Margaret Thatcher

IMPORTANT ADMISSION FACTORS

Academic GPA, extracurricular activities, recommendation(s), talent/ability, volunteer work

Average HS GPA	3.34
Range ACT	20–24
Minimum TOEFL (paper/computer)	550/213

APPLICATION DEADLINES

Regular admission	8/20
Regular notification	rolling
# of transfer applicants	453
% of transfer applicants accepted	18

ACADEMICS

Student/faculty ratio	16:1
% faculty teaching undergraduates	100
% of classes taught by graduate students	0

MOST POPULAR MAJORS

- Agricultural business and management
- Business administration/management
- Elementary education and teaching

EDUCATION REQUIREMENTS

Arts/fine arts, computer literacy, English (including composition), history, humanities, math, philosophy, sciences (biological or physical), social science

BANG FOR YOUR BUCK

The real cost of full-time tuition at College of the Ozarks is approximately $15,400 per year. The college pays 100 percent of this amount for each full-time student by using earnings from the mandatory work-study program and by accepting federal and state student-aid grants and gifts from other sources. Therefore, students pay exactly $0 for tuition each year. Financial aid only decreases for students if their financial need decreases, and students are responsible to pay for everything else that is not tuition. A year of room and board, books, and miscellaneous fees is $5,230. Students can pay for room and board fees by working on campus during the summer. These Summer Work Scholarships cover room and board charges for the summer and the following year's charges. Some College of the Ozarks students do take out loans, but these amounts are negligible compared to the loans taken out by students at most other colleges and universities.

GETTING IN

College of the Ozarks reviews high school transcripts, ACT or SAT scores, the results of a physical, a FAFSA, and two reference letters when making its admissions decision. Additionally, an interview is required of all applicants who meet admission criteria. There is no application fee. The most important factors for admission to College of the Ozarks are your academic record and a demonstration of financial need. Academically, students need to be in the top half of their high school graduating class and score at least a 19 on the ACT or a 910 on the SAT. If possible, students should take rigorous high school courses, and try to get excellent grades in English classes. Residents from certain counties in Arkansas, Missouri, Illinois, Oklahoma, or Kansas get somewhat preferred admissions treatment.

What do Graduates Do?

About 10 percent of all graduates attend graduate or professional schools. Eventually, a little more than 20 percent of all graduates obtain an advanced degree. Major industries in which graduates find employment include agriculture, aviation, business, education, and U.S. government. Employers that recruit on camps include AFLAC, the Boy Scouts of America, Fed Ex, Leggett & Platt, Inc., the Missouri State Highway Patrol, Murphy Farms, Tyson Foods, Walgreens, and Wal-Mart.

The Bottom Line

College of the Ozarks meets over 80 percent of each student's financial need. The average value of a financial aid award received—when you add up money from all sources—is nearly $12,000. Students make even more money by working on campus during the summer. During an academic year, students can expect to pay a little over $5,200 for room and board, books, fees, and personal expenses, not including transportation. Commuter students who borrow money accrue an average debt of $4,648 over a four-year period. The monthly payment on $4,648 in loan debt at an interest rate of 6 percent is about $24.

Fun Facts

College of the Ozarks has been in the fruitcake business for over half a century. Student workers produce more than 40,000 of the delicacies each year. About half of them are given to friends and donors.

College of the Ozarks may not be home to many swimming pools or movie stars, but the Ralph Foster Museum on campus is home to the original Beverly Hillbillies car (or truck, or jalopy, or whatever you want to call it). For a nominal fee, visitors sit in the driver's seat and have their picture taken.

FINANCIAL INFO

Tuition	$0
Room & board	$4,100
Average book expense	$800
Required fees	$280
Average freshman need-based grant	$12,016
% of graduates who borrowed	4.9
Average indebtedness	$4,648

FINANCIAL AID FORMS

Students must submit FAFSA.

POSTGRAD

% going to graduate school	35
% going to law school	1
% going to business school	7
% going to medical school	1

CAREER SERVICES

Alumni network, alumni services, career/job search classes, career assessment, internships, on-campus job interviews. Off-campus job opportunities are excellent.

COLLEGE OF THE SOUTHWEST

6610 Lovington Highway, Hobbs, NM 88240
www.CSW.edu • Admissions: 505-392-6563
Fax: 505-392-6006 • E-mail: admissions@csw.edu • Financial Aid: 505-392-6561

STUDENTS

Religious affiliation
                              No Affiliation
Academic year
   calendar   semester
Undergrad
   enrollment   504
% male/female   40/60
% Asian   1
% Black, non-Latino   4
% Latino   38
% Native American   2
% international   4
% from out of state   20
% freshmen return for
sophomore year   54
% freshmen graduate
   within 4 years   11

STUDENT LIFE

% of students living
   on campus   23

ADMISSIONS

of applicants   2,015
% accepted   50
% enrolled   24

VERY IMPORTANT ADMISSION FACTORS

Academic GPA, class rank,
   standardized test scores

Average HS GPA   3.18
Range SAT Verbal   370–500
Range SAT Math   370–540
Range ACT   15–20
Minimum TOEFL
   (paper/computer) 550/218

APPLICATION DEADLINES

Regular notification rolling
# of transfer applicants 176
% of transfer applicants
   accepted   69

ABOUT COLLEGE OF THE SOUTHWEST

Christianity is at the heart of the College of the Southwest, and faculty and administrators keep their faith and values at the center of the school's teaching and business operations. Although the school's mission makes its "Christ-centered values" explicit, administrators say the campus is accepting of other faiths. Students are not required to attend chapel each week or participate in any religious rites.

Students enjoy the familial learning environment where professors are caring and instruction is personalized. They say small class sizes and one-on-one instruction set the college apart. The liberal arts school attracts both traditionally college-age students as well as a number of older students who return to school after long absences or work while seeking degrees. Education is by far the most popular major among the friendly and outgoing student body. One in three students enters the program of study in the hopes of becoming a teacher. A quarter of students enroll in the school's business program which has specialties including marketing, accounting, management, and even sports management.

Students use words like "wholesome," "healthy," and "quiet" to describe the social side of the college. Free time is often spent playing board games, participating in intramural sports, and watching movies. Campus rules are strict, and resident assistants conduct room checks and enforce the school's zero-tolerance alcohol policy.

BANG FOR YOUR BUCK

The College of the Southwest does not guarantee full funding for every student who needs assistance, but it does work creatively to bridge the gap between the cost of attendance and a family's means. The college awarded just over $2 million in need- and merit-based aid for the 2005–2006 school year. About 80 percent of students received need-based aid, and the school met an average of 62 percent of their need. The average financial aid package totaled about $8,437.

The college directs students to merit-based and need-based scholarships as well as work-study programs and student loans. The school also offers athletic, theater, and debate team scholarships as well as academic scholarships that range from $1,000 to $4,000 annually.

"It is a Christian college that believes in the power of an education. The professors and staff at College of the Southwest believe in their students and what they are trying to do with their lives."

GETTING IN

The admissions staff at the College of the Southwest accepts about half of those who apply to the school and 20 percent of them accept the invitation, keeping enrollment at around 500 students. The school doesn't bother with essays, interviews, and recommendations. The majority of those accepted graduated in the top half of their high school or equivalent classes and scored at least a 910 on the SAT or a 19 on the ACT.

WHAT DO GRADUATES DO?

Business, criminal justice, and elementary education are the most popular majors at the College of the Southwest. Accordingly, many graduates take teaching positions at area schools, enter the corporate world, or become law enforcement officers for local, state, and federal agencies.

THE BOTTOM LINE

Tuition for the College of the Southwest costs $10,500, while room and board and books and supplies average $6,200. Transportation and personal expenses add another $1,550. In total, the school costs about $18,250 per year. The average student leaves with about $12,420 in student debt at graduation.

ACADEMICS

Student/faculty ratio 12:1
% faculty teaching
  undergraduates 100
% of classes taught by
  graduate students 0

MOST POPULAR MAJORS

- Business administration/ management
- Criminal justice/police science
- Elementary education and teaching

EDUCATION REQUIREMENTS

Arts/fine arts, computer literacy, English (including composition), history, humanities, math, sciences (biological or physical), social science; must complete 6 semester hours of religion classes.

FINANCIAL INFO

Tuition	$10,500
Room & board	$5,400
Average book expense	$800
Average freshman need-based grant	$5,166
Average freshman need-based loan	$2,465
% of graduates who borrowed	66
Average indebtedness	$12,420

FINANCIAL AID FORMS

Students must submit FAFSA, institution's own financial aid form.

Financial Aid filing deadline	6/2

POSTGRAD

% going to graduate school	30

CAREER SERVICES

Off-campus job opportunities are good.

FUN FACTS

The College of the Southwest accommodates the different lifestyles of older students with separate housing options. The Daniels and Adams apartments near campus are internet-ready and have basic cable like the dorms, but lack the noise and social disturbance likely to be found in a less mature crowd.

A Success Center devoted entirely to aiding student achievement is nestled within the Scarborough Memorial Library on campus. Students head to the center for homework help, study guidance, time management tips, and plain old moral support.

The dining hall staff spices things up with special events that feature student-pleasers like an ice cream sundae bar and an elaborate buffet. Plus, they are open to student suggestions for new menu items.

For three years running, the College of the Southwest has won recognition from the Red River Athletic Conference for having the highest grade point average for student-athletes among the 14 schools that are members. The Mustang's cumulative GPA was 3.04 for the 2004–2005 school year.

COLORADO STATE UNIVERSITY

Spruce Hall, Fort Collins, CO 80523-8020
www.ColoState.edu • Admissions: 970-491-6909
Fax: 970-491-7799 • E-mail: admissions@colostate.edu • Financial Aid: 970-491-6321

STUDENTS

Religious affiliation
No Affiliation
Academic year
calendar semester
Undergrad
enrollment 20,584
% male/female 48/52
% Asian 3
% Black, non-Latino 2
% Latino 6
% Native American 1
% international 1
% from out of state 18
% freshmen return for
sophomore year 82
% freshmen graduate
within 4 years 34

STUDENT LIFE

% of students living
on campus 30
% in fraternities 8
% in sororities 9

ADMISSIONS

of applicants 10,770
% accepted 88
% enrolled 41

HIGH SCHOOL UNITS REQUIRED

4 English, 3 math, 2
science, 2 social studies, 3
academic electives, 1
science or social studies

HIGH SCHOOL UNITS RECOMMENDED

4 English, 4 math, 3
science, 2 foreign language,
3 social studies, 2 academic
electives

ABOUT COLORADO STATE UNIVERSITY

Colorado State University is a land-grant institution that excels in areas that have both immediate and profound practical applications. Offerings in agricultural science, biological and physical sciences, business, engineering, health and exercise science, and veterinary medicine all serve students admirably—at a very affordable price to boot. Like most large universities, CSU is not a touchy-feely place; undergrads who thrive here are those who can work independently. The exceptions are those in the honors program, where smaller classes allow students plenty of access to professors.

CSU's student body is a mix of residents and locals who split time between campus and home. Outdoorsy types—characteristic of Colorado in general—abound. Minority representation is low, with Hispanics making up the single largest non-majority group. The campus and its surroundings offer undergrads a satisfying mix of social opportunities, outdoor recreation, and a drop-dead gorgeous natural setting. The Greek system here is active but not overwhelming, and those who choose to avoid the whole Greek scene will still find plenty here to entertain them. Hometown Fort Collins is widely regarded as idyllic; *Men's Journal* recently ranked the city fourth among the fifty best places to live in the U.S. Vail and Steamboat Springs (can you say ski country?) are both within easy driving distance, as are a number of other colleges and universities.

BANG FOR YOUR BUCK

The greatest financial lure of a Colorado State education is its low price tag, especially for Colorado residents. But the school also does a good job of providing financial aid to those who need it, offering both merit-based and need-based scholarships, loans, work-study, and other employment opportunities.

A wide variety of merit-based scholarships are available to CSU students. Some are sponsored by the university at large, others by specific departments, others still by outside agencies, such as the military or state government. Applicants qualify for some scholarships simply by applying to CSU; other scholarships require a separate application. The school's financial aid website (http://sfs.colostate.edu/) contains all pertinent information.

VERY IMPORTANT ADMISSION FACTORS

Academic GPA, class rank, rigor of secondary school record, standardized test scores

IMPORTANT ADMISSION FACTORS

Application essay, recommendation(s)

Average HS GPA   3.5
Range SAT Verbal 500–610
Range SAT Math   510–620
Range ACT   22–26
Minimum TOEFL
(paper/computer) 525/197

APPLICATION DEADLINES

Regular admission   7/1
# of transfer
applicants   2,393
% of transfer applicants
accepted   85

ACADEMICS

Student/faculty ratio   18:1
% faculty teaching
undergraduates   97
% of classes taught by
graduate students

MOST POPULAR MAJORS

• Biology/biological sciences
• Kinesiology and exercise science
• Psychology

GETTING IN

Colorado State considers each application on its own merits, although, like most schools that must process many thousands of applications each year, it applies cutoffs and formulas to winnow the field. The middle fiftieth-percentile of entering freshmen has a high school GPA between 3.3 and 3.8 and composite ACT scores of 22–26 or composite SAT I scores of 1020 to 1210. (Remember that 25 percent of all admitted students fall below these levels, so don't give up just because you're below one or all of the ranges specified above.) Extracurricular involvement, strong letters of recommendation, and diversity considerations all can increase an applicant's chances for admission.

WHAT DO GRADUATES DO?

More than 200 companies conduct over 5,000 job interviews each year on the Colorado State campus. Two annual career fairs further assist students in their search for postgraduate employment. CSU's greatest strengths lie in the sciences, and it is in these areas that the school is most successful at sending students on to careers and/or graduate study.

THE BOTTOM LINE

For 2006–2007, in-state tuition totaled $3,466; out-of-state tuition was $14,994. Estimated expenses for all students included: living expenses (i.e., room and board), $6,602; additional expenses (e.g., personal expenses), $2,000; books and supplies, $900. CSU provided financial assistance to 82 percent of all students who demonstrated financial need. Forty-nine percent of those students had their demonstrated need fully met. On average, all aid recipients had 82 percent of their need met (this calculation excludes PLUS loans, private alternative loans, and unsubsidized loans). The average total financial aid package received totaled $8,188, of which $4,914 consisted of grants and scholarships.

FUN FACTS

Colorado State students are ardent supporters of their Rams teams, but they get especially riled up for games against Wyoming. Contests between the two schools are dubbed "Border Wars." Games against University of Colorado, known as "Rocky Mountain Showdowns," are just as intense.

Colorado State has a serious football program. During the 2004 season, six former Rams were playing in the National Football League. The baseball program wasn't bad either, having produced three successful major league pitchers (Tippy Martinez, Mark Huismann, and Mark Knudson), but the school dropped it due to funding problems and Title IX requirements.

You don't have to wait until you've left Colorado State to enjoy your first class reunion. Every spring, the Student Alumni Connection hosts an event called Zerunion (the "zero-year reunion," get it?) to honor graduating seniors.

Homecoming weekend is a huge event at Colorado State, complete with a bonfire and a "Yell Like Hell" competition among various student organizations.

EDUCATION REQUIREMENTS

Arts/fine arts, English (including composition), humanities, math, sciences (biological or physical), social science, health/wellness, critical thinking

FINANCIAL INFO

In-state tuition	$3,466
Out-of-state tuition	$14,994
Room & board	$6,602
Average book expense	$900
Required fees	$1,251
Average freshman need-based grant	$5,707
Average freshman need-based loan	$3,318
% of graduates who borrowed	52
Average indebtedness	$16,887

FINANCIAL AID FORMS

Students must submit FAFSA.

POSTGRAD

CAREER SERVICES

Off-campus job opportunities are excellent.

THE COOPER UNION FOR THE ADVANCEMENT OF SCIENCE AND ART

30 Cooper Square, Office of Admissions and Records, New York, NY 10003
www.Cooper.edu • Admissions: 212-353-4120
Fax: 212-353-4342 • E-mail: admissions@cooper.edu • Financial Aid: 212-353-4130

STUDENTS

Religious affiliation
               No Affiliation
Academic year
  calendar   semester
Undergrad
  enrollment   920
% male/female   64/36
% Asian   27
% Black, non-Latino   6
% Latino   8
% international   9
% from out of state   41
% freshmen return for
  sophomore year   93
% freshmen graduate
  within 4 years   77

STUDENT LIFE

% of students living
  on campus   20
% in fraternities   10
% in sororities   5

ADMISSIONS

of applicants   2,600
% accepted   10
% enrolled   77
# of early decision/action
  applicants   445
% accepted early
  decision/action   15

HIGH SCHOOL UNITS REQUIRED

4 English, 1 math, 1
science, 1 social studies, 1
history, 8 academic
electives

ABOUT THE COOPER UNION FOR THE ADVANCEMENT OF SCIENCE AND ART

There are three major programs at the Cooper Union for the Advancement of Science and Art: architecture, art, and engineering. In all three of these majors, Cooper Union's eccentric, dorky, creative, and exceptionally motivated students enjoy fantastic academic facilities and small classes taught by a dedicated and truly world-class faculty. The ultra-tiny student population is also a big draw. With so few students, professors can help confused students outside of class, which makes it possible for classes to be much more advanced and challenging. And trust us, students do get confused. Academically, Cooper Union is really difficult. The intense academic atmosphere hardens the resolve of some and drives others to tears. A substantial core curriculum is required for each major. Sleep is rare. Good grades are rarer.

On the plus side, students struggle together. They endure, knowing that their programs are very helpful in terms of finding jobs. Cooper Union is made up of four buildings smack-dab in the middle of a busy intersection in the heart of the East Village in New York City. Although the curriculum is rigorous, with students logging many hours in the studios and labs, all have the opportunity to participate in to participate in sports and a wide variety of student clubs, including professional organizations, ethnic and cultural events, and fraternities. Being in New York City allows students to intern or have jobs during the semester.

BANG FOR YOUR BUCK

Cooper Union was founded in 1859 by Peter Cooper, who became a millionaire industrialist and inventor, although he had less than a year of formal schooling. He designed and built America's first steam locomotive and the first washing machine. It offers one of the most undeniably best deals for higher education. Every student gets a full-tuition scholarship valued at $30,000. Students eligible for additional federal and institutional financial aid receive assistance for books, supplies, housing, and personal expenses. Cooper Union strives to provide the greatest possible assistance to all students with financial need. Students also receive funds as resources permit. The general rule is that Cooper Union provides 40 percent of your demonstrated need and you provide the remaining 60 percent.

Students Say

"Academic intensity. Strong work ethic. Free tuition. Easily accessible by subway."

One thing Cooper Union doesn't pay for is a student's room and board or other personal expenses. Interested candidates should definitely take this into account because the cost of living in New York City is pretty extraordinary. When you add everything up, non-tuition expenses total over $19,000 each year. However, around 45 percent of students receive financial aid to defray these costs. Additionally, students in the architecture and art schools must purchase supplies.

GETTING IN

Cooper Union receives about 2,600 applications a year (600 for architecture, 1,200 for art, and 800 for engineering) and admits about 300 students (35 for architecture, 65 for art, and 200 for engineering). Suffice it to say that when students apply, they compete against students of exceptional ability and talent. Students must apply for a specific major. For art, students need to submit a portfolio and take an at-home test. For architecture, students also need to take an at-home test. For engineering, students need stellar grades, high SAT scores, and high scores on the SAT II in Math and Physics or Chemistry. For applicants to the architecture and art programs, the most important admission factor is the at-home test; the academic requirements are somewhat more flexible.

WHAT DO GRADUATES DO?

Cooper Union sends a substantial number of its graduates to graduate and professional schools. In an average year, at least 50 percent of graduating seniors in engineering accept research fellowships at major universities throughout the country. Many artists and architects prefer to go straight to work before eventually pursuing an advanced degree. Graduates work in aerospace, animation, architectural and structural engineering firms, financial services, manufacturing, pharmaceuticals, software, and telecommunications. Major employers include Credit Suisse First Boston, Exxon, Lockheed Martin, Microsoft, the Naval Surface Warfare Center, Symbol Technologies, and the U.S. Army Corp of Engineers.

HIGH SCHOOL UNITS RECOMMENDED

4 English, 4 math, 4 science (3 science lab), 2 foreign language, 4 social studies

VERY IMPORTANT ADMISSION FACTORS

Rigor of secondary school record, standardized test scores, talent/ability

IMPORTANT ADMISSION FACTORS

Academic GPA, application essay, extracurricular activities, recommendation(s)

Average HS GPA	3.6
Range SAT Verbal	600–700
Range SAT Math	640–770
Minimum TOEFL (paper/computer)	600/250

APPLICATION DEADLINES

Early decision	12/1
Early decision notification	12/23
Regular admission	1/1
Regular notification	4/1
# of transfer applicants	536
% of transfer applicants accepted	10

ACADEMICS

Student/faculty ratio	7:1
% faculty teaching undergraduates	100
% of classes taught by graduate students	0

MOST POPULAR MAJORS

- Architecture (BArch, BA/BS, MArch, MA/MS, PhD)
- Electrical, electronics and communications engineering
- Fine arts and art studies

EDUCATION REQUIREMENTS

English (including composition), history, humanities, social science

FINANCIAL INFO

Tuition*	$30,000
Room & board	$13,360
Average book expense	$1,800
Required fees	$15,000
Average freshman need-based grant	$3,325
Average freshman need-based loan	$1,848
% of graduates who borrowed	32
Average indebtedness	$11,617

FINANCIAL AID FORMS

Students must submit FAFSA, CSS/financial aid profile.

Financial Aid filing deadline	6/1

POSTGRAD

% going to graduate school	60
% going to law school	6
% going to business school	10
% going to medical school	3

CAREER SERVICES

Alumni network, alumni services, career/job search classes, career assessment, internships, on-campus job interviews. Off-campus job opportunities are excellent.

THE BOTTOM LINE

The average student spends $16,735 for books, supplies, room and board, and other personal expenses. Students with financial need receive grants and are able to borrow additional funds to cover their non-tuition expenses. Students from more affluent families rely on their parents. Many students leave Cooper Union with no debt. Students who do borrow money graduate with an average debt of $11,617; this is a small amount considering the education and cachet with which students graduate from Cooper Union.

FUN FACTS

The list of Cooper Union alumni reads like a who's who of industry. Notable graduates include Dr. Albert Carnesale, formerly Dean of Harvard's John F. Kennedy School of Government; Joshua Lionel Cowen, inventor of Lionel trains; Thomas Edison, an inventor you may have heard of; and Felix Frankfurter, former associate justice of the United States Supreme Court.

The founder of Daniel Libeskind Studio (the architectural firm chosen to redesign the World Trade Center site) is a 1970 architecture alumnus of Cooper Union. Cooper Union had representation on five of the six teams announced to be competing for the World Trade Center site commission.

Founder Peter Cooper is best known for designing and building America's first steam locomotive; however, he also made a far more important, historical, and long-lasting contribution to society: gelatin dessert, which later became JELL-O.

Cooper Union's Foundation Building was the first building in the United States to be supported by rolled structural beams and the first thoroughly fireproof structure in New York.

Cooper Union's project-based approach to teaching yields results ranging from the annual egg-drop contest, sponsored by the Albert Nerken School of Engineering, which challenges students to create a container that will protect the contents—a raw egg—from breaking when dropped from the top of the engineering building, to many rigorous undergraduate research initiatives.

Despite the slogan of "No gym, no courts, no fields, no pool, no horses, no time . . . no excuses," Cooper Union's athletic teams compete in Division II games and tournaments. Its basketball team was featured in *The New York Times* and on HBO's *Real Sports with Bryant Gumbel* and has touted an average 3.75 GPA and win-loss record of 12–2 over the past two seasons.

*Every student receives a full-tuition scholarship valued at $30,000.

DARTMOUTH COLLEGE

6016 McNutt Hall, Hanover, NH 03755
www.Dartmouth.edu • Admissions: 603-646-2875
Fax: 603-646-1216 • E-mail: admissions.office@dartmouth.edu • Financial Aid: 603-646-2451

STUDENTS

Religious affiliation
               No Affiliation
Academic year
  calendar   quarter
Undergrad
  enrollment   4,100
% male/female   50/50
% Asian   14
% Black, non-Latino   7
% Latino   6
% Native American   3
% international   5
% from out of state   96
% freshmen return for
sophomore year   98
% freshmen graduate
  within 4 years   84

STUDENT LIFE

% of students living
  on campus   82
% in fraternities   37
% in sororities   37

ADMISSIONS

of applicants   12,756
% accepted   17
% enrolled   49
# of early decision/action
  applicants   1180
% accepted early
  decision/action   34

HIGH SCHOOL UNITS RECOMMENDED

4 English, 4 math, 4
science, 3 foreign language,
3 social studies

ABOUT DARTMOUTH COLLEGE

Professors at Dartmouth know their stuff and know how to teach it, and that's a factor that contributes greatly to students'enjoyment of campus life. Academics, comparable with other Ivy League schools, are demanding, but Dartmouth students feel they are up to the challenge. Outside of the classroom, the campus community is generally relaxed, accepting, a bit outdoorsy, and usually bundled up under eight layers of clothing to get through the New Hampshire winters. Across the board, students agree it's a good place to be.

Dartmouth's 4,100 undergraduate students enjoy the college's strong reputation as a member of the Ivy League, and high-quality academics in 29 subjects and 10 interdisciplinary majors. Dartmouth has four top-notch graduate schools in arts and sciences, medicine, business, and engineering. Unlike many of the other Ivies, though, the student/faculty ratio of 4:1 favors the undergrads, who find graduate assistants in their classes to have the same open willingness to help them learn as the regular professors do. Majors range from African American studies to computer science to human biology to music; undergraduates may also join in selected faculty research projects and specialized programs in leadership training and cross-disciplinary studies. During the second and third years, students may take part in a variety of off-campus study programs, both in the United States and in international locations.

The campus, which is about two hours north of Boston and five hours from New York, is organized around an open green space where ice sculptures (among other things) can be found during the college's annual winter carnival. All incoming freshmen live in residential housing clusters located throughout the campus, and more than 80 percent of upperclassmen choose to do so as well. Almost all of the student body comes from outside the college's New Hampshire base; the First Year Office helps to make the transition to college life go smoothly on both academic and personal fronts. Either this effort is working really well or it's not needed: Dartmouth students simply get along. Ranging from the politically conservative to the very liberal, from the outdoorsy to the nature-phobic, they all accept each other. Outside of class, students can participate in academic groups, ethnically focused organizations, political groups (political awareness is quite strong on campus), arts organizations, and sports teams. Greek groups add to the social mix, students feel, because everyone is welcome to attend fraternity and sorority parties and events. The Dartmouth Outing Club, a long-standing and rather famous outdoors-oriented group, offers hiking and other trips specifically aimed at first-years. It's just one of the things that contribute to the most valued aspect of Dartmouth: a strong and accepting sense of community.

VERY IMPORTANT ADMISSION FACTORS

Academic GPA, application essay, character/personal qualities, class rank, extracurricular activities, recommendation(s), rigor of secondary school record, standardized test scores

IMPORTANT ADMISSION FACTORS

Talent/ability, volunteer work

Average HS GPA	3.75
Range SAT Verbal	670–770
Range SAT Math	680–780
Range ACT	29–34
Minimum TOEFL (paper/computer)	600/250

APPLICATION DEADLINES

Early decision	11/1
Early decision notification	12/15
Regular admission	1/1
Regular notification	4/10
# of transfer applicants	312
% of transfer applicants accepted	12

ACADEMICS

Student/faculty ratio	8:1
% faculty teaching undergraduates	100
% of classes taught by graduate students	0

MOST POPULAR MAJORS

- Economics
- Psychology
- Sociology

BANG FOR YOUR BUCK

All incoming freshmen who are found to have financial need by the college have their need met. That holds true across the years, too: Once a student qualifies and maintains good standing, the college continues to meet his or her financial need. The average scholarship amount awarded in 2005–2006 amounted to $25,633, while the average amount of self-help aid was $6,225 and loan funds were $5,993.

GETTING IN

Dartmouth is quite selective, admitting about 17 percent of those who apply. Strong emphasis is placed on all academic parameters for admission, including rigor of academic program, GPA, class rank, essay, test scores, and recommendations, while among non-academic factors, character and extracurricular activities are weighed heavily when Dartmouth chooses its future students. Volunteer work and talent and ability are taken into account too. Also, as the college explains on its website, admissions officers look for evidence of "passion for ideas, dedication to learning, leadership, compassion, integrity, motivation, and sense of humor." Members of the freshman class scored an average of 1437 on the SAT and had a GPA of 3.75.

What do Graduates Do?

Sciences, medicine, engineering, and business, along with teaching, research, public service, and writing, are popular career fields for Dartmouth graduates. Most Dartmouth graduates enroll in a graduate program within five years of graduating, and these include studies in law, medicine, engineering, business, and the liberal arts. In 2002, 65 percent went into the workforce from college and nearly 22 percent went directly into graduate degree programs, while 3 percent chose volunteer work. D'Acres of New Hampshire Organic Farm and Educational Homestead, Dana-Farber Cancer Institute, The New England Center for Children, Axia Limited, Barclays Capital, Fidelity Investments, and many more, including top firms, are among those who recruit on campus.

The Bottom Line

Incoming freshmen at Dartmouth in 2006 could expect to pay $33,297 in tuition and $294 in required fees. On-campus room and board totaled $9,840. Check out the cost calculator and service financial aid calculators on its website. The average grant award for first-year students is $26,838, and the average job and loan award for first-year students is $4,201. In recent years, Dartmouth has increased scholarship funding to students whose family incomes are $45,000 and below, allowing for reduction in the loan portion of the financial aid these students receive from Dartmouth.

Fun Facts

Dartmouth's Cabin & Trail club maintains part of the Appalachian Trail which runs near campus.

Each spring since 1973 the Dartmouth Powwow, organized by a student group of Native Americans, takes place on campus, featuring traditional dance, crafts, and music. Part of Dartmouth's mission when it was founded in the eighteenth century was to provide for the education of Native Americans.

Daniel Webster, Nelson Rockefeller, and Robert Frost are Dartmouth alumni.

Education Requirements

Arts/fine arts, English (including composition), foreign languages, humanities, math, sciences (biological or physical), social science; one course in history, philosophy, or religion

FINANCIAL INFO

Tuition	$33,297
Room & board	$9,840
Average book expense	$1,217
Required fees	$200
Average freshman need-based grant	$26,838
Average freshman need-based loan	$3,138
% of graduates who borrowed	4
Average indebtedness	$19,305

Financial Aid Forms

Students must submit FAFSA, CSS/financial aid profile, noncustodial (divorced/separated) parent's statement, business/farm supplement, Current W-2 forms or federal tax returns.

Financial Aid filing deadline	2/1

POSTGRAD

Career Services

Alumni network, alumni services, career/job search classes, career assessment, internships, regional alumni, on-campus job interviews. Off-campus job opportunities are excellent.

DAVIDSON COLLEGE

PO Box 7156, Davidson, NC 28035-5000
www.Davidson.edu • Admissions: 704-894-2230
Fax: 704-894-2016 • E-mail: admission@davidson.edu • Financial Aid: 704-894-2232

STUDENTS

Religious affiliation	None
Academic year	
calendar	semester
Undergrad	
enrollment	1,683
% male/female	50/50
% Asian	2
% Black, non-Latino	6
% Latino	4
% international	3
% from out of state	82
% freshmen return for	
sophomore year	96
% freshmen graduate	
within 4 years	84

STUDENT LIFE

% of students living	
on campus	91
% in fraternities	40

ADMISSIONS

# of applicants	4,258
% accepted	27
% enrolled	40
# of early decision/action	
applicants	441
% accepted early	
decision/action	49

HIGH SCHOOL UNITS REQUIRED

4 English, 3 math, 2 science, 1 foreign language, 2 social studies and history

HIGH SCHOOL UNITS RECOMMENDED

4 Math, 4 science, 4 foreign language, 4 social studies and history

ABOUT DAVIDSON COLLEGE

Davidson is a relatively small school in small-town North Carolina. It's also a college whose academic reputation rivals that of Ivy League schools such as Yale and Princeton. Despite being consistently ranked among the top 10 liberal arts colleges in the United States by a number of evaluators, Davidson is neither ivory tower nor isolated. What it is, in fact, is a community of people interested and intrigued by learning. Classes are small and intense, often having fewer than 20 students. Science, English, business, psychology, and the arts are all popular majors.

Hard intellectual work is required, and undergraduates often contribute to faculty research, but forming friendships and making connections in this small community is just as important as, and even part of, the learning process. About 80 percent of students live on campus in dormitories and apartments, and they socialize through fraternities, eating houses (another type of social group), more than 200 campus organizations, and intercollegiate and intramural sports. Students also can become involved in social and service activities in nearby Charlotte, one of North Carolina's fastest-growing cities, which is about 20 miles away. College administrators take great care in pairing freshman roommates, and they must be doing something right: Most seniors count among their closest friends those whom they first knew in their freshman dorms.

Davidson began as a Presbyterian college, and while it still has strong theological ties, no one is obligated to participate in religious life. However, the honor code is mandatory. The honor code, a recognition and promise that honor, honesty, responsibility, and respect are guiding ideas and disciplines, frames all of campus life. As a result exams are self-scheduled, library stacks are open, and community bicycles are free to borrow.

Students Say

"I feel like I am always learning, even when I am not in the classroom. The atmosphere provided by my fellow classmates provides almost as many new intellectual experiences as my time in class."

Bang for Your Buck

Davidson's admission decisions are made without regard for financial status. Once a student is admitted, the school works to ensure that that student can afford to attend. Of the 160 freshman applicants found to have financial need in 2005 (out of 262 who requested aid), the college awarded enough to meet the full aid requirements of all 160 students. Davidson is loyal to these students too: Once qualified for aid, a student who remains in good standing may expect to have aid renewed each year. Of the upperclassmen qualifying for aid in 2005, Davidson again met 100 percent of need with combinations of scholarships, loans, and self-help awards. Approximately 35 percent of Davidson's students receive need-based aid in some form.

Getting In

Davidson is highly selective: Not for nothing is it compared to the Ivy League. But the idea of community plays a part too, and college admissions evaluators value recommendations and character as well as the rigor and accomplishment evident in a student's academic record. Volunteer work is also considered, as is evidence of talent and ability, extracurricular activities, and the quality of the student's application essay. The average SAT for accepted freshmen in 2005 was 1359 and the average ACT score was 29. The average high school GPA of all freshman students who submitted a GPA rank in 2005 was 3.96. Davidson also requires a college prep course and recommends that students add third and fourth years in science and in the same foreign language, continue mathematics through calculus, and take additional courses in history.

Very Important Admission Factors

Character/personal qualities, recommendation(s), rigor of secondary school record, volunteer work

Important Admission Factors

Application essay, extracurricular activities, talent/ability

Average HS GPA	3.96
Range SAT Verbal	640–750
Range SAT Math	650–740
Range ACT	28–32
Minimum TOEFL (paper/computer)	600/250

Application Deadlines

Early decision	11/15
Early decision notification	12/15
Regular admission	1/2
Regular notification	4/1
# of transfer applicants	63
% of transfer applicants accepted	17

ACADEMICS

Student/faculty ratio	10:1
% faculty teaching undergraduates	100
% of classes taught by graduate students	0

Most Popular Majors

- Biology
- English
- History
- Economics
- Psychology

EDUCATION REQUIREMENTS

Arts/fine arts, English (including composition), foreign languages, history, math, philosophy, sciences (biological or physical), social science, religion, cultural diversity

FINANCIAL INFO

Tuition	$29,119
Room & board	$8,590
Average book expense	$1,000
Required fees	$1,075
Average freshman need-based grant	$16,871
Average freshman need-based loan	$3,063
% of graduates who borrowed	34
Average indebtedness	$22,954

FINANCIAL AID FORMS

Students must submit FAFSA, CSS/financial aid profile, noncustodial (divorced/separated) parent's statement, business/farm supplement, parent and student tax returns and W-2 forms; corporate tax returns, if applicable.

POSTGRAD

% going to graduate school   25

CAREER SERVICES

Alumni network, alumni services, career/job search classes, career assessment, internships, on-campus job interviews. Off-campus job opportunities are excellent.

WHAT DO GRADUATES DO?

Many Davidson graduates enter public service, either through politics or in public-sector jobs in government. Law and medicine are also popular career choices for Davidson graduates. The career center hosts a number of career fairs during the year, both for a general range of employers as well as those for specific fields. Davidson graduates work with Children's Theatre of Charlotte, Blue Nine Partners, Bain & Company, TIAA-CREF, the Sierra Club, Bank of America, and Union Theological Seminary.

THE BOTTOM LINE

For the 2006–2007 academic year, students at Davidson will pay $29,119 for tuition and $1,075 other required fees. Room and board (most students, including all freshmen, live on campus) add about $8,500 to the annual cost of a Davidson education. Freshmen granted aid in 2005–2006 received an average of $3,063 in loans, $3,178 in self-help assistance, and $16,871 in scholarship aid.

FUN FACTS

The Royal Shakespeare Company from England is doing a teaching and performing residency at Davidson through 2008.

Dr. Karl "Skip" Barkley, the general practitioner for the Wildcats, the college sports teams, has taken part in medical mission trips to Belarus, Nicaragua, and Mexico.

Mystery and true crime author Patricia Cornwell is a Davidson alumna.

DENISON UNIVERSITY

PO Box 740, 100 Chapel Drive, Granville, OH 43023
www.Denison.edu • Admissions: 740-587-6276
Fax: 740-587-6306 • E-mail: admissions@denison.edu • Financial Aid: 740-587-6279

STUDENTS

Religious affiliation
No Affiliation
Academic year
calendar   semester
Undergrad
enrollment   2,287
% male/female   43/57
% Asian   3
% Black, non-Latino   5
% Latino   3
% international   5
% from out of state   63
% freshmen return for
sophomore year   88
% freshmen graduate
within 4 years   78

STUDENT LIFE

% of students living
on campus   98
% in fraternities   31
% in sororities   40

ADMISSIONS

of applicants   5,030
% accepted   39
% enrolled   30
# of early decision/action
applicants   132
% accepted early
decision/action   70

HIGH SCHOOL UNITS REQUIRED

4 English

HIGH SCHOOL UNITS RECOMMENDED

4 Math, 4 science, 3
foreign language, 2 social
studies, 1 history

ABOUT DENISON UNIVERSITY

A small school with a rigorous curriculum and accessible professors, Ohio's Denison University pushes its undergraduates to excel. The workload here is frequently heavy, and falling behind is actively discouraged. Involved professors expect daily attendance (they're keeping track, too) and consider homework assignments and papers essential to the learning process. In short, if you snooze, you lose. Fortunately, there is plenty of help available to keep you from falling away from the pack—such as free tutoring and a writing center with a helpful staff. Anthropology sociology, arts programs, English, and psychology remain big draws. The hard sciences also offer an outstanding experience, especially with the addition of a massive new science center.

Denison's Greek scene was once legendary; today it is more sedate—the result of tighter reigns on the Greek's social habits on behalf of the administration. The university also did away with off-campus housing, making house parties and the like a thing of the past. Still, students can keep occupied with a steady events calendar of comedians, bands, films, lectures, concerts, and movies that give a wide range of entertainment. There is also a great opportunity for fine arts entertainment with gallery openings, dance recitals, choir and orchestra concerts, and student recitals. Sleepy hometown Granville pushes some students to drive the half-hour into Columbus for a good time. The student body is notoriously preppy and well-groomed, but a small counterculture of arts and film kids (look for them in the coffeehouse) adds some diversity.

BANG FOR YOUR BUCK

Denison enjoys a strong endowment that allows the school to invest heavily in students, both in the form of academic scholarships and need-based grants. The school forcefully asserts that strong academic credentials are the single most important criteria for admission. They seek to recruit a student body with a diversity of exceptional talents, regardless of whether those students have financial need. Assistance comes in the forms of both academic scholarships and need-based grants.

Students Say

"This is a small, active campus with lots of student organizations and a strong feeling of community. Every student seems to be involved in at least three organizations and every organization seems to get more and more successful every year."

VERY IMPORTANT ADMISSION FACTORS

Academic GPA, application essay, class rank, recommendation(s), rigor of secondary school record, standardized test scores

IMPORTANT ADMISSION FACTORS

Extracurricular activities, interview, talent/ability

Average HS GPA   3.6
Range SAT Verbal 580–690
Range SAT Math   590–680
Range ACT   26–30
Minimum TOEFL
   (paper/computer) 550/213

APPLICATION DEADLINES

Early decision 11/1 and 1/1
Regular admission   1/15
Regular notification   4/1
# of transfer applicants   65
% of transfer applicants
   accepted   51

ACADEMICS

Student/faculty ratio   11:1
% faculty teaching
   undergraduates   100
% of classes taught by
   graduate students   0

MOST POPULAR MAJORS

• Communications and media studies
• Economics
• English language and literature

Even so, the school cannot guarantee that it will meet 100 percent of demonstrated federal need, in what the schools calls "high-need cases," and students who still find the price too steep may need to look to outside scholarships. Nearly half of all Denison students receive some form of need-based aid; 97 percent of undergraduates received some form of aid in 2005–2006, the last year for which such statistics were available.

Merit scholarships are available for stellar abilities in academics, leadership, and the arts. The school also offers some minority scholarships. All told, Denison offers approximately 45 full-tuition scholarships, unlimited half-tuition scholarships, and Denison National Merit Stipends to prospective students.

GETTING IN

Denison is a highly competitive school. High school transcript is the most important factor in the admissions decision; the school looks for strong grades achieved in a rigorous college-prep curriculum. Standardized test scores are important, but slightly less so. Essays and recommendations are considered, as are such intangibles as life experience, extracurricular activities, and diversity in all of its forms. Candidates are not required to apply separately to divisions within Denison; admission to the university constitutes admission to all programs offered.

WHAT DO GRADUATES DO?

Denison alumni work in profit and nonprofit organizations in a variety of career fields, including advocacy, banking, investment banking, consulting, insurance, management, sales, research, teaching, and more. Top campus recruiters include Abercrombie & Fitch, AC Nielsen, Americorps, Deloitte and Touche, Denver Publishing, Educational Resources Group, the Grass Roots Campaign, Morningstar, National City Bank, the Ohio Legislative Service Commission, the Ohio Public Interest Research Group, the Peace Corps, and Teach for America.

THE BOTTOM LINE

For 2006–2007, the approximate cost of attending Denison was $39,220; tuition costs were $29,860; $800 in additional fees; $8,560 in room and board; and $1,800 for personal expenses and books. Thanks to generous aid packages, the average out-of-pocket expense of aid-receiving families in 2005–2006 (the last year for which figures were available) was $13,473.

FUN FACTS

Denison boasts an impressive alumni list that includes actors Steve Carell, Jennifer Garner, and Hal Holbrook; former Disney CEO Michael Eisner; Senator Richard Lugar; ESPN President George Bodenheimer; and Indy Car legend Bobby Rahal.

The firm of Frederick Law Olmsted designed the scenic Denison campus. Olmsted is a legendary landscape architect best known for designing New York City's Central Park, Brooklyn's Prospect Park, and the Stanford University campus.

During the fall semester, thousands of buzzards circle Denison's campus each day and roost in trees and on campus buildings. Sometimes they sit, wings outstretched, on the corner of Swasey Chapel to warm their wings in the morning. Legend has it that they are looking for freshmen who have recently completed their first exams. The buzzard is considered the "unofficial mascot" by students at Denison University.

EDUCATION REQUIREMENTS

Arts/fine arts, English (including composition), foreign languages, humanities, sciences (biological or physical), social science

FINANCIAL INFO

Tuition	$29,860
Room & board	$8,560
Average book expense	$1,800
Required fees	$800
Average freshman need-based grant	$15,711
Average freshman need-based loan	$4,182
% of graduates who borrowed	46
Average indebtedness	$14,257

FINANCIAL AID FORMS

Students must submit FAFSA.

POSTGRAD

% going to graduate school	15
% going to law school	2
% going to business school	1
% going to medical school	2

CAREER SERVICES

Alumni network, alumni services, career assessment, internships, regional alumni, on-campus job interviews. Off-campus job opportunities are fair.

DEPAUW UNIVERSITY

101 East Seminary, Greencastle, IN 46135
www.DePauw.edu • Admissions: 765-658-4006
Fax: 765-658-4007 • E-mail: admission@depauw.edu • Financial Aid: 765-658-4030

STUDENTS

Religious affiliation

	Methodist
Academic year calendar	4-1-4
Undergrad enrollment	2,345
% male/female	45/55
% Asian	2
% Black, non-Latino	6
% Latino	3
% international	2
% from out of state	53
% freshmen return for sophomore year	90
% freshmen graduate within 4 years	71

STUDENT LIFE

% of students living on campus	99
% in fraternities	72
% in sororities	68

ADMISSIONS

# of applicants	3,440
% accepted	66
% enrolled	26
# of early decision/action applicants	55
% accepted early decision/action	89

HIGH SCHOOL UNITS RECOMMENDED

4 English, 4 math, 4 science
(2 science lab), 4 foreign
language, 4 social studies

VERY IMPORTANT ADMISSION FACTORS

Academic GPA, rigor of
secondary school record,
standardized test scores

ABOUT DEPAUW UNIVERSITY

With demanding academics and a dominant Greek scene, DePauw University is the quintessential "work hard, play hard" school. Undergraduates stream here for first-rate programs in business, which include the Management Fellows Program with its coveted internship opportunities. They're also drawn by top departments in computer science and technology, media studies, the sciences, and music. Distribution requirements lean heavily toward the humanities and communications, guaranteeing that undergrads will leave with a strong liberal arts education and will have endured a challenging, heavy workload. DePauw's Winter Program, a month-long inter-term sends many students abroad (and away from the blustery Midwestern weather) while allowing others to undertake independent research projects. Small, discussion-based classes are led by professors who hold their pupils firmly to high academic standards.

Of course, DePauw students love a good party too, and the huge Greek system here ensures plenty of those, running the gamut from formals to philanthropies. In fact, DePauw has one of the nation's most popular Greek scenes. The bustling frat and sorority scene helps take the sting off life in Greencastle, a small town with few social options. Kids road-trip to Indianapolis when they want some big-city fun, but most are content to hang around campus and study, party, and cheer on their Tigers, who compete in the NCAA's Division III Southern Collegiate Athletic Conference. Generally speaking, the typical DePauw undergrad is Caucasian, conservative, preppy, and driven to succeed in school. He or she is more likely to be a doer than a deep thinker, more often immersed in athletics, socializing, and community service than in contemplation and introspection.

BANG FOR YOUR BUCK

DePauw is especially strong in the area of merit-based awards. The merit-award program takes into consideration unweighted high school GPA; class rank; and SAT or ACT scores to provide grants of up to $15,000 per year. More than 79 percent of the scholarship assistance the school awards comes from institutional funds rather than state or federal sources. Need-based financial aid is calculated from information you provide on the DePauw University Application for Need-Based Assistance (available in December) and the Free Application for Federal Student Aid (FAFSA). Once a student is enrolled at DePauw University, the only awards recognizing outstanding achievement or special talent are tuition awards given through academic departments or administrative offices. Students may contact academic department chairs regarding departmental awards.

"DePauw offers students experiential learning, a challenging curriculum in the classroom, and a variety of leadership opportunities outside it."

Fifty-seven percent of all DePauw undergraduates receive need-based assistance; 59 percent of those students received grants averaging nearly $12,500. The other 41 percent receive their aid in the form of loans and employment.

GETTING IN

Admission at DePauw is highly selective. Over 60 percent of those admitted exceed a score of 600 on the SAT Math and/or the SAT Verbal; the median combined score is 1250. Eighty-five percent of successful applicants are in the top quarter of their high school graduating class. The school looks for "a rigorous high school academic program where the student has excelled, both in terms of GPA and rank, [and a] strong performance on the SAT I/ACT" in its applicants.

WHAT DO GRADUATES DO?

DePauw scatters its graduates throughout the professions—consulting, education, entertainment, financial services, government, medicine, nonprofit/social service, and science. Standard & Poor's ranks the school eighth among over 800 liberal arts schools as a producer of top business executives. The school's top-notch School of Music helps populate the music world, while its Information Technology Associates Program sends many grads out into the world of IT. Prominent on-campus recruiters include Eli Lilly & Co., Harris Nesbitt, IBM, and Starcom.

IMPORTANT ADMISSION FACTORS

Application essay, class rank, interview, recommendation(s)

Average HS GPA	3.66
Range SAT Verbal	560–660
Range SAT Math	570–670
Range ACT	24–29
Minimum TOEFL (paper/computer)	560/225

APPLICATION DEADLINES

Early decision	11/1
Early decision notification	1/1
Regular admission	2/1
Regular notification	4/1
# of transfer applicants	50
% of transfer applicants accepted	38

ACADEMICS

Student/faculty ratio	10:1
% faculty teaching undergraduates	100
% of classes taught by graduate students	0

MOST POPULAR MAJORS

- Economics
- English composition
- Mass communications/media studies

EDUCATION REQUIREMENTS

Arts/fine arts, English (including composition), foreign languages, history, humanities, math, philosophy, sciences (biological or physical), social science

FINANCIAL INFO

Tuition	$27,400
Room & board	$7,800
Average book expense	$700
Required fees	$380
Average freshman need-based grant	$14,841
Average freshman need-based loan	$3,745
% of graduates who borrowed	55
Average indebtedness	$15,635

FINANCIAL AID FORMS

Students must submit FAFSA, institution's own financial aid form.

Financial Aid filing deadline	2/15

POSTGRAD

% going to graduate school	23
% going to law school	5
% going to business school	1
% going to medical school	2

CAREER SERVICES

Alumni network, alumni services, career/job search classes, career assessment, internships, regional alumni, on-campus job interviews. Off-campus job opportunities are fair.

THE BOTTOM LINE

After factoring in all forms of aid and expenses, the average DePauw aid recipient and his or her family are responsible for $11,407 in out-of-pocket expenses. Although DePauw does not guarantee meeting full demonstrated need of all admitted students, in 2005–2006 the school fully met the need of 97 percent of its aid recipients and met, on average, 98 percent of the demonstrated need of all aid recipients.

FUN FACTS

DePauw's alumni rolls are crammed with famous folks. Among the best-known: former Vice President J. Danforth Quayle; civil rights leader Vernon Jordon; former U.S. House member and Vice Chair of the 9-11 Commission Lee Hamilton; ESPN founder Bill Rasmussen; Nitty Gritty Dirt Band member Jimmy Ibbotson; and novelist Barbara Kingsolver.

DePauw's Society of Professional Journalists, founded on the DePauw campus in 1909, has a rich tradition of graduating some of the nation's top journalists. Their ranks include: Bernard Kilgore '29, the former managing editor of the *Wall Street Journal*; John McWethy '69, ABC News Chief National Security Correspondent; Pulitzer Prize–winning investigative journalist and author James B. Stewart '73; and Brett Baier '92, FOX News Pentagon Correspondent.

DePauw is home to the nation's first sorority—Kappa Alpha Theta—which was founded here in 1870.

Forget about belly bombers and Big Macs. When DePauw students need a burger, they order a GCB (short for Garlic Cheeseburger) from Marvin's, a local eatery that also makes pizzas and burritos. Unlike the local White Castle or Mickey D's, Marv's, as it's affectionately known to students, will bring the burgers right to you.

DRURY UNIVERSITY

900 North Benton Avenue, Springfield, MO 65802
www.Drury.edu • Admissions: 417-873-7205
Fax: 417-866-3873 • E-mail: druryad@drury.edu • Financial Aid: 417-873-7319

STUDENTS

Religious affiliation

	Other
Academic year calendar	semester
Undergrad enrollment	1,606
% male/female	46/54
% Asian	2
% Black, non-Latino	1
% Latino	2
% Native American	1
% international	5
% from out of state	18
% freshmen return for sophomore year	78
% freshmen graduate within 4 years	48

STUDENT LIFE

% of students living on campus	52
% in fraternities	32
% in sororities	24

ADMISSIONS

# of applicants	1,519
% accepted	74
% enrolled	45

HIGH SCHOOL UNITS REQUIRED

4 English, 3 math, 3 science, 2 foreign language, 3 social studies

HIGH SCHOOL UNITS RECOMMENDED

4 English, 4 math, 3 science, 2 foreign language, 3 social studies

ABOUT DRURY UNIVERSITY

Drury University places an emphasis on quality academics and strives to make subjects relevant to students' future plans. As part of that initiative, about 75 percent of students participate in internships of some kind, and Drury's education majors are offered the opportunity for extensive classroom experience. Many undergrads here choose to major in architecture, communications, business, and psychology. Biology and theater are also popular. The Hammons School of Architecture is the first fully accredited architecture school on a liberal arts campus. Class sizes are small, with most comprising an agreeable 10 to 30 students. Students and faculty alike value the small class size and the opportunity for interaction and mentoring it allows. And this type of interaction is a key component in Drury's vision, as all first-year students must enroll in Alpha Seminar, a year-long course in which students are required to attend numerous speaking engagements related to a theme, such as sustainability or global security. First-year students may also apply to join "living and learning" communities, residential programs related to academic interests such as health care, sciences, the arts, and justice-related fields.

While Drury's student body of 1,606 full-time undergraduates is largely middle-class and from the Midwest, the school takes a worldly stance with its required Global Perspectives (GP21) courses—which means that each student graduates with a minor in global studies. It's a program intended to integrate liberal arts–based thinking and knowledge with the imminent international challenges of the twenty-first century. Additionally, the college offers study abroad programs in Greece, China, England, Malaysia, and a dozen other locations. An impressive 40 percent of Drury's students take part in study abroad programs.

Back home in Springfield, students find the campus pleasant, welcoming, and easy to navigate. The city offers ready access to lively nightlife, the arts, and sporting events. Greek culture and the Disciples of Christ church are strong presences on campus—but not to the exclusion of those who don't favor these approaches to campus life. Students from both these groups and those who don't affiliate with either are often involved in service projects on and off campus. Many actively support the school's athletic teams—the Panthers—in men's and women's basketball, cross country, soccer, and other sports.

"The small classrooms and personal relationships with other students and professors encourage rigorous, honest, and passionate learning. The professors all seem to really love it here and the students enjoy the dedication from their teachers."

VERY IMPORTANT ADMISSION FACTORS

Standardized test scores

IMPORTANT ADMISSION FACTORS

Academic GPA, application essay, character/personal qualities, class rank, recommendation(s)

Average HS GPA   3.76
Range SAT Verbal 500–630
Range SAT Math   490–630
Range ACT   22–27
Minimum TOEFL
  (paper/computer) 530/197

APPLICATION DEADLINES

Regular admission   3/4
Regular notification rolling
# of transfer applicants 244
% of transfer applicants
  accepted   151

ACADEMICS

Student/faculty ratio   13:1
% faculty teaching
  undergraduates   100
% of classes taught by
  graduate students   0

MOST POPULAR MAJORS

• Business administration/
  management
• Education
• Health/medical preparatory
  programs
• Architecture

BANG FOR YOUR BUCK

Drury awards financial aid through a combination of scholarships, self help, and loan aid. A large number of incoming freshmen needing financial assistance have all of their need met. More than 70 percent of all students at Drury qualify for aid of some sort, and most continue to receive it throughout their four years there.

GETTING IN

Drury relies heavily on standardized test scores in its evaluation of applicants. Required SAT or ACT scores weigh most heavily, followed by class rank, academic GPA, recommendations, and the application essay. Character and personal qualities are the chief non-academic criteria of importance. The rigor of a student's academic program follows in third place, along with volunteer work and work experience. Two years of algebra and one year of geometry are required for admission, and the college recommends at least four units of English along with courses in natural sciences, social studies, and a foreign language. The average GPA of student admitted to Drury in 2006 was 3.76. The average ACT score of those accepted was 25 and the average SAT was 1661.

What do Graduates Do?

Architecture, medical-related fields, and teaching, as well as business-related professions, are often pursued by Drury grads. Employers such as Wal-Mart, the City of Springfield, Bass PRO Shops, St. John's Health Systems, Kirkpatrick, Phillips and Miller, Northwestern Mutual, and Regions Bank regularly interview on campus, and the career center sponsors career fairs focused on both business and education.

The Bottom Line

Full-time undergraduate tuition at Drury is $15,173. Required fees for freshmen are $484. On-campus room and board totals $5,790 per academic year. For 2006–2007, $5,979 was the average scholarship award to incoming freshmen; the average self-help award was $4,482 and the average loan amount was also around $4,125.

Fun Facts

Drury is committed to being a green campus and urges students to turn off the lights, use bicycles or walk rather than drive, and support the use of fair-trade coffee on campus.

David Harrison, author of the popular children's books *The Boy with a Drum*, *The Mouse Was Out at Recess*, and *The Alligator in the Closet*, has a degree in biology from Drury.

Drury is listed as one of the 50 most wired small college campuses by Yahoo Internet Life.

Everyone's favorite game show host, Bob Barker, returned to his alma mater in 2007 to deliver the commencement address.

Education Requirements

Arts/fine arts, computer literacy, English (including composition), foreign languages, history, humanities, math, philosophy, sciences (biological or physical), social science, health and wellness

FINANCIAL INFO

Tuition	$15,173
Room & board	$5,790
Average book expense	$1,000
Required fees	$339
Average freshman need-based grant	$6,096
Average freshman need-based loan	$4,167
% of graduates who borrowed	42
Average indebtedness	$17,585

Financial Aid Forms

Students must submit FAFSA, institution's own financial aid form.

POSTGRAD

% going to graduate school	35
% going to law school	5
% going to business school	9
% going to medical school	15

Career Services

Alumni network, alumni services, career/job search classes, career assessment, internships, regional alumni. Off-campus job opportunities are excellent.

EAST CAROLINA UNIVERSITY

Office of Undergraduate Admissions, 106 Whichard Building, Greenville, NC 27858-4353
www.ECU.edu • Admissions: 252-328-6640
Fax: 252-328-6945 • E-mail: admis@mail.ecu.edu • Financial Aid: 252-328-6610

STUDENTS

Religious affiliation
　　　　　　　No Affiliation
Academic year
　calendar　　　semester
Undergrad
　enrollment　　　17,626
% male/female　　　41/59
% Asian　　　　　　　2
% Black, non-Latino　　15
% Latino　　　　　　　2
% Native American　　1
% from out of state　　14
% freshmen return for
sophomore year　　　76
% freshmen graduate
　within 4 years　　　25

STUDENT LIFE

% of students living
　on campus　　　　27
% in fraternities　　4
% in sororities　　　4

ADMISSIONS

of applicants　　11,628
% accepted　　　　74
% enrolled　　　　38

HIGH SCHOOL UNITS
REQUIRED

4 English, 4 math, 3 science
(1 science lab), 2 foreign
language, 2 social studies, 4
academic electives

HIGH SCHOOL UNITS
RECOMMENDED

1 Fine arts, 1 social studies
(must be U.S. History)

ABOUT EAST CAROLINA UNIVERSITY

To most Carolinians, East Carolina University (simply ECU to lo-cals) is all about the Pirates, the school's mascot for its wildly popular intercollegiate teams. Those who attend this public university, how-ever, know that athletics are just a side dish; academic opportunities are the main course. Among ECU's many assets are strong programs in business and premed program along with an excellent physical therapy sequence and nursing school. With one of the Southeast's best art programs, students flock to ECU to pursue their passions in dance, music, interior design, and theater. The overall academic vibe is laid-back. While professors and students form meaningful relation-ships, the reasonable workload allows students to succeed without keeping their noses glued to a book for four years straight.

Hometown Greenville is no pulsing metropolis, but the campus is active enough to offset Greenville's occasional dearth of activity. On campus, there's a full event calendar and a recreation center where students can run, lift, shoot some hoops, and tackle the climbing wall. It's no wonder that sports at ECU are huge, as is the active party scene. Students quickly become skilled in balancing their studies with opportunities to party and drink, along with other popular alterna-tives like church groups, Greek life, minority groups, dances, bingo, and movies. With Raleigh and the beach about an hour and a half drive away, road trips are not uncommon.

BANG FOR YOUR BUCK

The state constitution of North Carolina guarantees affordable higher education to state residents, thus ECU is able to offer a low tuition to its students. This is especially true for native Tar Heels. Out-of-staters, on the other hand, will probably think that this school's out-of-state tuition is competitive but not a steal compared to other public doctorate-research intensive institutions. (The out-of-state un-dergraduate tuition falls within the midrange of tuitions charged by peer institutions.)

Most aid at ECU is need-based, stemming from need-based federal and state programs. The majority of the university's state-appropri-ated funds are earmarked for need-based programs, in order to en-sure students are "held harmless" from tuition increases. Merit-based scholarships are limited due to low-endowment funds.

Students Say

"ECU is continuing to create a high academic profile that rivals other top universities in the South by breaking down barriers and stereotypical attitudes that others may have toward the school."

Available merit-based aid includes a variety of academic scholarships to students who are in the top 5 percent of their high school class and who have a minimum 3.5 high school grade point average. While the size of the scholarships varies, and the number of scholarships is limited, all applicants who meet these criteria should request information about how to apply for these scholarships from ECU. The school also offers athletic scholarships, leadership scholarships, and scholarships specific to academic programs.

GETTING IN

Academic record is the single most important component of an application to ECU. GPA, class rank, and quality of curriculum all factor into an admissions decision. Standardized test scores are also considered to be a very important ingredient to the admission equation. Other factors including extracurricular activities, alumni relations, and recommendations are weighed at a lesser extent. All applicants, regardless of major, must follow the same set of processes to gain admission to the university. Each school or department, however, may have a special set of requirements to declare a major in that particular program. Details are available on the school's website.

WHAT DO GRADUATES DO?

Many graduates choose to seek work in health care related fields. Over 75 health care companies recruit on the ECU campus each year, including Maxim Healthcare Services, Duke University Hospital, and numerous regional medical centers. Construction management is another popular field, with approximately 50 companies coming on campus to recruit graduates each year, including: Centex Homes, Hensel Phelps Construction Company, and James G. Davis Construction. The school also helps feed North Carolina's education and business work forces.

VERY IMPORTANT ADMISSION FACTORS

Class rank, rigor of secondary school record, standardized test scores

Average HS GPA	3.22
Range SAT Verbal	460–560
Range SAT Math	480–570
Range ACT	18–22
Minimum TOEFL (paper/computer)	550/213

APPLICATION DEADLINES

Regular admission	3/15
Regular notification	rolling
# of transfer applicants	2,636
% of transfer applicants accepted	85

ACADEMICS

Student/faculty ratio	21:1
% faculty teaching undergraduates	88
% of classes taught by graduate students	8

MOST POPULAR MAJORS

- Elementary education and teaching
- Fine/studio arts
- Nursing—registered nurse training (RN, ASN, BSN, MSN)

EDUCATION REQUIREMENTS

Arts/fine arts, English (including composition), humanities, math, sciences (biological or physical), social science, health and exercise and sport science

FINANCIAL INFO

In-state tuition	$2,335
Out-of-state tuition	$12,849
Room & board	$6,940
Average book expense	$900
Required fees	$1,668
Average freshman need-based grant	$8,843
Average freshman need-based loan	$5,391
% of graduates who borrowed	28
Average indebtedness	$19,614

FINANCIAL AID FORMS

Students must submit FAFSA.

POSTGRAD

CAREER SERVICES

Alumni services, career/job search classes, career assessment, internships, on-campus job interviews.

THE BOTTOM LINE

For 2006–2007, full-time in-state undergraduates at ECU could expect to spend $4,003 for the year in tuition and fees. Out-of-state students pay $14,517 annually in tuition and fees. Meal plans run from $1,125–$1,575 per semester; housing costs run from $3,760–$3,910 per year for freshmen, with suite housing available for upperclassmen at $4,275 per year. The good news from this school is that nearly all students who demonstrate need receive financial aid. Seventy-eight percent of assistance administered by the school is need-based scholarship or grant aid; 18 percent is need-based self-help aid, and only 17 percent is merit-based.

FUN FACTS

Well-known ECU alumni include film star Sandra Bullock; Kevin Williamson, the creator of *Scream* and *I Know What You Did Last Summer*; Rick Atkinson, historian and Pulitzer Prize winner; Earnest Byner, former all-pro running back; Bob Greczyn, CEO of Blue Cross and Blue Shield of North Carolina; and James Maynard, founder of the Golden Corral restaurant chain.

Housing options at ECU are plentiful. The campus offers a Leadership Hall, Honors Halls, and such special-interest housing lifestyle options such as a freshman experience hall, tobacco-free halls, community service halls, coed halls, and single-sex halls.

Several hours prior to every home football game, the team takes the "Pirate Walk," a five-minute stroll from the first-base side of the baseball stadium to their locker room. Cheerleaders accompany them and fans line the route to cheer on their gridiron heroes. When the game begins, the Pirates take the field to the tune of Jimi Hendrix's "Purple Haze" (because the Pirates' uniforms are purple).

EAST TENNESSEE STATE UNIVERSITY

ETSU Box 70731, Johnson City, TN 37614-0731
www.ETSU.edu • Admissions: 423-439-4213
Fax: 423-439-4630 • E-mail: go2etsu@etsu.edu • Financial Aid: 423-439-4300

STUDENTS

Religious affiliation
No Affiliation
Academic year
calendar   semester
Undergrad
enrollment   9,486
% male/female   42/58
% Asian   1
% Black, non-Latino   4
% Latino   1
% international   1
% from out of state   8
% freshmen return for
sophomore year   69
% freshmen graduate
within 4 years   15

STUDENT LIFE

% of students living
on campus   21
% in fraternities   7
% in sororities   6

ADMISSIONS

of applicants   3,601
% accepted   81
% enrolled   55

HIGH SCHOOL UNITS REQUIRED

4 English, 3 math, 2
science (1 science lab), 2
foreign language, 1 social
studies, 1 history, 1 visual/
performing arts

HIGH SCHOOL UNITS RECOMMENDED

4 Math, 3 science

ABOUT EAST TENNESSEE STATE UNIVERSITY

East Tennessee State University boasts 112 undergraduate programs and a reputation for generally small class sizes. You are likely to receive more individual attention here than you would receive at, say, your large, run-of-the-mill, impersonal state university. The nursing and health-related programs are reportedly excellent. The premed program is great, too. (If you stick around after graduation—and can get in—the medical school has a stellar reputation to boot.) The brand-new College of Pharmacy will admit its first students in Spring 2007. Students also speak highly of the outstanding choir and instrumental ensembles here. Those who make it into ETSU's Honors Scholars Program meet most of their general education requirements by participating in four interdisciplinary, highly interactive, yearlong seminars. They also complete a yearlong research project with a faculty mentor and a Senior Honors Thesis.

ETSU students are a reasonably diverse bunch. There are large numbers of returning and older students, who happen to blend in quite well with the traditional students. The surrounding town of Johnson City (population: just under 60,000) is a regional cultural center but not exactly a hub of urbanity. There are, however, plenty of good restaurants and a respected local music scene. If you are an outdoorsy type, the area is Nirvana: ETSU is situated in the picturesque southern Appalachian Mountains. Breathtaking views are commonplace, especially in the fall when the leaves are so gorgeous that it's distracting. World-class rock climbing, spelunking, fishing, mountain biking, kayaking, and white-water rafting are minutes from your door. And to get you in shape for all the rugged stuff, there's an impressive new 100,000-square-foot Center for Physical Activity, which offers virtually any exercise you can dream up, including the biggest climbing wall we've ever seen.

VERY IMPORTANT ADMISSION FACTORS

Academic GPA, standardized test scores

IMPORTANT ADMISSION FACTORS

Rigor of secondary school record

Average HS GPA	3.25
Range SAT Verbal	450–590
Range SAT Math	450–570
Range ACT	20–25
Minimum TOEFL (paper/computer)	500/173

APPLICATION DEADLINES

# of transfer applicants	2,011
% of transfer applicants accepted	62

ACADEMICS

Student/faculty ratio   17:1

MOST POPULAR MAJORS

• Criminal justice/law enforcement administration
• Multi/interdisciplinary studies
• Nursing—registered nurse training (RN, ASN, BSN, MSN)

EDUCATION REQUIREMENTS

Arts/fine arts, computer literacy, English (including composition), history, humanities, math, philosophy, sciences (biological or physical), social science

BANG FOR YOUR BUCK

ETSU students receive over $13 million in financial aid each year. Both need-based aid and merit-based scholarships are plentiful. The Honors Scholars Program provides a full-ride tuition to 20 first-year students. To be eligible, you need an ACT score of 29 (or an SAT Math and Verbal score of 1280) and a high school grade point average of 3.5 or better. You also need to show that you have participated in community and leadership activities. Both in-state and out-of-state students may apply. The Academic Performance Scholarship Program is the largest scholarship program on campus. Recipients receive $3,000 per academic year for four years. The program is comprised of Guaranteed Awards and Competitive Awards. To qualify for a Guaranteed Award, you need an ACT score of 28 (or a combined SAT Math and Verbal score of 1240) and at least a 3.5 GPA. To qualify for a Competitive Award, you need to graduate as valedictorian of your high school and to have an ACT score of 26 (or a combined SAT Math and Verbal score of 1140) and at least a 3.5 GPA.

ETSU students are eligible for a host of other scholarships as well. The Roan Scholars Leadership Program awards four scholarships that cover tuition, room, meals, and books. (Selected high schools nominate students for this one and you must maintain a 2.9 GPA at ETSU to keep it.) If you are a resident of the Volunteer State with good grades, you are eligible for a Tennessee Education Lottery Scholarship worth $3,000 annually. You need at least a 21 on the ACT (or a 980 on the SAT Math and Verbal) and a 3.0 high school GPA to be considered.

GETTING IN

If you are under 21, you need a high school GPA of at least 2.3 (on a 4.0 scale) or an ACT score of 19. You should also make sure to complete a solid college-prep curriculum.

What Do Graduates Do?

Among recent graduates of ETSU, about half find jobs in the local area and almost 75 percent hang their professional hats in the state of Tennessee. The median starting salary for graduates is a little over $30,000 per year. Many big-time companies recruit on campus each year including Sprint PCS, Northwestern Mutual, Wells Fargo, Cintas, and Wachovia.

The Bottom Line

Over the course of their undergraduate years, the average ETSU student receives about $18,800 worth of financial aid. According to our math, that's $4,700 per year (assuming you graduate in four years). The total cost for tuition, room and board, and books here is roughly $9,794 for in-state students and $19,458 for out-of-state students.

Fun Facts

East Tennessee is the Motherland of Country Music. Traditional mountain music, bluegrass, gospel—they all have their roots right here. It's fitting then that ETSU was the first modern university to offer a full-fledged program in Bluegrass and Country Music. Here you can learn about various bluegrass instruments and how to play them, vocal harmony, songwriting, and bluegrass music theory.

There are 57 computer labs for students on campus.

ETSU offers a summer program in which students can spend three weeks at beautiful Edinburgh University's School of Celtic and Scottish Studies. Participants learn about Scottish folklore and history, storytelling and literature, and music and the arts. They also venture deep into the Scottish Borders, Highlands, and Islands.

The Basler Challenge Course is the pride and joy of ETSU's outdoor-adventure program. It includes an Alpine Tower and a Carolina Straight Wall, which you can climb if you are feeling especially brave. All gear is provided.

ETSU graduates its student-athletes at an 87 percent clip. The national average is 60 percent.

Country music luminary Kenny Chesney and now-retired New York Jets defensive back Donnie Abraham attended ETSU.

FINANCIAL INFO

In-state tuition	$3,828
Out-of-state tuition	$13,522
Room & board	$5,024
Average book expense	$942
Required fees	$809
Average freshman need-based grant	$24,350
Average freshman need-based loan	$780
% of graduates who borrowed	28
Average indebtedness	$18,956

FINANCIAL AID FORMS

Students must submit FAFSA.

POSTGRAD

CAREER SERVICES

Alumni network, alumni services, career/job search classes, career assessment, internships, regional alumni, on-campus job interviews. Off-campus job opportunities are good.

EMPORIA STATE UNIVERSITY

1200 Commercial, Emporia, KS 66801-5087
www.Emporia.edu • Admissions: 620-341-5465
Fax: 620-341-5599 • E-mail: goto@emporia.edu • Financial Aid: 620-341-5457

STUDENTS

Religious affiliation
　　　　　　　No Affiliation
Academic year
　calendar　　　　semester
Undergrad
　enrollment　　　　4,458
% male/female　　　39/61
% Asian　　　　　　　1
% Black, non-Latino　　4
% Latino　　　　　　　5
% Native American　　1
% international　　　　2
% from out of state　　5
% freshmen return for
sophomore year　　　74
% freshmen graduate
　within 4 years　　　24

STUDENT LIFE

% of students living
　on campus　　　　22
% in fraternities　　12
% in sororities　　　9

ADMISSIONS

of applicants　　1,333
% accepted　　　　80
% enrolled　　　　72

HIGH SCHOOL UNITS REQUIRED

4 English, 3 math, 3
science, 3 social studies, 1
computer technology

HIGH SCHOOL UNITS RECOMMENDED

4 English, 3 math, 3
science, 3 social studies, 1
computer technology

ABOUT EMPORIA STATE UNIVERSITY

Students at Emporia State University call it a small school and a big school rolled into one, meaning benefits abound. From small classes, interesting professors, an undergraduate-oriented education to great career track programs, and strong music, theater, and visual arts departments, plus excellent facilities, many find a happy life at Emporia. The biggest draw, though, is the faculty, who are both approachable and devoted to their students. Those small class sizes help students get to know their teachers and make getting that perfect recommendation for grad school that much easier. Here, most of your teachers will know you by name. The education and business programs draw students from all over Kansas.

Your typical Emporia undergrad comes from a small town in Kansas, with a middle-class background, and spends at least two weekends a month at home with family. This doesn't exactly promote a great deal of diversity, but that comes in the form of adult and nontraditional students. The student body overall is tolerant. Just know that many students are fairly religious Christians, and it may be difficult for those of other faiths to find a place to worship.

ESU is definitely not a party school. Most of the partying begins and ends on Thursday nights, so you are on your own for the rest of the week. This dearth of weekend fun is largely because most students go home on weekends, leaving the campus empty. Games and performances are scheduled every week, however, and the Union Activities Council works diligently to fill the gaps. Coffee houses abound near campus, and there is access to all sorts of outdoor activities. A car can be a major boost to your social life, as wheels will give you access to the much livelier nearby cities of Lawrence, Kansas City, Topeka, and Witchita.

BANG FOR YOUR BUCK

By involving faculty and staff in their budgetary review process, Emporia is achieving its financial goals and providing students with quality academics at an affordable price. Its tuition is currently among the lowest in Kansas, and its flat-rate policy enables students to pay for only 10 hours of tuition regardless of how many "bonus" hours they are actually taking. Even nonresidents should find the cost of ESU more affordable than other comparable institutions. And if you are from Texas, Oklahoma, Colrado, Kansas, Missouri, or Nebraska special programs allow you to pay 150 percent of the in-state tuition rather than the total nonresident tuition.

ESU has scholarships worth looking into for all types of students. Among them are the Presidential Academic Award (PAAs), given to first-time freshmen and transfer students. Freshman students are eligible for scholarships based on their composite ACT scores, while transfer students may receive a PAA scholarship based on GPA. They range from $500–$1,200. The Guaranteed GPA Scholarships program provides continuing students with guaranteed scholarships for each of their remaining three years at ESU based on their GPA. Awards range from $500–$1,200. The Virginia Endly Scholars is the University's full-ride academic scholarship, covering the cost of in-state tuition and fees, residence hall fees, full meal plan, and the average cost of books and supplies. Departmental and athletic scholarships are also available for students who have special skills in art, athletics, debate, music, physical sciences, and theater.

GETTING IN

The ESU Admissions Office admits students through Qualified Admissions, which considers class rank, standardized test scores, and precollege classes. If you earn an ACT score of 21 or above or rank in the top one-third of your high school's graduating class or complete the precollege curriculum (as detailed at Kansasregents.org) with at least a 2.0 GPA, you will be admitted to ESU. ESU uses a rolling admission deadline, and students can be admitted for non-fall terms. Last year, ESU accepted 72 percent of its applicants.

WHAT DO GRADUATES DO?

ESU produces over a thousand high-quality graduates annually who find success in all manner of fields. Graduates have experienced placement rates as high as 99.6 percent. ESU students and recent graduates are heavily recruited for accounting management, and education majors, thanks in part to their superior career track programs in these areas. Some businesses that recruit and hire ESU students include Koch Industries, Sherwin Williams, Payless Shoe Source, and Newman Regional Health Center.

VERY IMPORTANT ADMISSION FACTORS

Academic GPA, class rank, standardized test scores

IMPORTANT ADMISSION FACTORS

Talent/ability

Average HS GPA	3.23
Range ACT	19–24
Minimum TOEFL (paper/computer)	450/133

APPLICATION DEADLINES

Regular notification	rolling
# of transfer applicants	1,086
% of transfer applicants accepted	83

ACADEMICS

Student/faculty ratio	18:1
% faculty teaching undergraduates	100
% of classes taught by graduate students	10

MOST POPULAR MAJORS

- Business administration/management
- Elementary education and teaching
- Biology

EDUCATION REQUIREMENTS

Arts/fine arts, computer literacy, English (including composition), history, humanities, math, sciences (biological or physical), social science, speech, cultural diversity, applied science, physical education

FINANCIAL INFO

In-state tuition	$2,862
Out-of-state tuition	$10,214
Room & board	$5,170
Average book expense	$900
Required fees	$724
Average freshman need-based grant	$1,923
Average freshman need-based loan	$2,465
% of graduates who borrowed	70
Average indebtedness	$16,005

FINANCIAL AID FORMS

Students must submit FAFSA, state aid form.

POSTGRAD

% going to graduate school	19

CAREER SERVICES

Alumni network, alumni services, career/job search classes, internships, on-campus job interviews. Off-campus job opportunities are excellent.

THE BOTTOM LINE

Tuition for a Kansas resident costs $2,862, while nonresidents pay $10,214. Room and board are an additional $5,170, and required fees add another $724 to the bill. Generally, Kansas residents will have a fall/spring budget of about $11,600, while a nonresident's budget will amount to $19,100. About 60 percent of students at ESU receive financial aid. Loans average $2,765, while need-based gifts provide an additional $1,788. This leaves a resident responsible for about $4,203 per year out-of-pocket, and a nonresident responsible for $11,555.

FUN FACTS

Emporia State University is the first and only university in the world to offer a four-year degree in Engraving Arts. It also offers the only Office Systems Management major in the state of Kansas, as well as the state's only glass-forming program.

The ESU Debate Team competes against all colleges and universities across the nation including all regents' schools, Harvard, Dartmouth, Michigan, University of California—Berkeley, and the Massachusetts Institute of Technology (MIT).

ESU offers multiple online degrees, including seven master's degrees, one bachelor's degree, and two certificates. ESU boasts a 95 percent completion rate in online courses, which compares to just 65 percent nationally.

ESU Summer Theater is the longest running Summer Stock theater in the Great Plains.

THE EVERGREEN STATE COLLEGE

2700 Evergreen Parkway Northwest, Office of Admissions, Olympia, WA 98505
www.Evergreen.edu • Admissions: 360-867-6170
Fax: 360-867-6576 • E-mail: admissions@evergreen.edu • Financial Aid: 360-867-6205

STUDENTS

Religious affiliation

No Affiliation

Academic year

calendar   quarter

Undergrad

enrollment   4,124

% male/female   45/55

% Asian   5

% Black, non-Latino   5

% Latino   5

% Native American   4

% from out of state   22

% freshmen return for

sophomore year   67

% freshmen graduate

within 4 years   44

STUDENT LIFE

% of students living

on campus   21

ADMISSIONS

of applicants   1,732

% accepted   88

% enrolled   38

HIGH SCHOOL UNITS REQUIRED

4 English, 3 math, 2 science (1 science lab), 2 foreign language, 3 social studies, 1 academic electives; 1 fine, visual, or performing arts elective (or other college prep elective from the areas above)

VERY IMPORTANT ADMISSION FACTORS

Academic GPA, rigor of secondary school record, standardized test scores

ABOUT THE EVERGREEN STATE COLLEGE

The Evergreen State College is a public, progressive liberal arts and sciences school located in Olympia, Washington. Things are a little bit different compared to most traditional state schools. Evergreen's curriculum is innovative, interdisciplinary, and collaborative. Programs, a collection of courses woven together, are taught by teams of professors. These programs are theme-focused, interactive, and aimed at building a holistic understanding of an area. Students are able to examine major academic topics and tackle philosophical questions (like the nature of democracy, for instance). There are no required classes. There are no grades. Instead, students design their own academic pathways and prepare annual academic plans with the guidance of faculty members. Instead of grades, students receive narrative evaluations of their work from their professors.

Outside the classroom, Evergreen is fairly rife with student activism. Alternative world views, nose rings, dreadlocks, and hippie chic are as common as Evergreen or GeoGear. On Evergreen's stunningly pristine campus, self-described misfits and outcasts from mainstream society convene to discuss big ideas, changing the world, and where to find the best latte. Social life is pretty mellow. The campus is somewhat removed from Olympia, a town with a great independent music scene, and there is no Greek system. Students often bike and hike in nearby forest trails (when the weather is accommodating) and generally take in the beauty of the Pacific Northwest.

BANG FOR YOUR BUCK

The Evergreen State College offers what most colleges cannot: private college amenities and class sizes at a public university price. Even better, that price is heavily and generously subsidized. Almost 65 percent of the students receive some form of financial aid, and the average aid package is $11,619 per academic year. This is a significant chunk of change when you consider the cost of in-state tuition for a year at Evergreen is less than $4,400. Nonresidents pay considerably more for tuition.

"My overall experience with the academics here is that those who help themselves by asking for help in understanding how best to utilize Evergreen for their specific needs will make it out of here with more bang for their buck than at any other institution."

IMPORTANT ADMISSION FACTORS

Application essay, first generation, level of applicant's interest

Average HS GPA	3.07
Range SAT Verbal	520–650
Range SAT Math	470–590
Range ACT	21–27
Minimum TOEFL (paper/computer)	550/213

APPLICATION DEADLINES

Regular admission	3/1
Regular notification	rolling
# of transfer applicants	1,526
% of transfer applicants accepted	86

ACADEMICS

Student/faculty ratio	21:1
% faculty teaching undergraduates	100
% of classes taught by graduate students	0

EDUCATION REQUIREMENTS

Evergreen does not have distribution requirements for specific course work, but students are expected to work toward the "Expectations of an Evergreen Graduate" which includes a range of interdisciplinary study and student learning outcomes.

Over 150 scholarships of all sizes—collectively worth nearly $500,000—are available to Evergreen students. Scholarships are awarded based on all kinds of different criteria, including academic achievement and musical talent. The Evergreen State College Foundation Scholarships, for example, cover every cent of undergraduate tuition for up to eighteen credits. The Foundation Scholarship Award is the equivalent of resident tuition and is awarded to students who have distinguished themselves in a wide range of areas, including academics, art, community service, journalism, and science. Newly enrolling evening and weekend students—and some other students—are eligible for a one-time partial tuition waiver.

GETTING IN

A grade point average of 3.1 or higher in a college preparatory curriculum and a minimum SAT score of 1100 (or an ACT score of 23) should get you admitted to Evergreen. If, for whatever reason, your grades or test scores are lower, you can still get into Evergreen by writing a polished and well-conceived essay about yourself, your educational achievements, and why you feel you're ready for college-level work. Our advice is that you write this essay as if your life depends on it because it does in many ways. Also, as the diversity of the student population is a very big deal on this campus, your chances of being admitted increase if you are a veteran of the Vietnam War, an adult who is 25 years or older, or if your parents have not graduated from college.

WHAT DO GRADUATES DO?

Approximately 40 percent of Evergreen's graduates attend graduate school within five years of receiving their diplomas. A little over one-third of all graduates find jobs in business, science, or computer-related occupations. About 6 percent of all graduates go into communications, a little fewer than 10 percent go into social sciences, and 15 percent work in education. Evergreen students who stay in Washington also work for Microsoft and Boeing. Evergreen alumni appear to have a fair number of entrepreneurs within their ranks.

THE BOTTOM LINE

The total cost for tuition, books, supplies, room and board, travel, and expenses is $15,621 for residents and $26,070 for nonresidents. Since the average financial aid package is about $11,619, the out-of-pocket cost is approximately $4,000 for residents and approximately $14,450 for nonresidents. Students who borrow money graduate with an average loan debt of about $13,800.

FUN FACTS

Matt Groening, the creator of *The Simpsons,* is an Evergreen alum. Some of his favorite places to eat in Olympia were The Ribeye, Bob's Big Burgers, and Spar Café.

Josh Blue, 2006 winner of NBC's *Last Comic Standing*, is an alum.

Evergreen's mascot is the geoduck (pronounced "gooeyduck"), a large, long-necked clam indigenous to the area.

The men's basketball team was ranked as high as sixth in the nation in 2002 and competed in the NAIA Division II championship tournament.

Sleater-Kinney guitarists Carrie Brownstein and Corin Tucker are alumnae.

Evergreen has its own beach on Puget Sound's Eld Inlet.

Evergreen grows food for its dining facilities at its Organic Farm, a student-run operation.

KAOS is the college radio station.

Olympia was named one of the best college towns in the nation by *Outside* magazine in 2003.

FINANCIAL INFO

In-state tuition	$4,371
Out-of-state tuition	$14,559
Room & board	$7,140
Average book expense	$924
Required fees	$490
Average freshman need-based grant	$5,335
Average freshman need-based loan	$2,922
% of graduates who borrowed	60
Average indebtedness	$13,818

FINANCIAL AID FORMS
Students must submit FAFSA, institution's own financial aid form.

POSTGRAD

% going to graduate school	28
% going to law school	1
% going to business school	2
% going to medical school	3

CAREER SERVICES
Alumni network, alumni services, career/job search classes, career assessment, internships. Off-campus job opportunities are good.

FLAGLER COLLEGE

74 King Street, PO Box 1027, St. Augustine, FL 32085-1027
www.Flagler.edu • Admissions: 800-304-4208
Fax: 904-826-0094 • E-mail: admiss@flagler.edu • Financial Aid: 904-819-6225

STUDENTS

Religious affiliation
No Affiliation
Academic year
calendar   semester
Undergrad
enrollment   2,253
% male/female   38/62
% Asian   1
% Black, non-Latino   2
% Latino   4
% international 1
% from out of state 35
% freshmen return for
sophomore year 76
% freshmen graduate within
4 years   53

STUDENT LIFE

% of students living
on campus   35

ADMISSIONS

of applicants 2,377
% accepted   26
% enrolled   76
# of early decision/action
applicants   634
% accepted early
decision/action 58

HIGH SCHOOL UNITS REQUIRED

4 English, 3 math, 2 science
(1 science lab), 2 social
studies, 1 history, 1
academic elective

HIGH SCHOOL UNITS RECOMMENDED

4 English, 4 math, 3 science
(2 science lab), 2 foreign
language, 3 social studies, 2
history, 2 academic
electives

ABOUT FLAGLER COLLEGE

Education, business administration, communication, sports management, and graphic design are among the specialized areas in which Flagler concentrates its efforts and excels. Students at this private liberal arts school in northeastern Florida benefit from the school's focused efforts, which allow it to cut waste and pass the savings on to undergrads and their families. In the classroom, the vibe is laid-back—professors sometimes wear floral shirts to class—but intense, with a tough curriculum and mandatory attendance policies (to help students resist the lure of the sun and ocean, no doubt). Flagler's innovative program in deaf education is one of the very few of its kind.

Flagler students tend to be fairly conservative and middle class, which detractors complain can make life here a little one-dimensional. International students make up the bulk of Flagler's minority presence. Women outnumber men by a three-to-two ratio. That's not quite Surf City, but they're not bad odds for a guy on the prowl. Speaking of which, surfing is reportedly the number one diversion among all Flagler students—known for their outgoing and welcoming demeanors. Other beach-related activities—swimming and tanning, for example—run a close second. Fairly strict social regulations, which among other things, forbid opposite-sex visits in the single-sex dorms, are regarded as onerous, but most accept the restrictions as part of the cost of a Flagler education. The area offers amazing weather (minus hurricane season) and the campus has no shortage of palm trees. Historic St. Augustine is cozy and friendly, although it is occasionally overrun by tourists.

BANG FOR YOUR BUCK

Flagler concentrates its resources on a limited number of academic programs, wisely choosing excellence in a few fields rather than mediocrity in many. This strategy, in combination with a healthy endowment and a conservative financial strategy allows Flagler to set tuition rates exceptionally low. In 2005–2006, a full year's tuition—not one semester's, mind you—was $9,450.

Most aid awarded at Flagler is need-based. The school reports that aid packages usually increase with grade level, with attendant increases in loan eligibility and state grants. Students typically borrow $2,625 their freshman year; $3,500 in their sophomore year; and $5,500 in each of their junior and senior years.

For fall 2006, just under 10 percent of all students received merit-based instructional scholarships of approximately $2,526 each.

Flagler participates in all state-funded programs, including Florida Bright Futures and Florida Resident Access Grant (FRAG). The Florida Prepaid Program can be transferred to Flagler as well.

GETTING IN

Admissions are most competitive for students who want to study business, communication, education, or graphic design. Education applicants must have a minimum combined SAT score of 1010 or a composite 21 on the ACT. The admissions office scrutinizes each applicant's transcript for grades and the quality of the curriculum. It also pays close attention to test scores, letters of recommendation, essay, and extracurricular involvement. Flagler accepts just over one-fourth of all applicants.

WHAT DO GRADUATES DO?

Flagler graduates are most likely to begin careers in accounting, broadcasting, education, graphic design, journalism, law, public relations, social work, and sports management. Top employers include Dow Jones Company, the Florida School for the Deaf and Blind, the Jacksonville Jaguars, Merrill Lynch, Northwestern Mutual, the Philadelphia Flyers, Reuters, the San Francisco Giants, *The St. Augustine Record*, *The Washington Times*, WAWS-TV Fox 30 News, and World Golf Village.

THE BOTTOM LINE

Tuition and fees at Flagler amount to a staggeringly low $9,450 per year; as the school claims, it truly costs little more to attend Flagler than it costs some in-state students to attend their state universities. Room and board adds an additional $5,760 per year, another very low figure. The school estimates an additional $3,800 per year in transportation, entertainment, books, and supply costs, bringing the grand total to $19,010 per year for students living on campus. Those who choose to live off campus should expect an additional $3,000 per year in housing costs.

VERY IMPORTANT ADMISSION FACTORS

Academic GPA, rigor of secondary school record, standardized test scores

IMPORTANT ADMISSION FACTORS

Application essay, character/personal qualities, extracurricular activities, recommendation(s)

Average HS GPA	3.17
Range SAT Verbal	520–610
Range SAT Math	510–590
Range ACT	22–26
Minimum TOEFL (paper/computer)	550/213

APPLICATION DEADLINES

Early decision	12/1
Early decision notification	12/15
Regular admission	3/1
Regular notification	3/30
# of transfer applicants	608
% of transfer applicants accepted	26

ACADEMICS

Student/faculty ratio	20:1
% faculty teaching undergraduates	100
% of classes taught by graduate students	0

MOST POPULAR MAJORS

- Business administration/management
- Communications, journalism, and related fields
- Elementary education and teaching

EDUCATION REQUIREMENTS

Computer literacy, English (including composition), humanities, math, social science

FINANCIAL INFO

Tuition	$9,450
Room & board	$5,760
Average book expense	$900
Average freshman need-based grant	$3,547
Average freshman need-based loan	$2,839
% of graduates who borrowed	55
Average indebtedness	$15,535

FINANCIAL AID FORMS

Students must submit FAFSA, institution's own financial aid form, state aid form.

Financial Aid filing deadline	4/1

POSTGRAD

% going to graduate school	20
% going to law school	2
% going to business school	4

CAREER SERVICES

Off-campus job opportunities are excellent.

After applying for all financial aid, the average aid recipient at Flagler must come up with between $5,400 and $5,500 out of pocket per year. A little better than 79 percent of Flagler students receive financial aid.

FUN FACTS

The nexus of the Flagler campus is the former Ponce de Leon Hotel, a historic structure built in 1887 by Henry Flagler, a founding partner of Standard Oil with John D. Rockefeller. The hotel features a columned rotunda with a towering dome and a dining room surrounded by Tiffany stained glass windows. The hotel now serves as a women's dorm; the dining room is used by students on the meal plan.

The Ponce is listed as a National Historic Landmark. Over twenty-three million dollars has been spent on restoration of the campus over the years.

Flagler is home to WFCF, a popular 10,000-watt FM radio station that can be heard from south of Jacksonville almost to Daytona Beach. The station recently began streaming on the Internet, meaning its DJs can now be heard anywhere around the world.

Flagler's Society for Advancement of Management team has won more undergraduate national titles than any other school—six.

In the past year, Flagler students have interned at the Cannes Film Festival, the White House, and Dateline NBC.

St. Augustine, Flagler's hometown, calls itself the nation's oldest city. The city was founded in 1565 by Spanish soldiers.

FLORIDA SOUTHERN COLLEGE

111 Lake Hollingworth Drive, Lakeland, FL 33801
www.FlSouthern.edu • Admissions: 863-680-4131
Fax: 863-680-4120 • E-mail: fscadm@flsouthern.edu • Financial Aid: 863-680-4140

STUDENTS

Religious affiliation	
	Methodist
Academic year	
calendar	semester
Undergrad	
enrollment	1,816
% male/female	39/61
% Asian	1
% Black, non-Latino	6
% Latino	6
% international	4
% from out of state	28
% freshmen return for	
sophomore year	67
% freshmen graduate	
within 4 years	49

STUDENT LIFE

% of students living	
on campus	66
% in fraternities	5
% in sororities	10

ADMISSIONS

# of applicants	1,829
% accepted	73
% enrolled	35
# of early decision/action	
applicants	43
% accepted early	
decision/action	98

HIGH SCHOOL UNITS REQUIRED

4 English, 3 math, 3 science, 3 social studies, 3 history, 2 academic electives

HIGH SCHOOL UNITS RECOMMENDED

2 Foreign language

ABOUT FLORIDA SOUTHERN COLLEGE

Florida Southern College is a primarily residential campus set amid 100 acres of greenery in the west-central Florida town of Lakeland. Located midway between the lively entertainment scene of the Orlando/Disney area and the growing metropolis of Tampa, the college is associated with the United Methodist Church, and while some students find this presence a bit too strong, many others participate in campus ministry activities. One thing all freshman students take part in is the one-credit-hour program known as EXL, an acronym for the "examined life." Students work in small groups of 15 or fewer with a faculty mentor for one semester exploring a topics such as "Restaurant Nation: The Menus Tell the Tale of Our American Culture" and "Everything I Need to Know About College, I Learned from Disney"—and more conventional classes geared toward time management, study habits, research, and other aspects of college life.

The college offers 38 majors for undergraduates as well as 4 graduate programs. Classes are small, and undergraduates are offered the chance to participate in faculty research projects in many areas. Florida Southern's study abroad program offers not only year- and semester-long international experiences, but also shorter four-week programs collectively called the May Option. Of the 1,800 students at Florida Southern, about half are from Florida. The other half comprises students from more than 40 other states and countries, providing a welcome diversity of backgrounds. About 80 percent of freshmen and 70 percent of upperclassmen choose to live on campus, which is famous for its concentration of buildings designed by architect Frank Lloyd Wright.

When it comes to majors, the arts reign supreme. The college has a strong theater program that typically allows students to participate in up to four productions a year. The music program, concentrating on classical and jazz performance and study, is also well respected. Both these departments and other campus organizations offer a variety of entertaining events open to the student population, but with the nightlife mecca of Orlando not too far away, competition for student attention is decidedly fierce. Students may participate in more than 80 campus organizations, and half of students also participate in either intramural or intercollegiate sports.

Students Say

"The size of the school is [a] huge strength. All of the departments on campus become little communities in which students can find lifelong friends."

VERY IMPORTANT ADMISSION FACTORS

Rigor of secondary school record, standardized test scores

IMPORTANT ADMISSION FACTORS

Academic GPA, application essay, character/personal qualities, extracurricular activities, recommendation(s)

Average HS GPA   3.53
Range SAT Verbal   470–580
Range SAT Math   480–590
Range ACT   20–26
Minimum TOEFL
  (paper/computer) 550/213

APPLICATION DEADLINES

Early decision   12/1
Early decision
  notification   12/15
# of transfer applicants 262
% of transfer applicants
  accepted   68

ACADEMICS

Student/faculty ratio   14:1
% faculty teaching
  undergraduates   100
% of classes taught by
  graduate students   0

MOST POPULAR MAJORS

- Biological and biomedical sciences
- Elementary education and teaching
- Marketing/marketing management

BANG FOR YOUR BUCK

About 90 percent of incoming freshmen who qualified for aid at Florida Southern in 2005 were granted some assistance; the college met 100 percent of aid for about half of those who qualified. The average financial aid award package was a fairly substantial $18,403, and in general, aid applicants saw about 70 percent of their aid requirements met by the college. The majority of this amount was funded by scholarships, but loans and self-help-based aid accounted for significant amounts of aid as well. About 10 percent of the student body received non-need-based aid.

GETTING IN

For the 2005–2006 year, Florida Southern chose to accept about one third of those who applied for admission as freshmen. A strong high school academic program and high scores on standardized tests (ACT or SAT scores are required for admission) are considered most important. Other factors which admissions evaluators look at closely include GPA, essay, and recommendations. The average SAT score for students accepted at Florida Southern in 2005 was 1072, and those who took the ACT averaged 23. The average GPA of accepted students was 3.53. Admissions advisors strongly recommend a college prep course in high school, and suggest four years of English, three years of math, history/social sciences, and natural sciences, and recommend two years of a foreign language.

WHAT DO GRADUATES DO?

Business-related fields account for about a third of the degrees conferred by Florida Southern each year, and many pursue careers in that area. Education is also a popular choice. Recent graduates have gone to work with Disney World, Walgreens, Bank of America, Chick-Fil-A, Publix Supermarkets, and American Express, among others.

Among those who choose to continue their education, Florida Southern graduates have attended Asbury Theological Seminary, Barry College of Law, Duke University, Clemson, Florida State University, Vanderbilt, and William & Mary.

The Bottom Line

Undergraduate tuition at Florida Southern is $19,700, with required fees adding another $475. On-campus room and board costs a bit over $7,000 on average. College aid, once awarded, is likely to be available through the degree course and often accounts for up to 75 percent of need as determined by the college.

Fun Facts

The campus is a National Historic Site because of the historic significance and large concentration of buildings designed by Frank Lloyd Wright.

Basketball player Tarra Blackwell Lawrence (1994–1998) is Florida Southern's all-time leading scorer with 2,037 points.

Among the college's offerings is a science-based degree with a major in citrus. Students in this program are never far from their subject as the campus landscape includes more than 80 varieties of citrus.

EDUCATION REQUIREMENTS

Arts/fine arts, computer literacy, English (including composition), history, humanities, math, sciences (biological or physical), social science, religion

FINANCIAL INFO

Tuition	$19,700
Room & board	$7,140
Average book expense	$1,000
Required fees	$475
Average freshman need-based grant	$14,611
Average freshman need-based loan	$4,331
% of graduates who borrowed	67
Average indebtedness	$16,072

FINANCIAL AID FORMS

Students must submit FAFSA, institution's own financial aid form.

Financial Aid filing deadline	8/1

POSTGRAD

% going to graduate school	20

FLORIDA STATE UNIVERSITY

2500 University Center, Tallahassee, FL 32306-2400
www.FSU.edu • Admissions: 850-644-6200
Fax: 850-644-0197 • E-mail: admissions@admin.fsu.edu • Financial Aid: 850-644-5871

STUDENTS

Religious affiliation
               No Affiliation
Academic year
   calendar   semester
Undergrad
   enrollment   30,206
% male/female   43/57
% Asian   3
% Black, non-Latino   12
% Latino   11
% international   1
% from out of state   13
% freshmen return for
sophomore year   89

STUDENT LIFE

% of students living
   on campus   14
% in fraternities   14
% in sororities   14

ADMISSIONS

of applicants   22,450
% accepted   62
% enrolled   43

HIGH SCHOOL UNITS REQUIRED

4 English, 3 math, 3 science
(2 science lab), 2 foreign
language, 1 social studies, 2
history, 3 academic
electives

HIGH SCHOOL UNITS RECOMMENDED

4 English, 4 math, 4 science
(2 science lab), 4 foreign
language, 1 social studies, 2
history, 3 academic
electives

ABOUT FLORIDA STATE UNIVERSITY

The 30,000 undergraduates at Florida State come in all shapes and sizes, from Florida-born, die-hard sports fanatics to interesting groups of international students and minorities. But these disparate groups all demonstrate traits common to most FSU students, starting with a strong and uniting sense of school spirit. They are also very involved in school activities, whether it is Greek life, student organizations, or athletics. Undergrads are a happy bunch, and they're skilled at juggling their good times with getting a great education. Most seem to find the discipline to focus on classes during the week, while sports, cultural events, and general socializing dominate weekends. There's always a party going on somewhere for those who are out to find one. Tallahassee also offers a wealth of shopping, community service, concerts, and entertainment.

FSU's large size makes for some impressive benefits, including great programs in biology, business, engineering, hospitality, and music. Students also brag about the 24-hour computer labs, eight libraries, excellent facilities, and Florida sunshine. Research centers include the National High Magnetic Field Laboratory, the Reading Research Center, and the School of Computational Science. If there are any drawbacks, it can be difficult to score one-on-one time with busy professors and advisors. Still, a motivated student can find plenty to take advantage of at FSU. Of course, a motivated socialite can too.

BANG FOR YOUR BUCK

Florida State University works carefully to meet student's financial needs holding tight to the philosophy that students should be focused on their studies, not their finances. Partly because this is a public institution established and supported by the State of Florida, in-state residents are afforded a tuition rate that is currently the second lowest in the nation. With tuition and fees set just over $100 per credit hour for undergraduate study, most students find it quite affordable to pursue a degree at this top-tier research university. To further reduce the educational expenses for its residents, the State of Florida provides plenty of opportunities for grants and scholarships. Expenses in hometown Tallahassee are moderate, and students will find many options for housing and employment.

"There is a great mix of students on campus, which provides everything from slow Southern hospitality to a fun hip-hop culture to a great Latin salsa vibe. Everyone is generally extremely nice and talkative, and it's always fun to hang out with every type of student when people come together on game day!"

Florida State University offers financial aid through many programs, some need-based, and others based on merit. In 2005–2006, the disbursement was over 10 million dollars in university need-based grants, over 7.5 million dollars in university merit scholarships, and over 50 million dollars in state merit scholarship funds to undergraduate students. All admitted students are considered for university merit scholarships and may receive scholarships for $500–$1,000 per term based on their academic standing and test scores.

Getting In

The major factor in the decision-making process for incoming freshmen is the applicant's academic profile (meaning, your high school GPA and the level of courses you choose) in combination with your performance on the ACT and/or SAT. Your essay, recommendations, and extracurricular activities are of secondary importance. For certain majors, talent and/or ability as demonstrated in an audition or portfolio are also important components of the application. Applicants interested in majoring in music; dance; the BFA degree program in theater; or motion picture, television, and recording arts (Film School) should contact those departments for additional requirements.

What Do Graduates Do?

FSU graduates are employed in virtually every industry. In 2004–2005, the top five employers of FSU graduates were Ernst & Young, LLP, PricewaterhouseCoopers, Cerner, Harris Corporation, and Burdines-Macy's.

FSU encourages organizations that wish to establish a high-profile recruiting presence at Florida State University to become Placement Partners. Joining with the Career Center, Placement Partners are a distinguished group of employers who directly support student career development and employment programs at Florida State University and who actively participate in the Career Center's recruitment activities. Currently, over 44 corporations have registered as Placement Partners at FSU.

Very Important Admission Factors

Academic GPA, rigor of secondary school record

Important Admission Factors

Class rank, standardized test scores, state residency, talent/ability

Average HS GPA	3.59
Range SAT Verbal	530–620
Range SAT Math	540–630
Range ACT	23–27
Minimum TOEFL (paper/computer)	550/213

Application Deadlines

Regular admission	3/1
# of transfer applicants	6,693
% of transfer applicants accepted	50

ACADEMICS

Student/faculty ratio	22:1
% faculty teaching undergraduates	100
% of classes taught by graduate students	32

Most Popular Majors

- Criminal justice/safety studies
- Finance
- Psychology

EDUCATION REQUIREMENTS

Arts/fine arts, computer literacy, English (including composition), history, humanities, math, sciences (biological or physical), social science. All students entering the university with less than 60 semester hours must complete a cross-cultural course and a diversity in Western culture course. All students entering the university with 60 semester hours or more must complete either a cross-cultural course or a diversity in Western culture course.

FINANCIAL INFO

In-state tuition	$2,465
Out-of-state tuition	$15,596
Room & board	$6,778
Average book expense	$856
Required fees	$842
Average freshman need-based grant	$2,817
Average freshman need-based loan	$2,160
% of graduates who borrowed	52
Average indebtedness	$16,597

FINANCIAL AID FORMS

Students must submit FAFSA.

POSTGRAD

% going to graduate school	42

CAREER SERVICES

Alumni network, alumni services, career/job search classes, career assessment, internships, regional alumni, on-campus job interviews. Off-campus job opportunities are excellent.

THE BOTTOM LINE

For 2006–2007, Florida state residents paid a paltry $2,465 in tuition while out-of-state residents paid $15,596. (Even so, note that Florida State University has consistently charged below the national average for out-of-state tuition and fees.) Students could expect another $6,778 for room and board, $842 in fees, and $856 in book costs. (Personal expenses and transportation costs tack on additional monies, which vary by student.) Thus, the total cost of attending FSU full time for a state resident living on campus was $10,941; out-of-staters are looking at $24,072. The average financial aid package for students, including scholarships, was $11,755. A Florida resident commuting from home could save a substantial amount and ending up attending for less than $5,000 a year.

FUN FACTS

FSU's campus is virtually wireless, with ongoing technological upgrades to improve capabilities.

Students can join FSU's own Flying High Circus with no experience necessary.

FSU is home to the $100 million National High Magnetic Field Laboratory and the world's most powerful magnets. The lab draws more than 600 world-class scientists each year to the university where they present their findings to students and faculty.

FSU hosts the annual "Seven Days of Opening Nights" arts festival known throughout the Southeast. The festival gives students, faculty and community members the opportunity to see performances and interact with world renowned performers, authors and artists such as Garrison Keillor, Joyce Carol Oates and Joshua Bell.

FSU's School of Motion Picture, Television and Recording Arts encompasses one of the largest and best equipped facilities devoted wholly to film education, while its undergraduate and graduate programs rank among the most highly regarded in the world. In 2004 alone, students nabbed five Television Academy Awards and two Student Oscars, a feat unmatched by any other film school in the country.

FSU's distinct garnet hue dates back to 1947, when purple and crimson, previously used as spirit colors for the university, were combined to form a whole new symbol of the Seminoles.

During the Depression, administrators often let students pay tuition through a barter system, allowing trade for items such as sweet potatoes and oranges for tuition and board.

Actress Faye Dunaway was a runner-up in the 1959 Miss FSU Contest.

FSU Creative Writing Professor Mark Winegardner was commissioned and completed the sequel to the book, *The Godfather.*

FRANKLIN W. OLIN COLLEGE OF ENGINEERING

Needham, MA 02492-1245
www.Olin.edu • Admissions: 781-292-2222
Fax: 781-292-2210 • E-mail: info@olin.edu • Financial Aid: 781-292-2364

STUDENTS

Religious affiliation
　　　　　　No Affiliation
Academic year
　calendar　　　semester
Undergrad
　enrollment　　285
% male/female
% Asian　　　　7
% Black, non-Latino　2
% Latino　　　　3
% international　　1
% from out of state　90
% freshmen return for
sophomore year　　99

STUDENT LIFE

% of students living
　on campus　　100

ADMISSIONS

of applicants　545
% accepted　　25
% enrolled　　57

HIGH SCHOOL UNITS REQUIRED

4 English, 4 math, 3 science
(3 science lab), 2 foreign
language, 2 social studies, 2
history

HIGH SCHOOL UNITS RECOMMENDED

2 Computing, engineering
design

ABOUT FRANKLIN W. OLIN COLLEGE OF ENGINEERING

Small, innovative, and populated with bright go-getter engineers, Franklin W. Olin College of Engineering may well be the most dynamic undergraduate institution in the country. By design, the school is set up to quickly incorporate any breaking innovations in math, engineering, and science into the curriculum. The school is even more adept at transforming student suggestions into classroom activity, with student-designed projects and problems constantly introduced as part of the curriculum. The road has sometimes been bumpy as the school perfects its innovative approach, but any setbacks are more than outweighed by the rewards of Olin's collaborative methods. The focus here is on business, engineering, and science, but arts, humanities, and social science courses are also required. Students may supplement the curriculum by taking classes at nearby Brandeis, Babson, and Wellesley.

Olin undergrads are frighteningly smart. Many are self-confessed, tech-school-type nerds, but there are plenty of non-mouth-breathers too. Students each hold their passions that go beyond schoolwork—whether it's sci-fi movies and video games, or, less predictably, politics, art, and dance. They are a small, tight group, as they need to be, given the number of projects on which they must cooperate. Olin's tough workload leaves little time for fun, but most manage to squeeze in the occasional party or night out in Boston.

BANG FOR YOUR BUCK

You can't get any simpler than the Olin deal; get yourself admitted and the school automatically grants you a scholarship covering your full tuition for all four years. The value of that scholarship currently tops more than $125,000. (Of course, due to the tiny size of the student body, only 15 percent of applicants are offered enrollment—so you need to be on top of your game to cash in on this incredible set up.)

This leaves students with living expenses and the cost of a mandatory laptop computer, which all students must purchase when they arrive. The cost of the laptop is spread out over the first four semesters in the form of an interest-free loan. Students are free to apply for need-based aid to help cover all additional expenses. Slightly more than 10 percent of students receive some need-based aid.

VERY IMPORTANT ADMISSION FACTORS

Academic GPA, application essay, character/personal qualities, extracurricular activities, level of applicant's interest, recommendation(s), rigor of secondary school record, talent/ability

IMPORTANT ADMISSION FACTORS

Class rank, interview, standardized test scores, volunteer work

Range SAT Verbal 700–770
Range SAT Math 740–800
Range ACT 31–34

APPLICATION DEADLINES

Regular admission 1/7
Regular notification 3/21

ACADEMICS

Student/faculty ratio 9:1
% faculty teaching
undergraduates 100
% of classes taught by
graduate students 0

MOST POPULAR MAJORS

• Electrical, electronics and communications engineering
• Engineering
• Mechanical engineering

EDUCATION REQUIREMENTS

Arts/fine arts, humanities, math, sciences (biological or physical), social science, engineering

The cost of living in Needham is well above the national average, but bargains can be found in Boston—if you can get away from the books and labs long enough to make the trip.

GETTING IN

Around 77 students, plucked from an applicant pool of approximately 600 extremely bright potential engineers, make up each rarefied entering class at Olin. Successful applicants must provide a record demonstrating academic excellence, with particular strength in math and science. They must also distinguish themselves with a solid extracurricular resume showing interests beyond the classroom, communication and teamwork skills, leadership potential, and an awareness of and enthusiasm for Olin's special mission. After winnowing the applicant field through traditional means (studying transcripts, test scores, essays, and the rest of the application), Olin invites 180 finalist candidates to campus for a two-day session of team-based design and construction projects, small group discussions, and individual interviews. Candidates are assessed by faculty and observers, who are not allowed access to the traditional application material (to ensure that evaluations are based solely on applicants' performances, not by previous accomplishments). About two-thirds of this group are granted admission, of whom typically 75 choose to attend Olin.

WHAT DO GRADUATES DO?

At the time of this printing, Olin College will have graduated its first class. Prior to graduation, the class of 2006 was almost evenly distributed between applying to the nation's top graduate programs and seeking employment at a wide range of organizations—from nationally recognized corporations to small start-up companies. To date, over 70 percent of all Olin College students have participated in an internship or summer research experience. Some of the organizations for which Olin students have worked include IBM, Raytheon, NASA JPL, Sensicast, and Radisys, as well as more than 20 National Science Foundation REU sites.

THE BOTTOM LINE

For 2005–2006, total costs at Olin were a remarkably low $15,900 of billed expenses that includes $4,100 for the meal plan, $1,250 for the first two payments on the laptop, $650 for health insurance (if needed), a $150 student activity fee, $7,500 for room, an estimate of $750 for books and supplies, and $1,500 for travel and incidentals. All admitted students receive their education tuition-free through a full tuition scholarship valued at more than $130,000. Students who demonstrate financial need may receive additional assistance to meet all other costs not related to tuition. It's a sweet deal, folks.

FUN FACTS

Olin encourages undergrads to design a Passionate Pursuit, a semester-long project focusing on a subject or activity that excites the student. This non-degree, credit-bearing venture can involve any activity—technical, artistic, entrepreneurial, humanist, philanthropic—that interests the student. Recent examples include trombone study, flute performance, glassblowing, GPS mapping research, exploration of product design, earning a private pilot's certificate, the study of welding, exploration in jewelry making, and the study of swing dancing and its variations.

Olin College is the first, new, freestanding engineering college in the United States in nearly half a century.

Wireless nodes placed around campus allow Olin students to connect to the Internet from just about anywhere on the grounds.

FINANCIAL INFO

Tuition	$32,100
Room & board	$11,600
Average book expense	$750
Required fees	$150
Average freshman need-based grant	$8,654

FINANCIAL AID FORMS

Students must submit FAFSA.
Financial Aid filing deadline 4/15

CAREER SERVICES

Career/job search classes, career assessment, internships, on-campus job interviews. Off-campus job opportunities are good.

GEORGIA COLLEGE & STATE UNIVERSITY

Campus Box 23, Milledgeville, GA 31061
www.GCSU.edu • Admissions: 478-445-5004
Fax: 478-445-1914 • E-mail: gcsu@mail.gcsu.edu • Financial Aid: 478-445-5149

STUDENTS

Religious affiliation
No Affiliation
Academic year
calendar   semester
Undergrad
enrollment   4,801
% male/female   41/59
% Asian   1
% Black, non-Latino   8
% Latino   1
% international   2
% from out of state   2
% freshmen return for
sophomore year   83
% freshmen graduate
within 4 years   22

STUDENT LIFE

% of students living
on campus   40
% in fraternities   9
% in sororities   13

ADMISSIONS

of applicants   3,236
% accepted   60
% enrolled   53

HIGH SCHOOL UNITS REQUIRED

4 English, 4 math, 3 science
(2 science lab), 2 foreign
language, 3 social studies

VERY IMPORTANT ADMISSION FACTORS

Academic GPA, rigor of
secondary school record,
standardized test scores

ABOUT GEORGIA COLLEGE & STATE UNIVERSITY

Georgia College & State University has been designated the official liberal arts college of the state's public university system. With an undergraduate student body comprising roughly equal numbers of refugees from big-city Atlanta and incomers from rural Georgia, along with a growing presence of international students, the school sees some diversity of interests and backgrounds. GCSU is located in Milledgeville, a central Georgia town between Atlanta and Macon which was once the state's capital.

Education, business, and health sciences are popular majors; nursing, chemistry, theater, and music therapy also claim the interest of many. Students pursue these fields on a central campus marked by traditional Old South columned architecture, including the Old Governor's Mansion, noted as one of the finest examples of High Greek Revival architecture in the nation. Many consider the town itself a bit small, but proximity to the weekend destinations of Macon and Atlanta makes up for that. Most students live in apartments on or near the campus. Interests here run the gamut both academically and socially. Some students come to party, while others appreciate the quieter things in life. That said, both groups coexist and study peaceably in what is generally considered to be a friendly and interesting campus atmosphere.

Students generally appreciate the small-school atmosphere, the friendly vibe on campus, and the intellectual challenge and opportunities both in and out of the classroom. One such opportunity is a two-way mentoring program: The college recruits many of Georgia's leaders in professional fields to work with students as occasional mentors and advisors; students, in turn, have the chance to try mentoring themselves by working with high school and elementary-age students in area schools. The college also offers certificate program in leadership, another one in nonprofit management, as well as courses in service leadership which are open to all students. The college also affords the opportunity to create a transcript that describes skills experiences gained through out-of-class involvement.

BANG FOR YOUR BUCK

GCSU found that about 40 percent of those who applied for financial aid as incoming freshmen in 2005 met the college's standards to qualify for assistance. Of those who did qualify, 99 percent received some form of aid. However—and it's a thing to take account of—less than five percent of those students had all their need for aid met by the college's resources. Sound a bit grim? It isn't. With rock-bottom tuition, the college meeting about a third of a student's need for aid, and the average amount of a financial aid package hovering around $5,253, the key to your collegiate spending is well within reach. Need-based awards are about evenly divided in amount among scholarship, loan, and self-help assistance. According to the college, about 80 percent of all GCSU students receive some sort of aid. The college also offers payment plans for students and parents as well as the option to apply for aid online.

GETTING IN

Georgia College looks first at the strength of the high school academic program, standardized test scores, and GPA when considering candidates for admission. Class rank, essays, extracurricular activities, talent, and recommendations are also important. About 60 percent of those who apply are admitted. The average SAT score for an incoming Georgia College freshman in 2005 was 1120, and for the ACT it was 22. Admissions evaluators wish, according to the school's website, "to discover students who will bring academic and creative achievements, elements of diversity, a proven commitment to community service and who have the potential to make significant contributions to society."

WHAT DO GRADUATES DO?

Teaching, health professions, and business are among the career fields of GCSU graduates. Georgia College regularly hosts recruiters from the Georgia Merit System, Carolina Holdings, Georgia Bureau of Investigation, State Farm, Wells Fargo, the Medical College of Georgia, Cherokee County Schools, and Savannah-Chatham County Schools.

IMPORTANT ADMISSION FACTORS

Application essay, class rank, extracurricular activities, recommendation(s), talent/ability

Average HS GPA	3.26
Range SAT Verbal	520–600
Range SAT Math	510–600
Range ACT	20–24
Minimum TOEFL (paper/computer)	500/173

APPLICATION DEADLINES

Regular admission	4/1
# of transfer applicants	1,048
% of transfer applicants accepted	63

ACADEMICS

Student/faculty ratio	16:1
% faculty teaching undergraduates	100
% of classes taught by graduate students	3

MOST POPULAR MAJORS

• Business administration/management
• Nursing—registered nurse training (RN, ASN, BSN, MSN)
• Psychology

EDUCATION REQUIREMENTS

Arts/fine arts, English (including composition), foreign languages, history, math, sciences (biological or physical), social science

FINANCIAL INFO

In-state tuition $3,642
Out-of-state tuition $14,570
Room & board $7,116
Average book
  expense $800
Required fees $782
Average freshman
  need-based grant $2,898
Average freshman
  need-based loan $2,306
% of graduates
  who borrowed   57
Average
  indebtedness $15,082

FINANCIAL AID FORMS

Students must submit
FAFSA.

POSTGRAD

CAREER SERVICES

Career/job search classes,
career assessment,
internships, on-campus job
interviews. Off-campus job
opportunities are good.

THE BOTTOM LINE

Georgia residents may expect to pay a staggeringly reasonable $3,642 in tuition for a full academic year of courses. Those who come to Georgia College from outside the boundaries of the "Peach State" will encounter a steeper charge of $14,570 in tuition. Both groups of students will pay about the same for room and board on campus, $7,116, roughly half for rent and half for meal expense. The college offers an estimate of around $800 per academic year for books and supplies and around $3,000 for transportation and other miscellaneous expenses.

FUN FACTS

Pecans were first grown in Milledgeville.

Author Flannery O'Connor, a graduate of Georgia College, is honored with a special collection in the library

The Natural History Museum on campus has a number of Ice Age fossils, including a complete bison skull unearthed in Brunswick, Georgia.

GRAND VALLEY STATE UNIVERSITY

1 Campus Drive, Allendale, MI 49401
www.GVSU.edu • Admissions: 616-331-2025
Fax: 616-331-2000 • E-mail: admissions@gvsu.edu • Financial Aid: 616-331-3234

STUDENTS

Religious affiliation
No Affiliation
Academic year
calendar   semester
Undergrad
enrollment   18,715
% male/female   39/61
% Asian   3
% Black, non-Latino 5
% Latino   3
% Native American 1
% international   1
% from out of state 4
% freshmen return for
sophomore year   82
% freshmen graduate
within 4 years   20

STUDENT LIFE

% of students living
on campus   29
% in fraternities 4
% in sororities   3

ADMISSIONS

of applicants   13,255
% accepted   68
% enrolled   38

HIGH SCHOOL UNITS RECOMMENDED

4 English, 4 math, 4
science (2 science lab), 2
foreign language, 3 social
studies, 1 computer
science, fine arts

VERY IMPORTANT ADMISSION FACTORS

Rigor of secondary school
record, standardized test
scores

ABOUT GRAND VALLEY STATE UNIVERSITY

Grand Valley State University offers its very career-oriented students nearly 70 undergraduate programs. Programs in health-related fields, education, and business are especially popular. Grand Valley also requires a strong core curriculum in the liberal arts and sciences for everyone, regardless of major. An outstanding faculty makes a strong backbone for the school, with professors always willing to help and who encourage students to visit during office hours. It's faculty members, too—not graduate students or teaching assistants—who teach all levels of classes. Undergrads here have the chance to participate in the kinds of research projects normally reserved for graduate students at other state schools. Small class sizes (in most everything but introductory courses) ensure personal, interactive learning. State-of-the-art facilities and housing also aim to please. The Grand Valley classrooms have cutting-edge technology and all of the academic buildings are wireless.

Allendale, Michigan (12 miles west of Grand Rapids) is home to the school's main campus. GVSU also has several smaller campuses and learning centers located throughout the region, including one in downtown Grand Rapids. On the gorgeous main campus, students tend to be friendly, generally conservative, and typically Midwestern. Many come from the Grand Rapids area and commute from home—which makes for a sizeable contingent of older, nontraditional students. There are over 240 student organizations on campus, and the top-notch cafeteria food and abundance of apartment-style dorms enhance the quality of life for students. Grand Rapids is no metropolis, but it does provide a decent number of diversions. The beaches and fabulous sunsets of Lake Michigan are nearby, as is some decent snowboarding and ski slopes.

BANG FOR YOUR BUCK

Nearly 73 percent of all full-time students at Grand Valley receive some kind of financial aid. Need-based aid is ample and merit-based scholarships absolutely abound. Highlights include the Presidential Scholarships, which are worth $3,000 to $7,000 each year. You're eligible if you have a high school grade point average of 3.8 and a 32 on the ACT. Faculty Scholarships require a 3.6 high school GPA and a 29 on the ACT. Recipients from Michigan receive up to $4,200 a year for up to four years; nonresident recipients receive up to $8,880 a year for up to four years. (For both Presidential Scholarships and Faculty Scholarships, GVSU will kick in up to two grand extra if you are a National Merit Scholarship finalist.) Freshman Students Awards for

"The campus is beautiful and everyone is really friendly. It's big enough to meet new people, but small enough [that] you don't feel overwhelmed."

IMPORTANT ADMISSION FACTORS

Application essay, class rank

Average HS GPA	3.5
Range ACT	21–26
Minimum TOEFL (paper/computer)	550/213

APPLICATION DEADLINES

Regular admission	5/1
Regular notification	rolling
# of transfer applicants	3,274
% of transfer applicants accepted	64

ACADEMICS

Student/faculty ratio	18:1
% faculty teaching undergraduates	90
% of classes taught by graduate students	0

MOST POPULAR MAJORS

• Business administration/management
• health services/allied health
• Psychology

EDUCATION REQUIREMENTS

Arts/fine arts, English (including composition), history, humanities, math, philosophy, sciences (biological or physical), social science, thematic studies group requirement

Excellence are four-year renewable scholarships worth $1,200 a year for in-state students and $6,290 per year for out-of-staters. You need a 3.5 GPA and an ACT score of at least 26 to qualify.

Quite a few full-tuition, ethnic diversity–based scholarships are also available here. You need a high school GPA of 3.3 and at least a 21 on the ACT to qualify. Wolverine State residents are eligible for Michigan Merit Awards. You have to score a Level 1 or Level 2 on four Michigan Educational Assessment Program (MEAP) tests and get at least a 24 on the ACT.

GETTING IN

Admission here is competitive but not crazy-competitive. If you want to apply to Grand Valley State, you should complete a solid college-prep curriculum that includes four years of English; three years each of hard science, social science, and math; and two years in the same foreign language. The middle 50 percent of first-year students have high school GPAs between 3.3–3.8 and ACT scores that fall between 21–26.

WHAT DO GRADUATES DO?

During their four years here, a slew of GVSU students participate in internships and cooperative education programs—almost 4,500 per year. Students are also afforded the opportunity to participate in a host of career fairs and hundreds of on-campus interviews. Maybe that's why about 94 percent of all GVSU graduates end up either employed or in graduate or professional school within a few months of graduation. Most graduates find jobs directly related to their majors. Over 40 percent are employed in business, and another large segment of graduates become teachers. A sampling of employers hiring Grand Valley graduates includes Northwestern Mutual, Bank One, Grand Rapids Public Schools, and Johnson Controls. Newly-minted Grand Valley alumni have attended graduate schools such as Case Western Reserve University, George Washington University, the University of Michigan, and Western Michigan University.

THE BOTTOM LINE

The total cost for Michigan residents to attend Grand Valley including full-time tuition, room and board, books, and cost-of-living expenses is $13,988. Out-of-state residents can expect a total cost of $19,910. The average aid award here is just over $7,300.

FUN FACTS

Grand Valley boasts several study abroad programs. Our favorite involves Art and Aesthetics in Florence, Italy—easily one of the most beautiful and exciting cities in the world. Participants in this six-week program study the philosophy of art in the cradle of the Renaissance, in the heart of Tuscany. Perks include excursions into the Chianti region.

The intercollegiate athletic teams at Grand Valley are called the Lakers. The mascot is Louie the Laker.

Grand Valley's Division II football team won national championships in 2002, 2003, 2005, and 2006.

In 2005, the school was crowned NCAA Division II Champions in football, women's basketball, and volleyball.

FINANCIAL INFO

In-state tuition	$6,220
Out-of-state tuition	$12,510
Room & board	$6,360
Average book expense	$800
Average freshman need-based grant	$4,190
Average freshman need-based loan	$2,638
% of graduates who borrowed	73
Average indebtedness	$16,606

FINANCIAL AID FORMS

Students must submit FAFSA.

POSTGRAD

% going to graduate school	35

GRINNELL COLLEGE

Office of Admission, 1103 Park Street, Second Floor, Grinnell, IA 50112-1690
www.Grinnell.edu • Admissions: 641-269-3600
Fax: 641-269-4800 • E-mail: askgrin@grinnell.edu • Financial Aid: 641-269-3250

STUDENTS

Religious affiliation
　　　　　No Affiliation
Academic year
　calendar　　　semester
Undergrad
　enrollment　　　1,546
% male/female　　46/54
% Asian　　　　　　6
% Black, non-Latino　4
% Latino　　　　　　4
% international　　　11
% from out of state　78
% freshmen return for
sophomore year　　92
% freshmen graduate
　within 4 years　　83

STUDENT LIFE

% of students living
　on campus　　　87

ADMISSIONS

of applicants　　3,121
% accepted　　　　45
% enrolled　　　　28
# of early decision/action
　applicants　　　144
% accepted early
　decision/action　70

HIGH SCHOOL UNITS
RECOMMENDED

4 English, 4 math, 4 science
(3 science lab), 4 foreign
language, 4 social studies

ABOUT GRINNELL COLLEGE

Grinnell was founded by a group of Iowa pioneers in 1843, and that pioneering spirit still informs the college's approach to education. All freshman students are required to take what is known as a tutorial, a writing-intensive course that introduces them to academic thinking and research. Beyond that, there are no subject matter requirements for gaining an undergraduate degree from Grinnell. No "three courses in science" or "two semesters in English"—students are free to design their own paths to graduation. And students are also largely new to Iowa, with eight out of ten coming from outside the college's home state. Like proverbial moths to the flame, they are drawn to Grinnell by a combination of academic rigor, intellectual challenge, and opportunities for self-direction in educational choices, set amid the "friscalating" cornfields of Middle America.

The sciences, social studies, and humanities each have a strong presence at Grinnell; interdisciplinary programs including American studies, technology, gender and women's studies, and environmental studies are featured as well. The College also has institutes in prairie studies, peace studies, and other disciplines. Students may also have the chance to collaborate with faculty on advanced research projects. Typical of the self-directed approach to education, students who wish to go beyond the college's offerings in foreign languages may participate in alternate language learning, which the college will support with tapes, books, and sessions with native speaker tutors. However, this smorgasbord of intellectual delights comes with a price: Classes are hard and demanding, the ability to handle a lot of reading and writing—and to make one's own decisions—is necessary, and undergrads often complete work that would be considered graduate level at other institutions. This isn't a problem with most students, however; many say that it's exactly what they came to college to do. Overall, students find the atmosphere to be cooperative, welcoming, and challenging.

When they aren't hitting the books, Grinnellians might drive to the bright lights of Des Moines or Iowa City (each about an hour away) or participate in Grinnell's outdoor recreation programs including a variety of on- and off-campus activities. Sports enthusiasts have both intercollegiate and intramural games, and there are organizations for every possible interest. There's a spate of arts programs on campus too, all of which are free to students.

"Grinnell is about learning to live as informed, passionate, critically thinking, sensitive, active, open-minded, and involved members of communities."

Bang for Your Buck

Grinnell's admission process doesn't include consideration of financial need. Once the college determines a student's need, it will meet it: 100 percent of the need of qualified incoming students in 2005 was met, and 100 percent of the need of qualified upperclassmen was met as well. Financial aid packages average $27,787, with more than half the amount typically coming in the form of scholarships.

Getting In

Grinnell admits about 40 percent of those who apply. A rigorous high school academic program, high GPA and standardized test scores, a high class ranking, and strong recommendations are highly valued. In the non-academic area, evidence of talent, ability, and a strong record in extracurricular activities also carry weight. More than 90 percent of admitted freshmen were in the top quarter of their high school classes, with more than 64 percent hitting the top 10 percent. Their median score on the SAT was 1390; on the ACT it was 31. More than half were members of the National Honor Society, and about half also participated in varsity athletics. Arts, music, and dance, also saw substantial involvement, and more than 80 percent had some community involvement experience; additionally, about 35 percent held down jobs during high school.

What do Graduates Do?

Many of them earn PhDs, law degrees, and advanced business degrees from schools such as Harvard, Yale, the University of Chicago, and Vanderbilt. From there, or directly from Grinnell, they go on to careers in teaching, research, social service, and business. The Career Development Office provides counseling, advice, and contacts to alumni as well as current students and sponsors GRINNELLINK, an on-campus program that matches alumni with students for informal contacts. Also, Grinnell is a member of the Selective Liberal Arts Consortium, a 12-college group which holds interview days for seniors in Boston, Chicago, New York, Philadelphia, and Washington with employers who are looking for liberal arts graduates.

Very Important Admission Factors

Academic GPA, class rank, extracurricular activities, recommendation(s), rigor of secondary school record, standardized test scores, talent/ability

Important Admission Factors

Application essay, interview, racial/ethnic status

Average HS GPA
Range SAT Verbal 640–750
Range SAT Math   640–730
Range ACT   29–33
Minimum TOEFL
  (paper/computer) 550/220

Application Deadlines

Early decision   11/20
Early decision
  notification   12/20
Regular admission   1/20
Regular notification   4/1
# of transfer applicants 122
% of transfer applicants
  accepted   30

ACADEMICS

Student/faculty ratio   9:1
% faculty teaching
  undergraduates   100
% of classes taught by
  graduate students   0

Most Popular Majors

- Biological and physical sciences
- Economics
- History

First-semester tutorial
focusing on writing

FINANCIAL INFO

Tuition	$28,566
Room & board	$7,700
Average book	
expense	$600
Required fees	$464
Average freshman	
need-based grant	$18,952
Average freshman	
need-based loan	$4,384
% of graduates	
who borrowed	61
Average	
indebtedness	$16,744

FINANCIAL AID FORMS

Students must submit
FAFSA, institution's own
financial aid form, noncustodial (divorced/separated)
parent's statement.
Financial Aid
filing deadline   2/1

POSTGRAD

% going to	
graduate school	25
% going to	
law school	3
% going to	
medical school	3

CAREER SERVICES

Career assessment,
internships, on-campus job
interviews. Off-campus job
opportunities are good.

THE BOTTOM LINE

Students at Grinnell paid $28,566 in tuition for the 2005–2006 academic year. All freshmen live in campus housing, which rings up another $7,700 for room and board. There is another $464 needed for required fees. The college estimates $600 will be needed for books and supplies, and $1000 for transportation and other miscellaneous expenses. Once the college determines a student qualifies for aid, it works to find ways to provide that. About 90 percent of Grinnell's students received some form of aid. In 2005–2006, Grinnell awarded approximately $27 million in scholarships, grants, work and loans; close to $23 million of that was gift aid.

FUN FACTS

Actor Peter Coyote and jazz musician Herbie Hancock attended Grinnell.

The Grinnell campus was a stop on the Underground Railroad that led slaves to freedom in Civil War days. Also, there is an actual physical railroad which crosses the campus still today.

In keeping with the college's history and spirit, its athletic teams are known as the Pioneers. They compete in the Midwest Conference and in recent years have been especially strong in swimming, diving, and cross-country running.

GROVE CITY COLLEGE

100 Campus Drive, Grove City, PA 16127-2104
www.GCC.edu • Admissions: 724-458-2100
Fax: 724-458-3395 • E-mail: admissions@gcc.edu • Financial Aid: 724-458-2163

STUDENTS

Religious affiliation
　　　　　　Presbyterian
Academic year
　calendar　　　semester
Undergrad
　enrollment　　　2,465
% male/female　　51/49
% Asian　　　　　　2
% international　　　1
% from out of state　52
% freshmen return for
sophomore year　　93
% freshmen graduate
within 4 years　　　75

Student Life

% of students living
　on campus　　　　93
% in fraternities　　15
% in sororities　　　17

ADMISSIONS

of applicants　　1,918
% accepted　　　　56
% enrolled　　　　62
# of early decision/action
　applicants　　　640
% accepted early
　decision/action　50

High School Units
Recommended

4 English, 3 math, 3 science
(2 science lab), 3 foreign
language, 2 social studies, 2
history

About Grove City College

Grove City College's beautiful campus is located on the edge of Grove City, Pennsylvania, a cozy hamlet of about 8,000 souls, an hour or so north of Pittsburgh. Class and chapel attendance are compulsory, and GCC is dedicated to combining a comprehensive, traditional core curriculum in the liberal arts with a strong commitment to Christian principles. Grove City also boasts small classes, a free laptop for every student, and a sticker price that makes it one of the best all-around bargains in higher education. If you are looking for a conservative and affordable private school with strong Christian values, passionate professors, and rigorous academic standards, you would be hard-pressed to find a better choice than Grove City College.

The students are homogenous, exceptionally goal-oriented, and politically conservative. Most Grovers have a sincere desire to live the Christian life, and most are looking to get hitched in the not-too-distant future. They also spend a lot of hours reading, writing, and preparing for exams. Tough classes and a host of required courses keep the students on their toes. Spiritual and moral character is also constantly stressed. Outside the classroom, you'll find a warm Christian environment and an atmosphere of safety, tradition, and family values. You'll also find a mega-structured code of conduct that, among other strictly governed things, forbids alcohol and premarital sex.

Bang for Your Buck

You would think that a nationally-recognized liberal arts school that accepts no money from the federal government would have to charge an arm and a leg for tuition. It doesn't. Tuition at Grove City is less than *half* of the national average for private colleges. Grove City is a very well-managed school. It operates virtually debt-free and it seeks to provide liberal and professional education of the highest quality that is within the reach of students and families with modest means. The low tuition (and room and board) costs provide a built-in scholarship for every student with the credentials to get admitted. A number of financial aid programs are also available, including the Trustee Academic Scholarship, the Presidential Scholarship, and the campus-based Grove City Student Loan Program. The college's utterly interest-free Tuition Payment Plan allows all students to spread all or part of their annual education expenses in equal monthly installments at no additional cost.

VERY IMPORTANT ADMISSION FACTORS

Application essay, character/personal qualities, extracurricular activities, interview, religious affiliation/commitment, rigor of secondary school record, standardized test scores

IMPORTANT ADMISSION FACTORS

Recommendation(s), talent/ability

Average HS GPA	3.75
Range SAT Verbal	579–698
Range SAT Math	582–698
Range ACT	25–30
Minimum TOEFL (paper/computer)	550/213

APPLICATION DEADLINES

Early decision	11/15
Early decision notification	12/15
Regular admission	2/1
Regular notification	3/15
# of transfer applicants	81
% of transfer applicants accepted	37

ACADEMICS

Student/faculty ratio	17:1
% faculty teaching undergraduates	100
% of classes taught by graduate students	0

We bet you'd like to know how and why Grove City College does it. What's the big deal about accepting federal funds? Well, all that government money comes with certain strings attached. Grove City maintains its independent status so that it doesn't have to get bossed around by the feds. By politely declining federal money, GCC is able to preserve the integrity of its founding mission, and thus provide a quality education in a thoroughly Christian environment at an affordable cost. Grove City is also one of the most prominent and respected bastions of free market economic theory in the country. By practicing what it preaches, the college maintains competitively low prices and an elite academic program.

GETTING IN

In terms of grades and test scores, Grove City is one of the most competitive undergraduate schools in the country. Less than half of all candidates that apply are accepted. You need to be in the top 20 percent of your high school class and score something very near a 1200 on the SAT to be admitted. Grove City College also requires two letters of recommendation. One must be from a teacher, guidance counselor, or principal. The other must be from a pastor, youth pastor, or someone who knows you well enough to provide a character reference. There are also two essays and some shorter, essay-type questions on the application. In order of importance, the admissions staff considers class rank, the rigor of your high school curriculum and the GPA you earned in it, SAT or ACT scores, the (highly recommended) interview, extracurricular activities, essays, and letters of recommendation.

WHAT DO GRADUATES DO?

Grove City's Career Services Office is definitely exceptional. Its mission is to identify the talents and the God-given calling of each student during their first year and then build a four-year strategy to help the student pursue a satisfying career. Services include self-assessment testing, internship opportunities, job shadowing, career fairs, mock interviews, and on-campus recruiting opportunities with over 180 on-campus recruiting visits. The big four accounting firms recruit on campus every year, as do Pfizer Pharmaceutical, Sherwin Williams, Bayer, and Westinghouse. Within five years of graduation 50 percent of all GCC graduates are pursuing a higher degree.

The Bottom Line

Grove City College is one of the least expensive private colleges in the nation. Total annual charges for all academic programs including tuition, a nifty tablet PC and printer, books, and room and board are $17,978. There are no hidden charges. Comparatively, the total cost at Duke is a little over $38,000. The total cost at Bucknell, which is three hours down the road from GCC, is about $33,500. Every student receives a substantial financial benefit thanks to GCC's low costs. Charges at GCC typically increase 3–5 percent each year.

Fun Facts

Check out the college's entrepreneurship major: "When you graduate, you will possess a thoroughly Christian understanding of what it takes to succeed in the market, a complete and professionally reviewed business plan, [and] a network of contacts."

All full-time students receive the use of a laptop computer and printer. Students who are full time when they graduate get to keep the equipment. The Repair Shop is staffed by certified computer technicians who provide on-site repairs for all college-provided equipment.

Most Popular Majors

- Business administration/ management
- Elementary education and teaching
- English language and literature

Education Requirements

Arts/fine arts, foreign languages, history, humanities, math, sciences (biological or physical), social science

FINANCIAL INFO

Tuition	$10,962
Room & board	$5,766
Average book expense	$900
Average freshman need-based grant	$5,171
% of graduates who borrowed	68
Average indebtedness	$22,532

Financial Aid Forms

Students must submit institution's own financial aid form.

Financial Aid filing deadline	4/15

POSTGRAD

% going to graduate school	20
% going to law school	1
% going to business school	2
% going to medical school	2

Career Services

Alumni network, alumni services, career/job search classes, career assessment, internships, regional alumni, on-campus job interviews. Off-campus job opportunities are good.

GUILFORD COLLEGE

5800 West Friendly Avenue, Greensboro, NC 27410
www.Guilford.edu • Admissions: 336-316-2100
Fax: 336-316-2954 • E-mail: admission@guilford.edu • Financial Aid: 336-316-2354

STUDENTS

Religious affiliation
Quaker

Academic year
calendar   semester
Undergrad
enrollment   2,682
% male/female   38/62
% Asian   1
% Black, non-Latino 23
% Latino   2
% Native American 1
% international   1
% from out of state 62
% freshmen return for
sophomore year   72
% freshmen graduate
within 4 years   44

STUDENT LIFE

% of students living
on campus   75

ADMISSIONS

of applicants   2,492
% accepted   63
% enrolled   26

HIGH SCHOOL UNITS REQUIRED

4 English, 3 math, 2
science, 2 foreign language,
2 social studies, 1 history, 2
academic electives

HIGH SCHOOL UNITS RECOMMENDED

4 English, 3 math, 3
science, 2 foreign language,
1 social studies, 1 history, 2
academic electives

ABOUT GUILFORD COLLEGE

Guilford is a Quaker school, and the practice of Quaker principles of responsibility, equality, respect, and social justice engagement is a unique aspect of the college's character and atmosphere that students find refreshing and stimulating. Students and faculty call each other by first names, and the classroom environment supports individual thought and contemplation. Classwork is intense and demanding, often requiring a substantial amount of reading and writing for each subject. Independent research and study is encouraged and may be fashioned into course projects with faculty approval. There is an honors program with most courses taught as seminars, and students may exempt courses through examination as well. At the beginning of their Guilford life, students are expected to enroll in a week-long program, the ominously-titled CHAOS, which offers experiential learning and bonding situations coupled with practical orientation to college academics and campus life during the second half.

There isn't one typical sort of student at Guilford. Some are politically left wing, but they are just as likely to be left-wing preppies as they are to be left-wing hippies, and there's a fair share of jocks, goths, cheerleaders, and most other sorts of personalities found on campus. They may not always agree with each other but they get along, in part by accepting that Quaker ideal of respect and, well, acceptance. That also puts the focus on learning and achievement rather than competition among students; most students feel that they are competing only with themselves to learn more, grow more, and improve themselves. Many study science, including forensics and psychology, English, education, political science, and business. The music, art, and theater departments, which present a variety of public events to the community, are small but strong, and their size assures most students of hands-on participation in arts projects.

Guilford is set on the western edge of Greensboro, North Carolina, a fast-growing city with a vibrant arts and social scene of its own. Students are free to take part in that, but many find the activities on campus so interesting that they make those their focus. About 65 per cent of Guilford's nearly 2,700 students come from outside North Carolina. All traditional first-year students are required to live on campus, and two-thirds of upperclass students live on campus. Some live in housing geared to themes and with some community service project requirements, and others live in familiar dorm-style housing. Outdoor activities such as drum circles and jamming on the campus grounds are popular ways to kick back.

BANG FOR YOUR BUCK

Guilford evaluators found that about two-thirds of incoming students who applied for financial aid were qualified to receive it. Of those qualified, 100 percent of them received aid of some sort, typically covering about 85 percent of their need. Scholarships formed the bulk of award money; loans and self help aid were also included. About one in four of the freshman class in 2006 had their total financial need met by the college.

GETTING IN

The two things that Guilford looks at first in its applicants are the strength of the high school record and the level of interest a student displays toward the college. Other academic markers such as test scores, GPA, and class rank are next most important, as are evidence of character and experience in volunteer work. The median GPA of incoming freshman was 3.14 in 2006; they scored an average of 1131 on the SAT, and ACT scores averaged 23.

WHAT DO GRADUATES DO?

Business careers, the sciences, and teaching are popular choices for Guilford graduates. Educational Resources Group, Teach for America, and the Peace Corps are among those who recruit on campus; the Career & Community Learning Center also offers students the ability to participate in career fairs in connection with the four other colleges in the Greensboro area as well as Guilford specific events.

VERY IMPORTANT ADMISSION FACTORS

Level of applicant's interest, rigor of secondary school record

IMPORTANT ADMISSION FACTORS

Academic GPA, application essay, character/personal qualities, class rank, recommendation(s), standardized test scores, volunteer work

Average HS GPA	3.1
Range SAT Verbal	520–640
Range SAT Math	500–620
Range ACT	20–25
Minimum TOEFL (paper/computer)	550/213

APPLICATION DEADLINES

Regular admission	2/15
Regular notification	rolling
# of transfer applicants	235
% of transfer applicants accepted	39

ACADEMICS

Student/faculty ratio	17:1
% faculty teaching undergraduates	100
% of classes taught by graduate students	0

MOST POPULAR MAJORS

- Biological and biomedical sciences
- Business administration/ management
- Psychology

EDUCATION REQUIREMENTS

Arts/fine arts, computer literacy, English, foreign languages, history, humanities, math, philosophy, sciences, social science, First Year Experience, Historical Perspectives, Interdisciplinary Capstone Course, exploration courses in intercultural studies, social justice/environmental responsibility, Diversity in the United States, breadth course in business and policy studies

FINANCIAL INFO

Tuition	$23,090
Average book expense	$800
Required fees	$330
Average freshman need-based grant	$13,772
Average freshman need-based loan	$4,695
% of graduates who borrowed	61
Average indebtedness	$20,150

FINANCIAL AID FORMS

Students must submit FAFSA, noncustodial (divorced/separated) parent's statement, business/farm supplement.

POSTGRAD

% going to graduate school	18
% going to law school	3
% going to business school	2
% going to medical school	1

CAREER SERVICES

Alumni network, alumni services, career/job search classes, career assessment, internships, on-campus job interviews. Off-campus job opportunities are good.

THE BOTTOM LINE

In 2006–2007 tuition at Guilford runs $23,090, with $330.00 for required fees. On-campus room and board costs $6,690. The college estimates that $800 will be needed for books and supplies. Incoming students are eligible for a variety of scholarships, and there are incentive grants available to those who do well academically. The average graduate leaves Guilford with $20,150 of cumulative debt.

FUN FACTS

There are five four-year colleges and universities in Greensboro (Guilford College, Bennett College, Greensboro College, University of North Carolina—Greensboro, North Carolina A&T State University) with a total enrollment of nearly 40,000 students.

Not so surprisingly, the college's athletic teams are called the Quakers.

The student-run college radio station, WQFS, is one of the few college radio stations which allows and welcomes the help of nonstudent community DJs, and it is consistently ranked as one of the top college stations in the country.

HAMPDEN-SYDNEY COLLEGE

PO Box 667, Hampden-Sydney, VA 23943-0667
www.HSC.edu • Admissions: 434-223-6120
Fax: 434-223-6346 • E-mail: hsapp@hsc.edu • Financial Aid: 434-223-6119

STUDENTS

Religious affiliation	Presbyterian
Academic year calendar	semester
Undergrad enrollment	1,060
% male/female	
% Asian	1
% Black, non-Latino	4
% Latino	1
% international	1
% from out of state	33
% freshmen return for sophomore year	83
% freshmen graduate within 4 years	58

STUDENT LIFE

% of students living on campus	95
% in fraternities	34

ADMISSIONS

# of applicants	1,376
% accepted	67
% enrolled	35
# of early decision/action applicants	89
% accepted early decision/action	67

HIGH SCHOOL UNITS REQUIRED

4 English, 3 math, 2 science (1 science lab), 2 foreign language, 1 social studies, 1 history, 3 academic electives

HIGH SCHOOL UNITS RECOMMENDED

4 Math, 3 science, 3 foreign language

ABOUT HAMPDEN-SYDNEY COLLEGE

Those wishing to return to the days of Southern gentility, honor codes, and education without the distraction of female classmates should consider Hampden-Sydney College, a small, all-male school in southern central Virginia. Founded in 1775, H-SC is a place where traditions reign supreme. One of the school's long-standing traditions is that the curriculum should be well-rounded and difficult. As being notoriously difficult to come by, students relish the challenge—it's a fair price to pay to enjoy small classes, devoted professors, and entry into a long-standing old-boy network that includes some powerful alumni. One unique aspect of the H-SC curriculum is its demanding rhetoric requirement, which helps students develop valuable writing and editing skills.

H-SC's well-mannered undergrads are a pretty homogeneous lot, with many very conservative, Christian white males whose favorite extracurriculars include fraternities and/or outdoor activity. Brotherhood is stressed, as students bond over traditional values, gentlemanly customs, and the desire to have a great time while maintaining a solid GPA. H-SC's rural setting takes some getting used to for those who grew up in more lively environments, but most students quickly adapt to the slower pace and the bucolic diversions it offers. Sunday through sundown on Thursday is given over to serious study, but Thursday night through Saturday night is fair game for team sports, hunting, fishing, golfing, and frat parties. H-SC is surrounded by schools, some all-women, others coed, so there's no dearth of potential female co-partiers.

BANG FOR YOUR BUCK

In the 2005–2006 academic year, Hampden-Sydney students received over $20 million in scholarship, grants, and loans. For the year, the average financial aid package per student totaled $17,891 (including scholarships, loans, and work-study). The average institutional award was $10,193. Total charges were $34,428, not including books and other expenses.

VERY IMPORTANT ADMISSION FACTORS

Character/personal qualities, recommendation(s), rigor of secondary school record, standardized test scores

IMPORTANT ADMISSION FACTORS

Academic GPA, class rank, extracurricular activities

Average HS GPA   3.32
Range SAT Verbal   520–630
Range SAT Math   530–640
Range ACT   21–27
Minimum TOEFL
  (paper/computer) 570/230

APPLICATION DEADLINES

Early decision   11/15
Early decision
  notification   12/15
Regular admission   3/1
Regular notification   4/15
# of transfer applicants   45
% of transfer applicants
  accepted   53

ACADEMICS

Student/faculty ratio   10:1
% faculty teaching
  undergraduates   100
% of classes taught by
  graduate students   0

MOST POPULAR MAJORS

- Economics
- History
- Political science and government

Aid includes both need- and merit-based scholarships. Merit awards, such as the Honors Scholarships and Achievement Awards, range from $2,000–$20,000 per year. Applicants who do not receive merit awards upon entry and who distinguish themselves academically during their time at H-SC are encouraged to apply for in-course merit awards. Also, while students' need-based scholarships are determined by the yearly filing of the CSS Profile, if a student exceeds the school's academic expectations, the grant component of his financial aid award package will increase and the loan component will decrease.

H-SC participates in the Army ROTC Scholarship Program, which can yield a scholarship for tuition and fees worth $80,000 over the course of a four-year college career. Georgia residents are eligible for a program that matches Georgia's HOPE Scholarship.

GETTING IN

It takes a special kind of student to want to go to Hampden-Sydney, so the school's high admit rate is misleading; H-SC *is* tough to get into. The school focuses primarily on applicants' high school performance as indicated by his transcript, recommendations from people who know him well, extracurricular activities, leadership abilities, and standardized test scores.

WHAT DO GRADUATES DO?

H-SC graduates typically wind up in banking, business, coaching, communications, consulting, financial services, fund-raising, health care, law, the military, the ministry, public service, research, real estate, teaching, and technology. Some top employers include AIG SunAmerica Securities, Anteon Corporation, BB&T Bank, C. Forbes Inc., Cambridge Associates, Citigroup, Commonwealth Commercial Partners, Core Consulting, DMG Securities, Geico, Genworth Financial, Ferguson Enterprises, Home Town Realty, James River Insurance, John Hancock Financial Services, The Martin Agency, Mark G. Anderson Consultants, McGuire Woods LLP, Merrill Lynch, M&T Bank, Morgan Keegan, Philip Morris, RBC Centura Bank, Signature Government Solutions, Sun Trust Bank, Thalhimer, U.S. Army, U.S. Marines, Virginia Port Authority, Wachovia Bank, Wachovia Securities, and Wells Fargo. Ultimately, over 50 percent of Hampden-Sydney graduates go on to earn a professional or graduate degree.

THE BOTTOM LINE

Tuition for 2005–2006 was $25,166; room and board was an additional $8,258. Students need to factor in another $2,004 for books and required fees, plus whatever they'll need for discretionary spending. A student funding this without aid has to budget at least $37,000 per year, probably more.

Fortunately, the number of students who fall into this category is relatively small. H-SC invests $9 million into aid to provide some form of assistance to over 80 percent of its undergraduates. According to the school, the average amount students contribute is difficult to calculate and depends on the amount of loans the student is willing to take, his state of residence (Virginia residents can receive an additional $2,500–$3,000 per year from a state-sponsored, tuition-assistance grant), and his demonstrated need. Top recruits may receive more generous financial aid offers. Hampden-Sydney does *not* reduce institutional aid if private scholarships are awarded; the school believes that families' efforts to find additional funding sources should be rewarded.

FUN FACTS

Undergrads recently spearheaded a campus-wide fund-raising event for the local National Guard unit, which was deployed to the Middle East.

Hampden-Sydney is a member of the Old Dominion Athletic Conference, one of the toughest conferences in Division III of the NCAA. Currently three of its eight varsity teams are ranked nationally—football, basketball, and lacrosse. About 80 percent of all undergrads participate in the intramural and club sports programs.

Feel free to bring your shotguns, rifles, muskets, and bows and arrows with you to Hampden-Sydney. The school's rural setting accommodates hunting, which the school encourages. Weapons are stored in a locker room when not in use.

SUVs outnumber conventional automobiles in the Hampden-Sydney parking lots. Many have john boats hitched to trailers.

Hampden-Sydney is known for a yearly week-long Symposium, addressing issues of national concern and attracting national speakers and media attention. In 2004 the school held "The War on Terrorism: 9-11, Three Years After." Among the distinguished speakers were General Bryan D. Brown, U.S. Commander, U.S. Special Operations Command; and Seymour Hersh, commentator, journalist, and author.

EDUCATION REQUIREMENTS

Arts/fine arts, English (including composition), foreign languages, history, humanities, math, philosophy, sciences (biological or physical), social science

FINANCIAL INFO

Tuition	$25,166
Room & board	$8,258
Average book expense	$1,000
Required fees	$1,004
Average freshman need-based grant	$15,444
Average freshman need-based loan	$2,974
% of graduates who borrowed	54
Average indebtedness	$19,818

FINANCIAL AID FORMS

Students must submit FAFSA, CSS/financial aid profile, state aid form.

Financial Aid filing deadline	5/1

POSTGRAD

% going to graduate school	30
% going to law school	15
% going to business school	5
% going to medical school	5

CAREER SERVICES

Alumni network, alumni services, career/job search classes, career assessment, internships, regional alumni, on-campus job interviews. Off-campus job opportunities are good.

HAMPTON UNIVERSITY

Office of Admissions, Hampton University, Hampton, VA 23668
www.HamptonU.edu • Admissions: 757-727-5328
Fax: 757-727-5095 • E-mail: admit@hamptonu.edu • Financial Aid: 800-624-3341

STUDENTS

Religious affiliation
No Affiliation
Academic year
calendar   semester
Undergrad
enrollment   5,235
% male/female   36/64
% Asian   1
% Black, non-Latino   96
% Latino   1
% from out of state   69
% freshmen return for
sophomore year   85

STUDENT LIFE

% of students living
on campus   59
% in fraternities   5
% in sororities   4

ADMISSIONS

of applicants   5,401
% accepted   77
% enrolled   29

HIGH SCHOOL UNITS REQUIRED

4 English, 3 math, 2 science
(2 science lab), 2 social
studies, 6 academic
electives

HIGH SCHOOL UNITS RECOMMENDED

2 Foreign language

VERY IMPORTANT ADMISSION FACTORS

Application essay, character/
personal qualities, rigor of
secondary school record,
standardized test scores

ABOUT HAMPTON UNIVERSITY

Hampton is a historically Black university with strong science, pre-med, and business concentrations. While its nearly 6,000 students have somewhat of a fun-loving reputation, academics are taken seriously. There are special programs in oceanography, a school of journalism and communications, a pharmacy program, a school of nursing, a physics department with an international reputation for excellence, and a liberal arts program. Make sure to dress the part and hit the books hard: The school enforces a dress code and requires a rigorous and traditional undergraduate curriculum. But never fear: Caring and dedicated professors are there to help when needed.

Hampton is located on the coast of Virginia, which puts it within striking distance of professional and personal opportunities in many East Coast cities. And students love its beautiful campus on the waterfront. Along with the dress code, students can expect a policy of limited visitation between men and woman in the campus living areas, prohibition of drugs and alcohol, and strict penalties—including expulsion—for violating these policies. Those who chafe under these rules find Hampton a difficult place to be, but by and large, the majority of students are willing to accept them. Hampton draws students from 49 states and more than 30 international locations, and they generally do well when they get there, gaining the school high marks in a variety of national rankings for academic excellence, for graduating African Americans who are highly qualified in a number of professional fields, and for building character.

BANG FOR YOUR BUCK

Hampton awarded aid to about 90 percent of those it found to have need for financial assistance in 2005–2006. That aid was primarily in the form of self-help-based programs: Nearly eight out of ten students who received aid received that type of award. Slightly less than half were awarded college-based scholarships and about two-thirds received assistance in the form of loans. About two-thirds of those students who qualified for aid found their need fully met by the college's resources. Non-need-based scholarships were awarded to about 10 percent of the incoming freshman class.

GETTING IN

The application essay and evidence of character are very important to admissions evaluators at Hampton, as are the rigor of a student's academic program and standardized test scores (the SAT or ACT is required). Next, class rank and recommendations are considered; lastly, extracurricular activities and alumni connections are factored in. Students who score a minimum of 1000 on the SAT or 20 on the ACT "receive the highest consideration" for admission, the college says; recent admission figures show an average SAT score of 1042 and an ACT of 20 for those who were accepted. Forty-five percent of those applying to Hampton in the fall of 2005 had a GPA of 3.75 or higher, and the average GPA of those admitted was 3.6. Thirty-two percent of those students were in the top 10 percent of their high school classes.

WHAT DO GRADUATES DO?

The sciences—both academic and applied to health care careers such as pharmacy, medicine, and nursing—are the choice of many Hampton graduates. Business, politics, and communications are popular choices as well. The Hampton career center maintains an electronic file of student and alumni resumes, and recruiting and interviewing schedules are available online to those who have registered with the center. These services are available to alumni as well, as is career-counseling advice. The college holds several career fairs throughout the year, featuring both employers and graduate and professional school representatives. Hampton graduates may be found working for companies such as Booz Allen Hamilton, Proctor & Gamble, L'Oréal, Deutsche Bank AG, and American Express.

IMPORTANT ADMISSION FACTORS

Class rank, recommendation(s)

Average HS GPA	3.2
Range SAT Verbal	478–622
Range SAT Math	464–599
Range ACT	19–25
Minimum TOEFL (paper/computer)	550/214

APPLICATION DEADLINES

# of transfer applicants	894
% of transfer applicants accepted	30

ACADEMICS

Student/faculty ratio	16:1
% faculty teaching undergraduates	98
% of classes taught by graduate students	0

MOST POPULAR MAJORS

- Business administration/ management
- Journalism
- Psychology

EDUCATION REQUIREMENTS

Arts/fine arts, computer literacy, English (including composition), foreign languages, history, humanities, math, sciences (biological or physical), social science, general education

FINANCIAL INFO

Tuition	$12,722
Room & board	$6,746
Average book expense	$750
Required fees	$1,460
Average freshman need-based grant	$1,800
Average freshman need-based loan	$2,066
% of graduates who borrowed	28
Average indebtedness	$3,646

FINANCIAL AID FORMS

Students must submit FAFSA.

POSTGRAD

% going to graduate school	40
% going to law school	2
% going to business school	5
% going to medical school	10

CAREER SERVICES

Alumni network, alumni services, career/job search classes, career assessment, internships, on-campus job interviews. Off-campus job opportunities are excellent.

THE BOTTOM LINE

Students at Hampton paid $12,722 in tuition for the 2005–2006 academic year. Required fees added $1,460. Those who chose to live on campus paid $3,508 for room and $3,508 for board. The school estimates a student will need to budget $750 for books and supplies. If students wish to load up on academics, they may enroll in a maximum of 17 credits per semester for the full-time tuition rate; a minimum of 10 hours is required. But let's get to the bottom line of the bottom line here: Hampton students find themselves with an average of $3,645.79 in loans after graduation—which is, in a word, amazing.

FUN FACTS

Booker T. Washington was a student, and later a teacher, at Hampton.

The Emancipation oak on campus is designated as one of the 10 Great Trees of the World by the National Geographic Society. In 1863, it was the site of the first Southern reading of President Lincoln's Emancipation Proclamation, and classes for Black children were taught under its shade.

Hampton athletic teams are called the Pirates. They compete in MEAC, the Mid Eastern Athletic Conference.

HANOVER COLLEGE

PO Box 108, Hanover, IN 47243-0108
www.Hanover.edu • Admissions: 812-866-7021
Fax: 812-866-7098 • E-mail: admission@hanover.edu • Financial Aid: 812-866-7021

STUDENTS

Religious affiliation
                      Presbyterian
Academic year
  calendar   4-4-1
Undergrad
  enrollment   999
% male/female   44/56
% Asian   3
% Black, non-Latino   1
% Latino   1
% international   5
% from out of state   33
% freshmen return for
sophomore year   77
% freshmen graduate
  within 4 years   68

STUDENT LIFE

% of students living
  on campus   94
% in fraternities   35
% in sororities   38

ADMISSIONS

of applicants   1,680
% accepted   70
% enrolled   23

HIGH SCHOOL UNITS REQUIRED

4 English, 3 math, 3 science
(2 science lab), 2 foreign
language, 2 social studies, 2
history, 2 academic
electives

HIGH SCHOOL UNITS RECOMMENDED

4 English, 4 math, 4 science
(3 science lab), 4 foreign
language, 3 social studies, 3
history, 3 academic
electives

ABOUT HANOVER COLLEGE

Hanover prides itself on being a place where learning and life are intertwined and where small-town serenity is informed by intellectual challenge, and that ethic seems to be working out both in and out of the classroom. Whatever their opinions of the town size (on the smaller side) and nightlife (ditto), it is the sense of community on campus that students feel marks a Hanover education as outstanding. With a student population of around 1,000 and 90 percent of students living on campus, it's safe to say that Hanover is more tightly knit that your grandma's scarves. Sartorial metaphors aside, the college is a great place for those who want to know and be known while gaining knowledge. Students revel in the quality of instruction from their professors, who also tend to live on or near campus. Located on 650 acres overlooking the Ohio River near the town of Madison, Indiana, it's little surprise the adjectives "beautiful" and "relaxing" are the first ones students use to describe their campus.

Professors here teach classes in more than 30 major subjects including Medieval and Renaissance studies, music, philosophy, and physics. Hanover has a strong interest in real-world learning too, with almost 90 percent of students participating in internship programs and more than 75 percent taking part in academically-based and service-learning programs in the United States and overseas. The college's one-month spring term in May allows for complete immersion in these sorts of experiences. As a bonus, Hanover allows scholarship money to be applied to overseas tuition and supports students with travel funds and board payments for approved overseas programs as well. Students may take part in programs in Australia, Belgium, France, Germany, Mexico, Spain, and Turkey, where the college has formal agreements with educational institutions and may arrange study abroad programs in other countries with the help of college staff. Be sure to check out Hanover's website: It has a collection of web pages designed especially to meet the needs and questions of first-year students, and it also sponsors orientation programs for students and parents prior to and at the beginning of a student's first year on campus.

Students socialize easily thanks to small classes and a surplus of more than 70 organized activities and groups for everything from religion to music to athletics. In addition, around 50 percent of Hanover students belong to a fraternity or sorority. There's also a regular schedule of music, theater, and dance programs on campus throughout the year. Some find the small-town location of the college limiting and the presence of fraternities and sororities too strong, while others enjoy the quiet and relative safety of the area and see the campus and town as full of interesting things to do.

"The professors and administration are always visible and available. Hanover is truly a community with a large portion of the faculty actually living on campus. Every member of the faculty with whom I have had contact (which is the majority of the faculty) has been friendly and willing to assist any student to the best of their abilities."

VERY IMPORTANT ADMISSION FACTORS

Academic GPA, class rank, rigor of secondary school record

IMPORTANT ADMISSION FACTORS

Recommendation(s), standardized test scores, talent/ability

Range SAT Verbal 540–650
Range SAT Math 550–650
Range ACT 23–29
Minimum TOEFL
(paper/computer) 550/213

APPLICATION DEADLINES

Regular admission 3/1
Regular notification rolling
# of transfer applicants 57
% of transfer applicants
accepted 53

ACADEMICS

Student/faculty ratio 10:1
% faculty teaching
undergraduates 100
% of classes taught by
graduate students 0

MOST POPULAR MAJORS

• Biology/biological sciences
• Business administration/
management
• Psychology

BANG FOR YOUR BUCK

Good news for those in need: All incoming students who were found by Hanover officials to have financial need were awarded some aid, with the bulk of that aid taking the form of scholarships; self-help and loan packages were also available. Generally the college met about 85 percent of a student's determined need for aid. Most of that aid could be applied to college-approved study abroad programs as well.

GETTING IN

Hanover looks for evidence of strong academic performance in applicants. GPA and class rank figure prominently in the decision process, along with recommendations, talent and ability, and standardized test scores. Specific high school courses are not mandatory, but the school does want to see at least a B-average in a range of challenging courses and will consider homeschooled students on a case-by-case basis. The average SAT score for incoming freshmen in 2005 was 1199, and the average ACT score was 26.

WHAT DO GRADUATES DO?

Hanover graduates find work in business, communications, health care, education, the arts, and ministry. The college offers a number of career-preparation guides to assist students in both academic and extracurricular exploration of various career fields. Companies fond of Hanover graduates include Progressive Insurance, General Motors, St. Gabriel Archangel School, and Howard W. Sams Publishing. And other students have attended graduate school at Urbana University, Northern Kentucky University, and the University of North Carolina.

The Bottom Line

Undergraduate tuition at Hanover in 2006 was $22,200. Almost all students live in on-campus housing, which includes both room and board at a cost of $6,800, and there is an additional $500 cost for required fees. The college expects that students will spend about $900 for books and supplies in the course of an academic year. Those who take advantage of financial aid have, on average, $16,514 of debt after graduation.

Fun Facts

Actor Woody Harrelson of *Cheers* fame is an alumnus of Hanover.

Historically connected to the Presbyterian Church, Hanover recently received a grant to start The Center for Church Leadership, which will assist both Hanover students and people from regional churches with issues of vocation.

The closest big city to Hanover is Louisville, Kentucky, which is about a 45-minute drive away.

EDUCATION REQUIREMENTS

Arts/fine arts, English (including composition), foreign languages, history, humanities, math, philosophy, sciences (biological or physical), social science, physical education, theology

FINANCIAL INFO

Tuition	$22,200
Room & board	$6,800
Average book expense	$900
Required fees	$500
Average freshman need-based grant	$14,421
Average freshman need-based loan	$2,765
% of graduates who borrowed	63
Average indebtedness	$16,514

FINANCIAL AID FORMS

Students must submit FAFSA.

POSTGRAD

% going to graduate school	29
% going to law school	7
% going to business school	1
% going to medical school	4

CAREER SERVICES

Alumni network, alumni services, career/job search classes, career assessment, internships, regional alumni, on-campus job interviews. Off-campus job opportunities are fair.

HARVARD COLLEGE

Byerly Hall, 8 Garden Street, Cambridge, MA 02138
www.fas.Harvard.edu • Admissions: 617-495-1551
Fax: 617-495-8821 • E-mail: college@fas.harvard.edu • Financial Aid: 617-495-1581

STUDENTS

Religious affiliation
                No Affiliation
Academic year
   calendar   semester
Undergrad
   enrollment   6,649
% male/female   53/47
% Asian   18
% Black, non-Latino   8
% Latino   8
% Native American   1
% international   7
% from out of state   84
% freshmen return for
sophomore year   96
% freshmen graduate
   within 4 years   83

STUDENT LIFE

% of students living
   on campus   96

ADMISSIONS

of applicants   19,609
% accepted   11
% enrolled   79

HIGH SCHOOL UNITS RECOMMENDED

4 English, 4 math, 4
science, 4 foreign language

VERY IMPORTANT ADMISSION FACTORS

Character/personal qualities,
extracurricular activities,
recommendation(s), rigor of
secondary school record,
talent/ability

ABOUT HARVARD COLLEGE

So what's a notoriously expensive university doing in the pages of a Best Value Colleges guide? Simply put, you're getting your money's worth at Harvard—and then some. World-class professors, arguably the best college library in the United States, a diverse student body from across the country and around the world, a large endowment which allows the college to support student and faculty research projects, a strong alumni network, a prestigious reputation that helps students get internships and graduates find jobs—okay, and unlimited bragging rights. In the heart of Cambridge, Massachusetts, across the Charles River from Boston, with more than 6,000 enrolled students, Harvard could easily qualify for its own city.

It's a big place, but Harvard does its best to create opportunities for community among incoming students. To start, there's a website with information and contacts for incoming and prospective students. All freshmen students live on campus and usually near Harvard Yard, and as Harvard guarantees housing to its students for all four years (and as rents in Cambridge and around Boston are quite high) many upperclass students choose to live on campus as well. All freshmen also eat in the same place, Anneberg Hall, and there are adult residential advisers living in the halls to help students learn their way around the resources of the college and the university. Classes tend to be small and with 1,500 of them to pick from, students note, they need all the advising they can get. Students may choose to major in subjects ranging from cell biology to comparative psychology to Celtic languages, and dozens of other areas and cross-disciplinary concentrations. As for the professors, well, let's just say the school doesn't have a problem attracting the rock stars of the academic world.

Harvard can handpick for diversity, and in the process of doing so, usually creates a successful mix of articulate, intelligent people who challenge each other (in a good way) with their differing backgrounds and interests. Overachievers in high school, many are relieved to be able to settle into the course work and the one or two extracurricular activities which really interest them. Those outside of class activities might be in the arts, business, sports, ethnic matters, social service, or dozens of other areas in campus organizations, and/or in the busy and active life of the city of Cambridge. Cambridge is known as Boston's Left Bank for its concentration of arts venues, music, and artists, and Boston itself is just a short ride across the Charles by subway (the Massachusetts Bay Transportation Authority, or T). Studying and academics are vital to a Harvard student's life, but students, faculty, and college staff agree that community connections and experiences, and the people you meet through them, are the best thing about life at Harvard, and the most lasting.

BANG FOR YOUR BUCK

In 2004–2005, the last year for which figures were available, Harvard determined that about of the 90 percent of those who requested financial aid qualified for it, and of those who qualified, 100 percent of need was met. This was achieved through a combination of loans, self help, and scholarships. Harvard extends that commitment for the full four undergraduate years. The average financial aid package for that year was $32,009.

GETTING IN

Harvard admitted about 20 percent of those who applied as incoming freshmen in 2005–2006. The admissions evaluators look at evidence of talent and ability, academic performance, extracurricular activities, recommendations, and personal character. Ninety percent of freshmen were in the top 10 percent of their high school classes, and 98 percent ranked in the top quarter. Harvard doesn't report average GPAs or test scores of its accepted class, but an article in the *Harvard Gazette* revealed that the pool they had to chose from for the class to be admitted in the fall of 2006 was fairly high quality, with more than 56 percent scoring 700 or more in the math SAT I and 49 percent scoring 700 on the verbal SAT I.

WHAT DO GRADUATES DO?

With the prestige of a Harvard education as reference, graduates can do just about anything they want. Many go into law or politics. Companies are more than happy to hire Harvard graduates, and the arts, higher education, the health professions, and social service are also homes for many Harvard grads. In the fall of 2004, more than 125 companies registered with the office of career services to recruit on campus.

IMPORTANT ADMISSION FACTORS

Application essay, class rank, interview, standardized test scores

Range SAT Verbal 700–800
Range SAT Math   700–790
Range ACT   30–34

APPLICATION DEADLINES

Regular admission   1/1
Regular notification   4/1
# of transfer
   applicants   1,153
% of transfer applicants
   accepted   6

ACADEMICS

Student/faculty ratio   8:1
% faculty teaching
   undergraduates   100
% of classes taught by
   graduate students   0

MOST POPULAR MAJORS

- Economics
- Political science and government
- Psychology

EDUCATION REQUIREMENTS

Arts/fine arts, English (including composition), foreign languages, history, humanities, math, philosophy, sciences (biological or physical), social science

FINANCIAL INFO

Tuition	$30,275
Room & board	$9,946
Average book expense	$2,522
Required fees	$3,434
Average freshman need-based grant	$29,950
Average freshman need-based loan	$2,816
% of graduates who borrowed	48
Average indebtedness	$8,769

FINANCIAL AID FORMS

Students must submit FAFSA, CSS/financial aid profile, noncustodial (divorced/separated) parent's statement, business/farm supplement, tax returns.

POSTGRAD

% going to graduate school	25
% going to law school	15
% going to business school	13
% going to medical school	20

CAREER SERVICES

Alumni services, career/job search classes, internships, on-campus job interviews. Off-campus job opportunities are excellent.

THE BOTTOM LINE

Tuition at Harvard runs $30,275 for the academic year, with $3,434 needed for additional required fees. Living accommodations on campus run $9,946 with board, and $5,328 for room only. The college estimates that books and supplies will require $2,522. Need for financial aid isn't a factor in admission to Harvard. Indeed, the college notes that "the Admissions Committee may respond favorably to evidence that a candidate has overcome significant obstacles, financial or otherwise."

FUN FACTS

Grammy-winning bluegrass and jazz banjo player, composer, and record company CEO Alison Brown is a Harvard alumna.

Bill Gates attended Harvard but did not graduate.

The statue of John Harvard in Harvard Yard (students and visitors traditionally rub the toe of his boot for luck) is not actually of seventeenth-century minister John Harvard, as no images of him exist. It's a nineteenth-century student who posed for the sculptor.

HASTINGS COLLEGE

Hastings College, 710 North Turner Avenue, Hastings, NE 68901
www.Hastings.edu • Admissions: 402-461-7403
Fax: 402-461-7490 • E-mail: mmolliconi@hastings.edu • Financial Aid: 402-461-7455

STUDENTS

Religious affiliation
Presbyterian
Academic year
calendar   4-1-4
Undergrad
enrollment   1,114
% male/female   52/48
% Asian   1
% Black, non-Latino   3
% Latino   2
% international   1
% from out of state   20
% freshmen return for
sophomore year   78
% freshmen graduate
within 4 years   51

STUDENT LIFE

% of students living
on campus   75
% in fraternities 16
% in sororities   32

ADMISSIONS

of applicants   1,413
% accepted   79
% enrolled   28

HIGH SCHOOL UNITS REQUIRED

3 English, 3 math, 3
science (3 science lab), 4
social studies, 3 history

HIGH SCHOOL UNITS RECOMMENDED

4 English, 4 math, 4
science (4 science lab), 2
foreign language, 4 social
studies, 4 history

ABOUT HASTINGS COLLEGE

Hastings, Nebraska, is not only the one-time home of Kool-Aid inventor Edward Perkins; it's also the native turf of Hastings College, a small liberal arts institution affiliated with the Presbyterian Church. Like Kool-Aid, Hastings College is often associated with smiling faces. In fact, a recent Noel-Levitz student satisfaction inventory found that Hastings undergrads are extremely happy with many aspects of their experience such as teaching, advising, course content, and the overall value for the money. Education, business, and psychology are among the most popular majors at Hastings. Regardless of academic concentration, nearly all students complete the Liberal Arts Program, which combines at least one major with a spectrum of courses selected from the general education roster. Another track, called the Personalized Program, is available for students who wish to create their own interdisciplinary course of study.

Though complaints about academics are rare, it's not unusual to hear a grumble or two about the town of Hastings. With a population of 25,000, this quaint Midwestern town offers few distractions, but the campus life more than makes up for this. Big-time speakers and touring entertainers stop at this south Nebraska campus several times a year. More than 70 student organizations—ranging from the Outdoor Club to the Sociology Club—offer plenty of opportunities to put free time to good use. The biggest extracurricular activities, though, come in the form of athletics. And not just *playing* sports. Football and women's basketball games always pack the bleachers, and nearly every sporting event sees a healthy turnout ("Go Broncos!" is a mandatory refrain). This student body—most of which hails from Nebraska and Colorado—is also known to let loose now and again. That said, most of the "letting loose" occurs anywhere but campus: Just like Texas, on-campus drinking policies are not to be messed with.

VERY IMPORTANT ADMISSION FACTORS

Academic GPA, class rank, recommendation(s), rigor of secondary school record, standardized test scores

IMPORTANT ADMISSION FACTORS

Character/personal qualities, extracurricular activities, talent/ability

Average HS GPA	3.2
Range SAT Verbal	460–600
Range SAT Math	490–590
Range ACT	20–26
Minimum TOEFL (paper/computer)	600/250

APPLICATION DEADLINES

Regular notification	rolling
# of transfer applicants	98
% of transfer applicants accepted	80

ACADEMICS

Student/faculty ratio	12:1
% faculty teaching undergraduates	100
% of classes taught by graduate students	0

MOST POPULAR MAJORS

- Business administration/ management
- Education
- Psychology

BANG FOR YOUR BUCK

In 2005, about 98 percent of all full-time undergraduates received some form of need- or merit-based aid. "Special skills" grants and scholarships are awarded in a number of areas: art, athletics, Christian ministry, communications, music, theater, and spirit squad. An array of small grants (such as funding for legacy students and assistance for families with two or more dependents enrolled) are also available. Academic scholarship recipients are assessed by standardized test scores and class rank. The most prestigious financial packages offered at Hastings are the Walter Scott and the Kessler scholarships, each of which are given to three incoming students per year. These annually renewable awards (if the student maintains a 3.0 GPA) provide full tuition remission. The application process can be rigorous and competitive.

GETTING IN

Hastings places a big emphasis on high school performance. This means class rank, GPA, and letters of recommendations will all be carefully considered. Standardized test scores weigh heavily too. Hastings also prizes applicants with extracurricular abilities and unique personalities—the kind of people who can contribute to life in and out the classroom. Though Hastings is affiliated with the Presbyterian Church, the college does not consider a candidate's religious background and, in fact, is home to a wide variety of religious persuasions.

WHAT DO GRADUATES DO?

Though it's not easy to predict what Hastings students will choose to do with liberal arts degrees, many move into fields such as education, business, and media/communications. Students commonly matriculate to grad school, med school, or law school. The career services office helps students locate internships and summer jobs, as well as negotiate any red tape that stands between the student and potential academic credit. Career Services also offers a wide range of interview, resume, and cover letter resources and sessions to help college students transform into stellar job and/or grad school applicants.

The Bottom Line

In 2006–2006, the cost of tuition was $17,572. In addition, room and board totaled around $5,100 and books, transportation, fees, and other expenses came to nearly $3,500. Because this is a private institution, the tuition cost for in-state and out-of-state students is the same. Full-time undergrads eligible for need-based aid in 2005–2005 received an average package amounting to $12,660. Non-need-based grant and scholarships averaged $4,800. Nearly 79 percent of Hastings students graduating between July 2004 and June 2005 took out student loans. Among these borrowers, the average debt accumulated over four (or, in rare cases, five) years was $14,598.

Fun Facts

Tom Osborne, the Republican congressman from Nebraska's third district, is a native of Hastings and a graduate of Hastings College.

Yes, Kool-Aid founder Edward Perkins spent a number of his formative years in Hastings. And though he never attended Hastings College, the institution does bear his legacy. The college's Perkins Library was named for this father of sugary snack drinks.

Hastings College has been dubbed an All-Steinway School by Steinway & Sons, the elite piano maker. As the titles suggests, this means that every piano on campus is guaranteed to be a Steinway, or else...

The women's basketball team won the NAJA Division II National Championship in 2002, 2003, and 2006.

Education Requirements

Arts/fine arts, computer literacy, English (including composition), foreign languages, history, humanities, math, philosophy, sciences (biological or physical), social science, health/wellness, physical education, speech

FINANCIAL INFO

Tuition	$17,572
Room & board	$5,148
Average book expense	$680
Required fees	$730
Average freshman need-based grant	$9,643
Average freshman need-based loan	$3,695
% of graduates who borrowed	79
Average indebtedness	$14,598

Financial Aid Forms

Students must submit FAFSA, institution's own financial aid form.

POSTGRAD

% going to graduate school	24

Career Services

Alumni network, alumni services, career/job search classes, career assessment, internships, regional alumni, on-campus job interviews. Off-campus job opportunities are fair.

HENDRIX COLLEGE

1600 Washington Avenue, Conway, AR 72032
www.Hendrix.edu • Admissions: 501-450-1362
Fax: 501-450-3843 • E-mail: adm@hendrix.edu • Financial Aid: 501-450-1368

STUDENTS

Religious affiliation
                             Methodist
Academic year
  calendar   semester
Undergrad
  enrollment   1,010
% male/female   44/56
% Asian   3
% Black, non-Latino   4
% Latino   3
% Native American   1
% from out of state   45
% freshmen return for
  sophomore year   81
% freshmen graduate
  within 4 years   55

STUDENT LIFE

% of students living
  on campus   85

ADMISSIONS

of applicants   1,086
% accepted   83
% enrolled   31

HIGH SCHOOL UNITS RECOMMENDED

4 English, 3 math, 2
science, 2 foreign language,
3 social studies

VERY IMPORTANT ADMISSION FACTORS

Academic GPA, application
essay, rigor of secondary
school record, standardized
test scores

ABOUT HENDRIX COLLEGE

Hendrix College has always been a hands-on, learn-as-you-do kind of place, but the school plans to take it to a whole other level in 2005 with the introduction of its Your Hendrix Odyssey Program—a curricular component that requires three participatory educational experiences. Approved Odyssey activities must relate to one or more of the following areas: artistic creativity, global awareness, professional and leadership development, service to the world, research, and special projects. This new emphasis on experiential learning is designed to help students connect abstract concepts learned in the classroom to real-life experience. Beyond Odyssey, Hendrix offers what you'd expect from a top-notch liberal arts school: a broad, demanding curriculum presented by a faculty that enjoys interaction with students and takes its responsibility to instruct and lead seriously.

Undergrads at Hendrix work hard, but they do find some time to blow off steam on the weekends. Alcohol is part of the equation, but so are visiting speakers, concerts, theatrical productions, and campus-wide festivals. Greek life is nonexistent on this campus. Hometown Conway—with a population of just 50,000—may not be a hotbed of nightlife, but it scores entertainment points in other areas. In the past few years, the largest open-air shopping center in the state opened here. New state laws have allowed private clubs to open recently and a bevy of restaurants are cropping up as well. Students also make the 30-minute drive to Little Rock when they're looking for a taste of the city. Overall, the largely liberal crowd here is known for their open-mindedness and acceptance of others.

BANG FOR YOUR BUCK

More than 9 in 10 Hendrix students receive achievement-based and/or need-based aid. Every applicant is automatically eligible for merit-based scholarships as well as the school's Odyssey Distinction Awards, given for extracurricular accomplishment in secondary school. In fact, the admission application doubles as a scholarship application for all merit scholarships.

Merit awards include the Hays Memorial Scholarship, which bestows the full comprehensive fee for attending to four entering students each year. GPA (minimum 3.6), standardized test scores (minimum 32 composite ACT or minimum 1410 combined SAT I), leadership, extracurricular activities, an on-campus interview, and letters of recommendation all figure into determining recipients of the award.

Middle-income families benefit from a generous gift from the Robert and Ruby Priddy Charitable Trust, which allows Hendrix to offer additional funds to students who do not receive large merit-based scholarships or federal grants, but who show exceptional promise for success at Hendrix and for leadership and service. The Voyager Fund, which provides interest-free loans during a student's tenure (they become low-interest loans after graduation), also helps those in all economic strata.

Hendrix costs about 10 percent less than several comparable schools around the country. The cost of living in Conway, Arkansas, is on par with or slightly below the national average. On-the-ball families who submit the FAFSA before February 15 are guaranteed at least a $1,000 financial aid package.

GETTING IN

Hendrix considers an applicant's high school transcript, test scores, and essay the most important components of the application package. Major consideration is also given to extracurricular and leadership activities; each plays a role in both the determination of admission and the distribution of Odyssey Distinction Awards. The ability to demonstrate how well-rounded you are may also help in the application process.

WHAT DO GRADUATES DO?

More than half of all Hendrix graduates enter graduate or professional school either immediately after graduating or in the following year. Ten percent go to medical school. Those not proceeding to grad school generally seek employment, with the vast majority reporting that they found a job within six months of graduation.

Hendrix attracts a wide range of employers seeking high-quality problem-solvers from a variety of disciplines. Companies engaged in on-campus recruitment seek students in various majors including: accounting, biology, business, chemistry, computer science, psychology, and sociology, as well as students with liberal arts degrees. Acxiom, Alltel, AmeriCorps, BKD, Deloitte and Touche, Ernst and Young, JET, The Peace Corps, Southwest Research Institute, and Youth Villages represent a few of the employers that recruit Hendrix students.

IMPORTANT ADMISSION FACTORS

Character/personal qualities, class rank, extracurricular activities, interview, recommendation(s)

Average HS GPA   3.6
Range SAT Verbal   590–700
Range SAT Math   560–670
Range ACT   25–30
Minimum TOEFL
   (paper/computer) 550/215

APPLICATION DEADLINES

Regular admission   8/1
Regular notification   rolling
# of transfer applicants   43
% of transfer applicants
   accepted   60

ACADEMICS

Student/faculty ratio   11:1
% faculty teaching
   undergraduates   100
% of classes taught by
   graduate students   0

MOST POPULAR MAJORS

• Biology/biological sciences
   • English language and
      literature
   • Psychology

Arts/fine arts, English, foreign language, history, humanities, math, philosophy, sciences, social science; all freshmen are required to take "Journeys", and to take "Explorations." Starting from 2005, all freshmen are required to participate in the academic program entitled "Your Hendrix Odyssey: Engaging in Active Learning." Graduation requirements inlcude the completion of an approved activity in at least three categories.

FINANCIAL INFO

Tuition	$22,616
Room & board	$6,738
Average book expense	$900
Required fees	$300
Average freshman need-based grant	$12,762
Average freshman need-based loan	$3,863
% of graduates who borrowed	79.7
Average indebtedness	$16,360

FINANCIAL AID FORMS

Students must submit FAFSA, state aid form.

POSTGRAD

% going to graduate school	32
% going to law school	6
% going to business school	3
% going to medical school	7

THE BOTTOM LINE

For 2006–2007, tuition at Hendrix will be $22,616. Room and board, books, and miscellaneous expenses amounted to another $9,841, bringing the grand total to $32,457.

Estimated out-of-pocket expenses for aid recipients vary greatly, depending on the amount of need-based aid the student receives, and the amount of merit scholarships awarded. The mean need-based grant to freshmen is about $10,000 per year; the mean freshman loan is slightly more than $5,000. Work-study and merit-based awards supplement these figures, leaving the average student with out-of-pocket expenses ranging from a few thousand dollars to $8,000 per year.

FUN FACTS

Hendrix has established and killed its football program three times in its history. Football was phased out for the last time—maybe—in 1960, when the school decided to concentrate its men's athletic program on basketball.

Dancing was forbidden on campus until 1936. It took five years of student protests to convince the administration to overturn the "no dancing" policy.

Hendrix alumni include the late Congressman Wilbur D. Mills, former chair of the powerful House Ways and Means Committee. Mills' political career ended in a scandal that often eclipses his 38 years of service to his state.

Students are tossed into the fountain in the middle of campus on their birthday by fellow students, perhaps in tribute to the means of Wilbur D. Mills' downfall. If you don't get the joke, try a Google.com search for "Wilbur D. Mills" and "Tidal Basin."

Other distinguished Hendrix alumni include Craig Leipold, owner of the NHL Nashville Predators, opera singer Susan Dunn, and Oscar-winning actress Mary Steenburgen.

HILLSDALE COLLEGE

33 East College Street, Hillsdale, MI 49242
www.Hillsdale.edu • Admissions: 517-607-2327
Fax: 517-607-2223 • E-mail: admissions@hillsdale.edu • Financial Aid: 517-437-7341

STUDENTS

Religious affiliation
No Affiliation
Academic year
calendar   semester
Undergrad
enrollment   1,304
% male/female   48/52
% international   2
% from out of state   56
% freshmen return for
sophomore year   87
% freshmen graduate
within 4 years   64

STUDENT LIFE

% of students living
on campus   86
% in fraternities   35
% in sororities   45

ADMISSIONS

of applicants   1,093
% accepted   82
% enrolled   41

HIGH SCHOOL UNITS RECOMMENDED

4 English, 4 math, 3 science
(1 science lab), 2 foreign
language, 1 social studies, 2
history

VERY IMPORTANT ADMISSION FACTORS

Academic GPA, character/
personal qualities, rigor of
secondary school record,
standardized test scores

ABOUT HILLSDALE COLLEGE

The emphasis is categorically on what is old and traditional—not what is new and trendy—at Hillsdale College, a bastion of the liberal arts strongly dedicated to conservative and free-market thought. This place is solely for undergrads (there are no grad programs), with an average class size of 21 students. Course work is steeped in Western civilization. Intensive core requirements guarantee that each student takes a class on the Constitution, Western Heritage, American Heritage, and the Great Books. You are unlikely to leave Hillsdale College without wrestling with the likes of Homer's *Odyssey*, Dante's *Inferno*, or the *Confessions* of Saint Augustine. You are also likely to receive training in *laissez faire* economics from some of its most eminent advocates. Popular majors include accounting, chemistry, economics, history, and political science. Education is also one of the big draws.

The typical student is very smart and fairly religious. In fact, it's common for students to go to church every Sunday. This campus also has a notable contingent of homeschoolers. Hillsdale College is located in a south-central Michigan hamlet surrounded by cornfields. It's definitely no suitcase school. About 90 percent of students live in the dorms. Greek life is very popular and, despite a well-enforced dry-campus policy, parties can be found off campus. Hillsdale's legendary and lively series of annual seminars have included such luminaries as former President Ronald Reagan, Reverend Jesse Jackson, Supreme Court Justice Clarence Thomas, and Green Party presidential candidate Ralph Nader. When students need a change of scenery, they often head to the coffee houses, bookstores, restaurants, and night clubs of Ann Arbor, about 50 minutes away.

BANG FOR YOUR BUCK

Here's how Hillsdale College tells it: In 1975, the federal government determined that colleges and universities ought to sign forms stating that they do not discriminate on the basis of gender. Signing such a form seemed silly to the Hillsdale brass because, in fact, Hillsdale was the first American college to guarantee equal opportunity to women and African Americans in its charter (dated 1853, by the way, eight years before the Civil War). Primarily, Hillsdale wanted to avoid what its directors saw as unnecessary federal encroachments on its independence. Hence, Hillsdale reaffirmed its private commitment to nondiscrimination and fought the feds in court. The Sixth Circuit Court of Appeals ruled that Hillsdale could avoid federal controls but, in doing so, it must not participate in federal grant and loan

"Everyone is nice and honorable. No one steals anything. Students leave their laptops lying around and no one cares! It's wonderful."

IMPORTANT ADMISSION FACTORS

Application essay, class rank, extracurricular activities, interview, recommendation(s), volunteer work, work experience

Average HS GPA	3.65
Range SAT Verbal	570–720
Range SAT Math	540–670
Range ACT	24–29
Minimum TOEFL (paper/computer)	550/200

APPLICATION DEADLINES

Early decision	11/15
Early decision notification	12/1
Regular admission	2/15
# of transfer applicants	68
% of transfer applicants accepted	74

ACADEMICS

Student/faculty ratio	11:1
% faculty teaching undergraduates	100
% of classes taught by graduate students	0

MOST POPULAR MAJORS

- Biology/biological sciences
- Business administration and management
- History

programs. After lots of additional legal wrangling, Hillsdale College ended all participation in all federal financial aid programs in 1985.

The upshot of Hillsdale's don't-tread-on-me attitude is a sweet bargain for you. How so? For starters, tuition at Hillsdale is substantially less than the national average for private colleges. Hillsdale also allocates several million dollars each year to financial aid, resulting in an average (privately-funded) aid package of about $10,000 per student. Amost 80 percent of the students receive financial aid in some form. The funds are provided by individuals, companies, and foundations. Hillsdale also offers a host of need-based scholarships, grants, and low-interest loans. Merit-based scholarships range in value from $1,000 to full tuition and are based on academic performance, extracurricular involvement, and ability in athletics and fine arts. To qualify for many academic scholarships, you need an ACT score in the neighborhood of 27 or better (or an SAT Math and Verbal score of 1220) and have earned a high school grade point average of at least 3.6. Stellar recommendations and extracurricular involvement are also a must.

GETTING IN

Hillsdale students are largely a self-selecting group and first-year students have impressively high numbers. The average GPA of incoming students is 3.7. The average ACT score is 27. The average SAT Math and Verbal score is about 1280. Almost 60 percent of all students come from outside the state of Michigan. As part of the application, you need to submit an essay and one academic letter of recommendation. You can, however, submit up to six optional recommendations or character evaluations.

WHAT DO GRADUATES DO?

Within six months of graduation, 98 percent of Hillsdale's graduates either have jobs or, as is very often the case, proceed to enroll in graduate and professional programs. Law school and medical school are frequent destinations. Each year, the school sees 50 to 60 on-campus recruiters (impressive for a school with only 1,200 students). There is also a huge network of alumni and donors waiting to give jobs to newly-minted grads. Access to prime internships is another plus. If you are politically conservative or a big believer in free trade, you'll find that several flagship organizations advocating these policies bestow internships on Hillsdale students.

The Bottom Line

Tuition alone is $17,000. The annual cost including tuition, room and board, and fees is $24,160. The average financial aid package is $13,000. Thus, the average graduate leaves Hillsdale about $16,000 in debt.

Fun Facts

Study abroad destinations for Hillsdale students include Spain, Germany, London, France, Scotland, and Oxford.

Hillsdale's website contains the complete writings of William F. Buckley Jr.

Hillsdale boasts one sitting member in the U.S. House of Representatives, Chris Chocola of Indiana. He was elected to the United States House of Representatives, joining another Hillsdale alumnus Phil Crane, who served in the House until 2004.

The salary of Hillsdale's president is approximately $500,000 per year, placing him among the top three highest paid presidents of liberal arts colleges in the country.

The Hillsdale Collegian is Michigan's oldest college newspaper.

Education Requirements

Arts/fine arts, English (including composition), foreign languages, history, humanities, math, philosophy, sciences (biological or physical), social science; two one-credit week-long CCA (Center for Constructive Alternatives) seminars.

FINANCIAL INFO

Tuition	$17,000
Room & board	$6,750
Average book expense	$850
Required fees	$410
Average freshman need-based grant	$6,800
Average freshman need-based loan	$3,000
% of graduates who borrowed	65
Average indebtedness	$16,000

Financial Aid Forms

Students must submit FAFSA, institution's own financial aid form, noncustodial (divorced/separated) parent's statement, business/farm supplement, FAFSA for state residents only.

POSTGRAD

% going to graduate school	35
% going to law school	9
% going to business school	14
% going to medical school	4

Career Services

Alumni network, alumni services, career/job search classes, career assessment, internships, regional alumni, on-campus job interviews. Off-campus job opportunities are good.

HOOD COLLEGE

401 Rosemont Avenue, Frederick, MD 21701
www.Hood.edu • Admissions: 301-696-3400
Fax: 301-696-3819 • E-mail: admissions@hood.edu • Financial Aid: 301-696-3411

STUDENTS

Religious affiliation
                No Affiliation
Academic year
   calendar   semester
Undergrad
   enrollment   1,136
% male/female   25/75
% Asian   2
% Black, non-Latino   12
% Latino   3
% international   3
% from out of state   19
% freshmen return for
   sophomore year   87
% freshmen graduate
   within 4 years   64

STUDENT LIFE

% of students living
   on campus   53

ADMISSIONS

of applicants   1,852
% accepted   51
% enrolled   25

HIGH SCHOOL UNITS REQUIRED

4 English, 3 math, 3 science
(2 science lab), 2 foreign
language, 3 social studies, 1
academic elective

VERY IMPORTANT ADMISSION FACTORS

Academic GPA, rigor of
secondary school record,
standardized test scores

ABOUT HOOD COLLEGE

Head to the heart of Frederick, Maryland, and you're likely to come across the picturesque campus of Hood College. This small school—just over 1,200 undergrads—was an all-women's college until 2003, when it began admitting full-time male students as well. Today, the ratio of women to men is about three to one. Women and men alike praise Hood's small classes, intelligent students, and faculty and administrators who are so accessible it should be illegal. Among the more popular academic programs are education, English, biology, psychology, social sciences, and business. Part of what makes the academic experience at Hood so favorable is the twin emphasis on liberal arts education *and* vocation-minded learning. Another upside of the college is the Hood Honor Code. All undergrads sign this code during new student orientation, pledging to maintain a high degree of academic and social integrity during their days at Hood. And yes, the undergrads take this pledge very seriously.

That's not to say there are no fun and games at Hood. Students like to get a little crazy now and then, whether at a friend's pad or out at one of Frederick's nightspots. But this is not a party school. On a Friday evening, Hood undergrads are as likely to have a volume of Plato in hand as they are to quaff a can of PBR. Frederick, a city of over 50,000, houses an assortment of odd museums, antique shops, thrift stores, restaurants, and bars. Both Baltimore and Washington, DC, are less than an hour away. And students with a few outdoorsy bones in their bodies love the fact that Hood sits just minutes from the foothills of the Blue Ridge Mountains and is an easy drive from any number of state parks. While many of Hood's undergrads are from Maryland, nearly 25 percent hail from out of state.

BANG FOR YOUR BUCK

During the 2005–2006 academic year, almost 80 percent of Hood's undergraduates received need-based financial aid. In addition, about 20 percent received merit-based aid. Together, this means that pretty close to 100 percent of the college's enrollees were given some sort of financial assistance. Needless to say, this commitment to students' (and parents') pocketbooks is one of Hood's big draws. Every year, the college dishes out more than $5 million in merit-based scholarships and determines recipients based on their class rank, GPA, and standardized test scores. Extracurricular activities, leadership experiences, and community service can affect decisions as well. The two largest scholarships offered are the Hodson Trust Academic Scholarship and the Hodson-Gilliam Scholarship, each worth $14,000 per student and awarded annually to numerous recipients. It's worth noting that Hood does not offer any scholarships specifically for athletes.

GETTING IN

Catching the eye of the admissions committee begins with presenting solid standardized test scores and a strong track record in high school (which means an impressive GPA and a challenging academic curriculum). But demonstrations of personal character, extracurricular interests, and unique talents can go a long way in setting an applicant apart from the pack. Legacy also matters at Hood. So if your grandmother attended the college back in the day, don't forget to mention it.

WHAT DO GRADUATES DO?

With a small student body characterized by diverse interests, it's difficult to find trends among Hood's recently graduated job-seekers. Business, communications, education, and scientific research are popular fields. Many students move on to graduate or professional schools as well. For instance, the college's top-notch biology department sees nearly half of its seniors grab their diplomas and head off to programs in graduate, veterinary, or medical schools. Hood's career center sponsors and cosponsors a range of job fairs that allow students to get a sense of what's out there. Alumni networking, mock interviews, and resume and cover letter tutoring are among the many additional services the career center provides.

IMPORTANT ADMISSION FACTORS

Alumni/ae relation, character/personal qualities, class rank, extracurricular activities, level of applicant's interest, talent/ability

Average HS GPA	3.31
Range SAT Verbal	510–600
Range SAT Math	500–600
Range ACT	20–25
Minimum TOEFL (paper/computer)	550/215

APPLICATION DEADLINES

Regular notification	rolling
# of transfer applicants	380
% of transfer applicants accepted	55

ACADEMICS

Student/faculty ratio	12:1
% faculty teaching undergraduates	100
% of classes taught by graduate students	0

MOST POPULAR MAJORS

- Biology/biological sciences
- Business administration and management
- Psychology

EDUCATION REQUIREMENTS

Arts/fine arts, computer literacy, English (including composition), foreign languages, history, humanities, math, philosophy, sciences (biological or physical), social science, physical education

FINANCIAL INFO

Tuition	$23,320
Room & board	$8,135
Average book expense	$800
Required fees	$335
Average freshman need-based grant	$16,092
Average freshman need-based loan	$3,819
% of graduates who borrowed	74
Average indebtedness	$16,295

FINANCIAL AID FORMS

Students must submit FAFSA.

POSTGRAD

% going to graduate school	39
% going to law school	4
% going to business school	4
% going to medical school	1

CAREER SERVICES

Alumni network, alumni services, career/job search classes, career assessment, internships, on-campus job interviews. Off-campus job opportunities are good.

THE BOTTOM LINE

The cost of tuition during the 2005–2006 academic year was $23,320. (This price is the same for in-staters and out-of-staters.) Room and board came to $8,135; fees were $335; and the combination of books, supplies, transportation, and other expenses was estimated at $1,900. The total cost was $33,690. The college was able to meet 87 percent of demonstrated financial need. The average need-based aid package totaled $18,020. Among the 20 percent of students who did not receive need-based aid but did receive merit-based aid, the average package came to $13,256. Around 74 percent of recent graduates left Hood with student loan debt. The average amount owed was just over $16,000.

FUN FACTS

During World War II, many Hood students proudly held membership in a group called WORMS. It's not as gross as it seems. WORMS actually stands for "Women Organized in Relief of the Manpower Shortage."

In the early 1900s, Hood undergrads would compose little ditties for submission in the Campus Day Weekend song competitions. Many of these were captured in the Hood College Songbook, published in 1925 by Hinds Hayden and Eldredge, Inc. One of the tunes, called "Oh Daddy Get Your Daughter Out of Debt," goes like this:

Oh Daddy get your daughter out of debt,
And reimburse your little pet.

They've been treating me so mean:
When the bills are overdue, they send them to the Dean.

Now I want a new dotted Swiss,
But I've more pressing needs than this—

My winter furs aren't paid for yet,
Oh Daddy get your daughter out of debt.

JAMES MADISON UNIVERSITY

Sonner Hall, MSC 0101, Harrisonburg, VA 22807
www.JMU.edu • Admissions: 540-568-5681
Fax: 540-568-3332 • E-mail: admissions@jmu.edu • Financial Aid: 540-568-7820

STUDENTS

Religious affiliation
                    No Affiliation
Academic year
  calendar   semester
Undergrad
  enrollment   15,653
% male/female   39/61
% Asian   5
% Black, non-Latino 3
% Latino   2
% international   1
% from out of state 30
% freshmen return for
sophomore year   91
% freshmen graduate
  within 4 years   62

STUDENT LIFE
% of students living
  on campus   38
% in fraternities   9
% in sororities   11

ADMISSIONS
of applicants   16,388
% accepted   68
% enrolled   34

HIGH SCHOOL UNITS
REQUIRED

4 English, 4 math, 3 science
(3 science lab), 3 foreign
language, 1 social studies, 2
history

HIGH SCHOOL UNITS
RECOMMENDED

4 English, 4 math, 4 science
(3 science lab), 4 foreign
language, 2 social studies, 2
history

ABOUT JAMES MADISON UNIVERSITY

With a warm, welcoming environment befitting its Southern locale, James Madison University is the type of school where it doesn't take students long to feel comfortable and right at home. Business and management programs are popular and well-regarded, as are health services majors and the school's tech disciplines, among which the innovative integrated science and technology major is a standout. Throughout the university, faculty value real-world preparation for real-world jobs, and look to take the learning process outside the classroom whenever possible.

Extracurriculars are another of JMU's strengths, both in terms of variety of activities and clubs, as well as a high percentage of student involvement and enthusiasm. Greek life has a sizable fan base, but remains just one of many options for socializing. While students here get their work done, once the books are put away, they have a knack for partying with gusto. This tends to take the form of smaller house and apartment parties instead of monstrous theme parties. Thursday is also a big night for going out. Though you'd expect a conservative lot, with Republicans dominating the campus, students' political views are evenly split between party lines.

BANG FOR YOUR BUCK

JMU strives to keep tuition rates affordable. Tuition increases in the last few years have been below state and national average increases. The school offers both need-based and merit-based aid. Most merit-based scholarships reward academic excellence; there are, however, also scholarships awarded for leadership, community involvement, geographic background, area of study, and career goals.

Perhaps the most prestigious of JMU's awards is its Centennial Scholars Program, which covers the full cost of attending JMU for four years for incoming freshmen and two years for transfer or graduate students. To qualify, students must complete the FAFSA and have very high need, as well as strong academic qualifications. If you get it, there are further requirements to keep it for your subsequent years.

Incoming freshmen may apply for Madison Achievement Scholarships, which are given to students who demonstrate academic poten-

"JMU is all about academics mixed with an atmosphere of friendly people who know how to have a good time."

VERY IMPORTANT ADMISSION FACTORS

Academic GPA, rigor of secondary school record

IMPORTANT ADMISSION FACTORS

Standardized test scores

Average HS GPA	3.67
Range SAT Verbal	530–620
Range SAT Math	540–630
Range ACT	21–26
Minimum TOEFL (paper/computer)	570/230

APPLICATION DEADLINES

Regular admission	1/15
Regular notification	4/1
# of transfer applicants	1,926
% of transfer applicants accepted	60

ACADEMICS

Student/faculty ratio	17:1
% faculty teaching undergraduates	100
% of classes taught by graduate students	1

MOST POPULAR MAJORS

• Communications studies/
speech communication and
rhetoric
• Marketing/marketing
management
• Psychology

tial through their high school course work, grades, and standardized test scores. Such students typically exceed a score of 1300 on the SATs and rank in the top 5 percent of their high school class. The school attempts to attract underrepresented populations with its Bluestone Scholarships, reserved for minority students with excellent academic records in high school.

GETTING IN

JMU looks most closely at applicants' high school grades and curriculum. Standardized test scores are also considered important. Despite the large number of applications it must process each year, JMU strives to closely consider all aspects of the application package, including recommendations, essays, and extracurricular activities.

Students interested in studying dance, music, and musical theater must audition. Aspiring art majors are strongly encouraged to submit a portfolio; likewise, potential theater majors are encouraged to audition, although an audition is not required. The Colleges of Business, Media Arts and Design, Nursing, Political Science, and Teaching Licensure programs all require students to apply separately after gaining admission to the university at large.

WHAT DO GRADUATES DO?

JMU is a big enough school to send students out into all fields of business, government, and academics. Top on-campus recruiters include Abercrombie and Fitch, Deloitte and Touche, Enterprise Rent-A-Car, Lockheed-Martin, Marriott International, numerous federal government agencies, PricewaterhouseCoopers, Ryan Homes, and school districts (both in-state and out-of-state). There are also numerous hospitals and health care agencies—including Duke University Hospital, Fairfax Hospital, Georgetown University Hospital, and the Memorial Sloan-Kettering Cancer Center.

THE BOTTOM LINE

For 2006–2007, in-state tuition at JMU totaled $6,290 per year. Additional fees accounted for another $250. Room and board cost $6,756 annually, bringing the total cost for a year (less personal expenses and books) at JMU to $13,296 for in-state students. Out-of-state students pay an additional $9,946 in tuition annually, bringing their annual cost to $23,242.

After applying all financial aid, the annual in-state aid recipient was responsible for only $6,474 in out-of-pocket expenses. The average out-of-state aid recipient was responsible for $11,088 in out-of-pocket expenses.

FUN FACTS

JMU will be 100 years old in 2008 and plans for its centennial celebration are already underway. A focus of the Centennial is a fund-raising campaign that should increase the number and value of scholarships.

The Dukes are what they call JMU's athletic teams. They are named after Samuel P. Duke, who was president of the school for 31 years. The school mascot is a bulldog (named Duke, of course).

JMU began its life as The State Normal and Industrial School for Women. The school changed its name to Madison College in 1938 to honor James Madison, an influential framer of the U.S. Constitution, a strong proponent of public education, and the fourth president of the United States. Madison College became James Madison University in 1977.

When the weather heats up in Harrisonburg, Virginia, students head to Kline's Dairy Bar, where the line for homemade ice cream often stretches out into the parking lot. Kline's has been a JMU tradition since 1943.

EDUCATION REQUIREMENTS

Arts/fine arts, computer literacy, English (including composition), history, humanities, math, philosophy, sciences (biological or physical), social science, speech communication, critical thinking, wellness, U.S. history/government

FINANCIAL INFO

In-state tuition $6,290
Out-of-state tuition $16,236
Room & board $6,756
Average book
   expense $820
Average freshman
   need-based grant $5,827
Average freshman
   need-based loan $2,904
% of graduates
   who borrowed   53
Average
   indebtedness $12,591

FINANCIAL AID FORMS

Students must submit FAFSA.

POSTGRAD

CAREER SERVICES

Off-campus job opportunities are good.

KENTUCKY WESLEYAN COLLEGE

3000 Frederica Street, PO Box 1039, Owensboro, KY 42302
www.KWC.edu • Admissions: 270-852-3120
Fax: 270-852-3133 • E-mail: admitme@kwc.edu • Financial Aid: 270-852-3120

STUDENTS

Religious affiliation
Methodist
Academic year
calendar   semester
Undergrad
enrollment   930
% male/female   55/45
% Black, non-Latino   10
% Latino   2
% international   1
% from out of state 20
% freshmen return for
sophomore year   67
% freshmen graduate
within 4 years   31

STUDENT LIFE

% of students living
on campus   49
% in fraternities   13
% in sororities   21

ADMISSIONS

of applicants   1,074
% accepted   77
% enrolled   25

HIGH SCHOOL UNITS REQUIRED

4 English, 3 math, 3
science, 3 social studies

HIGH SCHOOL UNITS RECOMMENDED

2 Foreign language

VERY IMPORTANT ADMISSION FACTORS

Rigor of secondary school
record

ABOUT KENTUCKY WESLEYAN COLLEGE

In western Kentucky, the Ohio River edges the town of Owensboro, the hometown of Kentucky Wesleyan College, a liberal arts institution with a professional bent and a Methodist affiliation. This small school—we're talking barely more than 900 undergrads—has a reputation for the caring and comfortable atmosphere that students discover when they walk onto campus. In fact, faculty attention and availability are hallmarks of a KWC education. Undergrads can choose from more than 40 majors (many with areas of concentration), more than 25 minors, 10 pre-professional programs, and 5 secondary education certificates—an impressive spectrum for such a modestly sized school. The favored majors at KWC include business administration, communications, criminal justice, and education. Regardless of what they major in, all students must complete the General Education Program, which gives them a foundation in analysis, communications, mathematics, computer technologies, and a self-selected foreign language.

Owensboro is Kentucky's third-largest city, but this is not to suggest that there's a whole lot to grab a college student's attention there. Some KWC undergrads grumble about this, while others shrug it off—it's easier to study without the distractions, after all. And if distractions are what students are after, they can find plenty of them on campus. The college has more than 40 student organizations, including Greek chapters, media outlets, and specialty-interest organizations. A range of campus ministries are available as well, reflecting the strong presence of Christian values at KWC. When campus life doesn't offer enough excitement, KWCers can embark on a road trip to Louisville or Nashville, each within two hours of campus.

BANG FOR YOUR BUCK

The 2005–2006 academic year saw nearly 85 percent of KWC's student body receive need-based financial aid (in total, 72 percent of established need was met). The same year, 14 percent of KWC undergrads earned merit-based aid. Add it all up, and approximately 99 percent of students benefited from some sort of financial aid package. When students highlight the finer aspects of a KWC education, they rarely fail to mention the generous financial support. Every applicant to the college is automatically considered for scholarships. Merit-based scholarships are given according to standardized test scores and high school GPA. Among the biggest prizes are the Trustee Scholarships and Presidential Scholarships, respectively worth $8,000 annually and $6,000 annually. Specialized scholarships and grants are also available for transfer students, legacy students, United Meth-

Students Say

"At KWC, we are like one big happy family. We have our disagreements, but we all try to work them out and help each other improve our intelligence."

odist Church members, family members of ordained Methodist ministers, athletes, and students with special talents in band, art, music, and theater.

GETTING IN

For the KWC Office of Admission, the most important aspect of an application is the secondary school record. This means that GPA and caliber of courses can have a big impact on an admissions decision. Other factors that carry weight include class rank, standardized test scores, extracurricular interests, and unique personal talents. The college does not ask applicants to submit an admissions essay. Though KWC doesn't require applicants to be members of the United Methodist Church, it's worth pointing out that this is a college very invested in its religious roots and caters especially well to students interested in Christian values and spiritual development.

WHAT DO GRADUATES DO?

Popular professional fields among KWC graduates include law enforcement, education, business, marketing, media, and ministerial work. As upperclassmen prepare to hit the workforce, they can take advantage of the career-oriented counseling, testing, workshops, and more offered through the Career Development and Community Service Center. Throughout their college years, students can go to the CDCS Center for assistance in finding internships and part-time jobs that will help them build their resumes.

IMPORTANT ADMISSION FACTORS

Academic GPA, character/personal qualities, class rank, extracurricular activities, standardized test scores, talent/ability

Average HS GPA	3.3
Range SAT Verbal	400–570
Range SAT Math	460–560
Range ACT	18–25
Minimum TOEFL (paper/computer)	500/173

APPLICATION DEADLINES

Regular admission	8/21
Regular notification	rolling
# of transfer applicants	207
% of transfer applicants accepted	58

ACADEMICS

Student/faculty ratio	15:1
% faculty teaching undergraduates	100
% of classes taught by graduate students	0

MOST POPULAR MAJORS

- Business administration/management
- Communications studies/speech communication and rhetoric
- Criminal justice/safety studies

Arts/fine arts, computer literacy, English (including composition), foreign languages, history, humanities, math, philosophy, sciences (biological or physical), social science, interdisciplinary requirement, multicultural requirement, physical education, oral communications

FINANCIAL INFO

Tuition	$13,200
Room & board	$5,750
Average book expense	$1,250
Required fees	$400
Average freshman need-based grant	$10,420
Average freshman need-based loan	$2,339
% of graduates who borrowed	75
Average indebtedness	$19,990

FINANCIAL AID FORMS

Students must submit FAFSA.

POSTGRAD

CAREER SERVICES

Alumni services, career/job search classes, career assessment, internships, on-campus job interviews.

THE BOTTOM LINE

In 2005–2006, the KWC tuition was $13,200 for in-state and out-of-state students. Room and board came to $5,750, and fees ranged from $400 to $525. Other estimated costs included $1,250 for books/supplies and $2,000 for miscellaneous expenses. The total adds up to around $22,600. The average need-based financial aid package was $11,381. The average merit-based package was $10,158. Nearly 75 percent of KWC's undergrads take out student loans for an average overall debt of $19,990 after graduation.

FUN FACTS

The fall of 2006 saw Kentucky Wesleyan College's largest incoming class since 1966—and a 28-percent increase in incoming students compared to 2005. This put the total enrollment at KWC at 911 full-time undergrads and 57 part-timers.

Have a hankering for intramural sports? So do many students at KWC. In the fall, students enjoy intramural competition in flag football, indoor soccer, volleyball, racquetball, putt-putt, and golf. And in the spring, the roster includes basketball, bowling, ultimate Frisbee, softball, and tennis.

On January 3, 2000, an F3 tornado hammered the Kentucky Wesleyan College campus. Despite the severe damage and unexpected setbacks, KWC managed to remain optimistic: This offered a good opportunity to fix up or simply replace rundown facilities—improvements that today's students benefit from.

KNOX COLLEGE

2 East South Street, Galesburg, IL 61401
www.Knox.edu • Admissions: 309-341-7100
Fax: 309-341-7070 • E-mail: admission@knox.edu • Financial Aid: 309-341-7149

STUDENTS

Religious affiliation
                     No Affiliation
Academic year
  calendar   3-3
Undergrad
  enrollment   1,205
% male/female   46/54
% Asian   5
% Black, non-Latino   4
% Latino   4
% international   7
% from out of state   45
% freshmen return for
sophomore year   85
% freshmen graduate
  within 4 years   67

STUDENT LIFE

% of students living
  on campus   95
% in fraternities   24
% in sororities   11

ADMISSIONS

of applicants   1,771
% accepted   76
% enrolled   24

HIGH SCHOOL UNITS RECOMMENDED

4 English, 4 math, 3 science
(2 science lab), 3 foreign
language, 2 social studies, 2
history

VERY IMPORTANT ADMISSION FACTORS

Academic GPA, rigor of
secondary school record

ABOUT KNOX COLLEGE

In west central Illinois, about 32 miles east of the mighty Mississippi River, you'll find a town called Galesburg and a college called Knox. Renowned for its sharp students and successful alums, Knox is a small liberal arts college that places a strong emphasis on academic freedom and personal exploration. Knox forgoes the mass of requirements often found at liberal arts institutions, opting instead for a looser system that allows students to stretch themselves as they see fit and engage in extracurricular, volunteer, and off-campus learning opportunities. In fact, the school's very motto is "Freedom to Flourish." With all this freedom, however, self-discipline is a must. The workload is heavy and expectations are omnipresent. Fortunately, each student benefits from the one-on-one guidance of an academic counselor, who helps the student shape a four-year educational plan and settle on an academic major. While nearly every department earns kudos from Knox undergrads, the most popular majors include creative writing, the arts, education, political science, and premed.

Students are as excited about their social lives at Knox as they are about academics. The campus is always bouncing with activity. The Knox calendar is packed with theatrical performances, concerts, guest speakers, literary readings, poetry slams, comedians, magicians, special occasions like Casino Nights—you name it. Sports draw a healthy following around here—especially when it's time to take on regional rival, Monmouth College. Knox is an NCAA DIII school with a combined number of 21 men's and women's athletic teams. And after the big game is over, it shouldn't be too hard to find a shindig. While Knox is by no means a party school, these students do know how to throw down now and again. The town of Galesburg itself doesn't offer much to be enthused about, and while some students complain about this, most just turn their attentions to campus.

"Most students call their professors by their first names. They may even call them at home. I think that says a lot. If you are serious about doing something, there is someone out there who will help you do it."

IMPORTANT ADMISSION FACTORS

Application essay, class rank, recommendation(s)

Range SAT Verbal 580–700
Range SAT Math   540–660
Range ACT   25–30
Minimum TOEFL
   (paper/computer) 550/213

APPLICATION DEADLINES

Regular admission   2/1
Regular notification   3/31
# of transfer applicants 99
% of transfer applicants
   accepted   62

ACADEMICS

Student/faculty ratio   12:1
% faculty teaching
   undergraduates   100
% of classes taught by
   graduate students   0

MOST POPULAR MAJORS

- Anthropology
- Creative writing
- Psychology

EDUCATION REQUIREMENTS

Arts/fine arts, foreign language, humanities, math, sciences (biological or physical), social science. Students must take a one term interdisciplinary preceptorial emphasizing writing and discussion skills. In addition, two writing intensive courses and one course emphasizing oral presentation are required. One course

BANG FOR YOUR BUCK

About 67 percent of the Knox student body received need-based aid during the 2005–2006 year. Add to that the 29 percent that was awarded as merit-based aid, and you quickly see that a whopping majority of the college's undergraduates are given significant reductions on the cost of a Knox education. As the financial aid folks at Knox put it, "Just as we are committed to providing you the best education possible, we are also committed to ensuring cost is not a barrier." Some of the top academic scholarships include the National Merit Scholarships, Lincoln, Muelder, and Scripps Academic Scholarships Transfer Student Scholarships, Visual and Performing Arts Scholarships, Knox Writers' Scholarships, Social Concerns Scholarships, and more than half a dozen others. Check out the college's financial aid web page for specific information on each of these opportunities.

GETTING IN

The first thing a Knox College admissions officer looks at is your high school record: A strong GPA, AP classes, and honors classes are the factors that will make the best impression. Knox also looks carefully at class rank, letters of recommendation, and the quality of the application essay. Though Knox is test optional, it can't hurt to knock those SATs and ACTs out of the park. Check out their website at www.knox.edu/admission for more information.

WHAT DO GRADUATES DO?

This is what Knox has to say on its FAQ web page: "The whole idea behind a Knox education is to provide you with the knowledge, skills, and capacity for independent thought and inquiry you need to thrive in any professional endeavor." In other words, what doesn't a Knox student do? In fact, a whopping 60 percent of Knox undergrads go on to grad school. Those who go into the workforce land in fields such as business, teaching, marketing, and communications.

THE BOTTOM LINE

A year's tuition at Knox came to $27,606 in 2006–2007. Further costs were $294 in fees and $5,295 for room and board. Knox estimates that students spend $900 per year for books, $400 for transportation, and $600 other expenses. The sum total comes to $34,801. This, of course, is before financial aid is factored in. In 2005–2006, the average need-based financial aid package came to $21,317. The average merit-based package amounted $10,011. Of recent graduates, around 68 percent had student loans to repay. The average debt was $19,642.

FUN FACTS

Approximately 92 percent of Knox undergrads say they plan to earn a degree beyond the bachelor's.

Early one morning every spring, music blares and bells ring across the Knox campus. When students, professors, and administrators hear these sounds, they know that the annual "Flunk Day" has begun. Only a handful of students, called "The Friars," know when Flunk Day will occur and what it will entail. The point of the all-day affair is to celebrate the advent of spring and to bring the community together. The 2006 celebration (which landed on April 11) included a campus breakfast, inflatable games, a mechanical bull, a dunk tank, karaoke, a student-faculty softball game, a big dinner, and a movie screening.

Feeling social? Try the Pumphandle. At the beginning of every school year, students, faculty, and staff line up to shake each others' hands – pumping the handle as it were.

focusing on diversity is also required, as well as documentation of a significant experiential learning project outside the classroom. Breadth requirements include one course each in the four areas of arts, humanities, math, and natural science and an additional field of concentration, minor or major, not in the department of the major. There are also foreign language and quantitative literacy requirements.

FINANCIAL INFO

Tuition	$27,606
Room & board	$5,925
Average book expense	$900
Required fees	$294
Average freshman need-based grant	$16,474
Average freshman need-based loan	$4,424
% of graduates who borrowed	68
Average indebtedness	$19,642

FINANCIAL AID FORMS

Students must submit FAFSA, institution's own financial aid form.

POSTGRAD

% going to graduate school	60
% going to law school	14
% going to medical school	15

CAREER SERVICES

Alumni services, career/job search classes, career assessment, internships, on-campus job interviews. Off-campus job opportunities are good.

LAKE FOREST COLLEGE

555 North Sheridan Road, Lake Forest, IL 60045
www.LakeForest.edu • Admissions: 847-735-5000
Fax: 847-735-6271 • E-mail: admissions@lakeforest.edu • Financial Aid: 847-735-5010

STUDENTS

Religious affiliation
                    Presbyterian
Academic year
  calendar   semester
Undergrad
  enrollment   1,422
% male/female   42/58
% Asian   5
% Black, non-Latino   4
% Latino   6
% international   8
% from out of state   57
% freshmen return for
  sophomore year   80
% freshmen graduate
  within 4 years   63

STUDENT LIFE

% of students living
  on campus   80
% in fraternities   9
% in sororities   19

ADMISSIONS

of applicants   2,197
% accepted   63
% enrolled   28
# of early decision/action
  applicants   755
% accepted early
  decision/action   60

HIGH SCHOOL UNITS REQUIRED

4 English, 3 math, 2
science (2 science lab), 2
foreign language, 2 social
studies, 1 history, 3
academic electives

ABOUT LAKE FOREST COLLEGE

An excellent combination of challenging academics, competitive Division III sports, and great financial aid sets small Lake Forest College apart from the pack of solid liberal arts colleges, to say nothing of its proximity to Chicago. You'll find many other great perks. Lake Forest boasts a gorgeous campus, good food (as far as college food goes), and committed professors who go well out of their way to make themselves accessible both in and out of the classroom. And there are tons of internships; almost 50 percent of every graduating class leaves with some real-world experience. In addition to LFC's glamorous International Internship Programs in Paris and Santiago, students in recent years have held internships with Bank One, the Chicago Board of Trade, Morgan Stanley, Motorola, and Da Chicago Bears.

Lake Forest is located about thirty miles north of Chicago in the swanky, mansion-filled suburb of Lake Forest. Like every suburban enclave on the North Shore, the town of Lake Forest offers little interest to college students and shuts down pretty early. To keep themselves busy, the student population fervently supports its athletic teams and attends parties and the numerous campus-sponsored events. When escape becomes necessary, the vitality of Chicago is just a cheap train ride away.

BANG FOR YOUR BUCK

Lake Forest College is affordable because it maintains a strong commitment to providing generous financial aid to qualified applicants. Best of all—and we think you'll agree—LFC doesn't overdo the student loan thing. While many colleges and universities award student loans first, Lake Forest awards up to $10,500 in grants first. Only after this rather significant chunk of free money is exhausted does LFC resort to loans. The average need-based student loan for a first-year student ends up being under $4,000. Also, students are admitted without regard to financial need. And once you are admitted, Lake Forest is committed to maintaining its grant aid for all four years. Of all first-year students, 89 percent receive financial aid. The average financial aid package is nearly $22,585 (including loans). The average grant/scholarship package that comes directly from the coffers of LFC is $15,635. About 40 percent of all financial aid applicants who come from families with household incomes over $100,000 still qualify for need-based aid.

"When you have a faculty to student ratio of 1:12, [you] get to know each other, and the education is very personal and immediate. That is the bedrock for liberal arts colleges and especially here at Lake Forest College."

In addition, a slew of scholarships are available to students with exceptional academic records; talent in the arts, foreign languages, music, theater; or an interest in science (including math and computers), or writing, or leadership. Can't decide if you want to study physics or play the flute? Not a problem. Students can receive one academic, and one talent or departmental scholarship. Academic scholarships range from $1,000 to full tuition—currently more than $25,500.

Getting In

The most important aspect of your application to Lake Forest College is your academic record, including the combination of courses you've taken, grades, and your record of achievement. The second most important thing is recommendations. Next in importance is the graded paper (which LFC uses *instead* of an essay). Choose a paper that shows you can write in a clear and disciplined way and that you have the ability to present a thesis and argue it well. You also need to document your extracurricular activities and significant employment. Standardized test scores are optional.

What do Graduates Do?

About one-third of all Lake Forest College graduates go directly to graduate or professional schools. You'll find Lake Forest graduates at the University of Minnesota's medical school, Georgetown University Law Center, Washington University's graduate program in engineering, and Stanford's PhD program for statistics. Major employers of LFC alumni include Abbott Laboratories, Bank One, Brunswick Corp., Federal Reserve Bank of Chicago, and SBC Communications. Notable alumni include actor Richard Widmark (called "the face of film noir"), Alan Carr (producer of the movie *Grease*), and Herbert Block (political cartoonist and three-time Pulitzer Prize winner). Lake Forest's tremendous Career Advancement Center does a lot—and we mean *a lot*—to help students find internships and jobs.

HIGH SCHOOL UNITS RECOMMENDED

4 English, 4 math, 3 science (3 science lab), 4 foreign language, 2 social studies, 2 history, 2 academic electives

VERY IMPORTANT ADMISSION FACTORS

Academic GPA, interview, recommendation(s), rigor of secondary school record

IMPORTANT ADMISSION FACTORS

Application essay, character/personal qualities, extracurricular activities, talent/ability

Average HS GPA	3.5
Range SAT Verbal	540–640
Range SAT Math	530–650
Range ACT	24–28
Minimum TOEFL (paper/computer)	550/220

APPLICATION DEADLINES

Early decision	12/1
Early decision notification	12/20
Regular admission	2/15
Regular notification	3/20
# of transfer applicants	240
% of transfer applicants accepted	34

ACADEMICS

Student/faculty ratio	12:1
% faculty teaching undergraduates	100
% of classes taught by graduate students	0

MOST POPULAR MAJORS

- Business/economics
- Communications
- Education
- Psychology

EDUCATION REQUIREMENTS

English (including composition), humanities, math, sciences (biological or physical), social science

FINANCIAL INFO

Tuition	$28,700
Room & board	$6,960
Average book expense	$700
Required fees	$464
Average freshman need-based grant	$18,566
Average freshman need-based loan	$3,938
% of graduates who borrowed	63
Average indebtedness	$17,978

FINANCIAL AID FORMS

Students must submit FAFSA, federal income tax return.

Financial Aid filing deadline	3/1

POSTGRAD

% going to graduate school	35
% going to law school	9
% going to business school	4
% going to medical school	3

CAREER SERVICES

Alumni network, alumni services, alumni mentor program, career/job search classes, career assessment, internships, on-campus job interviews. Off-campus job opportunities are excellent.

THE BOTTOM LINE

The total cost for tuition, fees, room and board, books, and expenses at Lake Forest College is $37,500. Over the course of an academic year, the actual out-of-pocket cost for an average student is roughly $14,000. Graduates leave LFC with approximately $18,000 in student loan debt. At an interest rate of 6.8 percent, the monthly payment on $18,000 in debt would be about $207.

FUN FACTS

Among the study-abroad destinations for students at Lake Forest College are Paris, Greece, Turkey, Italy, India, Japan, Russia, the Czech Republic, Chile (Santiago), Beijing, and Tanzania. Semesters in Chicago, Washington, DC, and the Oak Ridge National Laboratory in Tennessee are also available.

The Starrett brothers, Paul (class of 1887) and Theodore (class of 1884), were among the leading pioneers in creating the methodology for the construction of skyscrapers. Paul was in charge of the construction of the Empire State Building. The Starrett brothers also took on the construction of the Lincoln Memorial in Washington, DC.

Theodore Suess Giesel (aka Dr. Seuss) gave the 1977 commencement address for Lake Forest graduates. The address, titled "Uncle Terwilliger on the Art of Eating Popovers," is perhaps the shortest address ever given. The fourteen line speech is engraved on a rock on the college's Middle Campus.

Ralph Jones, Lake Forest's football coach in the 1930s and 1940s, is credited with devising the T-formation.

LOUISIANA STATE UNIVERSITY— BATON ROUGE

110 Thomas Boyd Hall, Baton Rouge, LA 70803
www.LSU.edu • Admissions: 225-578-1175
Fax: 225-578-4433 • E-mail: admissions@lsu.edu • Financial Aid: 225-578-3103

STUDENTS

Religious affiliation
                    No Affiliation
Academic year
  calendar   semester
Undergrad
  enrollment   25,301
% male/female   48/52
% Asian   3
% Black, non-Latino   9
% Latino   3
% international   2
% from out of state   13
% freshmen return for
sophomore year   83
% freshmen graduate
  within 4 years   27

STUDENT LIFE

% of students living
  on campus   23
% in fraternities   10
% in sororities   17

ADMISSIONS

of applicants   10,825
% accepted   73
% enrolled   63

HIGH SCHOOL UNITS REQUIRED

4 English, 3 math, 3
science, 2 foreign language,
3 social studies, 3 academic
electives

HIGH SCHOOL UNITS RECOMMENDED

4 Math

ABOUT LOUISIANA STATE UNIVERSITY

In some ways, LSU is a victim of its own success. The school devotes considerable efforts and resources to its football team, with consistently excellent results. Unfortunately, in the process, the university has created the impression that football is the alpha and omega of the LSU experience. Yet, nothing could be further from the truth. In reality, LSU is a major research institute with outstanding academic programs in many of the traditional land-grant university disciplines, agriculture, business and marketing, education, and natural science among them. Proximity to the Mississippi River and the Gulf of Mexico facilitates the university's first-rate marine studies programs. Campus facilities, from research labs to Internet connections to the recreation center, are all first rate.

LSU is big enough that students of every type and background will find a place. The place accommodating Caucasian, upper-middle-class, Southern conservatives happens to be the biggest, but everyone fits in somewhere. All differences among students disappear on game day, when Tiger fans meet up early for tailgates and make a full-day party of it. Greek life is another constant in the lives of many. Hometown Baton Rouge is student-friendly, with lots of shops, cheap eats, and bars.

BANG FOR YOUR BUCK

By any standard, tuition at LSU is low. A little less than half of all students receive some form of need-based aid. All told, the school administers nearly $40 million in federal, state, and institutional need-based aid to undergraduates.

In 2005–2006, LSU provided need-based assistance to 96 percent of all aid applicants who demonstrated need. Eighty-seven percent of need-based aid packages included some form of need-based grant or scholarship. On average, the school met 62 percent of aid recipients' demonstrated need. Fifteen percent of aid recipients had a full 100 percent of their demonstrated need met by the school.

Many need-based packages are supplemented by non-need-based awards. The school administers over $34 million in federal, state, and institutional non-need-based awards. Merit-based awards, which are based on standardized test scores and high school GPA, provide up to full tuition and fees. Other awards are available to those with special skills in athletics, music, the arts, specific academic areas, and leadership. ROTC cadets and relations of LSU alumni are also eligible for dedicated scholarships and grants.

Students Say

"Football, fun, and tradition, all while getting a top-notch education."

VERY IMPORTANT ADMISSION FACTORS

Academic GPA, rigor of secondary school record, standardized test scores

IMPORTANT ADMISSION FACTORS

Class rank

Average HS GPA	3.47
Range SAT Verbal	520–630
Range SAT Math	540–660
Range ACT	22–27
Minimum TOEFL (paper/computer)	550/213

APPLICATION DEADLINES

Regular admission	4/15
# of transfer applicants	2,005
% of transfer applicants accepted	57

ACADEMICS

Student/faculty ratio	22:1
% faculty teaching undergraduates	85
% of classes taught by graduate students	10

MOST POPULAR MAJORS

• Biology/biological sciences
• General studies
• Psychology

EDUCATION REQUIREMENTS

Arts/fine arts, computer literacy, English (including composition), foreign languages, humanities, math, sciences (biological or physical), social science

GETTING IN

Admission to LSU is formula driven, resulting in admissions decisions based on high school GPA and standardized test scores. Any entering freshman with a high school GPA of at least 3.0 (18 academic credits minimum) and a combined SAT I score of at least 1030 is guaranteed admission. Students who do not meet these criteria may still be guaranteed admission. A detailed table outlining how the formula is applied can be found at the LSU website. It's also important to note that each of the senior colleges at LSU has its own specific admissions requirements.

WHAT DO GRADUATES DO?

LSU graduates find work in Louisiana's top industries, which include chemical production, food processing, paper manufacturing, petroleum and coal production, tourism, and transportation manufacturing. As an aside, business services, construction, government, health services, and wholesale and retail trade are projected to be the fastest growing employers in Louisiana over the next decade.

THE BOTTOM LINE

Louisiana residents attending LSU full time in 2006–2007 paid $2,981 in tuition and an additional $1,438 in required fees. Room and board cost $6,498; books and supplies cost an estimated $1,500; transportation expenses totaled $940; and personal and miscellaneous expenses amounted to $1,632. Thus, the total cost of attending LSU for a Louisiana native was $14,989. Nonresidents of Louisiana paid an additional $8,300 in tuition and an additional $476 in transportation expenses, bringing their total cost to $23,765. In 2005–2006, the last year for which such figures were available, over 10,000 LSU undergraduates received some form of need-based or merit-based scholarship.

Fun Facts

LSU is the home of *The Southern Review*, one of the world's most prestigious literary journals. *The Southern Review* was established in the 1930s by Robert Penn Warren, Cleanth Brooks, and Charles Pipkin.

Notable LSU alumni and former students include U.S. Senators John Breaux and Mary Landrieu, NBA superstar Shaquille O'Neal, movie composer Bill Conti, and political strategist James Carville. In 2005, 32 former LSU Tigers were playing in the NFL.

LSU's mascot, Mike, is a royal Bengal tiger. Mike lives in a 15,000-square-foot tiger habitat with streams, trees, and a waterfall.

In 2004, LSU was named one of the nation's most entrepreneurial campuses .

FINANCIAL INFO

In-state tuition	$2,981
Out-of-state tuition	$11,281
Room & board	$6,498
Average book expense	$1,500
Required fees	$1,468
Average freshman need-based grant	$4,707
Average freshman need-based loan	$2,443
% of graduates who borrowed	49
Average indebtedness	$19,258

Financial Aid Forms

Students must submit FAFSA, institution's own financial aid form.

LUTHER COLLEGE

700 College Drive, Decorah, IA 52101-1042
www.Luther.edu • Admissions: 563-387-1287
Fax: 563-387-2159 • E-mail: admissions@luther.edu • Financial Aid: 563-387-1018

STUDENTS

Religious affiliation
Lutheran
Academic year
calendar 4-1-4
Undergrad
enrollment 2,466
% male/female 42/58
% Asian 2
% Black, non-Latino 1
% Latino 1
% international 3
% from out of state 65
% freshmen return for
sophomore year 84
% freshmen graduate
within 4 years 65

STUDENT LIFE

% of students living
on campus 84
% in fraternities 7
% in sororities 9

ADMISSIONS

of applicants 2,121
% accepted 75
% enrolled 40

HIGH SCHOOL UNITS RECOMMENDED

4 English, 3 math, 2
science (1 science lab), 2
foreign language, 3 social
studies

VERY IMPORTANT ADMISSION FACTORS

Academic GPA, class rank,
recommendation(s), rigor of
secondary school record,
standardized test scores

ABOUT LUTHER COLLEGE

Luther College, a small liberal arts institution affiliated with the American Evangelical Lutheran Church, lays its emphasis on "faith, leadership, and community service." The 2,500 undergrads at Luther have their pick of more than 60 academic major/minor programs, as well as 11 pre-professional and special programs. The programs that attract the most students include education, English, biology, psychology, social sciences, and management. Oh, and there's music, too—it's probably the most popular and most renowned program on campus. The college's PAIDEIA program (that's Greek for "education") ensures that all students immerse themselves in liberal arts learning, including a freshman-year, two-semester interdisciplinary course and a senior-year seminar on values. Luther aims to send all of its students into the world as well-educated leaders and contributors to their communities. The school's liberal arts foundation serves these aims well by giving each student a broad understanding of the world, its peoples, and its ideas.

The campus is tucked away among the limestone bluffs of northeastern Iowa. Its hometown, Decorah, has just 8,500 residents. And while students will be the first to admit that Decorah is not exactly bumping, very few of them take off when the weekend rolls around. Why? Well, because campus life *is* bumping. The Student Activities Council earns great praise for jamming the calendar with on-campus entertainment ranging from rock concerts to guest lecturers. This is also a school where music is big. That is, *big*. Luther is home to seven vocal ensembles and eight instrumental ensembles. Nary a week goes by when one of these groups isn't performing at Luther. Campus ministries are well supported, too. In fact, the ministries have 10 outreach teams that filter into the surrounding communities. There are over 100 student groups on campus, including a well-accepted GLBT activist group. Luther undergrads are quick to point out that all people are welcome and accepted in Decorah.

Students Say

"Luther is a very active campus. There is always something going on. Athletic events and clubs keep you busy and there are always things like dances or music events to keep you entertained. It's very hard to be bored here."

BANG FOR YOUR BUCK

In 2005–2006, about 71 percent of Luther's student population received need-based financial aid. Further, around 28 percent were given merit-based aid packages. In other words, just about everyone enrolled at Luther was awarded some sort of financial assistance. Merit-based scholarships through 10 institutional funds are available. Incoming students do not need to apply for these scholarships; financial aid officers will determine the recipients based on information culled from the Luther College application. The most lucrative award is the Regent Scholarship, which provides a student anywhere from $34,000 to $56,000 over a four-year period. Recipients are selected according to standardized test scores, class rank, high school curriculum, and extracurricular activities.

GETTING IN

Luther's admissions officers take a close look at four primary facets of an application: high school record (grades and rigor of curriculum), class rank, standardized test scores, and letters of recommendation. Application essays, extracurricular activities, unique skills, and a candidate's overall character also play a part. Luther is looking for interested and interesting students who are prepared to contribute to the academic, social, and spiritual communities on campus and beyond.

WHAT DO GRADUATES DO?

Luther grads move into many professional arenas, including the sciences, music, business, religion, education, and communications. The library at the college's career center has plenty of resources to help students make informed vocational decisions. The career center also operates internship and volunteer programs that allow undergrads to pad their resumes with hands-on experience. Graduate school advising is also available.

IMPORTANT ADMISSION FACTORS

Application essay, character/personal qualities, extracurricular activities, racial/ethnic status, talent/ability, volunteer work

Average HS GPA	3.6
Range SAT Verbal	550–670
Range SAT Math	550–670
Range ACT	22–28
Minimum TOEFL (paper/computer)	550/213

APPLICATION DEADLINES

Regular notification	rolling
# of transfer applicants	149
% of transfer applicants accepted	64

ACADEMICS

Student/faculty ratio	13:1
% faculty teaching undergraduates	100
% of classes taught by graduate students	0

MOST POPULAR MAJORS

- Biology/biological sciences
- Business administration/management
- Elementary education and teaching

EDUCATION REQUIREMENTS

Arts/fine arts, English (including composition), foreign languages, history, humanities, math, philosophy, sciences (biological or physical), social science, religion

FINANCIAL INFO

Tuition	$26,380
Room & board	$4,290
Average book expense	$830
Average freshman need-based grant	$16,413
Average freshman need-based loan	$3,846
% of graduates who borrowed	82
Average indebtedness	$18,271

FINANCIAL AID FORMS

Students must submit FAFSA, institution's own financial aid form.

POSTGRAD

% going to graduate school	21
% going to law school	1
% going to business school	1
% going to medical school	3

THE BOTTOM LINE

Luther's tuition was $26,380 during the 2006–2007 academic year. Additional costs came in the form of room and board ($4,290), books and supplies (estimated at $830), transportation (estimated at $1,020), and other expenses (estimated at $1,510). The total cost, then, was around $34,000 before financial aid. The average need-based financial aid package received by Luther undergrads was $20,302 and the average merit-based package was $8,692 ($8,774 for freshmen). Among students graduating between July 2005 and June 2006, around 82 percent had taken out student loans with an average debt of $18,271.

FUN FACTS

For 75 years, Luther College admitted only male students. This changed in 1936 when the college went coed. Today Luther's student population is about 40 percent male and 60 percent female.

Fred Smith, a student in Luther's 2007 graduating class, released *A Smart Student's Guide to Healthy Living* at the beginning of his senior year. The book, published by New Harbinger Press, Inc., was a mother-son collaboration. Smith's mother, M.J. Smith, is a registered dietician who wrote two of the book's five chapters. *A Smart Student's Guide to Healthy Living* gives college students a plethora of advice about everything from eating well to implementing organizational techniques in order to make those early days of college a little easier.

The Vesterheim Norwegian-American Museum in downtown Decorah is a 16-building complex that bills itself as "America's oldest and largest museum devoted to one immigrant group."

LYON COLLEGE

PO Box 2317, Batesville, AR 72503-2317
www.Lyon.edu • Admissions: 870-698-4250
Fax: 870-793-1791 • E-mail: admissions@lyon.edu • Financial Aid: 870-698-4257

STUDENTS

Religious affiliation
              Presbyterian
Academic year
  calendar   semester
Undergrad
  enrollment   484
% male/female   49/51
% Asian   1
% Black, non-Latino   4
% Latino   2
% Native American   1
% international   3
% from out of state   17
% freshmen return for
sophomore year   75
% freshmen graduate
  within 4 years   58

STUDENT LIFE

% of students living
  on campus   76
% in fraternities   10
% in sororities   13

ADMISSIONS

of applicants   470
% accepted   72
% enrolled   33

HIGH SCHOOL UNITS REQUIRED

4 English, 3 math, 3 science
(2 science lab), 2 foreign
language, 1 social studies, 2
history, 1 academic elective

ABOUT LYON COLLEGE

About 90 miles northeast of Little Rock you'll find Batesville, Arkansas, the hometown of Lyon College. An intimate school of less than 500 undergrads, Lyon is a liberal arts institution affiliated with the Presbyterian Church. Perhaps as an outgrowth of its religious roots, Lyon "emphasizes development of character as well as intellect." Students are able to implement this philosophy through their involvement in 40 student clubs, a half-dozen Greek organizations, a dozen sports teams, an intramural league, campus ministries, and any of the varied activities that make the Lyon campus a fun place to be. And it's a good thing that campus is so appealing, as Batesville (a town of under 10,000) doesn't tend to excite your typical undergrad—though that's not to say Super Wal-Mart doesn't have its charms.

Intellectual growth is facilitated by a well-rounded liberal arts education comprising 18 academic programs, unlimited self-designed majors, a handful of professional concentrations, and a core curriculum. This core curriculum ensures that students devote significant time to mathematics, foreign languages, and English literature and composition. In addition, each student must complete a range of courses chosen from classical subjects like biology, physics, philosophy, and theology. The most popular majors are English, biology, psychology, business, and the social sciences. Lyon's goal is to enable students to grow academically, socially, spiritually, and physically (yes, phys ed *is* required). A large component of growth in each of these areas involves maintaining a sense of integrity. For this reason, Lyon has an honors system in place that requires each student to maintain high academic and social standards.

BANG FOR YOUR BUCK

In 2005–2006, need-based aid was distributed to nearly 70 percent of the Lyon College student body. Another 27 percent received merit-based scholarships. The basic admissions application to Lyon College automatically enters a prospective student into the pool of academic scholarships. This said, students intent on competing for these scholarships are encouraged to arrange an official campus visit to through the Office of Admission and to submit all materials prior to the absolute deadline. Candidates for fine arts scholarships typically come to campus for an interview or a portfolio review. Athletic scholarships hopefuls should contact the coach of the sport they're interested in pursuing.

"Lyon College is about preparing you for all aspects of life, including academics, athletics, spirituality, and socially."

HIGH SCHOOL UNITS RECOMMENDED

4 English, 4 math, 4 science (2 science lab), 2 foreign language, 1 social studies, 2 history, 1 academic elective

VERY IMPORTANT ADMISSION FACTORS

Academic GPA, standardized test scores

IMPORTANT ADMISSION FACTORS

Rigor of secondary school record

Average HS GPA   3.51
Range SAT Verbal 500–710
Range SAT Math   530–650
Range ACT   23–28
Minimum TOEFL
   (paper/computer) 550/213

APPLICATION DEADLINES

of transfer applicants   92
% of transfer applicants
   accepted   74

ACADEMICS

Student/faculty ratio   10:1
% faculty teaching
   undergraduates   100
% of classes taught by
   graduate students   0

MOST POPULAR MAJORS

• Biology/biological sciences
• Business administration/
      management
• Psychology

GETTING IN

Find your copy of The Princeton Review's *Cracking the SAT* and get to work, because the first thing the Lyon admissions committee looks at is SAT or ACT scores. After standardized test scores, they factor in the strength of the high school curriculum (take those AP and honors classes!) and the grades earned. Extracurricular activities, individual skills, and volunteer/work experience are considered too—these "extras" can tip the balance on scholarship decisions.

WHAT DO GRADUATES DO?

When asked what fields Lyon graduates tend to go into, Dean of Students Bruce Johnson says, "It's really all over the map." This is in part because Lyon is a liberal arts college that emphasizes personal exploration as a part of the academic process. Anywhere from a quarter to a third of all graduates move on to professional or graduate school. Other popular choices include business and scientific research. In recent years, a growing (if still somewhat modest) percentage of the graduates have joined service-oriented groups such as the Peace Corps, Teach for America, and various missions operated by the Presbyterian Church.

THE BOTTOM LINE

Lyon's tuition for 2005–2006 came to $14,420. Other costs included $440 in fees and $6,270 for room and board. The college estimates that the cost books totaled $1,000, transportation $900, and other miscellaneous expenses $900. Add it all up and the bill, before financial aid, weighs in at just under $24,000. The average need-based financial aid package was $13,749. For merit-based aid, the average was $11,096. About 92 percent of recent Lyon graduates accrued loan debt during their time in college. The average amount owed upon graduation was $15,956.

Fun Facts

Scotland is the birthplace of the Presbyterian Church, which is an official affiliate of Lyon College, so it makes sense that Lyon would be the headquarters of the vibrant Scottish Heritage Program. The program has many components, including an undergraduate minor in music/Scottish arts, a scholarship program, a pipe band, an annual Scottish heritage festival, and outreach classes for both piping and Highland dancing.

Five members of Lyon's faculty were listed in the 2006 *Who's Who Among America's Teachers.*

Education Requirements

Arts/fine arts, English (including composition), foreign languages, history, humanities, math, philosophy, sciences (biological or physical), social science, physical education

FINANCIAL INFO

Tuition	$14,420
Room & board	$6,270
Average book expense	$1,000
Required fees	$440
Average freshman need-based grant	$10,531
Average freshman need-based loan	$3,464
% of graduates who borrowed	92
Average indebtedness	$15,956

Financial Aid Forms

Students must submit FAFSA.

POSTGRAD

% going to graduate school	21
% going to law school	1
% going to business school	3
% going to medical school	5

Career Services

Alumni network, alumni services, career/job search classes, career assessment, internships, regional alumni, on-campus job interviews. Off-campus job opportunities are good.

MASSACHUSETTS INSTITUTE OF TECHNOLOGY

MIT Admissions Office Room 3-108, 77 Massachusetts Avenue, Cambridge, MA 02139
http://web.MIT.edu • Admissions: 617-253-4791
Fax: 617-258-8304 • E-mail: admissions@mit.edu • Financial Aid: 617-253-4971

STUDENTS

Religious affiliation
No Affiliation
Academic year
calendar 4-1-4
Undergrad
enrollment 4,127
% male/female 56/44
% Asian 26
% Black, non-Latino 6
% Latino 12
% Native American 1
% international 9
% from out of state 92
% freshmen return for
sophomore year 98
% freshmen graduate
within 4 years 82

STUDENT LIFE
% of students living
on campus 97
% in fraternities 55
% in sororities 26

ADMISSIONS
of applicants 11,373
% accepted 13
% enrolled 66

HIGH SCHOOL UNITS RECOMMENDED

4 English, 4 math, 4
science, 2 foreign language,
2 social studies

VERY IMPORTANT ADMISSION FACTORS

Character/personal qualities

ABOUT MASSACHUSETTS INSTITUTE OF TECHNOLOGY

Massachusetts Institute of Technology—or just MIT—is one of the global heavyweights in science and technology. Known for the high caliber of its education and heft of its research (even undergrads get involved in serious research), MIT allows its students to pick from 36 major departments. Individualized and specialized options are available as well, including more than 50 centers, institutes, and programs geared toward interdisciplinary research. By far, engineering offers the most popular degree track at MIT. Other big players include computer science, biology, physics, math, and business. While MIT's 4,000-plus undergrads lean toward scientific learning, the school's core requirements make sure that all students leave college with a well-rounded education. These core requirements balance foundational courses in science and math with a selection of classes in the arts, humanities, and social sciences. And this seems to be a combination that works well. Students beam about the success of alums and the weight that those three letters—MIT—carry in the academic and professional worlds.

Students will also be the first to admit that MIT might have more than its fair share of, well, nerds. At midnight on a Friday night in Cambridge's Charles River Basin (MIT's turf), you're more likely to find an undergrad standing over a beaker than over a keg. And this is exactly why MIT's students are so satisfied. The school offers an atmosphere highly conducive to intellectual development and intelligent debate. This said, extracurricular activities are not hard to find. MIT is home to 41 varsity athletics clubs (just so you're aware, the teams are called the MIT Engineers) and more than 50 sporting clubs. Greek societies are also present on campus, as well as a slew of academic, social, and cultural organizations. And let's not forget that Cambridge and the rest of Boston offer distractions galore, from high art to baseball games to leisurely strolls down Newbury Street. Of course, who has time for distractions?

"MIT is one of the toughest things I will ever do in my life, but it has also been one of the most fun, and when I come out of this place I know I will be prepared for anything."

BANG FOR YOUR BUCK

Approximately 62 percent of MIT's undergrads received need-based financial aid in 2005–2006. In addition, the school is able to distribute a range of merit-based scholarships. These scholarships come from a variety of sources, such as gifts to the school, endowments, and institutional revenue. MIT meets 100 percent of a student's demonstrated financial need, allowing qualified students from a wide variety of backgrounds to take advantage of this high-priced education. Students must reapply for financial aid on an annual basis, though financial aid packages rarely change, barring drastic shifts in financial status. The Student Financial Aid office and the Student Employment Office assist students in exploring the "self-help" (or work-study) component of a financial aid package. One option is the highly touted Undergraduate Research Opportunities Program (UROP), which allows students to work with professors to earn invaluable research experience as well as a paycheck.

GETTING IN

MIT's admissions officers examine each application carefully, and what they're really looking for is a sense of personality—candidates that stand out as multi-dimensional, interesting, and unique individuals. Other factors that contribute to the admissions decisions include high school curriculum, GPA, class rank, SAT or ACT scores, extracurricular interests, individual talents, and interviews. MIT is a highly selective school. In recent years, only about 13 percent of the applicants found acceptance letters in their mailboxes.

WHAT DO GRADUATES DO?

Approximately 50 percent of MIT's undergrads matriculate to graduate school. Among those who hit the workforce in 2006, the highest percentage (around 31 percent) entered the finance field. Consulting firms, computer companies, investment bankers, and schools also saw large numbers of MIT graduates join their ranks. In 2005–2006, 430 companies came to the school's Careers Office for professional recruitment. In fact, 42 percent of the graduates that year landed jobs through on-campus recruitment drives. Students are also well prepared for the professional world, as 72 percent of recent MIT graduates landed internships while in college.

IMPORTANT ADMISSION FACTORS

Academic GPA, class rank, extracurricular activities, interview, recommendation(s), rigor of secondary school record, standardized test scores, talent/ability

Range SAT Verbal 670–770
Range SAT Math   730–800
Range ACT   30–34

APPLICATION DEADLINES
Regular admission   1/1
Regular notification   3/25
# of transfer applicants 290
% of transfer applicants
  accepted   7

ACADEMICS
Student/faculty ratio   8:1
% faculty teaching
  undergraduates   100
% of classes taught by
  graduate students   1

MOST POPULAR MAJORS

- Computer science
- Electrical engineering
- Mechanical engineering
- Chemical engineering

EDUCATION REQUIREMENTS

Arts/fine arts, humanities, math, sciences (biological or physical), social science, physical education requirement, communication requirement, laboratory requirement, Restricted Electives in Science and Technology (REST) requirement

FINANCIAL INFO

Tuition	$33,400
Room & board	$9,950
Average book expense	$1,100
Required fees	$200
Average freshman need-based grant	$30,869
Average freshman need-based loan	$2,792
% of graduates who borrowed	45
Average indebtedness	$17,956

FINANCIAL AID FORMS

Students must submit FAFSA, CSS/financial aid profile, noncustodial (divorced/separated) parent's statement, business/farm supplement, Parent's complete federal income tax returns from prior year.

Financial aid filing deadline	2/15

POSTGRAD

% going to graduate school	48
% going to law school	2
% going to medical school	2

CAREER SERVICES

Alumni network, alumni services, career/job search classes, career assessment, internships, regional alumni, on-campus job interviews. Off-campus job opportunities are excellent.

THE BOTTOM LINE

MIT's tuition for the 2006–2007 academic year was $33,400. Required fees came to $200 and room and board totaled $9,950. MIT estimates that students spent an additional $1,100 on books and $1,700 on other miscellaneous expenses. Thus, the final cost of an MIT education was $46,350 per year plus individual travel expenses. As mentioned earlier, MIT is committed to meeting 100 percent of a family's demonstrated financial need. Many financial aid packages include loans. Among recent grads, half had taken out loans; the average debt amounted to $17,956.

FUN FACTS

Take a look at the MIT community past and present and you'll discover 63 Nobel laureates. These include graduates, post-doctoral students, and professors.

On September 12, 2006, Heidemarie Stefanyshyn-Piper became the first MIT alum to walk in space. Involved in what are called "extravehicular activities," she left the space shuttle Atlantis for 13 total hours during her 12-day mission in space. Stefanyshyn-Piper has two degrees from MIT: She earned a bachelor's in mechanical engineering in 1984 and a master's in the same field in 1985.

MIT's recently formed Croquet Club says of the sport, "It has also been found to be greatly entertaining." The club holds "games on sunny days, usually weekly when the weather is nice."

MAYVILLE STATE UNIVERSITY

330 Third Street Northeast, Mayville, ND 58257-1299
www.MayvilleState.edu • Admissions: 701-788-4842
Fax: 701-788-4748 • E-mail: admit@mayvillestate.edu • Financial Aid: 701-788-4767

STUDENTS

Religious affiliation
No Affiliation
Academic year
calendar   semester
Undergrad
enrollment   912
% male/female   46/54
% Black, non-Latino   3
% Latino   2
% Native American   3
% international   6
% from out of state   28
% freshmen return for
sophomore year   58
% freshmen graduate
within 4 years   31

STUDENT LIFE

% of students living
on campus   30

ADMISSIONS

of applicants   307
% accepted   68
% enrolled   70

HIGH SCHOOL UNITS REQUIRED

4 English, 3 math, 3 science
(3 science lab), 3 social
studies

HIGH SCHOOL UNITS RECOMMENDED

2 foreign language

VERY IMPORTANT ADMISSION FACTORS

Academic GPA

ABOUT MAYVILLE STATE UNIVERSITY

Mayville State University strives to provide "academic excellence in a cooperative, enjoyable learning environment that anticipates and responds to individual needs." One of the ways the university attends to individual needs is by bestowing all students with a Gateway Tablet notebook-style PC when they arrive on campus. In fact, Mayville State was the first Tablet PC campus in the United States. And these days, the campus is a WiFi extravaganza. This emphasis on technology enhances the educational access and opportunities that Mayville State's undergrads enjoy. One-half of students at Mayville State study education, while one-fourth earn a degree in business. The computer information systems major is popular as well. In every major, professors are praised for their accessibility and the attention they lavish on the students. With around 670 full-time undergrads and 60 faculty members, Mayville State boasts a very intimate learning environment.

The majority of the students at this campus in eastern North Dakota have arrived from somewhere within the state (Minnesota sends most of Mayville State's out-of-state students). The majority of these students are athletic, too. The school's six official sports teams and dozen intramural clubs keep these students moving, and nearly 20 student organizations are active on campus. Even so, sometimes students need a little more to get their juices flowing. Fortunately, Fargo and Grand Forks are each less than an hour from the campus gates. On-campus living is a requirement for freshmen and sophomores under the age of 21 and optional for upperclassmen. There are four residence halls at Mayville State. Each room comes equipped with cable TV connections, a telephone with voicemail, and, of course, 24/7 internet. About 40 percent of the student body lives on campus.

BANG FOR YOUR BUCK

Mayville State strives to make its education financially available to any student who is qualified and interested—and this begins with an incredibly inexpensive price tag for in-state tuition. Minnesotans receive a notably low rate as well. In 2005–2006, about 65 percent of Mayville State's full-time undergraduates were granted need-based financial aid. In total, the university was able to meet 84 percent of full-time students' demonstrated need. Beyond need-based funding, 2 percent of Mayville State's undergraduates received academic merit-based scholarships and 9 percent were awarded athletic scholarships.

IMPORTANT ADMISSION FACTORS

Rigor of secondary school record, standardized test scores

Average HS GPA	2.93
Range ACT	17–22
Minimum TOEFL	
(paper/computer)	525/195

APPLICATION DEADLINES

Regular notification	rolling
# of transfer applicants	202
% of transfer applicants accepted	92

ACADEMICS

Student/faculty ratio	15:1
% faculty teaching undergraduates	100
% of classes taught by graduate students	0

MOST POPULAR MAJORS

• Business administration/ management
• Computer and information sciences
• Elementary education and teaching

EDUCATION REQUIREMENTS

Arts/fine arts, computer literacy, English (including composition), humanities, math, sciences (biological or physical), social science

GETTING IN

Mayville State University is looking for students with strong high school transcripts (in other words, respectable grades earned in a challenging college-prep curriculum) and a good showing on standardized tests (the average ACT score is 19). The admissions officers also consider interviews and other demonstrations of personal character. About 68 percent of the applicants are accepted.

WHAT DO GRADUATES DO?

Many of Mayville State's graduates go into the fields of education or business. Graduate school is also a popular option. The university's career services office helps students to prepare for that "next step" by offering resources for locating internships, job-shadowing opportunities, seasonal and part-time employment, and general career investigation.

THE BOTTOM LINE

In 2006–2007, the cost of tuition for North Dakota residents was $3,613. There are varying rates for out-of-staters, ranging from $3,888 for Minnesota residents to $5,421 for most out-of-staters, or $9,648 for non-U.S. or Canada enrollees. Costs also include $1,643 in required fees and $3,884 for room and board. Full-time students also spent an estimated $700 on books and $2,800 in travel and other expenses. Combined, this adds up to around $12,640 in total cost for in-state students. The average need-based aid package for full-time students came to $6,854. The average academic-merit package came to $929, while athletic scholarships averaged $1,162. A survey of recent graduates shows that 77 percent took out federal loans for an average debt of $18,190.

FUN FACTS

Mayville State University's annual Farmers Bowl is an all-day celebration of the agricultural heritage of the region. The 2006 Farmers Bowl, held in mid-September, was themed, "Show Your Comet Pride" (Mayville State's team nickname, by the way, is the Comets). A parade, a corn on the cob chowdown, and a charity auction were among the day's big events.

The name "Mayville State University" was approved by the State Board of Higher Education in 1987. Before that, the institution was known by several names. From the school's founding in 1889 until 1961, as the Mayville Normal School, it catered exclusively to educators-to-be.

According to the 2000 census, Mayville and its sister town of Portland have a combined population of 2,557.

FINANCIAL INFO

In-state tuition	$3,613
Out-of-state tuition	$5,421–$9,648
Room & board	$3,884
Average book expense	$700
Required fees	$1,643
Average freshman need-based grant	$2,752
Average freshman need-based loan	$2,848
% of graduates who borrowed	77
Average indebtedness	$18,190

FINANCIAL AID FORMS

Students must submit FAFSA.

POSTGRAD

% going to graduate school	6
% going to law school	1
% going to business school	1
% going to medical school	1

CAREER SERVICES

Alumni network, alumni services, career/job search classes, career assessment, internships, on-campus job interviews. Off-campus job opportunities are fair.

MERCER UNIVERSITY—MACON

Admissions Office, 1400 Coleman Avenue, Macon, GA 31207-0001
http://GoMercer.com/ • Admissions: 478-301-2650
Fax: 478-301-2828 • E-mail: admissions@mercer.edu • Financial Aid: 478-301-2670

STUDENTS

Religious affiliation
                                    Baptist
Academic year
   calendar   semester
Undergrad
   enrollment   2,355
% male/female   45/55
% Asian   5
% Black, non-Latino   16
% Latino   2
% international   2
% from out of state   24
% freshmen return for
sophomore year   80
% freshmen graduate within
4 years   35

STUDENT LIFE

% of students living
   on campus   66
% in fraternities   24
% in sororities   25

ADMISSIONS

of applicants   3,108
% accepted   80
% enrolled   25

HIGH SCHOOL UNITS REQUIRED

4 English, 4 math, 3 science
(2 science lab), 2 foreign
language, 1 social studies, 2
history

VERY IMPORTANT ADMISSION FACTORS

Academic GPA, level of
applicant's interest, rigor of
secondary school record,
standardized test scores

ABOUT MERCER UNIVERSITY—MACON

Deep in the heart of Georgia, about 2,300 undergraduates each year enjoy the benefits of knowledgeable professors who seem to absolutely love devoting themselves to their students. Mercer University, a Baptist-affiliated school with a liberal arts bent, boasts a 13:1 student/faculty ratio and average class size of 10 to 19 students. Mercer's most sought-after degrees are earned in the fields of business, education, engineering, health sciences, interdisciplinary studies, and public administration.

While these students know how to study with the best of 'em, they also know how to unwind. It's true that if you glance at the rule books, Mercer seems like a no-nonsense place—for instance, rigid anti-alcohol policies and curfews on dorm visits by members of the opposite sex. But students say that the rules hinder a good time much less than expected. In fact, the administration receives an A-plus for doing its best to keep up with the times and to place student concerns above its own. This is reflected in its recent split with the Georgia Baptist Convention—the end of 172-year relationship—because the convention took issue with the existence of an on-campus GLTB group. Today Mercer is an independent Baptist university affiliated with the Cooperative Baptist Fellowship.

Campus life is energized by a broad selection of clubs, with Greek societies and religious organizations among the most popular. The many extracurricular opportunities and the intimate academic setting combine to form a tight sense of community at Mercer. And this sense of community is strengthened by the fact that this is a Southern school in spirit as well as geography. In other words, Southern hospitality and good will are alive and well in Macon, Georgia.

BANG FOR YOUR BUCK

Mercer hasn't earned a reputation as one of the great educational bargains in the South for nothing. The Office of Student Financial Planning vows to find the right mix of federal, state, local, and institutional funding in order to make a Mercer education available to all qualified students. In 2005–2006, upwards of 64 percent of the student body received need-based financial aid. Of the remaining 36 percent, the vast majority were awarded either merit-based or athletic scholarships. In total, 91 percent of demonstrated financial need

Students Say

"Mercer has an incredibly beautiful campus and many divisions and offices that have nothing but the best intentions in taking care of the students."

was met. Non-need-based funding is available in many areas, including academic achievement, Baptist affiliation, and athletic ability. All institutional scholarships and grants are determined by the Office of University Admissions. Recipients can claim these funds for up eight semesters, as long as they remain in good academic standing. Institutional scholarships, however, may not be applied to the summer semester.

GETTING IN

Four admissions factors are given especially heavy consideration: the rigor of a candidate's high-school curriculum, GPA, SAT/ACT scores, and the level of specific interest a candidate shows in attending Mercer. Slightly less important are extracurricular activities, volunteer work, individual talents, and personal character. Class rank, letters of recommendation, employment experience, and (when applicable) interviews are also looked at, though they carry lighter weight. Religious affiliation is not a factor. Candidates do not need to submit an application essay. The application form can be completed online through the Office of University Admissions website.

WHAT DO GRADUATES DO?

Mercer's graduates move into a range of fields, including education, business, nursing, the ministry, the public sector, and scientific research. Many also opt to enroll in graduate school or professional school. On-campus recruiting includes annual Teacher Recruitment Day. In 2006, 43 regional school systems came to recruit teachers from the university's well-respected Tift College of Education. Career Services also hosts an annual Career Day. The 2006 event hosted more than 150 employers. Resume, cover letter, interview, and graduate school advising are available as well.

IMPORTANT ADMISSION FACTORS

Character/personal qualities, extracurricular activities, talent/ability, volunteer work

Average HS GPA	3.6
Range SAT Verbal	530–640
Range SAT Math	550–640
Range ACT	22–27
Minimum TOEFL (paper/computer)	550/213

APPLICATION DEADLINES

Regular admission	7/1
Regular notification	rolling
# of transfer applicants	319
% of transfer applicants accepted	96

ACADEMICS

Student/faculty ratio	13:1
% faculty teaching undergraduates	
% of classes taught by graduate students	0

MOST POPULAR MAJORS

- Business administration/ management
- Communications, journalism and related fields
- Engineering

EDUCATION REQUIREMENTS

Arts/fine arts, computer literacy, English (including composition), foreign languages, history, humanities, math, philosophy, sciences (biological or physical), social science, religion/Christianity

FINANCIAL INFO

Tuition	$25,056
Room & board	$7,710
Average book expense	$900
Required fees	$200
Average freshman need-based grant	$15,670
Average freshman need-based loan	$5,006
% of graduates who borrowed	63
Average indebtedness	$11,075

FINANCIAL AID FORMS
Students must submit FAFSA, institution's own financial aid form, state aid form.

POSTGRAD

% going to graduate school	20

CAREER SERVICES
Alumni network, alumni services, career assessment, internships, on-campus job interviews.

THE BOTTOM LINE

During 2005–2006, the cost of tuition at Mercer was $25,056. Other costs came in the form of fees ($200) and room and board ($7,710). Mercer estimates that undergrads spent $900 on books, $600 on transportation, and $800 on other random expenses. The 2005–2006 price tag totaled approximately $35,266. Fortunately, Mercer's generous financial aid goes a long way to defraying these costs. The average need-based package added up to $23,102. Scholarship packages averaged between $15,000 and $16,000. Around 63 percent of graduates between July 2004 and June 2005 had taken out loans while enrolled at Mercer. On average, the accrued debt came to $11,075.

FUN FACTS

The 2006 "Saviors of Our Cities" rankings placed Mercer 13th among nationwide urban universities that contribute to the strength of their surrounding communities. The rankings were compiled by Evan Dobelle, who is the president and CEO of the New England Board of Education.

Ever-opinionated CNN and Court TV commentator Nancy Grace is a graduate of Mercer University. Other accomplished alums include Pulitzer Prize-winning authors J. Buford Boone and Malcolm Johnson; founder of Capricorn Records, Phil Walden; and the poet laureate of the state of Georgia, David Bottoms.

MILLSAPS COLLEGE

1701 North State Street, Jackson, MS 39210-0001
www.Millsaps.edu • Admissions: 601-974-1050
Fax: 601-974-1059 • E-mail: admissions@millsaps.edu • Financial Aid: 601-974-1220

STUDENTS

Religious affiliation
                                    Methodist
Academic year
    calendar   semester
Undergrad
    enrollment   1,065
% male/female   51/49
% Asian   3
% Black, non-Latino   12
% Latino   1
% international   1
% from out of state   50
% freshmen return for
sophomore year   83
% freshmen graduate
    within 4 years   63

STUDENT LIFE

% of students living
    on campus   81
% in fraternities   54
% in sororities   52

ADMISSIONS

of applicants   1,008
% accepted   82
% enrolled   31

HIGH SCHOOL UNITS REQUIRED

4 English, 3 math, 3 science
(1 science lab), 2 social
studies, 2 history

HIGH SCHOOL UNITS RECOMMENDED

4 English, 4 math, 4 science
(1 science lab), 2 foreign
language, 2 social studies, 2
history, 2 academic
electives

ABOUT MILLSAPS COLLEGE

"Community" is a key word at Millsaps College, a small liberal arts school in Jackson, Mississippi. Affiliated with the United Methodist Church, Millsaps has a reputation for its highly active, socially conscious undergrads, many of whom work with volunteer organizations in Jackson and around the world. On campus, the most popular activities include Greek life, religious clubs, and piling into the stands for Millsaps Majors basketball games. (We should note, though, that the wild Greek parties of old are tougher to find these days, due to administrative policy shifts in recent years.)

Millsaps' strong sense of community pervades the classrooms too, where incredibly attentive and intelligent professors provide an atmosphere rife with discussion. Millsaps' liberal arts curriculum places a heavy emphasis on writing—meaning that incomers should be prepared to crank out well-constructed essays on a regular basis. Undergrads have their pick of 28 majors and 26 minors, as well as self-designed majors created under the guidance of a faculty advisor. The largest majors include business, biology, psychology, English, and political science. However, whatever students major in they can expect (as the college puts it) a "mind-opening" educational experience.

About half of the Millsaps student body comes from within the state. Though many Millsaps undergrads do identify themselves as Methodist, this is an accepting campus where students of all persuasions—religious and otherwise—are able to feel comfortable. Because Millsaps is home to such a small population (and because four out of every five students lives on campus), it seems that there are no strangers at the college. This also contributes to the tight community feel at Millsaps. But it has its downside as well: The rumor mill is robust and secrets are scarce.

VERY IMPORTANT ADMISSION FACTORS

Academic GPA, character/personal qualities, rigor of secondary school record, standardized test scores

IMPORTANT ADMISSION FACTORS

Application essay, class rank, extracurricular activities, interview, recommendation(s), talent/ability, volunteer work

Average HS GPA	3.55
Range SAT Verbal	538–683
Range SAT Math	540–650
Range ACT	23–30
Minimum TOEFL (paper/computer)	550/220

APPLICATION DEADLINES

Regular admission	6/1
Regular notification	rolling
# of transfer applicants	144
% of transfer applicants accepted	67

ACADEMICS

Student/faculty ratio	12:1
% faculty teaching undergraduates	100
% of classes taught by graduate students	0

MOST POPULAR MAJORS

- Biology/biological sciences
- Business administration and management
- Psychology

BANG FOR YOUR BUCK

Millsaps offers generous aid packages that include federal and state loans and grants, institutional merit-based and specialized scholarships, United Methodist scholarships, and various state-supported scholarships for students from other states. In 2005–2006, nearly 57 percent of all students received need-based aid. This same year, an additional 38 percent were awarded merit-based aid. Approximately 80 percent of demonstrated need was met. The most generous awards available to incoming freshman are the Presidential Scholarships, which range from $12,000 to $30,000 annually and are renewable as long as the recipient remains in good academic standing. Federal Perkins loans, subsidized Stafford loans, and unsubsidized Stafford loans may be part of financial aid packages.

GETTING IN

Millsaps places the largest emphasis on the heft of a candidate's high-school curriculum, GPA, standardized test scores, and strong personal character. Other factors that are also given a careful look include class rank, the application essay, letters of recommendation, an interview with an admissions officer, extracurricular activities, volunteer work, and any unique talents. Ultimately, Millsaps prefers students who are strong academically, good citizens, *and* interesting, well-rounded individuals. About 82 percent of all applicants are accepted.

WHAT DO GRADUATES DO?

In recent years, about 43 percent of Millsaps undergrads went straight into graduate or professional school. One popular option is the college's five-year MBA program, which allows students to complete both the undergraduate and graduate curricula in a streamlined fashion. Business, in fact, is a popular vocational arena for Millsaps graduates to enter. Education, media, and scientific research are just a few of the many fields that other graduates land in. As is often the case with liberal arts colleges, Millsaps sends its graduates into a diverse assortment of fields. The Millsaps College Career Center offers an array of services, including career counseling, employment databases, and assistance with alumni/professional/academic networking.

The Bottom Line

The price of Millsaps's tuition in 2006–2007 was $20,660 for in- and out-of-state students. The required fees ran $1,372 and room and board came to $7,956. The college estimates that its undergrads spent an additional $1,000 on books, $500 on transportation, and $1,000 on other miscellaneous expenses, thus leading to a grand total of $32,488. For first-year students in 2005–2006, the average need-based financial aid package weighed in at $18,185. For merit-based and specialty scholarship packages, that number was $15,061. Around 63 percent of recent grads took out loans for an average total debt of $22,285.

Fun Facts

The Helen Moyers Biocultural Reserve is "a 4,000-acre tropical forest biocultural reserve in the heart of the Yucatan peninsula" which is operated by Millsaps College. Students electing to study abroad in the college's Living in Yucatan program can take courses in archaeology, business, ecology, education, geology, history, literature, and socio-cultural anthropology.

An on-campus mausoleum contains the remains of the college's founding father, Reuben Webster Millsaps.

Jackson, the capital of Mississippi, is home to over 400 houses of worship.

EDUCATION REQUIREMENTS

Arts/fine arts, English (including composition), history, humanities, math, sciences (biological or physical), social science, Millsaps' writing proficiency requirement—students must obtain a rating of proficient on a portfolio of seven papers submitted by the end of the sophomore year.

FINANCIAL INFO

Tuition	$20,660
Room & board	$7,956
Average book expense	$1,000
Required fees	$1,372
Average freshman need-based grant	$14,618
Average freshman need-based loan	$3,544
% of graduates who borrowed	63
Average indebtedness	$22,285

FINANCIAL AID FORMS

Students must submit FAFSA, institution's own financial aid form.

POSTGRAD

% going to graduate school	48
% going to law school	6
% going to business school	8
% going to medical school	9

CAREER SERVICES

Off-campus job opportunities are good.

MISSISSIPPI STATE UNIVERSITY

PO Box 6305, Mississippi State, MS 39762
www.MsState.edu • Admissions: 662-325-2224
Fax: 662-325-7360 • E-mail: admit@admissions.msstate.edu • Financial Aid: 662-325-2450

STUDENTS

Religious affiliation
No Affiliation
Academic year
calendar   semester
Undergrad
enrollment   12,555
% male/female   52/48
% from out of state   18
% freshmen return for
sophomore year   80
% freshmen graduate
within 4 years   25

STUDENT LIFE

% of students living
on campus   30
% in fraternities   17
% in sororities   18

ADMISSIONS

of applicants   5,778
% accepted   69
% enrolled   49

HIGH SCHOOL UNITS REQUIRED

4 English, 3 math, 3 science
(2 science lab), 1 social
studies, 2 history, 2
academic electives

HIGH SCHOOL UNITS RECOMMENDED

4 English, 4 math, 4 science
(2 science lab), 1 foreign
language, 2 social studies, 2
history, 1 world geography,
2 academic electives

VERY IMPORTANT ADMISSION FACTORS

Academic GPA, standardized
test scores

ABOUT MISSISSIPPI STATE UNIVERSITY

Mississippi State University offers a reliable mix of solid academics and enjoyable extracurriculars to earn the appreciation of its 12,000-plus undergraduates. The focus of MSU is on professional training in such areas as agricultural science, architecture, business, education, engineering—the school's champion program—landscape architecture, and veterinary medicine. Research is a top priority, but not at the expense of undergraduate education. Professors are accessible and welcoming, and ambitious students can even get involved their professors' research projects.

Life at MSU offers numerous extracurricular options, but none so attractive to undergraduates as the intercollegiate athletics. Win or lose, MSU's Bulldogs earn their supporters' undying devotion; the baseball team is a perennial powerhouse. Other campus diversions include concerts, lectures, movies, plays, gallery shows, and plenty of parties—often centered around the school's Greek community. MSU's recreation center is a world-class facility appreciated by the school's many jocks. All of this campus activity helps alleviate the boredom of MSU's aptly named hometown of Starkville. Like many large public schools, MSU draws a diverse crowd representing all races, faiths, personality types, and sexual preferences.

BANG FOR YOUR BUCK

MSU administers over $3 million in institutional need-based aid and nearly $7 million in non-need based aid, including $2.5 million in athletic scholarships. In 2005–2006, the average aid recipient here received a package worth $8,916, including PLUS loans and private or unsubsidized loans.

MSU provides need-based assistance to 98 percent of all aid applicants who demonstrate need. Eighty-six percent of need-based aid packages include some form of need-based grant or scholarship. On average, the school meets 70 percent of aid recipients' demonstrated need and is able to meet 100 percent of demonstrated need for 45 percent of aid recipients.

Notable merit-based awards include the Schillig Scholarships, which provide up to $50,000 over four years to students with a minimum score of 29 on the ACT (or 1280 on the SAT) and an outstanding high school record; Presidential Endowed Scholarships, which provide up to $50,000 over four years to students with a minimum score of 29 on the ACT (or 1280 on the SAT) and an outstanding high school record; and Engineering Excellence Scholarships, which are worth up to $12,000 over four years to incoming engineers and computer scientists with exceptional high school records and high standardized test scores (29 on the ACT or 1280 on the SAT).

GETTING IN

Admissions at MSU are formula-driven. Admissions Officers study an applicant's high school grades and standardized test scores, crunch the numbers, and make a decision. Entering students must achieve either a minimum GPA of 3.2 in required high school courses; a minimum GPA of 2.5 and a combined SAT score of at least 760; or a minimum GPA of 2.0 and a combined SAT score of 860. There is some leeway in the process, however. Students who demonstrate special talents or who show potential to contribute to the campus community may gain admission even if they don't meet the above requirements. MSU offers conditional admissions for others who don't meet the above requirements. Students admitted conditionally must successfully complete remedial work before gaining full admission. Admission to many programs (e.g., the College of Engineering) is relatively competitive, and general admission to MSU as an undeclared major does not ensure admission to these programs.

WHAT DO GRADUATES DO?

With over 12,000 undergraduates, MSU sends alumni into just about every professional field. Popular pre-professional disciplines include accounting, architecture, computer science, education, engineering, forestry, golf and sports turf management, industrial engineering, insurance, marketing, real estate, and wildlife management.

IMPORTANT ADMISSION FACTORS

Class rank

Average HS GPA	3.18
Range ACT	19–27
Minimum TOEFL (paper/computer)	525/195

APPLICATION DEADLINES

Regular notification	rolling
# of transfer applicants	2,807
% of transfer applicants accepted	67

ACADEMICS

Student/faculty ratio 14:1

MOST POPULAR MAJORS

- Business administration/ management
- Elementary education and teaching

EDUCATION REQUIREMENTS

Arts/fine arts, computer literacy, English (including composition), history, humanities, math, sciences (biological or physical), social science

FINANCIAL INFO

In-state tuition $4,596
Out-of-state tuition $10,552
Room & board $6,331
Average book
  expense $950
Average freshman
  need-based grant $3,665
Average freshman
  need-based loan $2,651
% of graduates
  who borrowed 49
Average
  indebtedness $18,230

FINANCIAL AID FORMS

Students must submit
FAFSA, State grant/
scholarship application.

POSTGRAD

CAREER SERVICES

Alumni services, career/job
search classes, career
assessment, internships,
on-campus job interviews.
Off-campus job opportuni-
ties are good.

THE BOTTOM LINE

In 2006–2007, Mississippi residents attending MSU full time paid $4,596 in tuition and fees. Room and board cost an additional $6,331; books and supplies cost an estimated $950; and personal and transportation expenses amounted to $1,030. Thus, the total cost of attending MSU for an in-state student was $12,907. Nonresidents of Mississippi paid an additional $5,956 in tuition, bringing their total cost to $18,863. More than half of all students at MSU receive some form of need-based aid.

FUN FACTS

Incoming MSU students are welcomed to the campus during Dawg Daze, a celebration that offers organized activities during the week prior to the start of classes. Events include a barbecue, a game of Capture the Flag, an ice-cream social, and a free concert.

No MSU sporting event is complete without hordes of Bulldog fanatics clanging their cowbells. (Cowbells are officially banned by the SEC, but fans don't observe the ban very well.)

MSU's baseball program has produced many superstars, including first basemen Will Clark and Rafael Palmeiro, relief pitcher Bobby Thigpen, and manager Buck Showalter. Other notable alumni include author John Grisham and comedian Jerry Clower.

MSU admitted its first African American student in 1965. Today the school's student body is approximately 20 percent African American.

MISSOURI STATE UNIVERSITY

901 South National, Springfield, MO 65897
www.MissouriState.edu • Admissions: 417-836-5517
Fax: 417-836-6334 • E-mail: info@missouristate.edu • Financial Aid: 417-836-5262

STUDENTS

Religious affiliation
No Affiliation
Academic year
  calendar   semester
Undergrad
  enrollment   14,463
% male/female   44/56
% Asian   1
% Black, non-Latino   2
% Latino   1
% Native American   1
% international   2
% from out of state   7
% freshmen return for
sophomore year   73

STUDENT LIFE

% of students living
  on campus   24

ADMISSIONS

of applicants   6,866
% accepted   77
% enrolled   50

HIGH SCHOOL UNITS REQUIRED

4 English, 3 math, 2 science
(1 science lab), 3 social
studies, 3 academic
electives

VERY IMPORTANT ADMISSION FACTORS

Class rank, rigor of secondary
school record, standardized
test scores

Average HS GPA   3.57
Range ACT   21–26
Minimum TOEFL
  (paper/computer) 500/173

ABOUT MISSOURI STATE UNIVERSITY

As the state's public affairs university, Missouri State University offers its undergraduates unique academic opportunities. The school, fresh off its centennial year in 2005, is driven toward imparting a broader world view to students, and encourages them to become more civic-minded. In case you think the Missouri State is only about delivering new generations of public policy advocates, there are a myriad of programs such as the professional writing degree and graphic design programs, which prepare students for a variety of engaging careers. Despite a relatively large student body, many undergrads are quick to state that professors make themselves accessible to students, oftentimes even helping them establish contacts within their particular field of interest.

Missouri State students are generally a laid-back and casual lot. However, don't let their nonchalance fool you—they know how to kick back and have a good time. Greek life is very prominent on campus and parties are thrown in abundance. Of course, even college kids need a respite from drinking every now and then, and nearby lakes and rivers provide ample opportunity for boating, swimming, and fishing. Springfield also supplies entertainment for students whether they want to catch a movie, drive go carts, bowl, or go dancing. As a requisite for any college town, there are plenty of coffee shops and public parks to help students unwind.

BANG FOR YOUR BUCK

Missouri State has mastered the art of providing a top-quality education while remaining highly affordable. Tuition is substantially lower than many other Missouri schools and comparable public institutions. Additionally, the school offers numerous scholarship options to students, with a high number being merit-based. For example, the Presidential Scholarship covers all mandatory student fees (valued at $11,742 per year for Missouri residents, $16,662 for those out-of-state). This particular scholarship requires incoming freshmen to have been in the top 10 percent of their graduating class and have earned a minimum of either 30 on the ACT or 1320 on the SAT. Interviews are also required.

Relax, there are less stringent scholarships available, too. The Academic Scholarship requires students to have been in the top 20 percent of their class and have scored either 26 on the ACT or 1170 on the SAT. This scholarship is valued at $2,250 per year for Missouri residents and $5,750 per year for out-of-state students. The Recognition Scholarship, valued at $1,125 for in-state and $4,625 for out-of-state, stipulates that students who graduate in the top 10 percent of their class earn test scores of either 24 (ACT) or 1090 (SAT).

APPLICATION DEADLINES

Regular admission   7/20
# of transfer
   applicants   1,853
% of transfer applicants
   accepted   83

ACADEMICS

Student/faculty ratio   18:1
% faculty teaching
   undergraduates   94
% of classes taught by
   graduate students   9

MOST POPULAR MAJORS

- Elementary education and teaching
- Management information systems
- Psychology

EDUCATION REQUIREMENTS

Arts/fine arts, computer literacy, English (including composition), history, humanities, math, sciences (biological or physical), social science

GETTING IN

As is the case with many state schools, admissions officers rely heavily on hard data to determine acceptance. Therefore, your secondary school record, class rank, and standardized test scores hold the most weight. Missouri State expects its students to have taken four years of English, threes years of math, three years of social science, two years of science (including a lab science), one year of visual/performing arts as well as several elective courses. Looking at the 2006–2007 freshman class, 83.3 percent of those who enrolled were in the top half of their graduating class and had an average ACT score of 23.8. Therefore, merely meeting these course requirements isn't enough. Students must show some academic achievement if they want an acceptance letter.

WHAT DO GRADUATES DO?

Career success begins early for Missouri State students as the campus attracts a number of corporations for recruiting. Companies and organizations that have recruited include AmeriCorps National Service, Commerce Bank, Deloitte & Touche, Annheuser-Busch, Topeka Public Schools, The John F. Kennedy Center for the Performing Arts, AT&T, Hallmark, KSPR-TV, and PricewaterhouseCoopers (just to give a small but impressive sampling).

THE BOTTOM LINE

Both Missouri residents and those students who attend from out of state will find Missouri State a relative bargain. Tuition and required dees for the 2006-2007 academic year cost in-state students $5,738 and out-of-state students $10,658. Room and board ran $5,078 and it's estimated that books and supplies cost roughly $800. Therefore, Missouri residents faced a total bill of $11,616 while nonresidents paid $16,536.

Freshmen who applied for need-based aid saw 64 percent of their needs met, while undergraduates overall had 58 percent of their needs met. The average need-based financial aid package that freshmen received during 2006–2007 was $6,080. The average for undergraduates overall was $6,160. This excludes PLUS loans, unsubsidized loans, and private alternative loans.

FUN FACTS

Noted Missouri State University alumni include David D. Glass, 1960 graduate and owner, chairman, and CEO of the Kansas City Royals Baseball Organization, and former chairman of the Executive Committee of the Wal-Mart Stores, Inc.; John Goodman, 1975 graduate and film and television star; Kathleen Turner, a film and stage actor who attended Missouri State University; and Tess Harper, 1972 graduate and film and television star. Others include actor/director Sterling Macer; 2005 National League Most Valuable Player Ryan Howard, first baseman for the Philadelphia Phillies; and 2003 American League batting champ, Bill Mueller, third baseman for the Los Angeles Dodgers.

In 2005, as part of its year-long Centennial Celebration, Missouri State hosted its inaugural Public Affairs Conference, bringing to campus significant leaders from a variety of disciplines to discuss topics relevant for a (twenty-first century democracy. Additionally, a series of speakers, including Nobel Peace Prize winners F.W. de Klerk and Elie Wiesel; former U.S. Senator Bill Bradley; 1997 Inaugural Poet Miller Williams; and senior editor of *The Wall Street Journal* Joseph N. Boyce, have given addresses on the Springfield campus. Missouri State University's extended campus has an array of distance learning technologies and delivery systems, including audio conferencing; radio; television (interactive video, telecourses, and microwave); satellite transmission; audio cassette and video cassette programs; and a variety of computer-based systems (including synchronous computer conferencing). Approximately 2,500 students are served through this virtual setting each year.

FINANCIAL INFO

In-state tuition	$5,190
Out-of-state tuition	$10,110
Room & board	$5,294
Average book expense	$800
Required fees	$540
Average freshman need-based grant	$4,907
Average freshman need-based loan	$2,613
% of graduates who borrowed	66
Average indebtedness	$16,003

FINANCIAL AID FORMS
Students must submit FAFSA.

POSTGRAD

% going to graduate school	20
% going to law school	2
% going to business school	10
% going to medical school	2

CAREER SERVICES
Alumni network, alumni services, career/job search classes, career assessment, internships, regional alumni, on-campus job interviews.

MONTANA TECH OF THE UNIVERSITY OF MONTANA

1300 West Park Street, Butte, MT 59701
www.MTech.edu • Admissions: 406-496-4178
Fax: 406-496-4710 • E-mail: admissions@mtech.edu • Financial Aid: 406-496-4212

STUDENTS

Religious affiliation
No Affiliation
Academic year
  calendar   semester
Undergrad
  enrollment   1,913
% male/female   56/44
% Asian   1
% Latino   1
% Native American   2
% international   3
% from out of state   10
% freshmen return for
sophomore year   66
% freshmen graduate
within 4 years   8

STUDENT LIFE

% of students living
  on campus   17

ADMISSIONS

of applicants   414
% accepted   98
% enrolled   98

HIGH SCHOOL UNITS REQUIRED

4 English, 3 math, 2
science (2 science lab), 3
social studies, 2 combined
years of foreign language,
visual and performing arts,
computer science, or
vocational education units

ABOUT MONTANA TECH OF THE UNIVERSITY OF MONTANA

Perched on the side of Big Butte, Montana Tech's tree-shaded campus can be seen for miles. It includes the charming and historical buildings of the school's past as well as those that have undergone a recent facelift—a $20 million dollar renovation project was recently finished on the north side of campus. Prior to 1951, Montana Tech awarded Bachelor of Science degrees in only five areas of study, but with its current amount of academic programs, clubs, and organizations, Montana Tech offers its students immense opportunity and has rightfully earned a reputation as one of the finest science, engineering, and technical colleges in the world. There are over 40 academic programs and more than 38 clubs and organizations in which students can participate. In fact, students can earn certificates and degrees in fields as varied as automotive technology and nursing.

Clubs and organizations at Montana Tech are as diverse as its degree programs. Students are encouraged to get involved in campus life by joining one or more of the athletic, service, religious, and special-interest organizations to meet their needs and expand their group of friends. Students are also welcome in what is known as the "Digger Den," an area which houses a big-screen TV, pool tables, video games, a ping-pong table, a stereo-video system, and conversation/study areas. For those students who like off-campus entertainment and who crave outdoor adventure, take heart: Montana Tech is located in one of the most stunning parts of the United States. Nestled between both Yellowstone National Park and Glacier Park, its location provides ample opportunities for all kinds of recreation including skiing, hiking, camping, and word-class fishing. Snow shoes are optional.

BANG FOR YOUR BUCK

Of the 1,600 students in the 2005–2006 academic year who applied for financial aid, 75 percent were awarded funds, half of which were fully met. In addition to federal- and state-sponsored aid, Montana Tech offers $900,000 in new student scholarships and $1.5 million in continuing scholarships. However, the amount of money available varies from program to program. The Montana Mining Association has generously set up scholarships for Montana residents who attend Montana Tech and major in mining engineering, metallurgical engineering, geological engineering, environmental engineering, and geophysical engineering.

"It's not unusual for students to gather in small groups on weekends to partake in activities that they each enjoy. School sports usually bring together a large crowd of people and everyone is invited to join in."

GETTING IN

Admission to Montana Tech is based on academic record and ranking. Prospective students must rank in the upper half of their graduating class or have achieved a 2.5 GPA or higher. ACT and SAT scores are also considered. Transfer students must have at least a 2.0 GPA.

WHAT DO GRADUATES DO?

Montana Tech graduates tend to find work in the engineering and science fields. Over the last decade, the average rate of placement for graduates has exceeded 96 percent. Montana Tech offers its graduates great industry relations and strong internship programs that aid students in making those ever-important professional contacts which, in turn, lead many students to have job offers before they graduate.

THE BOTTOM LINE

Montana Tech provides a nationally ranked education at a very affordable price. For 2005–2006, in-state tuition was $5,606 with an additional $5,594 in room and board and $800 for books. Out-of-state tuition rang in at $14,766. Students who took advantage of financial aid graduated on average with a cool $19,000 in cumulative debt.

HIGH SCHOOL UNITS RECOMMENDED

4 English, 4 math, 4 science (2 science lab), 2 foreign language

Average HS GPA	3.2
Range SAT Verbal	470–600
Range SAT Math	490–630
Range ACT	21–27
Minimum TOEFL (paper/computer)	525/195

APPLICATION DEADLINES

Regular notification	rolling
# of transfer applicants	211
% of transfer applicants accepted	78

ACADEMICS

Student/faculty ratio	16:1
% faculty teaching undergraduates	100
% of classes taught by graduate students	0

MOST POPULAR MAJORS

- Business administration/ management
- Engineering
- Petroleum engineering

EDUCATION REQUIREMENTS

English (including composition), foreign languages, history, humanities, math, sciences (biological or physical), social science, communications

FINANCIAL INFO

In-state tuition	$5,606
Out-of-state tuition	$14,766
Room & board	$5,594
Average book expense	$800
Average freshman need-based grant	$2,000
Average freshman need-based loan	$2,500
% of graduates who borrowed	80
Average indebtedness	$19,000

FINANCIAL AID FORMS

Students must submit FAFSA.

POSTGRAD

% going to graduate school	14

CAREER SERVICES

Alumni network, alumni services, internships, on-campus job interviews. Off-campus job opportunities are good.

FUN FACTS

In the spring of 1910, three graduating seniors (August Grunert, Walter H. Jensen, and William Stuewe Jr.) took on the project of building a 75-foot-by-91-foot "M" on Big Butte. With the help of 35 other enrolled students, they placed an estimated 441 tons of rhyolite in the shape of the giant letter over the expanse of a few weeks. On the first M-Day (May 20, 1910) all 50 of the enrolled students hauled buckets of water and lime to the site to make their school pride tangibly visible. Go Orediggers!

Situated on the Montana Tech campus is the Mineral Museum. It overlooks what is called "The Richest Hill on Earth." Prize specimens in the Montana collection include the Highland Centennial Gold Nugget which was recovered in1989 from a mine south of Butte. Also on display is a 400-lb. smoky quartz crystal affectionately referred to as "Big Daddy."

NEW COLLEGE OF FLORIDA

5800 Bay Shore Road, Sarasota, FL 34243-2109
www.NCF.edu • Admissions: 941-487-5000
Fax: 941-487-5010 • E-mail: admissions@ncf.edu • Financial Aid: 941-487-5001

STUDENTS

Religious affiliation
No Affiliation
Academic year
calendar   4-1-4
Undergrad
enrollment   761
% male/female   39/61
% Asian   3
% Black, non-Latino   2
% Latino   10
% international   5
% from out of state   17
% freshmen return for
sophomore year   80
% freshmen graduate
within 4 years   57

STUDENT LIFE

% of students living
on campus   68

ADMISSIONS

of applicants   684
% accepted   60
% enrolled   53

HIGH SCHOOL UNITS REQUIRED

4 English, 3 math, 3 science
(2 science lab), 2 foreign
language, 3 social studies, 3
academic electives

HIGH SCHOOL UNITS RECOMMENDED

4 English, 3 math, 3 science
(2 science lab), 2 foreign
language, 3 social studies, 5
academic electives

ABOUT NEW COLLEGE OF FLORIDA

A combination of academic freedom, hands-on learning, and rigorous standards makes New College of Florida stand out from other elite American colleges and universities. NCF is a public honors college where students enter into academic contracts enabling them to work closely with individual faculty members; hence, in addition to sitting in traditional classrooms, students help organize seminars, attend tutorials, conduct independent research, and participate in off-campus experiences. The unconventional nature of NCF doesn't end there. All courses are pass/fail and professors assess students with written evaluations. To graduate, every student must present a thesis to a Faculty Committee of three and pass an extensive oral examination. There's also a four-week January term during which students complete intensive and often creative independent study projects (either alone or in small groups).

Course work at NCF is intense and can be stressful. You'll receive plenty of personal attention from dedicated, passionate, and accessible professors; but if you are a slacker, you just won't be able to make the cut. The smart, creative, open-minded, and left-leaning students of NCF's 140-acre bay front campus are as nonconformist as the school they attend. They live in dormitories with individual entrances, private baths, and central air-conditioning, and they enjoy a pretty hopping campus party scene. They are also able to study outdoors almost all year round.

BANG FOR YOUR BUCK

Out-of-state tuition is about 40 percent less than the national average for private university tuition—and you are essentially getting a private school education. Low tuition and the distinctive nature of NCF's rigorous, individualized academic program make it a tremendous value for both in-state and out-of-state students. The Financial Aid Office tries to optimize both quality and quantity by awarding aid to as many eligible students as possible while simultaneously providing attractive aid offers to individual students. NCF attempts to utilize institutional funds to supplement each student's scholarship, grants, and other awards. On average, New College of Florida is able to meet 94 percent of each student's demonstrated financial need.

Thanks to a significant pool of private scholarship funding, NCF boasts an effective program of grants and scholarships for in-state and out-of-state students. In fact, New College offers more scholarships than we could possibly mention. Recent changes to New College's financial aid-funding formula means that all admitted first-year students are guaranteed scholarship funding, beginning with

"New College is a wonderful place. I don't think I could have had a better overall college experience anywhere else."

VERY IMPORTANT ADMISSION FACTORS

Application essay, academic GPA, standardized test scores, rigor of secondary school record

IMPORTANT ADMISSION FACTORS

Character/personal qualities, standardized test scores, recommendation(s)

Average HS GPA   3.96
Range SAT Verbal 630–720
Range SAT Math   580–670
Range ACT   25–29
Minimum TOEFL
   (paper/computer) 560/220

APPLICATION DEADLINES

Regular admission
            12/1, 2/15, 4/15
Regular notification
            1/15, 4/1, 4/25
# of transfer applicants 153
% of transfer applicants
   accepted   46

ACADEMICS

Student/faculty ratio   11:1
% faculty teaching
   undergraduates   100
% of classes taught by
   graduate students   0

MOST POPULAR MAJORS

- Anthropology
- Psychology
- Sociology

the 2005–2006 academic year. Levels for this funding are based upon an institutional rating, which takes into account a student's high school grade point average and standardized test scores. In addition, special scholarship funding is allocated for students who are designated as National Merit, National Achievement, and National Hispanic Scholars; these students may receive scholarship funding worth up to 100 percent of the cost of tuition and room and board. In-state students are also eligible for the state of Florida's Bright Futures Program, which covers tuition costs based upon high school performance and standardized test scores.

GETTING IN

Admission is difficult. About 90 percent of the enrolled first-year students who took the SAT scored over 1200. Over 75 percent of the enrolled first-year students who took the ACT scored 27 or higher. Grade point averages of admitted students go through the roof.

The most important thing you can do to improve your chances of getting admitted to New College of Florida is to get really good grades in really challenging high school classes. Don't take media studies. Don't take archery. Take Advanced Placement and other rigorous college-preparatory courses, and do well in them. Standardized test scores are very important, too. You should also dazzle the NCF admissions folks when completing the substantial writing components of the admissions application. This is a writing-intensive place. Show them that you are already a capable writer. Finally, you are required to submit one letter of recommendation. An on-campus interview is recommended, but optional. Make sure to schedule one if you can.

What do Graduates Do?

Out of all the graduates in NCF's 30 year history, 25 percent have gone into education, 23 percent into business, 21 percent into professions, and 10 percent into the arts. About 12 percent have earned PhD degrees. In the natural sciences, 28 percent of biology majors and 38 percent of chemistry majors have earned PhD degrees. In the last ten years, NCF has cranked out twenty Fulbright scholars. Notable NCF alumni include Gregory DuBois (a Rhodes scholar who graduated at the age of sixteen and is now a physics professor at Cal Tech), Sharon Matola (founder of the Belize Zoo), Carol Flint (executive co-producer of the TV show *ER*), and U.S. Representative Lincoln Diaz-Balart (R., Miami). Diaz-Balart's brother, Jose, an anchor for NBC6 and Telemundo in Miami is also an alum.

The Bottom Line

The average yearly out-of pocket cost for tuition, room and board, fees, and expenses is roughly $12,700. Keep in mind that approximately 80 percent of students at NCF are residents. If you are an out-of-state student, you are going to pay more. Don't forget that independent study projects and senior theses may involve additional costs for travel, research expenses, and equipment. You should take these additional factors into account when planning your budget.

Fun Facts

Recent examples of independent study projects by students at NCF include archeological digs in Ethiopia, internships at the Smithsonian Museum of Natural History, volunteering at an Indian orphanage, researching and building an ancient Roman ballista (that's a catapult used to fire big rocks), photographing and interviewing bicycle messengers in New York City, studying the physics behind breaking boards in martial arts, and tracking turkey vultures all over Florida.

Nice RAK—Nice Random Acts of Kindness—is a student group that plans and executes surprise good deeds, like handing out free bus passes downtown or taking over campus custodial duties for the day.

Bugeating 101: A group of NCF students worked with a professor to design a tutorial on the nutritional content of insects (as a possible way of addressing food shortages).

As part of their senior thesis, two NCF students made a three-ton Winnebago run on biodiesel extracted from used french fry oil. It got 25 miles to the gallon.

Education Requirements

Humanities, sciences (biological or physical), social science. Student must receive credit for the satisfactory completion of eight courses in the liberal arts curriculum of the college. These courses must include at least one course in each of the three divisions: humanities (including fine arts), social sciences (including behavioral sciences and history), and natural sciences (including mathematics).

FINANCIAL INFO

In-state tuition	$3,734
Out-of-state tuition	$19,964
Room & board	$6,564
Average book expense	$800
Average freshman need-based grant	$8,439
Average freshman need-based loan	$2,215
% of graduates who borrowed	38
Average indebtedness	$12,252

Financial Aid Forms
Students must submit FAFSA.

POSTGRAD

Career Services
Alumni network, alumni services, career assessment, internships, regional alumni, on-campus job interviews. Off-campus job opportunities are good.

NEW MEXICO INSTITUTE OF MINING & TECHNOLOGY

Campus Station, 801 Leroy Place, Socorro, NM 87801
www.NMT.edu • Admissions: 505-835-5424
Fax: 505-835-5989 • E-mail: admission@admin.nmt.edu • Financial Aid: 505-835-5333

STUDENTS

Religious affiliation
No Affiliation
Academic year
calendar   semester
Undergrad
enrollment   1,184
% male/female   73/27
% Asian   3
% Black, non-Latino   1
% Latino   20
% Native American   3
% international   3
% from out of state   12
% freshmen return for
sophomore year   68

STUDENT LIFE
% of students living
on campus   59

ADMISSIONS

of applicants   428
% accepted   81
% enrolled   81

HIGH SCHOOL UNITS REQUIRED

4 English, 3 math, 2 science
(2 science lab), 2 social
studies, 1 history, 3
academic electives

HIGH SCHOOL UNITS RECOMMENDED

4 English, 4 math, 4 science
(3 science lab), 2 foreign
language, 3 social studies, 1
history

ABOUT NEW MEXICO INSTITUTE OF MINING & TECHNOLOGY

New Mexico Institute of Mining & Technology is an intense school that specializes in science and engineering. New Mexico Tech's small size enables its students to participate in cutting-edge research conducted in laboratories and on the field. Students can get immediately involved in research projects like the Mount Erebus Volcano Observatory (which conducts real-time studies of an active volcano in Antarctica) or the Langmuir Laboratory for Atmospheric Research (where you can prepare for your career as a producer of The Weather Channel's *Storm Stories* by studying hail, lightning, and rain). New Mexico Tech's professors are immensely helpful and dispense homework at a hectic pace.

The very dedicated and tremendously intelligent students are science geeks and math nerds who are proud of that reputation. About 55 percent of the student population is male. Clubs and activities abound on campus, intramural sports are popular, and students enjoy hiking, rock climbing, and spelunking. There's not much of a party scene and the smallness of the surrounding town of Socorro (population approximately 9,000) definitely presents a challenge for creative minds. Students who need to spend some time in the glare of big city lights can drive about an hour north to Albuquerque.

BANG FOR YOUR BUCK

Like most public schools, New Mexico Tech is affordable for residents. Unlike most public schools, it is a great bargain even if you aren't from the Land of Enchantment. At about $8,700 for an academic year, New Mexico Tech is extremely affordable for nonresidents, especially when compared to out-of-state tuition at other science and engineering schools of its academic caliber. Out-of-state students at Colorado School of Mines, for example, are charged about $18,800 per year; Michigan Tech and Missouri-Rolla each cost over $14,000 a year for nonresidents. Tuition at New Mexico Tech for both residents and nonresidents is among the lowest in the nation, particularly when you take into account the quality and hands-on nature of the education.

New Mexico Tech students don't need to take out many loans because tuition is low and aid is readily available. Almost 80 percent of all the students receive financial aid in the form of school funded academic scholarships, grants, campus jobs (many of which are in labs and research facilities), and loans. There are five different merit scholarships for first-time students from New Mexico and one merit scholarship specifically for nonresident, first-time students. When you apply for admission, your application is automatically reviewed for a merit scholarship. You automatically receive a merit scholarship if you meet the requirements. A merit scholarship is also automatically renewed every year as long as you keep your grades up.

Getting In

When you apply for admission to New Mexico Tech you need to submit a completed application form, your high school transcripts, and your standardized test score (preferably the ACT). A grade point average of 3.5 or higher in a solid college-preparatory curriculum and an ACT score of 26 will make you a competitive candidate.

What do Graduates Do?

New Mexico Tech graduates get plum jobs in science and engineering making anywhere from $45,000 to $65,000 upon graduation. Many graduates do top secret stuff for national laboratories (i.e., Sandia National Labs, Los Alamos National Laboratory, and Lawrence Livermore National Lab) and for government contractors at defense facilities (i.e., White Sands Missile Range, the Nevada Test Site, and the China Lake Naval Station). Approximately 30 percent of all graduates go to graduate or professional schools soon after graduating.

Very Important Admission Factors

Academic GPA, rigor of secondary school record, standardized test scores

Average HS GPA	3.6
Range SAT Verbal	560–670
Range SAT Math	570–680
Range ACT	24–29
Minimum TOEFL (paper/computer)	540/207

Application Deadlines

Regular admission	8/1
Regular notification	rolling
# of transfer applicants	77
% of transfer applicants accepted	86

Academics

Student/faculty ratio	11:1
% faculty teaching undergraduates	85

Most Popular Majors

• Computer and information sciences
• Electrical, electronics and communications engineering
• Physics

Education Requirements

English (including composition), humanities, math, sciences (biological or physical), social science

FINANCIAL INFO

In-state tuition	$3,439
Out-of-state tuition	$10,873
Room & board	$5,090
Average book expense	$800
Required fees	$532
Average freshman need-based grant	$3,975
Average freshman need-based loan	$3,407
% of graduates who borrowed	58
Average indebtedness	$7,292

FINANCIAL AID FORMS

Students must submit FAFSA, institution's own financial aid form.

Financial aid filing deadline	3/1

POSTGRAD

% going to graduate school	30

CAREER SERVICES

Career/job search classes, career assessment, on-campus job interviews. Off-campus job opportunities are poor.

THE BOTTOM LINE

A year of tuition, room and board, books, fees, and all other expenses for residents is around $13,570. For nonresidents, the total cost is not much over $26,600. If you are an out-of-state applicant with good grades and ACT scores, you might receive a President Scholarship worth $2,700, federal grants worth $4,000, a work-study award of $1,860, and loans totaling about $4,360—this would leave you with an affordable out-of-pocket cost of around $5,800.

New Mexico Tech students graduate with an average debt totaling $9,500. At a 6 percent interest rate, your student loan monthly payment would be about $105; your should keep in mind that the Stafford Loan variable interest rate is currently less than 4 percent.

FUN FACTS

New Mexico Tech is a world leader in many areas, including hydrology, astrophysics, atmospheric science, geophysics, homeland security, geosciences, and petroleum recovery.

Students get to legally blow things up. The university's Energetic Materials Research and Testing Center is arguably *the* authority in theoretical and applied explosives engineering. Much of the research at Tech involves exploding things and investigating the technology used to do that; after all, it *is* what you do in mining. Students quickly become oblivious to the loud booms and thuds coming from the mountainous area just west of the main campus.

The men's rugby club team is called the Pygmies. The women's rugby club team is called the Pygmy Queens.

NORTH CAROLINA STATE UNIVERSITY

Box 7103, Raleigh, NC 27695
www.NCState.edu • Admissions: 919-515-2434
Fax: 919-515-5039 • E-mail: undergrad_admissions@ncsu.edu • Financial Aid: 919-515-2421

STUDENTS

Religious affiliation
No Affiliation

Academic year
calendar   semester

Undergrad
enrollment   20,546
% male/female   58/42
% Asian   5
% Black, non-Latino   10
% Latino   2
% Native American   1
% international   1
% from out of state   7
% freshmen return for
sophomore year   89
% freshmen graduate
within 4 years   36

STUDENT LIFE

% of students living
on campus   34
% in fraternities   8
% in sororities   10

ADMISSIONS

of applicants   13,610
% accepted   66
% enrolled   47

HIGH SCHOOL UNITS REQUIRED

4 English, 4 math, 3 science
(1 science lab), 2 foreign
language, 1 social studies,
1 history, 1 academic
electives

ABOUT NORTH CAROLINA STATE UNIVERSITY

Science and technology are a big deal at North Carolina State University, which also has nationally reputable major programs in architecture, design, textiles, management, engineering, agriculture, humanities and social sciences, education, physical & mathematical sciences, natural resources, and veterinary medicine. The College of Engineering and the College of Agriculture and Life Sciences form the backbone of the academic program. Professors are generally well prepared to work inside the classroom, and students must often be prepared to work outside the classroom; an important part of NC State's undergraduate curriculum is its cooperative education program, which allows students to work in the real world for college credit. The university's First Year College is also notably good at helping undecided students select a major.

Students are a very open, friendly, and tight-knit group, especially considering they attend one of the nation's larger schools. Of course, when upward of 30,000 graduate and undergraduate students congregate in the same place, it's a given that great people who have common interests will get along. Atlantic Coast Conference sports are a major part of life. On-campus food and dorms aren't that great, but a majority of NC State students live off campus and almost all of them go outside of campus to find fun things to do. The campus is big but not too spread out, and its location in the heart of Raleigh allows access to lots of shopping. The bars on Hillsborough Street are also very popular. Raleigh is home to many local bands; hence, students enjoy a happening music scene.

BANG FOR YOUR BUCK

North Carolina State has an annual budget of approximately $915 million and an endowment valued at more than $342 million. Annual expenditures for research and industry-sponsored programs exceed $440 million. The university is ranked 16th among national research universities that conduct nonfederally funded research and 35th nationally in its total expenditures for research and development. It is also ranked 2nd in total state and local research funding among (big-time) research universities. The bottom line is that there is a lot of research going on and a lot of money funding it.

Despite recent tuition increases, NC State continues to be a bargain. The average scholarship and grant packages have increased along with tuition; perhaps more importantly, the average loan debt of students has decreased. Tuition for residents is incredibly low. Out-of-state tuition rates are good, but not great—NC State is not always affordable for

High School Units Recommended

4 English, 4 math, 4 science (1 science lab), 2 foreign language, 1 social studies, 1 history, 4 academic electives

Very Important Admission Factors

Academic GPA, class rank, rigor of secondary school record, standardized test scores

Average HS GPA	4.07
Range SAT Verbal	530–620
Range SAT Math	560–660
Range ACT	23–27
Minimum TOEFL (paper/computer)	550/213

Application Deadlines

Regular admission	2/1
Regular notification	rolling
# of transfer applicants	3,478
% of transfer applicants accepted	38

ACADEMICS

Student/faculty ratio	16:1
% faculty teaching undergraduates	100
% of classes taught by graduate students	6

Most Popular Majors

• Biology/biological sciences
• Business administration and management
• Mechanical engineering

nonresidents with a high financial need. The university offers a number of merit-based scholarships, including about 50 Park Scholarships. These scholarships cover full tuition for four years and are awarded on the basis of scholarship, character, leadership, and service. In addition, several hundred merit scholarships are awarded to undergraduates each year, many of which are based on your major. Financial need is a requirement for the allocation of a large percentage of scholarships and grants. The philosophy is to offer loans as a last resort and to first exhaust all scholarship, grant, and work funds.

Getting In

The average SAT score for incoming first-year students at NC State is 1193. You need to submit your current high school transcript (NC State may request your grades from the first semester of your senior year, so don't slack off until you get accepted). The College of Design requires you submit a portfolio and encourages prospective candidates to load up on high school art classes. Some of NC State's undergraduate colleges are called "selective" and others are "highly selective." For selective colleges you need to have a B-plus grade point average and be in the top 25 to 30 percent of your high school class. Taking very demanding courses and getting good standardized test scores will help, too. For highly selective colleges, you need to take even harder classes, be in the top 10 to 15 percent of your high school class, and have slightly better grades and test scores. The most important factor that will affect your admission is your overall high school academic record. Extracurricular activities, including leadership and community service, may receive consideration, but theses factors are not weighed nearly as heavily as your academic record.

What do Graduates Do?

Something like 31 percent of all North Carolina State graduates attend graduate school within five years of receiving their diplomas. Graduates who go to work do so in a plethora of industries, including agriculture and agribusiness, banking (North Carolina is a banking mecca), biotechnology, manufacturing, software development, and telecommunications. Many big companies recruit on campus, including IBM Electric, GlaxoSmithKline, Northrop Grumman, the "Big Four" accounting firms, and the Naval Surface Warfare Center. Students in the College of Textiles and the College of Agriculture and Life Sciences have their own Career Services resources, both of which do good things for their respective undergraduates.

THE BOTTOM LINE

A year of tuition, fees, room and board, books, and all other expenses is approximately $14,453 for residents and $26,651 for nonresidents. Financial need notwithstanding, there is a huge difference between what residents and nonresidents will have to pay out of pocket. Maybe that's why only 7 percent of NC State's domestic undergraduate students hail from outside the Old North State. About 52 percent of all NC State students take out loans—students who borrow money graduate with an average loan debt of roughly $14,505.

FUN FACTS

Hey! Is your last name Gatlin or Gatling? If so, you are in luck. North Carolina State offers the John T. Gatling grant, which provides scholarship assistance to students who were born with the surname Gatlin or Gatling. Priority for the Gatling Scholarship is given to students, based on need, who are from North Carolina and who attend NC State. Gatling Scholarships may also be awarded to nonresidents who attend other colleges elsewhere if sufficient funds are available. (They usually aren't.)

Pardon our pun, but a *glowing* tradition at NC State is lighting the Bell Tower red to celebrate academic and athletic accomplishments.

With almost 30,000 students, NC State is the largest university in the state of North Carolina.

North Carolina State is ranked 17th among all colleges and universities when it comes to launching start-up companies. The university has received over 350 patents for beneficial technologies developed by its faculty.

EDUCATION REQUIREMENTS

Arts/fine arts, computer literacy, English (including composition), foreign languages, history, humanities, math, sciences (biological or physical), social science

FINANCIAL INFO

In-state tuition	$3,530
Out-of-state tuition	$15,728
Room & board	$7,040
Average book expense	$900
Required fees	$1,253
Average freshman need-based grant	$6,216
Average freshman need-based loan	$2,208
% of graduates who borrowed	52
Average indebtedness	$14,505

FINANCIAL AID FORMS

Students must submit FAFSA, institution's own financial aid form.

POSTGRAD

% going to graduate school	31
% going to law school	7
% going to business school	19
% going to medical school	7

OGLETHORPE UNIVERSITY

4484 Peachtree Road Northeast, Atlanta, GA 30319
www.Oglethorpe.edu • Admissions: 404-364-8307
Fax: 404-364-8491 • E-mail: admission@oglethorpe.edu • Financial Aid: 404-364-8354

STUDENTS

Religious affiliation
               No Affiliation
Academic year
  calendar   semester
Undergrad
  enrollment   1,018
% male/female   36/64
% Asian   4
% Black, non-Latino   20
% Latino   1
% international   6
% from out of state   29
% freshmen return for
sophomore year   87
% freshmen graduate
  within 4 years   48

STUDENT LIFE

% of students living
  on campus   68
% in fraternities   35
% in sororities   24

ADMISSIONS

of applicants   1,236
% accepted   64
% enrolled   29

HIGH SCHOOL UNITS REQUIRED

4 English, 3 math, 2
science, 3 social studies

HIGH SCHOOL UNITS RECOMMENDED

2 Foreign language

VERY IMPORTANT ADMISSION FACTORS

Academic GPA, application
essay, interview, rigor of
secondary school record,
standardized test scores

ABOUT OGLETHORPE UNIVERSITY

Oglethorpe University is an independent, highly selective liberal arts school located in the cultural and social hotbed of Atlanta. Its student body consists of students from more than 31 different countries and 34 different states, meaning that diversity isn't hard to come by. Add to that mix the allure and benefit of big-city life and it's no wonder why students report having such a broad range of experiences and interests at Oglethorpe. On campus, students can expect a traditional college education, which is balanced and even enhanced by the sights, sounds, experiences, and inspiration of the city that surrounds it.

With its academically rigorous programs in the liberal arts and sciences, Oglethorpe University offers its students a superior educational experience. The university faculty work in close collaboration with their students, providing them with individual attention and encouragement. They are committed to creating a true learning environment in the university's core programs of business administration, and the liberal arts and sciences.

As a largely residential school, Oglethorpe University is known for its devotion to caring about each and every student by placing importance on the individual. There are many opportunities for Oglethorpe students to interact with the community. The OUr Atlanta program connects incoming first-year students with many of the world-class businesses and organizations in the Atlanta area and provides the opportunity for students to experience Atlanta's arts, business, and athletic enterprises.

BANG FOR YOUR BUCK

The financial aid office at Oglethorpe University makes a substantial effort to supply the best and least painful solutions to all financial matters surrounding students working towards a degree in the liberal arts or business. There are quite a few endowed scholarships available to Oglethorpe scholars; no less than 49 are listed on the school's website. Also available are federal and state financial aid funds. There is even a financial aid program designed to assist students who would like to experience studying abroad. Of those who applied for financial aid funds, 84 percent received funds and a little less than one half of those needs of those were fully met.

Students Say

"Oglethorpe is all about fostering individuality and creative thought through a rigorous curriculum of very unique classes."

GETTING IN

Admissions officers at Oglethorpe University are a tough lot to impress. Entrance into the institution is based on a number of criteria. It is recommended that applicants complete a secondary school program that includes courses in English, social studies, mathematics, and science. Rigor of secondary school record, class rank, academic GPA, standardized test scores, application essays, recommendations, and interviews are all considered. The average GPA of applicants is 3.5. Successful candidates are likely to excel in all of the above areas.

WHAT DO GRADUATES DO?

A degree from Oglethorpe University opens the door to many different career paths. The jobs available to graduates are diverse: Marine architect, art director, and chemist are just a few of the careers pursued by graduates. In addition, many graduates continue their education to get postgraduate degrees. The university offers a career services center with fantastic resources for students interested in their own career development, including workshops and individual counseling available for those who want it. The office also connects students with many of Atlanta's finest corporations and prospective employers who conduct interviews on campus for potential employees.

THE BOTTOM LINE

For the 2005–2006 academic year, tuition cost $23,310 for both in-state and out-of-state students. Moreover, administrators estimated that students spent an additional $600 on school supplies and books and $200 for required fees. An additional $8,870 room and board charge is added for those students who choose to live on campus. Overall, the average student graduates from Oglethorpe with $14,260 in cumulative debt.

IMPORTANT ADMISSION FACTORS

Class rank, level of applicant's interest, recommendation(s)

Average HS GPA	3.5
Range SAT Verbal	500–630
Range SAT Math	470–610
Range ACT	21–27
Minimum TOEFL (paper)	550

APPLICATION DEADLINES

# of transfer applicants	170
% of transfer applicants accepted	55

ACADEMICS

Student/faculty ratio	13:1
% faculty teaching undergraduates	100
% of classes taught by graduate students	0

MOST POPULAR MAJORS

- Business administration/ management
- English language and literature
- Psychology

EDUCATION REQUIREMENTS

Arts/fine arts, computer literacy, English (including composition), foreign languages, history, humanities, math, philosophy, sciences (biological or physical), social science

FINANCIAL INFO

Tuition	$23,310
Room & board	$8,870
Average book expense	$600
Required fees	$100
Average freshman need-based grant	$15,840
Average freshman need-based loan	$2,150
% of graduates who borrowed	72
Average indebtedness	$14,260

FINANCIAL AID FORMS

Students must submit FAFSA, institution's own financial aid form, state aid form.

POSTGRAD

% going to graduate school	40
% going to law school	9
% going to business school	10
% going to medical school	2

CAREER SERVICES

Alumni network, alumni services, career/job search classes, career assessment, internships, on-campus job interviews. Off-campus job opportunities are excellent.

FUN FACTS

Oglethorpe's collegiate coat of arms is emblazoned with three boars' heads and the inscription *Nescit Cedere,* which means, "He does not know how to give up."

In February, the college celebrates the anniversary of James Edward Oglethorpe's founding of the colony of Georgia. The annual "Petrels of Fire" race, an homage to Trinity College's "Great Court Run" portrayed in the movie *Chariots of Fire*, features students attempting to run the 270-yard perimeter of Cambridge's Academic Quad before the Lupton Hall bell tower finishes its noon chimes.

In March of 2002, ESPN's David Lloyd named the Stormy Petrel as one of the most memorable college mascot names of all time.

OKLAHOMA BAPTIST UNIVERSITY

500 West University, Shawnee, OK 74804
www.OKBU.edu • Admissions: 800-654-3285
Fax: 405-878-2046 • E-mail: admissions@okbu.edu • Financial Aid: 800-654-3285

STUDENTS

Religious affiliation
               Southern Baptist
Academic year
  calendar   4-1-4
Undergrad
  enrollment   1,441
% male/female   40/60
% Asian   1
% Black, non-Latino   3
% Latino   2
% Native American   4
% international   3
% from out of state   42
% freshmen return for
  sophomore year   68
% freshmen graduate
  within 4 years   45

STUDENT LIFE

% of students living
  on campus   78
% in fraternities   12
% in sororities   5

ADMISSIONS

of applicants   1,144
% accepted   73
% enrolled   44

HIGH SCHOOL UNITS
RECOMMENDED

4 English, 3 math, 3 science
(2 science lab), 2 foreign
language, 1 social studies, 2
history, 2 academic
electives, 1 fine arts

VERY IMPORTANT ADMISSION
FACTORS

Academic GPA, rigor of
secondary school record

ABOUT OKLAHOMA BAPTIST UNIVERSITY

At Oklahoma Baptist University, all undergraduates complete a broad-based liberal-arts core curriculum en route to preparing for careers in business, education, health services, ministry, and the sciences. The core, naturally, incorporates a heavy measure of religious instruction; it also exposes students to study in fine arts, foreign language, history, literature, mathematics, philosophy, science, and writing. Teaching focuses on the interrelation of these disciplines, helping students place what they've learned in context. The core does limit students' elective choices, which some see as a drawback. It should be noted, however, that the small size of the school would place similar limitations on elective options anyway.

OBU undergrads are predominantly Caucasian, Christian, and conservative. Native Americans constitute the largest minority group. Students tend to be very active in both extracurricular activities and community service. The immediate surrounding community of Shawnee is pretty small, though greater opportunities for both service and fun exist in Oklahoma City, west of OBU. On campus, students enjoy movies, clubs, working out, Bible study, or just hanging out with friends. Intramural sports are big; in intercollegiate sports, the men's NAIA Division I basketball team is consistently competitive.

BANG FOR YOUR BUCK

Each year, OBU administers a little over $300,000 in institutional need-based aid and over $6 million in institutional merit-based aid, which includes nearly $1 million in athletic scholarships. These funds, in combination with federal loans, allow OBU to reduce the cost of attending for 90 percent of its student body.

OBU provides need-based assistance to 100 percent of all aid applicants who demonstrate need, and 90 percent of need-based aid packages include some form of need-based grant or scholarship. On average, the school meets 70 percent of aid recipients' demonstrated need. More than 51 percent of aid recipients will see 100 percent of their demonstrated need met by the school

IMPORTANT ADMISSION FACTORS

Character/personal qualities, class rank, extracurricular activities, recommendation(s), standardized test scores

Average HS GPA	3.67
Range SAT Verbal	510–650
Range SAT Math	500–630
Range ACT	21–28
Minimum TOEFL (paper/computer)	500/173

APPLICATION DEADLINES

Regular admission	8/1
Regular notification	9/1
# of transfer applicants	207
% of transfer applicants accepted	62

ACADEMICS

Student/faculty ratio	14:1
% faculty teaching undergraduates	100
% of classes taught by graduate students	0

MOST POPULAR MAJORS

- Bible/biblical studies
- Elementary education and teaching
- Nursing—registered nurse training (RN, ASN, BSN, MSN)

OBU offers incoming freshmen a number of academic scholarships based on their standardized test scores and high school GPA. (Renewal is then based on the student's GPA at OBU.) The top award, for students with an ACT composite score of at least 32 (or an SAT score of at least 1450) and a high school GPA of 3.75, covers the full cost of tuition. Any student with an ACT composite score of at least 23 (or an SAT score of at least 1060) and a high school GPA of 3.0 is eligible for a scholarship of at least $1,500 annually.

GETTING IN

Admission requirements for incoming freshmen at OBU include an ACT composite score of at least 20 (or a re-centered SAT score of at least 950) and either a weighted high school GPA of at least 3.0 or a ranking in the upper half of one's high school class. Conditional admission can be granted to students with ACT composite scores between 17 and 19 (or re-centered SAT scores between 800 and 940) and either a weighted high school GPA of at least 3.0 or ranking in the upper half of one's high school class. Those who do not meet these requirements may petition the committee for reconsideration of their application with a statement of purpose and provide two letters of recommendation from recent teachers. Homeschooled students are admitted on the basis of ACT or SAT scores and written assessment of homeschool achievements. The school may require homeschool applicants to take special assessments or to accept special class placements.

WHAT DO GRADUATES DO?

One in four OBU students majors in philosophy, religion, or theology in preparation for a career serving the Baptist community. Many graduates find work as teachers; about one in seven students here majors in education. About 40 percent of all OBU alumni undertake advanced academic work within five years of graduation.

The Bottom Line

In 2006–2007, OBU students paid $13,654 in tuition and an additional $1,012 in required fees. Room and board added another $4,330, bringing the direct cost of attending the school to $18,996. Students should anticipate an additional $1,000 in expenses for books and supplies, $1,400 in transportation expenses, and $1,400 in personal and miscellaneous expenses. Approximately two-thirds of all OBU undergraduates receive some form of need-based aid. A full 70 percent of all students receive some form of aid (need-based, merit-based, or both).

Fun Facts

By tradition, all freshmen and first-year transfer students at OBU wear beanies during orientation and during the first week of classes.

During basketball games, OBU fans and cheerleaders chant a nonsense cheer called Ka-Rip. It goes, in part: "Ka-rip Ka-rap Ka-piplo typlo tap/Oh! Oh! Rincto lincto hio-totimus…" It goes on like that for a while.

OBU's biggest annual event is the Harvest Festival, celebrated in early November. Homecoming Weekend is part of the festival. Each year, a Harvest Festival court is elected, consisting of the Harvest King and Queen, the Best All-Around Man and Woman, and the Most Servant-Like Man and Woman.

Education Requirements

Arts/fine arts, computer literacy, English (including composition), foreign languages, history, humanities, math, philosophy, sciences (biological or physical), social science, religion, speech, health concepts, health activity

FINANCIAL INFO

Tuition	$13,654
Room & board	$4,330
Average book expense	$1,000
Required fees	$1,012
Average freshman need-based grant	$3,843
Average freshman need-based loan	$3,209
% of graduates who borrowed	57
Average indebtedness	$16,614

Financial Aid Forms

Students must submit FAFSA.

POSTGRAD

% going to graduate school	37
% going to law school	1
% going to business school	1
% going to medical school	2

Career Services

Alumni network, alumni services, career/job search classes, career assessment, internships, regional alumni, on-campus job interviews. Off-campus job opportunities are fair.

OKLAHOMA STATE UNIVERSITY

324 Student Union, Stillwater, OK 74078
www.OKState.edu • Admissions: 800-233-5019
Fax: 405-744-5285 • E-mail: admit@okstate.edu • Financial Aid: 405-744-7440

STUDENTS

Religious affiliation
               No Affiliation
Academic year
  calendar   semester
Undergrad
  enrollment   18,773
% male/female   52/48
% Asian   2
% Black, non-Latino   4
% Latino   2
% Native American   9
% international   4
% from out of state   15
% freshmen return for
sophomore year   79
% freshmen graduate
  within 4 years   26

STUDENT LIFE

% of students living
  on campus   37
% in fraternities   13
% in sororities   17

ADMISSIONS

of applicants   6,533
% accepted   88
% enrolled   58

HIGH SCHOOL UNITS REQUIRED

4 English, 3 math, 2 science
(2 science lab), 2 social
studies, 1 history, 3
academic electives

HIGH SCHOOL UNITS RECOMMENDED

2 Foreign language, 1
computer science

ABOUT OKLAHOMA STATE UNIVERSITY

Oklahoma State University's student body boasts 19,000 Cowboys. Not many schools can say that! Undergrads are friendly, helpful, and down-to-earth. Many are Caucasian and middle-class, but there is a great deal of diversity in religion, language, and personal preference. Traditional and nontraditional students mix well together and are united by a love of OSU and of Cowboy athletics, particularly basketball, which is a perennial division I powerhouse in the Big XII Conference.

OSU offers a top-notch education in any of a wide variety of majors. Agricultural and animal science are the most popular majors (this is Oklahoma, after all), but students are drawn to the excellent engineering department and the Honors College as well—a program for students of exceptional ability. Study abroad programs, plus research and internship opportunities are all at your fingertips. And for such a large school, professors are reportedly motivated, accessible, and devoted to supporting their students. Another plus are the stream of upgrades, including a new alumni center, new suite-style dormitories, and a renovated basketball arena. A football stadium is soon to follow.

Oklahoma State has a safe campus, load of school spirit, and tons of activities. There are 300 campus organizations, and an incredibly active Greek scene, in addition to casino nights, biweekly concerts, Texas Hold'em Tournaments, and intramural games. All are appreciated in this aptly named small town of Stillwater where most of OSU's social scene takes place on campus.

BANG FOR YOUR BUCK

Oklahoma State University is very affordable due to relatively low tuition and fees and low cost of living in the community. For the 2005–2006 academic year, Oklahoma State University significantly enhanced its already solid scholarship programs available to entering first-year students and transfer students.

Oklahoma State University scholarships are awarded to students on both a merit and need basis. Oklahoma State Regents for Higher Education Academic Scholars receive substantial assistance in the form of cash and tuition scholarships. Minorities with at least a 3.3 GPA and demonstrated leadership abilities through participation in community service, extracurricular or other activities Gates Millennium Scholarship if they meet the Federal Pell Grant eligibility criteria.

More than one-third of the student body receives need-based financial aid; more than a quarter receive non-need-based scholarships.

GETTING IN

The most important components of the OSU are your high school transcript, class rank, and standardized test scores. Students do not need to apply to a specific college or department. In 2005–2006, a solid 91 percent of incoming freshmen had a high school GPA of 3.0 or higher.

WHAT DO GRADUATES DO?

OSU's student body is divided among six academic colleges that represent diverse opportunities across multiple industries. Many of our students combine multiple degree areas at the major and minor levels to enhance their skill-set across industry lines. Graduates are well-represented in the following fields: agriculture, architecture, banking and financial services, consulting, consumer products, creative/design, education, energy, engineering, family services, government, health care, hospitality, journalism/media, manufacturing, retail, technology, veterinary medicine, and many other areas. OSU Career Services connects with more than 2,600 national, regional, and local employers, 500 of which recruit through on-campus interviewing, mock interviews, career fairs, and on-campus informational sessions/workshops.

BOTTOM LINE

State residents in 2006–2007 paid just $3,262.50 in tuition to SUU. Out-of-state students paid a significantly more but a still reasonable price of $11,835. Once you factor in $1,734.30 in fees, $6,015 in room and board, $910 for books and supplies, and another $3,970 for travel and personal expenses, Oklahoma residents living on campus paid an estimated $15,891.80 before financial aid, loans, and/or grants and scholarships. Out-of-state students paid an estimated $24,464.30. The average financial aid package for those who demonstrated need was $8,782, plus another average of $3,517 in need-based scholarships or grant aid, for a total of $12,299 need-based aid for the average aid recipient.

VERY IMPORTANT ADMISSION FACTORS

Academic GPA, class rank, standardized test scores

Average HS GPA	3.53
Range SAT Verbal	500–610
Range SAT Math	510–620
Range ACT	22–27
Minimum TOEFL (paper/computer)	500/173

APPLICATION DEADLINES

Regular notification	rolling
# of transfer applicants	2,739
% of transfer applicants accepted	85

ACADEMICS

Student/faculty ratio	19:1
% faculty teaching undergraduates	77
% of classes taught by graduate students	12

MOST POPULAR MAJORS

- Animal sciences
- Elementary education and teaching
- Marketing/marketing management

EDUCATION REQUIREMENTS

English (including composition), history, humanities, math, sciences (biological or physical), social science, American Government and International Dimension

FINANCIAL INFO

In-state tuition $3,263
Out-of-state tuition $11,835
Room & board $6,015
Average book
  expense $910
Required fees $1,734
Average freshman
  need-based grant $3,869
Average freshman
  need-based loan $2,722
% of graduates
  who borrowed   56
Average
  indebtedness $17,719

FINANCIAL AID FORMS

Students must submit FAFSA.

POSTGRAD

CAREER SERVICES

Career/job search classes, career assessment, internships, on-campus job interviews. Off-campus job opportunities are good.

FUN FACTS

OSU offers a degree in Fire Protection and Safety Technology, which is only offered at two universities in the nation.

OSU has won 46 NCAA National Championships.

This very campus is where the parking meter, the peanut butter slice, and the watermelon thumper were invented.

Each year OSU takes home at least one award from the Association of Student Advancement Programs for Homecoming activities, which include philanthropic events, house decorations, street painting, and a parade. Over 45,000 alums return to Stillwater for this event!

There are two philanthropic events on campus, "Into the Streets" and the "Big Event," every fall and spring. At these events, students go out into the community for a day and conduct community service projects for the elderly.

PRESBYTERIAN COLLEGE

503 South Broad Street, Clinton, SC 29325
www.Presby.edu • Admissions: 864-833-8230
Fax: 864-833-8481 • E-mail: admissions@presby.edu • Financial Aid: 864-833-8290

STUDENTS

Religious affiliation

	Other
Academic year calendar	semester
Undergrad enrollment	1,171
% male/female	48/52
% Asian	1
% Black, non-Latino	5
% Latino	1
% from out of state	37
% freshmen return for sophomore year	83
% freshmen graduate within 4 years	67

STUDENT LIFE

% of students living on campus	95
% in fraternities	44
% in sororities	36

ADMISSIONS

# of applicants	1,194
% accepted	77
% enrolled	39
# of early decision/action applicants	59
% accepted early decision/action	91

HIGH SCHOOL UNITS REQUIRED

4 English, 3 math, 2 science (2 science lab), 2 foreign language, 2 history, 2 academic electives

HIGH SCHOOL UNITS RECOMMENDED

3 Foreign language, 3 science, 4 math, honors, AP, 1B classes

ABOUT PRESBYTERIAN COLLEGE

The Presbyterian College school motto, *Dum Vivimus Servimus*, or "While we live, we serve," is widely recognized and encouraged by both the community surrounding the institution and its faculty. Hand in hand with this commitment to service is the school's honor code, updated in 2006. It states, "On my honor, I will abstain from all deceit. I will neither give nor receive unacknowledged aid in my academic work, nor will I permit such action by any member of this community. I will respect the persons and property of the community, and will not condone discourteous or dishonest treatment of these by my peers. In my every act, I will seek to maintain a high standard of honesty and truthfulness for myself and for the College." Each annual Opening Convocation begins with students and faculty promising to adhere to the aforementioned principles. Just as membership has its privileges, following an honor code can result in several benefits, as many students do not feel the need to lock their dorm rooms, and students and faculty are considered to be trustworthy by default.

Academics at PC are rigorous and challenging, and the school rightly prides itself on the attentive and dedicated professors it employs. There are 84 full-time professors and 29 different majors available at the college. The average class sizes are small with 13 to 15 students. It also has three Cooperative and Dual-Degree Programs in engineering (with Clemson, Auburn, and Vanderbilt Universities), religion (with Union Theological Seminary), and forestry and environmental science (with Duke University). Also of note is the college's Maymester study abroad program, which features a series of academic programs in a variety of different disciplines and exotic locales during a few weeks in May. In 2006 destinations included Morocco, China, and the Galapagos Islands!

When it comes to the social scene, everything's Greek to Presbyterian. It has six national fraternities and three national sororities. A whopping 44 percent of the students are members, and each fraternity has a separate house in Fraternity Court, the center of the weekend social scene. Also keep in mind that over 90 percent of all students live on campus, meaning that the residence halls are an equal, if not greater, hotbed of good friends and good times. And all this is great news as Clinton, while charming and quaint, isn't known for its energetic nightlife.

Students Say

"The Honor Code is a huge part of PC. We all take great pride in upholding it. Also, the size of our school and the relationships between students and professors are a huge strength."

VERY IMPORTANT ADMISSION FACTORS

Academic GPA, application essay, character/personal qualities, standardized test scores

IMPORTANT ADMISSION FACTORS

Alumni/ae relation, class rank, extracurricular activities, first generation, recommendation(s), rigor of secondary school record

Average HS GPA	3.33
Range SAT Verbal	500–610
Range SAT Math	500–620
Range ACT	21–26
Minimum TOEFL (paper/computer)	550/200

APPLICATION DEADLINES

Early decision	11/15
Regular notification	rolling
# of transfer applicants	53
% of transfer applicants accepted	94

ACADEMICS

Student/faculty ratio	13:1
% faculty teaching undergraduates	100
% of classes taught by graduate students	0

MOST POPULAR MAJORS

- Biology/premed
- Business administration/ management
- History

BANG FOR YOUR BUCK

Presbyterian College runs on an endowment of $92 million dollars which allows it to invest in both need-based grants and academic scholarships. With that in mind, investing in a private school can be a strain on anyone's budget, which is why 90 percent of the students at PC receive some type of financial aid. The average financial aid package for fall 2006 was estimated at $19,000. Financial aid at Presbyterian College is divided into two separate categories, self help and gift aid. Gift aid comes in the forms of grants and/or scholarships and is not required to be paid back. Self-help financial aid comes in the form of loans and work-study grants. Students may be able to work on campus to help with college costs. Low-interest loans are also available, and most don't require payment back until after the student graduates.

GETTING IN

The Admission Office at PC is mostly interested in a potential student's high school transcript. Academic GPA, standardized test scores, and an applicant's entrance essay are all scrutinized, as are letters of recommendation. Thirty-one percent of applicants graduated in the top 10 percent of their class. On average, applicants maintained a high school GPA of 3.3. Extracurricular activities and character and personal qualities are taken under heavy consideration as well.

WHAT DO GRADUATES DO?

Presbyterian College graduates are sought by leading businesses and educational institutions and have a high acceptance rate into schools of medicine, law, and religion and graduate programs at major universities. The career center does a good job of setting up interested students with internships (sometimes paid, but always for credit) and these go a long way toward securing a job after graduation (even sometimes before). They also work with students to prepare them for the job market, streamline their resumes, and hone their interviewing skills.

THE BOTTOM LINE

In 2006–2007 tuition at Presbyterian College was reported to cost $22,484; required fees totaled $2,142, and it is estimated that students spent $1,110 on books and supplies, $1,390 on transportation, and $2,774 for other miscellaneous expenses. The good news is that if students prefer to live on campus they have a few options. Students can either pay for both room and board which costs $7,246 or they can separate the costs. A room without a meal plan costs $3,540 and a meal plan costs $3,706. On average, students left Presbyterian with $21,517 in cumulative debt.

FUN FACTS

PC currently has the largest bronze statue in the world, a Scotsman named Cyrus.

Presbyterian's campus has six buildings on the National Historic Registry including Doyle Hall, Laurens Hall, Jacobs Hall, President's House, Neville Hall, and the Bell Tower located between Neville Hall and Smyth Dormitory.

The PC mascot is a Blue Hose or a Scotsman with blue stockings.

EDUCATION REQUIREMENTS

Arts/fine arts, English (including composition), foreign languages, history, humanities, math, sciences (biological or physical), social science, religion

FINANCIAL INFO

Tuition	$22,484
Room & board	$7,246
Average book expense	$1,110
Required fees	$2,142
Average freshman need-based grant	$22,807
Average freshman need-based loan	$2,554
% of graduates who borrowed	55
Average indebtedness	$21,517

FINANCIAL AID FORMS

Students must submit FAFSA, institution's own financial aid form.

POSTGRAD

% going to graduate school	25
% going to law school	2
% going to business school	3
% going to medical school	4

CAREER SERVICES

Career assessment, internships, on-campus job interviews.

PRESCOTT COLLEGE

220 Grove Avenue, Admissions, Prescott, AZ 86301
www.Prescott.edu • Admissions: 928-350-2100
Fax: 928-776-5242 • E-mail: admissions@prescott.edu • Financial Aid: 928-776-5168

STUDENTS

Religious affiliation
No Affiliation
Academic year
calendar   semester
Undergrad
enrollment   752
% male/female   37/63
% Asian   1
% Black, non-Latino   1
% Latino   6
% Native American   3
% from out of state   67
% freshmen return for
sophomore year   68
% freshmen graduate
within 4 years   23

STUDENT LIFE

% of students living
on campus   0

ADMISSIONS

of applicants   147
% accepted   88
% enrolled   42

HIGH SCHOOL UNITS RECOMMENDED

4 English, 3 math, 2
science, 3 foreign language,
1 social studies, 2 history, 1
arts

VERY IMPORTANT ADMISSION FACTORS

Application essay,
recommendation(s), rigor of
secondary school record

ABOUT PRESCOTT COLLEGE

At Prescott College, faculty and students are very familiar with the adage, "learning by doing." In fact, learning by experience is just as important at the school as reading and discussing. As a student at Prescott College, you will experience a hands-on education; the college prides itself on its student activism. Principally, Prescott College is known for its environmental studies program, but other popular majors include cultural and regional studies: religion and philosophy, sustainability education, peace studies, cultural studies, political economy, Latin American studies, international studies, human development, education, adventure recreation, English, visual arts and psychology. The college is also part of what is known as the Eco League consortium, an alliance with six other colleges with strong environmental studies programs. Students can study for two semesters at any of the following colleges at no additional cost: Antioch College, Alaska Pacific University, Green Mountain College, College of the Atlantic, and Northland College.

Prescott does not have on-campus housing, but because it is the largest supplier of apartment-renters in the area, relations between the college and area landlords are friendly—meaning that a place to call your own is never too hard to find. And this is more than handy, as 95 percent of students are not from the area. The former mining town still has a lot of life in it, and students make the most of it, whether by taking advantage of the school's impressive roster of clubs and organizations, hanging out at the saloons of Whiskey Row, or attending one of the countless events—everything from Shakespeare to bluegrass to cowboy poetry—sponsored by the city every year.

BANG FOR YOUR BUCK

Prescott College offers a few scholarships, some of which are automatically available to incoming freshman who have high scores on their SATs or ACTs. There are also scholarships available to students for their subsequent years of study. Juniors can apply for The Frederick and Frances Sommer Fellowship which assists the academic and artistic endeavors of a senior Arts and Letters student. The institution also has other financial aid options in the forms of low-interest federal loans or loans from private lenders. Currently, 43 percent of students who applied received financial aid, with the average financial aid package totaling $9,839.

Getting In

The admissions administrators at Prescott College are more interested in a prospective student's personal merits than their test scores. While they do look at an applicant's GPA and standardized test scores, admissions are highly based on the applicant's entrance essays, personal recommendations, and the rigor of a secondary school record. Both ACT and SAT scores are accepted and the average GPA of students applying to Prescott College is 2.97.

What do Graduates Do?

With their new PhD program in education, many Prescott College graduates end up as some of the country's finest educators and administrators. Prescott graduates also work in various environmental fields, as the school is widely known for its environmental studies program. A fair number pursue graduate studies in the arts and sciences. The school's career center does an exemplary job of helping current students and alumni connect—simply put, they take care of their own.

The Bottom Line

In 2005–2006, Prescott College reported tuition costs of $18,576. Students could expect another $935 in required fees, $900 for books and supplies, $2,000 to $3,000 for transportation (depending on a student's proximity to campus), and around $2,500 for other expenses. Room and board can get a bit pricey with a cost of approximately $11,000. Recent graduates left Prescott with $18,235 in cumulative debt, on average.

IMPORTANT ADMISSION FACTORS

Academic GPA, character/personal qualities, extracurricular activities, interview, level of applicant's interest, standardized test scores, talent/ability

Average HS GPA	2.97
Range SAT Verbal	540–680
Range SAT Math	490–610
Range ACT	20–28
Minimum TOEFL (paper/computer)	500/173

APPLICATION DEADLINES

Early decision	12/1
Early decision notification	12/15
Regular admission	8/15
Regular notification	rolling
# of transfer applicants	156
% of transfer applicants accepted	85

ACADEMICS

Student/faculty ratio	7:1
% faculty teaching undergraduates	83
% of classes taught by graduate students	0

MOST POPULAR MAJORS

- Elementary education and teaching
- Environmental science
- Parks, recreation, leisure and fitness studies

EDUCATION REQUIREMENTS

English (including composition), math

FINANCIAL INFO

Tuition $18,576
Required fees $935
Average freshman
  need-based grant $4,627
Average freshman
  need-based loan $2,501
% of graduates
  who borrowed   68
Average
  indebtedness $18,235

FINANCIAL AID FORMS

Students must submit
FAFSA.

POSTGRAD

CAREER SERVICES

Career/job search classes,
career assessment,
internships. Off-campus job
opportunities are good.

FUN FACTS

Every semester, Prescott College hosts a series of Brown Bag Lunch lectures. Students are encouraged to bring their own lunch as well as something to share. Food fights are, however, discouraged.

Alligator Juniper, the name of Prescott College's literary journal, was named for a tree in the juniper family whose bark resembles the skin of an alligator. The tree, which is indigenous to both Arizona and New Mexico, has nothing to do with real alligators, so those who have alligator phobias need not fear—the reptiles do not roam the campus.

RAMAPO COLLEGE OF NEW JERSEY

505 Ramapo Valley Road, Mahwah, NJ 07430-1680
www.Ramapo.edu • Admissions: 201-684-7300
Fax: 201-684-7964 • E-mail: admissions@ramapo.edu • Financial Aid: 201-684-7550

STUDENTS

Religious affiliation
No Affiliation
Academic year
calendar   semester
Undergrad
enrollment   4,906
% male/female   40/60
% Asian   5
% Black, non-Latino   6
% Latino   8
% international   3
% from out of state   10
% freshmen return for
sophomore year   88
% freshmen graduate
within 4 years   48

STUDENT LIFE

% of students living
on campus   61
% in fraternities   8
% in sororities   5

ADMISSIONS

of applicants   4,430
% accepted   46
% enrolled   40

HIGH SCHOOL UNITS REQUIRED

4 English, 3 math, 3 science
(3 science lab), 3 foreign
language, 3 social studies, 2
academic electives

VERY IMPORTANT ADMISSION FACTORS

Academic GPA, class rank,
rigor of secondary school
record, standardized test
scores

ABOUT RAMAPO COLLEGE OF NEW JERSEY

Located right on the New York–New Jersey state line in Mahwah, Ramapo College has achieved a level of success in 37 years that some older colleges have yet to grasp. With 192 full-time faculty members and 5,500 students, the educational experience is an intimate one. Disciplines are broken into five colleges: The School of American and International Studies, The Anisfield School of Business, The School of Contemporary Arts, The School of Social Science and Human Services, and The School of Theoretical Science and Applied Science. Its caring and devoted faculty charge themselves with getting the best out of each and every student while stressing the "four pillars" of undergraduate education: international education, interdisciplinary curriculum, experiential learning opportunities, and intercultural understanding. The most popular majors are business administration and management, communications, and psychology.

The Greek system is alive and well, but be forewarned: The college maintains a strict policy on partying. And while the nightlife of Mahwah is not exactly explosive, Ramapo offers over 100 clubs and student organizations, and New York City is less than an hour away. And come autumn, basketball is king. Students claim that they have the best dorms in the country: Rooms come complete with microwaves, refridgerators, cable television and high-speed internet access. The campus's two best-known features are the Birch Mansion and the Havemeyer Arch. The Birch Mansion is a red brick, Queen Anne–style mansion located on a prominent spot in the main quad. Despite rumors of it being haunted, it is used for events and office space. The Havemeyer Arch is also located in the main quad. Its deep red coloring lends itself to the Ramapo College colors, and it is widely known as a gathering and hangout spot for students.

BANG FOR YOUR BUCK

Being a state institution, Ramapo College enjoys the benefits of offering its students a comparatively affordable price. There are three ways in which a student can apply for funding: grants, loans, and work-study programs. In 2005–2006, 64 percent of students who applied for financial aid received funds. The average financial aid packaged offered to students was $9,850. Ramapo also offers a few scholarships that are heavily based on academic merit. The Presidential Scholarship includes full fees, tuition, and room and board. The Ramapo Scholarship provides the student with full tuition and fees. In addition to these scholarships, Ramapo College offers the Dean's Scholarship and Merit Scholarship in the respective amounts of $5,000 and $2,000. Scholarship awards are maintained for an entire four years provided that the student maintains the required GPA.

"Ramapo has a beautiful campus and is not too spread out. A lot of clubs are offered. The faculty is always there to help you."

IMPORTANT ADMISSION FACTORS

Application essay, character/personal qualities, extracurricular activities, recommendation(s), talent/ability

Average HS GPA	3.5
Range SAT Verbal	530–620
Range SAT Math	540–640
Minimum TOEFL (paper/computer)	550/213

APPLICATION DEADLINES

Regular admission	3/1
# of transfer applicants	1,313
% of transfer applicants accepted	73

ACADEMICS

Student/faculty ratio	17:1
% faculty teaching undergraduates	100
% of classes taught by graduate students	0

MOST POPULAR MAJORS

- Business administration/management
- Communications studies/speech communication and rhetoric
- Psychology
- Nursing

GETTING IN

Every year, Ramapo College welcomes around 800 new freshmen. Before this point, administrators scrutinize many transcripts and applications. They consider the difficulty of classes taken in high school, academic GPA—the average for students admitted in 2005–2006 was 3.5—and SAT scores. Several of the programs, such as business administration, international business, information systems, and accounting have specific requirements and can be looked up on the college's website.

WHAT DO GRADUATES DO?

Ramapo College's Cahill Center assists students in making career decisions after they have graduated. The school draws over 50 representitives from professional and graduate schools to recruit students for postgraduate studies. Many graduates go on to work as accountants, business administrators, lawyers, psychologists, or nurses.

THE BOTTOM LINE

The tuition costs for the 2006–2007 academic year were $6,579 for in-state students and $11,890 for out-of-state students. Room and board adds another $9,924 to the total, along with required fees of $2,917, $1,200 for books and supplies, around $2,200 for transportation, and anywhere from $2,250 to $3,000 for miscellaneous expenses. The average graduate leaves Ramapo with $15,937 in cumulative debt.

FUN FACTS

Every spring at Ramapo College brings students the entertaining activities of Greek Week. Many of the students enjoy the annual pickle-eating contest as well as the mattress race.

Ramapo's men's basketball team has some mad skills. In the 2002–2003 season, the team reached the Elite 8. In 2003–2004, they won the ECAC Metro Championship. In 2004–2005, they won their first ever New Jersey Athletic Conference (NJAC) Championship and reached the Sweet 16 in the NCAA Tournament. They are coached by Chuck McBreen and normally wear very attractive warm-up suits.

Of the many clubs and organizations at Ramapo College, the school especially boasts about its Science Fiction and Comic Book Club.

EDUCATION REQUIREMENTS

Computer literacy, English (including composition), foreign languages, history, humanities, math, sciences (biological or physical), social science; a course in Values, Ethics and Aesthetics as well as in Global/Multicultural Disciplines; Senior Seminar—to be taken in appropriate major required for graduation

FINANCIAL INFO

In-state tuition	$6,579
Out-of-state tuition	$11,890
Room & board	$9,924
Average book expense	$1,200
Required fees	$2,917
Average freshman need-based grant	$9,075
Average freshman need-based loan	$2,594
% of graduates who borrowed	37
Average indebtedness	$15,937

FINANCIAL AID FORMS
Students must submit FAFSA.

POSTGRAD

CAREER SERVICES
Alumni network, alumni services, career/job search classes, career assessment, internships, on-campus job interviews.

REED COLLEGE

3203 Southeast Woodstock Boulevard, Portland, OR 97202-8199
web.Reed.edu • Admissions: 800-547-4750
Fax: 503-777-7553 • E-mail: admission@reed.edu • Financial Aid: 800-547-4750

STUDENTS

Religious affiliation
                      No Affiliation
Academic year
  calendar   semester
Undergrad
  enrollment   1,407
% male/female   45/55
% Asian   9
% Black, non-Latino   3
% Latino   6
% Native American   2
% international   8
% from out of state   87
% freshmen return for
sophomore year   90
% freshmen graduate
  within 4 years   75

STUDENT LIFE

% of students living
  on campus   59

ADMISSIONS

of applicants   3,049
% accepted   40
% enrolled   31
# of early decision/action
  applicants   216
% accepted early
  decision/action   60

HIGH SCHOOL UNITS RECOMMENDED

4 English, 3–4 foreign
language, 3–4 math, 3 lab
science, 3–4 history or
social science

VERY IMPORTANT ADMISSION FACTORS

Application essay, rigor of
secondary school record

ABOUT REED COLLEGE

More than 87 percent of students here have flocked to Reed from beyond the state of Oregon. The allure? Let's start with a prized academic experience that focuses on the liberal arts and sciences by catering to independent minds that thrive in an interactive environment. Small classes are filled with bold discussions led by engaging professors (or the students themselves). The typical Reedie can be liberal to a fault, but that works at this forward-thinking school: Undergraduates are encouraged to design their own majors and students do not receive grade reports unless they want to. But don't be fooled: learning is king. Juniors must pass a comprehensive exam in their major and seniors must complete a thesis and defend it before a faculty panel. The small student body is comprised of self-proclaimed geeks who take their academics seriously—and it's evident: The school ranks first among U.S. liberal arts colleges for the percentage of graduates going on to earn doctoral degrees and third among all institutions of higher education.

The progressive methods at Reed don't end in the classroom. Here, you'll find no Greek organizations, no varsity sports, and no campus organizations that aren't student created and student run. Instead of NCAA sports, students get their kicks from campus athletic facilities, student-coordinated teams (rugby, ultimate Frisbee, basketball, soccer, sailing, etc.), and the great outdoors. Hiking and kayaking are big, but so is the local music scene. The Oregon Coast sits an hour to the west, with Mt. Hood an hour to the east (where students can spend the weekend at the school's own ski cabin).

In addition to the fierce academic environment and nontraditional campus life, students find the proximity (only 15 minutes by bus) to downtown Portland—and its rustic natural beauty, artsy coffee shops, independent bookstores, organic cafes, and cultural community events—appealing. Students spend loads of time together too (whenever they're not studying). Most choose to live on or close to campus in small residence halls built for 7 to 30 students.

BANG FOR YOUR BUCK

Approximately one-half of Reed students receive financial assistance. That may not sound like a large figure, but for the 2006–2007 school year, 100 percent of those who applied for need-based financial aid and were determined to have financial need received it. Out of the 680 students who did, all of them found that their need was fully met. Reed's website states that the school "meets 100 percent of demonstrated need for every admitted student who meets all admission and financial aid application deadlines."

To attract students from a wide range of economic backgrounds, Reed's grants are entirely based on need; the school offers no merit-based grants or scholarships. On- and off-campus opportunities to earn a little extra money include regular student employment and federal work-study (FWS) employment. The typical working student takes on 5 to 10 hours each week, earning about $1,000 per year.

Getting In

An ambitious roster of high school courses—including honors and advanced courses—will get you off to a good start. The essay is also given significant consideration. An interview, which can make as strong an impression as class rank, standardized test scores, or recommendations, is recommended. That's because the admissions commitee is looking for excellence of character, self motivation, intellectual curiosity, individual responsibility, and social consciousness. This small school can afford to be choosy: The average high school GPA for 2006–2007 admission was 3.9 (very few who are wait listed will be admitted).

What do Graduates Do?

With such a large percentage of students going on to pursue advanced degrees, graduates often find work in business and as professors/administrators, with smaller fractions becoming doctors, lawyers, and the like. Institutions of higher education are the top employers of Reed grads in the nation. Other popular fields include social services, journalism, and entrepreneurship. Campus career fairs have been held for students looking for jobs with the City of Portland, in sales and management, and in nonprofit management. For those interested in the corporate world, Americorps, Microsoft, Intel, Boeing, and Kaiser Permanente are among current employers. Check out Web.Reed.edu for more info.

Important Admission Factors

Class rank, interview, recommendation(s), standardized test scores

Average HS GPA	3.9
Range SAT Verbal	660–750
Range SAT Math	620–710
Range ACT	28–32
Minimum TOEFL (paper/computer)	600/259

Application Deadlines

Early decision	11/15
Early decision notification	12/15
Regular admission	1/15
Regular notification	4/1
# of transfer applicants	196
% of transfer applicants accepted	41

ACADEMICS

Student/faculty ratio	10:1
% faculty teaching undergraduates	100
% of classes taught by graduate students	0

Most Popular Majors

- Psychology
- Biology/biological sciences
- English language and literature

Education Requirements

Arts/fine arts, English (including composition), foreign languages, humanities, philosophy, sciences (biological or physical), social science

FINANCIAL INFO

Tuition	$34,300
Room & board	$9,000
Average book expense	$950
Required fees	$230
Average freshman need-based grant	$27,387
Average freshman need-based loan	$2,684
% of graduates who borrowed	60.9
Average indebtedness	$17,175

FINANCIAL AID FORMS

Students must submit FAFSA, institution's own financial aid form, CSS/ financial aid profile, noncustodial (divorced/ separated) parent's statement.

Financial aid filing deadline	1/15

POSTGRAD

% going to graduate school	65
% going to law school	6
% going to business school	4
% going to medical school	5

CAREER SERVICES

Alumni network, alumni services, career/job search classes, career assessment, internships, regional alumni, on-campus job interviews. Off-campus job opportunities are good.

THE BOTTOM LINE

In 2006–2007, Reed students were looking at $34,300 for tuition, regardless of whether they lived in or out of state. Fees tacked on another $230, plus room and board which was $9,000. Students spent about $950 on books. Before transportation and other personal expenses, the bill came to $43,530. The school reports that the average net cost for tuition and fees, after aid, is $1,405. The average financial aid package—including grants, loans, and work opportunities—was approximately $29,582. After all is said and done, students currently graduate from Reed with a debt of just over $18,600.

FUN FACTS

Renn Fayre is an annual weekend-long celebration that kicks off with the Thesis Parade, a grand march where graduating seniors deliver their theses to the registrar. Champagne, fireworks, art installations, contests, costumes, and other merry-making are standard fare.

The campus is bisected by Reed Canyon, a 26-acre natural area that holds a wildlife habitat right in the midst of the city.

Reed College ranks in the top three of all U.S. colleges and universities for the percentage of graduates who earn PhDs in all fields. In the life sciences, Reed produces more PhDs than any other institution of higher learning.

RICE UNIVERSITY

MS 17 PO Box 1892, Houston, TX 77251-1892
www.Rice.edu • Admissions: 713-348-7423
Fax: 713-348-5952 • E-mail: • Financial Aid: 713-348-4958

STUDENTS

Religious affiliation
                 No Affiliation
Academic year
   calendar   semester
Undergrad
   enrollment   2,988
% male/female   52/48
% Asian   16
% Black, non-Latino   7
% Latino   12
% Native American   1
% international   3
% from out of state   47
% freshmen return for
sophomore year   96
% freshmen graduate
within 4 years   76

STUDENT LIFE

% of students living
   on campus   69

ADMISSIONS

of applicants   8,776
% accepted   24
% enrolled   34
# of early decision/action
   applicants   596
% accepted early
   decision/action   29

HIGH SCHOOL UNITS REQUIRED

4 English, 3 math, 2 science
(2 science lab), 2 foreign
language, 2 social studies,
3 academic electives

ABOUT RICE UNIVERSITY

At Rice University—the "Ivy of the South"—you will find small classes and an array of varied and challenging academic programs. Refreshingly, however, you won't find the intense and unpleasant academic competition that often accompanies schools of its stature. The 2,900 or so undergraduates are very smart, ultra-talented, and nerdy. Rice students are also go-getters. They spend their undergraduate careers studying relentlessly (four to five hours a day), seeking out internships and great summer jobs, and generally padding their resumes. Rice is most famous for its world-class engineering and science programs; about one-fourth of all the students major in engineering. The formidable School of Architecture is arguably one of the top five undergraduate architecture schools in the nation. And, if you can carry a tune (really, really well), the Shepherd School of Music is one of the nation's most prestigious music programs.

All in all, Rice's tree-lined campus is an oasis of architectural beauty. Inside the tall hedges that separate Rice's campus from the never-ending bustling sprawl of Houston, social life is defined by a unique system of nine residential colleges. If you go to Rice, you will be randomly assigned to one of these colleges, which will serve as your dorm, your dining hall, your coed fraternity/sorority—basically, the root of your social identity for your entire undergraduate career. Virtually all first-year students and more than 70 percent of all undergraduates reside at their associated colleges. Off campus, just beyond the hedges, lies a neat little area full of stores and restaurants called the Village. Houston—the fourth largest city in the United States—offers plenty to see and do. Conveniently, a METRO light rail stop is located across the street from Rice's main entrance, providing access to downtown within ten minutes.

BANG FOR YOUR BUCK

Rice University charges the lowest annual tuition of any highly selective private college or university in the United States—thousands less than Harvard or Duke. There are no excessive fees. Room and board charges are reasonable. In fact, over the years Rice has been known for holding down student tuition and fees, which currently run about 32 percent less than Rice's top private college competition.

Students Say

"Rice's endowment is one of the largest in the world, and they use this to discount tuition for all students."

HIGH SCHOOL UNITS RECOMMENDED

4 English, 4 math, 4 science (3 science lab), 4 foreign language, 2 social studies, 2 academic electives

VERY IMPORTANT ADMISSION FACTORS

Academic GPA, application essay, character/personal qualities, class rank, extracurricular activities, recommendation(s), rigor of secondary school record, standardized test scores, talent/ability

Range SAT Verbal 650–760
Range SAT Math   680–780
Range ACT   30–34
Minimum TOEFL
   (paper/computer) 600/250

APPLICATION DEADLINES

Early decision   11/1
Early decision
   notification   12/15
Regular admission   1/10
Regular notification   4/1
# of transfer applicants 379
% of transfer applicants
   accepted   27

ACADEMICS

Student/faculty ratio   5:1
% faculty teaching
   undergraduates   91
% of classes taught by
   graduate students   8

But wait! There's more! Rice graduates have far and away the lowest debt burden among graduates of highly selective schools in the United States. For the Rice class of 2008, Rice students will graduate with no more than $10,500 in need-based debt. Many students will graduate with no debt at all. And we're not talking only about fabulously wealthy billionaire heirs and heiresses, either. Students of ordinary means can walk away from Rice virtually debt-free. There is an annual limit of $2,625 on need-based borrowing for the class of 2008. Beyond that, admission is need blind and Rice guarantees to meet 100 percent of a student's demonstrated need for four years. For example, a member of the class of 2008 with a demonstrated need of $12,000 would be eligible for a loan of $2,625 and work-study aid of $1,700. The remaining $7,675 would be provided in grants and scholarships. How can this relatively tiny school afford to be so generous? Rice is completely loaded. The endowment-per-student ratio is about $780,000. Among undergraduate universities, only Princeton, Harvard, and Yale can top that.

GETTING IN

The most important thing to remember about applying to Rice is that you must indicate an intended school of study from among the six schools with undergraduate programs: architecture, engineering, humanities, music, natural sciences, or social sciences. You aren't bound by your decision, but your choice is really significant because entrance requirements make some of these schools more difficult to get into than others. For example, it's difficult to get admitted to Rice, but it's really, really difficult to get admitted to the school of music. No matter which school you choose, you need spectacular grades and outstanding standardized test scores (SAT or ACT *and* three SAT Subject Tests scores). You also need a well-rounded extracurricular record and stunning recommendations that will really set you apart. If you want to get into the school of music, you need to arrange an on-campus audition (during the winter or spring). If you want to get into the school of architecture, you need to put together a portfolio of slides or high-quality copies of your very best drawings, paintings, sculptures, photography, etc. Rice strongly recommends an interview with a faculty member in the school of architecture.

What do Graduates Do?

A degree from Rice is a pretty reliable meal ticket, especially in Texas and *especially* in Houston. The Career Services Center facilitates over 1,000 interviews and works with approximately 100 companies on- and off-campus, including Texas Instruments, Hewlett-Packard, and Motorola. Energy-related companies like BP, ChevronTexaco, and ExxonMobil hire oodles of Rice graduates each year. Not interested in getting a real job? That's cool, too. If you graduate from Rice, you can be reasonably certain that a graduate or professional school will accept you. About 70 percent of Rice graduates who apply to graduate and professional schools are accepted by their first choices.

The Bottom Line

A year of tuition, fees, room and board, books, transportation, and various living expenses is about $38,914. Rice's average aid award is a approximately $13,000. Keep in mind that family contributions vary widely. For example, your individual family's yearly contribution can be over $19,000 or as little as $3,000, depending on your financial circumstances. The great thing about Rice is that if you are eligible for need-based aid, the loan you will get with your aid package will average less than $3,000 per year, and you can choose to borrow more money to reduce your family contribution. The school covers all other need-based costs. If you graduate in four years, and you have to borrow the maximum allowable amount, you will have accumulated less than $14,000 in packaged student loans.

Fun Facts

Seventeen magazine's October 2002 issue ranked Rice University as the coolest college in the United States (and, presumably, the world) in its list of the "50 Coolest Colleges." Rice is "near the top in every category," including "academics, great shopping, vibrant campus life," and "cute boys of all stripes."

Beginning in 2004, Rice's president instituted a program for all Rice students called the Passport to Houston. The Passport to Houston is a pass allowing Rice students free access to ride Houston's light rail as well as access to many of the city's cultural and entertainment venues, including free admission to Houston's Fine Arts Museum, Natural Science Museum, and the Houston Zoo.

Most Popular Majors

- Biology/biological sciences
- Economics
- Political science and government

Education Requirements

12 Semester hours are required in each of three areas of study: humanities, social sciences, and natural sciences/engineering.

FINANCIAL INFO

Tuition	$26,500
Room & board	$9,590
Average book expense	$800
Required fees	$474
Average freshman need-based grant	$21,157
Average freshman need-based loan	$1,276
% of graduates who borrowed	28
Average indebtedness	$14,166

Financial Aid Forms

Students must submit FAFSA, CSS/financial aid profile, noncustodial (divorced/separated) parent's statement, business/farm supplement.

POSTGRAD

% going to graduate school	43
% going to law school	6
% going to business school	2
% going to medical school	13

RIPON COLLEGE

300 Seward Street, PO Box 248, Ripon, WI 54971
www.Ripon.edu • Admissions: 920-748-8114
Fax: 920-748-8335 • E-mail: adminfo@ripon.edu • Financial Aid: 920-748-8101

STUDENTS

Religious affiliation
No Affiliation
Academic year
calendar   semester
Undergrad
enrollment   945
% male/female   50/50
% Asian   2
% Black, non-Latino   2
% Latino   2
% Native American   1
% international   1
% from out of state   25
% freshmen return for
sophomore year   84

STUDENT LIFE

% of students living
on campus   81
% in fraternities   27
% in sororities   16

ADMISSIONS

of applicants   976
% accepted   81
% enrolled   33

HIGH SCHOOL UNITS REQUIRED

4 English, 2 math, 2
science, 2 social studies

HIGH SCHOOL UNITS RECOMMENDED

4 math, 4 science, 2 foreign
language, 4 social studies

VERY IMPORTANT ADMISSION FACTORS

Interview, rigor of secondary
school record

ABOUT RIPON COLLEGE

This small, friendly, Midwestern liberal arts school offers academics and the life-at-college experience on a personal level to each of its students. No student is left behind when there are less than a thousand of them, and the community spirit and outgoing nature of those who choose to attend this private school only add to the overall feeling of belonging. One hour a week is now reserved for an all-campus event to promote togetherness. In addition to a hardy Greek scene and popular sports teams to join (as more than 30 percent of students do) or support, the school has a knack for keeping students happy with a full calendar of events. (They're especially big on musical performances, with eight vocal and instrumental groups that perform regularly on campus, in addition to the national acts that are booked.)

Education, business administration, history, and biology are popular majors, but class discussion and an emphasis on good communication will be a big part of the four years here no matter what you study. Involvement in Ripon's classrooms extends to involvement outside of it. The Ripon mindset is that of a doer, someone who throws him- or herself into student government, clubs, Greek life, sports, study abroad, volunteer work, and anything else that comes his or her way. Many Red Hawks have a natural desire to lead and the school's leadership studies program and newly established ethical leadership program help to further hone those skills. Students are known for holding a wide range of interests, which is evident from the fact that about 40 percent of students tackle and complete double or triple majors; others create special majors of their own design. The rural campus doesn't bother this happy clan. The majority of students are from Wisconsin and accustomed to making the most of small-town life.

BANG FOR YOUR BUCK

Between need-based and non-need-based scholarships and grants, Ripon College awards more than $12.5 million to its 945 students. Scholarships range in amount from $2,000 to $15,000. One full-ride scholarship is given each year. Certain scholarships are earmarked for students with demonstrated interest in forensics, art, theater, music, history, community service, and Latin. A legacy scholarship (for those whose father, mother, brother, sister, grandmother, and/or grandfather graduated from Ripon) is also offered. Additionally, the school has an Army ROTC program and offers federal work-study to qualified students.

About 80 percent of Ripon students receive need-based financial aid. In 2005–2006, nearly every student who was determined to have financial need received assistance. The average aid package covered about 94 percent of the student's family's need. Ripon College also offers a separate scholarship program for incoming transfer students who have earned a 3.0 or above.

GETTING IN

Take impressive high school classes (and do well in them), opt to interview as part of the admission process, and you'll be on the road to Ripon. The school's Admissions Committee also smiles upon significant extracurricular involvement and those who are active in community service. Applicants are encouraged to provide any additional information they consider helpful. The vast majority of applicants choose to submit ACT scores (though SATs are also accepted)—incoming freshmen have an average score of 24.

WHAT DO GRADUATES DO?

Ripon grads become teachers, journalists, therapists, scientists, and businesspeople. They are also drawn to careers in health care, exercise, government, music, and communications.

BOTTOM LINE

Students attending in 2005–2006 were met with a tuition bill of $22,162. Required fees rang in at $275, with room and board at $6,060 for the school year. Add an estimated $750 for books, and $1,000 for transportation and other expenses and the Ripon education came to a grand total of $30,247 before any financial aid or scholarships were applied. About 90 percent of families take advantage of loan programs. When the average Ripon grad walks across the stage at graduation, he or she owes about $16,500.

IMPORTANT ADMISSION FACTORS

Character/personal qualities, class rank, extracurricular activities, recommendation(s), standardized test scores

Average HS GPA	3.39
Range SAT Verbal	480–650
Range SAT Math	500–620
Range ACT	21–27
Minimum TOEFL (paper/computer)	550/220

APPLICATION DEADLINES

Regular notification	rolling
# of transfer applicants	58
% of transfer applicants accepted	69

ACADEMICS

Student/faculty ratio	13:1
% faculty teaching undergraduates	100
% of classes taught by graduate students	0

MOST POPULAR MAJORS

- Biology/biological sciences
- Business administration/ management
- History

EDUCATION REQUIREMENTS

Arts/fine arts, English (including composition), foreign languages, humanities, math, sciences (biological or physical), social science, physical education, global studies

FINANCIAL INFO

Tuition	$22,162
Room & board	$6,060
Average book expense	$750
Required fees	$275
Average freshman need-based grant	$14,360
Average freshman need-based loan	$4,156
% of graduates who borrowed	90
Average indebtedness	$16,492

FINANCIAL AID FORMS

Students must submit FAFSA.

POSTGRAD

% going to graduate school	10
% going to law school	1
% going to business school	2
% going to medical school	2

CAREER SERVICES

Career/job search classes, career assessment. Off-campus job opportunities are good.

FUN FACTS

Ripon alumni include Harrison Ford (who did not graduate), Spencer Tracy (class of 1924), and jazz vocalist and Grammy award–winner Al Jarreau. As a student at Ripon, Jarreau was on the basketball team and performed locally with a vocal group called The Indigos. He graduated with a bachelor's degree in psychology in 1962 and has remained connected to the college, serving a term as a trustee, performing the College's "Alma Mater" on stage, and welcoming fellow alumni and friends backstage. He has also performed benefit concerts at the school to raise financial aid monies.

A recent addition to a healthy list of student organizations is Flying Hands, a sign language club.

Toward the beginning of Ripon's roots, students were required to attend two church services each Sunday. The first six presidents of the school had backgrounds in the clergy.

SAMFORD UNIVERSITY

800 Lakeshore Drive, Birmingham, AL 35229
www.Samford.edu • Admissions: 205-726-3673
Fax: 205-726-2171 • E-mail: admiss@samford.edu • Financial Aid: 800-888-7245

STUDENTS

Religious affiliation

	Baptist
Academic year calendar	4-1-4
Undergrad enrollment	2,811
% male/female	35/65
% Asian	1
% Black, non-Latino	6
% Latino	1
% from out of state	54
% freshmen return for sophomore year	84

STUDENT LIFE

% of students living on campus	65
% in fraternities	29
% in sororities	34

ADMISSIONS

# of applicants	1,952
% accepted	88
% enrolled	39

HIGH SCHOOL UNITS REQUIRED

4 English, 3 math, 3 science (2 science lab), 2 social studies, 2 history

HIGH SCHOOL UNITS RECOMMENDED

2 Foreign language

VERY IMPORTANT ADMISSION FACTORS

Application essay, character/personal qualities, recommendation(s), religious affiliation/commitment, rigor of secondary school record, standardized test scores

ABOUT SAMFORD UNIVERSITY

Life at Samford has been described as a calm, quiet, Christian bubble, and while that may be overstating the case a bit, the Southern Baptist faith and values do permeate the campus and student body. Many Samfordians love it—their peers are well-mannered, educated, tactful Southern gentlemen and belles. While a polite and friendly student body certainly has a pretty huge upside, it can come at the cost of diversity. Most students are white, conservative, and Baptist, and it can be hard for people from different backgrounds to fit in.

Still, for those that do fit in, Samford can be a pretty wonderful place to learn. Classes are small and discussion-oriented—teachers go out of their way to get to know each and every student. The academic environment can be challenging, but teachers at Samford want their students to succeed, both in the classroom and beyond—at grad school and in their careers. Pharmacy, nursing, and business programs are among those most consistently praised, in addition to journalism and communication.

When not studying, Samford students take advantage of the growing number and variety of diversions in increasingly cosmopolitan Birmingham, filled as it is with its lovely parks, coffee shops, theaters, and art galleries. Some Samfordians even take advantage of the city's club and bar scene, though most abstain. On campus, events of all types are available in abundance, including concerts, games, performances, and bonfires. The active fraternity and sorority scene is known for its root beer keggers—remember, this is a Baptist university. Not surprisingly, alcohol drinkers must do their imbibing in secret at this conservative campus. The same goes for mingling with the opposite sex after 10:00 P.M.; dorms are all single sex.

BANG FOR YOUR BUCK

Samford works hard to make its unique brand of college experience available to everyone regardless of financial means. It does so by offering a wide variety of supplements to help students meet their financial obligations. This includes institutional scholarships and loans, on-campus job opportunities, federal and state aid in the form of grants and loans, and alternative loans. The loan and need-based gift amounts offered to incoming freshman are quite hefty, averaging $6,948 in loans and a whopping $8,149 in gift aid which comes from institutional funds. Samford reports that 43 percent of its undergraduates receive need-based financial aid.

Students Say

"Samford is a very academic university in a strong Christian community."

IMPORTANT ADMISSION FACTORS

Alumni/ae relation, class rank, extracurricular activities, interview

Average HS GPA   3.62
Range SAT Verbal 500–620
Range SAT Math   510–610
Range ACT   22–28
Minimum TOEFL
  (paper/computer) 550/213

APPLICATION DEADLINES

Regular notification rolling
# of transfer applicants 318
% of transfer applicants
  accepted   68

ACADEMICS

Student/faculty ratio   12:1
% faculty teaching
  undergraduates   72
% of classes taught by
  graduate students   0

MOST POPULAR MAJORS

• Business administration/
  management
• Journalism
• Nursing—registered nurse
  training (RN, ASN, BSN,
  MSN)

EDUCATION REQUIREMENTS

Arts/fine arts, English
(including composition),
foreign languages, history,
humanities, math, sciences
(biological or physical),
social science, religion,
physical education

Additionally, merit-based scholarships and financial assistance are available and awarded for academic achievement, state and district residency, achievement in leadership, religious affiliation, excellence in music, drama, or athletics, and for ROTC participation.

GETTING IN

Samford judges secondary school records to be very important, although recommendations, standardized test scores, and essays receive nearly equal consideration. Class rank is important, but less so. Because of its conservative Christian heritage, the school also deems character and personal qualities to be of top importance, as is a candidate's religious affiliation or commitment. An applicant's state residency and minority status are also considered, as is volunteer work and practical work experience. The average high school GPA of admitted freshman is 3.62. A third of freshmen were in the top 10 percent of their high school classes, while nearly 90 percent of freshmen were in the top half of their high school classes.

WHAT DO GRADUATES DO?

Many Samford grads go on to pursue graduate degrees in a variety of fields. Those that jump straight into careers tend to gravitate towards business, journalism, and nursing. Religion is also a popular course of study at Samford and theological work is, not surprisingly, also frequently pursued.

The Bottom Line

A year's tuition at Samford will cost $16,000 dollars this year. As the school is private, in-staters and out-of-staters will pay the same price. Additionally, students will be paying between $1,175 and $1,545 per semester for housing and between $940 and $1,485 for the school's board plan. Book and supply expenses will add another $1,050 to the total annual cost, bringing it to approximately $22,840 per year. Freshmen receive an average loan of $6,948. On average, the need-based gift they receive is $8,149. After loans and gift aid, students are looking at an average out-of-pocket cost of approximately $7,743. Work-study programs can reduce this number still further.

Fun Facts

Founded in 1841, Samford University is the largest independently supported university in the state of Alabama.

Notable alumni include Bobby Bowden, Hall of Fame college football coach, and Deidre Downs, Miss America 2005.

Samford is the only private school in the Ohio Valley Conference.

FINANCIAL INFO

Tuition	$16,000
Room & board	$5,790
Average book expense	$1,050
Average freshman need-based grant	$8,149
Average freshman need-based loan	$3,169
% of graduates who borrowed	46
Average indebtedness	$17,532

Financial Aid Forms
Students must submit FAFSA.

POSTGRAD

Career Services
Off-campus job opportunities are excellent.

SCRIPPS COLLEGE

1030 Columbia Avenue, Claremont, CA 91711
www.ScrippsCollege.edu • Admissions: 909-621-8149
Fax: 909-607-7508 • E-mail: admission@scrippscollege.edu • Financial Aid: 909-621-8275

STUDENTS

Religious affiliation
                No Affiliation
Academic year
  calendar   semester
Undergrad
  enrollment   859
% male/female   0/100
% Asian   14
% Black, non-Latino   4
% Latino   6
% international   1
% from out of state   58
% freshmen return for
sophomore year   89
% freshmen graduate
  within 4 years   79

STUDENT LIFE

% of students living
  on campus   98

ADMISSIONS

of applicants   1,873
% accepted   45
% enrolled   26
# of early decision/action
  applicants   108
% accepted early
  decision/action   40

HIGH SCHOOL UNITS REQUIRED

4 English, 3 math, 3
science, 3 foreign language,
3 social studies

HIGH SCHOOL UNITS RECOMMENDED

4 English, 4 math, 4
science, 4 foreign language,
4 social studies and history

ABOUT SCRIPPS COLLEGE

A women's college set within a coeducational university environment, Scripps is an excellent choice for women seeking a combined single-sex/coed experience. As one of the Claremont Colleges, Scripps encourages students to take classes at any of the four other schools, which allows many options for courses. Or, they can take all their classes at Scripps, where there are plenty of opportunities for students to voice their opinions and professors are accessible both inside and outside the classroom. It's not uncommon to bump into teachers who are having lunch in Malott Commons. All students must complete a core curriculum that is tough as nails but a good bonding experience for all of the first-years who need to vent about it.

Scripps' campus is quiet, with hotel-like dorms that aren't conducive to loud, messy parties. It hardly matters, since there are four other colleges within spitting distance. Among the five colleges, there are parties six nights a week. Students also like to road trip to Los Angeles, about an hour away. Quicker respites from academia are enjoyed at local movie theaters and shopping centers. Social activism is *de rigueur* among these liberal, artsy, and philosophical women who won't be shy about sharing their opinions with you. The campus might be home to a bold queer population, but other students want you to know that just because they're outspoken doesn't mean they're the only ones at Scripps.

BANG FOR YOUR BUCK

Scripps is committed to assisting students and their families in accessing a premiere private liberal arts education through a financial aid program designed to remove the financial obstacles sometimes associated with a college education. The school's grant and scholarship program are designed to ensure that the young women who are admitted can have access to all that Scripps has to offer, regardless of their economic circumstances. Most awards are need-based, in fact, with the college meeting 100 percent of demonstrated financial aid. The school also ensures that the first $6,000 of demonstrated need each year is met with grants (rather than loans or work-study).

"Scripps is like a college-wide sorority that supports one another in academics and social life while still maintaining a high-level liberal arts education."

Scripps offers two merit-based scholarships. The James E. Scripps Scholarship (approximately 35 each year) is awarded at an amount equal to one-half of tuition and is automatically renewable for each of a student's four years at Scripps. The New Generation Scholarship (one per year) covers tuition, fees, room, board, three round-trip airfares annually, and a $3,000 summer research stipend to be used during the recipient's years at Scripps.

GETTING IN

The Admission Office at Scripps is most interested in an applicant's high school transcript. Admission Officers want to see fine grades in a solid college preparatory program. Evidence of advanced work through Advanced Placement, honors, and International Baccalaureate courses will enhance your application. Other factors include standardized test scores, letters of recommendation, extracurricular record, and evidence of writing skill, all which are carefully evaluated. Just less than half of all applicants are accepted.

WHAT DO GRADUATES DO?

Scripps alumnae pursue diverse career interests. You'll find them working in law firms; financial services companies; state, federal, and local government; NGOs; media and communications; health care systems and scientific research laboratories; educational institutions; and nonprofit/social service organizations. About one-fourth of each graduating class proceeds directly to graduate school.

More than 300 employers recruit on the Claremont campuses each year. Their ranks include Bear Sterns, Boston Consulting Group, Cisco Systems, Deloitte & Touche, the Gallup Organization, Google, JP Morgan, Merrill Lynch, Microsoft, the Peace Corps, the Securities & Exchange Commission, Teach for America, and the U.S. Department of State.

VERY IMPORTANT ADMISSION FACTORS

Academic GPA, alumni/ae relation, application essay, character/personal qualities, class rank, extracurricular activities, first generation, interview, racial/ethnic status, recommendation(s), rigor of secondary school record, standardized test scores

IMPORTANT ADMISSION FACTORS

Geographical residence

Average HS GPA	4.07
Range SAT Verbal	630–730
Range SAT Math	620–700
Range ACT	27–30
Minimum TOEFL (paper/computer)	600/250

APPLICATION DEADLINES

Early decision	11/1
Early decision notification	12/15
Regular admission	1/1
Regular notification	4/1
# of transfer applicants	79
% of transfer applicants accepted	46

ACADEMICS

Student/faculty ratio	11:1
% faculty teaching undergraduates	100
% of classes taught by graduate students	0

MOST POPULAR MAJORS

- Fine/studio arts
- Political science and government
- Psychology

Arts/fine arts, English (including composition), foreign languages, humanities, math, sciences (biological or physical), social science, women's studies, race and ethnic studies

FINANCIAL INFO

Tuition	$33,506
Room & board	$10,100
Average book expense	$800
Required fees	$194
Average freshman need-based grant	$25,927
Average freshman need-based loan	$2,910
% of graduates who borrowed	42
Average indebtedness	$12,071

FINANCIAL AID FORMS

Students must submit FAFSA, CSS/financial aid profile, noncustodial (divorced/separated) parent's statement, business/farm supplement, Verification worksheet, parent andstudent federal tax returns.

POSTGRAD

% going to graduate school	21
% going to law school	20
% going to business school	7
% going to medical school	40

THE BOTTOM LINE

For 2006–2007, the total cost of attending Scripps College was $45,600. A student with a family income of under $40,000 might need to come up with only $2,069 in out-of-pocket expenses; her aid package could cover the remaining $40,731, of which $35,931 will be in the form of grants. A student whose family income is $72,000 may find her out-of-pocket expenses total $13,878; the remaining $29,000 will be covered by aid, with $23,500 awarded in grant form. Even a student whose family earns six figures may receive financial assistance. So if you're planning to attend, it won't hurt to apply for financial aid, no matter what your circumstances.

FUN FACTS

Students can expect to enjoy a number of class-wide traditions throughout their tenure at Scripps. There's the "new student mugging" during orientation week; a candlelight dinner for sophomores; a "mocktail party" and etiquette dinner for juniors; and entry into the Graduates of the Last Decade (GOLD) organization prior to commencement.

At the end of the school year, seniors are encouraged to write their names and a message on Graffiti Wall. The wall has been a tradition at Scripps since the first class graduated in 1931.

The chocolate chip cookies served at Scripps' dining hall are legendary. Students line up at the commons to get them as they come fresh out of the oven. A total of 1,000 cookies (that's more than the total enrollment!) are baked continuously throughout the dinner hour—and they go fast.

SEWANEE—THE UNIVERSITY OF THE SOUTH

735 University Avenue, Sewanee, TN 37383-1000
www.Sewanee.edu • Admissions: 931-598-1238
Fax: 931-538-3248 • E-mail: collegeadmission@sewanee.edu • Financial Aid: 931-598-1312

STUDENTS

Religious affiliation
Episcopal
Academic year
calendar   semester
Undergrad
enrollment   1,402
% male/female   46/54
% Asian   2
% Black, non-Latino   4
% Latino   2
% international   2
% from out of state   79
% freshmen return for
sophomore year   88
% freshmen graduate
within 4 years   79

STUDENT LIFE

% of students living
on campus   94
% in fraternities 70
% in sororities   68

ADMISSIONS

of applicants   2,027
% accepted   67
% enrolled   31
# of early decision/action
applicants   157
% accepted early
decision/action   82

HIGH SCHOOL UNITS REQUIRED

4 English, 3 math, 2 science
(2 science lab), 2 foreign
language, 1 social studies, 1
history

ABOUT SEWANEE—THE UNIVERSITY OF THE SOUTH

Nestled atop the Cumberland Plateau and sprawling over 10,000 gorgeous acres, the University of the South (more commonly known as Sewanee) is a small liberal arts school with a longstanding reputation in the humanities and increasing stature in the sciences. The school's place in the literary universe was cemented in 1983—when the playwright Tennessee Williams bequeathed the rights to his works to the university—but had long been established by the school's role in promoting great writing (primarily through *The Sewanee Review*, America's oldest continuously published literary journal). Students benefit from the eloquent, enthusiastic professors but quickly learn that grade inflation is nonexistent. An "A" at Sewanee is truly hard-earned.

Geographic isolation (civilization is at least 45 minutes away by car) and Southern tradition combine to drive a whopping 68 percent of Sewanee undergrads into the Greek system. Unsurprisingly, alcohol is a popular social lubricant, but students find plenty to do besides study and party. The stately campus—rife with dignified stone buildings and rambling forest—lends itself to all manner of outdoor activities. Students can be found kayaking, rock climbing, caving, hiking, and swimming depending on the season. They frequently organize trips to nearby natural attractions and ski areas. Sewanee undergraduates usually hail from the South and are fairly well-to-do, white, conservative, and Episcopalian. Administration efforts to increase diversity have made some gains over the years, but still no one would confuse this place for a melting pot.

BANG FOR YOUR BUCK

Sewanee offers generous financial aid packages which greatly add to the benefits of attending the school. The school offers both need-based and merit-based scholarships and is currently working to increase the amount of its merit awards.

Current merit awards include the Benedict Scholarship, which covers full tuition, fees, and room and board up to four years. Wilkins Scholars receive half tuition regardless of need and receive more if need dictates. President's Awards range from $3,000–$6,000 annually. The school also offers scholarships directed to specific groups of students: the Regents' Scholars award, which provides half tuition (or more, if need dictates) to students of color; and the Freeman Scholars Award, which similarly rewards students in Asian studies.

HIGH SCHOOL UNITS RECOMMENDED

4 English, 4 math, 4 science (3 science lab), 4 foreign language, 2 social studies, 2 history

VERY IMPORTANT ADMISSION FACTORS

Recommendation(s), rigor of secondary school record

IMPORTANT ADMISSION FACTORS

Application essay, character/personal qualities, extracurricular activities, standardized test scores, volunteer work, work experience

Average HS GPA	3.62
Range SAT Verbal	588–670
Range SAT Math	570–660
Range ACT	25–29
Minimum TOEFL (paper/computer)	550/220

APPLICATION DEADLINES

Early decision	11/15
Early decision notification	12/15
Regular admission	2/1
Regular notification	4/1
# of transfer applicants	42
% of transfer applicants accepted	10

Sewanee offers a full range of financing options to assist families of all incomes in meeting their portion of the costs, including interest-free monthly payment plans and loan deferments during graduate schooling.

GETTING IN

All applicants to Sewanee are assessed by the same standards, regardless of their intended area of study. With such a small incoming class, the Admissions Office can afford to give each application careful scrutiny. Student essays are given especially close attention, as the school considers writing competency essential to success here. Recommendations, high school transcript, test scores, and record of extracurricular activity are also factors in the admissions decision. As at most private schools, alumni relations, minority status, and the ability to add geographical diversity all can impact positively on a candidate's chances.

WHAT DO GRADUATES DO?

The top fields among Sewanee graduates, in descending order, are education, law, religion, medicine, finance, banking, real estate, the environment, and government. Top employers include AmSouth, Bank of America, Credit Suisse First Boston, Merrill Lynch, Morgan Keegan, Morgan Stanley, Smith Barney, SunTrust, Coca-Cola, and Vanderbilt University.

The Bottom Line

For the 2006–2007 academic year, Sewanee charged tuition and fees totaling $28,750. Room and board cost an additional $8,160, bringing the total cost to $38,320 plus books, supplies, and personal expenses. Sewanee does not provide average grant and loan amounts, which it considers misleading. Average loan amounts range from $2,600–$6,100 per year. The school rewards academic excellence by decreasing loan amounts for qualified students after their first year and ensures that loan expectations never increase from one year to the next unless the financial situation of the student and his or her family changes significantly.

Fun Facts

The university's faculty members teach in academic gowns. Honor students, who automatically join the Order of Gownsmen, also wear gowns to class as part of a longstanding Sewanee tradition.

Traditionally, students touch the roof of their cars as they leave campus grounds. It's their way of summoning a "Sewanee Angel" to protect them while they're away. Students release their angels by touching the roof again as they return to campus.

Notable University of the South alumni include country singer/songwriter Radney Foster, *Newsweek* editor John Meacham, soccer great Kyle Rote, former Surgeon General William Crawford Gorgas, and former U.S. Senator Howard Baker.

University of the South is home to the prestigious Sewanee Writers' Conference, funded by a portion of playwright Tennessee Williams' estate. The two-week event convenes top American writers and young authors to discuss and study the craft of creative writing.

ACADEMICS

Student/faculty ratio	11:1
% faculty teaching undergraduates	100
% of classes taught by graduate students	0

Education Requirements

Arts/fine arts, English (including composition), foreign languages, history, humanities, math, philosophy, sciences (biological or physical), social science, physical education

FINANCIAL INFO

Tuition	$28,528
Room & board	$8,160
Average book expense	$600
Required fees	$222
Average freshman need-based grant	$17,663
Average freshman need-based loan	$3,182
% of graduates who borrowed	36
Average indebtedness	$14,926

Financial Aid Forms

Students must submit FAFSA, institution's own financial aid form.

POSTGRAD

% going to graduate school	38
% going to law school	6
% going to business school	4
% going to medical school	4

Career Services

Off-campus job opportunities are fair.

SHORTER COLLEGE

315 Shorter Avenue, Box 1, Rome, GA 30165
www.Shorter.edu • Admissions: 706-233-7319
Fax: 706-233-7224 • E-mail: admissions@shorter.edu • Financial Aid: 706-233-7227

STUDENTS

Religious affiliation
　　　　　Southern Baptist
Academic year
　calendar　　　　semester
Undergrad
　enrollment　　　1,046
% male/female　　50/50
% Asian　　　　　1
% Black, non-Latino　9
% Latino　　　　　2
% international　　4
% from out of state　9
% freshmen return for
sophomore year　　71
% freshmen graduate
　within 4 years　　39

STUDENT LIFE

% of students living
　on campus　　　62
% in fraternities　　7
% in sororities　　32

ADMISSIONS

of applicants　　1,454
% accepted　　　　75
% enrolled　　　　32

HIGH SCHOOL UNITS REQUIRED

4 English, 4 math, 3
science, 2 foreign language,
3 history

VERY IMPORTANT ADMISSION FACTORS

Academic GPA, standardized
test scores

ABOUT SHORTER COLLEGE

Shorter is a small, Southern Baptist school dedicated to bringing up Christian scholars. The small student body is somewhat homogenous—many students are very religious Christians, and most are from the South. They are also heavily involved in academics and extracurriculars at Shorter. It isn't uncommon for an undergrad to take seventeen hours worth of classes and be simultaneously involved in two or three additional sports, activities, or clubs.

At this well-rounded little school Shorter's music program gets excellent grades from students, as do the arts, sciences, and theater programs. The school's size lends itself to an intimate academic environment in which professors have the time and energy to really help students. Shorter's professors are always willing to go the extra mile to make students feel welcome and accepted. Administrators are equally helpful and have a visible presence on campus. Students come to this school for the chance to have fun and get a fantastic education while honoring God. They are challenged mentally and spiritually, but there is a support system of teachers, students, and friends that make overcoming these challenges possible.

Life at Shorter isn't all challenges, though. Students apply their energies to all sorts of groups and sports, in addition to their academics. The school's excellent music program ensures that music is important on campus, whether you are a musician or just someone who likes to listen. Greek life is also important, even though there are only two fraternities and two sororities. Religious groups and student government are another way students choose to get involved. When it comes to off-campus activities, hometown Rome doesn't provide much to do, so students often take weekend trips to Atlanta. This may be in part to escape the on-campus rules that are considered strict and rigid, even for a Baptist institution.

BANG FOR YOUR BUCK

Shorter is a school that works diligently year after year to keep the cost of tuition relatively low. As one sign of this, they have reorganized their financial aid to cover more of students' financial need. The school's Financial Aid Office provides a comprehensive Assistance Program that includes scholarships, grants, loans, and part-time campus employment. You can rest easy when you apply and know that every student enrolled full-time at Shorter College receives some form of financial assistance. An average of 61 percent of a student's need is met through the aid package, but a quarter of aid recipients have their needs met 100 by the school.

While many scholarships that are offered in academics, athletics, and the arts are merit-based, need-based remains the driving force. The school's competitive Scholarship Program provides a limited number of full tuition scholarships and, in very limited cases, full tuition plus room and board scholarships to eligible recipients. There are GPA and SAT/ACT requirements for the competitive Scholarship Program along with essay and interview requirements.

Once enrolled, students will notice that the cost of living in Rome, Georgia, is well below the national average. For college students especially, Rome is an inexpensive place to live and makes for an attractive small city of about 30,000.

Getting In

The Shorter Admissions Committee will first look at your academic GPA, test scores, and class rank when considering your application. Talent and the application essay are also important. Looking at incoming students in 2005–2006, 69 percent had a GPA of 3.0 or higher in high school, and nearly a third of them were in the top tenth of their high school's graduating class. Applicants for the arts programs must submit portfolios (for art) or audition (for music and theater).

What Do Graduates Do?

Graduates who don't continue on to graduate school, tend to enter the fields of accounting, banking, business, education, and health care, or they find positions that are connected to a certain church. Because of the school's small size, they team up with other schools nearby to host multi-institution recruitment fairs, giving their small student body maximum exposure.

IMPORTANT ADMISSION FACTORS

Application essay, class rank, rigor of secondary school record, talent/ability

Average HS GPA	3.26
Range SAT Verbal	460–570
Range SAT Math	460–560
Range ACT	17–23
Minimum TOEFL (paper/computer)	500/173

APPLICATION DEADLINES

Regular notification	rolling
# of transfer applicants	257
% of transfer applicants accepted	76

ACADEMICS

Student/faculty ratio	11:1
% faculty teaching undergraduates	100
% of classes taught by graduate students	0

MOST POPULAR MAJORS

- Biology/biological sciences
- Business/commerce
- Elementary education and teaching
- Business/business administration
- Music/theater/ musical theater

EDUCATION REQUIREMENTS

Arts/fine arts, computer literacy, English (including composition), history, math, sciences (biological or physical), social science, religion

FINANCIAL INFO

Tuition	$14,000
Room & board	$6,600
Average book expense	$1,000
Required fees	$300
Average freshman need-based grant	$9,685
Average freshman need-based loan	$2,470
% of graduates who borrowed	59
Average indebtedness	$16,193

FINANCIAL AID FORMS

Students must submit FAFSA, institution's own financial aid form, state aid form.

POSTGRAD

% going to graduate school	30

CAREER SERVICES

Career/job search classes, career assessment. Off-campus job opportunities are good.

THE BOTTOM LINE

For 2006–2007, annual tuition at Shorter is $14,000. Other expenses included $300 in fees, $6,600 in room and board, around $1,000 for books, plus another $5,400 for travel and personal expenses. Before any aid is applied, a student and his or her family would be facing $27,300 per academic year. All students who were determined to have need were given financial aid as well as aid in the form of scholarships and/or grants. The average financial aid package including scholarships and grant aid that students received was more than $18,000, reducing out-of-pocket expenses to $9,300 even before loans are factored into the equation.

FUN FACTS

Last fall the school fielded their first ever football team. The fledgling team won two of the first four games and is still going strong (as of the time of this publication).

When the school placed a new statue of a very windblown young lady next to their flagpole at the top of the hill that the college occupies, it was immediately clear that students have taken a shine to her. She has since been dressed up by her fans in a variety of ways—from amusing to high-style.

SONOMA STATE UNIVERSITY

1801 East Cotati Avenue, Rohnert Park, CA 94928
www.Sonoma.edu • Admissions: 707-664-2778
Fax: 707-664-2060 • E-mail: admitme.@sonoma.edu • Financial Aid: 707-664-2389

STUDENTS

Religious affiliation
                    No Affiliation
Academic year
  calendar   semester
Undergrad
  enrollment   7,112
% male/female   37/63
% Asian   1
% Black, non-Latino 2
% Latino   11
% Native American   1
% international   0
% from out of state 1
% freshmen return for
sophomore year   79
% freshmen graduate
within 4 years   22

STUDENT LIFE

% of students living
  on campus   34
% in fraternities   6
% in sororities   5

ADMISSIONS

of applicants   9,611
% accepted   74
% enrolled   21

HIGH SCHOOL UNITS REQUIRED

4 English, 3 math, 2
science (1 science lab), 2
foreign language, 1 history,
3 academic electives, 1
visual/performing arts, U.S.
government

VERY IMPORTANT ADMISSION FACTORS

Rigor of secondary school
record, standardized test
scores

ABOUT SONOMA STATE UNIVERSITY

A diverse mix of traditional students, part-timers, and commuters attend midsize Sonoma State University, which bills itself as California's premier public liberal arts and sciences college. Sonoma State offers a broad and challenging education at a bargain rate and accessible professors who are very willing to meet with students outside of class. The integration of technology into every nook and cranny of campus is a very big deal, and classes are pretty small. Business administration and psychology are the most popular majors at Sonoma State; the departments of environmental studies and English, and the Hutchins School of Liberal Studies are also big draws.

Sonoma State is located at the foot of the Sonoma Hills in the heart of Northern California's wine country. If you want to be involved in campus life, there are plenty of opportunities. Intramural sports and outdoor activities such as hiking, are popular; the Pacific Ocean is a short 40-minute drive away. The Greeks provide lots of the campus entertainment. The potential drawback is that—although the administration is working hard to make SSU more residential—34 percent of the students live on campus. On the plus side, campus housing is apartment style, and students have access to swimming pools and spas (upperclass students live in apartments where each bedroom has its own bathroom). Off campus, the surrounding town of Rohnert Park doesn't seem to notice that it is home to a university; however, undergraduates can head to San Francisco, which is about fifty miles to the south.

BANG FOR YOUR BUCK

Sonoma State administers a variety of federal and state financial aid programs; for programs with limited funding, awards are based on a highest-need, first-come, first-served philosophy. If you apply for need-based aid, you'll probably get more of it if you meet Sonoma State's January 31 early applicant deadline for filing the Free Application for Federal Student Aid (FAFSA) form. Nonresidents, who pay an additional $339 per credit, have access to a variety of grant, loan, and work-study programs. Each year, many students from outside of California (and not just the well-to-do ones) are able to afford to attend Sonoma State using a combination of financial aid, scholarships, and family resources.

Students Say

"The faculty is awesome, and it's a good education for less money than a U.C."

IMPORTANT ADMISSION FACTORS

Geographical residence, racial/ethnic status, state residency

Average HS GPA	3.23
Range SAT Verbal	470–570
Range SAT Math	470–570
Range ACT	19–24
Minimum TOEFL (paper/computer)	500/173

APPLICATION DEADLINES

Regular admission	1/31
Regular notification	rolling
# of transfer applicants	1,590
% of transfer applicants accepted	81

ACADEMICS

Student/faculty ratio	22:1
% faculty teaching undergraduates	98
% of classes taught by graduate students	1

MOST POPULAR MAJORS

- Business administration/ management
- Liberal arts and sciences studies and humanities
- Psychology

EDUCATION REQUIREMENTS

Arts/fine arts, English (including composition), history, humanities, math, sciences (biological or physical), social science, U.S. and California government and ethnic studies

Institutionally-funded financial aid is primarily merit-based at Sonoma State. The University Scholarship Program provides more than 250 annual awards ranging from $250–$2,500. Various academic departments and the athletic department also offer merit-based awards. If you've got a 4.0 high school grade point average, you're eligible for the President's Scholarship worth $1,000 annually and renewable for four years as long as you maintain an A or A-minus average.

GETTING IN

To apply to Sonoma State University, you must fill out the application form for the California State University system; electronic applications are preferred (visit Csumentor.edu). First-time freshman applicants must provide either SAT or ACT scores and high school transcripts. Transfer applicants—and there are quite a few of them—must provide complete transcripts for all postsecondary work completed and in progress. If you are a high school student looking to get admitted to Sonoma State, take college-preparatory courses in high school, get decent grades, and do well on the SAT or ACT. You need about a 1000 on the SAT and a B average to be competitive. Transfer students need to have good grades in core college courses (eq., math, composition).

WHAT DO GRADUATES DO?

Sonoma State graduates often get jobs in the fields of banking, business and management, education, health, high tech industries, and insurance. At some point in their lives, a little more than one-fifth of the students eventually obtain graduate degrees.

THE BOTTOM LINE

An academic year of tuition, room and board, and personal expenses costs $22,217. You can, however, expect a significant reduction in that total once you take grants and loans into account, particularly if you are a California resident. The average graduate who has taken out loans at Sonoma State University accumulates $15,030 of student loan debt.

FUN FACTS

The name of the retrieval system for the entire collection at the Jean and Charles Schulz Information Center is the Snoopy Library Catalog. Cartoonist Charles Schulz, creator of the *Peanuts* comic strip and his wife, were huge donors. The library features art deco style alabaster chandeliers and Charlie Brown's Cafe, which serves delicious snacks.

The Sonoma State University Seawolves men's soccer team won the 2005 CCAA league championship and the 2002 Division II NCAA national championship.

On Sonoma State's campus, you'll find a twisted column of metal. Some people call it a sculpture. Others call it "Bacon and Eggs" because it looks like a huge portion of bacon and eggs. A Starbuck's-run food kiosk located next to Bacon and Eggs is aptly named "Toast."

The entire Adlai Stevenson Hall was built around one magnolia tree to preserve the tree, which still stands today, 45 years later.

FINANCIAL INFO

In-state tuition	$0
Out-of-state tuition	$10,170
Room & board	$8,465
Average book expense	$1,314
Required fees	$3,648
Average freshman need-based grant	$6,329
Average freshman need-based loan	$2,574
% of graduates who borrowed	71
Average indebtedness	$5,030

FINANCIAL AID FORMS

Students must submit FAFSA.

POSTGRAD

CAREER SERVICES

Alumni services, career/job search classes, career assessment, internships, on-campus job interviews. Off-campus job opportunities are good.

SOUTHERN ILLINOIS UNIVERSITY— CARBONDALE

MC 4710, Carbondale, IL 62901
www.SIU.edu • Admissions: 618-536-4405
Fax: 618-453-4609 • E-mail: joinsiuc@siu.edu • Financial Aid: 618-453-4334

STUDENTS

Religious affiliation
　　　　　　　　No Affiliation
Academic year
　calendar　　　　semester
Undergrad
　enrollment　　　16,617
% male/female　　57/43
% Asian　　　　　2
% Black, non-Latino　17
% Latino　　　　　4
% Native American　1
% international　　2
% from out of state　14
% freshmen graduate
　within 4 years　　19

STUDENT LIFE

% of students living
　on campus　　　30
% in fraternities　　5
% in sororities　　5

ADMISSIONS

of applicants　　9,285
% accepted　　　　77
% enrolled　　　　34

HIGH SCHOOL UNITS REQUIRED

4 English, 3 math, 3 science
(3 science lab), 3 social
studies, 2 academic
electives

HIGH SCHOOL UNITS RECOMMENDED

2 Foreign language

ABOUT SOUTHERN ILLINOIS UNIVERSITY—CARBONDALE

Southern Illinois University—Carbondale is a large state school but, overall, class sizes are very manageable. Almost half of SIUC's classes have 19 or fewer students. Only 12 percent of classes, in fact, enroll more than 40 students. Also, while teaching assistants teach many classes, you'll also find dedicated, accessible, and very often entertaining instructors across the board. A required 40-hour core curriculum emphasizes Western civilization and the liberal arts and sciences. Once students fulfill their core requirements, they can major in an array of commendable majors. Notable programs include aviation, communication, engineering, and forestry. We especially dig Southern's McNair Scholars Program, which prepares first generation, low-income students and students from traditionally underrepresented groups for graduate school and careers in teaching and research.

SIUC is home to a big segment of students from the Chicagoland area as well as a number of rural students from the Southern Illinois area. There is also a surprisingly large international population and a decent number of nontraditional students. These 16,000-plus undergraduates range from party animals to bookworms. For fun, students often head to "The Strip," a cool area with an eclectic mix of bars, stores, cafes, and restaurants; it is also a good scene for live music. The nearby Shawnee National Forest offers plenty for nature lovers, including hiking, camping, mountain biking, and mountain climbing. A favorite spot among students is called the Spillway; it's the summer place to cliff-jump, jet-ski, and get a tan.

BANG FOR YOUR BUCK

About three-fourths of all students at SIUC receive some form of financial aid, which annually totals $150 million. SIUC also receives federal, state, foundational, corporate, and other grants and contracts to the tune of over $62 million annually. The top-of-the-line scholarship is the Presidential Scholarship, which covers tuition, mandatory fees, and room and board for a total of four years. As you might imagine, selection is competitive. You even have to interview on campus.

"Even though Southern Illinois is a large school, it seems as though every student gets some sort of individual attention, whether it be from a teacher or administration."

To be eligible, you need an ACT score of at least 29 (or a Math and Verbal score of 1300) and a high school grade point average of 3.75. Chancellor's Scholarships pay tuition and fees for up to four years and also require a 29 on the ACT, an on-campus interview, and a ranking in the top 10 percent of your high school class. Dean's Scholarships are worth $3,000 for your first two years at SIUC. Students in the Honors Program are eligible for three scholarship programs, which range in value from $1,000 to full-tuition waivers.

The Illinois legislature has added some nifty incentives for students. Those who begin their undergraduate careers at SIUC and complete their degrees in four years will receive $500 in their last semesters of study. Those same students are eligible for an additional $1,000 toward graduate school at SIUC or $2,000 toward Southern's Schools of Law or Medicine. Not long ago, the Land of Lincoln also passed a law that mandates a guaranteed tuition rate. Under this "Finish in Four" law, the tuition rate you pay during your first undergraduate year will be what you pay for four continuous academic years (unless you change to a major with a different tuition rate).

GETTING IN

A little over two-thirds of the students graduated in the top half of their high school graduating classes. The average ACT score for first-year students is roughly 22. If you have an ACT score of 22, or an SAT Math and Verbal score of at least 980, and you can say that you graduated in the top three-fourths of your high school class, you should be able to gain admission at SIUC without much of a problem.

WHAT DO GRADUATES DO?

With SIUC offering a myriad of academic programs, it's no wonder that alumni are working for leading corporations within a number of fields. SIUC graduates have found employment with such organizations as American Airlines, General Motors Northwest Aviation, Lockheed Martin, Proctor & Gamble, The Walt Disney Company, and the U.S. Department of Agriculture Forest Service.

VERY IMPORTANT ADMISSION FACTORS

Class rank, standardized test scores

IMPORTANT ADMISSION FACTORS

Academic GPA, rigor of secondary school record

Average HS GPA
Range SAT Verbal 450–590
Range SAT Math   460–580
Range ACT   19–24
Minimum TOEFL
  (paper/computer) 520/190

APPLICATION DEADLINES

Regular admission   8/17
Regular notification   rolling
# of transfer
  applicants   5,051
% of transfer applicants
  accepted   84

ACADEMICS

Student/faculty ratio   17:1
% faculty teaching
  undergraduates   80
% of classes taught by
  graduate students   30

MOST POPULAR MAJORS

• Industrial technology/
  technician
• Occupational safety and
health technology/technician
• Trade and industrial teacher
  education

EDUCATION REQUIREMENTS

Arts/fine arts, English
(including composition),
math, sciences (biological
or physical), social science,
human health

FINANCIAL INFO

In-state tuition	$5,310
Out-of-state tuition	$13,276
Room & board	$6,138
Average book expense	$900
Required fees	$1,987
Average freshman need-based grant	$6,609
Average freshman need-based loan	$3,439
% of graduates who borrowed	39
Average indebtedness	$14,708

FINANCIAL AID FORMS

Students must submit FAFSA.

POSTGRAD

% going to graduate school	30

CAREER SERVICES

Alumni network, alumni services, career/job search classes, career assessment, internships, regional alumni, on-campus job interviews.

BOTTOM LINE

The typical cost for a full-time student from the state of Illinois who lives in a residence hall, eats on campus, and pays fees is $16,752. Books and expenses add to that total. The average financial aid package at SIUC is a little over $10,000. Upon graduation, students leave SIUC with an average loan debt of about $14,708.

FUN FACTS

SIUC's team mascot is the Saluki dog, a breed of dog with roots in ancient Egypt. Salukis look like greyhounds except they have longer fur and long, fluffy ears.

Famous alumni who once graced the hallowed halls of SIUC include NYPD Blue actor Dennis Franz, comedian Jim Belushi, basketball legend and sports announcer Walt Frazier, African American astronaut Joan E. Higginbotham, and Major League Baseball's Steve Finley.

An eccentric genius named Buckminster Fuller taught at SIUC for many years. The geodesic dome is one of his many fascinating inventions. A geodesic dome is an almost spherical structure composed of a network of triangular elements lying on the surface of a sphere. It is the only structure made by humans that gets stronger as it increases in size. Several geodesic domes can be found around campus and the city of Carbondale.

SOUTHERN UTAH UNIVERSITY

Southern Utah University, Admissions Office, 351 West University Boulevard, Cedar City, UT 84720
www.SUU.edu • Admissions: 435-586-7740
Fax: 435-865-8223 • E-mail: adminfo@suu.edu • Financial Aid: 435-586-7735

STUDENTS

Religious affiliation
Academic year
  calendar   semester
Undergrad
  enrollment   7,029
% male/female   44/56
% Asian   2
% Black, non-Latino   1
% Latino   3
% Native American   2
% international   1
% from out of state   14
% freshmen return for
sophomore year   60
% freshmen graduate
  within 4 years   18

STUDENT LIFE

% of students living
  on campus   13
% in fraternities   4
% in sororities   3

ADMISSIONS

of applicants   2,483
% accepted   80
% enrolled   54

HIGH SCHOOL UNITS RECOMMENDED

4 English, 3 math, 3 science
(1 science lab), 2 foreign
language, 3 social studies

ABOUT SOUTHERN UTAH UNIVERSITY

Walk around campus at Southern Utah University, and you'll be amazed at how many smiles and hellos you receive. Everyone is very friendly—studious but fun, and with a lot of school pride. If SUU feels like a small town, it's probably because many of the students are from small towns themselves. Hard work and outdoorsman qualities abound in the student body, which is also largely Caucasian, middle class, and Mormon. SUU lures in much diversity with their fantastic School of Performing and Visual Arts. Performances are frequent, as are talks by multicultural and minority groups to help foster tolerance and respect.

One in four SUU students graduates with an education degree, as the school's education department is one of the best in Utah. Students can major in elementary, physical, or special education and choose any of a wealth of related minors. In addition to churning out teachers, SUU's business and criminal justice departments are tops. Small classes and plenty of individual attention from professors are trademarks of SUU. Discussions in class are more common than lectures, and the professors are at SUU to teach, not just to publish.

SUU's location allows unfettered access to the outdoors (including several National Parks), and students are quick to take advantage of the nearby skiing, hiking, mountain biking, ice climbing, and camping. The University also puts on tons of activities from games to dances, and there are a wide variety of clubs to join. While some say that SUU has something for everyone, many of the school's activities do revolve around religion, reflecting the Mormon nature of the school. But hey, if it's alternative fun you are after, Las Vegas is only two-and-a-half hours away.

BANG FOR YOUR BUCK

Southern Utah University is very affordable because of a comparatively low tuition rate for students around the country. SUU encourages students to borrow wisely, so many of them make a concentrated effort to get by without loans. Fortunately, the school is affordable enough that this goal is possible.

More than half of all students receive some sort of financial aid. On average, the school is able to meet 80 percent of a student's demonstrated need. Need-based federal funds are disbursed and need-based scholarships are available. (These are generally awarded on a case-by-case basis at the request of the Student Success Center.) There are also several scholarships awarded to students based on academic merit, talent, or leadership skills. Leadership Scholarships recognize

Very Important Admission Factors

Academic GPA, standardized test scores

Average HS GPA	3.4
Range SAT Verbal	440–560
Range SAT Math	430–560
Range ACT	18–24
Minimum TOEFL (paper/computer)	500/1

Application Deadlines

Regular admission	8/1
# of transfer applicants	1,141
% of transfer applicants accepted	77

ACADEMICS

Student/faculty ratio   23:1

Education Requirements

Arts/fine arts, computer literacy, English (including composition), history, humanities, math, philosophy, sciences (biological or physical), social science

students for the service they contribute to their community and school. As a high school student, the Governor's Honors Academy is a great opportunity to participate in leadership activities and earn funds for education.

SUU also offers a number of scholarships to help single parents start or continue their education and to Sterling Scholar regional winners throughout the area.

In 2005–2006 SUU awarded 1,649 undergraduates with scholarships, which amounted to about 38 percent of the total student body.

Students who live within 100 miles of campus (but in another state) are eligible to participate in the Senate Bill 20 waiver or Good Neighbor waiver. This waiver covers approximately 35 percent of nonresident tuition. The school's participation in the Western Undergraduate Exchange Program allows students in certain majors from most western states to attend while paying approximately 1.5 times resident tuition.

Getting In

Admissions officers give careful attention to your official high school transcript and ACT and/or SAT scores. No essays or letters of recommendation are required, though certain schools within the University have a supplemental set of admission requirements. Those hoping to major in education must complete certain prerequisites after arrival and maintain a 2.85 college GPA. Nursing students also must complete certain prerequisites after arrival. Those who wish to pursue the athletic training major must complete certain prerequisites before admission to the program.

What do Graduates Do?

Founded as a Teacher Training institution in 1897, SUU still places a strong emphasis on producing high-quality teachers to influence the young people in the west. Approximately 25 percent of all graduates enter the teaching profession. Other popular fields for graduates are accounting, biological sciences, computer science and information systems, criminal justice, engineering, finance and banking, graphic arts, communication, and nursing. Accounting firms (e.g., Bradshaw Smith & Co.; Deloitte & Touche; Ernst & Young), CPAs and advisors, and local school districts are among the major employers of Southern Utah grads. An influx of well-known companies also recruits on campus each year, ranging from Utah State Tax Commission, New York Life, and Northwestern Mutual Financial Network to Walgreens, Wal-Mart, Target, and Sherwin-Williams Company to the Utah Division of Parks and Recreation and the Utah Division of Wildlife Resources.

THE BOTTOM LINE

Talk about bargain hunting in the South: Resident undergraduate tuition at SUU is $3,060 a year. Nonresidents pay $10,098 a year in undergraduate tuition. General student fees are $504.50 a year. Room, board, and books add another $5,160 onto the bill, adding up to $8,724.50 for state residents and $15,762.50 for out-of-state residents.

In 2005–2006 (the last year for which figures are available), the average need-based financial aid package awarded was $4,438, with another $2,851 (on average) awarded in need-based scholarships and / or grant aid, for a total of more than $6,000. Students who borrowed for their education and graduated in that year, did so with an average cumulative debt of $11,239.

FUN FACTS

SUU does an excellent job in helping students understand financial responsibilities and how to successfully repay their loans. The national cohort default rate on student loans is 4.5 percent. SUU's default rate is 2.9 percent, down from 3.4 percent last year.

Southern Utah University is host to the Tony Award–winning professional theater company—the Utah Shakespearean Festival—as well as one of the most successful Olympics-style athletic competitions in the nation—the Utah Summer Games.

The school is currently hosting a web log "reality show" where current students comment online daily and then anyone else watching and reading about it can vote for or against them.

Here you'll find a rapidly-growing Outdoor Recreation Program that takes advantage of being situated in the middle of some of the most spectacular national parks, recreation, and wilderness areas in the nation—Zion, Bryce, Lake Powell, Lake Mead, Canyonlands, Arches, Grand Staircase-Escalante, and Cedar Breaks.

A new Bachelor of Science degree in Outdoor Recreation was introduced in Fall 2006.

FINANCIAL INFO

In-state tuition	$3,060
Out-of-state tuition	$10,098
Room & board	$4,124
Average book expense	$1,036
Required fees	$505
Average freshman need-based grant	$2,530
Average freshman need-based loan	$2,966
% of graduates who borrowed	64
Average indebtedness	$11,239

FINANCIAL AID FORMS

Students must submit FAFSA, institution's own financial aid form.

POSTGRAD

CAREER SERVICES

Alumni services, career/job search classes, career assessment, on-campus job interviews. Off-campus job opportunities are good.

SOUTHWESTERN UNIVERSITY

Admissions Office, PO Box 770, Georgetown, TX 78627-0770
www.SouthWestern.edu • Admissions: 512-863-1200
Fax: 512-863-9601 • E-mail: admission@southWestern.edu • Financial Aid: 512-863-1259

STUDENTS

Religious affiliation
                    Methodist
Academic year
  calendar   semester
Undergrad
  enrollment   1,296
% male/female   41/59
% Asian   5
% Black, non-Latino   3
% Latino   14
% Native American   1
% from out of state   7
% freshmen return for
sophomore year   89
% freshmen graduate
  within 4 years   67

STUDENT LIFE

% of students living
  on campus   80
% in fraternities   29
% in sororities   31

ADMISSIONS

of applicants   1,760
% accepted   67
% enrolled   28
# of early decision/action
  applicants   74
% accepted early
  decision/action   78

HIGH SCHOOL UNITS REQUIRED

4 English, 4 math, 3 science
(2 science lab), 2 foreign
language, 2 social studies, 2
history

ABOUT SOUTHWESTERN UNIVERSITY

Southwestern University is a small, private liberal arts college located in sleepy little Georgetown, Texas. Southwestern happens to be the state's oldest university. Most SU students have a few things in common: they hail from Texas, they are politically active, and they are smart. Beyond that, they run the gamut from white Republican Christians to liberal tree-huggers and from preps to jocks to geeks. With so many interests represented here, there is a niche at Southwestern for everyone, a rare trait for a school so small. Students report that it is easy to feel comfortable, no matter who you are.

With fewer than 1,300 students, Southwestern is able to go above and beyond when it comes to personalized attention, both from professors and administrators. Students love how approachable the faculty is—it isn't unheard of for a freshman to be having lunch with the university president! At SU, students find the academic experience challenging but rewarding, regardless of the number of hours spent in the library. And the rewards keep coming after graduation: Grad schools and employers are both aware of the high caliber of graduate that SU produces.

Situated in a small, historical town half an hour from Austin, Southwestern students don't have much to do around town. Even on campus, the nightlife isn't exactly hopping if you aren't in a frat, though the Greeks at Southwestern do throw some mighty good parties on Wednesdays and weekends. The Cove, an on-campus student facility, is a popular gathering place where people can hang out with friends, shoot some pool, and get food. Still, students wish there were more to do on campus, and many tend to head home on the weekends or make the 30-mile drive to Austin when they look for cosmopolitan distractions like concerts, shows, and clubs.

BANG FOR YOUR BUCK

If everything's bigger in Texas, that includes the efforts Southwestern University makes to deliver an academically rich education at an affordable price. A winning combination of scholarships, grants, and fellowships—and a variety of both need-based and non-need-based opportunities—is a blessing for students and their families looking for a strong, liberal arts education in the Lone Star State.

Southwestern offers a college education that is $10,000 to $15,000 lower than what you would expect of a liberal arts college of its academic caliber. Nearly 52 percent of students get need-based financial aid averaging a little more than $17,849 a year, with another 32 percent receiving merit scholarships averaging $7,781 a year. The fact that roughly only half of all students take out a loan to cover the cost of their SU education is telling. For a private university, that number is incredibly low.

GETTING IN

Above all else, admissions officials seek a strong academic record of great grades, tough classes, and solid test scores on the SAT and/or ACT. They specifically note that they will factor the writing component of the new SAT into admission and scholarship evaluations. Your application essay, extracurricular activities, recommendations, and personal interview (not required but highly recommended by the school) are also important. The office is looking for highly motivated students who enjoy an academic challenge and possibly have their sights set on grad school. Roughly half of all entering freshman for the 2005–2006 school year ranked in the top 10 percent of their high school class.

WHAT DO GRADUATES DO?

As communications, social sciences, and business are popular majors, many students gravitate toward related careers. The school's pre-professional programs in athletic training, law, medicine, and theology lead a number of students to pursue graduate work and careers in these fields as well. This liberal arts school places emphasis on intellectual development and intercultural learning, and many students look for careers that incorporate these characteristics.

HIGH SCHOOL UNITS RECOMMENDED

4 English, 4 math, 4 science (2 science lab), 3 foreign language, 2 social studies, 2 history

VERY IMPORTANT ADMISSION FACTORS

Academic GPA, application essay, class rank, recommendation(s), rigor of secondary school record, standardized test scores

IMPORTANT ADMISSION FACTORS

Alumni/ae relation, character/personal qualities, extracurricular activities, first generation, geographical residence, interview, level of applicant's interest, talent/ability

Range SAT Verbal 560–670
Range SAT Math 570–660
Range ACT 24–29
Minimum TOEFL
(paper/computer) 570/230

APPLICATION DEADLINES
Early decision 11/1
Early decision
notification 12/1
Regular admission 2/15
Regular notification 4/1
# of transfer applicants 111
% of transfer applicants
accepted 59

ACADEMICS

Student/faculty ratio   10:1
% faculty teaching
   undergraduates   100
% of classes taught by
   graduate students   0

MOST POPULAR MAJORS

- Business administration/
   management
- Communications studies/
   speech communication and
   rhetoric
- Psychology

EDUCATION REQUIREMENTS

Arts/fine arts, computer
literacy, English (including
composition), foreign
languages, humanities,
math, sciences (biological
or physical), social science

FINANCIAL INFO

Tuition $23,650
Room & board $7,815
Average book
   expense $1,000
Average freshman
   need-based grant $16,275
Average freshman
   need-based loan $2,760
% of graduates
   who borrowed   52
Average
   indebtedness $18,446

FINANCIAL AID FORMS

Students must submit
FAFSA.
Financial aid
   filing deadline   3/1

POSTGRAD

% going to
   graduate school   26
% going to
   law school   6
% going to
   medical school   5

CAREER SERVICES

Off-campus job opportuni-
ties are good.

BOTTOM LINE

Earnings from endowment at Southwestern are put towards the cost of student tuition. This means that students will be charged only about half the cost of their annual tuition—the rest is picked up by this "hidden scholarship" automatically, without so much as a financial aid application! For 2007–2007, tuition and fees for Southwestern will total $23,650. Room and board will add another $6,700 to $8,628 to the total bill. Half of SU's students get need-based aid averaging $17,849, while another third of students receive merit scholarships averaging $7,781. When you add this aid up and take into consideration the $45,000 price tag at similar private universities, you can see why Southwestern is such a bargain.

FUN FACTS

Southwestern's large, research-quality reflecting telescope at the school's Fountainwood Observatory was donated to the Physics Department by a local engineer and builder who was also an amateur astronomer. Periodic viewing nights are free and open to the public.

Southwestern University has been sending its old computers to Honduras for the past five years through a donation program it calls "Hardware for Honduras." In all, it has sent more than 120 computers to the Central American country to help adults in rural families learn skills to support their families and children broaden their skills and their horizons through the Internet.

Getting around this campus is a breeze: Just hop on one of the university's bright yellow bikes that are scattered around campus. Students, faculty, and staff may ride them within University property, and then park them to leave a ride for the next person.

ST. ANDREWS PRESBYTERIAN COLLEGE

1700 Dogwood Mile, Laurinburg, NC 28352
www.SAPC.edu • Admissions: 910-277-5555
Fax: 910-277-5087 • E-mail: admissions@sapc.edu • Financial Aid: 910-277-5560

STUDENTS

Religious affiliation
                        Presbyterian
Academic year
  calendar   semester
Undergrad
  enrollment   775
% male/female   38/62
% Black, non-Latino   9
% Latino   2
% Native American   1
% international   4
% from out of state 51
% freshmen return for
sophomore year   67
% freshmen graduate
  within 4 years   37

STUDENT LIFE

% of students living
  on campus   85

ADMISSIONS

of applicants   859
% accepted   76
% enrolled   29

HIGH SCHOOL UNITS RECOMMENDED

4 English, 3 math, 3
science, 2 foreign language,
2 social studies, 2 academic
electives

IMPORTANT ADMISSION FACTORS

Academic GPA, class rank,
extracurricular activities,
standardized test scores

ABOUT ST. ANDREWS PRESBYTERIAN COLLEGE

Diversity isn't just a buzz word for the brochures at this small, private school located a short distance from where the Carolinas meet. The school's interesting mix of strengths—including top-notch facilities for equine studies, a popular business administration program, some serious Division II sports teams, and an amazingly handicapped-accessible campus—make for an equally interesting mix of students. Students who choose St. Andrews for various reasons blend together well, and professors willing to lend an ear and help their students add to the feel of a community of individuals who are all on the same page.

St. Andrews boasts a spacious, scenic lakeside campus where professors might spontaneously decide to hold class outside under a blooming dogwood tree. The campus was constructed with wide doorways and hallways, ramps, elevators, and special restroom modifications to be handicapped accessible, and the list of services also extends to those with learning disabilities. The schools offers three semester-abroad programs and is home to the nation's first undergraduate press, the St. Andrews Press. An undergraduate magazine and award-winning literary journal carry on the publishing tradition. Favorite majors are education, English, and—topping the list—business administration, which is offered with many areas of concentration. A nationally recognized riding program welcomes riders at every level. Those looking for a related career might be interested in choosing a path in equine business management, therapeutic horsemanship, and pre-veterinary studies. In addition to riding horses, athletes gravitate toward the many competitive sports opportunities. Life in a small, rural town can have its drawbacks, but entertainment and activities fill the campus events calendar.

Another unusual distinction of St. Andrews? The big, bold sound that comes from one of the top competing pipe bands in the southern United States, whose members proudly wear the Earl of St. Andrews tartan.

Average HS GPA   3.0
Range SAT Verbal 590–576
Range SAT Math   460–460
Minimum TOEFL
  (paper/computer) 550/280

APPLICATION DEADLINES

Regular notification rolling
# of transfer applicants 187
% of transfer applicants
  accepted   72

ACADEMICS

Student/faculty ratio   14:1
% faculty teaching
  undergraduates   100
% of classes taught by
  graduate students   0

MOST POPULAR MAJORS

• Business administration/
  management
• Elementary education and
  teaching
• English language and
  literature

EDUCATION REQUIREMENTS

Arts/fine arts, computer
literacy, English (including
composition), foreign
languages, history,
humanities, math, sciences
(biological or physical),
social science

BANG FOR YOUR BUCK

St. Andrews is like your favorite grandmother in that it is a skilled and generous giver with always enough coin to go around. The school has sizeable monies set aside for both need-based and non-need-based awards. At a school with fewer than 800 students, 618 of them received financial aid in 2004–2005. On average, the school met more than 70 percent of these students' need through financial aid packages that averaged around $12,000 and need-based scholarships that averaged around $9,650.

If you graduate in the top 35 percent of your high school class and choose to attend St. Andrews, you will earn a merit-based scholarship worth one-quarter to one-half the cost of your tuition. Awards are renewable for all four years as long as you're making satisfactory academic progress. Scholarships are also available for musically talented students who show leadership potential and who participate in the College Choir or Bagpipe Band. Finally, St. Andrews offers scholarships for 18 athletic teams in NCAA Division II competition and for those who are accepted into the honors program.

GETTING IN

Class rank, GPA, standardized test scores, and extracurriculars (especially when they demonstrate leadership, volunteerism, and a commitment to service) help admissions officers begin the evaluation process but are not definitive factors. Southwestern takes pride in individual assessment, admitting more than three-quarters of all applicants. The average high school GPA of entering freshmen is a 3.0. Those with a nervous disposition will find relief in the rolling admissions process: St. Andrews notifies applicants of their decision within two weeks of receiving all application components.

WHAT DO GRADUATES DO?

St. Andrews grads often become teachers, professors, administrators, or take jobs in other areas of education (such as special education). Many also obtain their goal of landing careers that involve work with horses, at nonprofits, or in various sectors of business. Some choose the grad school route to pursue veterinary medicine.

BOTTOM LINE

In 2005–2006, students at St. Andrews paid $17,162 in tuition and $7,540 in room and board. The school estimates that the average student spent another $1,000 on books, $2,000 on transportation expenses (commuters spent only about $1,000), and $1,798 in other expenses. Thus, total expenses came to about $29,500 for on-campus residents and $28,500 for students commuting from home before loans, financial aid, and scholarships are applied.

FUN FACTS

St. Andrews' Asian Studies Program offers an immersion in selected cultures, languages, history, literature, politics, and economics of Asia and is one of only a few programs like this in the Southeast U.S. Professors have not only researched and written about Asia, but have also lived, taught, and studied there, and also traveled there often, usually with groups of students.

St. Andrews was one of the first colleges in the country to design a campus with wheelchair access in mind. The school's driver Evaluation/Training program was designed to serve people with disabilities who have the physiological potential to master the operation of a motor vehicle with the support of specialized instruction and adapted vehicles.

FINANCIAL INFO

Tuition	$17,162
Average book expense	$1,000
Average freshman need-based grant	$9,601
Average freshman need-based loan	$2,259
% of graduates who borrowed	70
Average indebtedness	$12,325

FINANCIAL AID FORMS
Students must submit FAFSA, state aid form.

POSTGRAD

% going to graduate school	40

ST. MARY'S COLLEGE OF MARYLAND

Admissions Office, 18952 East Fisher Road, St Mary's City, MD 20686-3001
www.SMCM.edu • Admissions: 240-895-5000
Fax: 240-895-5001 • E-mail: admissions@smcm.edu • Financial Aid: 240-895-3000

STUDENTS

Religious affiliation
No Affiliation

Academic year
calendar   semester
Undergrad
enrollment   1,879
% male/female   43/57
% Asian   4
% Black, non-Latino   9
% Latino   5
% international   1
% from out of state   17
% freshmen return for
sophomore year   87
% freshmen graduate
within 4 years   70

STUDENT LIFE

% of students living
on campus   80

ADMISSIONS

of applicants   2,255
% accepted   56
% enrolled   34
# of early decision/action
applicants   169
% accepted early
decision/action   54

HIGH SCHOOL UNITS
REQUIRED

4 English, 3 math, 3
science (2 science lab), 3
social studies, 7 academic
electives

ABOUT ST. MARY'S COLLEGE OF MARYLAND

Founded in 1840, St. Mary's College of Maryland is one of the country's few (and Maryland's only) public honors colleges. Though it is a public school, it is not part of the University of Maryland system—St. Mary's chose to opt out of the system in 1992. As an honors college, St. Mary's offers its small student body (around 2,000 students) the rigorous, personalized education of a private school at a bargain price. In fact, its public school prices are so low for the quality of education it offers that it is routinely recognized as one of the best values in education. With such a small student body and correspondingly small classes, students often get to know their professors on a first-name basis, exchanging home phone numbers and e-mail addresses. Though the college is currently experiencing some growing pains because of increased enrollment, it has taken steps to correct this temporary problem. Even so, students regard their education as challenging and stimulating.

Students at SMCM are an open, down-to-earth bunch. Though they have a tendency to be liberal, they embrace people with all sorts of beliefs and from all sorts of backgrounds. Closed-mindedness is one of the few things that isn't tolerated on campus. That said, the student body is predominantly white and wealthy—if anything, students at SMCM would like to see more diversity.

Overall, life at St. Mary's is pretty balanced. The campus, located on the St. Mary's River in the Chesapeake Bay Region, is quite lovely, with much to do to keep its students busy. Political activism, environmentalism, athletics (both intramural and varsity), and all sorts of outdoor activities and water sports provide entertainment. Though historic St. Mary's City adjoins the campus, there isn't much to do in town. For a more urban experience, students need to make the two-hour drive to Washington, DC.

"The school is located on a beautiful campus, on the corner of two rivers. Many students enjoy using local nature for fun, sailing, walking in the woods, exploration. The first capital of Maryland is also located near campus and many students enjoy the feeling of history."

BANG FOR YOUR BUCK

Proud to offer a private-school-caliber academic experience at a public school, St. Mary's is also proud of their reasonable, public-school price tag. According to the school's website, "Of the students in the entering class of 2006, 84 percent received some form of financial aid (100 percent of those who filed the FAFSA) and 64 percent received a grant and/or scholarship from St. Mary's." A tuition payment plan can help families manage the costs of a college education.

All applicants are considered for scholarships on an individual basis by the scholarship review committee—no need to fill out a separate application to be considered. Students with outstanding academic achievements and standardized test scores, an engaging essay, shining recommendations, and steady involvement in co-curricular activities may receive a merit scholarship without regard to financial need. (The scholarships cannot, however, exceed the value of in-state tuition.)

GETTING IN

This school seeks high achievers who take active responsibility for their education. The essay is considered a very important part of the application, along with the requisite standardized test scores and an impressive academic record in high school. Recommendations, extracurricular involvement, and talent are also given weight by admissions officials. It helps to be able to demonstrate a love for self-motivated learning, as many students design their own majors and plan to pursue an advanced degree after St. Mary's.

WHAT DO GRADUATES DO?

St. Mary's College does its part to prepare the more than 50 percent of St. Mary's grads who attend graduate or professional school at places like Cambridge, MIT, Stanford, Georgetown, Johns Hopkins, and Yale. (Not surprising when you look at their mentors: 98 percent of St. Mary's professors hold the highest degree in their field.) The lauded premed, pre-law, and other pre-professional programs prep students to apply and get in. The Health Sciences Advisory Committee advises students considering careers in medicine, dentistry, veterinary medicine, osteopathy, optometry, podiatry, or other health sciences, while the Pre-Law Advisory Network helps students plan for law school. Politics, teaching, business, and science are other popular career paths.

HIGH SCHOOL UNITS RECOMMENDED

4 English, 4 math, 4 science (3 science lab), 4 foreign language, 3 social studies, 3 history

VERY IMPORTANT ADMISSION FACTORS

Academic GPA, application essay, rigor of secondary school record, standardized test scores

IMPORTANT ADMISSION FACTORS

Extracurricular activities, recommendation(s), talent/ability

Average HS GPA   3.50
Range SAT Verbal 570–680
Range SAT Math   560–660
Minimum TOEFL
  (paper/computer) 550/260

APPLICATION DEADLINES

Early decision   12/1
Early decision
  notification   12/31
Regular admission   1/15
Regular notification   4/1
# of transfer applicants 224
% of transfer applicants
  accepted   53

ACADEMICS

Student/faculty ratio   12:1
% faculty teaching
  undergraduates   100
% of classes taught by
  graduate students   0

- Economics
- Political science and government
- Psychology

EDUCATION REQUIREMENTS

Arts/fine arts, English (including composition), foreign languages, history, humanities, math, philosophy, sciences (biological or physical), social science

FINANCIAL INFO

In-state tuition	$9,498
Out-of-state tuition	$19,340
Room & board	$8,505
Average book expense	$1,000
Required fees	$1,920
Average freshman need-based grant	$3,500
Average freshman need-based loan	$2,625
% of graduates who borrowed	69
Average indebtedness	$17,125

FINANCIAL AID FORMS

Students must submit FAFSA.

Financial aid filing deadline	3/1

POSTGRAD

% going to graduate school	32
% going to law school	3
% going to business school	1
% going to medical school	1

CAREER SERVICES

Alumni network, alumni services, career/job search classes, career assessment, internships, on-campus job interviews. Off-campus job opportunities are good.

BOTTOM LINE

The comprehensive cost of attending St. Mary's includes the direct expenses of tuition and fees ($11,418 for a Maryland resident; $21,260 for nonresidents), room ($4,820), and board ($3,685); as well as indirect expenses for books, supplies, personal needs, and travel. Direct costs for the 2006–2007 school year come in at $19,923 for Maryland residents, while nonresidents paid $29,765. The average freshman loan is about $2,625, and the average freshman need-based gift is $3,000. This means a state resident is looking at an average aid of $5,625. When federal and state loans, merit scholarships, and general loans are added into the mix, this amount can grow substantially.

FUN FACTS

In 1840, the school was founded as St. Mary's Female Seminary. Men were welcomed on campus by 1965, and despite the school's current name, "Maryland's public honors college" no longer has a religious affiliation.

The school has a unique waterfront campus along the St. Mary's River in Southern Maryland where students enjoy sailing and kayaking.

Come prepared to partake in tradition. Students take a dip in the pond on their birthday, bid on humorous items and experiences during the Christmas in April annual fundraising event, and gather around a bonfire before camping out on the lawn (or in a cardboard box when it rains) during Hunger and Homelessness Awareness Week. They are also served a third-world ration serving for dinner one evening.

ST. OLAF COLLEGE

1520 St. Olaf Avenue, Northfield, MN 55057
www.StOlaf.edu • Admissions: 507-646-3025
Fax: 507-646-3832 • E-mail: admissions@stolaf.edu • Financial Aid: 507-646-3019

STUDENTS

Religious affiliation
Lutheran

Academic year
calendar 4-1-4
Undergrad
enrollment 3,041
% male/female 44/56
% Asian 5
% Black, non-Latino 1
% international 1
% from out of state 42
% freshmen return for
sophomore year 93
% freshmen graduate
within 4 years 84

STUDENT LIFE

% of students living
on campus 96

ADMISSIONS

of applicants 3,529
% accepted 65
% enrolled 35
# of early decision/action
applicants 112/2,034
% accepted early
decision/action 84/30

HIGH SCHOOL UNITS REQUIRED

4 English, 2 math, 2 science
(1 science lab), 2 foreign
language, 1 social studies, 1
history, 2 academic electives

HIGH SCHOOL UNITS RECOMMENDED

4 English, 4 math, 4 science
(2 science lab), 4 foreign
language, 2 social studies, 2
history, 4 academic electives

ABOUT ST. OLAF COLLEGE

Life on the hilltop that is St. Olaf—where a toasty scent wafts up from the nearby Malt-O-Meal factory—is as cozy as it sounds. At this small private school in Minnesota, students—many of whom are musically talented, athletically inclined, and/or looking to make a difference—enjoy each other, a life centered around the campus, and resplendent expanses of limestone buildings, woods, wetlands, an open prairie, and a bluebird trail maintained by students.

Socially conscious, keenly political, and with an active concern for the greater good, Oles are willing to work hard to achieve results that tie into their beliefs. A student-run organic garden grows socially responsible produce to supply the school's food services department. Oles are the studious sort (many have sights set on grad school and premed programs) but, after class, are nearly as involved in sports as they are with music, dance, theater, and visual arts. Before they graduate, a typical student may have completed countless hours of volunteer work, played at least one sport, joined an organization, played in a music group, and contributed to the betterment of the school somehow. In the classroom, most popular majors include English, psychology, biology, economics, mathematics, chemistry, and physics. Study abroad experiences are wildly popular; more than 800 students a year hop on a plane to study internationally. If they don't do so during a semester or over the summer, a January interim allows time for the intellectually curious to enrich themselves either domestically or abroad in an off-campus study program.

Though the school is affiliated with the Evangelical Lutheran Church—and students appreciate its faith-based approach—more than 30 religious denominations are represented by the 3,000 students. Adding to the pervasive unified feel here, more than 95 percent of students call one of the college's 11 residence halls, 10 service and honor houses, 6 academic language houses, or 1 diversity house home.

"There are really no social classes here other than grade level. We're a closely-knit community. There's always something going on, and mostly people don't think about it, because someone will always invite them."

VERY IMPORTANT ADMISSION FACTORS

Academic GPA, application essay, rigor of secondary school record

IMPORTANT ADMISSION FACTORS

Character/personal qualities, extracurricular activities, recommendation(s), standardized test scores, talent/ability

Average HS GPA   3.67
Range SAT Verbal 580–700
Range SAT Math   590–700
Range ACT   25–30
Minimum TOEFL
   (paper/computer) 550/213

APPLICATION DEADLINES

Early decision   11/1
Early decision
   notification   12/1
Regular
   notification   2/15 rolling
# of transfer applicants 169
% of transfer applicants
   accepted   18

ACADEMICS

Student/faculty ratio   13:1
% faculty teaching
   undergraduates   100
% of classes taught by
   graduate students   0

MOST POPULAR MAJORS

• Biology/biological sciences
   • English language and
      literature
      • Psychology
      • Mathematics

BANG FOR YOUR BUCK

To make the school financially attractive and affordable, St. Olaf offers need-based aid, merit-based aid, and financing/payment plans to students and their families. As reported on the school's website: "83 percent of all first-year students who applied for need-based aid received assistance. The average award was $19,071. One hundred percent of applicants with family incomes below $72,000 received financial aid if they applied. For those recipients, the average financial aid package was $24,739." For 2005–2006, all 2,352 students who were determined to have financial need had their need fully met. Few schools can boast that kind of assistance.

Need-based grants can range up to as much as $22,000 per year. These funds are awarded to students whose need is not otherwise reasonably met with government grants, student loans, student work, and St. Olaf scholarships. Merit-based scholarships reward students who had stellar high school grades and served as leaders to their church or community.

GETTING IN

The difficulty of your high school classes (AP and honors classes will boost your desirability) and the grades you received are of top importance. Admissions officers prefer to see lower grades in tougher classes than very high grades in easier classes. Leadership positions and dedication to sports, community service, or music and the arts are also a plus. Because musical studies are a big draw, those applying for admission to the St. Olaf Academic (or for music scholarships) must apply early decision or early action.

WHAT DO GRADUATES DO?

For a school so fueled by musical performance and the thrill of team competition, St. Olaf produces relatively few celeb-level musicians or professional athletes. Instead, may grads look toward careers that serve—whether in international service, teaching, ministry, nonprofits, civic leaders, or through music and the arts. Many students arrive already focused on getting into grad, law, business or med school after they graduate.

BOTTOM LINE

Because the school makes such a concerted effort to aid students who have financial need, the numbers should not scare those who will be able to demonstrate that they need assistance. For 2005–2006, St. Olaf tuition was $28,200, with room and board costing another $7,400. Add an estimated $900 for books and $800 for other expenses and the experience cost each student about $37,300.

FUN FACTS

St. Olaf College was founded in 1874 by a group of Norwegian-American immigrant pastors and farmers.

Of the many musical performance opportunities on campus, one of the newer and more exotic ensembles is the St. Olaf Taiko Club. Taiko drumming is characterized by traditional, high-energy Japanese rhythms that one member has described as "more of a martial art than a musical ensemble." Rehearsals for this physical, full-body art form begin with jumping jacks, arm strengthening exercises, and drills to instill proper technique.

The St. Olaf women's hockey team advanced to the MIAC playoff tournament the past two years having only been an intercollegiate team since 2000.

EDUCATION REQUIREMENTS

Arts/fine arts, English (including composition), foreign languages, history, humanities, math, philosophy, sciences (biological or physical), social science, religion, physical activity

FINANCIAL INFO

Tuition	$28,200
Room & board	$7,400
Average book expense	$900
Average freshman need-based grant	$16,844
Average freshman need-based loan	$3,820
% of graduates who borrowed	62
Average indebtedness	$23,993

FINANCIAL AID FORMS

Students must submit FAFSA, CSS/financial aid profile, St. Olaf non-custodial parent statement. Financial aid filing deadline 2/1

POSTGRAD

% going to graduate school	26
% going to law school	3
% going to business school	2
% going to medical school	5

CAREER SERVICES

Alumni network, alumni services, career/job search classes, career assessment, internships, regional alumni, on-campus job interviews. Off-campus job opportunities are fair.

STANFORD UNIVERSITY

Undergraduate Admission, Monteg Hall, 355 Galvez Street, Stanford, CA 94305
www.Stanford.edu • Admissions: 650-723-2091
Fax: 650-725-2846 • E-mail: admission@stanford.edu • Financial Aid: 650-723-3058

STUDENTS

Religious affiliation
No Affiliation
Academic year
calendar   quarter
Undergrad
enrollment   6,391
% male/female   52/48
% Asian   24
% Black, non-Latino   10
% Latino   11
% Native American   2
% international   6
% from out of state   56
% freshmen return for
sophomore year   98

STUDENT LIFE

% of students living
on campus   90

ADMISSIONS

of applicants   22,333
% accepted   11
% enrolled   67

HIGH SCHOOL UNITS RECOMMENDED

4 English, 4 math, 3 lab
science, 3 foreign language,
2 social studies, 1 history

VERY IMPORTANT ADMISSION FACTORS

Academic GPA, application
essay, character/personal
qualities, class rank, recommendations, rigor of
secondary school record,
standardized test scores

IMPORTANT ADMISSION FACTORS

Extracurricular activities,
talent/ability

ABOUT STANFORD UNIVERSITY

Situated right next to Palo Alto, California on the world's second largest university campus (8,180 acres), Stanford University is a private university established in 1891 by Leland Stanford, governor of California and railroad tycoon, and his wife, Jane. Over the last 115 years, Stanford has developed into one of the world's elite educational institutions, considered by many to be the West Coast's answer to the Ivy League. Academics are simply top notch; despite the fact that this is a research-driven university, professors are seriously interested in getting to know their undergrads. That's not to say that there is a lot of hand-holding going on. Teachers are among the top minds in their respective fields, as are the visiting lecturers and speakers. Despite the rigor of Stanford academics, students are laid back and happy, something they feel distinguishes them from their peers back east.

While it may be the California weather, the "work hard, play hard" attitude may be a factor too. Weekends mean parties all over campus, trips to the local bars, great sports events, or even a trip into San Francisco, just 37 miles away. The perfect weather and setting also lend themselves to all sorts of outdoor activities, everything from hiking, biking, and surfing to sunbathing. Stanford students are fit and athletic. They pack the bleachers at the games for their sports teams, many of which have perennial national rankings. If sports aren't your thing, there is an astounding number of clubs and organizations to join—more clubs than there are students to fill them.

Never mind how busy they are: Stanford students are able to maintain a laid-back exterior. Despite their myriad talents, their drive, and their long list of achievements, you won't find students bragging or competing with each other. Simply put, they know they have it all: serious academics and athletics, and a calm California vibe.

BANG FOR YOUR BUCK

There are exciting changes in store for future Stanford applicants. Beginning in academic year 2006–2007, parents of undergraduate financial aid applicants whose total annual income is less than $45,000 will not be expected to pay for their children's educational costs at Stanford. Parents with income between $45,000 and $60,000 can expect a prorated reduction in their expected parent contribution.

This policy reflects Stanford's commitment to making its world-class education (which costs about $47,000 annually, all inclusive) available to talented and well-prepared students from lower-income families. Furthermore, Stanford has a need-blind/need-based financial aid system for U.S. citizens and permanent residents, which means that an applicant's financial status will not affect the admission decision, and that financial aid is distributed according to student need. Currently, about half of all students attending Stanford receive financial aid.

GETTING IN

Just how selective is Stanford? The school accepts about 12 percent of those who apply. A great recommendation or slick essay won't cut the mustard if you spent much more than 30 seconds slacking off in high school. In 2005–2006, 93 percent of those admitted had a GPA of 3.75 or above. Applicants must be cream of the crop, academically as well as personally. Public and community service are a big part of the Stanford experience for many, and dedication to such may give a boost to applications that already have a good shot at acceptance.

WHAT DO GRADUATES DO?

Pretty much whatever pleases them. Politicians, Supreme Court justices, presidents of top universities, astronauts, inventors, entrepreneurs, artists, musicians, authors, journalists, and professional athletes (from John McEnroe to Tiger Woods) have all called themselves Cardinals. Law and medicine are popular career choices for the roughly one-third of all seniors who head to graduate school after leaving Stanford. As is the Ivy League way, Stanford grads are privy to a connected alumni network. Before they graduate, Stanford's career services are on hand to assist in the job search, with an October career fair that attracts recruiters from more than 300 employers.

Average HS GPA	3.9
Range SAT Verbal	660–760
Range SAT Math	680–780
Range ACT	28–33

APPLICATION DEADLINES

Regular admission	12/15
Regular notification	4/1
Single-choice early action	11/1
Early notification	12/15
# of transfer applicants	1,407
% of transfer applicants accepted	5

ACADEMICS

Student/faculty ratio	6:1
% faculty teaching undergraduates	98
% of classes taught by graduate students	2

MOST POPULAR MAJORS

- Biology/biological sciences
- Economics
- Political science and government

EDUCATION REQUIREMENTS

English (including composition), foreign languages, humanities, math, sciences (biological or physical), social science. Undergrads complete at least 180 units. Engineering and applied sciences, humanities, mathematics, natural sciences, and social studies (one course in each); Ethical Reasoning, Global Community, American Cultures, and gender studies (two courses in any).

FINANCIAL INFO

Tuition	$32,994
Room & board	$10,367
Average book expense	$1,290
Average freshman need-based grant	$26,639
Average freshman need-based loan	$1,950
% of graduates who borrowed	46
Average indebtedness	$15,758

FINANCIAL AID FORMS

Students must submit FAFSA, CSS/ profile.

POSTGRAD

% going to graduate school	35

CAREER SERVICES

Alumni network, alumni services, career/job search classes, career assessment, internships, regional alumni, on-campus job interviews. Off-campus job opportunities are excellent.

BOTTOM LINE

For 2006–2007, the total cost for a year at Stanford University was $47,026. This cost includes $32,994 in tuition, $425 in additional fees for freshmen; $10,367 for room and board; $1,935 for personal expenses and $1,290 for books and supplies. The average freshman need-based loan is $1,950, and the average total need-based gift aid is an astounding $26,639. This means that even with the high cost of a Stanford education, students are paying less than $20,000 a year on average. And families with a combined income of less than $45,000 a year will not have a parent contribution.

FUN FACTS

The 50,000-seat Stanford Stadium, the 14-court Taube Family Tennis Stadium, and the 4-pool Avery Aquatic Center (home to swimming, diving, water polo, and synchronized swimming) are part of the extensive athletic facilities on Stanford's campus. There's also a rowing and sailing center, rugby stadium, equestrian center, fencing center, squash courts, wrestling and martial arts room, and climbing wall.

As per the "full moon on the quad" tradition, freshmen students are kissed at midnight by seniors under the first full moon of Autumn Quarter. Students from all classes show up for the event though, and the kissing is not necessarily limited to the original senior-freshmen variety.

The fact that freshmen may not bring cars to school may contribute to the estimated 12,000 bicycles in use on the sprawling Stanford campus.

STATE UNIVERSITY OF NEW YORK AT BINGHAMTON

PO Box 6001, Binghamton, NY 13902-6001
www.Binghamton.edu • Admissions: 607-777-2171
Fax: 607-777-4445 • E-mail: admit@binghamton.edu • Financial Aid: 607-777-2428

STUDENTS

Religious affiliation
_____ No Affiliation
Academic year
  calendar   semester
Undergrad
  enrollment   11,065
% male/female   52/48
% Asian   15
% Black, non-Latino   5
% Latino   6
% international   7
% from out of state   6
% freshmen return for
sophomore year   90
% freshmen graduate
  within 4 years   67

STUDENT LIFE

% of students living
  on campus   58
% in fraternities   8
% in sororities   9

ADMISSIONS

of applicants   21,658
% accepted   43
% enrolled   24

HIGH SCHOOL UNITS REQUIRED

4 English, 3 math, 2
science, 3 foreign language,
2 social studies

HIGH SCHOOL UNITS RECOMMENDED

4 math, 4 science, 3 foreign
language, 3 history

ABOUT STATE UNIVERSITY OF NEW YORK AT BINGHAMTON

Binghamton makes its students a very attractive promise: It is a top-rated school that is more competitive than most of the Northeast's private schools, and available at a state-school price. For the most part, Binghamton has delivered on its promise, and its student body is made up of over 11,000 undergraduates attracted primarily from all over New York State. Binghamton still manages to be a diverse campus, with active Black and Latino Student Unions and large Jewish and Asian populations. Students from Long Island and New York City sometimes feel like they come from a different planet than their upstate classmates. Though all groups don't exactly mix and mingle, there is certainly no tension among them, either.

Although the quality of a Binghamton education depends upon which school within the University you attend, top-notch departments include a good management program, a strong science department (especially in biology, premed, and psychology), stellar political science and philosophy programs, and a law program that yields high law school acceptance rates. Engineering and nursing programs provide good real-world prep. Professors run the gamut from research-minded to student-focused but many are challenging teachers who demand the best.

By most reports, the town of Binghamton doesn't provide much to do besides the same bars, frats, and other hangouts, which can eventually lose their luster. Still, there are tons of clubs, activities, and events to take part in. And the Bearcats, Binghamton's new mascot and image as a Division I sports team, looks to raise school spirit to new heights.

BANG FOR YOUR BUCK

As a state institution, Binghamton's students benefit from state support that keeps tuition low. When all is said and done, Binghamton's baccalaureate experience will cost a student literally one-third of what they can expect to pay at other comparable schools. Value not only comes in the form of the average need-based financial aid and grant/scholarship packages of more than $11,000 but also in student opportunities for experiential education through research, study abroad, and internships, along with the third highest four-year graduation rate in the nation for public institutions.

"Delivering Ivy League academics and a good social experience at a state school price."

Academic GPA, rigor of secondary school record, standardized test scores

IMPORTANT ADMISSION FACTORS

Application essay, class rank, extracurricular activities

Average HS GPA   3.7
Range SAT Verbal 560–660
Range SAT Math   600–690
Range ACT   25–29
Minimum TOEFL
   (paper/computer) 550/213

APPLICATION DEADLINES
Regular notification rolling
# of transfer
   applicants   3,381
% of transfer applicants
   accepted   47

ACADEMICS

Student/faculty ratio   21:1
% faculty teaching
   undergraduates   90
% of classes taught by
   graduate students   9

MOST POPULAR MAJORS

• Business administration/
   management
• English language and
   literature
• Psychology

EDUCATION REQUIREMENTS

Arts/fine arts, English (including composition), humanities, math, sciences (biological or physical), social science, physical education

Binghamton's tuition, even for out-of-state students, is exceedingly affordable when compared to its peer institutions. Most of Binghamton's peers charge tuition and fees that are two and a half times higher than Binghamton's tuition and fees. Over a four-year period, such a cumulative difference in tuition and fees can amount to almost $90,000.

As a relatively young public institution, Binghamton targets the vast majority of its funding to recognize students' scholastic achievement while at the same time recognizing the students' ability to pay. (Students who demonstrated financial need saw an average of 81 percent of that need met by the school.) If you receive an award, the school makes every effort to offer you a similar financial aid package in subsequent years as long as your ability to pay remains unchanged.

In addition, there are also a limited number of awards given to students regardless of their ability to pay. The Binghamton Scholars Program is a selective all-university four-year honors program for students of exceptional merit. During a student's third year of participation as a Binghamton Scholar, funds are made available to support various academic, research, internship and other experiences that can complement the student's educational experience.

GETTING IN

High school transcripts including the rigor of courses taken and grades achieved, SAT/ACT scores, leadership activities, and extracurricular involvement are the most relevant data for this Admissions Committee. Essays, recommendations, and other factors are considered secondary. The average high school GPA for incoming freshman is an eyebrow-raising 3.6.

WHAT DO GRADUATES DO?

Those who don't head to graduate school most often find employment in the accounting, business, education fields, engineering, legal, medical, and nursing. Among the companies who recruit on this campus are Deutsch bank, Ernst and Young, KPMG, Lord & Taylor, and PricewaterhouseCoopers.

The Bottom Line

For 2006–2007, in-state students paid $4,350 in tuition, while out-of-staters paid $10,610. All students living on campus saw additional expenses (on average) of $1,560 in fees, $8,588 for room and board, and $800 for books. This amounted to $15,208 for in-state students and $21,558 for out of state students before adding the costs of transportation and personal expenses. The typical out-of-pocket costs that an in-state family can expect to pay are approximately $4,129 annually.

Binghamton students find numerous opportunities for on- and off-campus employment as well. And because the vast majority of Binghamton students graduate in four years, they are not saddled with an additional year of tuition and fees.

Fun Facts

Ludacris, Green Day, Dashboard Confessional, and Lewis Black recently performed on campus. The America East Conference men's basketball championships were also held on campus in 2005 and the America East Conference women's basketball championships will be played in the university's Events Center in 2007.

Where can you find an electronic nose? In Omowunmi Sadik's lab. As a professor of chemistry, Sadik's groundbreaking research focuses on microelectrode biosensors that are able to detect even trace amounts of organic materials. Myriad applications for this "electronic nose" technology include drug detection (in the place of drug-sniffing dogs) and bomb detection.

Looking out for the little guys, the school has built ramps from the nature preserve across the road and into the adjacent woods to allow salamanders the ability to navigate the curbs to get to their mating habitat.

FINANCIAL INFO

In-state tuition	$4,350
Out-of-state tuition	$10,610
Room & board	$8,588
Average book expense	$800
Required fees	$1,560
Average freshman need-based grant	$4,874
Average freshman need-based loan	$2,957
% of graduates who borrowed	60
Average indebtedness	$14,734

FINANCIAL AID FORMS

Students must submit FAFSA, state aid form.

POSTGRAD

% going to graduate school	38
% going to law school	7
% going to business school	2
% going to medical school	9

CAREER SERVICES

Alumni network, alumni services, career/job search classes, career assessment, internships, regional alumni, on-campus job interviews. Off-campus job opportunities are excellent.

STATE UNIVERSITY OF NEW YORK— BROCKPORT

350 New Campus Drive, Brockport, NY 14420
www.Brockport.edu • Admissions: 585-395-2751
Fax: 585-395-5452 • E-mail: admit@brockport.edu • Financial Aid: 585-395-2501

STUDENTS

Religious affiliation
　　　　　　No Affiliation
Academic year
　calendar　　　　semester
Undergrad
　enrollment　　　　6,852
% male/female　　　43/57
% Asian　　　　　　1
% Black, non-Latino　5
% Latino　　　　　　3
% international　　　1
% from out of state　1
% freshmen return for
sophomore year　　83
% freshmen graduate
　within 4 years　　29

STUDENT LIFE

% of students living
　on campus　　　　37
% in fraternities　　1
% in sororities　　　2

ADMISSIONS

of applicants　　7,816
% accepted　　　　46
% enrolled　　　　27

HIGH SCHOOL UNITS REQUIRED

4 English, 3 math, 3 science
(1 science lab), 4 social
studies, 4 academic
electives

HIGH SCHOOL UNITS RECOMMENDED

3 Foreign language

ABOUT STATE UNIVERSITY OF NEW YORK—BROCKPORT

Unlike many of its better-known cousins in the SUNY system, Brockport offers a small-school experience, something students appreciate. Brockport doesn't skimp on academic variety either, despite its relatively small size. Students brag about their school's unique programs in computational science, physical education, and dance; career-track majors such as criminal justice, education, psychology, and nursing are also popular and well-regarded. An Honors Program, open to highly qualified applicants, gives ambitious undergraduates that extra challenge they crave and a little extra personal attention, while the DELTA (Distinctive Education and Leadership Training Advantages) College allows students to immerse themselves in integrative learning and professional development. The DELTA approach helps students decide if they've chosen the right major by encouraging them to take on related internships before graduation.

Hometown Brockport is hardly a bustling metropolis, but most who attend this upstate New York school don't mind. It's still a nice location, close enough to Rochester to make internships and jobs fairly available, yet far enough away to have the peaceful calm of a small town. Drinking is quite popular from Thursday through Saturday, since a number of local bars aren't hard to reach. Off-campus house parties are also popular. Brockport's sports teams, the Golden Eagles, earn the enthusiastic support among students, with football as a particular favorite. The student population even includes a number of jocks, due to the rock-solid physical education major and this small school's efforts to populate its 23 Division III intercollegiate teams.

BANG FOR YOUR BUCK

Because of increased institutional- and campus-based aid, the College at Brockport is slightly more affordable than its peer institutions. Three-quarters of all undergraduates receive some form of need-based aid, and over 75 percent of need-based aid recipients receive some form of grant money as part of their aid package.

Students Say

"We have the jocks, the cheerleaders, and the punks—and everyone fits in rather nicely."

Brockport also administers several merit-based awards. The Distinguished Scholar-in-Residence offers close to a full ride, valued at more than $51,000 over four years. The award is open to valedictorians or salutatorians who have a 96 or better high school average, and 1250 or higher SAT or 27 ACT score. This scholarship includes full in-state tuition, room, partial board (meal plan), and all standard mandatory fees each year. The Presidential Scholar-in-Residence is available to incoming freshmen with a high school average of 93 or higher, ranking in the top 20 percent of the class, and a 1200 or higher SAT or 26 ACT score. The award is a grant providing free room for up to four years for freshmen, with a top value of $20,240. The Dean's Scholar-in-Residence Award has total value of $10,000. Incoming freshmen are eligible for this award if they are in the top 25 percent of their class, have a 90 or higher average, and 1100 or higher SAT or 24 ACT score. On-campus residency is required.

GETTING IN

The most important components of an application to Brockport are the quality of the high school program and the high school GPA, rank, and the student's standardized test scores. Recommendations, essays, and extracurriculars are also considered. Because Brockport admits students to the college rather than to a specific major, students generally do not need to apply separately to specific programs. The exceptions are the Departments of Dance and Theater, in which students must audition and may also be required to provide a portfolio for review.

WHAT DO GRADUATES DO?

Brockport graduates find themselves employed in a wide range of fields. Nearly one in three enters finance and marketing; about one-quarter find jobs in education; and slightly more than one in ten winds up in health care. Major employers include Eastman Kodak Company, Excellus BlueCross BlueShield, Paychex, Inc., Rochester City School District, Walt Disney World Resorts, and Xerox Corporation.

VERY IMPORTANT ADMISSION FACTORS

Academic GPA, class rank, rigor of secondary school record, standardized test scores

IMPORTANT ADMISSION FACTORS

Application essay, extracurricular activities, recommendation(s), talent/ability

Average HS GPA	3.4
Range SAT Verbal	500–600
Range SAT Math	480–570
Range ACT	20–25
Minimum TOEFL (paper/computer)	530/197

APPLICATION DEADLINES

Regular notification	rolling
# of transfer applicants	2,966
% of transfer applicants accepted	59

ACADEMICS

Student/faculty ratio	19:1
% faculty teaching undergraduates	95
% of classes taught by graduate students	0

MOST POPULAR MAJORS

- Business administration and management
- Criminal justice/safety studies
- Physical education teaching and coaching

Arts/fine arts, computer literacy, English (including composition), foreign languages, history, humanities, math, sciences (biological or physical), social science

FINANCIAL INFO

In-state tuition	$4,350
Out-of-state tuition	$10,610
Room & board	$7,830
Average book expense	$1,000
Required fees	$1,006
Average freshman need-based grant	$3,782
Average freshman need-based loan	$4,216
% of graduates who borrowed	81
Average indebtedness	$19,083

FINANCIAL AID FORMS

Students must submit FAFSA, state aid form.

POSTGRAD

% going to graduate school	23
% going to law school	2
% going to business school	4
% going to medical school	1

THE BOTTOM LINE

For 2006–2007, in-state students could expect to pay $13,186 to attend Brockport full time ($4,350 in tuition, $5,060 in room, $2,770 in board, and the remainder in fees and expenses). Out-of-state students pay an additional $10,610 in tuition annually, bringing the total cost of attending to $22,840

According to the school, "The average out-of-pocket expense for an undergraduate student that is registered full time for the fall and spring semesters is $3,095 (based on the 2005–2006 academic year). This does not include work-study, which is not used as a deferral against the bill. The rest is covered by a combination of grants, scholarships, loans, and employment.

FUN FACTS

The population of the village of Brockport doubles when students, faculty, and staff arrive for the school year.

Brockport was founded in 1841 as the Brockport Collegiate Institute. In 1866 it became the Brockport State Normal School; like other Normal schools, Brockport took its name from a popular approach to teacher training. The school entered the SUNY system when that system was established in 1948.

During the summer of 1979, Brockport hosted the fifth International Special Olympics.

Brockport's baseball team always hopes to find nearby Hilbert College on the schedule. Over the years, Brockport has beaten the Hilbert Hawks 16 times without incurring a single loss.

STATE UNIVERSITY OF NEW YORK—FREDONIA

178 Central Avenue, Fredonia, NY 14063
www.Fredonia.edu • Admissions: 716-673-3251
Fax: 716-673-3249 • E-mail: admissions.office@fredonia.edu • Financial Aid: 716-673-3253

STUDENTS

Religious affiliation
　　　　　　　No Affiliation
Academic year
　calendar　　　　semester
Undergrad
　enrollment　　　　5,043
% male/female　　　42/58
% Asian　　　　　　　2
% Black, non-Latino　2
% Latino　　　　　　　3
% Native American　　1
% from out of state　　2
% freshmen return for
sophomore year　　　81
% freshmen graduate
　within 4 years　　　49

STUDENT LIFE

% of students living
　on campus　　　　50
% in fraternities　　　5
% in sororities　　　　3

ADMISSIONS

of applicants　　　5,902
% accepted　　　　　55
% enrolled　　　　　32
# of early decision/action
　applicants　　　　87
% accepted early
　decision/action　　60

HIGH SCHOOL UNITS REQUIRED

4 English, 3 math, 3
science, 3 foreign language,
4 social studies

ABOUT THE STATE UNIVERSITY OF NEW YORK—FREDONIA

Founded in 1826 as a state teachers' college specializing in music education, SUNY Fredonia now offers its 5,000 undergrads a range of degree options, from education to communication, though music remains one of the most popular majors. The music and art majors draw lots of artsy, creative, hippie types to Fredonia, though there is also a healthy mix of white, suburban frat kids. Students here find each other friendly and easy to get along with, though some are interested in bringing greater diversity to campus. One thing that does tend to divide the student body is its approach to education—many students come here to work hard and focus on education, while others come to drink beer and party.

Both groups have plenty to occupy them. Academically, Fredonia offers a great education—particularly in the music and education programs, the school's traditional strength. Graphic arts, history, psychology, and business programs are also highly regarded. Professors are friendly and their quality is generally high, if a bit inconsistent from school to school. The academic environment is overwhelmingly nurturing and positive: Professors treat their students with respect and want them to learn and understand. Fortunately for students who come to Fredonia to party, there is plenty of fun to be had on campus too. Students have varied social lives, but in general, Greek life, the surprisingly good local bars, and the wealth of student organizations means that Fredonia can offer its undergrads a fair helping of distractions. In addition, the music program's prominence on campus means there is always a musical event to check out.

BANG FOR YOUR BUCK

Fredonia gets creative in making education affordable, starting with the "Fredonia in 4" guarantee. First-time freshmen dedicated to graduating in four years are eligible. If a student's graduation is delayed due to the school's inability to provide the appropriate courses, the university will chip in tuition dollars and course-related fees required to complete the degree. And don't forget that 22 school departments have their own list of scholarship opportunities including those for students studying music, art, athletics, communication, computer science, education, history, physics, and theater. (Some scholarships require recipients to live in college residence halls.)

Students Say

"The administration seems to care about us, and my professors all are very knowledgeable on their topics. I am doing well in college and it isn't just because of me."

HIGH SCHOOL UNITS RECOMMENDED

4 English, 4 math, 4 science, 3 foreign language, 4 social studies

VERY IMPORTANT ADMISSION FACTORS

Academic GPA, rigor of secondary school record

IMPORTANT ADMISSION FACTORS

Class rank, extracurricular activities, recommendation(s), standardized test scores

Average HS GPA	3.43
Range SAT Verbal	520–600
Range SAT Math	520–600
Range ACT	21–26
Minimum TOEFL (paper/computer)	500/173

APPLICATION DEADLINES

Early decision	11/1
Early decision notification	12/1
Regular notification	rolling
# of transfer applicants	1,421
% of transfer applicants accepted	54

ACADEMICS

Student/faculty ratio	20:1
% faculty teaching undergraduates	100
% of classes taught by graduate students	0

That said, the majority of Fredonia students borrow money to help cover their educational expenses before they graduate, and the average student graduates with loans of about $12,500—a low-end figure for today's college degree. That's because Fredonia combines its modest tuition rate (especially for New York state residents) with a sizable number of need-based awards and merit scholarships that help many families make a good dent in the overall bill. A prestigious one-year merit scholarship for $3,000 goes to 30 entering freshmen each year, and another 60 freshmen and transfer students earn $1,000 scholarships for their academic achievement, leadership, and school or community involvement. The Fredonia Award for Excellence is a renewable $2,500 award given to high school students who graduate first or second in their class.

GETTING IN

Great high school grades and an impressive list of classes are the most desirable attributes of a SUNY Fredonia applicant. Of course, the Admissions Committee also looks at your class rank, standardized test scores, recommendations, and how you used your time when not in class when making their decision. Your application essay is also considered, but to a lesser extent. Only 13 percent of freshmen who arrived on campus in the fall of 2005 had earned below a 3.0 in high school. This entering class held an average high school GPA of 3.43. Not too shabby!

WHAT DO GRADUATES DO?

With more than a third of Fredonia grads earning a degree in education, teaching remains a very popular career choice, and that includes students who combine their love of performing music with teaching it. Communication, business, music, and the performing arts are also fields where students find their calling after graduation. (Many grads who do not choose a full-time career in music still pursue it as a hobby.) Nearly a third of Fredonia students decide to keep hitting the books and go on to grad school.

Bottom Line

In-state undergraduates at SUNY Fredonia should expect to spend $4,350 per year in tuition and fees—a bargain anywhere. Out-of-state students pay $10,610. Room and board adds an additional $7,880. Students will spend about $1,000 in books and supplies, and $1,132 in required fees. This brings the total for the year up to about $14,362 for New York residents. Out-of-staters have a total cost of $20,622. And what's more, at Fredonia the low costs are just the beginning. Over 60 percent of undergrads receive financial aid. Freshmen loans average $2,944 per year, and need-based gifts average $3,541. Add these up and state residents will pay, on average, only $7,877 for a year at SUNY Fredonia. Not bad at all.

Fun Facts:

In July 2006, SUNY Fredonia began construction on $3.3 million project to upgrade the athletic fields and build a fancy new soccer and lacrosse stadium. The improvements include a new natural grass playing field for the men's and women's soccer teams, an artificial turf field for varsity practices, club teams and intramural competitions, improved bleacher seating for 1,000 spectators, lights for night games, and enhanced drainage that will allow the team to host NCAA competitions.

World-renowned architect, I.M. Pei, with partner Henry N. Cobb, designed the master plan for the modernized Fredonia campus in 1968. Many buildings are considered exceptional examples of modern architecture.

SUNY Fredonia was originally one of the New York state teachers' colleges traditionally specializing in music education.

Most Popular Majors

- Business administration/ management
- Elementary education and teaching
- Music teacher education

Education Requirements

Arts/fine arts, English (including composition), foreign languages, history, humanities, math, sciences (biological or physical), social science

FINANCIAL INFO

In-state tuition	$4,350
Out-of-state tuition	$10,610
Room & board	$7,880
Average book expense	$1,000
Required fees	$1,132
Average freshman need-based grant	$3,541
Average freshman need-based loan	$2,888
% of graduates who borrowed	81
Average indebtedness	$12,500

Financial Aid Forms

Students must submit FAFSA, state aid form. Financial aid filing deadline   5/15

POSTGRAD

% going to graduate school   29

Career Services

Alumni network, alumni services, career/job search classes, career assessment, internships, regional alumni, on-campus job interviews. Off-campus job opportunities are good.

STATE UNIVERSITY OF NEW YORK AT GENESEO

1 College Circle, Geneseo, NY 14454-1401
www.Geneseo.edu • Admissions: 585-245-5571
Fax: 585-245-5550 • E-mail: admissions@geneseo.edu • Financial Aid: 585-245-5731

STUDENTS

Religious affiliation
    No Affiliation
Academic year
    calendar   semester
Undergrad
    enrollment   5,293
% male/female   41/59
% Asian   5
% Black, non-Latino   2
% Latino   3
% international   3
% from out of state   1
% freshmen return for
sophomore year   90
% freshmen graduate
    within 4 years   64

STUDENT LIFE

% of students living
    on campus   56
% in fraternities   10
% in sororities   12

ADMISSIONS

of applicants   10,448
% accepted   41
% enrolled   24
# of early decision/action
    applicants   281
% accepted early
    decision/action   59

HIGH SCHOOL UNITS RECOMMENDED

4 English, 4 math, 4
science, 4 foreign language,
4 social studies

ABOUT THE STATE UNIVERSITY OF NEW YORK—GENESEO

The most selective of the 13 universities in the State University of New York (SUNY) system, Geneseo is regarded as the SUNY honors college and boasts a professionally focused education that is on par with the educational experience at many of the nation's finest private universities. At Geneseo, all the state-school stereotypes are thrown out the window; the school is small (fewer than 5,500 students), the academics emphasize undergraduate teaching, and the campus is lovely. There are also enough programs, clubs, and opportunities to make a private school blush. Professors not only have impressive resumes but also care about their students and are always willing to help. And unlike many state schools, Geneseo offers few classes taught by TAs. Students here work hard and take pride in it.

That's not to say life at Geneseo is all study halls and trips to the library. Because the campus is "in the middle of nowhere," students are adept at creating their own entertainment and fun. Clubs and organizations are extremely active, and there are always events to attend at little or no cost. Intramural sports are also big, as is the campus party scene. Students also take advantage of the nearby hills to sled and mud-slide. Camping, hiking, and biking in the local state park and surrounding countryside are popular.

Another important note to Geneseo life: Female students outnumber their male counterparts nearly two to one, a statistic that is often joked about among the student body. The dearth of minority students is no joking matter, though, with many students wishing for a more diverse student body. Still, with its impressive academics, high quality of life, and low price tag, Geneseo should be attractive to students of all types.

BANG FOR YOUR BUCK

Talk about a reasonable tuition sticker: In-state students—who face a mere $4,350 in tuition—will actually drop more on room and board than they will on the price of the education itself. (If they live at home, they get an even more incredible deal.) More than 40 percent of freshmen receive need-based financial aid, and the average amount of need-based gift aid rings in at more than half the in-state tuition price tag: $2,036. On average, those students who are determined to have financial need find that 75 to 85 percent of their need is met through aid. In 2005–2006, more than 2,300 students had 100 percent of their need met.

Students Say:

"Geneseo is about the Ivy League education but with public school expenses."

Another 495 students who had no financial need were awarded merit scholarships. Academic scholarships are, of course, up for grabs. But awards for creative talent, leadership, citizenship, hailing from a certain county or high school, honors program enrollees, and minority students are also available. Each department at the school also offers its own set of scholarships that are available to high-achieving students in the program.

GETTING IN

The most academically finicky SUNY school doesn't mess around with their admissions process. To be one of the lucky ones admitted (not even half of all applicants are admitted), you need to show them that you don't mess around either. Present a high school transcript of substantive classes, a top rank in your class, and a smart score on the SAT or ACT. Freshmen in the entering class of 2005–2006 toted an average GPA of 3.8.

WHAT DO GRADUATES DO?

About 44 percent of Geneseo grads go on to graduate programs; the school hosts plenty of related workshops and events to prepare students for advanced study. SUNY Geneseo also makes efforts to interest grads in federal and public-service jobs both in the U.S. and overseas. Even so, nearly 80 percent of recent grads accept jobs in New York State. Business and education are among the most popular fields.

VERY IMPORTANT ADMISSION FACTORS

Class rank, rigor of secondary school record, standardized test scores

IMPORTANT ADMISSION FACTORS

Academic GPA, application essay, extracurricular activities, racial/ethnic status, recommendation(s), talent/ability

Average HS GPA	3.8
Range SAT Verbal	600–670
Range SAT Math	600–670
Range ACT	26–29
Minimum TOEFL (paper/computer)	525/234

APPLICATION DEADLINES

Early decision	11/15
Early decision notification	12/15
Regular admission	1/15
Regular notification	rolling
# of transfer applicants	1,529
% of transfer applicants accepted	42

ACADEMICS

Student/faculty ratio	19:1
% faculty teaching undergraduates	100
% of classes taught by graduate students	0

MOST POPULAR MAJORS

- Biology/biological sciences
- Business administration/management
- Elementary education and teaching

EDUCATION REQUIREMENTS

Arts/fine arts, English (including composition), foreign languages, history, humanities, math, sciences (biological or physical), social science, critical writing and reading, non-Western traditions, numeric and symbolic reasoning, U.S. history

FINANCIAL INFO

In-state tuition	$4,350
Out-of-state tuition	$10,610
Room & board	$7,788
Average book expense	$800
Required fees	$1,210
Average freshman need-based grant	$2,450
Average freshman need-based loan	$3,495
% of graduates who borrowed	75
Average indebtedness	$16,000

FINANCIAL AID FORMS

Students must submit FAFSA, state aid form.

Financial aid filing deadline	2/15

POSTGRAD

% going to graduate school	41
% going to law school	3
% going to business school	19
% going to medical school	3

CAREER SERVICES

Alumni services, career/job search classes, career assessment, on-campus job interviews. Off-campus job opportunities are fair.

BOTTOM LINE

In-state undergraduates at SUNY Geneseo should expect to spend $4,350 per year in tuition and fees—a bargain anywhere. Out-of-state students pay $10,610. Room and board adds an additional $7,788. Tack on $800 in books and supplies and $1,210 in fees, and the total for the year is $14,148 for New York residents. Out-of-staters have a total cost of $20,408. And now the good news: Nearly half of students receive financial aid. Freshman loans average $4,010 per year, and need-based gifts average $2,036. Add these up and, on average, state residents will pay only $8,102 for a year at Geneseo. Take into account the quality of the education here, and that is quite a bargain.

FUN FACTS

Geneseo has the highest four-year graduation rate of any public undergraduate college in the nation.

Men's ice hockey games have recently become major campus events. Packed stands of noisemaker-toting crowds are not unusual, and the team has its own pep band.

The campus is home to two unusual trees. The "painted tree" or "Greek tree" has been covered for decades in layers of paint by fraternity and sorority members (among others) who spray and brush on personal messages and promotions for events. The "Seuss Tree" is a twisting, spiral-shaped pine that resembles a drawing from one of the famous children's books. It is said to grow that way as a result of the effects of one particularly harsh winter that weighed it down with snow and ice.

STATE UNIVERSITY OF NEW YORK— STONY BROOK UNIVERSITY

Office of Admissions, Stony Brook, NY 11794-1901
www.StonyBrook.edu • Admissions: 631-632-6868
Fax: 631-632-9898 • E-mail: enroll@stonybrook.edu • Financial Aid: 631-632-6840

STUDENTS

Religious affiliation
No Affiliation

Academic year
calendar   semester
Undergrad
enrollment   14,851
% male/female   50/50
% Asian   22
% Black, non-Latino   9
% Latino   9
% international   6
% from out of state   4
% freshmen return for
sophomore year   87
% freshmen graduate
within 4 years   37

STUDENT LIFE

% of students living
on campus   53
% in fraternities   1
% in sororities   1

ADMISSIONS

of applicants   21,292
% accepted   47
% enrolled   27

HIGH SCHOOL UNITS REQUIRED

4 English, 3 math, 3
science, 2 foreign language,
4 social studies

HIGH SCHOOL UNITS RECOMMENDED

4 English, 4 math, 4
science, 3 foreign language,
4 social studies

ABOUT STATE UNIVERSITY OF NEW YORK—STONY BROOK UNIVERSITY

Thanks to a national reputation in the sciences, mathematics, and engineering, Stony Brook University has, over the past several decades, become one of the best-known schools in New York's State University system. Undergraduates come here for the chance to study cutting-edge material, help with important research, and earn a degree that opens doors in the real world. They don't come for the fabulous, cuddly teachers, though. Professors, while uniformly brilliant, often lack honed teaching skills or even an interest in developing those skills. Students who succeed at Stony Brook are those with a knack for teaching themselves. A high endurance for heavy workloads is also a huge asset.

Stony Brook attracts a sizeable international student body. Native New Yorkers make up the vast majority of the rest of the population. About half the students commute, creating a divide between those who are at the university 24/7 and those who come and go for classes only. Many of the residents head home on Friday after classes, leaving a pretty quiet campus on weekends. Those who stick around enjoy an active club and organization community, lots of music and theater performances, and a healthy party scene. Intercollegiate sports provide what is perhaps the sole rallying point for the entire student body (the Roth Pond Regatta is the other possible candidate—see below). Beyond campus are the towns of Long Island's north shore. Nearby Port Jefferson offers plenty of shopping as well as numerous bars and restaurants.

BANG FOR YOUR BUCK

Remarkably low tuition makes a Stony Brook education extremely affordable for all. The school's out-of-state tuition is almost 40 percent below the median for public AAU universities. For students who need additional help, the university provides more than $88 million in the form of institutional scholarships, federal and state grants, institutional and federally funded work opportunities, and federal loans to undergraduate students.

Stony Brook provides need-based assistance to 98 percent of all aid applicants who demonstrate need, with 81 percent of need-based aid packages including some form of need-based grant or scholarship. On average, the school meets 68 percent of aid recipients' demonstrated need, but only 10 percent of aid recipients will see 100 percent of their demonstrated need met by the school.

"Stony Brook University is a combination of a research and learning school in which professionals and pre-professionals come to work in areas ranging from medicine to teaching."

VERY IMPORTANT ADMISSION FACTORS

Rigor of secondary school record, standardized test scores

IMPORTANT ADMISSION FACTORS

Class rank

Average HS GPA	3.6
Range SAT	
Writing	520–620
Range SAT Math	590–680
Minimum TOEFL	
(paper/computer/IB)	
	550/213/80

APPLICATION DEADLINES

Regular notification	2/1
# of transfer	
applicants	4,972
% of transfer applicants	
accepted	58

ACADEMICS

Student/faculty ratio	16:1
% faculty teaching	
undergraduates	88

MOST POPULAR MAJORS

• Biology/biological sciences
• Business administration/ management
• Psychology

EDUCATION REQUIREMENTS

Arts/fine arts, English (including composition), foreign languages, history, humanities, math, philosophy, sciences (biological or physical), social science

Stony Brook University's commitment to excellence is demonstrated through various merit scholarship programs. Special scholarships are offered to those admitted to the Honors College and Women in Science and Engineering Programs, as well as to Intel Science Talent Research and National Merit Scholarship Competition Finalists and Semifinalists, valedictorians, and salutatorians. Presidential and Provost Scholarships, awarded to incoming freshmen who arrive with at least a 90 unweighted high school average and a 1300 composite on the critical reading and math sections of the SAT (or 31 ACT composite score), range in value from $1,000 to full tuition and fees.

GETTING IN

Admissions Officers at Stony Brook look most closely at applicants' high school grades, especially in college-preparatory courses. Successful applicants should have completed a rigorous high school curriculum. Additionally, those interested in studying engineering or technological disciplines at Stony Brook should have taken all available advanced math and science courses. Standardized test scores and co-curricular activities are also considered. Prospective music majors must audition to earn a spot within the Music Department.

WHAT DO GRADUATES DO?

Stony Brook graduates work in a broad range of professions and industries, including health care, computers, information technology, engineering, banking and finance, business management, education and human services, life and physical sciences, government, and the arts. Top employers of Stony Brook graduates include Alanta, Enterprise Rent-A-Car, Ford, Goldman Sachs, Lehman Brothers, Memorial Sloan Kettering Cancer Center, Northrop Grumman, Northwestern Mutual, Teach for America, Turner Construction, the state and federal governments, and Wells Fargo Financial.

The Bottom Line

In 2006–2007, New York residents paid $4,350 in tuition to attend Stony Brook full-time. Required fees added another $1,281 to their expenses. Room and board cost $8,450; books and supplies cost an estimated $900; transportation cost about $500; and personal and miscellaneous expenses totaled about $1,292. Thus, a resident who did not receive any aid could expect to spend approximately $16,773 to attend Stony Brook. Out-of-state students paid an additional $6,260 in tuition to bring their total costs to $23,033. The school reports that the average out-of-pocket expenditure for a student receiving aid was $4,112.

Fun Facts

Undoubtedly the oddest highlight of the Stony Brook school year is the Roth Pond Regatta, during which students, faculty, and staff fashion racing boats from cardboard, duct tape, and paint. Competitors strive to create the most original sea craft, typically focusing more on innovation than practicality (with predictable results, most boats and their creators sink in the pond).

Notable Stony Brook alumni include radio shrink Laura Schlessinger; *The View* host Joy Behar; New York State Supreme Court Justice Barry Cozier; and Carolyn Porco, the leader of the imaging team for the Cassini mission to Saturn. Members of the rock band Blue Oyster Cult met while attending Stony Brook.

FINANCIAL INFO

In-state tuition	$4,350
Out-of-state tuition	$10,610
Room & board	$8,450
Average book expense	$900
Required fees	$1,281
Average freshman need-based grant	$5,815
Average freshman need-based loan	$2,952
% of graduates who borrowed	59
Average indebtedness	$14,952

FINANCIAL AID FORMS

Students must submit FAFSA.

Financial aid filing deadline	3/1

STERLING COLLEGE (KS)

125 West Cooper, Sterling, KS 67579
www.Sterling.edu • Admissions: 620-278-4275
Fax: 620-278-4416 • E-mail: admissions@sterling.edu • Financial Aid: 620-278-4226

STUDENTS

Religious affiliation	Presbyterian
Academic year calendar	4-1-4
Undergrad enrollment	559
% male/female	51/49
% Asian	1
% Black, non-Latino	10
% Latino	6
% Native American	2
% international	1
% from out of state	54
% freshmen return for sophomore year	76
% freshmen graduate within 4 years	40

STUDENT LIFE

% of students living on campus	90

ADMISSIONS

# of applicants	932
% accepted	65
% enrolled	43

HIGH SCHOOL UNITS RECOMMENDED

4 English, 3 math, 3 science (1 science lab), 2 foreign language, 1 social studies, 2 history, 1 academic electives, 2 computer information/technology, physical education

VERY IMPORTANT ADMISSION FACTORS

Character/personal qualities, rigor of secondary school record, standardized test scores

ABOUT STERLING COLLEGE

Sterling College, known for its affiliation with the Presbyterian Church, is a Christ-centered college of approximately 600 students. It tends to attract students who are either strong Christians or people who want an education that will explore, relate to, or enhance their faith. As such, conservatives from small Kansas towns are the general rule, and people who don't fit this stereotype may have difficulty finding a place to fit in, though students insist that they get along with all types of people.

Academically, Sterling is unique in its service-focused curriculum, and in its efforts to integrate faith into its curriculum. The idea of servant leadership is taught in every class; students are encouraged to focus on improving the lives and work of those around them. One of the benefits of such a small student body is the close relationships forged between peers, and between students and professors—who have an excellent record of being available outside the classroom.

Both academically and socially, Sterling is a community where everyone knows one another. Living in a tiny town in "the middle of nowhere" (30 minutes from movies, shopping, and restaurants) with very few diversions means activity necessarily focuses on the campus. And because school policy is very strict with respect to alcohol, tobacco, and dorm visitation, campus life at Sterling takes a little getting used to. Once adjusted, though, many students love it, embracing the karaoke and bingo nights, bonfires, and barn dances. This environment fosters a love for and appreciation of the relationships you develop with your peers; students routinely comment on the amazing relationships they develop at Sterling. A final note for you party animals: The administration's rules regarding partying apply to on-campus behavior only. If you crave a brew, you can do so without restriction off campus.

"Sterling College is a totally awesome college that upholds Christian values, remains true to its beliefs, cares about each student, and makes sure that every person who leaves here with a degree will be going somewhere."

BANG FOR YOUR BUCK

At Sterling, financial aid consists of scholarships, grants, awards, loans, and employment, which are awarded to students alone or combined. In selecting a financial aid recipient, special consideration is given to an applicant's academic promise. A full 85 percent of students receive some form of need-based aid. Additionally, every student admitted to Sterling College receives a single Sterling College scholarship. For students not interested in participating in an activity, the Sterling College scholarship is based solely on academics. For arts students (theater, communication, art, music) scholarships are based on arts interest and academic record. Student athletes are awarded scholarships designated by coaches in consideration of athletic potential and academic record. Some Presbyterian scholarships are also available.

GETTING IN

Good grades on a high school record with challenging classes. Above-average standardized test scores. A solid character with some volunteer work to show for it. If you can check those off, you should present a strong showing before the Sterling Admissions Committee. More than half of all applicants are admitted, with the average incoming freshman having averaged a 3.32 GPA in high school. Gifted high school students completing 11th grade may apply for early admission to Sterling College with strong approval from a high school administrator.

WHAT DO GRADUATES DO?

A number of Sterling grads continue on to other classrooms—as teachers. Others join the ministry, practice medicine, go into business, government, journalism, health care, or find careers in the arts.

IMPORTANT ADMISSION FACTORS

Academic GPA, application essay, extracurricular activities, interview, level of applicant's interest, recommendation(s), religious affiliation/commitment, volunteer work

Average HS GPA	3.32
Range ACT	19–25
Minimum TOEFL (paper/computer)	520/190

APPLICATION DEADLINES

Regular notification	rolling
# of transfer applicants	168
% of transfer applicants accepted	55

ACADEMICS

Student/faculty ratio	11:1
% faculty teaching undergraduates	100
% of classes taught by graduate students	0

MOST POPULAR MAJORS

- Business administration/management
- Elementary education and teaching
- Health and physical education

EDUCATION REQUIREMENTS

Arts/fine arts, computer literacy, English (including composition), history, humanities, math, philosophy, sciences (biological or physical), social science, religion, exercise science

FINANCIAL INFO

Tuition	$14,300
Room & board	$6,086
Average book expense	$600
Required fees	$100
Average freshman need-based grant	$7,932
Average freshman need-based loan	$3,736
% of graduates who borrowed	79
Average indebtedness	$16,251

FINANCIAL AID FORMS
Students must submit FAFSA.

POSTGRAD

% going to graduate school	10
% going to law school	1
% going to business school	2
% going to medical school	2

CAREER SERVICES
Off-campus job opportunities are fair.

BOTTOM LINE

Tuition and fees for a year at Sterling College costs $14,300. Housing ranges between $2,400 and $3,000, and board adds an additional approximately $3,400 to $3,800. This puts annual costs at between $20,100 and $21,100.

For needy students, the financial aid office can help significantly toward meeting these financial obligations. The average freshman loan is about $2,625, and the average freshman need-based gift is $7,932. This puts the average assistance for students at $10,557, and reduces annual out-of-pocket expense to around $10,000. Depending upon the student, this amount can grow quite substantially, and tuition payment plans can help ease the burden by spreading the cost out over the entire year.

FUN FACTS

Student chaplains take on the role of encouraging and nurturing spiritual formation to other students, especially those in their residence hall. This is one of many ways students choose to serve the Sterling community.

The Christian Motorcyclists Association recently formed a partnership with Sterling College to reach college-age bikers and bring enhanced technology to their ministry training program. This is the first CMA chapter on a college campus.

It's all relative! Over the last ten years, 14 percent of students have come to Sterling because a family member also attended the college.

SWARTHMORE COLLEGE

500 College Avenue, Swarthmore, PA 19081
www.Swarthmore.edu • Admissions: 610-328-8300
Fax: 610-328-8580 • E-mail: admissions@swarthmore.edu • Financial Aid: 610-328-8358

STUDENTS

Religious affiliation

No Affiliation

Academic year
  calendar   semester
Undergrad
  enrollment   1,461
% male/female   48/52
% Asian   16
% Black, non-Latino   9
% Latino   10
% Native American   1
% international   6
% from out of state   83
% freshmen return for
sophomore year   96
% freshmen graduate
  within 4 years   86

STUDENT LIFE

% of students living
  on campus   95
% in fraternities   7

ADMISSIONS

of applicants   4,852
% accepted   19
% enrolled   40
# of early decision/action
  applicants   425
% accepted early
  decision/action   37

VERY IMPORTANT ADMISSION FACTORS

Academic GPA, application
essay, character/personal
qualities, class rank,
recommendation(s), rigor of
secondary school record

ABOUT SWARTHMORE COLLEGE

Swarthmore College is among the most prestigious liberal arts schools in the country, and its students embrace their good fortune in gaining entry here. They are also constantly reminded how smart and capable they are supposed to be, by a workload that can at times appear unmanageable. Most do manage, however, with the help of extremely supportive professors and administrators. And when they graduate, they know that they have passed a challenge by fire, and that they are well-tempered to face life's challenges. Swarthmore students enjoy an unusual degree of freedom, receiving both the encouragement and the resources to pursue whatever interests them.

Free time, as you might suspect, is in short supply at Swarthmore. Most undergrads pile on extracurricular commitments—philanthropy, student organizations, athletics—atop their heavy academic loads. When they can find the time, students love to grab a cup of joe and discuss the hot topics of the day with their classmates. They find time to party on campus after class and some like to blow off steam in nearby Philadelphia, which is easily accessible by public transportation. Swarthmore students are an extremely bright and creative lot, with political stances that swing to the left.

BANG FOR YOUR BUCK

About half of all Swarthmore undergraduates receive need-based aid every year. The school meets 100 percent of the demonstrated need of all U.S. citizens and permanent residents.

Available awards include the Philip Evans Scholarship Program, which meets recipients' full demonstrated financial need without loans. Evans Scholars also receive a one-time computer purchase allowance and an annual opportunity grant to create a personalized series of learning experiences outside the classroom (e.g., international travel, professional internships, independent research, community service). The awards are given to those whose achievements demonstrate integrity, intelligence, the potential to take advantage of the scholarship's offerings, and a commitment to give back to the community as involved citizens.

"Swarthmore is all about using the knowledge we gain from the classroom to change the world, whether it be discovering a cure for cancer or increasing voter registration in low-income neighborhoods or educating women from developing nations about birth control. Everyone wants to make a difference."

HIGH SCHOOL UNITS RECOMMENDED

4 English, 3 math, 3 science, 3 history, 3 social studies, foreign language, art and music

IMPORTANT ADMISSION FACTORS

Extracurricular activities, standardized test scores

Range SAT Verbal 660–770
Range SAT Math   660–760

APPLICATION DEADLINES

Early decision   11/15
Early decision
   notification   12/15
Regular admission   1/2
Regular notification   4/1
# of transfer applicants   105
% of transfer applicants
   accepted   26

ACADEMICS

Student/faculty ratio   8:1
% faculty teaching
   undergraduates   100
% of classes taught by
   graduate students   0

MOST POPULAR MAJORS

• Biology/biological sciences
• Economics
• Political science and government

EDUCATION REQUIREMENTS

Foreign languages, humanities, sciences (biological or physical), social science

Eugene Lang Opportunity Scholars are selected during the fall semester of sophomore year on the basis of their demonstrated commitment to civic engagement, advocacy, and activism. Scholars receive financial aid based on financial need, without loan or work-study requirements, as well as a summer internship and a budget of up to $10,000 to design and carry out a substantial and innovative social action project.

The National McCabe Scholarship goes to students who demonstrate ability, character, personality, leadership, and service to school and community. The amount awarded is based on a student's demonstrated financial need and all need is met with this scholarship.

Swarthmore even provides aid for study abroad, making this enriching opportunity available to all students.

GETTING IN

Swarthmore is among the most competitive colleges in the United States. The school looks closely at secondary school record, class rank, recommendations, standardized test scores, essay, character/personal qualities, and extracurricular activities. Successful candidates are likely to excel in all of these areas.

WHAT DO GRADUATES DO?

Swarthmore does a great job of graduating professionals. Many leave here and proceed directly to law school, medical school, teacher's colleges, engineering schools, or PhD programs. Many others enter the workforce for a while, then return to school to earn an MBA Swarthmore grads are most likely to wind up in public service, nonprofit organizations, community and international development, research institutes, think tanks, financial services, investment banking, or education. Top employers include Accenture Consulting, Goldman Sachs, National Economics and Research Associates (NERA), the National Institutes of Health (NIH), the Peace Corps, and the World Bank.

THE BOTTOM LINE

Tuition at Swarthmore for 2006–2007 was $32,912. Room and board plus the student activity fee amounted to an additional $10,620, bringing the comprehensive fee to $43,532. Students should figure on at least another $2,068 for books and incidental expenses—more if they plan to fly back home more than once or twice a year. In 2005–2006, the average aid package left students and their families with out-of-pocket expenses amounting to $16,886 per year. Swarthmore practices need-blind admissions and ensures that it will meet 100 percent of demonstrated need for all U.S. citizens and permanent residents. Don't assume you won't receive aid because your family is too well-off. Get this—in 2003–2004, 50 percent of aid recipients came from families earning more than $80,000 per year.

FUN FACTS

Swarthmore has been coed since its founding in 1864. It was one of the first coeducational colleges in the United States.

Swarthmore's alumni ranks include five Nobel Prize winners (chemist Christian Anfinsen, physicist John Mather, economist Ed Prescott, and biologists David Baltimore and Howard Temin); two famous novelists (James A. Michener and Jonathan Franzen); a former governor and presidential candidate (Michael Dukakis); and a whacked-out classical composer (Peter Schickele, sometimes known as P.D.Q. Bach).

Every year the Swarthmore men's and women's rugby team participate in the Dash for Cash, during which they streak down the main hall of Parrish Hall, grabbing donations from onlookers to fund the rugby program. For those who weren't around in the 1970s, "streaking" basically entails running around in the buff. Shoes and masks are generally allowed.

The McCabe Mile is another Swarthmore racing tradition. Students run a mile-long race around the stacks in McCabe Library, which is named after Thomas B. McCabe (class of 1915), the former director of the Scott Paper Company. The winner is awarded a roll of toilet paper.

(Note: Figures in the columns on these two pages represent the school's updated figures for 2006–2007.)

FINANCIAL INFO

Tuition	$32,912
Room & board	$10,300
Average book expense	$1,048
Required fees	$320
Average freshman need-based grant	$26,824
Average freshman need-based loan	$2,199
% of graduates who borrowed	36
Average indebtedness	$12,413

FINANCIAL AID FORMS

Students must submit FAFSA, institution's own financial aid form, CSS/financial aid profile, state aid form, noncustodial (divorced/separated) parent's statement, business/farm supplement, federal tax return, W-2 Statements, year-end paycheck stub.

Financial aid filing deadline	2/15

POSTGRAD

% going to graduate school	21
% going to law school	3
% going to business school	0
% going to medical school	3

CAREER SERVICES

Off-campus job opportunities are good.

TENNESSEE TECHNOLOGICAL UNIVERSITY

PO Box 5006, Cookeville, TN 38505
www.TNTech.edu • Admissions: 931-372-3888
Fax: 931-372-6250 • E-mail: admissions@tntech.edu • Financial Aid: 931-372-3073

STUDENTS

Religious affiliation
                No Affiliation
Academic year
  calendar   semester
Undergrad
  enrollment   7,167
% male/female   54/46
% Asian   1
% Black, non-Latino   4
% Latino   1
% international   1
% from out of state   4
% freshmen return for
  sophomore year   73
% freshmen graduate
  within 4 years   13

STUDENT LIFE

% of students living
  on campus   25
% in fraternities   12
% in sororities   8

ADMISSIONS

of applicants   3,292
% accepted   75
% enrolled   58

HIGH SCHOOL UNITS REQUIRED

4 English, 3 math, 2 science
(1 science lab), 2 foreign
language, 1 social studies, 1
history, 1 visual/performing
art

ABOUT TENNESSEE TECHNOLOGICAL UNIVERSITY

Despite the technological focus its name suggests, Tennessee Tech isn't simply an engineering and science school (although it does excel in both those areas). Actually, less than one-fifth of the student body pursues engineering degrees. Teaching and business administration are both more popular, the arts and sciences division is also robust, and TTU's nursing program is top tier. This is not your run-of-the-mill state university, with tons of students just barely gliding by. TTU professors expect students to work, and to work hard. Engineering and technology classes stress practical applications but don't skimp on the theory; students need to prepare for deep immersion in calculus and chemistry. An excellent Honors Program serves the crème de la crème.

Tech students tend to be religious, conservative, and open to a good time. In other words, they tend to be your typical middle-class, Caucasian Tennesseans. Minorities make up less than 10 percent of the student body. The school draws a fair number of representatives from the political left. There's a large jock population that helps drive the popular intramural sports scene. Undergraduates tend to bail out of town on weekends, but not before blowing off some steam on Thursday nights. Greek parties are popular, while the few bars in town are less so. The Cookeville area is accommodating to outdoorsy types through abundant local options for hiking, rock climbing, kayaking, and caving.

BANG FOR YOUR BUCK

Tennessee Tech offers more than 400 scholarships rewarding a variety of skills and personal attributes. These awards include scholarships not only for skill in athletics, academics, the arts, drama, leadership, and music but also for minority scholarships, ROTC scholarships, and awards to students with alumni connections. To help students keep all these awards straight, TTU offers ScholarWeb, an online tool that allows undergraduates to identify scholarships for which they are eligible.

"This is a very challenging school that must be taken seriously. Those who have graduated from here find that their degree from Tech prepared them better for the workplace than if they had gone elsewhere to study."

In 2005–2006, nearly every student who demonstrated financial need received some form of need-based aid. Sixty-three percent of those students received a scholarship or grant as part of their aid package. On average, TTU aid packages met 78 percent of demonstrated need; a quarter of all aid recipients were pleased to find that the school met 100 percent of their need.

TTU offers academic merit scholarships to new freshmen who are Tennessee residents and who have an ACT composite score of at least 28 and a high school grade point average of at least 3.5. These scholarships range in amounts from $2,500–$5,000 per year, and may be combined with any Tennessee Educational Lottery (HOPE) Scholarships a student might receive. The university also offers scholarships to students from traditionally underrepresented areas within the state of Tennessee, and it partners with Coca-Cola to offer full-tuition scholarships to some first-generation college students.

GETTING IN

High school record and standardized test scores are the most important aspects of any application to TTU. The school also sets minimum standards for certain programs. Engineer hopefuls, for example, must have a high school academic core GPA of at least 2.35 and an ACT Math sub-score of 20. Prospective nursing majors must have a high school academic core GPA of at least 3.0 and an ACT composite score of at least 20. Other pre-professional programs impose minimums similar to the one required by the nursing program.

WHAT DO GRADUATES DO?

Major industries recruiting TTU engineers include defense contractors, the automotive industry, and automotive parts manufacturing. The accounting program attracts numerous accounting firms and also sends many graduates on to MBA programs. Retail management, marketing/sales and financial services are all popular career choices among TTU alumni. Top on-campus recruiters include Denso, Eastman Chemical, Procter & Gamble, Kroger, State Farm, and U.S. Air Force Civilian Careers.

VERY IMPORTANT ADMISSION FACTORS

Academic GPA, rigor of secondary school record, standardized test scores

Average HS GPA	3.24
Range SAT Verbal	490–600
Range SAT Math	500–630
Range ACT	20–26
Minimum TOEFL (paper/computer)	500/173

APPLICATION DEADLINES

Regular admission	8/1
Regular notification	rolling
# of transfer applicants	1,825
% of transfer applicants accepted	70

ACADEMICS

Student/faculty ratio	18:1
% faculty teaching undergraduates	99
% of classes taught by graduate students	1

MOST POPULAR MAJORS

- Business administration/ management
- Elementary education and teaching
- Mechanical engineering

EDUCATION REQUIREMENTS

Computer literacy, English (including composition), history, humanities, math, sciences (biological or physical), social science, speech or professional communication

FINANCIAL INFO

In-state tuition	$3,828
Out-of-state tuition	$14,284
Room & board	$5,964
Average book expense	$1,200
Required fees	$762
Average freshman need-based grant	$3,476
Average freshman need-based loan	$1,477
% of graduates who borrowed	37
Average indebtedness	$18,286

FINANCIAL AID FORMS

Students must submit FAFSA.

POSTGRAD

CAREER SERVICES

Alumni network, alumni services, career/job search classes, career assessment, internships, on-campus job interviews. Off-campus job opportunities are excellent.

THE BOTTOM LINE

In 2006–2007, in-state tuition at TTU was $3,828; room and board cost $5,964; and books and supplies cost an additional $1,200. Thus, direct expenses totaled $1,992. Out-of-state tuition exceeded in-state tuition by $10,456, bringing total costs for out-of-state students to $21,448. Students in both categories must anticipate additional costs such as personal expenses and travel. Estimated post-aid out-of-pocket expenses vary widely from case to case; aid packages are based on demonstrated need. Some packages include both need-based and merit-based awards.

FUN FACTS

The first home team basket in any TTU Golden Eagle basketball game is greeted by a "blizzard" of confetti. Originally this torrent of "snowflakes" consisted of square tissue sheets (known as "Tech squares") used in dormitory restrooms. The school discontinued the use of the squares years ago, so now students must make their own confetti.

Carillon bells ring each quarter-hour on the TTU campus. On special occasions, the carillon plays selected musical pieces. It never plays "Carillon My Wayward Son," however.

Stroll by the fire hydrant on the Main Quad to see a unique site: a grave marker for Dammit, the beloved dog of a former TTU president.

TTU Homecoming wouldn't be complete without the Kazoo Band, populated entirely by costumed members of the Phi Gamma Delta fraternity.

TEXAS A&M UNIVERSITY— COLLEGE STATION

Admissions Counseling, College Station, TX 77843-1265
www.TAMU.edu • Admissions: 979-845-3741
Fax: 979-847-8737 • E-mail: admissions@tamu.edu • Financial Aid: 979-845-3236

STUDENTS

Religious affiliation
No Affiliation
Academic year
calendar   semester
Undergrad
enrollment   36,227
% male/female   51/49
% Asian   4
% Black, non-Latino   3
% Latino   11
% international   1
% from out of state   4
% freshmen return for
sophomore year   91
% freshmen graduate
within 4 years   35

STUDENT LIFE

% of students living
on campus   25
% in fraternities   3
% in sororities   6

ADMISSIONS

of applicants   17,871
% accepted   70
% enrolled   57

HIGH SCHOOL UNITS REQUIRED

4 English, 3 math, 3 science
(2 science lab), 2 foreign
language, 2 social studies, 1
history

ABOUT TEXAS A&M UNIVERSITY—COLLEGE STATION

For most students who attend this icon of the Lone Star State, Texas A&M (TAMU) is more than a school. It's a way of life. Sure, students seek out and receive a solid education and a respected degree, but students choose this school because they know and love the many deep-rooted traditions that make up A&M culture. Twelfth man, Midnight Yell, Reveille: If you're Aggie material, you already know what all these terms mean. Academically, TAMU excels in pre-professional areas, with agricultural science and marketing, business, education, and engineering among its top disciplines. Despite the school's large size, professors are easy to contact and very helpful. That's just the Aggie way.

The sound of students saying "Howdy!" reverberates across the A&M campus. This is one friendly place (it's a tradition, of course). Students work hard during the week then start their weekends on Thursday nights by hitting the local bars and clubs. In the fall, the action builds toward game day, complete with tailgating parties and raucous support for the gridiron Aggies. Otherwise, College Station is relatively quiet. (The city isn't hopping, as say, Austin.) Undergraduates are predominantly Caucasian, conservative Christians, with Hispanics making up the single largest minority population.

BANG FOR YOUR BUCK

TAMU provides need-based assistance to 98 percent of all aid applicants who demonstrate need. An impressive 99 percent of need-based aid packages include some form of need-based grant or scholarship. On average, the school meets 87 percent of aid recipients' demonstrated need with need-based aid and works like mad to meet 100 percent of demonstrated need for 56 percent of aid recipients. Much of TAMU's assistance is classified as non-need based, as the school supplements many of its need-based packages with non-need-based awards.

The Corps of Cadets awards scholarships ranging in value from $1,000–$10,000. These scholarships carry no military obligation. Most Corps scholarships for nonresidents of the state qualify the student for a nonresident tuition waiver.

Students Say

"The Aggie Spirit, the Aggie Traditions, the Aggie way of life—there's no way to explain it."

HIGH SCHOOL UNITS RECOMMENDED

4 English, 3 math, 3 science
(2 science lab), 2 foreign
language, 2 social studies, 1
history, 1 computer course

VERY IMPORTANT ADMISSION FACTORS

Class rank, extracurricular
activities, rigor of secondary
school record, standardized
test scores, state residency,
talent/ability

IMPORTANT ADMISSION FACTORS

Application essay, volunteer
work, work experience

Range SAT Verbal 530–640
Range SAT Math   560–670
Range ACT   23–28
Minimum TOEFL
   (paper)   550

APPLICATION DEADLINES

Regular admission   2/15
Regular notification rolling
# of transfer
   applicants   3,021
% of transfer applicants
   accepted   62

ACADEMICS

Student/faculty ratio   20:1
% faculty teaching
   undergraduates   75
% of classes taught by
   graduate students   25

Numerous departmental scholarships are available at TAMU, as are general scholarships for those who excel in athletics, academics, the arts, music, drama, and leadership. ROTC scholarships are available, too, as are scholarships for students with alumni relations and for dependents of TAMU employees.

GETTING IN

All Texas residents and out-of-state students enrolled in a recognized Texas school and who are ranked in the top 10 percent of their graduating high school class are automatically admitted to TAMU. Priority in choice of major is given to students who complete their applications early. Students who rank in the top 25 percent of their high school class and score at least 1300 on the SAT (with a minimum score of 600 in each component test) are also automatically admitted. Such applicants may not be admitted to the major of their choice, however. Other applicants are considered on a case-by-case basis; admissions decisions are made primarily on the basis of standardized test grades, class rank, and difficulty of curriculum undertaken. Personal essays and evidence of extracurricular activities, leadership, community work, employment, and family background are all considered in borderline cases.

WHAT DO GRADUATES DO?

A&M graduates enter careers in the following areas, among many others (with their average starting salaries in parentheses): accounting ($43,835); aerospace chemical engineering ($57,713); agricultural development ($36,664); construction science ($44,363); education ($33,331); engineering ($49,337); financial services ($37,525); IT ($44,077); marketing ($38,036); mechanical engineering ($50,014); and veterinary technician ($29,801). Many members of the Corps of Cadets move on to positions in the U.S. military.

THE BOTTOM LINE

In 2006–07, Texas residents attending Texas A&M full time paid $4,371 in tuition and an additional $2,595 in required fees. Room and board cost $7,660; books and supplies cost $1,280; transportation cost approximately $796; and personal and miscellaneous expenses totaled $1,756. Thus, the total cost of attending Texas A&M for a Texan was $18,458. Out-of-state students paid an additional $8,250 in tuition, bringing their total cost to $26,708. In 2005–2006, the last year for which such figures were available, TAMU administered $329 million in financial aid. Eighteen percent of that money was awarded in the form of scholarships, 14 percent in grants, 8 percent in tuition waivers, 22 percent in employment, and 38 percent in loans.

FUN FACTS

Texas A&M is famous for its many traditions. One such tradition is Muster, an Aggie reunion that occurs every April 21 at locations around the world.

The Aggies' mascot is Reveille, an American collie. Reveille holds the highest rank in the University's Corps of Cadets.

The George Bush Presidential Library and Museum is located on the Texas A&M campus.

Among A&M's best-known alumni are actor Rip Torn, former HUD secretary Henry Cisneros, and musician/actor Lyle Lovett.

Texas A&M is one of only three schools with a full-time Corps of Cadets Program leading to commissions in all branches of military service: Army, Air Force, Navy, and Marine Corps.

MOST POPULAR MAJORS

- Biological and physical sciences
- Multi/interdisciplinary studies
- Operations management and supervision

EDUCATION REQUIREMENTS

Arts/fine arts, computer literacy, English (including composition), foreign languages, history, humanities, math, philosophy, sciences (biological or physical), social science

FINANCIAL INFO

In-state tuition	$4,371
Out-of-state tuition	$12,621
Room & board	$7,660
Average book expense	$1,280
Required fees	$2,595
Average freshman need-based grant	$8,723
Average freshman need-based loan	$3,726
% of graduates who borrowed	32
Average indebtedness	$16,027

FINANCIAL AID FORMS

Students must submit FAFSA, institution's own financial aid form, Financial Aid Transcripts (for transfer students).

POSTGRAD

CAREER SERVICES

Alumni network, alumni services, career/job search classes, internships, on-campus job interviews. Off-campus job opportunities are excellent.

THOMAS AQUINAS COLLEGE

10000 North Ojai Road, Santa Paula, CA 93060
www.ThomasAquinas.edu • Admissions: 805-525-4417
Fax: 805-525-9342 • E-mail: admissions@thomasaquinas.edu • Financial Aid: 800-634-9797

STUDENTS

Religious affiliation
                     Roman Catholic
Academic year
  calendar   semester
Undergrad
  enrollment   359
% male/female   49/51
% Asian   3
% Latino   7
% Native American   1
% international   7
% from out of state   55
% freshmen return for
  sophomore year   91
% freshmen graduate
  within 4 years   84

STUDENT LIFE
% of students living
  on campus   99

ADMISSIONS
of applicants   196
% accepted   81
% enrolled   64

HIGH SCHOOL UNITS REQUIRED

4 English, 3 math, 2 foreign language, 2 history

HIGH SCHOOL UNITS RECOMMENDED

4 English, 4 math, 3 science, 2 foreign language, 2 history, 3 academic electives

ABOUT THOMAS AQUINAS COLLEGE

No textbooks. No lectures. No majors. No minors. No electives. If this sounds like your idea of college the way it was meant to be, you should take a closer look at Thomas Aquinas College. So how does learning actually take place at this tiny (359 students) Catholic college? One thing is for sure: This isn't your standard college. At TAC, the college's curriculum focuses on the study of the Great Books. Which books? The books written by the minds that have shaped the development of Western thought: Aristotle, Homer, Euclid, T. S. Eliot, Albert Einstein, and, of course, St. Thomas Aquinas himself. Over the course of their four years at TAC, students meet in seminars with their professors—called tutors—to discuss readings in subjects ranging from grammar, logic, rhetoric, arithmetic, geometry, music, astronomy, science, and philosophy. These seminars are small, and each member of the class is expected to contribute. It is also important to note that there are no electives or choices—all students take the exact same courses over their four years at TAC; the goal is to connect these subjects to the grander study of theology. For their part, professors go out of their way not only to guide students in class, but to really get to know them outside the classroom as well.

Though its approach to education is hardly traditional, Thomas Aquinas has a predominantly conservative student body, the majority of whom are white. These students take their faith and their intellectual life very seriously, even to the point of discussing questions posed in seminars during the week on Friday and Saturday nights. On campus, officially sanctioned parties like formal dances and banquets are designed to complement the academic program. That isn't to say that no one goes off to drink in the woods—it happens. The proximity of the Los Padres National Forest provides all manner of outdoorsy distractions, while Santa Barbara and Los Angeles are close, offering the culture and diversions of big cities. Some students do take issue with the strict rules governing conduct and dress code, while others wish the school was large enough to support sports teams. But most are happy with the chance to explore their faith and receive a solid education in the process.

Students Say

"Our school is about returning to the certainty of truth and the pilgrimage to it in the old tradition of Western thought."

BANG FOR YOUR BUCK

Some types of financial aid available at other schools are not available here because the college receives no federal campus-based funds or contracts. To compensate, the college has its own aid program funded through generous contributions from TAC's benefactors. You won't find athletic or music scholarships here, and though 85 percent of students take out an education loan before they graduate, they are, overall, very satisfied with both the quality of the education and the level of assistance they receive to help cover it.

More than most, this school puts students in charge of their own college learning experience. Fittingly, the first type of financial assistance provided by the college is on-campus employment. Students awarded a full "service scholarship" put in 13 hours a week in areas such as food service, buildings or grounds maintenance, the library, or clerical work. In exchange, a $3,180 credit is given against room and board.

GETTING IN

For such an unusual school, the admission process at Thomas Aquinas is fairly standard and straightforward. Your high school class choices, grades, standardized test scores, and essay are all considered to be very important. The average GPA of incoming freshmen hovers around a 3.68. A school with this kind of unique perspective and methods of teaching and learning tends to be self-selecting. While the Admissions Office receives relatively few applications—a total of 196 in 2005–2006—a full 159 of them were invited to enroll (102 accepted). About 50 wait listed students each year are admitted. Apply as early in your senior year as possible if you are serious about attending. (On a side note, homeschooled students have fared well at Thomas Aquinas College.)

WHAT DO GRADUATES DO?

Because there are no majors or academic areas of concentration, grads end up in a wide cross-section of fields. Many proceed to law or med school or earn advanced degrees in fields like philosophy, theology, mathematics, and the classics. Eleven percent of alumni have entered religious life. According to the school's website, "Graduates are teachers, doctors and dentists and nurses, engineers and research scientists, lawyers and political activists, priests . . . postmen and handymen and contractors, businessmen, architects, fathers and mothers, computer scientists and robotics experts, playwrights and composers and journalists."

VERY IMPORTANT ADMISSION FACTORS

Application essay, character/personal qualities, level of applicant's interest, recommendation(s), rigor of secondary school record, standardized test scores

IMPORTANT ADMISSION FACTORS

Academic GPA, religious affiliation/commitment

Average HS GPA	3.68
Range SAT Verbal	630–740
Range SAT Math	570–650
Range ACT	24–29
Minimum TOEFL (paper/computer)	570/230

APPLICATION DEADLINES

Regular notification   rolling

ACADEMICS

Student/faculty ratio	10:1
% faculty teaching undergraduates	100
% of classes taught by graduate students	0

EDUCATION REQUIREMENTS

English (including composition), foreign languages, history, humanities, math, philosophy, sciences (biological or physical), social science, theology, music, logic, rhetoric

FINANCIAL INFO

Tuition	$19,300
Room & board	$6,000
Average book expense	$450
Average freshman need-based grant	$11,949
Average freshman need-based loan	$2,519
% of graduates who borrowed	85
Average indebtedness	$14,000

FINANCIAL AID FORMS

Students must submit FAFSA, institution's own financial aid form, state aid form, tax return, noncustodial parent statement.

POSTGRAD

% going to graduate school	20
% going to law school	8
% going to business school	2

CAREER SERVICES

Alumni network, alumni services, career/job search classes, career assessment, internships, regional alumni, on-campus job interviews. Off-campus job opportunities are fair.

BOTTOM LINE

For 2006–2007, the school reports a tuition of $19,300, room and board expenses of $6,000 and approximately $450 in other costs like books and supplies. This brings the total cost per school year to about $25,750. About 75 percent of freshmen receive need-based financial aid, with the average aid package totaling $15,806. Overall, students who were awarded any need-based aid at all found that their need was met 100 percent.

FUN FACTS:

One of the student organizations on campus, named "The Bushwhackers," consists of a group of volunteers who work to maintain many of the hiking trails in the Los Padres National Forest, which borders campus. As a reward for a hard day's work, the group likes to camp out on a mountaintop under the stars with a high-resolution telescope in tow.

St. Thomas, Patron of Thomas Aquinas College, was born near Naples, Italy, in 1225 and devoted his life to the knowledge of God. He is known for advising a student Brother: "Do not try to plunge immediately into the ocean of learning, but go by way of little streams; for difficult things are more easily mastered once you have overcome the easier ones."

TRANSYLVANIA UNIVERSITY

300 North Broadway, Lexington, KY 40508-1797
www.Transy.edu • Admissions: 859-233-8242
Fax: 859-233-8797 • E-mail: admissions@transy.edu • Financial Aid: 859-233-8239

STUDENTS

Religious affiliation
            Disciples of Christ
Academic year
  calendar   other
Undergrad
  enrollment   1,117
% male/female   42/58
% Asian   2
% Black, non-Latino   2
% Latino   2
% from out of state   18
% freshmen return for
sophomore year   88
% freshmen graduate
  within 4 years   60

STUDENT LIFE

% of students living
  on campus   77
% in fraternities   50
% in sororities   50

ADMISSIONS

of applicants   1,286
% accepted   83
% enrolled   27

HIGH SCHOOL UNITS REQUIRED

4 English, 3 math, 3
science, 2 social studies

HIGH SCHOOL UNITS RECOMMENDED

4 English, 4 math, 4
science, 2 foreign language,
2 social studies, 1 history, 1
academic electives

ABOUT TRANSYLVANIA UNIVERSITY

Students who enroll in Transylvania University find they are welcomed into an extremely friendly and intimate community. Indeed, walking about the campus feels as if everyone knows your name. Fortunately, this sentiment permeates the classroom as well. The small size of the student body (roughly 1,100 matriculated) means small classes—in fact, many have fewer than 10 students. This allows for more personal attention and lets students develop close relationships with their professors.

Transylvania's academic calendar also provides some impressive opportunities. They operate on a 4-4-1 system, which means there are two 14-week semesters, followed by a "short term" held in May. The short term offers students the opportunity to explore interests they might not be able to indulge in during the regular semester. Moreover, a number of the May term classes are held off campus or overseas.

Transylvania's location (in the heart of bluegrass country) certainly adds to its appeal. This growing city of nearly a quarter-million people is just blocks away from downtown Lexington and offers commerce and culture that serves to enrich students' education. Students have ready access to shopping, movies, live entertainment, and restaurants. They also take advantage of this proximity by finding internships and part-time jobs with a variety of organizations and companies located downtown. Are you planning to choose a research-heavy major? A shuttle bus transports students between Transylvania's library and libraries on the University of Kentucky's campus. Additionally, the Lexington Public Library is within walking distance. Should Lexington ever lose its attraction, both Louisville and Cincinnati are only a little more than an hour away.

BANG FOR YOUR BUCK

Transylvania makes a substantial effort to supply an affordable education to its undergraduates. Students find there are numerous options for financial assistance available. Among those are merit-based scholarships that reward academic and leadership achievement, as well as grant loans and campus work—all of which are distributed based upon need.

"I chose Transy because of the close community feeling of a home away from home. Everyone is so nice on campus—I love it."

VERY IMPORTANT ADMISSION FACTORS

Rigor of secondary school record, standardized test scores, high school GPA

IMPORTANT ADMISSION FACTORS

Application essay, class rank, extracurricular activities, recommendation(s)

Average HS GPA   3.5
Range SAT Verbal 540–650
Range SAT Math   535–645
Range ACT   23–28
Minimum TOEFL
   (paper/computer) 550/213

APPLICATION DEADLINES

Regular admission   2/1
Regular notification rolling
# of transfer applicants 49
% of transfer applicants
   accepted   63

ACADEMICS

Student/faculty ratio   13:1
% faculty teaching
   undergraduates   100
% of classes taught by
   graduate students   0

MOST POPULAR MAJORS

• Biology/biological sciences
• Business/commerce
• Psychology

The smartest of the smart cookies will be pleased to know that each year, the university awards 20 William T. Young Scholarships to outstanding incoming freshmen. This covers all tuition and fees, a value that flirts with $85,000. Additionally, there are a number of other scholarships given out for stellar test scores and grade point averages. Among them are the President's Scholarships ($10,000 per academic year); the Morrison Scholarship ($9,000 per year); and the Pioneer Scholarship, which offers $8,000 for the year.

GETTING IN

Admissions counselors appreciate well-rounded candidates. High school transcripts, SAT and ACT scores, letters of recommendation, and extracurricular activities all hold some importance. Applicants are expected to be enrolled in college preparatory courses and should have taken no less than four units of English, three units of mathematics, three units of science, and two units of social science. A background in foreign language will also earn you points. Understand, however, that merely passing these classes won't win you an acceptance letter. Nearly two-thirds of the incoming freshmen graduated in the top 10 percent of their class, so you'll need to hit the books if you want to see a positive result.

WHAT DO GRADUATES DO?

With such a diverse choice of majors, ranging from exercise science to music to business administration, you can be assured that Transylvania graduates can be found in a myriad of industries. The university offers unparallel preparation and advising for all pre-professional programs including dentistry, engineering, law, medicine, ministry, pharmacy, physical therapy, and veterinary medicine. This probably helps to explain why 50 percent of Transylvania's alums go on to graduate or professional school. Roughly one-third of those attend medical or law school. And why shouldn't they? The medical school acceptance rate is better than 90 percent, while the law school acceptance hovers around 100 percent.

THE BOTTOM LINE

For the 2006–2007 academic year, tuition and fees ran $20,950, with room and board totaling $6,850. Moreover, administrators estimate that students spent roughly $750 on books and class supplies. Tack on another $500 in travel costs (what the average student spends) and $1,250 for personal expenditures. The approximate grand total for the year was $30,300 per student.

Around 90 percent of Transylvania's students receive scholarships or some form of aid. Of those who applied for need-based aid, applicants saw 87 percent of their need met on average; the average need-based financial aid package freshmen received during 2006-2007 totaled $18,056. (This figure excludes PLUS loans, unsubsidized loans, as well as private alternative loans.)

FUN FACTS

Transylvania is a Latin word meaning "across the woods." The heavily forested territory of western Virginia that became Kentucky in 1792 was originally called Transylvania, and it became the school's name when the college was founded in 1780.

Many Transylvania alumni have gone on to have successful political careers. Among the distinguished graduates are two U.S. vice presidents, one Supreme Court Justice, 50 U.S. senators, 101 U.S. representatives, 36 governors, and 34 ambassadors.

Transylvania was the 16th college in the United States and the first college west of the Allegheny Mountains.

The University administration building, Old Morrison, is a registered National Historic Landmark that is featured prominently on the official seal of the City of Lexington.

EDUCATION REQUIREMENTS

Arts/fine arts, English (including composition), foreign languages, humanities, math, sciences (biological or physical), social science, Non-Western Cultural Traditions, Western Cultural Traditions

FINANCIAL INFO

Tuition	$20,120
Room & board	$6,850
Average book expense	$750
Required fees	$830
Average freshman need-based grant	$12,719
Average freshman need-based loan	$3,080
% of graduates who borrowed	58.6
Average indebtedness	$14,773

FINANCIAL AID FORMS

Students must submit FAFSA.

Financial aid filing deadline	3/1

POSTGRAD

% going to graduate school	37
% going to law school	6
% going to business school	3
% going to medical school	4

CAREER SERVICES

Alumni network, alumni services, career/job search classes, career assessment, internships, regional alumni, on-campus job interviews. Off-campus job opportunities are excellent.

TRINITY INTERNATIONAL UNIVERSITY

2065 Half Day Road, Deerfield, IL 60015
www.TIU.edu • Admissions: 847-317-7000
Fax: 847-317-8097 • E-mail: tcadmissions@tiu.edu • Financial Aid: 847-317-8060

STUDENTS

Religious affiliation
	Other
Academic year calendar	semester
Undergrad enrollment	1,247
% male/female	40/60
% Asian	2
% Black, non-Latino	12
% Latino	3
% international	1
% from out of state	36
% freshmen return for sophomore year	75
% freshmen graduate within 4 years	60

STUDENT LIFE
% of students living on campus	58

ADMISSIONS
# of applicants	466
% accepted	81
% enrolled	44

HIGH SCHOOL UNITS REQUIRED

3 English, 2 math, 2 science (1 science lab), 2 foreign language, 2 social studies, 3 academic electives

VERY IMPORTANT ADMISSION FACTORS

Academic GPA, rigor of secondary school record, standardized test scores

ABOUT TRINITY INTERNATIONAL UNIVERSITY

Trinity International University, the only Evangelical Free Church of America university in the United States, is a school founded on the belief that all wisdom lies in Jesus Christ and dedicated to preparing students to serve God, regardless of what their major may be. It shouldn't come as a shock, then, that many students come to Trinity on the way to entering the ministry. Other students come to Trinity seeking matrimony—it is said that 85 percent of students find their mates here. Students here are predominantly white, suburban, Protestant-Evangelical, and from traditional, conservative homes. Though some students claim to celebrate diversity on campus, others call for more diversity, not just racially but in terms of opinion and experience. No matter how divergent their backgrounds, all TIU students work to integrate faith into everything they do.

Professors at Trinity International have a genuine love for their students and get to know them more closely by going on outings and talking with them. The learning environment is collaborative, and the classes—particularly the higher level courses—are small, allowing for individual attention and improvement. Students here feel that their teachers work hard to make their classes worthwhile, though some argue that the standards could be set a bit higher.

When they aren't in class, Trinity students list hanging out with friends, discussing religious issues, watching movies, playing video games, shopping, and going to church as some of their favorite activities. The surrounding Forest Preserve also provides opportunities for hiking or lakeside volleyball, and the local area offers restaurants and other diversions. The vibe on campus is social but low-key. For a more high-energy destination, students can always hop on the train and head right to downtown Chicago.

BANG FOR YOUR BUCK

Over 70 percent of Trinity students receive financial assistance, with the average financial package covering between half and two-thirds of tuition, fees, room, and board. In 2006–2007, all students who were determined to have financial need received aid in some form. The average financial aid package was close to $18,000. The school distributes financial aid on the basis of financial need as well as scholastic achievement, and athletic and musical ability. Another perk for students whose church offers to donate funds toward their college education: Trinity will match that donation up to $1,000 for each academic year.

"My school is tightly knit—even with the graduate and seminary side. There are a lot of people that are willing to bridge gaps, and a great sense of togetherness is evident."

Are you a pastor's kid? A new Ordained Family Scholarship Program doles out $12,500 in total gift aid to eligible sons and daughters of ordained Evangelical Free Church of America pastors, staff, and missionaries. The school explains it this way: "A qualifying student with no other financial aid would receive a scholarship of $12,500. A student receiving a $9,000 football scholarship would see an increase in gift aid to a total of $12,500." Students are eligible each year that they remain full-time undergrad status.

GETTING IN

Trinity International looks for academic promise in its applicants, as evidenced through strong grades throughout high school and a fine score on the SAT or ACT. But you don't need to be a genius to have a good shot of getting in. Only 22 percent of Trinity freshmen were in the top 10 percent of their high school class. A student's motivation and Christian commitment also come into play as the admissions staff considers your case, and a favorable letter of recommendation from a pastor is required. Generally speaking, more than 80 percent of those who apply are admitted to Trinity.

WHAT DO GRADUATES DO?

Nearly a quarter of TIU students graduate with a major in education. Naturally, many are then called to the head of the class after they graduate. A number of students arrive with another kind of calling—the intent to enter the ministry. Many do. Others find work in counseling or in business, or they prepare for a second degree in grad school.

IMPORTANT ADMISSION FACTORS

Application essay, character/personal qualities, recommendation(s), religious affiliation/commitment

Average HS GPA	3.31
Range SAT Verbal	490–630
Range SAT Math	470–620
Range ACT	20–27
Minimum TOEFL (paper/computer)	530/197

APPLICATION DEADLINES

Regular notification	rolling
# of transfer applicants	192
% of transfer applicants accepted	67

ACADEMICS

Student/faculty ratio	13:1
% faculty teaching undergraduates	51
% of classes taught by graduate students	0

MOST POPULAR MAJORS

- Business administration/management
- Elementary education and teaching
- Pastoral studies/counseling

EDUCATION REQUIREMENTS

Arts/fine arts, English (including composition), foreign languages, history, humanities, math, philosophy, sciences (biological or physical), social science, Bible

FINANCIAL INFO

Tuition	$19,880
Room & board	$6,550
Average book expense	$910
Required fees	$306
Average freshman need-based grant	$9,778
Average freshman need-based loan	$1,814
% of graduates who borrowed	75
Average indebtedness	$17,794

FINANCIAL AID FORMS

Students must submit FAFSA.

BOTTOM LINE

For 2006–2007, the total cost for a year at Trinity International University is $29,800. This cost includes $19,800 in tuition, $306 in additional fees, $6,550 for room and board, and $910 for books and supplies. Transportation is estimated at $1,130, and other expenses are around $1,000. Seventy-four percent of the freshman class receives some needs based financial aid. The average freshman need-based loan is $3,070, and the average total need-based gift aid is an astounding $5,897. This all translates to an out-of-pocket cost of less than $21,000 per year. Individual scholarships can reduce this amount still further. For example, the Carol Thor Memorial Scholarship offers two awards of $3,750 to students already in the education program who are planning on teaching in an urban school system.

FUN FACTS

TIU lore has it that 85 percent of students find their future mate on campus and get married either during college or shortly after graduation.

Student organizations include a gospel choir, a dance team that performs at halftime during football and basketball games, an orchestra (that includes community members), a handbell choir, and Kids on Kampus, a ministry to the children who live on the TIU campus.

Those who major in Christian ministries can choose from six different areas of emphasis: camping/outdoor education ministries, children's ministries, counseling/social services, intercultural ministries, pastoral ministries, and youth ministries.

TRUMAN STATE UNIVERSITY

McClain Hall 205, 100 East Normal Street, Kirksville, MO 63501
http://Admissions.Truman.edu • Admissions: 660-785-4114
Fax: 660-785-7456 • E-mail: admissions@truman.edu • Financial Aid: 660-785-4130

STUDENTS

Religious affiliation
            No Affiliation
Academic year
  calendar   semester
Undergrad
  enrollment   5,478
% male/female   42/58
% Asian   2
% Black, non-Latino   4
% Latino   2
% international   3
% from out of state   23
% freshmen return for
sophomore year   86
% freshmen graduate
  within 4 years   41

STUDENT LIFE

% of students living
  on campus   51
% in fraternities   31
% in sororities   22

ADMISSIONS

of applicants   4,912
% accepted   82
% enrolled   36

HIGH SCHOOL UNITS REQUIRED

4 English, 3 math, 3 science
(2 science lab), 2 foreign
language, 3 social studies, 1
fine arts

HIGH SCHOOL UNITS RECOMMENDED

4 English, 4 math, 3 science
(2 science lab), 2 foreign
language, 3 social studies, 1
fine arts

ABOUT TRUMAN STATE UNIVERSITY

Truman State University is arguably the premier public liberal arts school in the Midwest and almost certainly the best one in the Show-Me State. For the intelligent, friendly, middle-class Midwesterners who populate its campus, Truman offers small classes, tremendous pre-professional programs, a demanding honors program, and one of the nation's most rigorous and most highly praised liberal arts core curriculums. In addition to the courses in their majors, every student must complete massive quantities of course work in the arts and humanities, communications, mathematics, science, and social sciences. Truman has interesting, caring, and demanding professors. The academic atmosphere is serious, and a profusion of out-of-class work is the norm.

On Truman's beautiful and tranquil campus, you'll find tons of clubs and intramural sports. Christian organizations are also abundant, and fraternities and sororities at Truman manage to maintain a high profile without dominating social life. Kirksville—the small Missouri town that surrounds the campus—offers a reasonably lively bar scene, mixed with college-town book and gift shops, coffeehouses, restaurants, and a multiplex movie theater. Nearby Thousand Hills State Park offers great camping, boating, hiking, and fishing.

BANG FOR YOUR BUCK

Truman provides an affordable alternative to a private liberal arts institution. And we're not just parroting the admissions staff. Tuition is reasonable for Missouri residents and especially discounted for non-residents. Need-based financial aid is as plentiful as you would expect at a state university. Sophomores, juniors, and seniors with decent grades who demonstrate financial need and have exhausted all other sources of funds can borrow an additional $3,000 each year through Truman. Truman's cool Student Computer Purchase Loan Program allows students who have completed at least twelve credit hours to borrow up to $2,000 toward the purchase of a computer, printer, and related software. Truman also offers a limited number of $4,000 cultural loans for students who want to spend a semester abroad.

"Truman State University is about allowing students to receive an Ivy-League education without going into enormous debt in the process."

VERY IMPORTANT ADMISSION FACTORS

Academic GPA, class rank, rigor of secondary school record, standardized test scores

IMPORTANT ADMISSION FACTORS

Application essay

Average HS GPA	3.76
Range SAT Verbal	570–670
Range SAT Math	560–660
Range ACT	25–30
Minimum TOEFL (paper/computer)	550/213

APPLICATION DEADLINES

Regular admission	3/1
Regular notification	rolling
# of transfer applicants	317
% of transfer applicants accepted	62

ACADEMICS

Student/faculty ratio	15:1
% faculty teaching undergraduates	98
% of classes taught by graduate students	2

MOST POPULAR MAJORS

• Biology/biological sciences
• Business administration/ management
• Psychology

EDUCATION REQUIREMENTS

Arts/fine arts, computer literacy, English (including composition), foreign languages, history, humanities, math, philosophy, sciences (biological or physical), social science

Merit-based aid also abounds at Truman. There are twelve renewable and ultra-competitive Pershing Scholarships—named in honor of General John J. Pershing, a Truman alumnus—that cover tuition, room and board, and study abroad costs. Recipients get a faculty mentor and become members of the Pershing Society. If you have really good grades and a confirmable leadership track record, check out the Truman Leadership Award—named in honor of the University's namesake, Harry S. Truman. This award covers full tuition, room and board, and recipients receive leadership training that includes a seminar on the Seven Habits of Highly Effective People™. Other sources of aid are also available.

GETTING IN

The most important components of your application to Truman are your high school grades, college-preparatory courses, class rank, and SAT or ACT scores. Average ACT scores usually hover around 27 and the mean grade point average of incoming students is roughly 3.75. In addition to your academic numbers, Truman will seriously review your application essay, extracurricular activities, volunteer activities, and work experience. If you are interested in majoring in nursing, you need to complete a separate application through the nursing program. Auditions are required for students interested in majoring in music.

WHAT DO GRADUATES DO?

Nearly 45 percent of all Truman graduates go straight to graduate and professional school. Other graduates go to work for small businesses, large corporations, medical research firms, government service, and a variety of other industries. Over 200 different companies and organizations recruit on campus each year. Some major employers of Truman alums include Boeing, Caterpillar, Edward Jones, the May Department Stores Company, KPMG, Ernst & Young, IBM, Sprint, Target Stores, SBC, and various hospitals and medical centers.

THE BOTTOM LINE

Residents pay $11,540 for tuition and room and board, and nonresidents pay about $15,970. If you don't think you can afford that, don't get too worried; over 80 percent of all first-year students receive some form of financial assistance. Fifty-nine percent of Truman's students graduate without borrowing a dime. Students who borrow money rack up an average loan debt of approximately $16,546 by the time they graduate.

FUN FACTS

General John J. Pershing is almost certainly Truman's most accomplished alumnus. Pershing had an exemplary military career and was instrumental in bringing about the racial integration of the United States Army.

The women's swim team recently won their fifth consecutive NCAA Division II National Championship by the largest margin in NCAA Division II history. The women's volleyball team finished second at the Division II National Championships.

Each year, more than 500 Truman students study abroad in programs offered around the world. Truman offers summer, semester, and year-long programs and internships abroad. Students study in over 50 different countries annually.

In 1996, Truman State changed its name. It used to be Northeast Missouri State University. Truman State University has had six different names since its establishment in 1867, including Northeast Missouri State Teachers College and the North Missouri Normal School and Commercial College.

Truman's annual Lyceum Series brings a variety of cultural events to campus. Past events have included the Kansas City Symphony, Peking Acrobats, Nobel Laureate Lech Walesa, and the St. Louis Brass Quintet.

FINANCIAL INFO

In-state tuition	$5,970
Out-of-state tuition	$10,400
Room & board	$5,570
Average book expense	$900
Required fees	$122
Average freshman need-based grant	$2,906
Average freshman need-based loan	$3,110
% of graduates who borrowed	43
Average indebtedness	$16,546

FINANCIAL AID FORMS

Students must submit FAFSA, institution's own financial aid form.

POSTGRAD

% going to graduate school	45
% going to law school	4
% going to business school	1
% going to medical school	5

CAREER SERVICES

Career/job search classes, career assessment, internships, on-campus job interviews. Off-campus job opportunities are excellent.

UNITED STATES AIR FORCE ACADEMY

HQ USAFA/ RRS, 2304 Cadet Drive, Suite 200, USAF Academy, CO 80840-5025
www.AcademyAdmissions.com • Admissions: 719-333-2520
Fax: 719-333-3012 • E-mail: rr_webmail@usafa.af.mil

STUDENTS

Religious affiliation
　　　　　No Affiliation
Academic year
　calendar　　　semester
Undergrad
　enrollment　　　4,325
% male/female　　82/18
% Asian　　　　　7
% Black, non-Latino　4
% Latino　　　　　6
% Native American　2
% international　　1
% from out of state　95
% freshmen return for
sophomore year　　92
% freshmen graduate
within 4 years　　　83

STUDENT LIFE

% of students living
　on campus　　　100

ADMISSIONS

of applicants　　9,601
% accepted　　　　18
% enrolled　　　　80

HIGH SCHOOL UNITS RECOMMENDED

4 English, 4 math, 4
science (4 science lab), 2
foreign language, 3 social
studies, 3 history, 1
academic electives, 1
computer

VERY IMPORTANT ADMISSION FACTORS

Character/personal
qualities, interview, rigor of
secondary school record,
standardized test scores

ABOUT UNITED STATES AIR FORCE ACADEMY

At the United States Air Force Academy, cadets endure painfully hard academics, military instruction, and an overall strictly regimented existence. The workload is monstrous—more than most human beings could possibly complete, really. Character and ethics reign supreme. If you can make it through this four-year gauntlet, an Air Force diploma is an awesome credential. The professors are very accessible and committed to their students. An extensive core curriculum covers a broad spectrum of classes in engineering, the humanities, and sciences. Cadets get to work with electron microscopes, nuclear magnetic resonance, and real cadavers. Majors—there are thirty-two to choose from—tend to be of the engineering and science variety, but there are exceptions, like English, geography, and management. The curriculum also includes classes in character development and leadership. During the summer, cadets go skydiving and glider-flying.

The Air Force Academy has its share of geeks, athletes and power-hungry twits. While everyone is extremely competitive, the intense academic and extracurricular pressures force cadets to work together. All cadets are subjected to training evaluations, military inspections, mandatory athletics, and frequent training sessions. You either learn time management, or you leave. Social bonds also form quickly, and they are tight.

BANG FOR YOUR BUCK

While life inside and outside the classroom at the air force academy is a monumental challenge, the financial aspects are downright cushy. It doesn't cost a dime to attend. As a cadet, you'll receive full tuition, room and board, medical care, and even a $700 paycheck every month. You also get $5.75 per day to pay for food served at the Cadet Dining Hall. Don't get overly excited about getting paid, though. The stipend that cadets receive mostly covers the costs associated with attending, like uniforms and books. After you pay for all the stuff you are required to buy, you will probably have some cash left over for petty spending, but not much. You also get free medical and dental care. You'll be issued a personal computer, and the Academy will provide you with all kinds of leadership skills, whip you into top-notch physical shape, and even teach you how to forage for food and build your own shelter by way of a three-week survival trek through the Rocky Mountains.

Students Say

"It's one of the most academically challenging, ethically stringent, and affordable universities in the world, one that our country should be proud of."

In exchange for your salary and your education, Uncle Sam expects a serious commitment and quite a bit of blood, sweat, and tears in return. Academy graduates are awarded a bachelor of science degree and a commission in the United States Air Force. You will have a commitment to serve on active duty for at least five years after graduation—longer if you make it through pilot training. In addition to flying state-of-the-art aircraft, several different career tracks are available. You can, among other things, be an air traffic controller, maintain missiles, or get into the very cool field of space operations. Air Force officers receive 30 days of paid vacation annually and can retire with a full pension after completing twenty years of active service.

Getting In

The Air Force Academy is one of the nation's most highly selective colleges. To get admitted, you need a stellar record of academic and leadership achievement. There's a demanding physical fitness test that all candidates for admission must pass, too. You also need to be between the ages of 17 and 23, a citizen of the United States, have an exceptional moral character, and be unmarried with no children. There's also a nomination process. More often than not, your nomination should come from one of your United States senators or representatives, or from the current vice president. On the academic front, take as many honors and advanced placement math and lab science courses as you possibly can, and get excellent grades in them. Load up on English, too. About 13 percent of the cadets were high school valedictorians or salutatorians. Pretty much everyone graduated high school in the top 25 percent of their class. Math scores on the SAT and Math and Science scores on the ACT scores count a great deal. Shoot for a 650 on the SAT in Math or a 29 on the ACT in both Math and Science. Candidates who score below 580 in Verbal and 560 in Math on the SAT (and below 25 in Math/Science reasoning and 24 in English/Reading on the ACT) probably won't be admitted.

Important Admission Factors

Academic GPA, application essay, class rank, extracurricular activities, talent/ability, volunteer work, work experience

Average HS GPA	3.6
Range SAT Verbal	590–670
Range SAT Math	610–700

Application Deadlines

Regular admission	1/31
Regular notification	rolling

ACADEMICS

Student/faculty ratio	8:1
% faculty teaching undergraduates	100
% of classes taught by graduate students	0

Most Popular Majors

- Business administration/management
- Engineering
- Social sciences

Education Requirements

Computer literacy, English (including composition), foreign languages, history, humanities, math, philosophy, sciences (biological or physical), social science, physical education, flight, military arts and sciences

FINANCIAL INFO

In-state tuition $0
Out-of-state tuition $0

FINANCIAL AID FORMS
Students must submit

POSTGRAD

% going to
  graduate school   5
% going to
  business school   1
% going to
  medical school   1

CAREER SERVICES
Career assessment.

WHAT DO GRADUATES DO?

You will not be shocked to learn that all cadets obtain a solid background in all phases of aviation during their academic careers at the academy. Obviously, many cadets want to be fighter pilots and competition for spots in all levels of flight training (e.g., airlift, bomber, transport) is fierce. The salary and the perks of newly-minted officers compare favorably with starting salaries in virtually every industry. There are many opportunities for advanced education through the Air Force, and at civilian colleges and universities. Among graduating Air Force cadets, 18 percent go into operations, 38 percent enter scientific and technical areas, 20 percent enter logistics, and 24 percent go into mission support.

THE BOTTOM LINE

The Air Force Academy is free. Once you decide to attend, there is an initial $2,400 down payment. First-year cadets are paid over $9,000 per year, and the Academy will simply garnish a portion of your monthly salary each month for several months until the $2,400 is paid. In exchange for a free education and a nominal salary, students agree to serve as an active duty officer in the United States Air Force for at least five years.

FUN FACTS

Over half of Academy graduates may be selected for flight training.

The 18,000-acre campus of the Air Force Academy is located eight miles north of Colorado Springs and 55 miles south of Denver.

Each year, roughly 85 percent of all admitted applicants earned a varsity letter in high school athletics.

You'll take aquatic classes while at the Academy. If want to attend and you don't already know how to swim, learn.

UNITED STATES COAST GUARD ACADEMY

31 Mohegan Avenue, New London, CT 06320-8103
www.CGA.edu • Admissions: 800-883-8724
Fax: 860-701-6700 • E-mail: admissions@cga.uscg.mil • Financial Aid:

STUDENTS

Religious affiliation
No Affiliation
Academic year
calendar   semester
Undergrad
enrollment   1,012
% male/female   72/28
% Asian   5
% Black, non-Latino   3
% Latino   4
% Native American   1
% international   1
% from out of state   94
% freshmen return for
sophomore year   94
% freshmen graduate
within 4 years   68

STUDENT LIFE

% of students living
on campus   100

ADMISSIONS

of applicants   1,597
% accepted   26
% enrolled   73

HIGH SCHOOL UNITS REQUIRED

4 English, 4 math, 3
science (3 science lab)

VERY IMPORTANT ADMISSION FACTORS

Academic GPA, character/
personal qualities, class rank,
extracurricular activities,
rigor of secondary school
record, standardized test
scores

ABOUT UNITED STATES COAST GUARD ACADEMY

Set on hills overlooking the Thames River, the United States Coast Guard Academy is an elite professional college educating future Coast Guard officers. It is also one of the best bargains in higher education. Cadets receive a full scholarship and a monthly stipend, and complete college in four years, debt-free. Graduates get guaranteed positions of leadership as commissioned officers in the United States Coast Guard. Founded in 1876, the Coast Guard Academy is the smallest United States federal service academy. The entire student body ("Corps of Cadets") has fewer individuals than a single graduating class of the academies for the Army, Navy, or Air Force. Life here is disciplined and highly structured. Cadets must attend all classes, lectures, and military training, wear a uniform every day, and abide by a strictly enforced honor code. Coast Guard cadets form a highly supportive group. They are not competing against one another so much as they are working side by side to get through an extremely demanding life experience. Coast Guard classes are small and very challenging. Faculty are student-focused and include a mix of distinguished military officers and civilians. There are 13 programs of study within eight majors, including engineering, math, management, and government. There are no "easy" majors and all cadets study math, science, nautical science, and liberal arts.

The Academy follows a traditional two-semester schedule with summers devoted to professional and military training. "Swab Summer" transforms incoming students from civilians to cadets. Remaining summers may involve training aboard ship or at a Coast Guard station, attending flight school or tactical training, or working with another government agency domestically or abroad. Forty-five days of leave are provided throughout the year.

BANG FOR YOUR BUCK

The Coast Guard Academy provides a four-year bachelor of science program with a full scholarship covering 100 percent tuition for each student. You also receive a stipend ($734 per month to start), and you get a sweet deal on a state-of-the-art computer (which is replaced every two years). Part of the monthly stipend is a spending allowance that increases as cadets approach graduation. Sophomores receive an additional $80 per month; juniors receive an additional $185; and seniors receive an additional $270. The remainder of the monthly stipend goes toward books and uniforms. Any funds that you are able to save over the course of four years will belong exclusively to you upon graduation. Additionally, cadets are eligible for a car loan at an interest rate of about 1 percent. Acad-

IMPORTANT ADMISSION FACTORS

Application essay, recommendation(s), talent/ability

Average HS GPA   3.72
Range SAT Verbal 590–680
Range SAT Math   620–690
Range ACT   25–29
Minimum TOEFL
   (paper/computer) 560/220

APPLICATION DEADLINES

Regular admission   3/1
Regular notification   rolling

ACADEMICS

Student/faculty ratio   9:1
% faculty teaching
   undergraduates   100
% of classes taught by
   graduate students   0

MOST POPULAR MAJORS

• Engineering
• Oceanography, chemical and physical
• Political science and government

EDUCATION REQUIREMENTS

Computer literacy, English (including composition), foreign languages, history, humanities, math, philosophy, sciences (biological or physical), social science, nautical sciences; engineering requirements

emy graduates earn a bachelor of science and a commission as an officer in the Coast Guard. They depart the campus entirely debt-free with one of the most adventurous jobs in the nation—and a car!

The Coast Guard Academy is much smaller than the other service academies, with a cadet corps of less than 1,000. Just like at ritzy liberal arts schools, the cadets receive a lot of personal attention. After graduation, cadets become officers and are eligible for a wide range of fully funded postgraduate study opportunities. There's also flight school. Unlike some service academies we could name, the Coast Guard places no restrictions on assignments based on gender.

GETTING IN

The Coast Guard Academy offers admission solely on the basis of merit; there are no congressional nominations or geographic quotas involved. Applicants must be United States citizens between 17 and 22 years of age upon entering the Academy. Roughly 90 percent of the Coast Guard Academy corps of cadets graduates in the top 25 percent of their high school classes. Median SAT scores range from 1200–1330 (a 27 on the ACT will make you competitive). If you want to get into the Academy, take a strong college-preparatory program that includes chemistry, high-level math, and physics. You need to demonstrate leadership potential and the ability to contribute to campus life. Admissions will look at athletic accomplishment, essays, recommendations, and ask you to take a medical examination. Poor vision, color blindness, and asthma are frequent causes for medical disqualification.

Applicants are required to apply by March 1.

WHAT DO GRADUATES DO?

Academy graduates go straight to active duty as Ensigns, the entry-level rank for Coast Guard commissioned officers. Graduates must serve a minimum of five years past graduation, and many choose to serve longer. First duty assignments are usually two years as a deck officer aboard a Coast Guard cutter. After a successful first tour, other duty assignments are available, including command positions in as little as two years. It is worth noting that Academy graduates who majored in engineering can apply for *any* duty assignment in the Coast Guard. Academy graduates work in careers that include aviation, engineering, marine environmental safety, environmental protection, law enforcement, homeland security, finance, intergovernmental operations, intelligence, and communications.

Every junior officer can apply for advanced education at civilian universities at Coast Guard expense. These programs require an additional service commitment of two months for every month spent in school. While in graduate school, Coast Guard officers are considered full-time students and they continue to receive full pay and benefits.

THE BOTTOM LINE

Coast Guard cadets receive full scholarships covering tuition, fees, and room and board, plus a monthly stipend for books, uniforms, and personal spending. The stipend increases each year and any funds that a cadet does not spend are transferred to the cadet upon graduation. Every cadet also gets an exceptional deal on a state-of-the-art notebook computer, which is replaced every two years.

Applicants who earn an appointment and decide to attend are required to make a one-time deposit of $3,000 into a savings account. This pays for the computer and first uniforms. Whatever is left over remains in a cadet's individual account under his or her control. Individuals who cannot afford the $3,000 deposit can arrange to have the amount deducted in increments from the monthly stipend. All graduates of the Coast Guard Academy are awarded a Bachelor of Science degree and a commission in the Coast Guard, where they must serve at least five years.

FUN FACTS

The Coast Guard is America's humanitarian maritime military service. It is the only U.S. armed service dedicated solely to protecting America's homeland and citizens.

The Coast Guard Academy was the first U.S. service academy to admit women, which it did by choice. The other service academies admitted women only after Congress required it. Women comprise 30 percent of Coast Guard cadets, a much higher percentage than the other service academies. The Coast Guard is America's only military service in which *all* duty assignments are open to women.

Graduates of the Coast Guard Academy choose to serve beyond their five-year commitment at a much higher rate than graduates of the other service academies. According to the Coast Guard, "our humanitarian mission becomes so much a part of our graduates that they choose to continue in the Coast Guard family."

Instead of waiting tables or bagging groceries back home, Coast Guard cadets spend their summers training in the operational Coast Guard. For example, all cadets serve aboard the barque *Eagle,* the only tall ship in America's armed forces.

Every cadet plays on an intercollegiate, club, or intramural team. About 75 percent play an intercollegiate sport—a higher percentage than most civilian colleges and *much* higher than all the other U.S. military academies. There are 23 intercollegiate sports: 11 men's, 9 women's, and 3 coed.

Marine and environmental science, government, and four engineering disciplines.

UNITED STATES MERCHANT MARINE ACADEMY

Office of Admissions, Kings Point, NY 11024-1699
www.USMMA.edu • Admissions: 516-773-5391
Fax: 516-773-5390 • E-mail: admissions@usmma.edu • Financial Aid: 516-773-5295

STUDENTS

Religious affiliation
No Affiliation
Academic year
calendar   trimester
Undergrad
enrollment   1,007
% Asian   3
% Black, non-Latino   2
% Latino   5
% international 2
% from out of state   87
% freshmen return for
sophomore year 92

STUDENT LIFE

% of students living
on campus   100

ADMISSIONS

of applicants   1,797
% accepted   21
% enrolled   77

HIGH SCHOOL UNITS
REQUIRED

4 English, 3 math, 3 science
(1 science lab), 8 academic
electives

ABOUT UNITED STATES MERCHANT MARINE ACADEMY

The United States Merchant Marine Academy is a year-round national service academy that promises to make you into a leader and prepare you for a career at sea—either in the commercial maritime industry or in the armed forces. It's one of the nation's better-kept academic secrets. Kings Point is the place to be if you like the water, if you want very strong academics, and if you crave a military lifestyle. The well-rounded core curriculum is demanding and extremely comprehensive. It includes computer science, heavy doses of math and the liberal arts, and naval warfare. You'll also take courses in aquatic survival, basic firefighting, and self-defense. Students (called midshipmen) can major in marine transportation (if you want to work on the bridge of a ship) or marine engineering (if you want to work in the engine room). Each major offers three specialized areas. Regardless of your major, you will also complete rigorous physical training and spend approximately one year at sea (called sea year) working for commercial shipping companies and visiting exotic ports all over the world. Graduates of the academy receive a bachelor of science, a license as a merchant marine officer (issued by the Coast Guard), and an appointment as a commissioned officer in a reserve component of one of the branches of the United States armed forces.

Midshipmen can participate in many activities on the academy's storied waterfront campus, including sailing, power boating, crew, and windsurfing. But be warned: Life is regimented. Just like at all the other service academies, the men and women who become midshipmen undergo a difficult, challenging, and exasperatingly hectic experience. Midshipmen cram about as much activity into one day as the average college student does in one week. Sharing in an intense academic and regimental program creates a sense of camaraderie amongst midshipmen not found at most colleges.

"Cheap education, traveling the world, and making big bucks after graduation. What more could you want?"

Bang for Your Buck

This place is such an amazing bargain because the cost of tuition and room and board are paid entirely by Uncle Sam. Keep in mind though, that midshipmen are required to cover the cost of purchasing notebook computers and certain associated hardware and software. They must also pay various activity and licensing fees. More specifically, first-year plebes must pay an initial fee of about $6,200 (mostly for buying the mandatory laptop). Sophomores must pay about $1,800; juniors pay $1,700; and seniors pay $2,600. If you can't afford to pay these fees up front, Stafford Loans and PLUS loans are available, just as they are at any other college, and Pell Grants are available for the neediest students. Midshipmen receive no pay while in residence at the Academy. When they are assigned for sea year, however, they receive $764 per month. Speaking of sea year, it takes place for four months during sophomore year and eight months during junior year. Midshipmen are assigned in pairs to apprentice as operators on United States merchant ships. They typically will visit 18 foreign ports around the globe during this period while they study and do shipboard work. The world is their campus!

While graduates of West Point must go into the Army and Naval Academy graduates must go into the navy and so on, a USMMA graduate may enter any branch of the armed forces as an officer (or as a reserve officer).

Getting In

If you want to get admitted to Kings Point, you need to obtain a nomination from your United States representative or one of your senators, and must submit SAT or ACT test results, high school transcripts, recommendations, and the results of a physical examination, and security clearance. Particularly important are standardized scores (you need a 1200 or better on the SAT to be competitive), class rank (about 80 percent of those admitted applicants rank in the top 40 percent of their high school classes), and extracurricular activities that show your leadership ability. It is very important to have a track record of leadership in high school. Examples of what the Admissions folks are looking for include being a varsity sport's team captain, the newspaper or yearbook editor, or president of a club.

High School Units Recommended

4 English, 4 math, 4 science (2 science lab), 2 foreign language, 4 social studies

Very Important Admission Factors

Character/personal qualities, rigor of secondary school record, standardized test scores

Important Admission Factors

Application essay, class rank, extracurricular activities, geographical residence, recommendation(s), talent/ability

Average HS GPA	3.6
Range SAT Verbal	570–690
Range SAT Math	590–670
Range ACT	25–31
Minimum TOEFL (paper/computer)	550/213

Application Deadlines

Early decision	11/1
Early decision notification	12/31
Regular admission	3/1
Regular notification	rolling

ACADEMICS

Student/faculty ratio 11:1
% faculty teaching undergraduates

- Engineering
- Naval architecture and marine engineering
- Transportation and materials moving services

EDUCATION REQUIREMENTS

Computer literacy, English (including composition), history, humanities, math, sciences (biological or physical). Sea Year—All students must complete at least 300 days aboard ship during their sophomore and junior years.

FINANCIAL INFO

In-state tuition	$0
Out-of-state tuition	$0
Required fees	$2,606
Average freshman need-based grant	$2,711
Average freshman need-based loan	$2,414
% of graduates who borrowed	36
Average indebtedness	$9,423

FINANCIAL AID FORMS

Students must submit FAFSA, institution's own financial aid form.

Financial aid filing deadline	5/1

POSTGRAD

% going to graduate school	3
% going to law school	2

CAREER SERVICES

Alumni network, alumni services, career/job search classes, career assessment, internships, on-campus job interviews. Off-campus job opportunities are poor.

WHAT DO GRADUATES DO?

By law, Kings Point graduates are required to serve for five years at sea on a United States flag merchant vessel and participate in the United States naval reserve for eight years. Entering a branch of the military on active duty also fulfills this obligation, and a little over one-quarter of all graduates choose active military duty in the Navy, Coast Guard, Air Force, Army, and the Marine Corps. Typically, about 45 percent of graduates sail as merchant marine officers on United States cargo ships. Another 30 percent work on dry land in shipyard management and shipping company operations. Virtually all graduates get jobs within six months of commencement. Most have offers of employment before graduation day. More than 70 percent of all Kings Point graduates remain in the maritime industry for at least 30 years after graduation.

THE BOTTOM LINE

Tuition and room and board cost nothing at the Academy. In addition to the initial fee of $6,606 and annual fees thereafter (ranging from $1,800 to $2,600), annual expenses are around $500 per year (you don't leave campus much). Since the student body at Kings Point represents all the fifty states and United States territories, travel expenses widely vary. If you were to apply student loans toward all fees (about $12,300 total), your monthly student loan payment would be $151, assuming the highest possible annual rate (8.25 percent) for Stafford Loans.

FUN FACTS

The United States Merchant Marine Academy is often called Kings Point because of its location on the shores of the Long Island Sound in Kings Point, New York.

The Regimental Band is popular, with about 80 students participating out of an overall student body of 950. The band has played in the Macy's Thanksgiving Day Parade, at the opening ceremonies of the U.S. Open, at Shea Stadium, at the opening of the D-Day Museum in New Orleans, and at many other venues.

Major annual social activities are a ring dance in August when the seniors receive their class rings, a formal holiday ball in December, and a formal graduation ball in June.

UNITED STATES MILITARY ACADEMY

646 Swift Road, West Point, NY 10996-1905
www.USMA.edu • Admissions: 845-938-4041
Fax: 845-938-3021 • E-mail: admissions@usma.edu • Financial Aid: 845-938-3516

STUDENTS

Religious affiliation
                    No Affiliation
Academic year
    calendar   semester
Undergrad
    enrollment   4,231
% male/female
% Asian   7
% Black, non-Latino   6
% Latino   7
% Native American   1
% international   1
% from out of state   92
% freshmen return for
sophomore year   92

STUDENT LIFE

% of students living
    on campus   100

ADMISSIONS

of applicants   10,778
% accepted   14
% enrolled   77

HIGH SCHOOL UNITS RECOMMENDED

4 English, 4 math, 4 science
(2 science lab), 2 foreign
language, 3 social studies, 1
history, 3 academic
electives

VERY IMPORTANT ADMISSION FACTORS

Academic GPA, application
essay, character/personal
qualities, class rank, extracurricular activities,
recommendation(s), rigor of
secondary school record,
standardized test scores,
talent/ability

ABOUT UNITED STATES MILITARY ACADEMY

It's all about leadership on the beautiful and fabled campus of the United States Military Academy (better known as West Point), a first-class university where the motto is duty, honor, country, and where students face a broad and daunting core curriculum that includes three engineering courses, two information technology courses, several liberal arts courses, and four math courses. Classes are engaging and discussion-oriented, and they tend to be very small, which means professors know your name. And to put it simply, the student body is diverse. Cadets come from many different backgrounds—ethnically and economically—and from every corner of the country. They all get along with one another quite well, if perhaps only because teamwork is mandatory.

There is more to life than academics at West Point. In four years, students must be molded into military officers. To that end, life is strict, rigorous, regimented, and vastly different from the typical experience at an elite undergraduate university. Life at West Point is defined by study, exercise, and plenty of drilling. Basically, the West Point approach is to cram as much activity into one day as is humanly possible. Sleep is often hard to come by. For their first two years, students have virtually no free time. Intercollegiate athletic events are well attended, even when the army's teams are not that competitive. We should also mention that all cadets who are not on varsity teams are required to play intramural sports.

BANG FOR YOUR BUCK

Attending West Point is entirely free. In fact, starting from your first day, you'll earn an annual salary of a little over $9,000. You won't see much of the money, though. Instead, you'll use it to pay for books, laundry, shoe repair, activities fees, uniforms, and a laptop computer. By the time you are a senior, you should actually be taking home about $500 per month. That's not a lot, but it's not chump change, either.

IMPORTANT ADMISSION FACTORS

Geographical residence, interview, level of applicant's interest, racial/ethnic status, volunteer work

Average HS GPA	3.75
Range SAT Verbal	570–670
Range SAT Math	600–690
Range ACT	21–36

APPLICATION DEADLINES

Regular admission	2/28
Regular notification	rolling

ACADEMICS

Student/faculty ratio	7:1
% faculty teaching undergraduates	100
% of classes taught by graduate students	0

MOST POPULAR MAJORS

- Economics
- History
- Political science and government

EDUCATION REQUIREMENTS

Computer literacy, English (including composition), foreign languages, history, humanities, math, philosophy, sciences (biological or physical), social science, military science, engineering, information technology, physical education, geography, law

In exchange for your salary and education, the Army expects a five-year commitment after graduation and quite a bit of sweat. The summer before your first year at West Point, you'll undergo basic training—road marches, rappelling, training with live ammunition, and the whole works. During the summer between your first and second years, you'll learn about tanks and artillery, build bridges, blow stuff up, and study different kinds of warfare. The next two summers will be devoted to internships and leadership experiences, which could involve training new cadets, leading a platoon in the army, air assault or combat diving training, an internship at a foreign military academy or at a U.S. embassy, or research at a Department of Defense laboratory. West Point graduates are awarded bachelor of science degrees and a commission as a second lieutenant in the army. You must serve a minimum of five years on active duty.

GETTING IN

Applying to West Point is free. Admission revolves around something called a whole candidate score, which is 60 percent academics, 30 percent leadership, and 10 percent physical preparation. Our advice regarding academics is to start early and do well. Take physics and math at least up through calculus. Take several years of the same foreign language. Get A's and score above 1200 on the SAT. Leadership means being a recognized leader selected by your peers, such as being the president or captain of anything, Girl or Boy Scout, newspaper editor, or even a drum major in a marching band. Being an Eagle Scout or all-state at anything is also a serious plus. Physical preparation involves winning varsity letters in team-oriented sports, and a five-event physical aptitude exam that includes a standing long-jump, a 300-yard shuttle run, push-ups, and a kneeling basketball throw. We're not done. You must also be nominated by one of your state's United States senators or representatives. You need three letters of recommendation, and you'll need to write a few essays.

What do Graduates Do?

In the fall of their senior year, cadets select from a number of officer specialties according to the current needs of the army. Selections are awarded according to class rank. Each graduate is commissioned as a second lieutenant. After five years, about 40 percent of all West Point graduates decide to remain on active duty (though the percentage can fluctuate based on the national economy and the needs of the military). Graduates who leave the military are pretty well prepared for leadership in the private sector. Business, graduate, law, and medical schools are also common destinations for West Point graduates once they retire from the military.

The Bottom Line

West Point is free. Once you decide to attend, there is an initial deposit of $2,400 to defray first-year expenses. If you can't afford it, don't fret; you will be advanced the money from your annual pay. First-year cadets at West Point are paid over $9,000 per year, and the Academy will simply garnish a portion of your monthly salary each month until the debt is paid. In exchange for a free education and a nominal salary, students agree to serve as an active duty officer in the army for five years.

Fun Facts

Graduates of the United States Military Academy include two United States presidents, a multitude of ambassadors, state governors, legislators, judges, cabinet members, educators, astronauts, engineers, and corporate executives. Moreover, Ulysses S. Grant, Jefferson Davis, Robert E. Lee, Dwight D. Eisenhower, and Edwin E. "Buzz" Aldrin all graduated from West Point.

After five years as an officer in the army, the average West Point graduate will become a captain and will earn roughly $72,000 total compensation per year.

FINANCIAL INFO

In-state tuition	$0
Out-of-state tuition	$0

POSTGRAD

% going to graduate school	100
% going to medical school	2

UNITED STATES NAVAL ACADEMY

117 Decatur Road, Annapolis, MD 21402
www.USNA.edu • Admissions: 410-293-4361
Fax: 410-295-1815 • E-mail: webmail@usna.com • Financial Aid:

STUDENTS

Religious affiliation
No Affiliation
Academic year
calendar   semester
Undergrad
enrollment   4,422
% male/female   82/18
% Asian   5
% Black, non-Latino   6
% Latino   9
% Native American   2
% international   1
% from out of state   95
% freshmen return for
sophomore year   96
% freshmen graduate
within 4 years   86

STUDENT LIFE

% of students living
on campus   100

ADMISSIONS

of applicants   11,259
% accepted   13
% enrolled   81

HIGH SCHOOL UNITS RECOMMENDED

4 English, 4 math, 2
science (1 science lab), 2
foreign language, 2 history,
1 introductory computer
and typing courses

ABOUT UNITED STATES NAVAL ACADEMY

The very challenging United States Naval Academy is the undergraduate college of the navy and Marine Corps. The future naval and marine officers—known as midshipmen—undertake a total immersion program that blends academics, mandatory extracurricular activities, physical conditioning, and professional and leadership training. The academy dictates all first-year classes and virtually all other courses, too, so you do not get to choose a major. Professors are focused on teaching and couldn't be more accessible. The Administration, while efficient, is big on tradition, paperwork, and micromanagement; but that's life at a service academy.

Midshipmen start their academy stints with eight weeks of basic training. During the summer after your plebe (first) year, you'll go to sea for six weeks for what is euphemistically known as a summer cruise. The next summer can only be described as the coolest thing ever. You get to fly navy aircraft in Pensacola, dive in a nuclear-powered submarine off the coast of Florida, and attack mock enemy positions in the forests of Virginia with real marines. There's also another cruise. In the final summer, you join a navy or Marine Corps operational unit and do the things a junior officer does. During the school year, you don't get much free time. Life for intelligent, goal-oriented, type-A students is hard and Spartan. The restricted lifestyle creates leaders and workaholics, and ends all opportunities for sleep. Free tuition, room and board, and a guaranteed job upon graduation make the hassles bearable. A very palpable sense of camaraderie among the midshipmen is also helpful. In the rare moments when they are allowed to have fun, midshipmen head to the bars of Annapolis, visit nearby colleges, or take in a movie at the mall. Local sponsor families provide relief for students, mostly in the form of home-cooked meals.

BANG FOR YOUR BUCK

Tuition and room and board are free. The navy also pays for medical and dental care, and midshipmen are allowed to fly on a space-available basis in military aircraft around the world. Another great perk is that you get paid to be a midshipman. The stipend that midshipmen receive mostly covers the costs associated with attending, such as books and services (e.g., haircuts, laundry, tailoring, getting shoes fixed). After you pay for all the stuff you are required to buy, you will probably have some cash left over for petty spending. You can also sign up for the Midshipmen Investment Fund (MIF), which allows you to invest a portion of your monthly pay into mutual funds. You get to keep more of your stipend after each completed year.

After graduation, you make a five-year service commitment. Several different career tracks are available. You can, among other things, specialize in surface warfare, enter the submarine service, fly all different kinds of aircrafts (including helicopters or jet fighters), work with nuclear propulsion systems, command Marines, or become a Navy SEAL.

Getting In

It's competitive and convoluted, and there are many hoops to jump through. There's an interview. You need a nomination from a representative or senator (from the federal government, not your state), or from the vice president. You also need to have a clean rap sheet and be between the ages of 17 and 23, unmarried, childless, and (with a few narrow exceptions) a United States citizen. There's a medical examination and a physical aptitude test. If you meet all of these qualifications, we can talk about grades and test scores. They need to be really good. If you want to get admitted to the academy, don't take any blow-off courses in high school. Pile on the college-preparatory course work, and focus on math and science. You need to be in the top 20 percent of your high school class to merit serious consideration, and you need an outstanding SAT score. The average SAT score among incoming plebes is 1300.

What do Graduates Do?

Base pay for newly-minted naval officers is about $3,900 per month. Basic allowance for housing (in Norfolk, Virginia) is $872 for singles and $1,014 for married people. Among the members of the class of 2001, 242 chose aviation. Around 150 (all men) chose submarine warfare, and sixteen chose Navy SEAL training. Roughly 40 midshipmen chose surface warfare with a special focus on nuclear power. Each year, a few midshipmen also get to go to graduate school at prestigious universities; the navy pays. From year to year, over 90 percent of all graduates were able to pursue their first career choice.

VERY IMPORTANT ADMISSION FACTORS

Application essay, character/personal qualities, class rank, extracurricular activities, interview, level of applicant's interest, recommendation(s), rigor of secondary school record, standardized test scores

IMPORTANT ADMISSION FACTORS

Talent/ability

Average HS GPA
Range SAT Verbal 570–680
Range SAT Math   620–700
Minimum TOEFL
(computer)   200

APPLICATION DEADLINES

Regular admission   1/31
Regular notification   rolling

ACADEMICS

Student/faculty ratio   7:1
% faculty teaching
undergraduates   100
% of classes taught by
graduate students   0

MOST POPULAR MAJORS

• Economics
• Political science and government
• Systems engineering

EDUCATION REQUIREMENTS

English (including composition), history, humanities, math, sciences (biological or physical), social science, engineering, naval science, military law, ethics, leadership

FINANCIAL INFO

In-state tuition	$0
Out-of-state tuition	$0
Average book expense	$1,000

FINANCIAL AID FORMS

Students must submit FAFSA.

POSTGRAD

% going to graduate school	2
% going to medical school	1

CAREER SERVICES

Alumni network

THE BOTTOM LINE

It's free and you get paid a small stipend from day one. You do make a commitment to be a naval officer for five years after graduation. You should be aware that there is a $2,500 entrance fee that you are required to pay once you are accepted and decide to attend the Academy. If you can't pay the fee up front, it's not a big deal. There are two options. You can pay the entrance fee in full by the end of your second year, or the academy can take a little bit from your stipend each month over the course of your last two years until the fee is paid.

FUN FACTS

In 1893, a live goat debuted as the navy's mascot at the fourth army-navy game. That goat was named El Cid. At around the turn of the century, after an 11–7 victory over Army, a different goat was the mascot and it was dubbed Bill. The next year a new goat, Bill II, was called upon to assume the role of navy mascot. In 1905, a large Angora from New Jersey was given the name of Bill III. The next year saw another goat called Bill (whose name was eventually changed to "Three-to-Nothing Jack Dalton" and whose mounted remains—reared on his hind legs in a fighting pose—can be seen today in a glass case in the foyer of the Academy's Halsey Field House). In 1916, after several consecutive defeats at the hands of their rival, an ad was run in an Annapolis newspaper: "Wanted: the meanest and fiercest goat possible . . . would like to see same before purchasing." Many, many goats later, Bill XXXI is the current mascot of the navy and is trotted out annually for the army-navy football game.

Notable alumni include former United States President Jimmy Carter, future NBA Hall-of-Famer David Robinson, corporate bigwig and billionaire H. Ross Perot, Senator John McCain, and former Dallas Cowboys quarterback Roger Staubach.

Eighteen majors are offered, including aerospace and electrical engineering, chemistry, computer science, economics, English, history, naval architecture, physics, and political science.

THE UNIVERSITY OF ALABAMA AT BIRMINGHAM

Office of Undergraduate Admissions, HUC 260, 1530 Third Avenue South, Birmingham, AL 35294-1150
www.UAB.edu • Admissions: 205-934-8221
Fax: 205-975-7114 • E-mail: undergradadmit@uab.edu • Financial Aid: 205-934-8223

STUDENTS

Religious affiliation
No Affiliation
Academic year
calendar   semester
Undergrad
enrollment   11,060
% male/female   39/61
% Asian   3
% Black, non-Latino 32
% Latino   1
% international   2
% from out of state 6
% freshmen return for
sophomore year   77
% freshmen graduate
within 4 years   15

STUDENT LIFE

% of students living
on campus   14
% in fraternities 6
% in sororities   6

ADMISSIONS

of applicants   4,255
% accepted   88
% enrolled   43

HIGH SCHOOL UNITS REQUIRED

4 English, 4 math, 4 science
(2 science lab), 1 foreign
language, 4 social studies

VERY IMPORTANT ADMISSION FACTORS

Academic GPA, standardized
test scores

ABOUT UNIVERSITY OF ALABAMA AT BIRMINGHAM

Established in the late 1960s, the University of Alabama at Birmingham is a young university that emphasizes academics and a diverse student population. At UAB students from all ages, religions, and social and ethnic backgrounds contribute to an atmosphere that adds a wealth of social experience to the classroom learning. Students come from so many walks of life, in fact, that it is impossible to feel left out. Everyone finds his or her place within a student body that is eager to make friends. UAB students are also busy. It isn't unusual for an undergrad to work 30 hours a week and still find time to do well in classes and enjoy life.

Academically, UAB has reason to be proud. Its campus houses an internationally known research hospital, and has fantastic premed and pre-nursing programs. The business school also boasts a very high job-placement rate. It doesn't hurt that Birmingham is the largest city in Alabama, offering plenty of opportunities for internships. Professors here know their stuff, and most are armed with PhDs. Even so, most of them are highly accessible outside of class. The school's consistent efforts to improve everything from their facilities and sports teams to student activities are a boon for students too.

UAB's location in the heart of Birmingham means that students are within walking distance of lots of clubs, shops, and restaurants. Weekends usually mean choosing between campus parties and Birmingham's packed clubs and busy nightlife. Sporting events bring enthusiastic fans and school spirit, while a busy Entertainment Committee sponsors movies, comedians, cookouts, and concerts in the mini-park.

BANG FOR YOUR BUCK

First off, UAB participates in the Common Market agreement whereby neighboring states exchange reciprocity for programs not offered in their particular state. Academic scholarships for freshmen students are awarded on a first-come/first-serve basis with priority given to those students who are admitted to UAB by November 1 of their senior year in high school.

Students Say

"The Administration from the president on down has an open-door policy with an appointment. It's a major research university in the middle of a city with a big heart."

IMPORTANT ADMISSION FACTORS

Rigor of secondary school record

Average HS GPA	3.31
Range ACT	20–26
Minimum TOEFL (paper/computer)	500/173

APPLICATION DEADLINES

Regular admission	3/1
# of transfer applicants	2,523
% of transfer applicants accepted	91

ACADEMICS

Student/faculty ratio 18:1

MOST POPULAR MAJORS

- Biology/biological sciences
- Communications studies/ speech communication and rhetoric
- Psychology

EDUCATION REQUIREMENTS

Arts/fine arts, computer literacy, English (including composition), foreign languages, history, math, philosophy, sciences (biological or physical), social science, literature

UAB is intentional in its commitment to make scholarship assistance available to a wider range of outstanding students rather than focusing all funds on the upper 5–10 percent of students, as is the case at many institutions. Academic scholarships are awarded to students on a standard set of merit-based criteria (regardless of need), including both GPA and standardized test scores. These merit-based scholarships are renewable at the same amount (or higher if the scholarship is for "full tuition") in each subsequent year if the student maintains the prescribed GPA, credit hours per term, and continuous enrollment.

Available scholarships include the University Scholar Awards, which cover in-state tuition and fees, plus a $1,000 book stipend annually; Academic Excellence Scholarships for $8,000 per year; the Charles W. Ireland Endowed Scholarship and the McCallum Presidential Scholarship are each valued at $10,000 per year; and the Am-South Academic Scholarship for $12,500 per year.

More than half the students are awarded need-based financial aid.

GETTING IN

Academic credentials and strength of the high school curriculum taken are most important for applications to this school. Standardized test scores are also given a keen appraisal. Students planning to major in biomedical engineering must present a higher ACT/SAT test score than is required for admission to the university. Students majoring in nursing and business are admitted to those respective schools only after having completed prerequisite core courses with a specific GPA. In 2005–2006, 77 percent of all incoming freshmen were ranked in the top half of their high school's graduating class.

WHAT DO GRADUATES DO?

Business, engineering, and nursing are popular fields for these grads. While still in school, students can take advantage of a pre-nursing shadowing program, a mentoring program, professional career counselors, on-campus interviews, co-op and internship programs, and an online resume referral service that sends students' credentials to potential employers. The school's Corporate Partners who hire grads include Honda, ABC, Enterprise Rent-A-Car, New South Federal Savings Bank, and Southland National Insurance Companies.

The Bottom Line

For 2006–2007, the in-state tuition at UAB was $3,960; out-of-state was $9,900. Fees tacked on another $832, in addition to $7,111 for room and board, $900 for books, and an average of $2,800 for travel and other expenses. The average need-based financial aid package awarded at UAB was $14,145 with another $3,265 on average that is awarded in the form of need-based scholarships and/or grants. The average in-state student who demonstrated financial need ended up with zero out-of-pocket expenses.

Fun Facts

A state of the art campus recreation center opened in May 2006 and currently averages over 2,000 users per day.

A new 750-bed freshman residence hall and dining commons opened in fall 2006.

The Science & Technology Honors Program for elite, entering freshmen interested in advanced research welcomed its first class in the fall 2005 term.

UAB participates in the "Tuition Pay" Program, allowing students and their families to schedule tuition payments monthly for better and more affordable budgeting purposes.

FINANCIAL INFO

In-state tuition	$3,960
Out-of-state tuition	$9,900
Room & board	$7,111
Average book expense	$900
Required fees	$832
Average freshman need-based grant	$3,265
Average freshman need-based loan	$2,637
% of graduates who borrowed	53
Average indebtedness	$17,650

Financial Aid Forms

Students must submit FAFSA, institution's own financial aid form.

POSTGRAD

Career Services

Alumni network, alumni services, career/job search classes, career assessment, internships, regional alumni, on-campus job interviews. Off-campus job opportunities are good.

THE UNIVERSITY OF ALABAMA IN HUNTSVILLE

301 Sparkman Drive, Huntsville, AL 35899
www.UAH.edu • Admissions: 256-824-6070
Fax: 256-824-6073 • E-mail: admitme@email.uah.edu • Financial Aid: 256-824-2761

STUDENTS

Religious affiliation
                No Affiliation
Academic year
  calendar   semester
Undergrad
  enrollment   5,232
% male/female   51/49
% Asian   3
% Black, non-Latino   14
% Latino   2
% Native American   1
% international   4
% from out of state   13
% freshmen return for
  sophomore year   75
% freshmen graduate
  within 4 years   13

STUDENT LIFE

% of students living
  on campus   16
% in fraternities   5
% in sororities   4

ADMISSIONS

of applicants   1,698
% accepted   87
% enrolled   45

HIGH SCHOOL UNITS REQUIRED

4 English, 3 math, 3
science, 4 social studies, 6
academic electives

ABOUT UNIVERSITY OF ALABAMA IN HUNTSVILLE

The University of Alabama in Huntsville boasts Colleges of Business, Liberal Arts, Nursing, and Science. Nursing is particularly noteworthy, and you'll find a host of excellent majors across the board. Let's be honest, though: Engineering is really "the thing" at UAH. The first-rate undergraduate engineering programs here include chemical, civil, computer, electrical, industrial, mechanical, and optical engineering. UAH ranks sixth in the United States in NASA-funded research and reliably ranks among the top 20 nationally in producing female engineering graduates. Like every other school where engineering is "the thing," course work ranges from challenging to absolutely grueling. At least professors at UAH offer a great deal of support. Students also value the training, tutoring, job placement assistance, and advising they receive.

Approximately 80 percent of all students come from Alabama. They are very professionally oriented. They want good, respectable careers and the financial certainty that goes along with them. Something like geek-chic flourishes at UAH. Students are generally very studious, but you'll find a little bit of everything, from partiers to Bible-thumpers and all manners of nontraditional and international students. Many students live at home and commute to school. Many others are traditional students who live off campus. Students who are happiest with their social lives find their own niches. When they put down their books (for some, a very rare experience), they often head out to fraternity parties or to the array of bars and clubs in downtown Huntsville.

BANG FOR YOUR BUCK

UAH's very low in-state tuition is a fraction of the cost of comparable schools. For students with financial need, the Alabama Student Assistance Program (ASAP) provides grants ranging from $300–$2,500 per academic year to Alabama residents. Just under half all entering first-year students receive scholarship offers. These awards are both need- and merit-based and they range from funds for textbooks to full-ride tuition scholarships. Merit-based scholarships seem to flow like water and UAH offers a lot more than we could possibly list. National Merit, Achievement, and Hispanic Finalists get four-year full rides. Semi-Finalists get four-year half-rides. Presidential and Academic Excellence Scholarships are renewable and range in value from $600–$7,600. If you graduated as the valedictorian of your high school, UAH will throw in an extra one-time scholarship of $1,000.

The Cooperative Education Program at UAH is awesome and available to all qualified students regardless of major. Co-op students supplement their education with paid, practical work experience by working a minimum of three terms. Co-ops currently earn between $6,500 and $14,000 per year and frequently alternate semesters of full-time enrollment at UAH with semesters of full-time paid employment in a field related to their major. Over 95 percent of co-ops work in Huntsville or the surrounding area and, naturally, many students receive job offers from their employers. As a bonus, co-op employment at UAH often involves cutting-edge technology (and has included working on projects that will fly on space shuttle missions).

GETTING IN

UAH is tough to get into. Entering first-year students have an average high school GPA of 3.4 or higher. The middle 50 percent have ACT scores ranging from 21–27 and SAT Math and Verbal scores ranging from 1030–1240. Grades and standardized test scores are the whole ball of wax for the Admissions staff, or at least most of the ball of wax. Hence, the most important things you can do if you want to attend UAH is to make good grades in as many academically challenging courses as possible and get competitive standardized test scores.

WHAT DO GRADUATES DO?

UAH graduates are highly recruited and are very often able to grab plum jobs in their major fields. Alums have been known to do everything from accounting to technical writing, web design and electrical engineering. Importantly, UAH's Career Services works diligently to provide students with numerous application opportunities. They periodically hold career fairs attracting such companies as Boeing, DirecTV, General Electric, Liberty Mutual, Aerospace Testing Alliance, FedEx, Verizon Wireless and the Alabama Department of Revenue.

VERY IMPORTANT ADMISSION FACTORS

Academic GPA, rigor of secondary school record, standardized test scores

Average HS GPA   3.4
Range SAT Verbal 520–630
Range SAT Math   510–650
Range ACT   22–28
Minimum TOEFL
  (paper/computer) 500/173

APPLICATION DEADLINES
Regular admission   8/15
# of transfer applicants 989
% of transfer applicants
  accepted   94

ACADEMICS
Student/faculty ratio   16:1
% faculty teaching
  undergraduates   100
% of classes taught by
  graduate students   3

MOST POPULAR MAJORS

• Electrical, electronics and communications engineering
• Management information systems
• Nursing—registered nurse training (RN, ASN, BSN, MSN)

EDUCATION REQUIREMENTS

Arts/fine arts, computer literacy, English (including composition), history, humanities, math, sciences (biological or physical), social science

FINANCIAL INFO

In-state tuition	$4,848
Out-of-state tuition	$10,224
Room & board	$5,970
Average book expense	$720
Average freshman need-based grant	$4,222
Average freshman need-based loan	$2,551
% of graduates who borrowed	53
Average indebtedness	$17,043

FINANCIAL AID FORMS

Students must submit FAFSA, institution's own financial aid form.

Financial aid filing deadline	6/1

POSTGRAD

CAREER SERVICES

Alumni services, career/job search classes, career assessment, internships, on-campus job interviews.

THE BOTTOM LINE

In-state resident full-time tuition per academic year at UAH is $4,848. Out-of-state students pay $10,224. Room and board is $5,970 per academic year. Books and supplies cost about $700 per year. The grand total is $11,518 for Alabama residents and $16,894 for everyone else. The average financial aid package is roughly $6,064. Graduates leave UAH with an average debt of approximately $17,000.

FUN FACTS

In recent years, UAH researchers have performed over $200 million in contracts and grants, received 11 patents, and created almost $1 million in licenses and royalty fees.

When in Huntsville, don't miss the U.S. Space and Rocket Center, a museum housing more than 1500 pieces of rocket and space hardware from the U.S. Space Program. Exhibits include a Saturn V rocket, a Skylab simulator, and the Apollo 16 command module "Casper." The museum also features interactive science exhibits, space-themed rides, and one of the original IMAX theaters called the "Spacedome." The Center is the final resting place of Able and Baker, the two monkeys who flew on test flights for the Jupiter rocket.

UAH is a Space Grant university and Huntsville is internationally renowned for its high technology industry and its ties to the U.S. Space Program. UAH has a long history of cooperation with NASA at the nearby Marshall Space Flight Center. UAH also has extensive partnerships with the U.S. Army's Aviation and Missile Command and the Strategic Missile and Defense Command.

THE UNIVERSITY OF ALABAMA AT TUSCALOOSA

Box 870132, Tuscaloosa, AL 35487-0132
www.UA.edu • Admissions: 205-348-5666
Fax: 205-348-9046 • E-mail: admissions@ua.edu • Financial Aid: 205-348-6756

STUDENTS

Religious affiliation
                No Affiliation
Academic year
  calendar   semester
Undergrad
  enrollment   17,372
% male/female   47/53
% Asian   1
% Black, non-Latino   12
% Latino   2
% Native American   1
% international   1
% from out of state   20
% freshmen return for
sophomore year   86
% freshmen graduate
within 4 years   35

STUDENT LIFE

% of students living
  on campus   26
% in fraternities   21
% in sororities   27

ADMISSIONS

of applicants   10,707
% accepted   72
% enrolled   48

HIGH SCHOOL UNITS REQUIRED

4 English, 3 math, 3 science
(2 science lab), 1 foreign
language, 3 social studies,
1 history, 5 academic
electives

ABOUT UNIVERSITY OF ALABAMA AT TUSCALOOSA

The University of Alabama at Tuscaloosa is one of the premier flagship state universities in the South. It's a very big, research-oriented school that is made to feel a little smaller by traditionally strong bonds between students and professors, along with a palpable sense of community and school pride. It also helps that gargantuan-sized classes are few and far between. Undergraduates can choose from dozens of majors in nine educational divisions: arts and sciences, commerce and business administration, communication, education, engineering, nursing, human environmental sciences, social work, and a unique, independent-study program: New College. The bigger colleges within the university have nicer facilities and equipment; the smaller colleges offer more student-faculty interaction and support for individual students.

Bama's ambling, tree-lined campus is home to very friendly, overwhelmingly conservative students. There's ethnic diversity at UA; however, people tend to clot together by skin color. Socially, the fraternities and sororities run this place, end of subject. The party scene is robust and healthy across the student body. Everyone seems to have a good time—from bars and frat parties to tailgating before, during, and after football games. Recreational facilities are dreamy and students are fervent about their Crimson Tide sports teams, especially football. Roll Tide! Roll!

BANG FOR YOUR BUCK

Merit-based academic scholarships are more than plentiful at the University of Alabama. Over 29 percent of all undergraduates receive one. There is no separate application for scholarships. When you send in your admission application, you automatically get considered for all scholarships in your educational division (e.g., arts and sciences, business). Recipients of the Academic Elite Scholarships typically have grade point averages of 3.8 or higher and ACT scores of at least 32 (or an SAT of at least 1400). You also need to write essays and to have a record of extracurricular activity, service, and leadership achievements. These scholarships are worth the value of in-state or out-of-state tuition for four years. The university also kicks in a laptop computer. National Merit or Achievement Finalists get a full ride including on-campus housing for four years. (Just list Alabama as your college of choice with the National Merit Corporation and register for Bama Bound orientation by June 1 so you can get a laptop.) With at least a 27 on the ACT or a 1200 on the SAT (Math and Verbal) and a 3.7 GPA, you are eligible to receive $1,250 per year for four years.

"The strength of UA is its friendliness. Everyone loves to interact and it's easy to feel at home. Football is great too."

HIGH SCHOOL UNITS RECOMMENDED

4 English, 3 math, 3 science (2 science lab), 1 foreign language, 3 social studies, 1 history, 5 academic electives

VERY IMPORTANT ADMISSION FACTORS

Academic GPA, rigor of secondary school record, standardized test scores

IMPORTANT ADMISSION FACTORS

Class rank

Average HS GPA	3.4
Range SAT Verbal	500–630
Range SAT Math	500–630
Range ACT	21–27
Minimum TOEFL (paper/computer)	500/173

APPLICATION DEADLINES

Regular notification	rolling
# of transfer applicants	2,626
% of transfer applicants accepted	65

ACADEMICS

Student/faculty ratio	19:1
% faculty teaching undergraduates	72
% of classes taught by graduate students	12

If you aren't planning to get a scholarship because of your grades (or because you are a music prodigy, or whatever), don't worry: Approximately two-thirds of the undergraduates receive some type of financial aid. All the normal avenues of need-based aid—Pell grants and all manner of subsidized and unsubsidized student loans—are available at UA, just like everywhere. Alabama residents who demonstrate exceptional need are also eligible to receive varying amounts of funding from the Alabama Student Assistance Program.

GETTING IN

Generally, if you've stayed out of serious trouble and have taken a solid and well-rounded college-prep curriculum in high school, you'll get admitted with a grade point average of 2.5 and either a 20 on the ACT or a 950 on the SAT. If you have the grades but not the test scores, or vice versa, then you may or may not get in UA. The minimum high school course requirements for regular admission are four years of English, four years of history and social science, three years of math, at least one year of foreign language, and three years of science.

WHAT DO GRADUATES DO?

While a solid percentage of graduates find their way to grad school, law school, and medical school each year, the student population is mainly very career-focused. An Alabama diploma is a well-respected credential throughout the Southeast. Companies that frequently recruit on campus include BearingPoint, Chevron Texaco, Georgia-Pacific, Honda, Kimberly-Clark, Northrop Grumman, U.S. Steel, and Wal-Mart. Alabama's Career Center also has its own private careerbuilder.com, an online recruiting system called CrimsonCareers. This free service gives students the ability to browse for job opportunities and to post resumes online.

The Bottom Line

For Alabama residents, full-time tuition at Bama plus housing, meals, books, and supplies can total about $11,608. Out-of-state students pay $21,124 for the same package. Room and board costs are $5,380. On average, students receive about $3,732 per year in grants, $5,151 per year in scholarships, and $4,895 per year in loans. The average federal work-study amount per year is roughly $2,900.

Fun Facts

In 2005, the University of Alabama led the nation with five students named to the 2005 *USA Today* All-USA College Academic Team. Alabama's football team won national championships in 1925, 1926, 1930, 1934, 1941, 1961, 1964, 1965, 1973, 1978, 1979, and 1992. The women's gymnastics program captured national championships in 1988, 1991, 1996, and 2002.

For some time now, the University of Alabama has been one of the top public universities in the Southeast in enrollment of African American students. In fall 2004, African Americans comprised 9 percent of all first-year students, 12 percent of the entire undergraduate enrollment, and 12 percent of the overall student population.

Like fish? The internationally recognized University of Alabama Ichthyological Collection is home to one of the largest educational and research collections of fish in the southeastern United States. You'll find more than one million preserved, skeletal, and frozen specimens here.

The University of Alabama owns the rights to six logos for the school. Four of them contain an elephant; five contain the letter "A" at least once.

Most Popular Majors

- Business administration/management
- Elementary education and teaching
- Nursing—registered nurse training (RN, ASN, BSN, MSN)

Education Requirements

Arts/fine arts, computer literacy, English (including composition), foreign languages, history, humanities, math, philosophy, sciences (biological or physical), social science

FINANCIAL INFO

In-state tuition	$5,278
Out-of-state tuition	$15,294
Room & board	$5,380
Average book expense	$950
Average freshman need-based grant	$3,847
Average freshman need-based loan	$3,367
% of graduates who borrowed	50
Average indebtedness	$18,545

Financial Aid Forms

Students must submit FAFSA.

POSTGRAD

Career Services

Off-campus job opportunities are fair.

UNIVERSITY OF ALASKA—FAIRBANKS

PO Box 757480, Fairbanks, AK 99775-7480
www.UAF.edu • Admissions: 907-474-7500
Fax: 907-474-5379 • E-mail: admissions@uaf.edu • Financial Aid: 907-474-7256

STUDENTS

Religious affiliation
No Affiliation
Academic year
calendar   semester
Undergrad
enrollment   4,862
% male/female   43/57
% Asian   3
% Black, non-Latino 3
% Latino   3
% Native American   19
% international   3
% from out of state 13
% freshmen return for
sophomore year   68
% freshmen graduate
within 4 years   6

STUDENT LIFE

% of students living
on campus   29

ADMISSIONS

of applicants   1,777
% accepted   78
% enrolled   72

HIGH SCHOOL UNITS REQUIRED

4 English, 3 math, 3 science
(1 science lab), 3 social
studies, 3 academic
electives

HIGH SCHOOL UNITS RECOMMENDED

2 Foreign language

ABOUT UNIVERSITY OF ALASKA—FAIRBANKS

People come to Alaska from all over the country, and even the world, to brave the below-zero temperatures and study at UAF. Any university described as the furthest north university in the world is bound to attract a certain type of student, and it shows—typical undergrads are Caucasian, male, casual, and with an outdoor edge. But you would expect nothing less from those choosing to take part in Alaska's rough-and-tumble way of life. Though there could of course be more diversity in the student body, this type of undergrad contributes to a laid-back environment filled with kind, though cold, people.

These students aren't the type to get downhearted in Fairbanks' long winters. Instead, they embrace the cold, taking part in skiing, snowboarding, backpacking, camping, and other outdoor activities. Intense intramural sports programs take students' minds off of the weather, as does the school's natural setting. With Mt. McKinley in the distance and the aurora borealis shining bright, the views at UAF are unsurpassed. There is also plenty of opportunity to hit the sled hill on campus. Others get involved in volunteer work, organizations related to their major, accessible leadership positions, or with an on-campus job to earn some extra cash.

It isn't just the views and the frontier spirit that bring students to UAF. The engineering and physical science programs are excellent, and the math and language programs are strong to boot. Combine that with extreme affordability with lots of scholarships to be had, and you have a pretty impressive package. With less than 5,000 students, UAF boasts accessible professors and small classes. This formula combines to ensure that the low tuition price doesn't reflect a low quality education. If you want a chance to get a great value education, and to learn in a rugged setting of great natural beauty, UAF may be a school to check out, just don't forget your parka.

BANG FOR YOUR BUCK

Low tuition prices and a high-quality education make UAF a real value. Students are engaged at every level in opportunities for research and/or hands-on training and still pay a tuition rate that is lower than the institution's peer average. UAF participates in the Western Undergraduate Exchange Program, which significantly reduces nonresident tuition costs for students from participating states. The availability of the Alaska Supplemental Loan Program to nonresidents augments other financial aid. In addition, there are scholar-

Students Say

"The greatest strengths are the availability of activities, especially in winter. Also UAF is one of the only universities that has specialized programs for northern studies in areas such as engineering."

ship and federal work-study opportunities are available to nonresident students. Approximately 1,000 undergraduate and graduate students are employed at UAF.

Financial aid awards are based on both need and merit. UAF instituted the Horizon Grant (a need-based financial aid program) two years ago, which awards tuition assistance of $800 per year to qualified students. The school has also designated an Admissions Outreach Coordinator to assist students in identifying and applying for scholarship opportunities. This coordinator works closely with representatives in the Financial Aid office to provide students the best possible service.

Scholarships and grants are earmarked for students pursuing specific majors, Alaska natives, and other criteria. Scholarship awards range from $800–$8,000 a year. Of note, the state of Alaska offers the UA Scholars Program, a four-year tuition waiver, to Alaska resident high school graduates with demonstrated academic excellence. And for the first time ever, summer sessions have begun offering in-state tuition to out-of-state students.

GETTING IN

All baccalaureate applicants are considered for admission on equal terms. The engineering and science programs have higher levels of academic preparation for entry into their programs, however. To apply, you'll need to submit your high school GPA and ACT and/or SAT scores. Note, however, that ACT and/or SAT scores are strictly used for course placement. The average GPA for incoming freshmen is a 3.11.

WHAT DO GRADUATES DO?

The number one employers for this school—and in Alaska in general—are the State of Alaska and the federal government. Large employers of graduates within the private sector include the resource industry, especially oil and mining, the service industry, fishing and tourism.

VERY IMPORTANT ADMISSION FACTORS

Academic GPA, standardized test scores

Average HS GPA	3.11
Range SAT Verbal	450–600
Range SAT Math	450–580
Range ACT	17–24
Minimum TOEFL (paper/computer)	550/213

APPLICATION DEADLINES

Regular admission	8/1
# of transfer applicants	872
% of transfer applicants accepted	75

ACADEMICS

Student/faculty ratio   11:1

MOST POPULAR MAJORS

• Biology/biological sciences
• Business administration and management
• Psychology

EDUCATION REQUIREMENTS

Arts/fine arts, English (including composition), history, humanities, math, philosophy, sciences (biological or physical), social science

FINANCIAL INFO

In-state tuition	$3,825
Out-of-state tuition	$12,195
Room & board	$5,580
Average book expense	$1,100
Required fees	$693
Average freshman need-based grant	$3,768
Average freshman need-based loan	$5,690
% of graduates who borrowed	49
Average indebtedness	$23,994

FINANCIAL AID FORMS

Students must submit FAFSA.

POSTGRAD

CAREER SERVICES

Alumni services, career/job search classes, career assessment, internships. Off-campus job opportunities are good.

THE BOTTOM LINE

In 2006–2007, in-state tuition for first-year students was $3,825, while out-of-state students paid $12,195. (At this school, the tuition rate rises slightly for both sets of students after the first year.) Fees added $693, plus $5,580 for room and board, $1,100 for books, $2,574 for other expenses, and a student's additional costs for travel and personal needs. This left Alaska residents with $13,772 before aid, and out-of-state students with $22,142. The average financial aid package awarded to those who have demonstrated need is $8,557, making for a substantial savings even before need-based scholarships, merit scholarships, and/or loans are factored in.

FUN FACTS:

Are you ready for this weather? Check out the following temperatures and hours of sun:

*July average temperature: 72F

*January average temperature: -4F

*Hours of sun, June 21 (summer solstice): 21:49

*Hours of sun, December 21 (winter solstice): 3:42

At this school, a growing emphasis is on generating opportunities for undergraduate students to engage in organized research.

UAF participates in electronic funds transfer and encourages completion of online loan applications. UAF offers emergency loans to purchase books should financial aid be delayed, as well as a payment plan option for students.

Gaining residency for the purposes of paying in-state tuition takes two-years of living in-state (during which the student may be going to school). After one year of living in-state, the student may apply for state residency and the Alaska Permanent Fund Dividend, an annual sum that varies between $850 and $1,900.

For those who prefer to keep their interactions with the cold to ice cream cones, UAF has an outstanding summer sessions program. Temperatures in July in Fairbanks average 72 degrees. And with close to 24 hours of sunlight, students have no problem staying awake to do their homework. Summer classes take advantage of the university's unique geographic location and include week-long field trip painting courses at nearby mountain ranges, gold prospecting, and a wilderness writing course at Denali National Park. Another bonus? No matter where students are from, all summer sessions students pay the extremely low in-state tuition rate.

UNIVERSITY OF CALIFORNIA—BERKELEY

Office of Undergraduate Admissions, 110 Sproul Hall #5800, Berkeley, CA 94720-5800
www.Berkeley.edu • Admissions: 510-642-3175
Fax: 510-642-7333 • E-mail: ouars@uclink.berkeley.edu • Financial Aid: 510-642-6442

STUDENTS

Religious affiliation
	No Affiliation
Academic year calendar	semester
Undergrad enrollment	23,447
% male/female	46/54
% Asian	41
% Black, non-Latino	4
% Latino	11
% Native American	1
% international	3
% from out of state	10
% freshmen return for sophomore year	97
% freshmen graduate within 4 years	58

STUDENT LIFE

% of students living on campus	35
% in fraternities	10
% in sororities	10

ADMISSIONS

# of applicants	36,989
% accepted	27
% enrolled	42

HIGH SCHOOL UNITS REQUIRED

4 English, 3 math, 2 science (2 science lab), 2 foreign language, 2 social studies, 2 history, 1 academic electives, 1 visual or performing arts

ABOUT UNIVERSITY OF CALIFORNIA—BERKELEY

Among the top schools in one of the nation's top public university systems, University of California—Berkeley enjoys a cache that few other best-buy schools can match: think Tiffany's, but at Target prices. Berkeley is best known for research; seven Nobel laureates currently grace the faculty list, bringing the historical total of Nobelists with Berkeley ties to nineteen. That's all well and good, but what does it mean for undergraduates? Fortunately for them the quality of instruction at Berkeley is just fine, with professors who see teaching as a privilege rather than a chore. Berkeley's engineering program is both stellar and popular, claiming more than 10 percent of the student body. Biological and life sciences and social sciences and history are also a draw for students. Opportunities to get in on the cutting-edge research at Berkeley abound.

Most disciplines at Berkeley impose tough academic demands, leaving students with little free time during the semester. When students can break free of the books, a world of options awaits them both on campus and off. The school is home to numerous student organizations, a hopping party scene, a beloved football team, and plenty of outlets for political activism. Then there's Berkeley, with its amazing variety of restaurants, and, of course, San Francisco is just down the road. The social scene is hampered somewhat by residential restraints. The Berkeley area is too expensive for most students, so many commute from far away, leaving them less leisure time on campus than they might desire. Asian students constitute the majority, making up nearly 40 percent of the student body.

BANG FOR YOUR BUCK

Every year Berkeley administers over $100 million in federal, state, and institutional need-based grants and scholarships. About half of the undergraduates receive some form of need-based financial aid.

Berkeley provides need-based assistance to 98 percent of all aid applicants who demonstrate need, with almost all of its need-based aid packages including some form of need-based grant or scholarship. On average, the school meets 89 percent of aid recipients' demonstrated need and has found a way to meet 100 percent of demonstrated need for a stunning 56 percent of aid recipients.

HIGH SCHOOL UNITS RECOMMENDED

4 English, 4 math, 3 science (3 science lab), 3 foreign language, 2 social studies, 2 history, 1 academic electives, 1 visual or performing arts

VERY IMPORTANT ADMISSION FACTORS

Academic GPA, application essay, rigor of secondary school record, state residency

IMPORTANT ADMISSION FACTORS

Character/personal qualities, extracurricular activities, standardized test scores, talent/ability, volunteer work, work experience

Average HS GPA   3.9
Range SAT Verbal 590–710
Range SAT Math   630–740
Minimum TOEFL
   (paper/computer) 550/213

APPLICATION DEADLINES

Regular admission   11/30
# of transfer
   applicants   10,439
% of transfer applicants
   accepted   29

ACADEMICS

Student/faculty ratio   15:1
% faculty teaching
   undergraduates   100
% of classes taught by
   graduate students   0

Berkeley awards about 5,000 scholarships annually. These prizes and honors supplement the non-merit aid administered to undergraduates. Merit-based scholarships are drawn from the Cal Bears, Cal Opportunity (reserved for underprivileged students), and the prestigeous Regent's and Chancellor's Scholarship. There are also prizes to reward achievements in film and video, folklore, Greek and Latin translation, Jewish studies, music composition, philosophy, photo-imaging, poetry, political science, and prose.

GETTING IN

Berkeley is a highly selective university in which more than 30,000 eager undergraduates apply each year. The school works hard to give each application its due consideration: Trained admissions readers evaluate each application individually in the comprehensive review process. High grades and test scores are both very important factors, but the school also looks for evidence that students have challenged themselves both academically and in their extracurricular activities. Applicants' personal essays are also considered a very important element of the total application.

WHAT DO GRADUATES DO?

Traditionally about one-quarter of all Berkeley graduates proceed to graduate school within a year of matriculation. Students majoring in chemistry, engineering, and natural resources are most likely to pursue a graduate degree immediately after graduation. (Those who will ultimately wind up in MBA programs, on the other hand, typically work for two to three years before returning to school.) About half the student body finds full-time employment, most often in business (57 percent); followed by industry (14 percent); education (12 percent); nonprofit organizations (9 percent); and government (7 percent). About three-fifths of Berkeley graduates find jobs in the Bay Area. One in 10 takes a job in or around Los Angeles. Another 14 percent find work outside the United States.

The Bottom Line

In 2006–2007, California residents attending Berkeley full-time paid $6,558 in tuition and mandatory fees. Room and board cost $13,074; books and supplies cost an estimated $1,326; transportation expenses averaged $684; and personal and miscellaneous expenses added an additional $1,388. Thus, the cost of attending Berkeley as a California resident in 2006–2007 was $23,030. Nonresidents paid an additional $18,684 in tuition and fees to bring their total to $41,714. The average financial aid package to Berkeley aid recipients totaled $15,203. The average need-based scholarship was $10,937; the average need-based self-help award was $6,146; and the average need-based loan was $5,058.

Fun Facts

Berkeley has been the springboard for many a career in entertainment. Alums include actor Bill Bixby, Counting Crows singer Adam Duritz, Bangles singer Susanna Hoffs, actor Gregory Peck, and *Star Trek* star George Takei.

More than a few famous authors have trod the Berkeley campus as well. Former Berkeley undergrads include Beverly Cleary (*Ramona the Pest*), Joan Didion (*The White Album*), Jack London (*Call of the Wild*), Terry McMillan (*How Stella Got Her Groove Back*), and Irving Stone (*The Agony and the Ecstasy*).

Still not impressed? Berkeley's alumni rolls also include former Chief Justice of the United States Supreme Court, Earl Warren and Apple Computer cofounder Steve Wozniak.

Most Popular Majors

- Computer engineering
- English language and literature
- Political science and government

Education Requirements

Arts/fine arts, English (including composition), history, philosophy, sciences (biological or physical), social science, American cultures, international studies

FINANCIAL INFO

In-state tuition	$0
Out-of-state tuition	$18,684
Room & board	$13,074
Average book expense	$1,326
Required fees	$6,558
Average freshman need-based grant	$12,021
Average freshman need-based loan	$4,254
% of graduates who borrowed	47
Average indebtedness	$13,171

Financial Aid Forms

Students must submit FAFSA, state aid form. Financial aid filing deadline 3/2

POSTGRAD

Career Services

Alumni services, career/job search classes, career assessment, internships, on-campus job interviews. Off-campus job opportunities are excellent.

UNIVERSITY OF CALIFORNIA—DAVIS

178 Mrak Hall, 1 Shields Avenue, Davis, CA 95616
www.ucdavis.edu • Admissions: 530-752-2971
Fax: 530-752-1280 • E-mail: undergradadmissions@ucdavis.edu • Financial Aid: 530-752-2390

STUDENTS

Religious affiliation
　　　　　No Affiliation
Academic year
　calendar　　　　quarter
Undergrad
　enrollment　　　23,458
% male/female　　45/55
% Asian　　　　　　41
% Black, non-Latino　3
% Latino　　　　　　11
% Native American　　1
% international　　　1
% from out of state　2
% freshmen return for
sophomore year　　91
% freshmen graduate
　within 4 years　　42

STUDENT LIFE

% of students living
　on campus　　　　27
% in fraternities　　9
% in sororities　　　8

ADMISSIONS

of applicants　32,437
% accepted　　　　68
% enrolled　　　　25

HIGH SCHOOL UNITS REQUIRED

4 English, 3 math, 2 science
(2 science lab), 2 foreign
language, 2 social studies, 1
academic electives, 1 visual
and performing arts

ABOUT UNIVERSITY OF CALIFORNIA—DAVIS

Boasting the largest campus in the University of California system at over 5,300 acres, the University of California—Davis is a large public university that has come a long way from its agrarian roots. Today, its rigorous academics, vibrant campus community, and location near the state capital and the Bay Area draw students from all over the world; and for those that report that Davis wasn't their top choice, the majority are glad they came. Davis has approximately 23,450 undergraduates, so there is a group or niche for everyone. That said, students tend to be predominantly white or Asian.

UC Davis is known as a world-class research university, offering some of the best undergraduate research opportunities anywhere. Its life sciences division also receives top marks—in fact, the school claims to have more biology majors than any other campus in America. Professors are regarded as excellent despite the occasional bad egg, but students need to take the initiative and make the first move—there are, after all, 23,450 undergraduate peers that also require attention. Psychology, economics, and biological sciences are the most popular majors on campus.

When not studying, Davis students can often be found taking advantage of all the outdoor activities available in the area. Undergrads here have a reputation for being environmentally friendly, so the proximity to hiking, backpacking, camping and skiing is a big plus, as is the beautiful campus. Though the town of Davis itself is small and closes early, the campus is large enough that students always find something to do, such as attend movies, sports events, and performances. The move up into Division I for college athletics also promises future excitement on campus, and San Francisco and Sacramento are only a short drive away.

Students Say

"A top-rated, academically oriented school on par with many of the top private institutions but at a public university price."

BANG FOR YOUR BUCK

As a public institution and a member of perhaps the most preeminent state university system in the world, state support allows UC Davis to provide high-quality, low-cost education to its students, particularly if they are state residents. The variety of need-based financial aid resources are designed to meet the needs of a diverse student population. Most financial aid at Davis is targeted toward the students who need it the most. The University of California system provides substantial university grant funding for its most needy students, often up to the full education cost. More than half the student body here receives some form of need-based financial aid. Scholarships based on merit are also awarded, and UC Davis also provides the full array of student and parent loans, deferred payment plans, and a variety of student job opportunities, both on campus and off.

GETTING IN

Admission to the University of California—Davis is no cakewalk. The average high school GPA for incoming freshmen is 3.70, with 95 percent of the student body in the top 10 percent of their high school classes. The schools of the UC system are known for attracting the top 13 percent of high school graduates in California, the cream of the state's academic crop. An applicant's secondary school record is of primary importance, as are standardized test scores. An applicant's essays, character, extracurricular activities, and special talents are also considered, albeit less so.

HIGH SCHOOL UNITS RECOMMENDED

4 English, 4 math, 3 science (3 science lab), 3 foreign language, 2 social studies, 1 academic electives, 1 visual and performing arts

VERY IMPORTANT ADMISSION FACTORS

Academic GPA, rigor of secondary school record, standardized test scores

IMPORTANT ADMISSION FACTORS

Application essay, character/personal qualities, extracurricular activities, first generation, talent/ability

Average HS GPA   3.70
Range SAT Verbal   500-630
Range SAT Math   560-670
Range ACT   21-27
Minimum TOEFL
  (paper/computer) 550/213

APPLICATION DEADLINES

Regular admission   11/30
Regular notification   3/15
# of transfer
  applicants   7,557
% of transfer applicants
  accepted   58

ACADEMICS

Student/faculty ratio   19:1
% faculty teaching
  undergraduates
% of classes taught by
  graduate students

MOST POPULAR MAJORS

- Biology/biological sciences
    - Economics
    - Psychology

EDUCATION REQUIREMENTS

English (including composition), 3 arts and humanities,
3 science and engineering,
3 social sciences, 1 social-
cultural diversity

FINANCIAL INFO

In-state tuition $0
Out-of-state tuition $26,984
Room & board $11,239
Average book
  expense $1,514
Required fees $8,299
Average freshman
  need-based grant $9,655
Average freshman
  need-based loan $4,425
% of graduates
  who borrowed   50
Average
  indebtedness $12,701

FINANCIAL AID FORMS

Students must submit
FAFSA, state aid form.

POSTGRAD

% going to
  graduate school   40
% going to
  law school   4
% going to
  business school   1
% going to
  medical school   12

WHAT DO GRADUATES DO?

UC Davis students and graduates benefit from the Internship and Career Center (ICC), which provides work experience through involvement in one of hundreds of businesses, industries, community service organizations, governmental agencies, and research laboratories. Additionally, Davis's proximity to the state capital of Sacramento provides incredible opportunities in law and government. Internships are a very important part of the Davis experience, and critical in the development of a career path for graduates. Apple, Delloitte and Touche, Genentech, the Federal Bureau of Investigation, Gap Inc., Industrial Light and Magic, Intel Corporation, the U.S. Department of State, the U.S. Forest Service, and Walt Disney Imagineering are among the companies that have sponsored internships at Davis. Wells Fargo, Intel, Lockheed Martin, and Kaiser Permanente are among the leading employers of Davis graduates.

BOTTOM LINE

In-state fees for California residents is currently $8,299, while out-of-staters were responsible for a total of $26,984, including $18,169 of nonresident tuition. All students need to add an additional $11,239 for room and board if they intend to live on campus and use a meal plan, as well as $1,514 for books and supplies. The average need-based gift awarded to freshmen is $9,655, while $3,300 is awarded in loans, on average. This means that California residents are looking at around $6,600 out of pocket each year. Though if you aren't a California resident, that additional $18,000 dollars of tuition makes the deal a wee bit less palatable.

FUN FACTS

The Department of Viticulture and Enology (concerning the scientific study of grape-growing and winemaking) at Davis has been and continues to be responsible for significant advancements in winemaking utilized by many Californian wineries.

The UC Davis bus service, Unitrans, operates trademark London K double-decker buses. It has been in operation since 1968 and is believed to be the only non-sightseeing transit system in the U.S. to operate vintage double-deck er buses in daily service. The system is operated and managed entirely by students.

UNIVERSITY OF CALIFORNIA— LOS ANGELES

405 Hilgard Avenue, Box 951436, Los Angeles, CA 90095-1436
www.UCLA.edu • Admissions: 310-825-3101
Fax: 310-206-1206 • E-mail: ugadm@saonet.ucla.edu • Financial Aid: 310-206-0400

STUDENTS

Religious affiliation
No Affiliation
Academic year
calendar   quarter
Undergrad
enrollment   24,811
% male/female   44/56
% Asian   38
% Black, non-Latino   3
% Latino   15
% international   4
% from out of state   5
% freshmen return for
sophomore year   97
% freshmen graduate within
4 years   57

STUDENT LIFE

% of students living
on campus   35
% in fraternities   15
% in sororities   11

ADMISSIONS

of applicants   42,227
% accepted   27
% enrolled   39

HIGH SCHOOL UNITS REQUIRED

4 English, 3 math, 2 science
(2 science lab), 2 foreign
language, 2 history, 1
academic electives, 1 visual
and performing arts

ABOUT UNIVERSITY OF CALIFORNIA LOS ANGELES

Home to nearly 36,000 undergraduate and graduate students, UCLA is not a place for people who easily get lost in a crowd. Those who can fend for themselves, though, will find everything they seek in this academic equivalent of a big-box store. Just about every discipline imaginable, taught by more experts than you can fathom, with access to just about every type of research facility ever created are all here, just waiting for you to go find them. Strong areas include—are certainly not limited to—the arts, chemistry, engineering, English, film, history, and premedical studies. Discussions and teacher-student interactions here most often occur in TA-led labs and study sessions; classes themselves tend to be large, impersonal, and lecture-based. A quarterly academic calendar keeps things hopping and the workload intense.

Look around the UCLA campus and you'll find everyone from seriously competitive scholars to overachieving b-school types to performance artists and party animals. Students unsurprisingly socialize in smaller, more manageable cliques including fraternities and sororities. They fan out into the area surrounding campus for food and mild diversion, but for more intense fun they head into greater LA, especially to trendy hot spots in Santa Monica and Hollywood. The beach and promenade are only ten minutes from campus; a couple of hours drive in the opposite direction lands you in some primo ski territory or the desert (such as Palm Springs). College athletics are practically a religion here, with basketball and football accounting for many of the high holy days.

BANG FOR YOUR BUCK

UCLA keeps tuition low for in-state students. Roughly half of all students receive some form of need-based financial assistance through the school. The UCLA Scholarship Resource Center offers counseling and guidance to direct students to outside scholarships to supplement their school-sponsored aid.

Students Say

"UCLA is an awesome school with great weather, a good social scene, and great education in a tight city."

HIGH SCHOOL UNITS RECOMMENDED

4 English, 4 math, 3 science (3 science lab), 3 foreign language, 2 history, 1 academic electives, 1 visual and performing arts

VERY IMPORTANT ADMISSION FACTORS

Academic GPA, application essay, rigor of secondary school record, standardized test scores, talent/ability

IMPORTANT ADMISSION FACTORS

Extracurricular activities, volunteer work, work experience

Average HS GPA	4.13
Range SAT Verbal	570–690
Range SAT Math	600–720
Range ACT	24–30
Minimum TOEFL (paper/computer)	550/220

APPLICATION DEADLINES

Regular admission	11/30
Regular notification	rolling
# of transfer applicants	13,189
% of transfer applicants accepted	38

Undergraduates are eligible for a number of merit-based and directed scholarships. Regents Scholarships reward academic achievement with an annual $5,500 award. Alumni scholarships do the same, to the tune of $1,000–$10,000 per year. Other scholarships serve students with special talents, who meet certain demographic criteria or who receive sponsorship from a particular organization.

Financial aid eligibility is reevaluated each year. Students whose family circumstances remain relatively unchanged from year to year can expect similar aid packages over their course of their tenure here.

Located just two miles from ritzy and celebrity-studded 90210-ville, you can bet your bottom dollar that the cost of living here is above the national average.

GETTING IN

UCLA receives nearly 47,000 applications a year. It is inconceivable that the school could process so many applicants without applying some cut-off formulas. That said, the school does a good job of looking closely at all reasonable candidates, especially those applying to such specialty programs as those in the arts, film, television, and theater. Factors in all admissions decisions include academic GPA and quality of secondary school curriculum, standardized test scores, and quality and difficulty of senior-year course work. Evidence of leadership ability, exceptional achievement in extracurriculars, and compelling personal stories (e.g., overcoming socioeconomic obstacles or personal tragedy to succeed in school) may also influence the admissions decision.

WHAT DO GRADUATES DO?

What *don't* they do? With over 300,000 alumni, UCLA has graduates in just about every field imaginable, and usually lots of them. Plenty head off to graduate school, while others find their way into all types of jobs. The school's spring job fairs bring in more than 60 recruiting companies to campus; the autumn job fair attracts more than 110 employers; and more than 30 companies attended the Internship and Summer Job Fair.

THE BOTTOM LINE

For 2006–2007, the suggested total budget for California residents was $23,293; this figure includes all academic fees, books and supplies, room and board, transportation, insurance, and personal expenses. Nonresidents needed to pony up an additional $18,684 per year in additional tuition. During 2005–2006, the last year for which figures were available, UCLA offered some form of aid to every student who demonstrated need. The school met the need of approximately half those students; on average, the school met about 83 percent of demonstrated need for all aid recipients. Aid recipients who graduated in 2004 left the school with an average loan total of $14,431.

FUN FACTS

UCLA's student body includes representatives from all 50 states and 125 foreign countries.

The UCLA Film and Television Archive is the second-largest collection of its kind. The largest is housed at the Library of Congress.

UCLA's athletic teams have won 99 NCAA titles and 120 team titles in 19 different sports. No other school can match the Bruins' record of accomplishment.

Notable UCLA alumni include baseball legend Jackie Robinson, basketball legend Kareem Abdul-Jabbar, tennis legend Arthur Ashe, Internet legend Vinton Cerf, and moviemaking legend Francis Ford Coppola. And four Nobel laureates, too!

UCLA leads the pack in providing innovative undergraduate programs that extend beyond the traditional classroom. These include special support research by undergraduates, interdisciplinary freshmen "clusters," and a community learning center that links civic activism with academic work.

ACADEMICS

Student/faculty ratio 18:1
% faculty teaching
undergraduates 100
% of classes taught by
graduate students 0

MOST POPULAR MAJORS

- Economics
- Political science and government
- Psychology

EDUCATION REQUIREMENTS

Arts/fine arts, English (including composition), foreign languages, history, humanities, math, philosophy, sciences (biological or physical), social science

FINANCIAL INFO

In-state tuition $6,522
Out-of-state tuition $25,206
Room & board $12,312
Average book
expense $1,554
Required fees $381
Average freshman
need-based grant $11,802
Average freshman
need-based loan $4,744
% of graduates
who borrowed 52
Average
indebtedness $14,431

FINANCIAL AID FORMS

Students must submit FAFSA.

POSTGRAD

CAREER SERVICES

Off-campus job opportunities are good.

UNIVERSITY OF CALIFORNIA— RIVERSIDE

1120 Hinderaker Hall, Riverside, CA 92521
www.UCR.edu • Admissions: 951-827-3411
Fax: 951-827-6344 • E-mail: discover@ucr.edu • Financial Aid: 909-787-3878

STUDENTS

Religious affiliation
No Affiliation
Academic year
calendar   quarter
Undergrad
enrollment   14,792
% male/female   48/52
% Asian   41
% Black, non-Latino   7
% Latino   25
% international   2
% from out of state   1
% freshmen return for
sophomore year   86
% freshmen graduate
within 4 years   39

STUDENT LIFE

% of students living
on campus   28
% in fraternities   4
% in sororities   4

ADMISSIONS

of applicants   19,982
% accepted   83
% enrolled   18

HIGH SCHOOL UNITS REQUIRED

4 English, 3 math, 2 science
(2 science lab), 2 foreign
language, 2 history, 2
academic electives

ABOUT UNIVERSITY OF CALIFORNIA—RIVERSIDE

With its beautiful campus, excellent learning environment, and caring professors, the University of California—Riverside now stacks up quite favorably against its more famous sisters in Berkeley and Los Angeles. Its appeal is widespread and draws about as diverse a group of students as can be assembled, both from within California and abroad. By University of California standards, its size is fairly small, allowing the place to feel comfortable and homey while still offering all the opportunities of a major university. Students find a diverse peer group and a community that's just small enough for people to really get to know one other.

Academics at UCR are tough to beat, and when combined with the attractive financial aid packages, they make for a remarkable value. The computer science program is particularly excellent. Most departments boast accessible professors, particularly in upper-level courses. Some big-school problems do creep in— professors can be too distracted by research opportunities to focus on undergrads, and space in lab sections can be tight. Still, for such a large place, strong efforts are made to cater to students' needs, and there is lots of interaction between students, faculty, and the Administration.

UCR boasts a great campus environment with scores of extracurricular activities, many of which will help students land jobs down the road. Socially, the Greek scene is a dominant and uniting force, bringing fun by the keg-load to campus. Students with wheels escape Riverside for recreation in LA and the beach cities, not much more than an hour away.

BANG FOR YOUR BUCK

As a public institution, state support allows UC Riverside to provide high-quality, low-cost education. The variety of need-based financial aid resources meet the needs of a diverse student population, with most financial aid directed to financially needy students. The University of California provides substantial University grant funding for those with the most need. Need-based UC Riverside grants can range up to $12,000, coupled with Federal Pell Grants of up to $4,050. In 2005–2006, 70 percent of the student body received some form of financial aid.

Students Say

"UCR's campus provides for the full 'college life,' yet its small size creates this . . . essence of togetherness."

Sizeable four-year merit scholarships are awarded each year to the top-ranked incoming freshmen, without regard to need. The merit-based Regents and Chancellor's Scholarships, for example, can cover up to full fees for four years of attendance.

UC Riverside also provides a full array of student and parent loans, deferred payment plans, and a variety of student job opportunities, both on and off campus.

GETTING IN

UC Riverside is competitive, and it shows. In 2005–2006, 94 percent of entering freshmen were ranked in the top 10 percent of their high school's graduating class. Grades, test scores, and high school courses are the most important factors in admission. Extracurricular activities, volunteer work, and work experience are also considered, but to a lesser extent. Freshmen and transfer applicants to the art (studio) major submit a portfolio as part of the admission process.

WHAT DO GRADUATES DO?

Graduates from UC Riverside often find work in sectors including accounting, consumer products and services, engineering, financial services, government, health care, manufacturing and industry, as well as retail and transportation. UC Riverside has partnered with Fortune 500 companies and other employers that hire students, including Johnson & Johnson, Merck & Co., Eli Lilly, GlaxoSmithKline, Pfizer Inc., Amgen, and PacifiCare Health Systems Inc. The school's engineering and science graduates have been hired by big names like Microsoft, Boeing, and Unisys. Graduates moving into accounting, financial services, and consumer products have been snatched up by PricewaterhouseCoopers, Lehman Brothers Holdings, Merrill Lynch, New York Life Insurance Company, Anheuser-Busch Companies Inc., Target, Wal-Mart Stores Inc., Wells Fargo & Company, American Express, and many departments within local, state, and federal government.

HIGH SCHOOL UNITS RECOMMENDED

4 math, 3 science (3 science lab), 3 foreign language

VERY IMPORTANT ADMISSION FACTORS

Academic GPA, application essay, class rank, rigor of secondary school record, standardized test scores

IMPORTANT ADMISSION FACTORS

First generation

Average HS GPA	3.43
Range SAT Verbal	440–560
Range SAT Math	470–610
Range ACT	18–23
Minimum TOEFL (paper/computer)	550/220

APPLICATION DEADLINES

Regular admission	11/30
Regular notification	rolling
# of transfer applicants	4,857
% of transfer applicants accepted	72

ACADEMICS

Student/faculty ratio	18:1
% faculty teaching undergraduates	100
% of classes taught by graduate students	0

MOST POPULAR MAJORS

- Biology/biological sciences
- Business administration/ management
- Psychology

Arts/fine arts, English (including composition), foreign languages, history, humanities, math, philosophy, sciences (biological or physical), social science, ethnic studies

FINANCIAL INFO

In-state tuition	$0
Out-of-state tuition	$18,684
Room & board	$10,200
Average book expense	$1,700
Required fees	$6,591
Average freshman need-based grant	$12,306
Average freshman need-based loan	$4,007
% of graduates who borrowed	62
Average indebtedness	$14,965

FINANCIAL AID FORMS

Students must submit FAFSA, state aid form. Financial aid filing deadline 3/2

POSTGRAD

CAREER SERVICES

Alumni network, alumni services, career/job search classes, career assessment, internships, on-campus job interviews. Off-campus job opportunities are excellent.

THE BOTTOM LINE

In 2006–2007, in-state tuition was free for California residents, while those from out of state had to cough up a cool $18,684. All students need to add on another $6,591 in required fees; $10,200 for room and board (if they chose to live on campus); $1,700 for books and supplies; and up to $3,000 for transportation and other personal expenses. In-state residents were facing a sticker price of $22,217, and out-of-staters (who must really want to be here) were set to pay $40,901. The good news is that if you are able to demonstrate need, the school is able to meet an average of 89 percent of students' need for freshmen. The average need-based package awarded to those in need was $14,743 with an average of another $12,306 in need-based scholarship or grant aids.

FUN FACTS

In the hills above UCR is a yellow "C," which stands for "California" and is one of the largest block letters made of cement in the United States. The "C" was originally a gift to the campus from the graduating class of 1955 and still receives a yearly face-lift or new coat of paint. It is 132 feet high, 70 feet wide, and ranges from 10 feet to 28 feet thick. More than 50 cubic yards of concrete and 500 feet of reinforcing steel were used to construct the "C," which is currently yellow, one of the traditional UC colors, but has been painted white, green, pink, and striped like a zebra. It has been turned into a zero, a C-plus, and a C-minus. One time, it was painted a brownish-green color that made it disappear visually into the hillside by pranksters who left a ransom note. The "C" took three years to build and community leaders donated many of the materials.

Several movies, including *Boys And Girls* (starring Freddie Prinze Jr. and Jason Biggs) and *Slackers* (starring Devon Sawa) have been filmed in part on campus. In addition, Mercedes-Benz used the arches of the Rivera Library in its advertising campaign for its M-class luxury vehicles. Volkswagen also used the arches in their marketing campaign.

UC Riverside alumnus Richard R. Schrock won the 2005 Nobel Prize in Chemistry. Schrock graduated from UCR with a BA in Chemistry in 1967.

What's 161 feet high, has a 171-foot deep foundation, and contains 5,162 holes? The UCR Bell Tower. Aside from being a major meeting location at the UCR campus, the 161-foot tall tower is itself a weekly attraction with its live concert by the UCR Carillonneur, David Christensen. He is the third carillonneur at UCR and, since 1987, has performed more than 500 concerts of music from many genres.

UNIVERSITY OF CALIFORNIA— SAN DIEGO

9500 Gilman Drive, 0021, La Jolla, CA 92093-0021
www.UCSD.edu • Admissions: 858-534-4831
Fax: 858-534-5723 • E-mail: admissionsinfo@ucsd.edu • Financial Aid: 858-534-4480

STUDENTS

Religious affiliation
　　　　　No Affiliation
Academic year
　calendar　　　　quarter
Undergrad
　enrollment　　　21,369
% male/female　　48/52
% Asian　　　　　39
% Black, non-Latino　1
% Latino　　　　　11
% international　　3
% from out of state　2
% freshmen return for
sophomore year　　95
% freshmen graduate
　within 4 years　　54

STUDENT LIFE

% of students living
　on campus　　　33
% in fraternities　10
% in sororities　　10

ADMISSIONS

of applicants　40,518
% accepted　　　44
% enrolled　　　21

HIGH SCHOOL UNITS REQUIRED

4 English, 3 math, 2 science
lab, 2 foreign language, 2
history, 1 academic
electives, 1 visual and
performing arts

ABOUT UNIVERSITY OF CALIFORNIA—SAN DIEGO

Mathematics and the sciences reign supreme at the University of California—San Diego (UC San Diego), a school whose excellent reputation, huge research budgets, and idyllic climate have helped it attract eight Nobel laureates to its faculty. While research and graduate study garner most of the attention, undergraduates still receive a solid education that results in an impressive degree. How much they enjoy the process depends largely on what they study and how assertive they are when they need attention. The division of the undergraduate program into six smaller colleges helps take some of the edge off UC San Diego's big-school vibe, allowing students easier access to administrators. A quarterly academic calendar keeps things moving.

The typical UC San Diego undergrad is hardworking, a little antisocial, and extremely bright. These students populate the premed and engineering programs, and, when not working, they like to relax with a computer game. Surfers, stoners, and a sizeable hardcore Christian community round out the student body. Campus life is generally pretty quiet. Students are often too busy with schoolwork to have fun, and when they have free time, they find hometown La Jolla inhospitable. (The area's a little too upscale for most college students.) The town won't sanction a frat row either, so Greek life is practically dead. Students spend a lot of time at the beach or in competition, enjoying the school's healthy intramural sports programs. Downtown San Diego is hip, but without a car is tough to reach. Tijuana is also close by.

BANG FOR YOUR BUCK

Each year, UC San Diego administers over $92 million in federal, state, and institutional need-based scholarships and grants. Another $8.3 million in non-need-based scholarships and grants are also available.

Of all aid applicants who demonstrate need, UC San Diego provides financial aid assistance to 96 percent of them. Eighty-nine percent of need-based aid packages include some form of need-based grant or scholarship. On average, the school meets 84 percent of aid recipients' demonstrated need, with a quarter seeing 100 percent of their demonstrated need met by the school.

HIGH SCHOOL UNITS RECOMMENDED

4 English, 4 math, 3 science lab, 3 foreign language, 2 history, 1 academic electives, 1 visual and performing arts

VERY IMPORTANT ADMISSION FACTORS

Academic GPA, application essay, character/personal qualities, rigor of secondary school record, standardized test scores, state residency, talent/ability, volunteer work

IMPORTANT ADMISSION FACTORS

Extracurricular activities

Average HS GPA	3.94
Range SAT Verbal	550–660
Range SAT Math	600–710
Range ACT	23–29
Minimum TOEFL (paper)	550

APPLICATION DEADLINES

Regular admission	11/30
Regular notification	rolling
# of transfer applicants	9,291
% of transfer applicants accepted	64

UC San Diego offers numerous academic merit scholarships, too, including the prestigious Regents Scholarship, which provides an honorarium, priority registration, and extended housing and library borrowing privileges. The school also offers a number of restricted merit-based scholarships, such as the James Avery Scholarship (restricted to African American students in the performing or visual arts); the Bay Area Alumni Award (for Bay Area natives only); the Hispanic Scholarship Council Scholarship for Community Service; the Charmaine and Maurice Kaplan Scholarship, for students active in extracurricular activities; and the George Parker Memorial Scholarship, for students who were orphaned for at least three years prior to the age of 18.

GETTING IN

This crowd-pleaser of a school receives over 40,000 applications each year. Admissions decisions are based on a combination of academic and personal achievement factors, including adjusted high school GPA, quality of high school curriculum, and standardized test scores, as well as such factors as leadership qualities, volunteer and community service, family income and educational environment, and special circumstances or personal challenges.

WHAT DO GRADUATES DO?

UC San Diego's survey of students graduating in 2006 found that nearly 40 percent continued to graduate education. Top fields included education (15 percent); engineering and computer science (14 percent); law (15 percent); and medicine (17 percent). Most of the remaining 60 percent found jobs in the following fields (their average starting salaries are also included in parenthesis): communications and the arts (7 percent, $30,800); business (17 percent, $39,900); human services (17 percent, $30,100); life and health sciences (17 percent, $31,900); and technology (30 percent, $54,200).

The Bottom Line

California residents attending UC San Diego full time in 2006–2007 paid $6,685, plus $540 in mandatory fees. Room and board cost $9,657; books and supplies cost an estimated $1,504; transportation expenses averaged $1,965; and personal and miscellaneous expenses added an additional $1,594. Thus, the cost of attending UC San Diego as a California resident in 2006–2007 was $23,566. Nonresidents paid an additional $18,684 in tuition to bring their total to $35,565. The average financial aid package to UC San Diego aid recipients totaled $13,342. The average need-based scholarship was $9,504; the average need-based self-help award was $5,298; and the average need-based loan was $5,109.

Fun Facts

According to the National Science Foundation, UC San Diego is seventh in the nation in total federal research expenditures. The school's annual research funding is well over $700 million.

The UC San Diego faculty includes eight Nobel laureates and nine MacArthur fellows.

Beavis and Butthead and *King of the Hill* creator Mike Judge graduated from UC San Diego.

ACADEMICS

Student/faculty ratio   19:1
% of classes taught by
    graduate students   10

Most Popular Majors

- Economics
- Microbiology
- Political science and government

Education Requirements

Arts/fine arts, English (including composition), foreign languages, history, humanities, math, sciences (biological or physical), social science

FINANCIAL INFO

In-state tuition $6,685
Out-of-state tuition $18,684
Room & board $9,657
Average book
    expense $2,504
Required fees $540
Average freshman
    need-based grant $9,351
Average freshman
    need-based loan $4,489
% of graduates
    who borrowed   51
Average
    indebtedness $14,535

Financial Aid Forms

Students must submit FAFSA, state aid form.
Financial aid
    filing deadline   6/1

POSTGRAD

% going to
    graduate school   30
% going to
    law school   15
% going to
    business school   8
% going to
    medical school   16

UNIVERSITY OF CALIFORNIA— SANTA BARBARA

Office of Admissions, 1210 Cheadle Hall, Santa Barbara, CA 93106-2014
www.UCSB.edu • Admissions: 805-893-2881
Fax: 805-893-2676 • E-mail: appinfo@sa.ucsb.edu • Financial Aid: 805-893-2432

STUDENTS

Religious affiliation	No Affiliation
Academic year calendar	quarter
Undergrad enrollment	18,114
% male/female	45/55
% Asian	16
% Black, non-Latino	3
% Latino	17
% Native American	1
% international	1
% from out of state	5
% freshmen return for sophomore year	91
% freshmen graduate within 4 years	49

STUDENT LIFE

% of students living on campus	26
% in fraternities	8
% in sororities	10

ADMISSIONS

# of applicants	36,963
% accepted	53
% enrolled	20

HIGH SCHOOL UNITS REQUIRED

4 English, 3 math, 2 science (2 science lab), 2 foreign language, 2 social studies, 2 history, 1 visual and performing art, 1 academic elective

ABOUT THE UNIVERSITY OF CALIFORNIA—SANTA BARBARA

The College of Creative Studies at UCSB encompasses art, biology, biochemistry, literature, physics, and several other disciplines, an interesting pairing of fields that suggests the eclectic ambiance of the campus. UCSB also has a College of Letters and Science, a School of Environmental Science, and a College of Engineering, along with graduate programs and off-campus study. Students agree that one of the best things about UCSB, regardless of major, is the professors. They know how to teach and are genuinely interested in doing so. Because it's a research university, undergraduates may be offered the chance to work on research projects. Teaching assistants are also noted for being dedicated and helpful, especially in leading small discussion sections accompanying large lectures in introductory courses. Students also praise the wide range of subjects to study and the intellectual challenge of the classes. With a number of advanced study institutes on campus, the sciences are especially popular, and the humanities and social sciences have strong presences as well. More than 200 majors are offered; the top choices are business, economics, biology, communications, psychology, and engineering.

The campus is about 100 miles northwest of Los Angeles, with views of the Pacific Ocean and the mountains, and typically benevolent Southern California weather. Two-thirds of students are from Southern California, one-third is from the northern part of the state, and fewer than 7 percent of students hail from outside California. Though this makes for an overwhelmingly sun-sand-surf, So-Cal vibe, those from other states say the somewhat provincial atmosphere is that of a welcoming province, with everybody finding a comfortable niche in campus life. About half the students are Caucasian, although Asian and Hispanic students are also well represented. About 95 percent of incoming freshmen live in college housing; in addition to on-campus dorms, the college owns several nearby apartment-style accommodations, and there are private residence halls also. The small town of Isla Vista, where the majority of students live, is a social mecca renowned for its parties. Nearby Santa Barbara offers a variety of clubs, businesses, and activities for students. On campus there are more than 250 organizations including Greek, social activist, political, and environmental groups for students to look into.

Students Say

"A well-balanced system of partying and studying, designed to make the most of your college experience."

BANG FOR YOUR BUCK

As a major research university with a wide range of programs, award-winning scholars (especially in the sciences), and a place where even the teaching assistants are lauded for their commitment to student education, UCSB fuses good value and learning. It's a state school with a freshman class of more than 4,000, so some classes are large, and students must find their own way to community and friends. But with all the resources of a major research school and an enjoyable climate (both geographical and social), it's a bargain at zero tuition for California residents (required fees ring in at $7,010) and a relatively modest cost for out-of-staters.

GETTING IN

The rigor of one's high school academic program, the application, and the application essay are most important, followed by evidence of character, class rank, talent/ability, and extracurricular activities. All incoming freshmen for 2006 ranked in the top quarter of their high school classes. Their average GPA was 3.76. On the SAT the average score was 1182, and on the ACT it was 25. Note that competition for admission is intense, with more than 39,000 applications received in the fall of 2006. About 4,100 freshmen actually enrolled.

WHAT DO GRADUATES DO?

Quaker Oats, Oracle Software, ESPN, *Road & Track* magazine, the State University System of California, and a number of scientific, technical, and software firms employ UCSB graduates. More than 50 employers interview on campus each quarter.

HIGH SCHOOL UNITS RECOMMENDED

4 math, 3 science (3 science lab), 3 foreign language

VERY IMPORTANT ADMISSION FACTORS

Application essay, rigor of secondary school record

IMPORTANT ADMISSION FACTORS

Character/personal qualities, extracurricular activities, standardized test scores, talent/ability

Average HS GPA	3.76
Range SAT Verbal	530–650
Range SAT Math	560–670
Range ACT	22–28
Minimum TOEFL (paper/computer)	550/213

APPLICATION DEADLINES

Regular admission	11/30
Regular notification	3/15
# of transfer applicants	8,398
% of transfer applicants accepted	67

ACADEMICS

Student/faculty ratio   17:1

MOST POPULAR MAJORS

- Business
- Economics
- Psychology

EDUCATION REQUIREMENTS

Arts/fine arts, English (including composition), foreign languages, history, humanities, math, philosophy, sciences (biological or physical), social science, major requirements, minumum 2.0 GPA by time of graduation. Academic Residence Requirement: Students must be registered at UCSB for a minumum of 3 regular quarters, at least 35 of the final 45 units must be completed in the college/school in which the degree is to be awarded.

FINANCIAL INFO

In-state tuition	$0
Out-of-state tuition	$18,684
Room & board	$11,178
Average book expense	$1,505
Required fees	$7,010
Average freshman need-based grant	$11,328
Average freshman need-based loan	$5,515
% of graduates who borrowed	52
Average indebtedness	$15,297

FINANCIAL AID FORMS

Students must submit FAFSA.
Financial aid filing deadline   5/31

POSTGRAD

CAREER SERVICES

Career/job search classes, career assessment, internships, on-campus job interviews. Off-campus job opportunities are excellent.

THE BOTTOM LINE

California residents pay no tuition fees to attend UCSB. Out-of-state students pay $18,684. All students pay $7,300 in educational fees. In 2005, an on-campus room cost $11,178, and board was $2,380. The university estimates that $1,505 is needed for books and supplies. About 60 percent of those who were determined to have financial need were awarded some, and the university met 82 percent of student need on average. In general, award amounts were equally distributed between self help in the form of loans and work-study, and gift aid such as scholarships. The college also awarded non-need-based scholarship funds to about 100 students that year, with an average amount of $6,000.

FUN FACTS

Oceanographer Robert Ballard and astronaut Leroy Chiao are UCSB alumni, as is media personality Christine Craft.

The school teams are called the "Gauchos." Don't know what a gaucho looks like? Think Zorro. A number of UCSB alumni have gone on to the ranks of major league baseball.

UCSB is home to the Southern California Earthquake Research Center.

UNIVERSITY OF CALIFORNIA— SANTA CRUZ

Office of Admissions, Cook House, 1156 High Street, Santa Cruz, CA 95064
http://Admissions.UCSC.edu • Admissions: 831-459-4008
Fax: 831-459-4452 • E-mail: admissions@ucsc.edu • Financial Aid: 831-459-2963

STUDENTS

Religious affiliation
    No Affiliation
Academic year
    calendar   quarter
Undergrad
    enrollment   13,588
% male/female   46/54
% Asian   19
% Black, non-Latino   3
% Latino   15
% Native American   1
% international   1
% from out of state 4
% freshmen return for
sophomore year   89
% freshmen graduate
    within 4 years   42

STUDENT LIFE

% of students living
    on campus   45
% in fraternities   1
% in sororities   1

ADMISSIONS

of applicants   23,003
% accepted   75
% enrolled   17

HIGH SCHOOL UNITS REQUIRED

4 English, 3 math, 2 science
(2 science lab), 2 foreign
language, 1 social studies, 1
history, 1 academic
electives, 1 visual or
performing arts

ABOUT UNIVERSITY OF CALIFORNIA—SANTA CRUZ

The size of the undergraduate program at University of California—Santa Cruz has increased by about 50 percent over the past decade. In the process, UCSC has been transformed from a relatively small and unheralded school to a major national research center. UCSC has worked hard to maintain its "culture of teaching" over the years, but with this growth has come an inevitable decline in student-teacher interaction. Professors are still relatively accessible, but it just isn't the cozy academic Valhalla it once was. UCSC uses a residential-college system to abate the effects of expansion. The system breaks students into smaller groups that make it easier for them to make friends and form study groups. Psychology and business are the most popular programs, while biology (premed) is considered the strongest and most competitive.

Once a legendary bastion of hippies and surfers, UCSC now accommodates a broader population that includes science geeks, jocks, preps, ravers, and, of course, those hippies and surfers. Asian Americans and Pacific Islanders constitute the largest minority (nearly 20 percent); Hispanics are also well represented, constituting 14 percent of the undergraduate student body. Most students at UCSC are pretty chill, in accordance with local custom. The town reinforces the live-and-let-live vibe. Santa Cruz is a copasetic place where gorgeous natural surroundings have a pacifying effect on everyone. Downtown Santa Cruz has plenty to offer in the way of cafes, restaurants, shopping, galleries, and live music venues.

BANG FOR YOUR BUCK

The UCSC Office of Financial Aid is committed to helping all admitted students attend UCSC, regardless of economic circumstances. Approximately half of all full-time undergraduates receive some form of financial assistance through need- and merit-based scholarships, grants, loans, and part-time employment opportunities. The school administers over $50 million in federal, state, and institutional need-based scholarships and grants annually.

UCSC provides need-based assistance to 96 percent of all aid applicants who demonstrate need. Eighty-seven percent of need-based aid

Students Say

"Hippies, trees, biology, fog, bikes, an isolated campus, and you share the sidewalks with roaming deer."

HIGH SCHOOL UNITS RECOMMENDED

4 English, 4 math, 3 science (3 science lab), 3 foreign language, 1 social studies, 1 history, 1 academic electives, 1 visual or performing arts

VERY IMPORTANT ADMISSION FACTORS

Academic GPA, application essay, rigor of secondary school record, standardized test scores, state residency

IMPORTANT ADMISSION FACTORS

Character/personal qualities, class rank, extracurricular activities, first generation, geographical residence, talent/ability

Average HS GPA   3.51
Range SAT Verbal 520–630
Range SAT Math   530–640
Range ACT   21–27
Minimum TOEFL
  (paper/computer) 550/220

APPLICATION DEADLINES

Regular admission   11/30
Regular notification rolling
# of transfer
  applicants   5,023
% of transfer applicants
  accepted   70

ACADEMICS

Student/faculty ratio   19:1
% faculty teaching
  undergraduates   100
% of classes taught by
  graduate students   0

packages include some form of need-based grant or scholarship. On average, the school meets 84 percent of aid recipients' demonstrated need, yet the school manages to meet 100 percent of demonstrated need for 38 percent of aid recipients.

UCSC offers a number of academic scholarships that take financial need into account; students' financial aid applications serve as application for these awards. Regents Scholarships, which are strictly merit-based, provide recipients with either an honorarium or some form of tuition relief. UCSC undergrads are eligible for numerous restricted scholarships awarded on the basis of personal characteristic, hometown, and alumni relation.

GETTING IN

Admissions Officers at UCSC use an elaborate point system in which applicants are evaluated in 14 areas then awarded a composite score of up to 10,000 points. These 14 areas are as follows (maximum points available in area): adjusted GPA (4,400 points); standardized test scores (2,400 points); degree of difficulty of high-school curriculum (200 points); honors courses completed (200 points); eligibility in the local context (400 points); quality of senior-year program of study (200 points); outstanding performance in one or more subject areas (250 points); achievement in special projects (250 points); evidence of academic improvement (100 points); special talents, achievements, and awards (500 points); accomplishment in pre-collegiate programs (200 points); academic accomplishment within life experiences (700 points); achievement in spite of attending substandard schools (200 points); and geographic origin (100 points). Good luck!

WHAT DO GRADUATES DO?

A substantial number of UCSC graduates enter graduate programs soon after receiving their bachelor's degrees, while others enter the workplace. Top employers of UCSC graduates include the following: Americorps; Applied Signal Technology; Arthur Andersen LLP; Coastek InfoSys, Inc.; the Community Action Network; CrossWind Technologies, Inc.; CTB/McGraw-Hill; eBay, Inc.; Granite Rock Company; the Japan Exchange & Teaching (JET) Program; Metro Newspapers; Mutual of New York; the Peace Corps; Planned Parenthood; PricewaterhouseCoopers LLP; Providian Financial Corporation; Teach for America; Texas Instruments; and the U.S. military.

The Bottom Line

In 2006–2007, California residents attending UCSC full time paid $7,603 in tuition and fees. Room and board cost another $11,571; books and supplies cost an estimated $1,332; and personal and transportation expenses amounted to $2,223. Thus, the total cost of attending UCSC for an in-state student was $22,729. Nonresidents of California paid an additional $17,304 in tuition and an additional $7,603 in mandatory fees, bringing their total cost to $47,636. About half of all full-time undergraduates receive some form of need-based financial aid. The average need-based scholarship in 2006–2007 was $8,967; the average need-based self-help award was $5,849; and the average need-based loan was $4,672.

Fun Facts

UCSC has more than 65,000 alumni. Among them are astronaut Steven Hawley; actor Camryn Manheim; Los Angeles Opera conductor Kent Nagano; singer/songwriter Gillian Welch; and Marc Okrand, creator of the Klingon language for the *Star Trek* series.

The UCSC campus includes over 25 miles of hiking and jogging trails.

A highly regarded study entitled *The Rise of American Research Universities* ranked UCSC eleventh in the nation among public campuses for the research productivity of its faculty. The same study ranked UCSC first in the social sciences and sixth in the arts and humanities.

MOST POPULAR MAJORS

- Art/art studies
- Business administration/ management
- Psychology

EDUCATION REQUIREMENTS

Arts/fine arts, English (including composition), humanities, sciences (biological or physical), social science; a writing-intensive course and a U.S. ethnic minorities/non-Western society course are both required. Also, a senior examination or equivalent body of work is required of all seniors prior to graduation.

FINANCIAL INFO

In-state tuition	$0
Out-of-state tuition	$17,304
Room & board	$11,571
Average book expense	$1,332
Required fees	$7,603
Average freshman need-based grant	$8,889
Average freshman need-based loan	$4,196
% of graduates who borrowed	53
Average indebtedness	$13,419

FINANCIAL AID FORMS

Students must submit FAFSA.

Financial aid filing deadline	3/2

POSTGRAD

CAREER SERVICES

Alumni network, alumni services, internships. Off-campus job opportunities are excellent.

UNIVERSITY OF CENTRAL FLORIDA

PO Box 160111, Orlando, FL 32816-0111
www.UCF.edu • Admissions: 407-823-3000
Fax: 407-823-5625 • E-mail: admission@mail.ucf.edu • Financial Aid: 407-823-2827

STUDENTS

Religious affiliation
                No Affiliation
Academic year
  calendar   semester
Undergrad
  enrollment   37,568
% male/female   45/55
% Asian   5
% Black, non-Latino   9
% Latino   13
% international   1
% from out of state   5
% freshmen return for
sophomore year   83
% freshmen graduate
  within 4 years   30

Student Life

% of students living
  on campus   23
% in fraternities   11
% in sororities   9

ADMISSIONS

of applicants   20,265
% accepted   62
% enrolled   51

High School Units Required

4 English, 3 math, 3 science
(2 science lab), 2 foreign
language, 3 social studies, 4
academic electives

Very Important Admission Factors

Academic GPA, rigor of
secondary school record,
standardized test scores

About University of Central Florida

With a student body of magnificent proportions and a campus located in one of America's entertainment capitals, the University of Central Florida boasts diversity in every experience it has to offer. When it comes to academics, students find themselves driven to excel—thanks to a career-driven yet laid-back environment that places an emphasis on the future without forgoing the fun. The school maintains strong ties to the booming community to give its undergraduates in business, computer science, education, engineering, hospitality management, mass communications, and some good hands-on experience in their fields before they graduate. Because nearly 30 percent of the student body majors in business or marketing, the liberal and fine arts programs tend to suffer in comparison. However, there has been increased funding in this direction. To ensure student success in all areas of study, UCF has implemented several resources for free tutoring, and, through corporate partnerships, has wired its entire campus with wireless Internet and stocked every classroom with the latest and greatest in hardware.

With such a sizeable student body, there is hardly a "typical student," nor is there any limit to the amount of campus associations and activities you can join to meet like-minded folks, so you'll never feel lost in the mix. Between the school and Orlando at large, there is something to do every night of the week. From student government to intramural sports, UCF makes a point of organizing events, and the surrounding area boasts an endless supply of restaurants, shops, movie theaters, bars, bowling alleys, clubs, and, of course, theme parks. Students also flock to see their beloved Golden Knights take to the gridiron. Despite a less-than-stellar history, the team has recently been on the up-and-up.

Bang For Your Buck

UCF offers an array of merit- and need-based financial awards. As a bonus, all incoming freshmen are automatically considered for a merit scholarship. Considerations for these scholarships are high school course selection, grade point average, and ACT or SAT scores. Students should be quick to contact their academic departments too, as they also offer awards that require a separate application. An impressive 88 percent of undergraduates who apply for it received some form of need-based financial aid. Non-need-based awards are available to those who excel in academics, athletics, leadership, music, drama, or who have alumni affiliation. Minority scholarships and ROTC scholarships are available to boot.

Students Say

"UCF is all about letting their students have the freedom to grow and develop into the person they never knew they could become."

GETTING IN

With 75 degree programs in six academic colleges, the choice of study is endless. However, only half of students who apply are accepted, meaning UCF takes the application process very seriously. The proof is in the pudding: The freshman class of 2005, for example, posted average SAT scores of 1186, ACT scores of 26, and an average high school GPA of 3.5. Academic record, recommendations, standardized test scores, and essays are the main criteria considered for admission. Less important, but still taken into account, are class rank, an interview with the school, extracurricular activities, and work experience. Candidates are not required to apply separately to departments at UCF; admission to the university constitutes admission to all programs offered.

WHAT DO GRADUATES DO?

UCF starts early to help its students decide where they want to head professionally. By the time their four years are up, most students are headed with a clear direction off to grad school or into the workforce. The school's Career Services department works hard to offer an abundant supply of job fairs, job training, and career counseling. For the university, it's all about location and preparation: Seventy percent of UCF graduates stay on to live and work in Central Florida where they earn, on average, $63,000 per year, often accepting positions with such companies as the Walt Disney Co. and Lockheed Martin.

IMPORTANT ADMISSION FACTORS

Application essay

Average HS GPA	3.5
Range SAT Verbal	520–610
Range SAT Math	530–620
Range ACT	22–26
Minimum TOEFL (paper/computer)	550/213

APPLICATION DEADLINES

Regular admission	5/1
Regular notification	rolling
# of transfer applicants	9,356
% of transfer applicants accepted	61

ACADEMICS

Student/faculty ratio	27:1
% faculty teaching undergraduates	100
% of classes taught by graduate students	6

MOST POPULAR MAJORS

- Management information systems
- Marketing/marketing management
- Psychology

EDUCATION REQUIREMENTS

English (including composition), history, humanities, math, sciences (biological or physical), social science

FINANCIAL INFO

In-state tuition	$3,492
Out-of-state tuition	$17,017
Room & board	$8,000
Average book expense	$888
Required fees	$10
Average freshman need-based grant	$3,215
Average freshman need-based loan	$2,621
% of graduates who borrowed	43.6
Average indebtedness	$13,095

FINANCIAL AID FORMS

Students must submit FAFSA.

Financial aid filing deadline	6/30

POSTGRAD

% going to graduate school	21
% going to law school	5
% going to business school	7
% going to medical school	7

CAREER SERVICES

Career/job search classes, career assessment, internships, on-campus job interviews. Off-campus job opportunities are good.

THE BOTTOM LINE

State membership has its privileges—an academic year of tuition, room and board, and fees at UCF for a Florida resident is $11,502, while nonresidents will find themselves paying $25,027. Thanks to a generous system of scholarships and financial awards, students who receive aid manage to take an average of $4,669 per year off of that total. In 2006, graduates who took advantage of student loans left the school with $13,095 in cumulative debt, a reasonable sum as compared to peer universities.

FUN FACTS

The university has become a haven for the video game designers of tomorrow. In 2004, UCF, in collaboration with Electronic Arts, formed the School of Interactive Entertainment in downtown Orlando.

The university's first mascot was the "Citronaut"—part-fruit, part-astronaut, it was quickly done away with by students in favor of something less comical. Enter "Knightro," the Golden Knight, and his sidekick "Glycerine"—names to make the American Gladiator in all of us proud.

The school holds the Guinness Record for most number of people on a water bed—108.

UNIVERSITY OF CENTRAL MISSOURI

Office of Admissions, WDE 1401, Warrensburg, MO 64093
www.CMSU.edu • Admissions: 660-543-4290
Fax: 660-543-8517 • E-mail: admit@cmsuvmb.cmsu.edu • Financial Aid: 660-543-4040

STUDENTS

Religious affiliation
　　　　　　　　No Affiliation
Academic year
　calendar　　　　semester
Undergrad
　enrollment　　　　8,143
% male/female　　　45/55
% Asian　　　　　　　1
% Black, non-Latino　6
% Latino　　　　　　　2
% Native American　　1
% international　　　3
% from out of state　6
% freshmen return for
sophomore year　　　70
% freshmen graduate
　within 4 years　　20

STUDENT LIFE

% of students living
　on campus　　　　34
% in fraternities　　18
% in sororities　　　12

ADMISSIONS

of applicants　　3,544
% accepted　　　　　76
% enrolled　　　　　53

HIGH SCHOOL UNITS REQUIRED

4 English, 3 math, 2 science
(1 science lab), 3 social
studies, 3 academic
electives, 1 arts

HIGH SCHOOL UNITS RECOMMENDED

2 Foreign language

ABOUT UNIVERSITY OF CENTRAL MISSOURI

Laid-back and welcoming, the University of Central Missouri (formerly known as Central Missouri State University) has long been a popular choice among students seeking a beautiful residential campus, varied course offerings, and caring instruction in Missouri. But the school hopes to develop a more national reputation. It changed its name in September 2006 as a part of an effort to emerge as "a nationally recognized comprehensive university that delivers a world-class university education." The initiative also hopes to make the school more inclusive by increasing numbers of international and minority students. There's certainly room for diversity at the school where 94 percent of students are from Missouri and 84 percent are white.

The school's motto, "Education for Service," will continue to guide UCM's vast array of study programs. Students flock to aviation, education, criminal justice, and business programs and enjoy the personal attention that comes with small class sizes. They say professors are exceptionally supportive and invested in student success. Campus activities from intercollegiate sports to religious organizations also keep students busy. Greek life is strong at UCM, with 10 percent of students benefiting from friendships, national ties, and volunteer projects. Far from a distraction, Greek life seems to boost the academic achievement of involved students. Generally, fraternity and sorority members at UCM have higher grade point averages and graduation rates than the general population.

BANG FOR YOUR BUCK

UCM has one of the lowest student-debt ratios in the state, making it even more attractive to students who seek a quality education without breaking the proverbial bank. Affordable tuition coupled with strong scholarship and award programs makes this college a great value. The school even offers textbook rental programs to cut costs still further for bargain-hunting students. For the 2005–2006 school year, UCM gave more than $20 million in need- and merit-based grants and scholarships. Roughly 60 percent of undergraduates received need-based aid, and 90 percent of their need was met with average financial aid packages of $7,340.

VERY IMPORTANT ADMISSION FACTORS

Class rank, rigor of secondary school record, standardized test scores

Range ACT   19–24
Minimum TOEFL
   (paper/computer) 500/173

APPLICATION DEADLINES
Regular admission   8/20
Regular notification   rolling
# of transfer
   applicants   1,187
% of transfer applicants
   accepted   81

ACADEMICS
Student/faculty ratio   18:1
% faculty teaching
   undergraduates   100
% of classes taught by
   graduate students   4

MOST POPULAR MAJORS

• Criminal justice/law enforcement administration
• Education

EDUCATION REQUIREMENTS

Arts/fine arts, computer literacy, English (including composition), history, humanities, math, sciences (biological or physical), social science, Multicultural Education, speech, Personal Development, Integrative Studies

GETTING IN

The admissions staff at UCM gives the most consideration to prospective students' high school academic records, class rank and standardized test scores. The average ACT score of admitted students was 22. The average SAT score was not reported. Extracurricular activities and letters of recommendation from high school teachers and counselors are also reviewed. Essays and interviews are not a part of the admissions process at this school. Approximately 16 percent of students graduated within the top 10 percent of their high school classes. Three-fourths of applicants were accepted, and half of those enrolled.

WHAT DO GRADUATES DO?

UCM's career-exploration freshman seminar wins rave reviews from students who say instructors really care about students' futures and help them navigate the difficult path from major selection to career. The top employers for the class of 2006 were accounting, engineering, consulting, education, and financial services companies and organizations. The average job salary offer for students going into engineering was $49,160, with the starting salaries of consultants and accountants following closely behind. Aviation technology students become pilots, airport managers, and air traffic controllers. Criminal justice students move into law enforcement careers at the local, state, and national levels.

THE BOTTOM LINE

In-state students paid about $13,567 for the 2005–2006 school year while out-of-state students' expenses totaled $18,982. UCM in-state tuition was $5,835 and out-of-state tuition was $11,250. Required fees cost students $420 and room and board came to about $5,412. Books and supplies cost $500 and personal expenses totaled about $1,400 for the year. At graduation, the average undergraduate owes about $13,184 in cumulative debt.

FUN FACTS

The University of Central Missouri has a long history of name changes. It was founded as the State Normal School No. 2 in 1871. In 1919, it became Central Missouri State Teachers College, and by 1945 "teachers" was dropped making it Central Missouri State College. In 1972, the name was changed to Central Missouri State University before the latest name, University of Central Missouri, was adopted in September of 2006.

The college has a 260-acre farm with cattle and a historic barn. Horticulture students grow tomatoes and peppers. They hope to develop a "pick-your-own" community garden, horse stables and other attractions.

Homecoming is huge at UCM: Alumni flock from far and wide to cheer the Fightin' Mules on with current students. A pep rally, alumni breakfast, and parade round out the weekend, but the focus is, of course, on football.

FINANCIAL INFO

In-state tuition	$5,835
Out-of-state tuition	$11,250
Room & board	$5,412
Average book expense	$500
Required fees	$420
Average freshman need-based grant	$3,183
Average freshman need-based loan	$2,262
% of graduates who borrowed	68
Average indebtedness	$13,184

FINANCIAL AID FORMS

Students must submit FAFSA.

POSTGRAD

CAREER SERVICES

Alumni services, career/job search classes, career assessment, internships, on-campus job interviews. Off-campus job opportunities are good.

UNIVERSITY OF CHICAGO

1101 East Fifty-eighth Street, Suite 105, Chicago, IL 60637
www.UChicago.edu • Admissions: 773-702-8650
Fax: 773-702-4199 • Financial Aid: 773-702-8666

STUDENTS

Religious affiliation
          No Affiliation
Academic year
  calendar   quarter
Undergrad
  enrollment   4,671
% male/female   50/50
% Asian   14
% Black, non-Latino   4
% Latino   8
% international   7
% from out of state 70
% freshmen return for
sophomore year   95

STUDENT LIFE

% of students living
  on campus   56

ADMISSIONS

of applicants   9,011
% accepted   40
% enrolled   33

HIGH SCHOOL UNITS RECOMMENDED

4 English, 4 math, 4
science, 3 foreign language,
2 social studies, 2 history

VERY IMPORTANT ADMISSION FACTORS

Application essay, character/
personal qualities,
recommendation(s), rigor of
secondary school record,
talent/ability

ABOUT THE UNIVERSITY OF CHICAGO

Rigorous academic work, great intellectual challenge, and world-renowned experts as professors: a student will find all that and more at the University of Chicago. Task-oriented and intellectually driven, sharp, smart, and questioning are all qualities that could characterize students at Chicago. Thinking to a purpose and an attitude of sharp questioning seems to be the focus, rather than the more relaxed inquiry and rumination approach at some schools of equal intellectual repute. Many find a home and welcome challenges in the debates and discussions that define Chicago's campus atmosphere, though. "People at Chicago know what they care about most and what they enjoy most: learning, testing, critiquing, disputing, convincing, persuading, dissuading, explaining, and researching," the university says of itself.

Majors range from early Christian literature to media studies, history, linguistics, and math. In addition to the standard course descriptions in the college catalog there's also a website that features student evaluations of the classes in question. The university also supports about 50 tutors who meet with students one-on-one for additional help in course work for introductory-level classes in biology, chemistry, economics, mathematics, physics, and writing. Studying, thinking, and analysis is what Chicago is about. But there's a lot to experience outside the classroom as well. Those who enjoy learning new things and don't mind having all their ideas challenged regularly should thrive at the University of Chicago.

The campus is located in the Hyde Park neighborhood, about seven miles south of downtown Chicago. Some students find the neighborhood at bit too quiet, but others enjoy the community's eclectic and diverse atmosphere. About 60 percent of Chicago's professors and their families live in Hyde Park. Many undergraduates live on campus in dorms known as houses, each with its own identity, governance, traditions, and designated tables in the dining halls. For general socializing, the Reynolds club is a crossroads of campus life. There's also a center for student who live off campus. Classic Gothic style (that's Medieval Gothic, not the twenty-first century kind) is the architectural period of choice here, and these buildings shelter green spaces which in fair weather also become places to hang out, socialize, and study.

"The university offers lectures by Nobel laureates and renowned political figures, film screenings, and SCAV HUNT, in which students spend three days without food or sleep trying to do things like build a nuclear reactor."

BANG FOR YOUR BUCK

In academic rigor and reputation, Chicago ranks very high and that's a benefit for many. The analytical requirements and challenges may help prepare students for the rough-and-tumble professional world too. Financial need is not a factor considered in the admissions process; once the university determines that a student has financial need, it works to meet 100 percent of that need throughout the student's undergraduate years at Chicago. Financially speaking, just over half of all students who apply for need-based aid receive it—but those that receive it get an impeccable 100 percent of their need satisfied with an average aid package of $23,078.

GETTING IN

The University of Chicago admitted about 38 percent of those who applied in the fall of 2005. Most important to admissions evaluators were rigorous academics in high school, the application essay, the quality of a student's recommendations, and evidence of talent and ability along with personal character. Class rank, GPA, volunteer work, and extracurricular activities were considered next. 79 percent ranked in the top 10 percent of their high school classes, and 99 percent in the top half. On the SAT, 83 percent had scores of 1300 or better, and 64 percent scored 30 or better on the ACT. The university emphasizes the holistic nature of its process and offers resources for high school counselors on its website as well.

WHAT DO GRADUATES DO?

With Chicago's top-notch academic reputation, many employers are eager to talk with Chicago grads, and more than 200 firms scheduled recruiting visits to campus in 2005. More than 95 percent of those graduates who intended to go to work right after graduation found work; a number of others chose grad school or entered the Peace Corps. The Career and Placement Office helps in all these areas and holds a number of real-life and online career fairs during the year as well.

IMPORTANT ADMISSION FACTORS

Academic GPA, class rank, extracurricular activities, volunteer work

Average HS GPA	3.89
Range SAT Verbal	680–770
Range SAT Math	670–760
Range ACT	28–33
Minimum TOEFL (paper/computer)	600/250

APPLICATION DEADLINES

Regular admission	1/2
Regular notification	4/1
# of transfer applicants	571
% of transfer applicants accepted	23

ACADEMICS

Student/faculty ratio	6:1
% faculty teaching undergraduates	93
% of classes taught by graduate students	0

MOST POPULAR MAJORS

- Biology/biological sciences
- Economics
- English language and literature

EDUCATION REQUIREMENTS

Arts/fine arts, humanities, math, sciences (biological or physical), social science, civilizations

FINANCIAL INFO

Tuition	$33,336
Room & board	$10,608
Average book expense	$1,000
Required fees	$669
Average freshman need-based grant	$24,902
Average freshman need-based loan	$4,531
% of graduates who borrowed	50.5
Average indebtedness	$17,651

FINANCIAL AID FORMS

Students must submit FAFSA, institution's own financial aid form, CSS/financial aid profile, state aid form, business/farm supplement.

Financial aid filing deadline	2/1

POSTGRAD

% going to graduate school	35
% going to law school	8
% going to medical school	8

CAREER SERVICES

Off-campus job opportunities are excellent.

THE BOTTOM LINE

Tuition at the University of Chicago is $33,336 per year. On-campus room and board costs $10,608 per year, and there are additional fees totaling about $1,400 for first-year students. The college estimates around $2,000 a year will be needed for books and other personal expenses. On average, recent graduates left Chicago with $17,651 in cumulative debt.

FUN FACTS

If you see a flash of green up in the trees as you walk the streets of the Hyde Park neighborhood, it's probably a monk parakeet, one of a colony of the usually tropical birds which have lived in the area since 1973. Several agencies have tried to exterminate them over the years, while some neighborhood residents have rallied to support the birds.

Chris Howell, who graduated in 1975, is vintner and general manager at Cain Vineyard and Winery in Napa Valley, which produces about 1,800 cases of wine each year.

Clarence Darrow, famed for the "Monkey Trial" of 1925, lived in the Midway Apartment Hotel on Sixtieth Street near campus. During the trial, three university faculty members provided expert witness statements.

UNIVERSITY OF FLORIDA

201 Criser Hall, Box 114000, Gainesville, FL 32611-4000
www.UFL.edu • Admissions: 352-392-1365
Fax: 904-392-3987 • E-mail: ourwebrequests@registrar.ufl.edu • Financial Aid: 352-392-1275

STUDENTS

Religious affiliation
No Affiliation
Academic year
calendar   semester
Undergrad
enrollment   33,094
% male/female   47/53
% Asian   7
% Black, non-Latino   9
% Latino   12
% Native American   1
% international   1
% from out of state   4
% freshmen return for
sophomore year   94
% freshmen graduate
within 4 years   51

STUDENT LIFE

% of students living
on campus   22
% in fraternities   15
% in sororities   15

ADMISSIONS

of applicants   21,151
% accepted   57
% enrolled   60
# of early decision/action
applicants   4481
% accepted early
decision/action   50

ABOUT THE UNIVERSITY OF FLORIDA

The University of Florida is a state school—93 percent of its students come from within the borders of the Sunshine State—and it's big, with a total enrollment of 50,000-plus and a freshman class comprising about 7,000 students. The University of Florida has more than 20 colleges and offers more than 100 undergraduate majors. It's a school where academic excellence and varied learning opportunities are both valued and available. The faculty includes eminent scholars, Fulbright award winners, and national experts in almost every field. The campus houses the world's largest citrus research center, a world-renowned institute for the study of the brain, a public television and radio station, and one of the largest health centers in the Southeast. There are academics too. UF, as it is nicknamed, is strong in the hard sciences and has a medical school, as well as more than a hundred research centers and institutes and an administration committed to making it a Top 10 public university (it ranked 13th in a recent national listing). Students feel that emphasis on ranking may sometimes distract administrators from remembering issues important to students, but professors are generally seen as available and helpful. This is especially true for upperclass students. Freshman and sophomore classes are often big lecture sections with little interaction with professors, and they are far too often handled by teaching assistants, say those who have made it through them.

Those in search of social life have come to the right place. Whether it's a party or a Gators game, students show up with passion and in staggering numbers. There's a hefty club scene downtown and fraternity/sorority scene on campus, with about 30 percent of both men and women choosing to go Greek. Many students live in dorms or nearby campus in apartments they share with friends. The campus has a major art museum, radio and television stations, and one of the largest natural history museums in the Southeast, as well as a major medical center. There's also an on-campus lake with recreational equipment available and dozens of Greek organizations, social organizations, religious groups, and other activities for a student to investigate. Gainesville is a medium-sized town in north central Florida, so while one shouldn't expect surfboards and aerosols, the Gulf of Mexico is only a 45-minute drive to the west. The Atlantic Ocean is about an hour and a half east, while Disneyworld, Universal Studios, and related attractions are an hour or so south in Orlando—one of the world's true centers of nightlife.

HIGH SCHOOL UNITS REQUIRED

4 English, 3 math, 3 science (2 science lab), 2 foreign language, 3 social studies

Average HS GPA	3.9
Range SAT Verbal	570–670
Range SAT Math	590–690
Range ACT	25–29

APPLICATION DEADLINES

Early decision	10/1
Early decision notification	12/1
Regular admission	1/17
# of transfer applicants	5,456
% of transfer applicants accepted	39

ACADEMICS

Student/faculty ratio   23:1

MOST POPULAR MAJORS

• Business administration/management
• Finance
• Psychology

BANG FOR YOUR BUCK

With relatively low tuition and a strong program of scholarships for Florida residents, UF is especially good value for in-state students. Though out-of-state students pay almost three times as much to attend, they still receive the resources of a major academic institution in return, and there are financial aid resources available to them as well. Almost all Florida residents admitted to UF qualify for Bright Futures scholarships funded by proceeds from the Florida Lottery, and details of this program are on the university's website. The university met about 85 percent of the need of those incoming freshmen who were determined to have need in 2006. Most were awarded both scholarship and self-help aid, with packages averaging $4,317. Individual colleges at the university offer scholarships; these are detailed in the financial aid section of the school's website, as are a number of other financial aid resources.

GETTING IN

In 2006, the majority of freshmen admitted to UF had a GPA of 3.7 or above. The university, however, is quick to point out that it is not grades or academic rank alone that will ensure admission. They also consider "personal essays, academic awards, extracurricular activities, family background, and home community," all considered in relation to the strength of total the pool of applicants. A challenging slate of high school courses is also taken as a plus. On the reading and math section of the SAT, the majority of those admitted had scores in the 1200–1390 range.

WHAT DO GRADUATES DO?

Georgia-Pacific, Wachovia Corporation, Grant Thornton LLP, Aidman, Piser & Company, Vistakon/Johnson & Johnson, Bridgestone, Dillards, PriceWaterhouseCooper, and Lockheed are among those companies that interview regularly on campus. Agriculture, law, politics, education, communications, and health professions are choices of many UF graduates. The career resource center sponsors career fairs in these areas and offers a wide variety of services to students and alumni to assist them in job searching and in preparing for interviews, presenting credentials, and the like.

THE BOTTOM LINE

In-state tuition runs at a more-than-cool $3,206, while those from out of state pay $17,791. Room and board ring in at $6,590, books and supplies at $920, transportation at $520, and personal expenses round out at $3,010. The average graduate leaves with $14,835 in cumulative debt.

FUN FACTS

UF has begun a partnership with Spain to create the world's largest telescope, to be located in the Canary Islands. It is on track to be completed in 2007.

Radio announcer Red Barber, actress Faye Dunaway, football coach Steve Spurrier, country singer Mel Tillis, and home-improvement guru Bob Vila all attended college in Gainesville.

The chief sports (especially football) rivals of the University of Florida Gators are the University of Miami Hurricanes and the Florida State University Seminoles.

FINANCIAL INFO

In-state tuition	$3,206
Out-of-state tuition	$17,791
Room & board	$6,590
Average book expense	$920
Average freshman need-based grant	$4,317
Average freshman need-based loan	$2,792
% of graduates who borrowed	41
Average indebtedness	$14,835

FINANCIAL AID FORMS

Students must submit FAFSA.

POSTGRAD

CAREER SERVICES

Alumni services, career/job search classes, career assessment, internships, on-campus job interviews. Off-campus job opportunities are fair.

UNIVERSITY OF GEORGIA

Terrell Hall, Athens, GA 30602
www.UGA.edu • Admissions: 706-542-8776
Fax: 706-542-1466 • E-mail: adm-info@uga.edu • Financial Aid: 706-542-6147

STUDENTS

Religious affiliation
                No Affiliation
Academic year
  calendar   semester
Undergrad
  enrollment   24,791
% male/female   43/57
% Asian   5
% Black, non-Latino   5
% Latino   2
% international   1
% from out of state   12
% freshmen return for
sophomore year   93
% freshmen graduate
within 4 years   41

STUDENT LIFE

% of students living
  on campus   27
% in fraternities   18
% in sororities   23

ADMISSIONS

of applicants   12,326
% accepted   65
% enrolled   59

HIGH SCHOOL UNITS REQUIRED

4 English, 4 math, 3
science (2 science lab), 2
foreign language, 3 social
studies

HIGH SCHOOL UNITS RECOMMENDED

4 English, 4 math, 3
science (2 science lab), 3
foreign language, 1 social
studies, 2 history, 1
academic electives

ABOUT THE UNIVERSITY OF GEORGIA

Put close to 35,000 college-age students in a small Southern sports town, a Southern rock town, and a short drive away from the big-city lights of Atlanta, and what do you get? Stellar academic programs! Of course, the music, the sports, and the barbecue are all attractions, but the rigorous programs in journalism, science, agriculture, and literature, to name a few, are the backbone of the University of Georgia's increasingly attractive profile as a world-class research institution which draws top faculty and students. There's a full slate of on-campus, out-of-class activities, and many students say the town of Athens is one of the chief attractions of going to Georgia. There's a rock scene, a hippie scene, and a jock scene—to name just a few—and all seem welcome. Students often gather around that other constant of UGA, the Georgia Bulldogs. A football power in the Deep South, Georgia's other sport teams have rabid followers as well, and it also hosts strong programs in women's sports.

The University of Georgia's star is rising in academic reputation, as a result of notice from the popular press and the prestigious awards and grants bestowed on faculty and students. Some of the most popular majors include psychology, agriculture, business, and premed. Students make note of their committed and well-known professors, while also pointing out that many of the classes—especially in the first two years—are large, and that it is to a student's advantage to go beyond just showing up. Seek out and get to know the faculty, they advise, to prepare yourself for and make the most of the intensive classes in your third and fourth years. Honors classes are a good bet too, as they usually have a smaller student-faculty ratio. Students generally agree that you get a great education at Georgia, especially if you take the initiative to explore academic options and choose wisely among them.

BANG FOR YOUR BUCK

Most of the students are from Georgia and take advantage of the state's HOPE scholarship which makes the tuition even a better fit for the family budget. The scholarship, funded by proceeds from the Georgia Lottery, is available to Georgia residents attending in-state schools, and information on this may be found at UGA's website. Almost 99 percent of in-state incoming freshmen in 2005 received HOPE scholarships. Almost 74 percent of all students who apply for aid receive an average of $5,731 a year.

GETTING IN

The University of Georgia admitted slightly less than half of those who applied as incoming freshmen in the fall of 2005. There is an open admissions policy for most Georgia residents but class rank, GPA, and rigor of academic record are most strongly considered, followed by standardized test scores and the interview. The average GPA of these students was 3.74, the average SAT score was 1240, and the average ACT score was 27. Enrollment at UGA is becoming increasingly selective, with the university able to choose from among the best of the state's high school graduates and the cream of the crop from the rest of the Southeast. In 2005, UGA received three applications for every one it accepted.

WHAT DO GRADUATES DO?

Cintas, Enterprise, BB&T, Sun Trust, Protiviti, Wells Fargo, Ameriprise, and McKesson Healthcare are among those who interview on campus. Georgia graduates also go on to grad school at universities including Duke, Emory, The Medical College of Georgia, New York University, and Saint Louis University.

THE BOTTOM LINE

Georgia freshmen paid $10,184 on tuition in 2005, while those from out of state had to come up with $19,776. On-campus room charges ran $1,900, while board cost $1,200. The university estimates a student will require about $1,000 for books and supplies. Recent graduates left UGA with $13,422 in cumulative debt, on average.

VERY IMPORTANT ADMISSION FACTORS

Academic GPA, rigor of secondary school record

IMPORTANT ADMISSION FACTORS

Standardized test scores

Average HS GPA	3.74
Range SAT Verbal	560–660
Range SAT Math	570–670
Range ACT	24–28
Minimum TOEFL (paper/computer)	550/213

APPLICATION DEADLINES

Regular admission	1/15
Regular notification	2/15
# of transfer applicants	2,326
% of transfer applicants accepted	57

ACADEMICS

Student/faculty ratio	18:1
% faculty teaching undergraduates	79
% of classes taught by graduate students	18

MOST POPULAR MAJORS

- Art/art studies
- Biology/biological sciences
- Psychology

EDUCATION REQUIREMENTS

Arts/fine arts, computer literacy, English (including composition), history, humanities, math, sciences (biological or physical), social science, physical education, environmental literacy, cultural diversity

FINANCIAL INFO

In-state tuition	$3,820
Out-of-state tuition	$16,650
Room & board	$6,848
Average book expense	$800
Required fees	$1,072
Average freshman need-based grant	$6,148
Average freshman need-based loan	$2,558
% of graduates who borrowed	43
Average indebtedness	$13,422

FINANCIAL AID FORMS

Students must submit FAFSA.

POSTGRAD

% going to graduate school	10
% going to law school	15
% going to medical school	9

CAREER SERVICES

Off-campus job opportunities are excellent.

FUN FACTS

UGA was voted the nation's second-best college sports town by *Sports Illustrated* and ranked number one among "campus scenes that rock!" by *Rolling Stone*.

The University's Grady College of Journalism and Mass Communication administers the Peabody Awards program, often cited as the most prestigious award in electronic media.

Sports Illustrated ranks UGA sixth on its list of best colleges for women athletes. UGA has more than 250 female athletes on its 12 women's varsity teams, and also has 27 club sports for women.

UNIVERSITY OF HAWAII—MANOA

2600 Campus Road, QLCSS Room 001, Honolulu, HI 96822
www.Manoa.Hawaii.edu • Admissions: 808-956-8975
Fax: 808-956-4148 • E-mail: ar-info@hawaii.edu • Financial Aid: 808-956-7251

STUDENTS

Religious affiliation
　　　　　　　　No Affiliation
Academic year
　calendar　　　　semester
Undergrad
　enrollment　　　　13,831
% male/female　　　45/55
% Asian　　　　　　65
% Black, non-Latino　　1
% Latino　　　　　　2
% international　　　　3
% from out of state　　20
% freshmen return for
sophomore year　　　75

STUDENT LIFE

% of students living
　on campus　　　　　15

ADMISSIONS

of applicants　　6,896
% accepted　　　　68
% enrolled　　　　43

HIGH SCHOOL UNITS REQUIRED

4 English, 3 math, 3
science, 3 social studies, 4
academic electives, 5
electives

HIGH SCHOOL UNITS RECOMMENDED

2 Foreign language

VERY IMPORTANT ADMISSION FACTORS

Academic GPA, rigor of
secondary school record,
standardized test scores

ABOUT UNIVERSITY OF HAWAII—MANOA

The University of Hawaii—Manoa is among the nation's premier research institutions, with world-class facilities for the study of astronomy, marine biology, and Hawaiian studies, among numerous other areas. Unique programs abound in such disciplines as Asian theater, oceanography, Pacific cultural studies, tropical agriculture, and volcanology. Best of all, professors here generally are committed to undergraduate education, which is not always the case at research-oriented schools. Their involvement in cutting-edge research means that undergrads sometimes get the inside track on breaking discoveries and emerging technologies.

UHM is home to many Chinese, Filipino, Hawaiian, and Japanese students. Caucasians make up about one-quarter of the student body here. The school also has a large population of nontraditional students. Students are extremely friendly and easygoing but, because most commute, do not form an especially tight community. Even those who live on or near campus are more likely to head to the beach in their spare time than to stick around campus. Who wouldn't?

BANG FOR YOUR BUCK

Tuition and fees are below the national average at UHM, and they're downright cheap for in-state students. Out-of-state tuition is higher, but students from 14 states (Alaska, Arizona, California, Colorado, Idaho, Montana, Nevada, New Mexico, North Dakota, Oregon, South Dakota, Utah, Washington, and Wyoming) pay less than full out-of-state tuition for most programs. That's thanks to the Western Undergraduate Exchange (WUE) Scholarship Program, which allows residents of participating states to attend each others' state universities at 150 percent of the in-state tuition rate. Not all programs are eligible. Check the school's website or viewbook for more details.

UHM doesn't entirely deliver on the need-based aid (see "The Bottom Line"), but the school is so cheap that that's not a major issue for the majority of students. Most simply increase the amount of money they borrow or work harder over the summer to make up the difference. A limited number of merit awards are available; the best are for athletes, who receive an average scholarship of $10,777 per year.

IMPORTANT ADMISSION FACTORS

State residency

Average HS GPA   3.41
Range SAT Verbal   480–580
Range SAT Math   520–620
Range ACT   21–25
Minimum TOEFL
   (paper/computer) 500/173

APPLICATION DEADLINES

Regular admission   5/1
Regular notification   rolling
# of transfer
   applicants   5,473
% of transfer applicants
   accepted   67

ACADEMICS

Student/faculty ratio   12:1

MOST POPULAR MAJORS

• Art history, criticism and
   conservation
• Psychology
• Zoology/animal biology

EDUCATION REQUIREMENTS

Arts/fine arts, English
(including composition),
foreign languages,
humanities, math, sciences
(biological or physical),
social science

GETTING IN

UHM applies a straightforward formula to determine admission status. Freshmen who meet all of the following criteria are guaranteed admission: SAT 510 Verbal, 510 Math, or minimum ACT score of 22 on each section; rank among top 40 percent of graduating high school class; and GPA of 2.8 in a college preparatory curriculum including four units of English, three units of math (including Algebra II and Geometry), three units of science, three units of social studies, four additional college-prep units, and five elective units. Certain competitive programs require more stringent qualifications, such as higher GPA and SAT or ACT scores, or portfolios. The colleges and departments that are statistically competitive are Architecture, Business, Dental Hygiene, Education, and Engineering. International students must submit TOEFL scores.

WHAT DO GRADUATES DO?

Graduates of UHM—the flagship campus of the University of Hawaii system—flock to a wide variety of industries, with accounting and engineering chief among them. Accounting firms that recruit every semester are: PricewaterhouseCoopers, Deloitte and Touche, Ernst and Young, and KPMG. Engineering firms like Raytheon, Northrop Gumman, Pearl Harbor Naval Shipyard, and Boeing are regular recruiters at UHM as well. Other recruiters that come to campus include Aloha United Way, IBM Corporation, Kinko's, Kmart Corporation, Edward Jones, the U.S. Defense Intelligence Agency, the U.S. Department of Labor, and the U.S. Department of Defense.

THE BOTTOM LINE

For 2006–2007 (the last year for which complete data was available), in-state tuition at UHM was $4,320; out-of-state tuition was $12,192. Many out-of-state students, however, receive tuition waivers through the Western Undergraduate Exchange (WUE) Scholarship Program. Required fees totaled an additional $202.40. Discretionary costs included room and board, $6,690; books and supplies, $1,145; transportation, $360; and personal expenses, $1,189. Of the 4,109 students here who demonstrated need, UHM offered some form of aid to 64 percent of them. Thirty-two percent of those students had their need fully met; on average, all aid recipients had about 71 percent of their need met through university-dispensed financial aid. The average need-based scholarship totaled $3,655; the average need-based loan amounted to $3,797.

Fun Facts

University of Hawaii researchers were the first to use freeze-dried sperm to fertilize an egg, the first to clone a male mammal, and the first to clone multiple generations of mammals. The school's scientists developed Cryptophcin-52, an anti-cancer drug, as well as the first safe storage cells for hydrogen fuel.

A stroll across campus may lead you to discover some of its unusual features including an authentic Japanese tea house and garden, a Hawaiian taro patch, and a study center that replicates the throne hall of a Korean king.

The school was founded as the College of Agriculture and Mechanic Arts in 1907. When the College of Liberal Arts and Sciences was added in 1920, the name of the school was changed to University of Hawaii. As the UH system grew, the school was renamed again in 1972 as University of Hawaii — Manoa.

FINANCIAL INFO

In-state tuition	$4,320
Out-of-state tuition	$12,192
Room & board	$6,690
Average book expense	$1,145
Required fees	$202
Average freshman need-based grant	$3,690
Average freshman need-based loan	$2,435
% of graduates who borrowed	32.9
Average indebtedness	$12,575

FINANCIAL AID FORMS
Students must submit FAFSA.

POSTGRAD

CAREER SERVICES
Alumni services, career/job search classes, internships, on-campus job interviews. Off-campus job opportunities are good.

UNIVERSITY OF IDAHO

UI Admissions Office, PO Box 444264, Moscow, ID 83844-4264
www.UIdaho.edu • Admissions: 208-885-6326
Fax: 208-885-9119 • E-mail: admappl@uidaho.edu • Financial Aid: 208-885-6312

STUDENTS

Religious affiliation
　　　　　　No Affiliation
Academic year
　calendar　　　　semester
Undergrad
　enrollment　　　　8,978
% male/female　　　54/46
% Asian　　　　　　　2
% Black, non-Latino　1
% Latino　　　　　　　4
% Native American　　1
% international　　　　2
% from out of state　25
% freshmen return for
sophomore year　　　82
% freshmen graduate
　within 4 years　　　23

STUDENT LIFE

% of students living
　on campus
% in fraternities　　　16
% in sororities　　　　13

ADMISSIONS

of applicants　　4,444
% accepted　　　　　82
% enrolled　　　　　48

HIGH SCHOOL UNITS REQUIRED

4 English, 3 math, 3 science
(1 science lab), 1 foreign
language, 3 social studies, 2
academic electives

ABOUT UNIVERSITY OF IDAHO

In addition to providing a great education at a great price, the University of Idaho offers its students the chance to grow in all aspects of life. Its 9,000 students are a down-to-earth bunch from all over who get along famously regardless of their race or religion. In fact, the only dividing line on campus seems to be the fraternity and sorority system, which drives a playfully competitive wedge between Greeks and non-Greeks. Athletes and frat boys at UI can have a bit of an attitude, and there could perhaps be a bit more diversity on campus, but in general, the students get to know each other well and regard one another as cheerful and friendly.

UI's friendly, helpful administration keeps the school running like a well-oiled machine and is at least partly responsible for the bargain price, even if costs are on the rise a bit. Academics are solid, too, especially the music business, and natural resources program. Across all departments professors are knowledgeable and approachable. They obviously want to be where they are and want their students to succeed. What's more, they lack the superiority of many university professors, treating their students as equals.

In Moscow, Idaho, there isn't much to do besides hang out with friends at local coffee shops. UI itself, though, offers a mingle-happy on-campus atmosphere with outdoor recreational opportunities for hiking, camping, fishing, whitewater refting, and hunting. Also popular is UI's super-cool student recreation center, with its just-added climbing wall. It is packed with students working out and playing sports. Football and basketball games draw crowds, as does the Lionel Hampton Jazz Festival every February. Then there are always the requisite frat parties. Overall there is plenty to do socially on a campus that feels like home.

BANG FOR YOUR BUCK

The University of Idaho offers a private school education at a public school price, through low-cost tuition and fees and an $19 million dollar scholarship program. Over $80 million in scholarships and other financial aid is awarded to students annually. Awards are based on both need and merit.

UI's generous scholarship program helps nearly half of its students at one time or another. UI has several scholarships it guarantees to students who meet the minimum criteria. National Merit Finalists are awarded a minimum of $5,000 a year for four years. Students with a minimum 30 ACT and a 3.5 GPA are awarded $2,500, a Presidential Scholars Award renewable for four years. Students with a minimum 3.7 GPA receive Achievement Scholarships. On the national scholarship front, UI has a track record in helping students successfully garner such awards as Rhodes, Fulbright, National Science Foundation, and others. (Many undergrads see regular opportunities to work alongside the research faculty so they receive mentoring that proves essential in preparation for graduate education programs.)

For nonresident students, UI participates in the Western Undergraduate Exchange (WUE) programs, which allows students to pay 150 percent of in-state costs and waives out-of-state tuition. Students from WUE states are awarded a WUE if they have a minimum 20 ACT and 3.3 GPA. Additionally, Washington Reciprocity waives tuition for some Washington state students, and general out-of-state tuition waivers may apply for selected students.

GETTING IN

A good-looking high school grade point average and ACT/SAT test scores are the way to woo admissions officers. Solid recommendations won't hurt either. Admission standards are the same for all students regardless of major. (Those who enroll in the elite UI Honors Program must meet higher academic standards.) As students enter their junior year, each department has more detailed entry requirements for admittance to selected degree programs. Half of the record freshman class (1,715 students) last year were in the top 25 percent of their high school classes.

WHAT DO GRADUATES DO?

Hosting one of the largest career fairs in the Pacific Northwest, UI brings close to 150 employers to campus twice a year. Business and technology, government and state and educational agencies, natural resources, law, media, and design organizations attract the largest contingents of UI grads. While many other companies recruit on campus, some of the major employers are: Albertsons Corporation, Boeing, Bureau of Land Management, Chevron Corp., Hewlett-Packard, Micron Technologies, National Park Service, Simplot, state and federal departments of lands–Fish and Game Departments, Stryker Endoscopy, USDA Forest Service, Weyerhaeuser Corp., and other small and private companies and engineering firms.

VERY IMPORTANT ADMISSION FACTORS

Rigor of secondary school record, standardized test scores

Average HS GPA	3.36
Range SAT Verbal	490–610
Range SAT Math	490–610
Range ACT	20–26
Minimum TOEFL (paper/computer)	525/193

APPLICATION DEADLINES

Regular admission	8/1
# of transfer applicants	1,629
% of transfer applicants accepted	72

ACADEMICS

Student/faculty ratio	20:1
% faculty teaching undergraduates	70
% of classes taught by graduate students	20

EDUCATION REQUIREMENTS

Foreign languages, history, math, philosophy, social science, communications

FINANCIAL INFO

In-state tuition	$0
Out-of-state tuition	$9,660
Room & board	$5,696
Average book expense	$1,388
Required fees	$4,200
Average freshman need-based grant	$3,263
Average freshman need-based loan	$3,337
% of graduates who borrowed	69
Average indebtedness	$20,002

FINANCIAL AID FORMS
Students must submit FAFSA.

POSTGRAD

CAREER SERVICES
Career/job search classes, career assessment, internships, regional alumni, on-campus job interviews. Off-campus job opportunities are excellent.

THE BOTTOM LINE

In-state residents might initially wince at a price tag just under $14,000 for required fees/tuition ($4,200), room and board ($5,696), books ($1,388), and transportation and other personal expenses ($3,856), but it's almost never that much in reality. For those who demonstrate need, after they receive need-based financial aid and need-based scholarships, that figures comes down to more like $3,000 out of pocket, even before loans.

As of 2006–2007, nonresident tuition and fees per year at UI was $9,660, which is 17 percent lower than the $13,984 average tuition and fees at UI's peer group intuitions. Last year, 49 percent of full-time undergraduate students were in the WUE program, thus were paying only $5,952 per year in tuition and fees.

FUN FACTS

Have you ever tasted pina colada ice cream? A 20-year old undergraduate student major in food science and Spanish developed this new flavor during her summer internship with Schwan Food Company. The company's fleet of signature yellow trucks carry the new flavored ice cream to neighborhoods nationwide.

Known as "IBC bootcamp" for undergraduate business majors, the College of Business and Economics' nationally recognized Integrated Business Curriculum (IBC) provides real hands-on experience in business decision making with corporate case firms such as Boeing, Harley Davidson, Starbucks, Columbia Sportswear, Micron Technologies and Coldwater Creek. The college even offers a Professional Golf Management Program, one of 16 accredited in the nation, and golf is played year round at nearby locations.

UI students, employees and alumni are resourceful, as is shown by their "Found Money Fund." They have parlayed three cents into $187,112.67 (at last count) since 1981.

UI is home of the world's first equine clones—three cloned mules named Idaho Gem, Utah Pioneer, and Idaho Star—all of which are healthy, full brothers to a world champion racing mule. Gem and Star are being trained to race for 2006.

UI's Engineering Design Expo and Mars Rover Challenge showcase student innovation and inventions, as do UI's experimental vehicles that compete regionally each year.

UI has one of the largest study abroad programs in the Pacific Northwest.

As a residential campus, the UI recently constructed the "Living Learning Community" of eight "houses"—four major-themed units and four interdisciplinary. Each house includes a full kitchen, community living rooms, dining rooms, dens, and study areas with a fireplace housing two to five people per suite.

UNIVERSITY OF ILLINOIS AT URBANA-CHAMPAIGN

901 West Illinois Street, Urbana, IL 61801
www.UIUC.edu • Admissions: 217-333-0302
Fax: 217-244-0903 • E-mail: ugradadmissions@uiuc.edu • Financial Aid: 217-333-0100

STUDENTS

Religious affiliation
　　　　　　　　No Affiliation
Academic year
　calendar　　　　semester
Undergrad
　enrollment　　　31,242
% male/female　　　53/47
% Asian　　　　　　12
% Black, non-Latino　7
% Latino　　　　　　7
% international　　　5
% from out of state　11
% freshmen return for
sophomore year　　　93

STUDENT LIFE

% of students living
　on campus　　　　52
% in fraternities　　20
% in sororities　　　22

ADMISSIONS

of applicants　　22,367
% accepted　　　　65
% enrolled　　　　50

HIGH SCHOOL UNITS REQUIRED

4 English, 3 math, 2 science
(2 science lab), 2 foreign
language, 2 social studies, 2
academic electives

VERY IMPORTANT ADMISSION FACTORS

Academic GPA, application
essay, class rank, rigor of
secondary school record,
standardized test scores

ABOUT UNIVERSITY OF ILLINOIS AT URBANA-CHAMPAIGN

　While the majority of students are well-to-do from the Chicago sub-urbs, a large foreign student population and abundant supply of Mid-western friendliness keep things in balance for everyone U of I. (And it's put to perfect example in the university's LLCs—Living Learning Communities). Though the image of infinite cornfields can ring true, it certainly doesn't take away from a social atmosphere that rarely turns down a cold libation. (Around these parts, despite the legal drink-ing age of 21, you only have to be 19 to go to a bar or bartend, meaning that while the underage won't be able to imbibe, they won't be left out in the cold.) U of I has the largest intrafraternity system in the world, but those outside the frat and sorority houses won't feel left out of the proverbial loop with the plethora of sports, political, and academic groups. What's more, the university has taken the initiative to take up any slack by building a new Campus Recreation Center and creating Illinites Activities Nights, which offers open-air movie screenings. (It's like a drive-in, without driving.) And what would a classic Midwest-ern university be without a well-loved, but bottom rung, football team?

　But don't let the good times fool you: The students and faculty at the U of I take their studies seriously. The grading standards are set high, so expect a challenge especially for your first year where introductory classes are designed to separate the future graduates from the current partiers. There's a reason this is the largest university in Illinois—stu-dents may choose from an academic field of 150 programs of study in 16 colleges and schools. Business and engineering are the most popu-lar programs; accounting, agriculture, animal sciences, architecture, and psychology also receive props. Although the sheer volume of at-tention that goes into the more science-oriented departments often eclipses the liberal arts, even those programs are not without strengths. And every program can thank the university's academic stature. On reputation alone the school has no trouble attracting excellent profes-sors who welcome the opportunity to build solid connections with their students.

"There are so many kinds of students here at the University of Illinois so it is easy to find someone with similar interests. There are so many clubs and organizations that it is hard to not find your niche."

IMPORTANT ADMISSION FACTORS

Character/personal qualities, extracurricular activities, level of applicant's interest, talent/ability, volunteer work, work experience

Range SAT Verbal 540–670
Range SAT Math 620–740
Range ACT 25–30
Minimum TOEFL
  (paper/computer) 550/213

APPLICATION DEADLINES

Regular admission 1/2
Regular notification rolling
# of transfer
  applicants 2,595
% of transfer applicants
  accepted 47

ACADEMICS

Student/faculty ratio 15:1
% faculty teaching
  undergraduates 68
% of classes taught by
  graduate students 26

MOST POPULAR MAJORS

• Biology/biological sciences
  • Finance and business
    management
    • Psychology
    • Engineering

BANG FOR YOUR BUCK

The university provides a substantial range of programs at incredible prices. Seventy percent of undergraduates who applied received some form of need-based financial aid in 2005–2006, the most recent academic year for which figures are available. The university also has a bounty of private and institutional scholarships that must be applied for separately, but they are well worth the time it takes to complete the applications. If you're applying for need-based scholarships through the Office of Student Financial Aid, make sure to fill out the Undergraduate Scholarship Supplement Form, which can be filled out online. Once admitted, most departments will review students' academic records and select their scholarship recipients accordingly. Do check with your specific department, however, in case other forms may be required. (The College of Agricultural, Consumer and Environmental Sciences is one that often requires a supplemental form.) Merit-based awards are available to those who excel in academics, art, athletics, drama, leadership, music, or who have alumni affiliation. ROTC scholarships are also available; however, minority status is not considered.

GETTING IN

Ninety-six percent of the admitted freshmen of 2006 were in the top 25 percent of their class. Academic record, class rank, standardized test scores, and essays are the main criteria considered for admission. Less important, but still taken into account, are extracurricular activities, ability and talent, character, volunteer work, and work experience. Candidates are not required to apply separately to departments at U of I for admission; however, those applying to the Fine and Applied Arts department may need to submit a portfolio of their work for consideration.

WHAT DO GRADUATES DO?

Career Services at U of I does an impressive job of guiding students through the process of applying for and finding a job. Their website features a breakdown by major that explains what efforts you'll need to make to secure a job by the end of your fourth year. This preparation goes a long way toward students' confidence level and end success. Consider this: University alumni have created Netscape Communications, AMD, Paypal, Oracle Corporation, YouTube, and more. They are good people to know, indeed.

THE BOTTOM LINE

The large number of Illinois natives or residents at this school can be easily explained: An academic year of tuition, room and board, books and supplies, and fees at U of I for a resident is $18,579, while nonresidents will find themselves paying $32,684. Figure into this equation the average amount of financial aid students receive in their first year—$17,458—and things get much more comfortable. Graduates in 2006 who took advantage of student loans left the school with a cool $15,413 in cumulative debt.

FUN FACTS

The school was one of the original 37 public land-grant institutions created within 10 years of the signing of the Morrill Act by Abraham Lincoln in 1862.

To date, U of I alumni have 11 Nobel laureates and 18 Pulitzer Prizes in their ranks—one of whom was *A Heartbreaking Work of Staggering Genius* author Dave Eggers.

Other alumni include Hugh Hefner, Gene Hackman, Jesse Jackson, and Ron Popeil—the inventor of the infomercial.

Located next to the underground undergraduate library, the Morrow Plots are the country's oldest experimental agricultural fields in continuous use. Agriculture professor Manley Miles and first agriculture dean, George Morrow, began laying out the plots in 1876. The plots were designated a National Historic Landmark in 1968.

EDUCATION REQUIREMENTS

English (including composition), foreign languages, history, humanities, math, philosophy, sciences (biological or physical), social science, cultural studies

FINANCIAL INFO

In-state tuition	$7,708
Out-of-state tuition	$21,794
Room & board	$7,716
Average book expense	$1,000
Required fees	$2,174
Average freshman need-based grant	$6,996
Average freshman need-based loan	$3,554
% of graduates who borrowed	44
Average indebtedness	$15,413

FINANCIAL AID FORMS

Students must submit FAFSA.

POSTGRAD

% going to graduate school	31
% going to law school	3
% going to business school	7
% going to medical school	5

UNIVERSITY OF IOWA

107 Calvin Hall, Iowa City, IA 52242
www.UIowa.edu • Admissions: 319-335-3847
Fax: 319-333-1535 • E-mail: admissions@uiowa.edu • Financial Aid: 319-335-1450

STUDENTS

Religious affiliation
No Affiliation
Academic year
calendar — semester
Undergrad
enrollment — 19,566
% male/female — 47/53
% Asian — 4
% Black, non-Latino — 2
% Latino — 2
% international — 1
% from out of state — 30
% freshmen return for
sophomore year — 84
% freshmen graduate
within 4 years — 38

STUDENT LIFE

% of students living
on campus — 27
% in fraternities — 7
% in sororities — 12

ADMISSIONS

of applicants — 13,241
% accepted — 84
% enrolled — 35

HIGH SCHOOL UNITS REQUIRED

4 English, 3 math, 3 science,
2 foreign language, 3 social
studies

HIGH SCHOOL UNITS RECOMMENDED

4 Foreign language

ABOUT UNIVERSITY OF IOWA

Located in the very heart of America's heartland, UI prides itself on its friendliness, open-mindedness, and enthusiasm. There is no shortage of social contact, which tends to revolve around football games, various campus groups, and the local bar scene. The Greek system is dry, which is why the majority of nightlife occurs in Iowa City's impressive supply of eating and drinking establishments, coffee shops, and parks. Despite the well-documented joie de vivre, many of the Hawkeyes abstain from drink and still have fun with the constant theatrical, musical, and sporting events. While most of the university's diversity is supplied by the graduate student population, great strides have been recently taken to attract a more racially diverse undergraduate class.

Make no bones about it—UI is a big state school, which means that research is king. That said, with its small-town vibe comes a small-campus ease to form strong relationships with professors who are both passionate about the material and teaching. Simply put, no effort will go unrewarded, so the key component to academic success is your ambition. But just in case, university administrators are there to offer unparalleled advice, support, and guidance. The most popular majors are communications, English, and psychology. It's worth mentioning that UI has an excellent liberal arts college (the state's largest—57 majors, 53 minors, and 11 certificate programs), featuring one of the best writing programs in the nation.

BANG FOR YOUR BUCK

UI takes care of its own, delivering both high-quality education and rock-bottom prices. This bargain is furthered by the more than 350 merit- or need-based scholarships available per year for students, the best being The Presidential Scholarship that offers $13,000 a year for up to four years. First-year students with an ACT of 30 or above, a combined SAT of 1320 or above, a UI Admission Index of 150 or above, and a high school grade point average of 3.9, should make sure they apply. This and other scholarships must be applied to separately, but are well worth the effort made: Upon acceptance, you could effectively go to school free (check the school's website for details and forms). For the 2005–2006 year, 74 percent of freshmen who applied received some form of need-based financial aid. Non-need-based awards are available in academics, art, athletics, drama, leadership, music, and ROTC; minority status and state residency are also eligible for these awards.

GETTING IN

Those applying to UI must choose between the College of Liberal Arts and Sciences or the College of Engineering. Then during the second or third year, students can apply to the Colleges of Business, Education, Nursing, or Pharmacy. However, students with exceptional high school records will be considered in their first year for admission to the Colleges of Business or Nursing. The main criteria considered for admission are academic record, class rank, and standardized test scores. Less important, but still taken into account, are alumni relation, talent/ability, state residency, and minority status.

WHAT DO GRADUATES DO?

They pretty much do whatever they want—and successfully at that. Clearly, the odds are in the Hawkeyes' favor. For the 2003–2004 year, graduates of the Colleges of Business, Education, Engineering, Law, Liberal Arts and Sciences, Nursing, and Pharmacy all had at least a 90 percent rate of finding employment or acceptance to graduate programs.

VERY IMPORTANT ADMISSION FACTORS

Academic GPA, class rank, rigor of secondary school record, standardized test scores

Average HS GPA	3.56
Range SAT Verbal	520–650
Range SAT Math	540–660
Range ACT	22–27
Minimum TOEFL (paper/computer)	530/197

APPLICATION DEADLINES

Regular admission	4/1
Regular notification	rolling
# of transfer applicants	2,879
% of transfer applicants accepted	73

ACADEMICS

Student/faculty ratio	15:1
% faculty teaching undergraduates	100

MOST POPULAR MAJORS

- Communications studies/ speech communication and rhetoric
- English language and literature
- Psychology

EDUCATION REQUIREMENTS

English (including composition), foreign languages, history, humanities, math, sciences (biological or physical), social science

FINANCIAL INFO

In-state tuition	$5,110
Out-of-state tuition	$17,334
Room & board	$6,912
Average book expense	$860
Required fees	$1,025
Average freshman need-based grant	$4,361
Average freshman need-based loan	$2,885
% of graduates who borrowed	58
Average indebtedness	$17,259

FINANCIAL AID FORMS

Students must submit FAFSA, institution's own financial aid form.

THE BOTTOM LINE

The value of UI is truly exceptional. In 2006–2007, Iowa residents paid $5,110 in tuition while out-of-state residents paid $17,334. Students could expect another $6,912 for room and board, $1,025 in fees, and $860 in book costs. The average financial aid package for students, including scholarships, was $7,256—which drops in-state to $6,651 and out-of-state is $18,875. If a better deal were to be found, it would be illegal.

FUN FACTS

The university was founded in 1847, only 59 days after Iowa joined the statehood.

In what became a benchmark for higher education, UI was the first public university to admit both men and women equally.

UI is home to what had been the largest global Internet community (the ISCABBS), before the advent of the World Wide Web.

Famous literary alums: Mildred Wirt Benson, creator of Nancy Drew; Flannery O'Connor; Rita Dove; and Mona Van Duyn, the first female U.S. poet laureate.

UNIVERSITY OF KANSAS

Office of Admissions and Scholarships, 1502 Iowa Street, Lawrence, KS 66045
www.KU.edu • Admissions: 785-864-3911
Fax: 785-864-5017 • E-mail: adm@ku.edu • Financial Aid: 785-864-4700

STUDENTS

Religious affiliation
                    No Affiliation
Academic year
  calendar   semester
Undergrad
  enrollment   21,131
% male/female   49/51
% Asian   4
% Black, non-Latino   4
% Latino   3
% Native American   1
% international   3
% from out of state   24
% freshmen return for
  sophomore year   82
% freshmen graduate
  within 4 years   31

STUDENT LIFE

% of students living
  on campus   22
% in fraternities   12
% in sororities   18

ADMISSIONS

of applicants   10,030
% accepted   74
% enrolled   57

HIGH SCHOOL UNITS REQUIRED

4 English, 3 math, 3 science,
3 social studies, 1 computer
technology (1 unit)

HIGH SCHOOL UNITS RECOMMENDED

4 English, 4 math, 3
science, 2 foreign language,
3 social studies, 1 computer
technology (1 unit)

ABOUT UNIVERSITY OF KANSAS

A big school with big opportunities, the University of Kansas excels in diverse areas, from its top business school to its solid programs in communications, education, engineering, journalism, music, nursing, premedical sciences, and the social sciences. As at any large state school, you can also cruise through and pass your classes or you can grab at every opportunity—academic and otherwise—to make the most of your college career. Ambitious students should aim for greatness by seeking enrollment in the Honors Program. Classes are small and the top-notch professors really care about their students.

Among KU's 20,000-plus undergraduates you'll find Kansas farmers, city kids from Kansas City and St. Louis, and many international students. Different groups of students range from Greeks to hippies, but nearly everyone catches the infectious school spirit, especially during basketball season. From late October to April, the Final Four basketball is KU's favorite way to play. Even in the off-season, KU students love life at their school. Hometown Lawrence is college student-friendly with dozens of bars, great music venues, a rich culture, and tons of locally owned restaurants. While the university knows a good time when it sees one and has very popular Greek organization house parties every weekend, keep in mind that at this hulking school there are options for everyone, even teetotalers.

BANG FOR YOUR BUCK

KU students benefit from the school's sizeable endowment. The KU Endowment Association ranks nineteenth in size of endowment per student among public universities. One out of every four first-year students is on a scholarship. In 2005–2006, KU students received more than $160 million in financial aid resources. The endowment allows the school to supplement federal and state aid, making KU a perennial best buy. In fact, only four members of KU's peer group—the 34 public universities in the prestigious Association of American Universities—charge lower tuition and fees than KU. In the immediate region, KU costs significantly less than the universities of Missouri, Iowa, Nebraska, and Arkansas.

Students receive a variety of aid packages, including need-based grants, merit-plus-need scholarships, merit-only scholarships, fee waivers, and self-help aid such as work-study and loans.

VERY IMPORTANT ADMISSION FACTORS

Academic GPA, class rank, rigor of secondary school record, standardized test scores

Average HS GPA	3.4
Range ACT	22–27

APPLICATION DEADLINES

Regular admission	4/1
Regular notification	rolling
# of transfer applicants	2,808
% of transfer applicants accepted	75

ACADEMICS

Student/faculty ratio	20:1
% faculty teaching undergraduates	98
% of classes taught by graduate students	18

MOST POPULAR MAJORS

- Biology/biological sciences
- Business/commerce
- Psychology

EDUCATION REQUIREMENTS

English (including composition), foreign languages, humanities, math, sciences (biological or physical), social science, oral communication/logic, Western civilization, non-Western civilization

Distinctive scholarship opportunities include the Summerfield and Watkins-Berger scholarships, which are renewable awards totaling $4,500 a year. These awards are granted to the top 50 men and women in the state of Kansas. Students must have a 3.5 GPA and 31 ACT to be considered. National Merit, National Achievement, and National Hispanic Scholars can receive an award in the amount of $10,000 a year, which is renewable. This award is available to both state residents and out-of-state students. All together, KU offers more than $25 million in scholarships and grants to undergraduate and graduate students, to ensure access to the University of Kansas for those students with demonstrated financial need.

GETTING IN

At KU, your high school record, class rank, and standardized test scores are very important. Extracurricular activities and other factors are considered to a lesser degree. Students need to indicate their intended academic major on the application. Some of the undergraduate professional schools are competitive and have different application deadlines. As a new freshman, students can only enter into the School of Architecture, School of Engineering, School of Fine Arts and the College of Liberal Arts and Sciences. Of these, Architecture, Engineering, and Fine Arts are competitive.

WHAT DO GRADUATES DO?

Major employers of KU grads include Sprint, the Federal Reserve, Boeing, Raytheon, Cerner, and Philip Morris. Among the hundreds of companies that recruit each year on campus are Black & Veatch, Boeing Company, Cerner, Deloitte and Touche, ExxonMobil Corp., General Electric, Hallmark Cards, Koch Industries, Pepsi Bottling Group, Pulte Homes, Sprint, Target, Union Pacific, and Walgreens.

THE BOTTOM LINE

In 2006–2007, Kansas residents paid $16,262 to attend KU. They paid $5,513 in tuition, $640 in required fees, $5,747 in room and board, $750 for books and supplies, $1,472 in transportation expenses, and $2,140 in other expenses. Out-of-state students paid an additional $8,970 in tuition to bring the annual cost of attending KU to $25,232. The average financial aid award of those with demonstrated need was $7,025; need-based scholarships and/or grant added another $3,660, for a total of $10,685 off the sticker price for those with need.

FUN FACTS

KU has produced 25 Rhodes scholars, putting the university in the upper echelon of public universities. Five KU alumni have been selected for MacArthur Foundation "genius scholarships."

The only KU basketball coach to sport a losing record was James Naismith, who invented the game.

A steam whistle signals the end of the class hour on the KU campus. Some students fondly refer to it as "Tooty Toot."

Billing himself as the "Great Wessellini" and "The Great Lorenzo: The Human Cannonball," art student Dan Wessell entertained the KU student body in the early 1970s by attempting two ill-fated stunts: flying over Memorial Stadium in a homemade glider and rolling down the slope of Mount Oread in a giant Plexiglas bubble. In the climate of student strikes, anti-war demonstrations, and civil rights protests, his antics were a welcome respite from more serious issues.

FINANCIAL INFO

In-state tuition	$5,513
Out-of-state tuition	$14,483
Room & board	$5,747
Average book expense	$750
Required fees	$640
Average freshman need-based grant	$3,752
Average freshman need-based loan	$2,607
% of graduates who borrowed	42
Average indebtedness	$17,243

FINANCIAL AID FORMS

Students must submit FAFSA.

Financial aid filing deadline	3/1

POSTGRAD

% going to graduate school	28

CAREER SERVICES

Career/job search classes, career assessment, internships, on-campus job interviews. Off-campus job opportunities are excellent.

UNIVERSITY OF MARYLAND— COLLEGE PARK

Mitchell Building, College Park, MD 20742-5235
www.UMD.edu • Admissions: 301-314-8385
Fax: 301-314-9693 • E-mail: um-admit@uga.umd.edu • Financial Aid: 301-314-9000

STUDENTS

Religious affiliation
               No Affiliation
Academic year
  calendar   semester
Undergrad
  enrollment   24,876
% male/female   51/49
% Asian   14
% Black, non-Latino   13
% Latino   6
% international   2
% from out of state   24
% freshmen return for
sophomore year   92
% freshmen graduate
  within 4 years   50

STUDENT LIFE

% of students living
  on campus   43
% in fraternities   9
% in sororities   11

ADMISSIONS

of applicants   22,428
% accepted   49
% enrolled   38

HIGH SCHOOL UNITS REQUIRED

4 English, 3 math, 3 science
(2 science lab), 2 foreign
language, 3 social studies

HIGH SCHOOL UNITS RECOMMENDED

4 Math

ABOUT UNIVERSITY OF MARYLAND—COLLEGE PARK

University of Maryland—College Park has worked hard to undo its party-school reputation of years past, and it has succeeded spectacularly. Unlike its previous manifestation, today's Maryland is a highly competitive, highly respected institution of higher learning and cutting-edge research. Toss in a lovely campus, a diverse and talented student body, and great intercollegiate athletics and you begin to understand why so many undergraduates are clamoring to get in. Proximity to Washington, DC is another huge plus, especially for those seeking careers in government, public service, and general opinion shaping. The engineering and business programs are also big winners here.

Maryland's College Park campus is enormous, large enough to accommodate any and every activity under the sun. If you can imagine it, it's happening somewhere at the University of Maryland, and if it's not, it's certainly happening somewhere down the road in either Washington, DC or Baltimore. Metro trains and buses make traveling to either city a snap, and as an added bonus, they eliminate the nightmare of urban parking. Back on campus, Maryland athletics are practically a religion, with football and men's basketball inspiring the most devout followings. The student body represents a wide range of backgrounds. Most students stick within the comfort of their own groups, but everyone finds a place to fit in.

BANG FOR YOUR BUCK

In recent years, Maryland has pursued a business plan aimed at increasing affordable access while maintaining quality of education. The school's goal is to increase the percentage of demonstrated need met for all aid recipients.

The school focuses on its undergraduates who demonstrate need in a variety of ways. First, the Maryland Pathways Program provides a debt-free education to underprivileged Maryland resident students. The school's Incentive Awards targets Maryland students who have faced extreme hardship and overcome many challenges to enroll in college. It also provides recipients with full scholarships room, board, books and expenses, as well as tutorial support and mentoring. Finally, Maryland is building partnerships and collaborative programs with local two-year colleges to increase the likelihood of transfer from these less expensive schools.

Maryland provides need-based assistance to 94 percent of all aid applicants who demonstrate need, with 68 percent of need-based aid packages including some form of need-based grant or scholarship. On average, the school meets 68 percent of aid recipients' demonstrated need and has been able to meet 100 percent of demonstrated need for just over a quarter of all aid recipients.

Merit-based awards are widely available to students. The top 25 percent of each entering class is awarded some form of merit aid.

GETTING IN

All applications to Maryland are reviewed individually and holistically, with consideration given to more than two-dozen factors (e.g., curriculum, GPA, standardized test scores, references). While all components of the application are important, a student's prior academic achievement reviewed in the context of what was available to them is emphasized during the Admission Committee review. Certain majors limit enrollment, so apply early to avoid being closed out. It's also worth noting that most freshmen are accommodated in their first-choice major.

WHAT DO GRADUATES DO?

College Park has a huge undergraduate program with many standout divisions. Those who are matriculated proceed to all areas of the academic and professional worlds. Top employers of Maryland undergraduates include Baltimore Gas & Electric, Booz Allen Hamilton, CGI-AMS, the Central Intelligence Agency, General Electric, General Mills, IBM, Lockheed Martin, Microsoft Corporation, Northrop Grumman, NVR/Ryan Homes, Priority One Services, Target Corporation, and Verizon Communications.

VERY IMPORTANT ADMISSION FACTORS

Rigor of secondary school record, standardized test scores

IMPORTANT ADMISSION FACTORS

Application essay, class rank, recommendation(s), state residency, talent/ability

Average HS GPA	3.86
Range SAT Verbal	580–670
Range SAT Math	600–700
Minimum TOEFL (paper/computer)	575/233

APPLICATION DEADLINES

Regular admission	1/20
Regular notification	4/1
# of transfer applicants	6,059
% of transfer applicants accepted	64

ACADEMICS

Student/faculty ratio	19:1
% faculty teaching undergraduates	65
% of classes taught by graduate students	18

MOST POPULAR MAJORS

- Computer and information sciences
- Criminology
- Political science and government

Arts/fine arts, English
(including composition),
history, humanities, math,
sciences (biological or
physical), social science,
one diversity course, two
advanced studies courses
outside of one's major

FINANCIAL INFO

In-state tuition	$6,566
Out-of-state tuition	$20,005
Room & board	$8,422
Average book expense	$909
Required fees	$1,340
Average freshman need-based grant	$5,885
Average freshman need-based loan	$2,390
% of graduates who borrowed	47
Average indebtedness	$14,451

FINANCIAL AID FORMS

Students must submit
FAFSA.

POSTGRAD

CAREER SERVICES

Off-campus job opportuni-
ties are good.

THE BOTTOM LINE

In 2006–2007, annual full-time in-state tuition and fees at College Park totaled $7,906. Room and board was $8,422, depending on the type of room and meal plan. Thus, total direct costs for in-state students was $16,328. Students are advised to budget an additional $909 for books, $674 for transportation, and $2,022 for personal and miscellaneous expenses. Maryland strives to provide the greatest amount of need-based aid possible then offers families other non-need-based funding to bridge the gap between what the families can afford and the need or merit funding already awarded. Low-interest loans such as Parental Loans for Undergraduate Students (PLUS) and Alternative Education loans, in addition to the school's non-interest Terp Payment plan, help broaden students' options.

FUN FACTS

University of Maryland economist Tom Schelling recently won the Nobel Prize in Economics. He joins two other Maryland faculty members who have been named Nobel Prize winners.

The University of Maryland has produced its own ice cream since 1924. A delicious 25,000 gallons of ice cream are produced here annually.

The Commencement Address in 1996 was delivered by not one but two Muppets: Kermit and Elmo.

Queen Elizabeth II and Prince Philip attended a Terrapins football game on October 19, 1957, at which the Terps defeated the Tar Heels 21–7. The queen and prince probably noticed that the game did not at all resemble the football played in England.

UNIVERSITY OF MICHIGAN—FLINT

303 East Kearsley Street, 245 UPAV, Flint, MI 48502
www.UMFlint.edu • Admissions: 810-762-3300
Fax: 810-762-3272 • E-mail: admissions@umflint.edu • Financial Aid: 810-762-3444

STUDENTS

Religious affiliation
No Affiliation
Academic year
calendar   semester
Undergrad
enrollment   5,481
% male/female   37/63
% Asian   2
% Black, non-Latino   11
% Latino   3
% Native American 1
% international   1
% from out of state   1
% freshmen return for
sophomore year   80
% freshmen graduate
within 4 years   10

STUDENT LIFE

% of students living
on campus   0
% in fraternities 1
% in sororities   1

ADMISSIONS

of applicants   1,651
% accepted   85
% enrolled   41

HIGH SCHOOL UNITS REQUIRED

4 English, 3 math, 2
science, 3 social studies

HIGH SCHOOL UNITS RECOMMENDED

4 English, 4 math, 4 science
(2 science lab), 2 foreign
language, 3 social studies,
2 history

ABOUT THE UNIVERSITY OF MICHIGAN—FLINT

UM Flint is a commuter campus: There are no dorms and all students live in the surrounding communities. Education, health professions, and business majors make up more than half the student body, but there are programs in arts, humanities, science, and interdisciplinary studies along with a range of other topics. The school offers degrees in more than 60 undergraduate and 10 graduate areas, including a doctor of physical therapy, and has international courses in locations such as China, India, and the Dominican Republic. Professors are well respected in their fields and, thanks to a smaller campus, students get the opportunity to work with them one on one. The approximately 5,000 students at UM Flint value the quality of education—especially in nursing and biology—and the school's small size and association with the widely respected University of Michigan.

Flint itself is a midsized city in southeastern Michigan, about 60 miles from Detroit, Ann Arbor, and Lansing. Though some find the area a bit grim, most are quick to point out that there's much to do and a welcoming community that supports education. On campus, there are student government activities, service clubs and cultural, political, and religious groups. Though organizations are working to change this, most UM Flint students are on campus only for their classes or to use the resources of the library. Many work while going to school, and they value the university's ability to schedule classes at varying times throughout the day and evening to meet their needs. Students also praise the honors program, which allows closer contact with professors and the chance to participate in research.

Keep your eyes out for a parking space. With no on-campus dorms, everyone has to find a place to park. The campus, on the banks of the Flint River, is small and easy to get around. Many (but not all) of the students are people already residing in the area, but there's a mix of ages, ethnicities, and interests to offer differing perspectives. It's a commuter lifestyle without a great deal of on-campus socializing but with the quality of a University of Michigan education, a combination which suits the busy lifestyle of most UM Flint students.

VERY IMPORTANT ADMISSION FACTORS

Academic GPA, rigor of secondary school record, standardized test scores

IMPORTANT ADMISSION FACTORS

Extracurricular activities

Average HS GPA	3.2
Range SAT Verbal	435-540
Range SAT Math	400-550
Range ACT	18-24
Minimum TOEFL (paper/computer)	550/213

APPLICATION DEADLINES

Regular notification	rolling
# of transfer applicants	1,313
% of transfer applicants accepted	84

ACADEMICS

Student/faculty ratio	15:1
% faculty teaching undergraduates	100
% of classes taught by graduate students	0

MOST POPULAR MAJORS

- Business administration and management
- Education
- health services/allied health

EDUCATION REQUIREMENTS

Arts/fine arts, English (including composition), foreign languages, history, humanities, math, philosophy, sciences (biological or physical), social science

BANG FOR YOUR BUCK

The university determined that about half the incoming freshmen who requested aid in the fall of 2005 qualified for it, and they awarded some form of aid to almost all of those students. Fewer than 10 percent had their need fully met, however. The average financial aid package was $5,621, typically comprising loans, scholarships, and work-based awards. There are several scholarship programs including The Michigan Scholar and the Heritage Scholarship. Details may be found on the university's website.

GETTING IN

The University of Michigan—Flint considers three academic factors most strongly in selecting freshman students: rigor of high school curriculum, GPA, and standardized test scores. They next look at involvement in extracurricular activities. They'll also consider geographic location, alumni relations, and how a student does in an interview. Sixteen percent of the class admitted in 2005 were in the top 10 percent of their high school classes; 75 percent were in the top half. Their average high school GPA was 3.2 and average ACT score was 21.

WHAT DO GRADUATES DO?

Arbor Mortgage, Edward Jones Investments, LaSalle Bank, The Michigan Farm Bureau, New York Life, and Northwestern Mutual are among the business firms who recruit on campus; many health care and education related employers do also, especially at university sponsored career fairs. Bowling Green State University, the University of Central Michigan, Wayne State University, and the University of Michigan Ann Arbor are among the graduate schools that join in education-themed career fairs.

THE BOTTOM LINE

Those who qualify as Michigan residents pay $6,568 in tuition and $334 in required fees. Out-of-staters pay that same amount for required fees and $12,818 in tuition. As there is no on-campus living, the college does not offer estimates for room and board but suggests that off-campus students will need about $2,630 in meal expenses, slightly more than $4,000 in room cost, and $950 for books and supplies during an academic year. Transportation costs, no small thing at a commuter campus, will run about $2,100 per year.

FUN FACTS

Flint native, Michael Moore, put his hometown on the map in 1989. His documentary, *Roger & Me*, explained what happened to Flint, Michigan after General Motors closed its factories and opened new ones in Mexico.

UM Flint was first established as a senior college, with only junior and senior students. With the freshman class admitted in 1965, Flint College, as it was then known, became the first four-year University of Michigan program offered outside of Ann Arbor.

UM Flint Alumnus Avery Brand and alumna Liza (Lakes) Garza each received commercial Emmy nominations in the spring of 2006 for commercials promoting the university.

FINANCIAL INFO

In-state tuition	$6,568
Out-of-state tuition	$12,818
Required fees	$334
Average freshman need-based grant	$3,674
Average freshman need-based loan	$2,800
% of graduates who borrowed	66
Average indebtedness	$21,888

FINANCIAL AID FORMS

Students must submit FAFSA, institution's own financial aid form, institution's own financial aid form used in Spring/Summer Sessions only.

POSTGRAD

CAREER SERVICES

Alumni network, career assessment, internships, on-campus job interviews. Off-campus job opportunities are fair.

UNIVERSITY OF MINNESOTA—MORRIS

600 East Fourth Street, Morris, MN 56267
www.Morris.UMN.edu • Admissions: 320-589-6035
Fax: 320-589-1673 • E-mail: admissions@morris.umn.edu • Financial Aid: 320-589-6035

STUDENTS

Religious affiliation
　　　　　　　No Affiliation
Academic year
　calendar　　　semester
Undergrad
　enrollment　　　1,747
% male/female　　40/60
% Asian　　　　　　4
% Black, non-Latino　2
% Latino　　　　　　2
% Native American　10
% international　　　2
% from out of state　13
% freshmen return for
sophomore year　　86
% freshmen graduate
　within 4 years　　41

STUDENT LIFE

% of students living
　on campus　　　51

ADMISSIONS

of applicants　　1,233
% accepted　　　　80
% enrolled　　　　40

HIGH SCHOOL UNITS REQUIRED

4 English, 3 math, 3 science
(2 science lab), 2 foreign
language, 4 social studies, 4
history

HIGH SCHOOL UNITS RECOMMENDED

4 Math, 4 science, 3 foreign
language

ABOUT THE UNIVERSITY OF MINNESOTA—MORRIS

A good three hours west of the Twin Cities, set in rural Morris, Minnesota (population: 5,068), where seasons change (and not much else), the University of Minnesota—Morris could be the best kept secret of American colleges. Yes, UMM is one limb of the larger University of Minnesota, but its modest size and jam-packed student events calendar—not to mention its perennially high ranking among the nation's top public liberal arts colleges—are just a few things lending themselves to this bustling anomaly in stark, secluded Morris. With class sizes typically less than 20, led by attentive, generous faculty; with over 90 student-run organizations entertaining an active, diverse student body, UMM prides itself on being "close to home, far from ordinary."

The campus itself is over a century old: Originally, it was a Catholic boarding school for Native Americans; next, it reopened as an agricultural boarding school in 1910; finally, in 1960, it was reenvisioned as a liberal arts college for the University of Minnesota system. No matter the phase of this historically protected campus, Native American students have always been admitted to the school free of tuition, a policy in effect to this day. And it is this marriage of preservation and progressivism that help make UMM unique on a national level. Kind to the land and fond of alternative sources of energy, UMM recently installed a wind turbine east of campus, which now powers about 60 percent of the college. Two more turbines are in the works, as well as a biomass plant—to be both a research facility and the new source of about 80 percent of UMM's heat in the harsh winter.

Out on the prairie, UMM's 1,800 full-time students find harmony between class and play. Their professors, they say, hold them to high standards but are down-to-earth and sincerely dedicated to teaching. While English and biology majors are more numerous than any others, no area of study is far and away the most popular—a testament to the liberal arts ideal at UMM and the overall diversity of the student body. Self-described as a politically liberal campus (its GLBT student group enjoys the university's moral support), all views and ways of life are welcome. Student activities include the Media Services Department's production of "Prairie Yard and Garden," a nationally broadcasted PBS program, and the annual UMM Jazz Fest, which is so hugely popular that sometimes even the university chancellor can't get a ticket.

BANG FOR YOUR BUCK

Three-quarters of the student body applies for some form of financial aid, and on average 82 percent of a student's need is met. Slightly more money, however, comes from self-help-based aid such as loans or work study than from scholarships and grants. Nevertheless, UMM offers first-year students an extensive array of donor-funded scholarships; among them are the Bank of the West Scholarship and the Otter Tail Power Company Scholarship, each awarded based on academic merit and for living within that corporation's "service area."

GETTING IN

UMM's 80-percent acceptance rate might be lower if more than 1,232 applied each year, but luring students toward a public university experience in the middle of nowhere is understandably difficult. This shouldn't suggest, however, that applicants aren't exceptional kids. On the academic end of things, a student's high school curriculum is most scrutinized, as well as standardized test scores and overall class rank. UMM wants to see a good application essay, too. As for nonacademic criteria, the more well-rounded, the better. An admissions counselor understands that a high school senior may not have mastered the art of the interview, and so is forgiving, but good character and a history of extracurricular activities, especially volunteer work, are important.

WHAT DO GRADUATES DO?

According to its 2005 Graduate Exit Survey Report, 76 percent of the graduates said they planned to pursue postgraduate studies within three years of leaving UMM; in actuality, a still commendable 45 percent do. Companies and organizations known to frequently hire UMM grads include the famous Mayo Clinic in Rochester (MN), the renowned Guthrie Theatre in Minneapolis, the Target Corporation, IBM, and various elementary and secondary schools across the country.

VERY IMPORTANT ADMISSION FACTORS

Class rank, rigor of secondary school record, standardized test scores

IMPORTANT ADMISSION FACTORS

Application essay, character/personal qualities, extracurricular activities, recommendation(s), talent/ability, volunteer work, work experience

Range SAT Verbal 570–680
Range SAT Math 565–680
Range ACT 22–27
Minimum TOEFL
(paper/computer) 550/213

APPLICATION DEADLINES
Regular admission 3/15
Regular notification rolling
# of transfer applicants 190
% of transfer applicants
accepted 73

ACADEMICS
Student/faculty ratio 11:1
% faculty teaching
undergraduates 100
% of classes taught by
graduate students 0

MOST POPULAR MAJORS
• Elementary education and teaching
• Psychology

EDUCATION REQUIREMENTS

Arts/fine arts, computer literacy, English (including composition), foreign languages, history, humanities, math, sciences (biological or physical), social science, First-year Seminar, International Perspective, Ethical and Civic Responsibility

FINANCIAL INFO

In-state tuition	$8,720
Out-of-state tuition	$8,720
Room & board	$6,150
Average book expense	$900
Required fees	$1,592
Average freshman need-based grant	$6,839
Average freshman need-based loan	$6,650
% of graduates who borrowed	74
Average indebtedness	$20,942

FINANCIAL AID FORMS

Students must submit FAFSA.

POSTGRAD

% going to graduate school	48
% going to law school	11
% going to business school	3
% going to medical school	4

CAREER SERVICES

Alumni services, career/job search classes, career assessment, internships, on-campus job interviews. Off-campus job opportunities are good.

BOTTOM LINE

You won't find many public colleges charging resident and non-resident students the same amount to attend, but UMM does. Tuition rings in at an incredibly generous $8,720. In fact, the only thing more generous is the free tuition Native Americans receive. The school estimates room and board $6,150, required fees at $1,592, and books and supplies at an even $900.

FUN FACTS

In sports, UMM's football team ended its infamous 46-game losing streak on September 20, 2003, walloping Principia College 61–28.

Also, UMM is the first college in America to add women's wrestling as an official varsity sport, though it lasted only from 1993 to 2003.

Recently, a group of UMM students, staff, faculty, and supporters traveled to Las Vegas on a lark and won the coed division of the 2nd Annual Dodgeball World Championship.

THE UNIVERSITY OF NORTH CAROLINA AT ASHEVILLE

CPO #2210, 117 Lipinsky Hall, Asheville, NC 28804-8510
www.UNCA.edu • Admissions: 828-251-6481
Fax: 828-251-6482 • E-mail: admissions@unca.edu • Financial Aid: 828-251-6535

STUDENTS

Religious affiliation
　　　　　　　　　No Affiliation
Academic year
　calendar　　　　semester
Undergrad
　enrollment　　　　3,124
% male/female　　　42/58
% Asian　　　　　　　2
% Black, non-Latino　　2
% Latino　　　　　　　2
% international　　　　1
% from out of state　　14
% freshmen return for
sophomore year　　　76
% freshmen graduate within
4 years　　　　　　　28

STUDENT LIFE

% of students living
　on campus　　　　34
% in fraternities　　　3
% in sororities　　　　2

ADMISSIONS

of applicants　　2,362
% accepted　　　　63
% enrolled　　　　　32

HIGH SCHOOL UNITS REQUIRED

4 English, 4 math, 3 science
(1 science lab), 2 foreign
language, 1 social studies, 1
history

HIGH SCHOOL UNITS RECOMMENDED

4 Academic electives

ABOUT THE UNIVERSITY OF NORTH CAROLINA AT ASHEVILLE

Thanks to its growing academic reputation, the University of North Carolina at Asheville is no longer the well-kept secret it once was. Still, Asheville's draw remains mostly regional, attracting applicants primarily from nearby Georgia and Florida. Asheville offers the quality education of a private school at a public school price. The university provides students with numerous academic options, limits class sizes, and focuses strongly on the liberal arts and sciences. The professors are extremely approachable and—much to the chagrin of some students—will notice if you ditch class.

Asheville is an awesome, vibrant city, and the surrounding Blue Ridge Mountains are breathtaking. Students can go hiking, rock climbing, biking, whitewater rafting, or exploring in the tranquil wilderness of Appalachia. Closer to campus, there are tons of things to do, including concerts, theater, and community service. Greek organizations also provide a social nexus for many.

BANG FOR YOUR BUCK

Financial aid is readily available and there's a lot of one-to-one interaction between the folks in financial aid and individual students. The goal is to develop aid packages that allow students to graduate with the smallest possible debt. The university first seeks the highest possible amount of grant funds and then looks to loans. And the good news is that if you get an outside scholarship, UNC Asheville reduces your loan amount, not the amount of free money you receive. Ninety-eight percent of students who qualified redeived financial aid.

Asheville also offers a number of merit-based scholarships. University Laurels Academic Scholarships are awarded competitively to first-year students who are in the top 10 percent of their high school class and score a 1200 or higher on the SAT. Within the Laurels Scholarship Program are UNC—Asheville's sought-after and prestigious Undergraduate Research Fellowships. Applicants must plan on pursuing an undergraduate research project during their junior and senior years and can expect annual awards of up to $5,000. Environmental studies is one of the hottest majors and boasts several scholarship opportunities, including research fellowships valued at $3,000 each. Additional research scholarships worth between $3,000 and $6,000 are available to upperclassmen who work with faculty mentors to design and conduct original

VERY IMPORTANT ADMISSION FACTORS

Academic GPA, class rank, rigor of secondary school record

IMPORTANT ADMISSION FACTORS

Standardized test scores

Average HS GPA	3.8
Range SAT Verbal	540–660
Range SAT Math	540–640
Range ACT	22–27
Minimum TOEFL (paper/computer)	550/213

APPLICATION DEADLINES

Regular admission	2/16
Regular notification	3/23
# of transfer applicants	465
% of transfer applicants accepted	84

ACADEMICS

Student/faculty ratio	13:1
% faculty teaching undergraduates	100
% of classes taught by graduate students	0

MOST POPULAR MAJORS

- Business administration/ management
- English language and literature
- Psychology

environmental research. There is also the Western North Carolina Leadership Scholarship program, which is targeted to area students, and the North Carolina Teaching Fellows Program, which provides mostly full-tuition fellowships to in-state students who agree to teach upon graduation in North Carolina public schools.

GETTING IN

It's pretty basic. The components of UNC Asheville's application are your high school transcripts and SAT or ACT scores. The most important component is your high school curriculum. Load up on honors, Advanced Placement, and International Baccalaureate courses. To get accepted at UNC Asheville, you need a solid B average in a college-preparatory curriculum and an SAT score of about 1165; if you take the ACT, you will need a score of about 24. We should also note that out-of-state enrollment is capped at 18 percent of each incoming first-year class.

WHAT DO GRADUATES DO?

About 20 percent of all UNC Asheville students go on to graduate or professional schools upon graduation—often to places like the Art Institute of Chicago, the University of California at Berkeley, and Yale. Asheville graduates who decide to work upon graduation work at companies like Coca-Cola Company, Fox Television, The Weather Channel, and Microsoft. Asheville also has a number of very strong internship programs. Mass communication majors intern with regional media and ad agencies. Atmospheric science majors intern at the National Climatic Data Center—the world's largest active archive of weather data—which is located right in Asheville. Almost all management majors also intern in business administration, health care administration, or marketing. The environmental studies department has a dynamic internship program as well, and most of its students pursue internships with local, national, or international environmental organizations as part of their course work.

THE BOTTOM LINE

Residents pay an average of about $13,653 per year for tuition, room and board, and all other reasonable expenses, while nonresidents pay an average of about $23,768. The average aid award is about $8,152. On average, sophomores, juniors, and seniors receive a little more funding because they are eligible for much more in the way of research fellowships. Asheville's relatively low cost allows students to graduate without much debt. About half of all students graduate with an average loan debt of about $15,309.

Fun Facts

The current projects of UNC Asheville's Environmental Quality Institute include investigations of the water quality of western North Carolina, research regarding the presence of arsenic in pressure-treated lumber, a study of lead exposure from artificial Christmas trees, and exploring the potential for heavy metal contamination by way of Chinese herbal medicines.

One really cool resource that UNC Asheville has going for it career-wise is the North Carolina Center for Creative Retirement. A bunch of retired, high-achieving professionals volunteer at the Career Counseling Center. They are experts in fields ranging from education to nuclear science, and they help students with resumes, mock interviews, cover letters, and other general career advice.

Asheville students have interned at France's International Biological Control Agency looking for ways to control gypsy moths and saw flies; at the Tropical Research Foundation in Belize codifying medicinal plants with a local shaman in a forest reserve; and in southern Spain exploring the migration of tropical birds. Other students have participated in the study of endangered birds in Olympic National Forest, tracked large mammals in the Rocky Mountain States, and aided in fisheries biology in the Great Smoky Mountains.

Education Requirements

Arts/fine arts, computer literacy, English (including composition), foreign languages, humanities, math, sciences (biological or physical), social science, health and wellness

FINANCIAL INFO

In-state tuition	$2,172
Out-of-state tuition	$12,287
Room & board	$5,880
Average book expense	$850
Required fees	$1,710
Average freshman need-based grant	$3,119
Average freshman need-based loan	$2,456
% of graduates who borrowed	51
Average indebtedness	$15,309

Financial Aid Forms

Students must submit FAFSA.

POSTGRAD

% going to graduate school	21
% going to law school	1
% going to business school	1
% going to medical school	1

THE UNIVERSITY OF NORTH CAROLINA AT GREENSBORO

123 Mossman Building, Greensboro, NC 27402-6170
www.UNCG.edu • Admissions: 336-334-5243
Fax: 336-334-4180 • E-mail: admissions@uncg.edu • Financial Aid: 910-334-5702

STUDENTS

Religious affiliation

No Affiliation

Academic year calendar	semester
Undergrad enrollment	12,172
% male/female	32/68
% Asian	3
% Black, non-Latino	20
% Latino	2
% international	1
% from out of state	7
% freshmen return for sophomore year	78
% freshmen graduate within 4 years	38

STUDENT LIFE

% of students living on campus	32

ADMISSIONS

# of applicants	8,987
% accepted	60
% enrolled	45

HIGH SCHOOL UNITS REQUIRED

4 English, 3 math, 3 science (1 science lab), 2 foreign language, 1 social studies, 1 history, 1 academic elective

VERY IMPORTANT ADMISSION FACTORS

Academic GPA

ABOUT THE UNIVERSITY OF NORTH CAROLINA AT GREENSBORO

Chartered in 1891, the University of North Carolina at Greensboro is one of the three original institutions of the University of North Carolina system and home to six professional schools and two colleges, the College of Arts and Sciences and the Lloyd International Honors College. The former, which is larger by far, houses an impressive variety of departments and programs that include everything from African American studies to film and video production to drama to medical technology—all told, over 100 different courses of study. And for those with the proper qualifications who are looking to forge their own educational opportunities, the Lloyd International Honors College offers the opportunity to travel abroad, take on special research projects, and receive certain priorities, which include honors advising and library privileges.

But even though the variety of programs is legion, and the incoming classes are at record highs, (the fall 2005 freshman class clocked in at 2,424), students don't feel like just another brick in the wall. This has to do, in large part, with the intimate student-faculty ratio of 16:1, an average class size of under 30, and the fact that over 90 percent of classes are taught by the professors themselves. What's more, the professors are very accessible, offering not only extensive office hours, but commonly handing out their e-mail addresses and cell phone numbers so that they can offer additional help to students when necessary.

And speaking of brick, the picturesque 210-acre campus features 30 academic buildings and 24 residence halls set against lush green walks and trees. There is plenty of space not only for classes, but also for socializing and extracurricular activities, which is a good thing considering that there are over 140 student organizations, 16 intercollegiate athletic teams, and everything from dance troupes to a fishing club. And yet despite all the activity, the atmosphere is decidedly mellow and accepting, whether you're a Bach fanatic or a Gap devotee. Student backgrounds are as diverse as their interests, representing 49 states and over 81 countries. The dating scene might be a little tough on the ladies, since many of the undergraduate men are either spoken for or prefer their own company, but it's a bonus for the guys, since women outnumber men by over two to one.

Students Say

"UNCG is difficult to sum up in one sentence—it's about diversity, learning, growing, changing, partying, studying, helping others . . . UNCG is probably the most all-encompassing school in the Southeast."

BANG FOR YOUR BUCK

As with all state schools, it pays to be on the home team. North Carolina residents can expect to pay about $2,300 per year for tuition, while out-of-state residents can expect to pay about $13,500. But for both groups, UNCG provides significant financial aid. Over 99 percent of those who are found eligible receive financial aid, and the school meets over 83 percent of students' need. In addition, the school offers over 40 merit-based, renewable scholarships: Awards range from $2,500 to full tuition, fees, room, and board.

GETTING IN

Competition is far from fierce: The school accepts over 85 percent of applicants. Admissions officers look for students who have taken four years of English, math, and science, and two of history, social studies, and a foreign language. Close attention is given to difficulty of classes taken thus far, GPA, standardized test scores, the application essay, and recommendations, while class rank is not considered. And while extracurriculars, community service, and work experience are looked at, much greater emphasis is placed on the applicant's character and personality. The average incoming freshman has a 3.45 GPA and a composite SAT critical reading and math score of 1045.

WHAT DO GRADUATES DO?

UNCG provides regular PhD fairs and career fairs to help their graduates select and pursue either a higher degree or a job after graduating. In addition, campus recruiters regularly visit, and include mostly financial firms such as Wells Fargo, American Express, Mass Mutual, and Wachovia, which makes sense considering that business and marketing is the leading major. Other popular fields include education, English, psychology, the social sciences, health and related sciences, and visual and performing arts. Satisfaction is high among graduates, with the vast majority pursuing either higher degrees or careers within their chosen fields.

IMPORTANT ADMISSION FACTORS

Rigor of secondary school record, standardized test scores

Average HS GPA 3.48
Range SAT Verbal 470–580
Range SAT Math 470–580
Minimum TOEFL
(paper/computer) 550/1

APPLICATION DEADLINES

Regular admission 8/1
Regular notification rolling
# of transfer
  applicants 2,971
% of transfer applicants
  accepted 58

ACADEMICS

Student/faculty ratio 16:1
% faculty teaching
  undergraduates 100

MOST POPULAR MAJORS

- Business administration/ management
- Elementary education and teaching
- Nursing—registered nurse training (RN, ASN, BSN, MSN)

EDUCATION REQUIREMENTS

Arts/fine arts, English (including composition), foreign languages, history, humanities, math, philosophy, sciences (biological or physical), social science

FINANCIAL INFO

In-state tuition	$2,308
Out-of-state tuition	$13,576
Room & board	$5,513
Average book expense	$1,314
Required fees	$1,505
Average freshman need-based grant	$3,558
Average freshman need-based loan	$2,446
% of graduates who borrowed	60
Average indebtedness	$13,661

FINANCIAL AID FORMS
Students must submit FAFSA.

POSTGRAD

CAREER SERVICES
Alumni services, career/job search classes, career assessment, on-campus job interviews. Off-campus job opportunities are good.

THE BOTTOM LINE

The school provides need-based support to over 99 percent of eligible students, and meets over 80 percent of their need. The average need-based financial aid package weighs in at a hefty $8,400. In addition to tuition, students can expect to pay $1,500 in required fees, $5,500 for room and board, and $3,000 or so for books, travel, and miscellaneous personal expenses. North Carolina residents receive a steep discount of approximately $11,000 per year.

FUN FACTS

The Rock, a large boulder donated by the class of 1973, is spray-painted once a day and serves as a kind of giant message board.

The "Blue Crew," a club dedicated to cheering on the school's various athletic teams (collectively known as the Spartans), was recently joined by "the Ocho," eight young men who paint the word "S-P-A-R-T-A-N-S" on their chests.

History never tasted so sweet—Yum Yum's, the campus ice-cream parlor, has been drawing students since 1906.

Each year, new students are given a Spartan pin and a daisy. The flower's hues are the school's original colors (before blue was added): white and gold.

THE UNIVERSITY OF NORTH CAROLINA AT PEMBROKE

One University Drive, PO Box 1510, Pembroke, NC 28372
www.UNCP.edu • Admissions: 910-521-6262
Fax: 910-521-6497 • E-mail: admissions@papa.uncp.edu • Financial Aid: 910-521-6255

STUDENTS

Religious affiliation
                    No Affiliation
Academic year
   calendar   semester
Undergrad
   enrollment   5,158
% male/female   36/64
% Asian   2
% Black, non-Latino 26
% Latino   3
% Native American 20
% international   1
% from out of state 5
% freshmen return for
sophomore year   67
% freshmen graduate
   within 4 years 22

STUDENT LIFE
% of students living
   on campus   28

ADMISSIONS
of applicants   2,511
% accepted   84
% enrolled   38

HIGH SCHOOL UNITS REQUIRED

4 English, 3 math, 3 science
(1 science lab), 2 foreign
language, 1 social studies, 1
history

ABOUT THE UNIVERSITY OF NORTH CAROLINA AT PEMBROKE

Founded in 1887 as a school for the education of Native Americans, the University of North Carolina at Pembroke offers its 5,800 students a program of academic excellence, balancing teaching, research, and service. UNCP's current diversity reflects its original mission—it has become a true melting pot with the most diverse student body at any regional university in the South. Caucasians, minorities, and a still-prominent Native American population share the campus. UNCP students are generally down to earth, neither rich nor spoiled. They also accept and embrace all races, ages, political viewpoints, and sexual preferences. Nontraditional and adult students also make up a fairly large portion of the student body.

UNCP's small size offers academic benefits unparalleled at most public universities, with small class sizes and personal attention from accessible professors (many of whom are on a first-name basis with their students). Nearly 50-degree programs are available, including excellent programs in sciences, education, and business.

The town of Pembroke is growing right along with the University. A Super Wal-Mart and a number of locally owned restaurants and fast food joints have sprung up nearby. UNCP's campus is clearly separate from the town and feels like its own community. The result is that most entertainment takes place on campus, either via the active and social Greek scene, or at other campus parties. Since many students go home over the weekends, Thursday is the big party night. The administration is working to provide students with more to do on campus, offering lots of free events including speakers, plays, movies, and dances, in addition to the 60 clubs and organizations. The area in general is very rural, with the nearest major towns being Lumberton, which is close, and Fayetteville, which is about an hour drive away.

BANG FOR YOUR BUCK

UNCP is one of the 16 institutions that comprise the University of North Carolina (UNC). UNC is committed to ensuring access to higher education for all qualified individuals and keeping tuition affordable. The university provides need-based awards on a first come, first serve basis, according to the results of the FAFSA form. Financial aid awards are disbursed on the basis of need and merit.

VERY IMPORTANT ADMISSION FACTORS

Academic GPA, class rank, rigor of secondary school record, standardized test scores

Average HS GPA   3.07
Range SAT Verbal   420–510
Range SAT Math   430–520
Range ACT   16–20
Minimum TOEFL
(paper)   500

APPLICATION DEADLINES

Regular notification rolling
# of transfer applicants 602
% of transfer applicants
accepted   91

ACADEMICS

Student/faculty ratio   18:1
% faculty teaching
undergraduates   99
% of classes taught by
graduate students   0

MOST POPULAR MAJORS

• Business administration/
management
• Criminal justice/safety
studies
• Sociology

EDUCATION REQUIREMENTS

Arts/fine arts, computer literacy, English (including composition), history, humanities, math, philosophy, sciences (biological or physical), social science, physical education

A variety of academic scholarships are available to the student body. Scholarships are available in these categories: Alumni Sponsored Scholarships, General Scholarships Departmental Scholarships, and Specialized Scholarships.

In addition to incentive scholarships for new and transferring students, the UNC University Scholarship is a competitive scholarship available to outstanding North Carolina high school students who graduate with a 3.5 GPA or better. (The application deadline for most UNCP scholarships is March 1, but you'll want to check all deadlines well in advance.)

UNCP has been consistently ranked as a school whose graduates have the lowest loan debt in the Southeast. The school also has the fourth lowest default rate on loans in the UNC system.

GETTING IN

Admission to UNC Pembroke is based upon the applicant's cumulative GPA, SAT and/or ACT scores, class rank, quality of college preparatory classes, classroom work, and extracurricular activities. If you've done fairly well in high school and don't bomb the standardized tests, you should be set. Just about half of all incoming freshmen in 2004–2005 had a high school GPA of 3.0 or higher—the other half, obviously, had below that. Some majors require additional information that supplement the standard requirements set by the University.

WHAT DO GRADUATES DO?

Recent graduates work in the following areas: 37 percent work in education and 15 percent are employed in business and industry. The U.S. Department of Education, the Federal Bureau of Investigation, Walt Disney, Merck Pharmeceuticals, the CIA, the U.S. Census Bureau, and many others recruit students on campus and employ them following graduation.

THE BOTTOM LINE

If you're attracted to the UNC schools, it pays off big time to live in NC. At Pembroke, in-state tuition for 2006–2007 was $3,809; out-of-state students attending the same classes on the same campus paid $13,187. Room and board accounted for another $5,517, books for $1,000, and travel and other personal expenses for an estimated $3,902. On the bright side, more than 60 percent of students receive financial aid of some sort, and 74 percent of them see their need met fully by the school. In the end, the average out-of pocket expense for in-state, on-campus students at UNCP is $1,725.

FUN FACTS

UNC Pembroke's Athletic department is adding two new programs within the next two years, including football (kicking off September 2007) and women's golf.

New academic programs include undergraduate study in biotechnology, information technology management, and nursing.

UNC Pembroke was founded in 1887 as a normal school for Native American. While the university has changed, UNCP still has a strong connection to its heritage. Approximately 20 percent of UNCP's student body is Native American and 21 percent is African American. There is also a sizable population of international students on campus.

FINANCIAL INFO

In-state tuition	$3,809
Out-of-state tuition	$13,187
Room & board	$5,517
Average book expense	$1,000
Average freshman need-based grant	$4,144
Average freshman need-based loan	$2,552
% of graduates who borrowed	57
Average indebtedness	$14,423

FINANCIAL AID FORMS

Students must submit FAFSA.

POSTGRAD

% going to graduate school	18
% going to business school	2
% going to medical school	7

THE UNIVERSITY OF NORTH CAROLINA AT WILMINGTON

601 South College Road, Wilmington, NC 28403-5904
www.UNCW.edu • Admissions: 910-962-3243
Fax: 910-962-3038 • E-mail: admissions@uncw.edu • Financial Aid: 910-962-3177

STUDENTS

Religious affiliation
　　　　　　　No Affiliation
Academic year
　calendar　　　semester
Undergrad
　enrollment　　　10,249
% male/female　　　42/58
% Asian　　　　　　2
% Black, non-Latino　　5
% Latino　　　　　　2
% Native American　　1
% from out of state　　13
% freshmen return for
sophomore year　　　83
% freshmen graduate
within 4 years　　　41

STUDENT LIFE

% of students living
　on campus　　　　22
% in fraternities　　7
% in sororities　　　8

ADMISSIONS

of applicants　　8,820
% accepted　　　　61
% enrolled　　　　36

HIGH SCHOOL UNITS REQUIRED

4 English, 4 math, 3 science
(1 science lab), 2 foreign
language, 2 social studies, 1
history, 5 academic
electives

ABOUT THE UNIVERSITY OF NORTH CAROLINA AT WILMINGTON

Located in one of the Tar Heel state's most popular coastal towns, the University of North Carolina at Wilmington offers a relaxed environment in a town that's a mix of big city and old South. Students find this setting conducive to having fun while setting themselves up for a career. A big school with a smaller school feel, UNCW boasts a solid faculty that excels at the upper levels and isn't afraid to show their passion for the subject at hand. (One in five undergrads studies business and management.) Ambitious students should shoot for entry into the Honors Program, which opens up avenues of education and opportunities that are otherwise unavailable to the general college.

At Wilmington, the beach is right around the corner, and students take full advantage of its proximity. The Center for Marine Science is a great place to immerse yourself in research experience and high-tech scientific equipment. There's also a large surfing contingent of guys and gals alike! And they're not shy about throwing a shirt on over their swimsuits when they go to class so they can head to the beach the second the bell rings. The school's high-profile film program draws lots of arty types, but you probably won't see them on campus: many spend all their time involved in a local TV or movie production. Occasionally they take a break to watch someone else's movie, as the school library stocks a ton of DVDs, and Wilmington itself is a big film town. The student body is mostly Caucasian and shows a strong commitment to community service.

BANG FOR YOUR BUCK

The UNC system boasts one of the lower in-state tuitions in the country, a real bargain when coupled with the relatively high quality of instruction throughout the system. The school offers both need- and merit-based aid, with the majority of funds allocated to the needy. Need-based aid comes in the form of federal work-study, institutional employment, scholarships, grants, and loans. An upcoming fund raising campaign is designed to increase the number and value of merit scholarships.

"UNCW is where charm, location, and personable professors join in the making of a true college experience."

Merit-based awards include: the James Leutze Merit Scholarship, which provides approximately $9,000 to incoming freshmen, with the opportunity for renewal; the Honors Scholars Program, which offers incoming freshmen scholarships between $500 and the cost of in-state tuition and fees (currently about $4,000); athletic scholarships; diversity scholarships; Teaching Fellowships (35 such awards are available, each in the amount of $6,500 per year for four years, though recipients must commit to teaching in North Carolina for at least four years after graduation); and AmeriCorps scholarships for select students who complete 300 hours of community service in an academic year.

Students often choose to work while attending UNCW, as there are a wide variety of jobs available both on and off campus. Other cost-savers? Students are allowed to ride city buses at no cost by using their UNCW One Card. The school is pedestrian- and bicycle-friendly so cars are not a necessity. And students who arrive without a car will find it a positive impact on their finances.

Getting In

Like many state schools that must process numerous applications, UNCW relies on high school GPA, quality of high-school curriculum, and standardized test scores to winnow out unlikely candidates. The school also strongly considers class rank and state residency. Other factors, including recommendations, essays, extracurriculars, and minority status are considered but are not major factors in the admissions decision.

Specialized programs impose additional admissions requirements. Applicants to the Department of Music and to the schools of business, education, and nursing must apply to both the university and to the department/school; acceptance to the university does not ensure acceptance to the specific department/school. Music students must also audition.

What Do Graduates Do?

The most active recruiters on the UNCW campus come from banking, finance, business services; computers and technology; education; government; health care; hospitality; insurance; and public accounting.

VERY IMPORTANT ADMISSION FACTORS

Academic GPA, rigor of secondary school record, standardized test scores, state residency

IMPORTANT ADMISSION FACTORS

Application essay, class rank, recommendation(s)

Average HS GPA	3.62
Range SAT Verbal	520–600
Range SAT Math	540–610
Range ACT	21–25
Minimum TOEFL (paper/computer)	550/213

APPLICATION DEADLINES

Regular admission	2/1
# of transfer applicants	2,346
% of transfer applicants accepted	80

ACADEMICS

Student/faculty ratio	18:1
% faculty teaching undergraduates	100

MOST POPULAR MAJORS

- English language and literature
- Psychology
- Speech and rhetorical studies

EDUCATION REQUIREMENTS

Arts/fine arts, English (including composition), foreign languages, history, humanities, math, sciences (biological or physical), social science

FINANCIAL INFO

In-state tuition	$2,221
Out-of-state tuition	$12,156
Room & board	$6,722
Average book expense	$1,000
Required fees	$1,939
Average freshman need-based grant	$3,761
Average freshman need-based loan	$2,836
% of graduates who borrowed	51.5
Average indebtedness	$15,620

FINANCIAL AID FORMS

Students must submit FAFSA, institution's own financial aid form, Contact Financial Aid and Veterans Services Office for instructions.

POSTGRAD

% going to graduate school	9
% going to law school	1
% going to business school	1
% going to medical school	1

CAREER SERVICES

Alumni network, alumni services, career/job search classes, career assessment, internships, on-campus job interviews. Off-campus job opportunities are excellent.

THE BOTTOM LINE

For 2006–2007, the average out-of-pocket cost of attending UNCW for an in-state student was $13,882, which included the following: tuition and fees ($4,160); room and board ($6,722); and other expenses ($3,000). Out-of-state students can expect to spend $23,817 per year; the additional expense comes solely from the difference between in-state and out-of-state tuition. The cost of attendance at UNCW is reasonable but does include loans for most students and their parents. Students who ask for an aid increase to buy a computer, for example, should expect to take out a loan for that purpose. Families on financial aid who wish to participate in the book-buying program (through which students pay for all of their books before the start of the semester) may have to pay those funds up front, but the student refund check should include enough money to pay the family back, if they accept all of the available aid.

FUN FACTS

The UNCW Mascot is a Seahawk. For good luck, students rub the talon of the Seahawk sculpture located in front of the Warwick Center.

According to a campus legend, a student who walks under the campus clock tower prior to graduation will not graduate.

Recent performers on the UNCW campus include Dave Chappelle, JoDee Messina, Doc Watson, Ladysmith Black Mambazo, and Matchbox 20. Recent speakers include Andrew Sullivan, Eric Schlosser, Cornell West, Molly Ivins, Sister Helen Prejean, and Ken Burns.

The Film Studies Program benefits from the university's proximity to EUE Screen Gems studio. The UNCW campus is occasionally the backdrop for movies and TV shows, including *Dawson's Creek, One Tree Hill,* and *Surface* series.

UNIVERSITY OF NORTH FLORIDA

4567 St. Johns Bluff Road, South, Jacksonville, FL 32224-2645
www.UNF.edu • Admissions: 904-620-2624
Fax: 904-620-2299 • E-mail: admissions@unf.edu • Financial Aid: 904-620-2604

STUDENTS

Religious affiliation
　　　　　　　No Affiliation
Academic year
　calendar　　　semester
Undergrad
　enrollment　　　13,069
% male/female　　　42/58
% Asian　　　　　　5
% Black, non-Latino　10
% Latino　　　　　　6
% international　　　1
% from out of state　3
% freshmen return for
sophomore year　　75

STUDENT LIFE

% of students living
　on campus　　　　18
% in fraternities　　8
% in sororities　　　6

ADMISSIONS

of applicants　　9,147
% accepted　　　　62
% enrolled　　　　42

HIGH SCHOOL UNITS REQUIRED

4 English, 3 math, 3 science
(1 science lab), 2 foreign
language, 3 social studies,
4 academic electives

ABOUT UNIVERSITY OF NORTH FLORIDA

A budding state university on the fast track to prestige, the University of North Florida is a predominantly commuter-populated school boasting top programs for business, jazz, nursing, nutrition, and pre-med (complete with new science facilities). With over 12,000 undergraduates, UNF is just the right size for students, with enough people to make it interesting, but not so many that you feel lost or anonymous. Class sizes are smaller than at the larger state university, and the UNF professors love meeting with students outside of class and answering any and all of their questions with interest and enthusiasm.

UNF's diverse student body is a mixed lot: happy-go-lucky surfers and skateboarders, continuing-education adults who offer a different perspective to classroom discussions, and a sizable international student population who tend to fit in well with American students. Most students are locals who love the beach. A few have a reputation for loving school so much that they draw out their time, causing others to joke that they attend UNF, which stands for "You Never Finish." Just don't spend too much time in the sun and surf because those who do tend to be weeded out early on. Thursday night is party night and students know how to have a good time in low-key Jacksonville. Big-name bands find their way to campus for concerts, free movies are offered weekly, and Greek life is huge, as are sports events and a knockout fitness center. A number of students have part-time jobs or take part in volunteer work.

BANG FOR YOUR BUCK

UNF offers some of the lowest in-state tuition rates anywhere in the United States. That and the Bright Futures Scholarship Program which subsidizes much of the cost of tuition for large number of students make UNF a bargain for many who attend. (Bright Futures is a statewide lottery-funded scholarship program that served over 130,000 Floridians in 2004–2005.) The school awards both need- and merit-based aid, with the latter available for athletes, minorities, and performing artists, as well as for those who demonstrate outstanding skill in leadership and/or academics.

VERY IMPORTANT ADMISSION FACTORS

Academic GPA, rigor of secondary school record, standardized test scores

Average HS GPA   3.46
Range SAT Verbal 510–610
Range SAT Math   500–600
Range ACT   20–24
Minimum TOEFL
   (paper/computer) 500/213

APPLICATION DEADLINES

Regular admission   7/2
# of transfer
   applicants   3,385
% of transfer applicants
   accepted   62

ACADEMICS

Student/faculty ratio   22:1
% faculty teaching
   undergraduates   90
% of classes taught by
   graduate students   0

MOST POPULAR MAJORS

- Business administration and management
- Elementary education and teaching
- Mass communications/media studies

EDUCATION REQUIREMENTS

Arts/fine arts, computer literacy, English (including composition), foreign languages, history, humanities, math, philosophy, sciences (biological or physical), social science, cultural diversity

The school's most prized scholarship is the Guaranteed Scholarship, given to every student who applies by the deadline and who has a recalculated core GPA of 3.75 or greater with a minimum SAT of 1260 or an ACT of 28. Recipients are awarded $3,000 dollars a year for four years. If the student has a recalculated GPA of 4.0 and a minimum SAT of 1300 or ACT of 30, then the award goes up to $4,000 a year renewable for four years. The school also offers a variety of other four-year merit-based scholarships for which a particular recalculated GPA is the primary qualification.

GETTING IN

UNF's Admissions Office reviews applications the old-fashioned way: one student at a time. Each student is reviewed on an individual basis, so what is most important can vary from student to student depending on the particular circumstances. After looking over your high school transcript and standardized test scores, the school often moves on to the essay or even a personal, one-on-one conversation with an administrator to determine if you would be a good fit at UNF. The average high school GPA for entering freshman in 2005–2006 was a 3.46, and a full 80 percent of the freshman class arrived at UNF with a high school GPA of 3.0 or better. Applicants to the music program must audition.

WHAT DO GRADUATES DO?

UNF has several job fairs on campus each year. Major employers of UNF graduates include area hospitals, engineering companies, the financial services industry, and public schools.

THE BOTTOM LINE

In-state tuition for 2006–2007 at UNF was $2,211.30; fees totaled another $1,141.20; room and board was $6,640; and books, transportation, and other expenses totaled $4,283. The total expense for a Floridian living on campus was $14,275.50. Out-of-state students paid an additional $11,752.50 in tuition, bringing their total cost to $26,028. The typical out-of-state student may receive a fee waiver if they are academically sound and they apply early, but this may still leave their out-of-pocket expenses totaling $16,000 a year. On the other hand, that same caliber of student graduating from a Florida high school may receive 100 percent Bright Futures scholarship as well as have parents who planned ahead and purchased the Florida Pre-Paid College plan. In those cases, it is very possible that the student may have no out-of-pocket expense and actually receive money back!

FUN FACTS

UNF's mascot is the Osprey, but the university came close to having the armadillo as the mascot.

"Swooping" is how UNF enthusiasts show their school spirit (SWOOP actually stands for "Students With Outstanding Osprey Pride!"). Here's how to swoop: first, someone shouts: "What do Opsreys do?" then a crowd responds "Swoop!" while raising their arms in the formation of wings and then bending slightly forward, bringing the arms down and halfway back to emulate the flying wings of an Osprey.

Two UNF professors and 17 of their students boarded an Amtrak train during spring break 2005 and set off on a nine day, 7,000-mile field trip across the country. While on board, the students completed the course "Discover the U.S. on the Rails," which focused on the conceptual, contextual learning through the disciplines of anthropology and environmental science.

FINANCIAL INFO

In-state tuition	$2,211
Out-of-state tuition	$13,964
Room & board	$6,640
Average book expense	$800
Required fees	$1,141
Average freshman need-based grant	$1,018
Average freshman need-based loan	$778
% of graduates who borrowed	46
Average indebtedness	$16,707

FINANCIAL AID FORMS

Students must submit FAFSA, Financial aid transcript for transfer students.

UNIVERSITY OF OKLAHOMA

1000 Asp Avenue, Norman, OK 73019-4076
www.OU.edu • Admissions: 405-325-2252
Fax: 405-325-7124 • E-mail: admrec@ou.edu • Financial Aid: 405-325-4521

STUDENTS

Religious affiliation
No Affiliation
Academic year
calendar   semester
Undergrad
enrollment   20,967
% male/female   49/51
% Asian   5
% Black, non-Latino   5
% Latino   4
% Native American 7
% international   2
% from out of state   23
% freshmen return for
sophomore year   85
% freshmen graduate
within 4 years   19

STUDENT LIFE

% of students living
on campus   28
% in fraternities 14
% in sororities   23

ADMISSIONS

of applicants   7,388
% accepted   86
% enrolled   51

HIGH SCHOOL UNITS
REQUIRED

4 English, 3 math, 2 science
(2 science lab), 2 social
studies, 1 history, 3
academic electives

HIGH SCHOOL UNITS
RECOMMENDED

3 Foreign language, 1
computer science

ABOUT UNIVERSITY OF OKLAHOMA

More than 20,000 undergraduates reap the benefits that are found at the University of Oklahoma (OU), a longtime athletic powerhouse that has recently elevated its academic status from "regional" to "national." Like many large state universities, OU has improved its profile by investing in science and technology. The meteorology department here is world renowned, the life sciences departments are up and coming, and engineering programs enjoy a solid reputation, especially in the area of petroleum engineering. Throughout the university, experiential learning is stressed, and undergraduates are encouraged to conduct research and undertake internships and co-ops to supplement their classroom learning. One drawback: A tight state budget can make for crowded classes and stressful registration periods. Those who can get into the honors program should grab the opportunity. While the workload is more challenging, classes are smaller and registration is much easier.

A massive Greek scene consisting of 42 fraternities and sororities sets the pace on the OU campus. Wild parties are plentiful, but so are tamer options. The Greeks, it should be noted, are actively involved in community service. (There is indeed more to frat life than high-fiving around a keg.) Other on-campus events include weekly movies, regular concerts featuring big-name national acts, and, of course, intercollegiate athletics. Hometown Norman doesn't add much to the mix, but fortunately the more cosmopolitan Oklahoma City is just up the road. OU's student body exudes Bible-belt values; most students are very friendly and very conservative. The school has a substantial Native American population.

BANG FOR YOUR BUCK

OU has benefited from generous alumni donations in recent years. Notably, the school has raised more than $1 billion over the past decade and has plowed much of that money into its endowment. As a result, the number of endowed faculty positions has nearly quadrupled, increasing from 100 to more than 414, thus shifting the cost to retain and attract talented faculty members away from students. The school recently launched the largest scholarship fund-raising campaign in its history, with a goal to raise $100 million over the next five years, encompassing both need- and merit-based awards.

"OU is located in a college town where the Greek system is prominent, students have fairly conservative viewpoints, and there are a few crazies mixed in."

OU provides need-based assistance to nearly 100 percent of all aid applicants who demonstrate need. Thirty-three percent of need-based aid packages include some form of need-based grant or scholarship. In some cases, aid recipients received merit-based scholarships in lieu of need-based grants. On average, the school meets 84 percent of aid recipients' demonstrated need; the school meets 100 percent of demonstrated need for 45 percent of aid recipients.

In 2006–2007, students were be able to apply for and receive an estimate of federal, state, and institutional awards through the school's new Sooner Aid Analysis (SAA) Program. This information is made available to parents and students months earlier than the typical federal aid process because prior year tax information is used for the estimate.

GETTING IN

Academic transcripts and test scores (ACT, SAT, AP, CLEP, TOEFL) are the most important components of an OU application. International students must establish English proficiency and complete a confidential financial statement. Applicants to the architecture program must submit a portfolio for review. Prospective journalism majors must pass a language skills test. Fine arts majors must either audition or present a portfolio.

WHAT DO GRADUATES DO?

Many OU graduates work in accounting services, banking, consulting, the energy and petroleum industry, financial services, manufacturing, and wholesale . Major employers of OU graduates include American Airlines, BP, Chesapeake Energy, ConocoPhillips, Devon Energy, ExxonMobil, Ferguson, KPMG LLP, National Instruments, OGE, PricewaterhouseCoopers, Shell Companies, Raytheon, Target, Schlumberger, Wal-Mart, and Williams. More than 1,450 employers come to interview on OU's campus, attend OU's career fairs, post jobs online on OU's employment website, or access OU's students' online resume books.

VERY IMPORTANT ADMISSION FACTORS

Academic GPA, class rank, rigor of secondary school record, standardized test scores

Average HS GPA	3.63
Range ACT	23–28
Minimum TOEFL (paper/computer)	550/213

APPLICATION DEADLINES

Regular admission	4/1
# of transfer applicants	2,793
% of transfer applicants accepted	75

ACADEMICS

Student/faculty ratio	22:1
% of classes taught by graduate students	22

MOST POPULAR MAJORS

- Journalism
- Psychology
- Zoology/animal biology

EDUCATION REQUIREMENTS

Arts/fine arts, computer literacy, English (including composition), foreign languages, history, humanities, math, philosophy, sciences (biological or physical), social science, communication

FINANCIAL INFO

In-state tuition	$3,006
Out-of-state tuition	$11,295
Room & board	$6,863
Average book expense	$1,099
Required fees	$2,104
Average freshman need-based grant	$3,984
Average freshman need-based loan	$3,110
% of graduates who borrowed	45
Average indebtedness	$18,537

FINANCIAL AID FORMS

Students must submit FAFSA.

POSTGRAD

CAREER SERVICES

Alumni services, career/job search classes, career assessment, internships, on-campus job interviews. Off-campus job opportunities are excellent.

THE BOTTOM LINE

In 2006–2007, Oklahoma residents attending OU paid $5,109.50 in tuition and fees. Room and board cost an estimated $6,863 and books cost an additional $1,099. Thus, total direct costs for a resident attending OU were $13,071.50. Nonresidents paid an additional $8,289 in tuition, bringing their total direct costs to $24,360.50. All students should anticipate another $4,419 in transportation and other expenses. The average out-of-pocket expenses for students who receive aid is approximately $3,200 annually.

FUN FACTS

OU recently purchased 13 new Piper Warrior IIIs for student training in the Aviation Department. These new single-engine planes feature cutting-edge technology, such as Global Positioning Systems, that students need to learn to use to be competitive in the aviation industry.

The University of Oklahoma maintains one of the three most important collections of early manuscripts in the history of science in the United States. It includes Galileo's own copy of his work, with corrections in his own handwriting.

OU President David Boren, a former U.S. senator and governor of Oklahoma, teaches an introductory course in political science each semester, and keeps in close touch with students.

UNIVERSITY OF PITTSBURGH— JOHNSTOWN

157 Blackington Hall, 450 Schoolhouse Road, Johnstown, PA 15904
www.UPJ.Pitt.edu • Admissions: 814-269-7050
Fax: 814-269-7044 • E-mail: upjadmit@pitt.edu • Financial Aid: 814-269-7045

STUDENTS

Religious affiliation

No Affiliation

Academic year

calendar	semester
Undergrad	
enrollment	3,116
% male/female	52/48
% Asian	1
% Black, non-Latino	1
% from out of state	1
% freshmen return for sophomore year	73
% freshmen graduate within 4 years	36

STUDENT LIFE

% of students living on campus	67
% in fraternities	3
% in sororities	3

ADMISSIONS

# of applicants	2,589
% accepted	85
% enrolled	38

HIGH SCHOOL UNITS REQUIRED

4 English, 2 math, 2 science (1 science lab), 2 foreign language, 4 social studies

HIGH SCHOOL UNITS RECOMMENDED

3 Math, 2 science lab

ABOUT THE UNIVERSITY OF PITTSBURGH—JOHNSTOWN

Although it's one branch of a larger institution, the University of Pittsburgh—Johnstown (UPJ for short) has a pleasing, small-college feel. Nestled in the history-rich community of Johnstown, Pennsylvania, UPJ's over 3,000 students live mostly on campus, boast over 70 student-run organizations (from intramural sports to *WUPJ-TV*), and take notes from distinguished faculty who keep class sizes comfortably small. The most popular areas of study tend to be business and marketing, education, and the social sciences. By and large a haven for Pennsylvanians (all but one percent), UPJ has a way of growing on you in the best of ways.

Founded in 1927 as the nation's first regional campus of a major university, UPJ has had time to master the idea of a dynamic, rewarding college experience. Annual celebrations of homecoming, Greek Week, the Ethnic Festival, Winter Carnival, Black History Month and others are what keep students from packing a suitcase every weekend, not to mention the university's own built-in escapes: two-and-a-half miles of hiking, biking, and cross-country nature trails weaving through the streams and woodlands of the greater 40-acre Rocky Run Nature Area. And UPJ's impressive Pasquerilla Performing Arts Center, a cultural beacon and asset to all of Johnstown, houses every production of the UPJ Theatre Department—which is absolutely spoiled by its facilities—and regularly hosts the Johnstown Symphony Orchestra and the Pittsburgh Ballet Theatre.

BANG FOR YOUR BUCK

By virtue of being a public institution, UPJ offers a relatively low-cost education—tuition for in-state freshmen hovers around $10,000 a year—even before financial aid is factored in. In fact, over 80 percent of students receive financial assistance, including grants, scholarships, loans, and work-study employment, totaling more than $22 million. Essentially, anyone who applies for financial aid, whether need-based or non-need-based, receives it. And on average, the percentage of tuition covered by financial aid is 51 percent for full-time students. To break it down even further, UPJ doles out scholarship and grant monies—the kind of money that doesn't need to be repaid—totaling well over $8 million a year.

VERY IMPORTANT ADMISSION FACTORS

Academic GPA, class rank, rigor of secondary school record

IMPORTANT ADMISSION FACTORS

Interview, standardized test scores

Average HS GPA   3.27
Range SAT Verbal 470–560
Range SAT Math   470–570
Range ACT   18–23
Minimum TOEFL
   (paper/computer) 550/213

APPLICATION DEADLINES

Regular notification rolling
# of transfer applicants 204
% of transfer applicants
   accepted   74

ACADEMICS

Student/faculty ratio   19:1
% faculty teaching
   undergraduates   100
% of classes taught by
   graduate students   0

EDUCATION REQUIREMENTS

English (including composition), history, humanities, math, sciences (biological or physical), social science

GETTING IN

While it wouldn't be fair to say that UPJ is difficult to get into—with an 85 percent acceptance rate and no wait list—their ideal student isn't a slouch. Of utmost importance to admissions counselors are the quality of your high school curriculum, overall class rank and GPA. SAT and/or ACT test scores are looked at too, and prospective students should be prepared to impress during their admissions interview. Although it won't make or break your chances of getting in, good evidence of leadership ability, self-motivation, and extracurricular interests can't hurt.

WHAT DO GRADUATES DO?

UPJ graduates in business typically stay on that course toward jobs in accounting and finance (think Ernst & Young or Met Life), and, yes, education degree-holders pursue gigs in elementary or secondary education. The associate degree program in allied health, however, sends a generous number of students into emergency medical services (AKA paramedics) and surgical technologies careers. And actually, an allied health grad can rake in as much as $40,000 a year right out of college.

BOTTOM LINE

When tuition is added to fees, the typical first-year student isn't biting the bullet too hard. Per term, a dorm room's going rate is $1900, required fees are just under $700, and the average meal plan is $1200. Out-of-state students, on the other hand, are looking at $19,776 a year in tuition alone. So, at UPJ, it pays to be Pennsylvanian. And for the 83 percent of the student body who leave with loan repayments looming, their average cumulative debts are just under $19,000, which is pennies considering UPJ's hidden gem of an education.

Fun Facts

A couple of famous alumni are successful politicians: the outspoken Democratic U.S. Congressman, John Murtha; and the Pennsylvania state senator, John Wozniak.

Johnstown, Pennsylvania, is well known for two reasons in particular. It is home to the Johnstown Inclined Plane, the world's steepest vehicular inclined plane with a 70.9 percent grade. The Plane's funicular was built in the immediate aftermath of Johnstown's other claim to fame: the Great Flood of 1889. After heavy rainfall crippled Lake Conemaugh's South Fork Dam, 20 million gallons of water were unleashed onto Johnstown, killing 2,200 people. The disaster, as you might imagine, forced the community to consider settling higher ground.

FINANCIAL INFO

In-state tuition	$9,966
Out-of-state tuition	$19,570
Room & board	$6,200
Average book expense	$1,000
Required fees	$692
Average freshman need-based grant	$4,061
Average freshman need-based loan	$2,355
% of graduates who borrowed	83
Average indebtedness	$18,962

FINANCIAL AID FORMS

Students must submit FAFSA.

POSTGRAD

% going to law school	1
% going to business school	1
% going to medical school	2

CAREER SERVICES

On-campus job interviews. Off-campus job opportunities are excellent.

UNIVERSITY OF SAINT MARY (KS)

4100 South Fourth Street Trafficway, Leavenworth, KS 66048
www.StMary.edu • Admissions: 913-758-6118
Fax: 913-758-6140 • E-mail: admis@hub.smcks.edu • Financial Aid: 800-752-7043

STUDENTS

Religious affiliation	
	Roman Catholic
Academic year	
calendardiffers by program	
Undergrad	
enrollment	435
% male/female	44/56
% Asian	3
% Black, non-Latino	13
% Latino	11
% international	1
% from out of state	35
% freshmen return for	
sophomore year	60
% freshmen graduate	
within 4 years	28

STUDENT LIFE

% of students living	
on campus	42

ADMISSIONS

# of applicants	570
% accepted	45
% enrolled	33

HIGH SCHOOL UNITS REQUIRED

4 English, 2 math, 2 science, 2 history

HIGH SCHOOL UNITS RECOMMENDED

4 English, 4 math, 4 science (2 science lab), 2 social studies, 4 history, 2 academic electives, 2 computer programming

ABOUT UNIVERSITY OF SAINT MARY (KS)

The University of Saint Mary, a small Catholic school near the Missouri border, follows the educational philosophy of the sponsoring Sisters of Charity, who stress the integration of faith into a solid liberal arts–based curriculum. With fewer than 500 undergraduates, USM makes for a tiny community in which everyone can participate fully. Instruction centers on personal attention, with classes small enough for professors to tailor their lectures, discussions, and assignments to the talents and interests of the enrolled students. While some feel that the school's size too narrowly limits the breadth and number of available courses, the school's benefits far outweigh any drawbacks.

USM undergrads tend to be athletic and outgoing. Sports play a big role in most students' lives, although undergrads also save room in their extracurricular schedules for the arts, Bible study, and socializing. Dorms are homey and relaxing, terms that pretty much sum up campus life in general. While USM students like to hang out and toss back a few beers on the weekend, no one would mistake the social scene for the party environment at a large state school. Campus events like ice-skating, bowling, and movies supplement students' downtime activities. Downtown Kansas City is less than 30 miles away, so students always have easy access to urban entertainment and some of the world's best barbecue.

BANG FOR YOUR BUCK

The availability of generous scholarship and grant programs, coupled with a flexible payment plan, helps USM students finance this relatively inexpensive private education. USM offers both merit- and need-based grants and scholarships.

USM provides need-based assistance to 98 percent of all aid applicants who demonstrate need, and each one of their need-based aid packages include some form of need-based grant or scholarship. On average, the school meets 61 percent of aid recipients' demonstrated need; the school meets 100 percent of demonstrated need for 15 percent of aid recipients.

In 2005–2006, the average financial aid package at USM totaled $10,816. Need-based scholarships had an average value of $6,790. The value of the average need-based loan was $4,345.

Non-need-based grants and scholarships are available to students who excel in academics, athletics, the arts, music, drama, and leadership. Those seeking art, music, and theater scholarships must audition or present a portfolio. All Kansas residents who rank high in their class and earn high scores on the ACT or SAT are eligible for Kansas Tuition Grants and State Scholarships.

Getting In

Admission to USM is based on high school GPA, class rank, and ACT or SAT score. Interviews, record of extracurricular activities, special talents, evidence of strong character, and work experience are all factored into the admissions decision. The school traditionally admits 75 percent of all applicants.

What Do Graduates Do?

USM graduates find careers in business, education, entertainment, health care, journalism, law, medical research, politics, public relations, and state and federal government. Top employers of USM graduates include Booz Allen Hamilton, Commerce Bank, CBIZ, the Federal Aviation Administration, H&R Block, Hertz, the *Los Angeles Times*, Microsoft, UMB, Sprint, Gateway, and Shook, Hardy & Bacon (a law firm). Because of the school's size, USM piggybacks on other school's recruiting events; numerous career fairs are available to students through consortiums with other institutions.

VERY IMPORTANT ADMISSION FACTORS

Academic GPA, rigor of secondary school record, standardized test scores

IMPORTANT ADMISSION FACTORS

Character/personal qualities, extracurricular activities, interview, talent/ability, volunteer work, work experience

Average HS GPA	3.24
Range SAT Verbal	370–490
Range SAT Math	310–500
Range ACT	17–22
Minimum TOEFL (paper/computer)	500/

APPLICATION DEADLINES

Regular notification	rolling
# of transfer applicants	178
% of transfer applicants accepted	47

ACADEMICS

Student/faculty ratio	10:1
% faculty teaching undergraduates	100
% of classes taught by graduate students	0

MOST POPULAR MAJORS

- Business administration/ management
- Elementary education and teaching
- Psychology

Arts/fine arts, English (including composition), foreign languages, history, humanities, math, philosophy, sciences (biological or physical), social science, Common Learning Experiences

FINANCIAL INFO

Tuition	$16,100
Room & board	$5,850
Average book expense	$700
Required fees	$145
Average freshman need-based grant	$7,183
Average freshman need-based loan	$3,570
% of graduates who borrowed	71.9
Average indebtedness	$17,125

FINANCIAL AID FORMS

Students must submit FAFSA.

THE BOTTOM LINE

In 2006–2007, USM undergraduates paid $16,100 in annual tuition. Room and board cost an additional $5,850. Required fees added $145 in cost; the estimated annual expenditure for books is $700. Thus, the total cost of attending USM was $ 22,795, plus travel and personal expenses. Take heart in knowing that 64 percent of full-time undergraduates receive some form of financial aid. USM takes every measure to minimize your out-of-pocket expenses by offering a package of scholarships, grants, loans, and employment. It is currently restructuring its entire financial aid program to better meet the needs of students and become one of the most affordable private institution options in Kansas.

FUN FACTS

All incoming full-time freshmen receive a free laptop, which they keep upon graduation.

Trying to kick your nicotine habit? Enrolling at USM will help. The school prohibits the use of tobacco products, including smokeless tobacco, in all university buildings. Yes, that includes the dormitories!

Generations of students have passed on the legend that a nun lost her head when her scarf got caught in the doors of an old elevator, and today, she haunts USM. The "headless nun" occasionally appears at campus functions, and she was once spotted rollerblading through the dining hall.

THE UNIVERSITY OF SOUTH DAKOTA

414 East Clark, Vermillion, SD 57069
www.USD.edu • Admissions: 605-677-5434
Fax: 605-677-6323 • E-mail: admiss@usd.edu • Financial Aid: 605-677-5446

STUDENTS

Religious affiliation

No Affiliation

Academic year
  calendar   semester
Undergrad
  enrollment   5,728
% male/female   38/62
% Asian   1
% Black, non-Latino   1
% Latino   1
% Native American   2
% international   1
% from out of state   23
% freshmen return for
sophomore year   69
% freshmen graduate
  within 4 years   21

STUDENT LIFE

% of students living
  on campus   31
% in fraternities   9
% in sororities   8

ADMISSIONS

of applicants   2,829
% accepted   86
% enrolled   48

HIGH SCHOOL UNITS REQUIRED

4 English, 3 math, 3 science
(3 science lab), 3 social
studies, 1 fine arts

HIGH SCHOOL UNITS RECOMMENDED

4 English, 4 math, 4 science
(3 science lab), 2 foreign
language, 3 social studies, 1
fine arts

ABOUT THE UNIVERSITY OF SOUTH DAKOTA

The University of South Dakota, affectionately dubbed "The U" by students and faculty, is a small public university located in Vermillion, a small town in the southeast corner of the state. Vermillion takes great pride in its school, and rightfully so—USD offers highly regarded programs in media, law, political science, business, and pre-health majors with an emphasis on preparing students for their future careers. The quality and value of the education here is high; with only 6,000 undergrads, USD gives its students plenty of opportunity to learn hands-on, closely interact with faculty, and explore textbook material as it applies to real life.

Students come largely from small towns in South Dakota and its neighboring states. What the school lacks in diversity it makes up for in friendliness and tolerance, embracing students who visit on exchange programs from all over the world, as well as students from different cultural backgrounds or sexual orientations.

Though Vermillion is somewhat lacking in nightlife, the surrounding area is a virtual playground for hunting, fishing, and camping enthusiasts. Barring that, the campus provides the typical staples of smaller state universities: parties, coffee shops, bar-hopping, and fraternities and sororities. Because of the lack of options on weekends, many students either take road trips to Sioux Falls or Sioux City, or simply head home when they finish class.

"USD is the perfect place to not only discover who you are, but to become who you can [be], unlocking your potential and letting you maximize your abilities."

VERY IMPORTANT ADMISSION FACTORS

Class rank, rigor of secondary school record, standardized test scores

Average HS GPA	3.23
Range SAT Verbal	440–610
Range SAT Math	450–600
Range ACT	19–25
Minimum TOEFL (paper/computer)	550/213

APPLICATION DEADLINES

Regular notification   rolling

# of transfer applicants	1,591
% of transfer applicants accepted	67

ACADEMICS

Student/faculty ratio	15:1
% faculty teaching undergraduates	96
% of classes taught by graduate students	4

MOST POPULAR MAJORS

• Business administration/ management
• Psychology

EDUCATION REQUIREMENTS

Arts/fine arts, computer literacy, English (including composition), humanities, math, sciences (biological or physical), social science, interdisciplinary studies

BANG FOR YOUR BUCK

The University of South Dakota prides itself on offering educational value to both in-staters and out-of-staters. A substantial part of this stems simply from USD's low cost. In addition to simple affordability, South Dakota offers a wide range of scholarships, grants, loans, and work-study jobs. In fact, USD awards over $650,000 in aid/scholarships to incoming freshmen each year. What's more, last year over 90 percent of all students received some form of financial aid. Much of this financial aid was need-based, with over 60 percent of students receiving need-based assistance. The average need-based loan for freshmen was $3,076; and $2,996 was the average need-based grant. Additionally, merit-based scholarships are also available to exceptional students. These are offered for academic achievement, athletics, achievement in the creative arts, leadership, music/drama, minority status, and ROTC participation.

GETTING IN

A student's academic resume is the most important factor to admissions officers at South Dakota. This means GPA and class rank take top billing, with standardized test scores also regarded as very important. Extracurricular activities, essays, recommendations, special talents and abilities, and minority status are all considered in a candidate's application, but to a lesser degree. Admission procedures and standards are the same for all undergraduate applicants. Prospective students can take either the SAT or the ACT, but admissions recommends the ACT. In order to meet admissions requirements, students must have either an ACT of 19, a high school GPA of 2.6, or a top-50-percent ranking in their high school class.

WHAT DO GRADUATES DO?

Practical careers are popular at USD—business, pre-health, and law majors lead the list. The practical approach to teaching makes an education at the University of South Dakota very career oriented. Employers often describe USD students as critical thinkers with strong work ethics who are well prepared for their careers. Because of this, employers both in and out of South Dakota actively recruit students from USD. This is done by posting to Coyote Careers, an e-recruiting page created to link employers with job seeking students and graduates.

The Bottom Line

For the 2006–2007 school year, the school estimates that tuition for state residents is $10,677, including housing, books, and food. Of this number, housing runs about $2,388 and the meal plan costs $2,079.40. Remarkably, out-of-staters don't pay much more: Their tuition, at $11,948, is all-inclusive. With $650,000 in scholarships earmarked for the freshman class alone, and with financial aid of some sort provided to 90 percent of all students, there is plenty of value to be had.

Fun Facts

The Dakota Dome is host to all types of sporting events, and has a full gym, pool, tennis, and racquetball courts available to students.

USD has one of the top 10 Rural Medicine programs in the country.

FINANCIAL INFO

In-state tuition	$2,690
Out-of-state tuition	$7,569
Room & board	$4,964
Average book expense	$750
Required fees	$2,690
Average freshman need-based grant	$2,996
Average freshman need-based loan	$3,076
% of graduates who borrowed	80
Average indebtedness	$19,535

Financial Aid Forms

Students must submit FAFSA.

POSTGRAD

% going to graduate school	33
% going to law school	7
% going to business school	3
% going to medical school	19

UNIVERSITY OF SOUTH FLORIDA

4202 East Fowler Avenue, SVC-1036, Tampa, FL 33620-9951
www.USF.edu • Admissions: 813-974-3350
Fax: 813-974-9689 • E-mail: jglassma@admin.usf.edu • Financial Aid: 813-974-4700

STUDENTS

Religious affiliation
No Affiliation
Academic year
calendar   semester
Undergrad
enrollment   32,898
% male/female   41/59
% Asian   6
% Black, non-Latino   13
% Latino   11
% international   3
% from out of state   4
% freshmen return for
sophomore year   82

STUDENT LIFE

% of students living
on campus   13
% in fraternities 8
% in sororities   6

ADMISSIONS

of applicants   18,307
% accepted   58
% enrolled   40

HIGH SCHOOL UNITS
REQUIRED

4 English, 3 math, 3 science
(2 science lab), 2 foreign
language, 3 social studies, 3
academic electives

HIGH SCHOOL UNITS
RECOMMENDED

4 English, 3 math, 3 science
(2 science lab), 2 foreign
language, 3 social studies, 3
academic electives

ABOUT UNIVERSITY OF SOUTH FLORIDA

A relatively young school that is still carving out a niche for itself, the University of South Florida (founded in 1956) is an up-and-coming public university that's developing a higher profile year by year. New traditions continually pop up, school spirit is growing, and academics are on the up and up. As it stands now, the premed program is quite competitive, as are programs in communication, engineering, environmental science, and psychology. Those who qualify should take advantage of the Honors College, which boasts fabulous teachers who are easily accessible, classes that are small and interesting, and special privileges such as early registration for classes. Because USF is well-established in the Tampa Bay community, students can easily translate academics into career and internship opportunities in the city.

A campus of more than 30,000 undergraduates, USF can accommodate nearly every interest. Clubs run the gamut at USF. You'll find tons of clubs that peak your interest but may not actually have time to participate in all of them. The sense of community is strong, despite the fact that most students commute. That's due in part to the Marshall Center, where lots of students go to hang out, especially those under 21. The center also hosts bands, tournaments, get-togethers, and the like. Great weather doesn't hurt matters either, outdoor activities are popular year-round. Like many large schools, USF draws a diverse crowd; undergrads show a span of ages, looks, backgrounds, interests, beliefs, and gradations of suntans or paleness.

BANG FOR YOUR BUCK

In-state tuition at USF is ranked among the lowest in the country for state universities. In addition, almost half the full-time undergraduate population receives some form of financial aid; about 70 percent of them receive at least some of that aid in the form of grants and scholarships. USF awards both need- and merit-based grants. The merit-based grants are awarded for academic excellence, skill in art and athletics, proven leadership ability, minority status, and area of geographic origin.

USF offers particularly generous awards to National Merit Scholars. All designated Florida residents can receive a four-year grant worth $7,500 per year by making USF their first-choice school. Non-residents of Florida can receive full tuition and room and board ($69,628 total value) by earning National Merit Scholar status and designating USF as their first-choice school. Under this program, all students (in-state and out-of-state) also receive a laptop computer, priority housing and registration, and study abroad aid. Not too shabby!

GETTING IN

USF looks primarily at high school GPA in college preparatory classes, class rank, and standardized test scores to determine admissions. Recommendations, essays, and extracurriculars are considered primarily in borderline cases.

Those applying to the Honors Program must have at least a 3.7 high school GPA (as calculated by the school, using a formula that rewards students for work in honors and AP classes) and an SAT score of at least 1270 (with a minimum verbal score of 580) or a composite ACT score of 29 (with a minimum English score of 29).

WHAT DO GRADUATES DO?

Each year, USF sends its tens of thousands of graduates into every conceivable line of work, including accounting, communications, education, engineering, government, health care, social work, and technology. Major employers of USF grads include Ernst & Young, KPMG, AmSouth Bank, Target, USAA Insurance, Progress Energy, Raytheon, Verizon, and Proctor & Gamble.

VERY IMPORTANT ADMISSION FACTORS

Academic GPA, rigor of secondary school record, standardized test scores

IMPORTANT ADMISSION FACTORS

Class rank, talent/ability

Average HS GPA	3.54
Range SAT Verbal	510–600
Range SAT Math	520–610
Range ACT	21–26
Minimum TOEFL (paper/computer)	550/213

APPLICATION DEADLINES

Regular admission	4/15
Regular notification	rolling
# of transfer applicants	8,853
% of transfer applicants accepted	77

ACADEMICS

Student/faculty ratio	18:1
% faculty teaching undergraduates	85
% of classes taught by graduate students	15

MOST POPULAR MAJORS

- Curriculum and instruction
- Marketing/marketing management
- Social sciences

EDUCATION REQUIREMENTS

Arts/fine arts, English (including composition), foreign languages, history, humanities, math, sciences (biological or physical), social science

FINANCIAL INFO

In-state tuition	$3,416
Out-of-state tuition	$16,115
Room & board	$7,180
Average book expense	$800
Required fees	$74
Average freshman need-based grant	$4,541
Average freshman need-based loan	$1,849
% of graduates who borrowed	53
Average indebtedness	$17,995

FINANCIAL AID FORMS

Students must submit FAFSA.

POSTGRAD

% going to graduate school	21

CAREER SERVICES

Career/job search classes, internships, on-campus job interviews. Off-campus job opportunities are excellent.

THE BOTTOM LINE

In 2006–2007, Florida residents who attended USF full-time paid $3,416 in tuition; $7,180 in room and board; $74 in fees; $800 for books and supplies; and $4,170 in other expenses. Thus, the total cost of attending USF full-time for a state resident living on campus was $15,640. Nonresidents paid an additional $12,699 in tuition, bringing their total cost to $28,339. For 2006–2007, the average awards for students receiving financial aid and/or scholarships totaled $9,025.

FUN FACTS

Notable USF alumni include America's Cup winner Ed Baird; Disneyland International President and CFO Eddie Carpenter; soap opera stars Mark Consuelos and Drake Hogestyn; comedian Gallagher; major league baseball manager Tony LaRussa; Rick de Oliveira, producer of MTV's *Road Rules* and *The Real World*; Pulitzer Prize–winning journalist Richard Oppel; and NFL star J. R. Reed.

USF's Marching Band is called the Herd of Thunder. The name alludes to the school's mascot, Rocky the Brahman Bull.

The construction of a Special Events Center in 1990 cost the school a portion of its beloved Crescent Hill. Students, realizing that one wall of the new building offered a perfect movie projection screen, turned the loss into a gain by initiating the Movies on the Lawn Program. The program continues today, screening popular movies every Wednesday.

UNIVERSITY OF SOUTHERN INDIANA

8600 University Boulevard, Evansville, IN 47712
www.USI.edu • Admissions: 812-464-1765
Fax: 812-465-7154 • E-mail: enroll@usi.edu • Financial Aid: 812-464-1767

STUDENTS

Religious affiliation

No Affiliation

Academic year

calendar   semester

Undergrad

enrollment   9,252

% male/female   39/61

% Asian   1

% Black, non-Latino   5

% Latino   1

% international   1

% from out of state   8

% freshmen return for

sophomore year   64

% freshmen graduate

within 4 years   5

STUDENT LIFE

% of students living

on campus   32

% in fraternities   2

% in sororities   2

ADMISSIONS

of applicants   4,651

% accepted   92

% enrolled   49

HIGH SCHOOL UNITS RECOMMENDED

4 English, 4 math, 3 science, 2 foreign language, 2 social studies, 2 history, 2 academic electives

ABOUT THE UNIVERSITY OF SOUTHERN INDIANA

Just over 40 years old and based on the model of the "new American college," the University of Southern Indiana (USI) emphasizes strong teaching and the precious interaction between faculty and students. In its brief history, USI and its academic mission have had a profound influence on Southwestern Indiana's acceptance of the importance of postsecondary education. Since 1985, for example, the percentage of high school graduates going on to college in the area has risen from 33 percent to 81 percent. This is an extraordinary feat for a university in which more than 60 percent of students are southwestern Indianans, quite a few among them the first in their families to attend college.

Naturally, none of the university's buildings pre-date 1969, and with the enormous and continued support of state funding, USI continues to make significant strides in expanding its educational and athletic facilities. In 1990, the Orr Center (named for former Indiana governor, Robert Orr) became the spacious new home for the School of Business—leaving little wonder as to why business is USI's most popular major. Likewise, since 1990, new buildings for the liberal arts, nursing, and education programs—also among the most popular areas of study—have been added, and recently a new $27.5 million library opened with state-of-the-art technology. All of these infrastructural improvements go to show that USI refuses to let its "new American college" identity gather a single speck of dust.

BANG FOR YOUR BUCK

For its 10,201 students, USI brings every bit as much to the table in the form of scholarships and grants as it does in available student loan money. The university's annual endowment totals more than $15 million, doled out via a number of merit-based awards. The Departmental Scholarship waives a portion of tuition for students who ranked in the top 10 percent of their high school graduating class, who earned an Indiana Academic Honors Diploma, or who have been recognized for exceptional talents in theater, art, or creative writing. The Distinguish Scholar Award goes to National Merit winners and finalists, and the Presidential Scholarship is reserved for high school valedictorians and salutatorians—both awards covering full tuition. A hefty sum is also funneled into athletic scholarships. When it comes to financial aid, virtually every student who applies for need-based or non-need-based aid receives it, and the awards average $6,250 annually.

Students Say

"USI is a school where you are taught by qualified instructors who challenge you and push you to the edge, but at the same time . . . are there to help you at any time."

IMPORTANT ADMISSION FACTORS

Academic GPA, class rank

Average HS GPA   2.97
Range SAT Verbal 420–530
Range SAT Math   420–540
Range ACT   18–23
Minimum TOEFL
  (paper/computer) 525/197

APPLICATION DEADLINES
Regular admission   8/15
Regular notification rolling
# of transfer
  applicants   1,092
% of transfer applicants
  accepted   82

ACADEMICS
Student/faculty ratio   20:1
% faculty teaching
  undergraduates   100
% of classes taught by
  graduate students   0

MOST POPULAR MAJORS
• Business administration/
  management
• Elementary education and
  teaching
• Psychology

EDUCATION REQUIREMENTS
Arts/fine arts, computer literacy, English (including composition), history, humanities, math, philosophy, sciences (biological or physical), social science

Like most public institutions, USI caters more to its in-state applicants; however, because Evansville backs right up to the northwestern Kentucky border, students hailing from the Bluegrass State will find the specially designed tuition program and the USI Nonresident Grant to be friendly invitations to cross that Ohio River.

GETTING IN

Roughly 90 percent of USI applicants get in; the enrollment rate is just under 50 percent. USI doesn't place a high premium on the rigor of high school curricula, but applicants' class rank and overall GPA are highly considered. And though prospective students who were teenage hermits aren't penalized, the fine print will show that a good record of extracurricular activities is a definite bonus. The average incoming freshman scores a composite 950 on the SAT and a 20 on the ACT. The average first-year student's high school GPA was 2.97.

WHAT DO GRADUATES DO?

Nearly 75 percent of each year's graduating class remains in Indiana, a statistic that lines up well with the major economic expansion in the southern region of the state. Toyota, GE Plastics, Vectren Energy, Bristol-Meyers, and other manufacturing interests are nearby and increasingly provide employment opportunities to USI grads. The university's Career Services and Placement department has gone to great lengths to make jobs in a graduate's related field easy to search and apply for.

THE BOTTOM LINE

A year at USI, before financial aid but including housing, food and fees, costs a little under $11,000. Actually, room and board ($6,977) is costlier than tuition and fees ($4,775), which isn't all that unusual. Books and transportation and miscellaneous expenses can range from $800 to $1,700. All said, a USI graduating senior will owe an average of $15,724—a relatively shallow hole in the "real world" of college graduates.

FUN FACTS

Competing at the NCAA Division II level, USI's 15 sports teams have at one time or another competed in national tournaments or ranked nationally. In 1995, the men's basketball team won the national championship.

The first Sears department store was opened on October 5, 1925, in Evansville.

All exterior shots on the sitcom *Roseanne* are still pictures taken from in and around Evansville.

The university has a myriad of study abroad experiences including opportunities to live and learn in English castles or tour the world with a Semester at Sea.

FINANCIAL INFO

In-state tuition	$4,460
Out-of-state tuition	$10,631
Room & board	$6,972
Average book expense	$900
Average freshman need-based grant	$4,506
Average freshman need-based loan	$2,412
% of graduates who borrowed	60.1
Average indebtedness	$15,724

FINANCIAL AID FORMS

Students must submit FAFSA, institution's own financial aid form.

POSTGRAD

% going to graduate school	16

CAREER SERVICES

Alumni network, alumni services, career/job search classes, career assessment, internships, on-campus job interviews.

THE UNIVERSITY OF TEXAS AT AUSTIN

PO Box 8058, Austin, TX 78713-8058
www.UTexas.edu • Admissions: 512-475-7440
Fax: 512-475-7475 • E-mail: • Financial Aid: 512-475-6282

STUDENTS

Religious affiliation	No Affiliation
Academic year calendar	semester
Undergrad enrollment	36,878
% male/female	48/52
% Asian	17
% Black, non-Latino	4
% Latino	16
% international	3
% from out of state	5
% freshmen return for sophomore year	93
% freshmen graduate within 4 years	39

STUDENT LIFE

% of students living on campus	19
% in fraternities	9
% in sororities	13

ADMISSIONS

# of applicants	23,925
% accepted	51
% enrolled	56

HIGH SCHOOL UNITS REQUIRED

4 English, 3 math, 2 science, 2 foreign language, 3 social studies, 1.5 academic electives

HIGH SCHOOL UNITS RECOMMENDED

4 math, 3 science, 3 foreign language, 0.5 fine arts

ABOUT THE UNIVERSITY OF TEXAS AT AUSTIN

As you know, everything's bigger in Texas. So, naturally, the colossal and academically superb University of Texas at Austin is one of the largest universities in the United States based on total enrollment. The administration does an admirable job of coping with the numbers. Most services, from paying bills to renewing library books, are available online. The Web provides detailed ratings about professors from student-completed surveys, which helps undergraduates hone in on the best professors. Actually registering for classes is another story altogether (and often not a happy one, especially for first-year students). It's also hard to graduate in four years. Professors are brilliant and very willing to talk outside of class. It is difficult, however, to get individual attention *in* class. About fifty honors seminars are available to undergraduates. They are usually small and are taught by the best of the best professors.

Around 90 percent of the students come from Texas. Though they don't always hang out together, students from all manner of ethnic groups and social strata—from Abilene country folks to Dallas jetsetters—are well represented at the university and get along well. There are throngs of smart people who have genuine ambition, and you'll find no shortage of activity on campus. The awesome surrounding town of Austin also offers a ton of activities to students; Austin is the live music capital of the world and a very liberal city in a very conservative state. Nightlife includes theater, dance clubs, parties, public parks, and Sixth Street—a mile-long strip of watering holes. Greek life is gargantuan, too. Longhorn football has a legendary cult following at the University, even for students who aren't all that interested in sports.

BANG FOR YOUR BUCK

A combination of factors makes the University of Texas at Austin very affordable. To begin with, tuition is extremely low when you consider the wealth of resources available. In addition, living expenses are substantially lower in Austin than in major metropolitan areas on either the east or west coasts. There's also an excellent work-study program on campus and a perpetually booming student-based local economy that provides substantial work opportunities with very righteous wages for almost any student who wishes to work. More importantly, the university tries to meet the need of all students by offering a package of grants, loans, and scholarships to those who are eligible and can get in. A very large percentage of the aid available is need-based, and the Financial Aid Office makes a conscious effort to minimize loans, particularly for students who have few financial resources. The TEXAS Grant Program provides grants that cover tuition and fees for many Texas families who would have received little or no grant funding not so many years ago. If you aren't financially needy, there are also a vast number of non-need-based scholarships available.

Interestingly, out-of state tuition rates are based on the average of the out-of-state tuition rates at major public institutions in five other large states. Therefore, by pure power of logic, tuition for nonresidents is comparable to many other public competitive institutions (and significantly lower than tuition at virtually every competitive private school). If you are awarded a $1,000 competitive academic scholarship by the university, you are eligible to receive a nonresident fee waiver, which allows you to pay tuition at the in-state rate. A very large number of financially needy nonresident students receive these waivers as part of their aid package. All National Merit, National Achievement, and National Hispanic scholars who are from other states receive this award as part of their scholarship package, regardless of financial need.

GETTING IN

Want to be automatically admitted to the University of Texas at Austin? Move to Texas and graduate in the top 10 percent of your class at an accredited Texas high school. If that's not an option, or if you graduate from a high school in Texas somewhere in the bottom 90 percent, getting into the University is pretty competitive. A completed application includes SAT or ACT scores, high school transcripts, senior-year course schedule, two essays, a list of your extracurricular achievements, and (if you want) letters of recommendation. No matter how you slice it, your class ranking is the most important admissions component. Test scores are a close second. It will also help you considerably to take a challenging college-preparatory curriculum. After that, your essays and your extracurricular activities will make or break you.

VERY IMPORTANT ADMISSION FACTORS

Class rank, rigor of secondary school record

IMPORTANT ADMISSION FACTORS

Application essay, extracurricular activities, standardized test scores, talent/ability, volunteer work, work experience

Range SAT Verbal 540–670
Range SAT Math 570–690
Range ACT 23–29
Minimum TOEFL
(paper/computer) 550/213

APPLICATION DEADLINES

Regular admission 2/1
Regular notification rolling
# of transfer
applicants 7,108
% of transfer applicants
accepted 39

ACADEMICS

Student/faculty ratio 18:1
% faculty teaching
undergraduates 100

MOST POPULAR MAJORS

• Social sciences
* Business/marketing
• Communications/journalism

EDUCATION REQUIREMENTS

Arts/fine arts, English (including composition), foreign languages, history, humanities, math, sciences (biological or physical), social science

FINANCIAL INFO

In-state tuition	$7,630
Out-of-state tuition	$20,364
Room & board	$8,176
Average book expense	$800
Average freshman need-based grant	$6,750
Average freshman need-based loan	$3,650
% of graduates who borrowed	39
Average indebtedness	$16,850

FINANCIAL AID FORMS

Students must submit FAFSA.

WHAT DO GRADUATES DO?

With a degree from the university, you will be successful in pretty much any endeavor. There are several different Career Services divisions; essentially each college has its own Career Services staff that helps students find jobs and internships. Many graduates attend graduate and professional school each year; the graduate, law, and medical schools in Texas are excellent.

THE BOTTOM LINE

Full-time tuition is about $7,630 per year for residents of the Lone Star State and roughly $20,364 per year for nonresidents. More than half the student body receives some form of financial aid. The average need-based financial aid package for university undergraduates is $9,210 for an academic year.

FUN FACTS

Texas is big, and it's got a lot of big stuff. You can find the world's largest rocking chair in front of the Texas Hill Country Furniture and Mercantile in Lipan, Texas. There's Paisano Pete, the largest roadrunner in the world, at US-290 and Main Street in Fort Stockton, and Big Tex, the tallest cowboy in the world (52 feet) in Fair Park. If you like nuts, we suggest a visit to the Guadalupe County Courthouse in Seguin where you'll find the world's largest pecan.

The University of Texas at Austin owns The Watergate papers of *Washington Post* reporters Bob Woodward and Carl Bernstein. The University also is home to many costumes from *Gone with the Wind*.

An engineering professor at the university is helping the United States Air Force learn techniques to build better missile detectors by studying pit vipers. Pit vipers are very poisonous snakes with complicated heat-sensing systems that are so perceptive they can sense prey several yards away even in total darkness.

UNIVERSITY OF UTAH

201 South 1460 East, Room 250 S, Salt Lake City, UT 84112
www.Utah.edu • Admissions: 801-581-7281
Fax: 801-585-7864 • E-mail: admissions@sa.utah.edu • Financial Aid: 801-581-6211

STUDENTS

Religious affiliation
              No Affiliation
Academic year
  calendar   semester
Undergrad
  enrollment   22,155
% male/female   55/45
% Asian   5
% Black, non-Latino   1
% Latino   5
% Native American   1
% international   2
% from out of state   16
% freshmen return for
sophomore year   79
% freshmen graduate
  within 4 years   20

STUDENT LIFE

% of students living
  on campus   12
% in fraternities   1
% in sororities   1

ADMISSIONS

of applicants   6,770
% accepted   84
% enrolled   42

HIGH SCHOOL UNITS REQUIRED

4 English, 2 math, 3 science
(1 science lab), 2 foreign
language, 1 history, 4
academic electives

VERY IMPORTANT ADMISSION FACTORS

Academic GPA, rigor of
secondary school record,
standardized test scores

ABOUT UNIVERSITY OF UTAH

Like many large state universities, the University of Utah does an admirable job of offering excellent educational opportunities to a large undergraduate population—and at a very reasonable price. Also like its peer institutions, the U (as students affectionately call it) does little in the way of hand-holding; undergrads must be independent and enterprising to get the most out of all that is offered here. Classes are frequently taught by graduate students—which isn't necessarily a bad thing, since many of the full professors are more interested in research than in teaching. Things get better in the upper levels, where full professors are both more accessible and more engaged.

File this bit of info in the "dog bites man" category: There are lots and lots of Mormon students at University of Utah. Non-Latter-day Saints who are undergrads, however, have little trouble fitting in with the majority population, whom they describe as very accepting. As a bonus, the state's allure to Mormons far and wide means there's a huge and diverse international population here. Unfortunately, students don't get much chance to mingle, since the residential population is relatively small. With most students living off campus, school spirit lags and campus life can be awfully slow at times (except on fall weekends, when the powerful Utes play their home football games). The Greek scene is small but makes its presence known. The setting is lovely, with the surrounding Wasatch Mountains offering endless opportunities for skiing, hiking, and kayaking. And you can't complain about hometown Salt Lake City either, with its many shops, restaurants, theaters, and sports facilities—and, appropriately, only a smattering of bars.

BANG FOR YOUR BUCK

Whether you're from Utah or outside the state, tuition at the U is low. The school makes a good deal even better by providing both need-based and merit-based awards to undergraduates.

Many merit scholarships for incoming freshmen are awarded based on high-school GPA and standardized test scores. The school also offers a number of leadership and diversity scholarships. Incoming freshmen ready to declare a major may be eligible for departmental scholarships. Best of all are the Presidential Scholarships, which cover all tuition for four years and also include a stipend.

"The University of Utah gets underrated. It is a quality research university in a supportive community surrounded by amazing mountains."

IMPORTANT ADMISSION FACTORS

Talent/ability

Average HS GPA	3.52
Range SAT Verbal	500–630
Range SAT Math	500–640
Range ACT	21–27
Minimum TOEFL (paper/computer)	500/173

APPLICATION DEADLINES

Regular admission	4/1
# of transfer applicants	3,137
% of transfer applicants accepted	82

ACADEMICS

Student/faculty ratio	14:1
% faculty teaching undergraduates	74
% of classes taught by graduate students	10

MOST POPULAR MAJORS

• Economics
• Human development and family studies
• Mass communications/media studies

EDUCATION REQUIREMENTS

Arts/fine arts, English (including composition), history, humanities, math, sciences (biological or physical), social science

GETTING IN

Admission to University of Utah depends primarily on the quality of one's high school curriculum, GPA, and standardized test scores. Due to low high-school graduation rates in the state of Utah, anyone who excels in these three areas should have no trouble gaining admission. Marginal candidates can improve their chances by demonstrating non-academic talent, leadership abilities, and a strong resume of extracurricular activity. Different colleges and departments do impose some unique requirements; check with the school you wish to enter for details.

WHAT DO GRADUATES DO?

Utah graduates work in all major industries. Major employers include Ernst & Young, Wells Fargo, Ford Motor Company, Boeing, and the National Parks Service. Each year between 130 to 150 companies recruit on campus.

THE BOTTOM LINE

Tuition for Utah residents in 2006–2007 was $3,972 per year. Out-of-state students paid $13,902, although many paid less. Students living in the 14 states outside Utah that are covered by the WICHE compact (and who make up a large portion of the school's out-of-state population) can enroll in many programs and pay just 50 percent more than in-state tuition. Required additional fees totaled $690; room and board amounted to another $5,604. In addition, anticipated costs for books, supplies, and transportation added another $2,300 to the annual cost. In that same year, Utah provided aid to 99 percent of its students who demonstrated need through FAFSA filings. Only 15 percent of those who received aid had their full demonstrated need met, however. On average, the school met 56 percent of the demonstrated need for all aid recipients. According to the school, aid recipients living at home were left with out-of-pocket expenses of just $7,200. Students living on campus had $6,300 of out-of-pocket expenses, while for students living in off-campus apartments that figure rose to $15,300.

Fun Facts

University of Utah was the site of the opening and closing ceremonies for the 2002 Olympic Winter Games. As a legacy to those games, the Olympic Cauldron Park has been developed on campus and is open to the public. It includes a theater showing highlights from the games, the actual Olympic Cauldron, and other memorabilia from the games.

The Utah campus is within 30 minutes of seven world-class ski resorts.

University of Utah is a college football powerhouse. Its recent players include NFL Offensive Rookie of the Year running back Mike Anderson, Pro Bowl defensive lineman Luther Elliss, and Pro Bowl wide receiver/kick returner Steve Smith.

Other notable Utah alumni include U.S. Senator Robert F. Bennett; Pixar President Ed Catmull; Wells Fargo Chairman Spencer F. Eccles; U.S. Senator E.J. "Jake" Garn; inventor of the Jarvik-7 artificial heart Robert K. Jarvik; Pulitzer Prize winner Laurel Thatcher Ulrich; and speed-reading pioneer Evelyn Wood.

FINANCIAL INFO

In-state tuition	$3,972
Out-of-state tuition	$13,902
Room & board	$5,604
Average book expense	$1,100
Required fees	$690
Average freshman need-based grant	$4,342
Average freshman need-based loan	$3,401
% of graduates who borrowed	38.5
Average indebtedness	$13,741

FINANCIAL AID FORMS

Students must submit FAFSA, institution's own financial aid form.

POSTGRAD

CAREER SERVICES

Alumni network, alumni services, career/job search classes, career assessment, regional alumni, on-campus job interviews. Off-campus job opportunities are good.

UNIVERSITY OF VIRGINIA

Office of Admission, PO Box 400160, Charlottesville, VA 22906
www.Virginia.edu • Admissions: 434-982-3200
Fax: 434-924-3587 • E-mail: undergradadmission@virginia.edu • Financial Aid: 434-982-6000

STUDENTS

Religious affiliation
　　　　　　No Affiliation
Academic year
　calendar　　semester
Undergrad
　enrollment　　14,676
% male/female　45/55
% Asian　　　　10
% Black, non-Latino　8
% Latino　　　　4
% international　5
% from out of state　33
% freshmen return for
sophomore year　97
% freshmen graduate
　within 4 years　84

STUDENT LIFE

% of students living
　on campus　　45
% in fraternities　30
% in sororities　30

ADMISSIONS

of applicants　16,086
% accepted　　　37
% enrolled　　　51
# of early decision/action
　applicants　　2,311
% accepted early
　decision/action　41

HIGH SCHOOL UNITS REQUIRED

4 English, 4 math, 2
science, 2 foreign language,
4 social studies

HIGH SCHOOL UNITS RECOMMENDED

5 Math, 4 science, 5 foreign
language, 4 social studies

ABOUT UNIVERSITY OF VIRGINIA

Few schools can match University of Virginia's potent combination of phenomenal faculty, intelligent students, remarkable intercollegiate sports, *and* extraordinary academics. Indeed, students are continually impressed by the high caliber of opportunities available to them, both within the classroom and outside it. Notably, unlike other public institutions, there doesn't seem to be a tendency for UVA students to be lost amid the paperwork and bureaucracy. Professors are accessible and devoted; many go out of their way to ensure that students are comfortable with the material.

Of course, like any self-respecting student body, UVA students not only frequent the library but the frat houses as well. Greek life is very prominent at the university and one can always find someone, somewhere, who is throwing a party. Even if drinking doesn't appeal to you, you'll definitely be able to find your niche. UVA offers an enormous range of activities, and students can partake in everything from theater to a strong student government organization. Proving that education continues outside the confines of the classroom, UVA continually attracts some impressive speakers. Students have been able to hear speakers like Ralph Nader, the Dalai Lama, and Archbishop Desmond Tutu, just to give a small sampling. If all these on-campus activities still leave you wanting, Charlottesville is surrounded by outdoor adventure. The Blue Ridge Mountains are located about 20 miles away, so hiking is always a viable option. For those students with a penchant for rafting, the James River is roughly 40 minutes from campus. And an hour away you'll find Wintergreen Resort, where you can indulge in both skiing and golf.

BANG FOR YOUR BUCK

UVA exerts a tremendous effort to ensure its undergraduates have access to an affordable education. Between grants, loans, work-study, and numerous scholarships, students are able to find a means of financial support. AccessUVa is the university's financial aid program, designed to ensure that higher education is affordable for all admitted students, regardless of economic circumstance. AccessUVa offers loan-free packages for low-income students, caps on need-based loans for all other students, and a commitment to meet 100 percent of need for every student. By limiting debt—or eliminating it altogether, in the case of students with the most need—AccessUVa offers assurances to prospective students that if they make the grade, they can afford to attend the university. Many of the scholarships available are based upon need, academic achievement, and/or specific donor criteria. For example, the John Allen Love Scholarship is offered to students from Missouri. The Kaprielian Memorial Scholarship is open to students who are of Armenian descent. Scholarships abound for Virginia residents, including the Virginia Commonwealth Award, which gives recipients up to $3,000 per academic year. Preference is given to Pell Grant recipients. Out-of-state residents will also find plenty of scholarship opportunities. One such award is the Robert C. Byrd Honors Scholarship. These students receive up to $1,500 for their first year, and the scholarship is renewable for up to three years.

GETTING IN

As one of the premiere public universities in the country, UVA holds its applicants to high standards. Admissions Officers stress that candidates are more than the sum of their GPA or SAT scores and therefore don't set minimum requirements. That said, please note that the majority of accepted students have earned stellar marks both in high school and on the standardized tests. The average SAT score of incoming freshmen was 1325, and 88 percent of those who enrolled were in the top ten ranking of their class. Intellectual ability is paramount, so prospective students should have taken a rigorous course load in high school. Your personal essay and recommendations also hold weight. Students should be aware that geographical location and legacies can also play a significant role in the process, as Virginia residents and children of alums are given preference.

VERY IMPORTANT ADMISSION FACTORS

Academic GPA, alumni/ae relation, class rank, first generation, racial/ethnic status, recommendation(s), rigor of secondary school record, state residency

IMPORTANT ADMISSION FACTORS

Application essay, character/personal qualities, extracurricular activities, standardized test scores, talent/ability

Average HS GPA	4.07
Range SAT Verbal	600–710
Range SAT Math	620–720
Range ACT	26–31

APPLICATION DEADLINES

Early decision	11/1
Early decision notification	12/1
Regular admission	1/2
Regular notification	4/1
# of transfer applicants	2,255
% of transfer applicants accepted	37

ACADEMICS

Student/faculty ratio	15:1
% of classes taught by graduate students	15

MOST POPULAR MAJORS

- Business administration/management
- Economics
- Psychology
- History

English (including composition), foreign languages, history, humanities, math, sciences (biological or physical), social science, Non-Western Perspectives

FINANCIAL INFO

In-state tuition	$6,129
Out-of-state tuition	$24,053
Room & board	$6,909
Average book expense	$1,000
Required fees	$1,716
Average freshman need-based grant	$12,589
Average freshman need-based loan	$3,626
% of graduates who borrowed	31
Average indebtedness	$12,726

FINANCIAL AID FORMS

Students must submit FAFSA, institution's own financial aid form.

POSTGRAD

% going to graduate school	41
% going to law school	6
% going to medical school	2

CAREER SERVICES

Alumni network, alumni services, career/job search classes, career assessment, internships, on-campus job interviews.

WHAT DO GRADUATES DO?

The University of Virginia offers a plethora of majors and the diversity of subjects on campus is definitely reflected in the range of postgraduation employers. UVA alums can be found in such prestigious companies or organizations as Goldman Sachs, ESPN, the Central Intelligence Agency, Charlottesville Public Schools, JP Morgan, LexisNexis, and Memorial Sloan Kettering Cancer Center.

THE BOTTOM LINE

There is a large disparity here between tuition and fees for in-state versus out-of-state students. For the 2006–2007 academic year, Virginia residents paid a mere $7,845, whereas non-Virginians faced a bill of $25,945. Room and board cost students $3,639 and $3,270, respectively. It's estimated that all students paid around $1,000 for books and supplies while personal expenses ran roughly $1,754. While it's projected that Virginians spent around $220 for travel, out-of-staters spent between $355 and $1,255.

Impressively, 100 percent of applicants in need had their needs met. The average need-based financial aid package that freshmen received during 2006–2007 was $15,553. The average for undergraduates overall was $14,883. This excludes PLUS loans, unsubsidized loans, and private alternative loans.

FUN FACTS

Many notable figures have either attended and/or graduated from UVA. This distinguished group includes writer Edgar Allan Poe (who studied at UVA from 1826–1827); *Saturday Night Live* writer and performer Tina Fey (class of 1992); both Robert F. Kennedy and Edward M. Kennedy graduated from UVA Law School (class of 1951 and 1959, respectively); *Today Show* host Katie Couric (class of 1979); and New York Giants running back Tiki Barber (class of 1997).

Thomas Jefferson, who founded UVA, used to host students for dinner every Sunday at his Monticello home. The home, which sits just a few miles from campus, is now open for public tours of the house and gardens.

Unlike many other southern schools, UVA stayed open during the Civil War. When Union General George A. Custer marched into Charlottesville, he met with faculty and community leaders on the corner of university grounds, who convinced him not to destroy the school. Union soldiers camped on the lawn and marched on four days later without any bloodshed.

UNIVERSITY OF WEST GEORGIA

1601 Maple Street, Carrollton, GA 30118
www.WestGA.edu • Admissions: 678-839-4000
Fax: 678-839-4747 • E-mail: admiss@westga.edu • Financial Aid: 678-839-6421

STUDENTS

Religious affiliation
No Affiliation
Academic year
calendar   semester
Undergrad
enrollment   8,346
% male/female   40/60
% Asian   1
% Black, non-Latino   23
% Latino   2
% international   1
% from out of state   3
% freshmen return for
sophomore year   71
% freshmen graduate
within 4 years   9

STUDENT LIFE

% of students living
on campus   30
% in fraternities   3
% in sororities   3

ADMISSIONS

of applicants   5,175
% accepted   55
% enrolled   69

HIGH SCHOOL UNITS REQUIRED

4 English, 4 math, 3
science (2 science lab), 2
foreign language, 1 social
studies, 2 history

ABOUT UNIVERSITY OF WEST GEORGIA

The University of West Georgia's students give off a distinct Southern air to those who come from around the state to take advantage of UWG's academic excellence and personal environment. The atmosphere is friendly and supportive—students love one another, and there are plenty of smiles and hellos when you walk around campus. The only obstacle to meeting new friends comes from cliques, often groups of students who have come to UWG from the same high school. Diversity is a bit of a challenge—this is West Georgia, after all—but while some students stick to themselves, many others go out of their way to make minority students comfortable.

For a public school, UWG is small and personal. Professors take extra time out of their lives to help students, are happy to answer questions outside of class. Also helpful are the Learning Communities—groups of approximately 25 first-year students who share the same classes and dorms, which eases the freshman transition to college life. UWG's Honors College offers the university's best students a more competitive academic environment as well as the chance to live among their talented peers and take trips to New York City and the nation's capital.

Because most students leave campus to go home on the weekends, Thursday nights are when the parties begin, either at fraternities or student apartments. Greek life is fairly big, and, since Carrollton isn't exactly a bustling metropolis, most student activity takes place on campus, or on trips to Atlanta, a 40-minute drive away. Though UWG's football team is often a Division II powerhouse, the team lacks its own stadium. That doesn't detract much from a beautiful campus, though, or from a happy group of students who know when to play and when to work.

BANG FOR YOUR BUCK

As a public, state-supported university, the University of West Georgia is committed to containing costs. They offer low tuition, a full compliment of federal and state financial aid, and numerous scholarship opportunities for incoming and continuing students. UWG's out-of-state costs are similar to or less than many state's in-state tuition and fees, making it a great value for nonresidents as well.

Students Say

"A school that provides intimate learning and environments and listens to its students' opinions to determine how to best better the university."

VERY IMPORTANT ADMISSION FACTORS

Academic GPA, standardized test scores

Average HS GPA	3.04
Range SAT Verbal	470–560
Range SAT Math	460–550
Range ACT	18–22
Minimum TOEFL (paper/computer)	523/193

APPLICATION DEADLINES

Regular admission	7/1
Regular notification	rolling
# of transfer applicants	1,501
% of transfer applicants accepted	61

ACADEMICS

Student/faculty ratio	19:1
% faculty teaching undergraduates	90
% of classes taught by graduate students	0

MOST POPULAR MAJORS

• Biology/biological sciences
• Elementary education and teaching
• Nursing—registered nurse training (RN, ASN, BSN, MSN)

EDUCATION REQUIREMENTS

Arts/fine arts, computer literacy, English (including composition), foreign languages, history, humanities, math, sciences (biological or physical), social science

UWG's scholarships are based on both merit and need, while financial aid packages are based on student expected family contribution and need. UWG is dedicated to assisting students in making the best choices for financing their education. To this end, they provide peer financial aid counselors to help students make sound financial choices.

Many different scholarships are made available to ease the burden on students. Among the more exciting are: the State of Georgia Hope Scholarship, which covers full-time tuition and $150 per term for books, and the Presidential Scholarship, which covers $4,500 per year and is renewable.

GETTING IN

Secondary school record, high school academic GPA, standardized test scores, and class rank are the admissions factors of greatest importance to UWG Admissions Officers. In fact, they are the only factors considered. Admitted freshman averaged a GPA of 3.04 in high school and an SAT score of 1005 or ACT score of 20. Ninety-six percent of UWG students come from public high schools. Several majors at UWG restrict admission until certain academic criteria are met. Please consult the University Catalog for information about a specific major.

WHAT DO GRADUATES DO?

UWG graduates are well prepared for the working world, and often take jobs in accounting, business administration, and education. UWG trains many educators for Georgia's Public School System, and a wide range of companies in varied fields recruit West Georgia graduates.

THE BOTTOM LINE

In-state tuition at University of West Georgia is $2,560, while out-of-staters pay $10,242. Room and board is an additional $5,861 and additional fees cost $900. The total cost for a state resident is $9,321, with nonresidents owing $17,003. The average financial aid package received amounted to $6,441, with an additional $4,346 coming from need-based scholarships and grants. This totals $10,787 in aid.

Many students find that their yearly expenses are completely covered by a combination of federal financial aid and scholarships (including HOPE). Many students receive a refund of an overpayment and are able to use that money for living expenses and other educational expenses.

FUN FACTS

UWG is going through a process to change mascots as of January 1, 2006. The school will find a new mascot due to the NCAA restriction on mascots depicting Native American imagery.

In fall 2006, UWG opened its $21 Million Student Center, which will house student recreation and activities. The facility will have more than 129,000 square feet of space in addition to a 40-foot climbing wall.

Twenty-three percent of UWG's students are African American, and 63 percent are female.

Recently, four Honors physics students were selected by NASA to perform an experiment aboard its "Weightless Wonder" aircraft, and UWG beat Harvard, Northwestern, and Dartmouth at the UC—Berkeley Tournament. UWG has had more Honors student research proposals accepted for presentation at the annual meeting of the National Collegiate Honors Council than any other U.S. college or university for six of the past eight years.

FINANCIAL INFO

In-state tuition	$2,560
Out-of-state tuition	$10,242
Room & board	$5,861
Average book expense	$900
Required fees	$900
Average freshman need-based grant	$4,368
Average freshman need-based loan	$2,121
% of graduates who borrowed	60.7
Average indebtedness	$14,555

FINANCIAL AID FORMS

Students must submit FAFSA.

UNIVERSITY OF WISCONSIN— EAU CLAIRE

105 Garfield Avenue, Eau Claire, WI 54701
www.UWEC.edu • Admissions: 715-836-5415
Fax: 715-836-2409 • E-mail: admissions@uwec.edu • Financial Aid: 715-836-3373

STUDENTS

Religious affiliation
No Affiliation
Academic year
calendar   semester
Undergrad
enrollment   9,929
% male/female   41/59
% Asian   3
% Latino   1
% Native American   1
% international   1
% from out of state   23
% freshmen return for
sophomore year   83
% freshmen graduate
within 4 years   19

STUDENT LIFE

% of students living
on campus   40
% in fraternities   1
% in sororities   1

ADMISSIONS

of applicants   7,134
% accepted   70
% enrolled   41

HIGH SCHOOL UNITS REQUIRED

4 English, 3 math, 3
science, 2 foreign language,
3 social studies, 2 academic
electives

VERY IMPORTANT ADMISSION FACTORS

Class rank, rigor of
secondary school record

ABOUT UNIVERSITY OF WISCONSIN—EAU CLAIRE

The University of Wisconsin—Eau Claire is a challenging, midsize state university that offers an exceptional and very affordable education. There are less than 10,000 undergrads, giving UW Eau Claire the feel of a smaller college. Don't be fooled, though. In terms of its array of majors and minors, Eau Claire compares favorably with much larger schools. As one example, more than 700 students are involved directly in faculty research—an honor reserved for graduate students at most universities. Business, education, communications, nursing, and premedical sciences are among the most popular majors. UW Eau Claire professors are accomplished and are known for being accessible outside of class. You'll even find four Wisconsin Professor of the Year recipients on campus. And you certainly *won't* find anywhere near the number of teaching assistants here that you would see at a really big school like, just for example, UW Madison.

The average student is politically liberal, socially laid-back, and dedicated to schoolwork. The atmosphere on campus is a warm and welcoming one. Intramural sports are popular, while fraternities and sororities aren't a big deal. Lectures, concerts, and on-campus activities keep students busy too. Off campus, the city of Eau Claire (population: 62,000) is an ideal college town. Water Street and the downtown bar scene provide plenty of weekend options. Or, if you love the great outdoors, there are rugged trails and a lake nearby. The rolling (some would say quasi-mountainous) terrain also makes for some great running and biking. When students get the urge for something a little more cosmopolitan, the cities of Madison and Minneapolis are reasonably close.

BANG FOR YOUR BUCK

More than 65 percent of the students at UW Eau Claire receive grants, loans, scholarships, campus jobs, or some other kind of financial aid, and UWEC is able to find enough money for almost everyone who has financial need. Wisconsin Higher Education Grants are available to Wisconsin residents with considerable financial need. Another need-based award for in-state students is the Talent Incentive Program Grant, which is worth up to $1,800 per year. If you have at least one-quarter Native American blood ancestry or tribal affiliation, the Wisconsin Indian Assistance Program offers grants of up to $1,100 per year. You should also know that a reciprocity agreement between Minnesota and Wisconsin enables Minnesota residents to attend Wisconsin public schools at virtually in-state tuition.

UW Eau Claire awards over $250,000 in merit-based scholarships to first-year students. Scholarships range in value from $250 to $6,000 annually. If you are from the Badger State and a high school valedictorian, UWEC has a renewable Wisconsin Academic Excellence Scholarship valued at $2,250 just for you. Students in the top 6 percent of their class with an ACT score of at least 28 or an SAT (Math and Verbal) score of at least 1260 receive an automatic $1,000 scholarship. If you graduate in the top 25 percent of your high school class with at least a 25 on the ACT, you may qualify for a $1,000 Chancellor's Scholarship. This is one school where good high school grades can really pay off.

GETTING IN

Admission to UW Eau Claire is based on your class rank and standardized test scores. It's a sliding scale. If you graduate in the top 25 percent of your high school class, you need an ACT of 22 (or comparable SAT Math and Verbal scores). If you graduate in the top half your class, you need an ACT of 23. If you don't have a class rank (or if you graduate in the bottom half of your class), you will probably need a high school grade-point average of 3.25 and at least a 23 on the ACT. It's also important to take college-prep courses in high school.

WHAT DO GRADUATES DO?

Within six months of graduation, right near 97 percent of UW Eau Claire graduates either have real jobs or are continuing their education in graduate and professional schools. The people in Career Services are concerned about students and are really on the ball. The Internship Office maintains a file of more than 4,000 internships. Firms that recruit on campus include 3M, Cargill, Hormel Foods, IBM, Grant Thornton, and the good folks at Harley-Davidson.

IMPORTANT ADMISSION FACTORS

Standardized test scores

Range SAT Verbal	520–630
Range SAT Math	540–640
Range ACT	22–26
Minimum TOEFL (paper/computer)	525/197

APPLICATION DEADLINES

Regular notification	rolling
# of transfer applicants	1,416
% of transfer applicants accepted	61

ACADEMICS

Student/faculty ratio	20:1
% faculty teaching undergraduates	100

MOST POPULAR MAJORS

- Business administration/ management
- Elementary education and teaching
- Marketing/marketing management

EDUCATION REQUIREMENTS

Arts/fine arts, computer literacy, English (including composition), foreign languages, history, humanities, math, philosophy, sciences (biological or physical), social science

FINANCIAL INFO

In-state tuition $5,502
Out-of-state tuition $12,977
Room & board $4,936
Average book
   expense $450
Average freshman
   need-based grant $3,643
Average freshman
   need-based loan $3,516
% of graduates
   who borrowed 65
Average
   indebtedness $16,953

FINANCIAL AID FORMS

Students must submit
FAFSA.

POSTGRAD

% going to
   graduate school 11

CAREER SERVICES

Alumni services, career/job
search classes, career
assessment, internships,
on-campus job interviews.
Off-campus job opportuni-
ties are good.

THE BOTTOM LINE

The total cost for Wisconsin residents to attend UW Eau Claire, in-cluding full-time tuition, fees, room and board, books, and cost-of-living expenses, is $13,702. Minnesota residents pay about $13,000. Other out-of-staters can expect a total cost of $21,177 annually. The average financial aid package is worth $6,967. Graduates leave cam-pus with great memories and an average debt of approximately $16,154.

FUN FACTS

If you visit UW Eau Claire, don't sound like a rube. "Eau Claire" is pro-nounced like "O'Clare." Trust us on this.

UW Eau Claire boasts study abroad programs in far-flung and exotic lo-cales including Bulgaria, Costa Rica, Denmark, Fiji, Ghana, Japan, Latvia, Malta, New Zealand, Nicaragua, Scotland, and Thailand.

You should consider UW Eau Claire if you like to swim competitively and are really good at it. The men's swim team has been conference champion 25 of the past 33 years. The women's swim team has been conference cham-pion 19 of the past 25 years.

UW Eau Claire's intercollegiate athletic teams are called the Blugolds. That's one word, with no "e," no hyphens, and no capital "G."

UNIVERSITY OF WISCONSIN— LA CROSSE

1725 State Street, LaCrosse, WI 54601-3742
www.UWLAX.edu • Admissions: 608-785-8939
Fax: 608-785-8940 • E-mail: admissions@uwlax.edu • Financial Aid: 608-785-8604

STUDENTS

Religious affiliation
　　　　　　　　No Affiliation
Academic year
　calendar　　　　semester
Undergrad
　enrollment　　　7,908
% male/female　　41/59
% Asian　　　　　3
% Black, non-Latino　1
% Latino　　　　　1
% Native American　1
% international　　1
% from out of state　16
% freshmen return for
sophomore year　　90
% freshmen graduate
within 4 years　　21

STUDENT LIFE

% of students living
　on campus　　　36
% in fraternities　1
% in sororities　　1

ADMISSIONS

of applicants　　6,347
% accepted　　　　67
% enrolled　　　　41

HIGH SCHOOL UNITS REQUIRED

4 English, 3 math, 3
science (2 science lab), 3
social studies, 4 academic
electives

ABOUT UNIVERSITY OF WISCONSIN—LA CROSSE

What's in a name? When it comes to the University of Wisconsin—La Crosse, it's sports, sports, and more sports. Whether varsity or recreational, everyone plays on this health-conscious but party-minded campus. The recreation center is a major hub of social activity; for UWL students, a fit body goes hand in hand with a fit mind. But on the weekend, parties abound and you need only listen for music to find a place to imbibe or unwind. Downtown La Crosse is stocked with nightlife options, movie theaters, music venues, and restaurants, while the nearby bluffs are a mainstay for local climbers and hikers. Then there's always the Mississippi River. What the school may lack in diversity it makes up for with a positive and open-minded outlook (students turned out in droves for the 2004 elections, casting their vote for the left) that is bolstered by required attendance at multicultural events.

With a student population of around 8,500, UWL offers a small-campus feel with a major university's funding and programs. Not surprisingly, it's the exercise and sports science programs at UWL that reign supreme. And thanks to the university's reputation as one of the fitness and athletic training field's leaders, students are quick to reap career-related rewards upon graduation. Other popular majors include biology, elementary education and teaching, and marketing/management. Professors lead great classes and are known for their helpfulness, building rapport with students by placing an emphasis on discussion rather than lecturing. An effective counseling service has students' interests and needs at heart. They do an outstanding job of preparing students for everything from a change in major to their future in the workforce.

BANG FOR YOUR BUCK

A very respectable 94 percent of undergraduates who applied received some form of need-based financial aid in 2005–2006. Merit-based awards are available to those who excel in academics, art, athletics, music, and drama. There are also awards for those with alumni affiliation, leadership skills, minority status, or ROTC. All incoming freshmen with outstanding academic credentials are automatically considered for several merit-based scholarships. There is also a veritable bounty of other awards offered through each academic department, so make sure to investigate and apply as soon as possible.

HIGH SCHOOL UNITS RECOMMENDED

4 English, 4 math, 4 science (2 science lab), 3 foreign language, 4 social studies, 2 academic electives

VERY IMPORTANT ADMISSION FACTORS

Academic GPA, class rank, rigor of secondary school record, standardized test scores

IMPORTANT ADMISSION FACTORS

Application essay

Range SAT Verbal 500–610
Range SAT Math 520–660
Range ACT 23–27
Minimum TOEFL
  (paper/computer) 550/213

APPLICATION DEADLINES

Regular notification rolling
# of transfer
  applicants 1,003
% of transfer applicants
  accepted 67

When it comes to keeping costs down, there are two very helpful offers worth mentioning. The first is a textbook rental service that, for $74.31 per semester (included in tuition costs), students can rent all the books they need, instead of the usual system of buying high and reselling low. The second is the highly beneficial Four-Year Graduation Agreement that UWL offers to entering freshmen. Provided the student agrees to graduate within four years of enrollment and satisfies the conditions of this agreement, the school will pay for the student's tuition for any courses that still need to be taken beyond the four-year mark. As a result, you'll find yourself on the proverbial fast track to success, and if there's a slight hitch along the way, you won't be paying for it.

GETTING IN

For the 2004–2005 year (the last year this info was available), 34 percent of admitted freshmen were in the top 10 percent of their high school class. The average combined SAT I score was 1139, and the average ACT score was 24. Academic record, class rank, standardized test scores, and essays are the main criteria considered for admission. Less important, but still taken into account, are the interview, recommendations, extracurricular activities, ability and talent, character, volunteer work, and work experience. Those with state residency or minority status are particularly encouraged to apply. Candidates are not required to apply separately to departments at UWL for admission. However, those applying with particular majors in mind (there are 85 to choose from) should check with their department of interest to ensure that no supplemental material is needed.

What Do Graduates Do?

A little help from the Career Services department goes a long way—training seminars, job fairs, and internships all play an integral part in securing work after commencement. For UWL's recent graduating classes, nearly 24 percent of students entered graduate programs. Of those who moved straight into the workforce, approximately 99 percent found successful employment in their field within six months of graduating, with an average salary of $32,895.

The Bottom Line

Simply put, it's the classic tale of big-time education at small-time costs—an academic year of tuition and room and board at UWL for a resident is $10,525, while nonresidents will find themselves paying $17,843. The average amount of financial aid students receive in their first year is $4,692. In 2005, graduates who took advantage of student loans left the school with a low $16,793 in cumulative debt.

Fun Facts

The school colors are maroon and gray, and the school mascot is the eagle.

Founded in 1909 as the La Crosse Normal School, it did not adopt its present name until it merged with the University of Wisconsin system in 1971.

ACADEMICS

Student/faculty ratio 22:1
% faculty teaching
    undergraduates 100
% of classes taught by
    graduate students 0

Most Popular Majors

- Elementary education and teaching
- Kinesiology and exercise science
- Marketing/marketing management

Education Requirements

Arts/fine arts, computer literacy, English (including composition), history, humanities, math, sciences (biological or physical), social science, health/wellness

FINANCIAL INFO

In-state tuition $5,555
Out-of-state tuition $12,873
Room & board $4,970
Average book
    expense $300
Average freshman
    need-based grant $4,117
Average freshman
    need-based loan $2,814
% of graduates
    who borrowed   63
Average
    indebtedness $16,793

Financial Aid Forms

Students must submit FAFSA, institution's own financial aid form.

POSTGRAD

% going to
    graduate school   21

UNIVERSITY OF WISCONSIN—MADISON

Armory & Gymnasium, 716 Langdon Street, Madison, WI 53706-1481
www.wisc.edu • Admissions: 608-262-3961
Fax: 608-262-7706 • E-mail: onwisconsin@admissions.wisc.edu • Financial Aid: 608-262-3060

STUDENTS

Religious affiliation
No Affiliation
Academic year
calendar   semester
Undergrad
enrollment   28,458
% male/female   46/54
% Asian   5
% Black, non-Latino   3
% Latino   3
% Native American   1
% international   3
% from out of state   30
% freshmen return for
sophomore year   94
% freshmen graduate
within 4 years   43

STUDENT LIFE

% of students living
on campus   26
% in fraternities   9
% in sororities   8

ADMISSIONS

of applicants   21,682
% accepted   68
% enrolled   42

HIGH SCHOOL UNITS REQUIRED

4 English, 3 math, 3 science, 2 foreign language, 3 social studies, 2 academic electives

HIGH SCHOOL UNITS RECOMMENDED

4 English, 4 math, 4 science, 4 foreign language, 4 social studies, 2 academic electives

ABOUT THE UNIVERSITY OF WISCONSIN—MADISON

Wisconsin is the quintessential public university, and Madison is the quintessential college town. Located in southern Wisconsin between Lakes Mendota and Monona, the flagship of the state's university system is so large that it's almost bewildering: There are 28,458 undergrads, and grad students push the total past 41,000. The campus is spread across 933 acres. There are 43 libraries. Among the 150 or so majors, there is just about everything one might want to study. We checked. There's cartography, Hebrew, real estate, and poultry science.

Despite the vastness of the school, it's hard to find a student body more loyal. On football game days, everything is about Badger pride. And if you run into an UW Madison alum, you hear almost universally good things about their experience there. There are hundreds of campus organizations tailored to every conceivable kind of student. The school has long been one of the best research institutions in the country. And there's plenty to do in Madison, a liberal town of 208,054.

UW Madison has a well-earned reputation as a party school: In The Princeton Review's *Best 361 Colleges* it was listed fourth in this category, behind University of Texas at Austin, Penn State and West Virginia University. UW Madison students surely must take this as a slap, especially considering their efforts on game days, when the partying begins well before the 11:00 A.M. kickoff. Freshmen must find *some* time for studies, however, as 94 percent of them come back for their sophomore year. There are gripes, however: Students complain about the high number of courses taught by TAs instead of professors. As far as racial breakdown, UW Madison is overwhelmingly white: Caucasian students comprise 82.8 percent of the student body, compared with 5.4 percent Asian American, 3.2 percent international, 2.8 percent Hispanic and just 2.5 percent African American. But there's something for everyone at this school, and for a strong all-around education and a wealth of opportunities, it's hard to find a better bargain than UW Madison.

Bang for Your Buck

There is such a flood of applicants seeking need-based aid that many are turned away. A total of 19,011 put in for such aid in 2005–2006, and only 10,530 were found to have a demonstrable financial need. Of those, 9,913 received some aid (5,068 students received a non-need-based scholarship or grant). However, the total aid package for undergrads is still $11,288. In 2005–2006 UW Madison handed out a total of $3.4 million in need-based scholarships and grants, compared with $9.3 million in other aid, and $7 million in athletic scholarships.

Getting In

There were 21,682 applications for the fall of 2005, and UW Madison accepted 14,768 (68 percent). A total of 6,118 enrolled. Their average GPA in high school was 3.66 and on the SAT verbal, the majority of students (44 percent) scored between 600–699. On the math, half were in the 600s. On the ACT, the vast majority (64 percent) were in the 24–29 range.

Beginning in the fall of 2007, all freshman applicants must submit results from either the new SAT or the ACT with the writing component. Students who took either test before February 2005 must take at least one of the exams again to be eligible for admission.

What do Graduates Do?

As mentioned, UW Madison is known as a research university, and the timeline of university history available on its website is peppered with references to breakthroughs in science and medicine (e.g., "1970: Nobel Prize–winning biochemistry professor Har Gobind Khorana synthesizes a gene for the first time in history."), and as you'd imagine, this is a field graduates tend to follow, whether as in graduate school or in the workforce. The school also has produced strong candidates in the engineering and business fields.

VERY IMPORTANT ADMISSION FACTORS

Academic GPA, class rank, rigor of secondary school record

IMPORTANT ADMISSION FACTORS

Application essay, standardized test scores, state residency

Average HS GPA	3.66
Range SAT Verbal	560–670
Range SAT Math	600–700
Range ACT	26–30
Minimum TOEFL (paper/computer)	550/213

APPLICATION DEADLINES

Regular admission	2/1
Regular notification	rolling
# of transfer applicants	3,763
% of transfer applicants accepted	54

ACADEMICS

Student/faculty ratio	13:1
% faculty teaching undergraduates	
% of classes taught by graduate students	21

MOST POPULAR MAJORS

- English language and literature
- Political science and government
- Psychology

EDUCATION REQUIREMENTS

English (including composition), foreign languages, humanities, math, sciences (biological or physical), social science, ethnic studies

FINANCIAL INFO

In-state tuition	$6,000
Out-of-state tuition	$20,000
Room & board	$6,920
Average book expense	$890
Required fees	$726
Average freshman need-based grant	$5,963
Average freshman need-based loan	$4,469
% of graduates who borrowed	45
Average indebtedness	$18,630

FINANCIAL AID FORMS

Students must submit FAFSA, institution's own financial aid form.

POSTGRAD

CAREER SERVICES

Off-campus job opportunities are excellent.

THE BOTTOM LINE

Considering UW Madison's high acceptance rate, and that in-state tuition is only $6,000, it's no wonder so many Wisconsinites choose to go here (70 percent are natives or residents). For out-of-staters, the tab is $20,000. Other expenses are relatively cheap too: $6,920 for room and board, $890 for books, and $726 for fees.

FUN FACTS

Bucky Badger, UW Madison's cartoon mascot, was first drawn by California illustrator Art Evans in 1940. Evans created other college logo characters, such as the Minnesota Gopher and the Purdue Boilermaker (also of the Big 10). In 1949, UW Madison held a contest to name its mascot. Reports say there were between "0 and 15 entries," but the committee chose its own name: Buckingham U. Badger.

Memorial Union Terrace, with its distinctive "sunburst" chairs of orange, green, and yellow, is a hub of social activity on campus, on the shore of Lake Mendota. Long ago, it was a gathering place for the Winnebago Indian tribe.

Notable alums include aviation pioneer Charles Lindbergh (1924), architect Frank Lloyd Wright (1890), author Joyce Carol Oates (1961), baseball Commissioner Bud Selig (1956), and glass artist Dale Chihuly (1967).

UNIVERSITY OF WYOMING

Dept 3435, 1000 East University Avenue, Laramie, WY 82071
www.UWYO.edu • Admissions: 307-766-5160
Fax: 307-766-4042 • E-mail: Why-Wyo@uwyo.edu • Financial Aid: 307-766-2116

STUDENTS

Religious affiliation	No Affiliation
Academic year calendar	semester
Undergrad enrollment	8,984
% male/female	48/52
% Asian	1
% Black, non-Latino	1
% Latino	4
% Native American	1
% international	1
% from out of state	30
% freshmen return for sophomore year	74

STUDENT LIFE

% of students living on campus	23
% in fraternities	5
% in sororities	5

ADMISSIONS

# of applicants	3,155
% accepted	95
% enrolled	47

HIGH SCHOOL UNITS REQUIRED

4 English, 3 math, 3 science (3 science lab), 3 Cultural Context Electives—Recommended—3 behavioral or social sciences, 3 visual or performing arts, 3 humanities or earth/space sciences

ABOUT THE UNIVERSITY OF WYOMING

Dirt-cheap tuition is just one of the qualities that make the University of Wyoming a great buy. While many of the degree programs reflect the state's long tradition of agriculture and mining, there's a wide array of undergraduate majors available, from art to nursing to Chicano studies to a respected economics and finance department. The student-faculty ratio is just 15:1, and professors and their TAs are down to earth and approachable. UW's whole vibe is one of unpretentiousness: Seventy percent of the 9,510 undergrads come from within the state, and many hail from very small towns. Issues of class and status are virtually nonexistent at UW, which makes the campus often feel like a tight-knit community.

Then again, part of the camaraderie comes from the shared misery of the brutal Laramie winters. At an elevation of 7,200 feet, the march to class across Prexy's Pasture on a January morning will feel like a polar expedition. But the elements also grace UW students with a wealth of outdoor activities: The Snowy Range Ski Area is 35 miles to the west, and during the gorgeous spring and fall some of the West's best rock climbing can be found at Vedauwoo (*veed*-uh-voo), 10 miles to the east. Out-of-staters might notice an extreme lack of racial diversity at UW, whose students are 84 percent white. But compared with the rest of Wyoming, Laramie feels like Berkeley or Boulder. There's diversity of ideas and opinions, which are freely shared beneath the taxidermic animal heads at the Buckhorn bar downtown.

BANG FOR YOUR BUCK

Wyoming's energy industry is booming again, and the state is flush with cash. The legislature created a $400 million endowment to fund a generous scholarship program named for Stanley K. Hathaway, the former governor who, in 1969, floated the idea of taxing mineral extraction, which has produced a $2.5 billion trust fund for the state. Beginning in the fall of 2006, Wyoming high school students can receive thousands in scholarship money, depending on their grades and test scores. There are three levels of scholarship: Students who carry a 3.5 GPA and got a 26 on the ACT (UW doesn't require the SAT) can get a Hathaway of up to $1,600 per semester for eight semesters, provided they keep up their grades. But at the first level, all it takes is a 2.5 GPA and a 19 on the ACT to score $800 a semester. As for need-based aid, on average, incoming freshmen who qualify receive $2,656. During the 2004–2005 school year, 74 percent of the full-time undergrads who put in for need-based aid got it.

HIGH SCHOOL UNITS RECOMMENDED

4 English, 3 math, 3 science (3 science lab), 2 foreign language

VERY IMPORTANT ADMISSION FACTORS

Academic GPA, rigor of secondary school record, standardized test scores

Average HS GPA	3.4
Range SAT Verbal	480–610
Range SAT Math	500–610
Range ACT	20–26
Minimum TOEFL (paper/computer)	525/197

APPLICATION DEADLINES

Regular admission	8/10
# of transfer applicants	1,825
% of transfer applicants accepted	94

ACADEMICS

Student/faculty ratio	15:1
% faculty teaching undergraduates	97
% of classes taught by graduate students	9

MOST POPULAR MAJORS

- Business administration and management
- Elementary education and teaching
- Nursing—registered nurse training (RN, ASN, BSN, MSN)

GETTING IN

Virtually everyone who applies to UW gets in. For the 2005–2006 school year, 3,155 prospective freshmen applied and of those, 3,008 were accepted (a populist 97 percent). The school says the most important factors for students are "rigor of secondary school record," GPA, and standardized test scores. But students have the option of taking either the SAT or ACT, and if it's the latter, the writing component isn't taken into consideration. Other things that UW doesn't care about: Where you ranked in your high school class, where you're from, and whether a relative is an alum. It's all very democratic—for the people, by the people, of the people, y'know?

WHAT DO GRADUATES DO?

Education and nursing are two of the more popular majors at UW, but in 2006, more graduates received their degrees in business or marketing (16.3 percent) than in any other field. In a state that goes through periodic cycles of boom and bust, graduates often leave the state when the economy is mired in a funk. But Wyoming needs people for work related to coal and natural gas. In 2006, UW opened the School of Energy Resources to educate students in techniques of energy exploration—including wind farming.

The Bottom Line

Did we mention that tuition is cheap? Try $9,360 for out-of-state residents, while in-staters, for whom an education at UW is practically a birthright, pay just $2,820. Tack on another $6,861 for room and board, plus $1,200 for books and $696 for fees, according to the school. Honestly, any cheaper and it'd be called stealing.

Fun Facts

One of Wyoming's favorite sons was the late, great sportscaster Curt Gowdy, who went to UW from 1940–1942 and played on the basketball team. The year after he left, the Cowboys, led by Kenny Sailors who is credited with inventing the modern jump shot, won the NCAA title.

Other noteworthy alumni include Vice President Dick Cheney (of course), Los Angeles Lakers owner Jerry Buss, and celebrity lawyer Gerry Spence.

Cheney received his masters in political science from UW in 1966. Here's the riveting title of his thesis: "Highway Acceleration in Wisconsin: A Case Study in Executive-Legislative Relations."

EDUCATION REQUIREMENTS

Arts/fine arts, English (including composition), humanities, math, sciences (biological or physical), social science. Also required are Intellectual Community; Oral Communication; U.S. and WY Constitutions; Physical Activity and Health; Information Literacy; Diversity in the U.S.; Global Awareness

FINANCIAL INFO

In-state tuition	$2,820
Out-of-state tuition	$9,360
Room & board	$6,861
Average book expense	$1,200
Required fees	$696
Average freshman need-based grant	$2,656
Average freshman need-based loan	$2,030
% of graduates who borrowed	45.8
Average indebtedness	$16,742

FINANCIAL AID FORMS

Students must submit FAFSA.

POSTGRAD

CAREER SERVICES

Off-campus job opportunities are good.

UTAH STATE UNIVERSITY

0160 Old Main Hill, Logan, UT 84322-0160
www.USU.edu • Admissions: 435-797-1079
Fax: 435-797-3708 • E-mail: admit@cc.usu.edu • Financial Aid: 435-797-0173

STUDENTS

Religious affiliation
No Affiliation
Academic year
calendar   semester
Undergrad
enrollment   12,530
% male/female   51/49
% Asian   1
% Black, non-Latino 1
% Latino   1
% international   3
% from out of state 27

STUDENT LIFE

% in fraternities 2
% in sororities   2

ADMISSIONS

of applicants   4,666
% accepted   94
% enrolled   47

HIGH SCHOOL UNITS REQUIRED

4 English, 3 math, 3 science
(1 science lab), 1 history, 4
academic electives,

HIGH SCHOOL UNITS RECOMMENDED

2 Foreign language

VERY IMPORTANT ADMISSION FACTORS

Academic GPA, standardized
test scores

ABOUT UTAH STATE UNIVERSITY

Founded in 1888 as an agricultural college, Utah State has broadened its curriculum considerably and now offers strong academics in a wide range of programs, (though it still boasts a wonderful College of Agriculture). Its students are predominantly Mormons from Utah who are down to earth and ready to learn. Many are working part- or full-time in addition to their course loads, and married couples are common on campus. The Church of Jesus Christ of Latter-day Saints is a dominant force at Utah State, with little to say to those outside the faith. The little diversity comes from the non-Mormon students from Utah and a small minority of students from the Middle East, India, and China. Most of these groups keep to themselves.

Besides the College of Agriculture, USU has an excellent college of engineering that boasts an aerospace program that sends more research into space than any other university. The school's pre-veterinary program is one of the nation's best, with very high acceptance rates into veterinary schools, and its college of natural resources prepares students for careers in conservation, ecology, forest ranging, and outdoor education. USU's education program also provides Utah with great teachers too. These and other programs are very relevant to the work world, helping students to find and succeed in their first jobs.

There are all sorts of activities to take part in at USU, from watching their top-notch Division I hoops team to any sort of student club you can imagine. The activity board is constantly dreaming up ways to keep its students entertained, from free movies to karaoke, and if you are feeling more adventurous, the Rocky Mountains offer all sorts of outdoorsy possibilities. Salt Lake City isn't far if it's big city life you crave.

BANG FOR YOUR BUCK

Utah State University tuition is 67 percent of the national average for four-year universities and 84 percent of the western states average. Why? Utah traditionally has been a low-tuition state, assuring access for in-state and out-of-state students alike. The school has all sorts of features built into the system to make sure this stays true.

First, their centralized scholarships are awarded at application; just fill out the application form for admission and you're automatically considered for scholarships. A Graduation Guarantee Program allows students to contract with the university to ensure that they do graduate on time—or the university pays the tuition. In addition, the school's "plateau tuition" allows a student to enroll for 13–18 credits—all at the same cost.

Intent-to-transfer agreements with two-year feeder institutions allow students to receive advising from both institutions simultaneously to ensure that every course taken at the two-year school counts.

Utah State has also adopted for more than a decade a philosophy of "meaningful academic employment." Why work at a fast-food restaurant or a grocery store when you can be enhancing your resume as an Undergraduate Teaching Fellow, an Honors Fellow, a Library Peer Mentor, a Rhetoric Associate, or a Research Fellow? These programs give students a financial boost for their studies and enable faculty to write stellar letters of reference for grad school.

USU students receive both need- and merit-based aid. Almost half of all students receive some sort of financial aid. Individualized financial aid counselors steward their students carefully to ensure they have the least amount of debt possible and the greatest support. In contrast to other institutions, USU students often increase in grant support as they progress through the institution

Getting In

Most important on your application are your standardized test scores, GPA, and high school curriculum. Professional programs (e.g., business, engineering) may have more stringent Admissions guidelines. For instance, the engineering program estimates that students will most likely be successful if they have an ACT score of 27 in Math; business grants give automatic admission based on academic achievement, but for those students not meeting those benchmarks, success in a set of gateway courses is required to matriculate into the business program. The Art department requires a portfolio for admission; music and theater arts may require auditions. The average GPA of freshmen entering Utah State in 2005–2006 was 3.54.

IMPORTANT ADMISSION FACTORS

Rigor of secondary school record

Average HS GPA 3.54
Range SAT Verbal 470–620
Range SAT Math 490–620
Range ACT 21–27
Minimum TOEFL
(paper/computer) 500/173

APPLICATION DEADLINES
of transfer
applicants 1,657
% of transfer applicants
accepted 93

ACADEMICS
Student/faculty ratio 17:1
% faculty teaching
undergraduates 95
% of classes taught by
graduate students 7

MOST POPULAR MAJORS

• Accounting
• Information science/studies
• Marketing/marketing
management

EDUCATION REQUIREMENTS

Arts/fine arts, computer literacy, English (including composition), history, humanities, math, sciences (biological or physical), social science. American Institutions—Collaborative Learning and Group Decision Making; depth in specified areas outside the major; interdisiplinary courses.

FINANCIAL INFO

In-state tuition	$3,228
Out-of-state tuition	$10,679
Room & board	$4,400
Average book expense	$1,080
Required fees	$571
Average freshman need-based grant	$2,800
Average freshman need-based loan	$2,600
% of graduates who borrowed	50
Average indebtedness	$12,430

FINANCIAL AID FORMS

Students must submit FAFSA, institution's own financial aid form.

POSTGRAD

% going to graduate school	23
% going to medical school	1

CAREER SERVICES

Alumni network, career/job search classes, career assessment, internships, on-campus job interviews. Off-campus job opportunities are good.

WHAT DO GRADUATES DO?

Accounting, aerospace industry, agribusiness, business, computing, education, engineering, environmental agencies, government, and insurance are some of the biggest career draws for graduating students. Regional school districts, Hewlett-Packard, Micron, and the state and federal government are some of the major employers seeking out new grads. Other recruiters include the FBI, CIA, Disney, Dell, Federal Aviation Association, Intermountain Farmers Association, Kennecott Copper Corporation, Internal Revenue Service, and Social Security Administration.

THE BOTTOM LINE

In-state tuition for 2006–2007 was $3,227.92. Out-of-staters paid $10,678.50. There was an additional $571 in fees, $4,400 for room and board, and $1,080 for books. After all things are considered (i.e., financial aid, scholarships), the average out-of-pocket expenses for resident students was $4,010. The average out-of-pocket expenses for nonresident students was $8,460. (These figures do not include discretionary costs of travel and personal expenses.) Utah State has been termed the second least expensive university in its class for out-of-state tuition. Many out-of-staters tell us it is cheaper to go out-of-state to USU than enroll at one of their state universities.

FUN FACTS

A car is not necessary; there are free campus and city bus systems.

Utah State is known for "free or inexpensive food," ranging from Walking Tacos to Aggie Ice Cream; Logger's Breakfast to the Ceramic Club's Annual Chili Bowl Sale—chili included.

The following are available for nonresidents who attend: Western Undergraduate Exchange (WUE), students pay 150 percent of resident tuition over the undergraduate education; National Student Exchange, students pay tuition at their home institution; 100-Mile Radius Waivers, waives the in-state portion of tuition for students who live within 100 miles of the border; Utah-Idaho Waivers, waives the out-of-state portion of tuition for students who live in Idaho but it is also based on academic merit.

The Aggies once held the World Record for most people simultaneously kissing (but it was broken six months later by a group in Canada).

Fall features the Jell-O Slide in which students compete on the Quad to see how far they can slide on a river of Jell-O. After all, Utah is famous for being the biggest consumer of green Jell-O, a flavor the company had to bring back after a short termination due to popular demand in this western state.

Engineering majors host the Concrete Canoe Race at the First Dam Lake below campus, taking on rival universities. Engineers are also known for the fastest edible toy car race and longest ski jump by a robot.

VANDERBILT UNIVERSITY

2305 West End Avenue, Nashville, TN 37203
www.Vanderbilt.edu • Admissions: 615-322-2561
Fax: 615-343-7765 • E-mail: admissions@vanderbilt.edu • Financial Aid: 615-322-3591

STUDENTS

Religious affiliation
　　　　　　No Affiliation
Academic year
　calendar　　　semester
Undergrad
　enrollment　　　6,402
% male/female　　48/52
% Asian　　　　　6
% Black, non-Latino　8
% Latino　　　　5
% international　　2
% from out of state　85
% freshmen return for
sophomore year　　96
% freshmen graduate
within 4 years　　83

STUDENT LIFE

% of students living
　on campus　　　83
% in fraternities　　34
% in sororities　　50

ADMISSIONS

of applicants　　12,162
% accepted　　　34
% enrolled　　　39
# of early decision/action
　applicants　　　1,329
% accepted early
　decision/action　　48

HIGH SCHOOL UNITS
REQUIRED

4 English, 3 math, 2
science (2 science lab), 2
foreign language, 2 social
studies

HIGH SCHOOL UNITS
RECOMMENDED

4 English, 4 math, 4
science (4 science lab), 2
foreign language, 4 social
studies

ABOUT VANDERBILT UNIVERSITY

All those swanky parties thrown by Vanderbilt Chancellor Gordon Gee have paid off handsomely—for the school and its students. Since the bowtie-wearing Gee took over in 2000, he has overseen a fundraising effort that has brought in a staggering $1.2 billion. Gee passed the collection plate at many a soiree thrown by him and his wife at Braeburn, the university-owned mansion where the Gees live, which was renovated at Gee's request. The tab for the improvements was a whopping $6 million, causing much consternation among the trustees. But no one can argue that the money Gee raised has helped propelled the Nashville, Tennessee–based private school from respected to elite status. In 2006, Vandy made *Newsweek*'s list of "New Ivies"—schools that are gaining on the Ivy League in accomplishment and prestige. And in the last *Times of London* World University Rankings, Vandy was No. 53, up 61 spots from the previous year. That placed it 23rd among U.S. schools—ahead of ivy-draped Brown and Dartmouth.

Vanderbilt's rising stock has allowed it to become more selective. In 2000, Vandy accepted 55 percent of applicants. In 2006, it was 33.7 percent. Students who get in surely must feel a bit cloistered: All unmarried undergrads are required to live in one of the 29 residence halls on campus. And although 50 percent of men and 34 percent of women belong to fraternities and sororities, freshmen aren't allowed to rush until the second semester. But Vandy looks out for its students too. The faculty-student ratio is a very cozy (and almost unheard-of) nine to one. The school takes seriously the notion of producing well-rounded students who can think for themselves. Vandy also estimates that it met 99.8 percent of the financial need of freshmen who received aid in 2005–2006. One more thing: The Sarratt Student center has everything but a mini-golf course.

BANG FOR YOUR BUCK

Vanderbilt has just 6,402 undergrads, and visitors might only see it as a salon for the extremely well-off. Sure, tuition is the usual nightmare for a top-flight private school ($32,620), but the vast majority of students get help. During the 2005–2006 school year, Vandy and its alumni doled out an incredible $66.7 million in need-based scholarships and grants (compared to Harvard's reported $58.5 million). Sixty percent of Vandy undergrads get some aid, while another 34 percent secure loans. Of those who were deemed deserving, over 99 percent of their need was met. Four percent of those who apply to Vandy are offered merit scholarships, but the bar is set high: 1500 SAT or 34 ACT.

Students Say

"The typical student at Vandy can easily talk about everything from current events to frat-party themes. Vandy students tend to be friendly, upbeat, and involved in many activities on campus. Although students seem to be more concerned with appearance than at the average college, most people here are dorks at heart (though they would never admit it)."

VERY IMPORTANT ADMISSION FACTORS

Academic GPA, class rank, extracurricular activities, rigor of secondary school record, standardized test scores,

IMPORTANT ADMISSION FACTORS

Application essay, recommendation(s)

Range SAT Verbal 640–730
Range SAT Math   660–740
Range ACT   29–33
Minimum TOEFL
   (paper)   570

APPLICATION DEADLINES

Early decision   11/1
Early decision
   notification   12/15
Regular admission   1/3
Regular notification   4/1
# of transfer applicants 379
% of transfer applicants
   accepted   25

ACADEMICS

Student/faculty ratio   9:1
% faculty teaching
   undergraduates
% of classes taught by
   graduate students   39

MOST POPULAR MAJORS

• Economics
• Biomedical engineering
• Human and organizational
   development

GETTING IN

As mentioned, Vandy is getting stingier about applicants. And the toughest of Vandy's four undergrad colleges to get into is also the most populous: Nearly two-thirds of Vandy students are enrolled in Arts and Science, but only 30 percent of A&S applicants were accepted in 2006. The other three colleges are the Blair School of Music (43 percent acceptance rate); Engineering (47 percent); and the Peabody College of Education and Human Development (46 percent). Of the 1,595 members of the freshman class of 2006–2007, 149 were National Merit Scholars.

Among the most important factors for applicants, Vanderbilt lists academic record, high school class rank, GPA, standardized test scores, and extracurriculars. Listed as "important" are the application essay and letters of recommendation. The tests required are the SAT Reasoning Test or the ACT; the writing portion is required for both.

WHAT DO GRADUATES DO?

While Arts and Science is the largest of Vandy's four undergrad colleges, the most popular major at Vandy is human and organizational development, which combines liberal arts with course work designed to prepare students for a "successful career focused on finding solutions to human problems in businesses, organizations, and communities." Vandy also is proud of its engineering school: Jacobs Hall, which houses labs, offices, and classrooms for civil, environmental, and electrical engineering, underwent a $28 million renovation in 2002.

THE BOTTOM LINE

Vandy estimates the total expense at $47,302, including $10,890 for room and board, $1,104 for books and $820 in fees. The average aid package for incoming freshmen is $32,265. Considering this, current graduates leave Vandy with $19,585 in cumulative debt—which is, all things considered, not too shabby.

FUN FACTS

Cornelius Vanderbilt, the New York shipping and railroad baron whose nickname, "Commodore," became Vandy's mascot name, never gave any money to philanthropy except for the $1 million he donated to get the university started in 1873.

The last Vandy football coach to have a winning record was Steve Sloan, who guided the 'Dores to a 12-9-2 mark during the halcyon seasons of 1973–1974. Between then and the 2005 season, the team went a combined 92-240-1.

Notable alums include newsman David Brinkley; former Vice President Al Gore's wife Tipper Gore; talk-show host Dinah Shore; Chicago Cubs pitcher Mark Prior; and Clear Channel Communications President and CEO Mark P. Mays.

EDUCATION REQUIREMENTS

English (including composition), foreign languages, humanities, math, sciences (biological or physical), social science

FINANCIAL INFO

Tuition	$32,620
Room & board	$10,890
Average book expense	$1,104
Required fees	$820
Average freshman need-based grant	$25,749
Average freshman need-based loan	$3,096
% of graduates who borrowed	31
Average indebtedness	$19,585

FINANCIAL AID FORMS

Students must submit FAFSA, CSS/financial aid profile, noncustodial (divorced/separated) parent's statement. Financial aid filing deadline 2/1

POSTGRAD

% going to graduate school	32
% going to law school	7
% going to business school	1
% going to medical school	4

CAREER SERVICES

Alumni network, alumni services, career/job search classes, career assessment, internships, regional alumni, on-campus job interviews. Off-campus job opportunities are excellent.

WABASH COLLEGE

PO Box 352, 301 West Wabash Avenue, Crawfordsville, IN 47933
www.Wabash.edu • Admissions: 765-361-6225
Fax: 765-361-6437 • E-mail: admissions@wabash.edu • Financial Aid: 765-361-6370

STUDENTS

Religious affiliation
　　　　　　　No Affiliation
Academic year
　calendar　　　semester
Undergrad
　enrollment　　　874
% male/female　　100/0
% Asian　　　　　3
% Black, non-Latino　6
% Latino　　　　　5
% international　　5
% from out of state　29
% freshmen return for
sophomore year　　89
% freshmen graduate
　within 4 years　　70

STUDENT LIFE

% of students living
　on campus　　　90
% in fraternities　　60

ADMISSIONS

of applicants　　1,319
% accepted　　　51
% enrolled　　　40
# of early decision/action
　applicants　　　47
% accepted early
　decision/action　75

HIGH SCHOOL UNITS RECOMMENDED

4 English, 4 math, 2 science
(2 science lab), 2 foreign
language, 2 social studies, 2
history

VERY IMPORTANT ADMISSION FACTORS

Class rank, rigor of
secondary school record

ABOUT WABASH COLLEGE

Wabash students are the last of a fading breed: Men who opt for single-sex education. While a dwindling but still substantial number of all-women's schools continue to thrive, the ranks of America's all-male undergraduate institutions have fallen into the low single digits. There's no danger of Wabash going the way of the dinosaur anytime soon, though; its solid reputation and even more solid endowment ensure that the tradition of quality, single-sex education will continue in central Indiana into the foreseeable future. Wabash undergrads adhere to the elegant, all-inclusive Gentleman's Rule, which simply requires them to behave as responsible citizens both on and off campus. The rule may seem maddeningly vague (and perhaps easier said than done), but it functions perfectly to moderate student behavior during their tenure. First-rate professors and a hands-on administration enhance the Wabash experience, which includes grueling academics capped with mandatory comprehensive oral and written exams.

Wabash men are typically very bright, very ambitious, and very conservative. Not all are religious, but those who are take their faiths quite seriously. The student body has grown more diverse in recent years, but don't come here expecting anything resembling the Democratic National Convention. Weeknights at Wabash are all about academics, while weekends are filled with big, big parties. Women from neighboring schools travel to Wabash, confident that their honor is protected by the Gentleman's Rule. Purdue, Ball State, Butler, and Indiana University are all within driving distance, should students crave the occasional away game. The men of Wabash love their athletics; the Greek system holds a strong allure too, snapping up well over half of all undergrads. Hometown Crawfordsville is small—housing only 15,000 permanent residents—but Indianapolis is less than fifty miles to the southeast. Chicago can be reached by car in less than three hours.

BANG FOR YOUR BUCK

Wabash ranks among the top 25 colleges and universities in the country in terms of endowment per student, which means the school can afford to distribute aid generously. So that's exactly what it does. Wabash is one of the few schools that still guarantees that it will meet 100 percent of students' demonstrated financial need.

Students Say

"Wabash is about creating gentlemen and training them to think critically, act responsibly, lead effectively, and live humanely."

Merit-based aid is also plentiful. The school famously offers $3 million worth of competitive academic scholarships on its Honor Scholarship Weekend, during which students travel to the school to take competitive exams (students outside a 300-mile radius of the school may be reimbursed for travel to and from the competition). Sixteen Fine Arts Fellowships are awarded annually to students who demonstrate excellence in the arts and creative writing. The school's Lilly Awards were among the first in the nation to offer full scholarships to students who demonstrate leadership, character, and personal achievement.

GETTING IN

Despite the limited appeal of an all-male college, Wabash draws a strong applicant pool every year, and so can afford to winnow its incoming classes carefully. The school looks closely at secondary school grades and the quality of the curriculum pursued, letters of recommendation, and the application essay. Standardized test scores are required. Alumni relations, geographical diversity, and record of extracurricular activity can also play a role in an admit/deny decision.

WHAT DO GRADUATES DO?

Two in five Wabash graduates remain in academia to immediately pursue graduate programs. Law school and medical school claim about 10 percent each, while graduate programs in the arts and sciences grab most of the rest. Within five years of graduation, nearly three-quarters of all Wabash grads will have pursued graduate work (as some graduate programs—b-schools, most notably—prefer candidates who accumulate some work experience between undergraduate and graduate school). Students who go directly to work are typically recruited by pharmaceutical companies, banks and financial planning institutions, management consulting firms, and similar concerns. About 5 percent go into secondary teaching.

IMPORTANT ADMISSION FACTORS

Academic GPA, character/personal qualities, extracurricular activities, interview, recommendation(s), standardized test scores, talent/ability

Average HS GPA	3.67
Range SAT Verbal	510–620
Range SAT Math	560–653
Range ACT	23–28
Minimum TOEFL (paper/computer)	550/213

APPLICATION DEADLINES

Early decision	11/15
Early decision notification	12/15
Regular notification	rolling
# of transfer applicants	42
% of transfer applicants accepted	9

ACADEMICS

Student/faculty ratio	10:1
% faculty teaching undergraduates	100
% of classes taught by graduate students	0

MOST POPULAR MAJORS

- English language and literature
- History
- Psychology
- Biology

EDUCATION REQUIREMENTS

Arts/fine arts, English (including composition), foreign languages, history, humanities, math, sciences (biological or physical), social science, freshman tutorial, cultures and traditions course

FINANCIAL INFO

Tuition	$24,342
Room & board	$7,064
Average book expense	$700
Required fees	$450
Average freshman need-based grant	$17,550
Average freshman need-based loan	$3,660
% of graduates who borrowed	71
Average indebtedness	$18,137

FINANCIAL AID FORMS

Students must submit FAFSA, CSS/financial aid profile, federal tax returns and W-2 statements.

Financial aid filing deadline	3/1

POSTGRAD

% going to graduate school	37
% going to law school	9
% going to medical school	9

CAREER SERVICES

Alumni network, alumni services, career assessment, internships, regional alumni, on-campus job interviews.

THE BOTTOM LINE

Very few students pay the full cost at Wabash. Most receive generous aid packages in excess of $20,000. In addition, recipients of such large awards are expected to take loans and work on campus to contribute to the cost of their educations. On average, aid recipients are left with annual out-of-pocket expenses amounting to about $7,500. That's only a small fraction of the estimated comprehensive annual cost of $33,556 per year (tuition, $24,342; room and board, $7,064; student activities fee, $450; estimated books and personal expenses, $1,700). An added bonus? Crawfordsville, Indiana has a very low cost of living.

FUN FACTS

Wabash is one of only three all-male, four-year colleges remaining in the United States. The other two are Morehouse and Hampden-Sydney. Saint John's University in Collegeville, Minnesota, is also technically all-male, although its close relationship with sister school the College of Saint Benedict puts it in the gray zone.

Wabash athletic teams are nicknamed the "Little Giants," and yes, they already know that that's an oxymoron. Nearly half of all undergrads participate in at least one varsity sport.

Wabash played and won the first intercollegiate baseball, football, and basketball games ever played in the state of Indiana.

Alumnus Thomas Riley Marshall, a U.S. Vice President, famously said "What this country needs is a good five-cent cigar."

Other famous Wabash alumni include Lew Wallace, Union general and author of *Ben Hur*; Robert Allen, one-time CEO of AT&T; and pro footballer Pete Metzelaars.

WASHINGTON STATE UNIVERSITY

PO Box 641067, Pullman, WA 99164-1067
www.WSU.edu • Admissions: 509-335-5586
Fax: 509-335-4902 • E-mail: admiss2@wsu.edu • Financial Aid: 509-335-9711

STUDENTS

Religious affiliation
                No Affiliation
Academic year
  calendar   semester
Undergrad
  enrollment   19,554
% male/female   48/52
% Asian   6
% Black, non-Latino   3
% Latino   4
% Native American   1
% international   3
% from out of state   11
% freshmen return for
sophomore year   82
% freshmen graduate
  within 4 years   34

STUDENT LIFE

% of students living
  on campus   33
% in fraternities   15
% in sororities   18

ADMISSIONS

of applicants   9,314
% accepted   77
% enrolled   40

HIGH SCHOOL UNITS REQUIRED

4 English, 3 math, 2 science
(1 science lab), 2 foreign
language, 2 social studies, 1
history, 1 academic
electives

ABOUT WASHINGTON STATE UNIVERSITY

You get ten schools for the price of one at Washington State University, a large public school on the southeastern part of the Evergreen State. That's because the University has subdivided into smaller colleges to foster a more personalized learning environment. Nine colleges are devoted to unique areas of study (e.g., agriculture, education, engineering); the tenth is the Honors College. All of the colleges administer their own scholarships in addition to centrally managed scholarship resources. Organizing the colleges this way allows WSU to keep class sizes reasonable and student-faculty contact fairly frequent. Top programs include the Edward R. Murrow School of Communication (within the College of Liberal Arts) and pre-professional programs.

Preppie types from the bigger cities fill out the ranks; minority students are less evident, although the Asian population is substantial. Students tend to be on the apolitical side, saving their enthusiasm for the football team, which is revered across campus. Intramural sports are also well loved. Most outdoor activities are confined to spring and fall, as winters can be bitterly cold. The Greek scene is big at Washington State, with a noticeable divide between the Greek and non-Greek communities.

BANG FOR YOUR BUCK

Among its peers, Washington State University is consistently one of the most affordable institutions for out-of-state students. The university's nonresident undergraduate tuition and fees were almost $3,000 below the average for its 22 national research university peers in 2006. Over the last five years, Washington State University tuition and fees have averaged more than $2,000 less than the peer average, resulting in a savings of more than $8,000 over a four-year undergraduate career.

Non-natives can save in other ways as well. Incoming freshmen with high GPAs and SAT/ACT scores are eligible to receive scholarships worth up to $7,200 per year. High-achieving freshmen and transfer students may also apply for other university scholarships ranging in value from $1,000 to $4,000 per year.

HIGH SCHOOL UNITS RECOMMENDED

4 English, 4 math, 2 science
(1 science lab), 2 foreign
language, 2 social studies, 1
history, 1 academic
electives

VERY IMPORTANT ADMISSION FACTORS

Academic GPA, application
essay, standardized test
scores

IMPORTANT ADMISSION FACTORS

Personal statement, rigor of
secondary school record

Average HS GPA   3.45
Range SAT Verbal 480–590
Range SAT Math   500–610
Minimum TOEFL
   (paper)   520

APPLICATION DEADLINES

Regular notification rolling
# of transfer
   applicants   4,039
% of transfer applicants
   accepted   83

ACADEMICS

Student/faculty ratio   14:1
% faculty teaching
   undergraduates   84
% of classes taught by
   graduate students   8

Washington State residents should look into the university's prestigious Regents Scholars Program, which allows every high school in the state to nominate two outstanding students to receive scholarships. All nominees who choose to attend receive a scholarship that covers a substantial portion of tuition, and 25 of the nominees receive four-year scholarships worth more than $54,000.

Need-based grants and scholarships were included in 66 percent of all of WSU's need-based awards in 2005–2006. On average, the school's aid packages met 78 percent of aid recipients' demonstrated need. Thirty-five percent of all students had their need fully met by need-based financial aid.

GETTING IN

WSU looks carefully at applicants' high school records, perusing them for solid grades in a curriculum that meets or exceeds high-school core requirements (and preferably includes academically challenging classes, such as AP courses). Standardized test scores are also important; the school accepts both the SAT and the ACT. WSU considers applicants' personal statements as well, with Admissions Officers turning a keen eye toward evidence of an applicant's potential contribution to the university community. Some WSU programs have special requirements that exceed the university's general admissions standards. These programs include communication, engineering, and nursing, among others.

WHAT DO GRADUATES DO?

WSU is a huge school, so its work is across the full range of industries and professions. Substantial programs in agriculture, the arts, business, communication, education, engineering, health sciences, the natural sciences, and the social sciences help feed all related professions in those areas. On-campus recruiters include Accenture, Battelle, Black and Decker, Deloitte & Touche, Enterprise Rent-A-Car, General Electric Company, Hilton Hotels, Micron Technology Inc., Microsoft, Target Stores, Walt Disney World, Washington Mutual, the Washington State Department of Fish and Wildlife, the Washington State Department of Natural Resources, and the Washington State Parks and Recreation Commission.

THE BOTTOM LINE

In 2006–2007, in-state tuition at WSU was $5,432. Room and board totaled $7,326, and fees added another $1,015. The estimated expense for books and supplies was $912; transportation cost an average of $1,434; and miscellaneous expenses amounted to an additional $2,108, bringing the total cost of attending WSU for an in-state student to $18,277. Nonresidents paid an additional $9,640 in tuition to bring their total cost to $27,867. The school reports that the average out-of-pocket cost for students receiving financial aid was approximately $6,900 in 2004–2005 (the last year for which figures were available).

FUN FACTS

The Washington State University Creamery is famed worldwide for its Cougar Gold, a rich, creamy cheese made with a secret culture and milk from the University's 135 Holstein cows. Cougar Gold won the top of its class (hard-pressed, non-cheddar cheeses) in the World Cheese Awards in England in 2000. Last year, the Creamery produced 375,000 pounds of cheese, in 200,000 cans. Most sales are by mail.

For the past 21 years, the university has offered an annual four-day cheese-making course, which draws cheese makers from around the country.

In the fall, WSU's Physics and Astronomy Club stages a rousing reenactment of Galileo's legendary Tower of Pisa physics experiment with its popular "Pumpkin Drop." In the name of science, future physicists observed as pumpkins large and small plummet from the roof of the tallest building on campus.

Smaller than a dime and thinner than a piece of paper, the world's tiniest engine was invented by WSU engineering professors David Bahr, Cecilia Richards, and Robert Richards. Someday the engine may replace batteries in portable electronics.

MOST POPULAR MAJORS

- Nursing
- Education
- Engineering
- Mass communications/ media studies
- Social sciences

EDUCATION REQUIREMENTS

Arts/fine arts, English (including composition), foreign languages, history, humanities, math, sciences (biological or physical), social science

FINANCIAL INFO

In-state tuition	$5,432
Out-of-state tuition	$15,072
Room & board	$7,326
Average book expense	$912
Required fees	$1,015
Average freshman need-based grant	$5,236
Average freshman need-based loan	$3,073
% of graduates who borrowed	64
Average indebtedness	$17,798

FINANCIAL AID FORMS

Students must submit FAFSA.

POSTGRAD

% going to graduate school	20

CAREER SERVICES

Alumni network, alumni services, career/job search classes, career assessment, internships, on-campus job interviews. Off-campus job opportunities are fair.

WEBB INSTITUTE

298 Crescent Beach Road, Glen Cove, NY 11542
www.Webb-Institute.edu • Admissions: 516-671-2213
Fax: 516-674-9838 • E-mail: admissions@webb-institute.edu • Financial Aid: 516-671-2213

STUDENTS

Religious affiliation
　　　　　　No Affiliation
Academic year
　calendar　　　semester
Undergrad
　enrollment　　　　　80
% male/female　　　80/20
% Asian　　　　　　　2
% Black, non-Latino　　1
% Latino　　　　　　　1
% from out of state　　76
% freshmen return for
sophomore year　　　92
% freshmen graduate
within 4 years　　　　65

STUDENT LIFE

% of students living
on campus　　　　　100

ADMISSIONS

of applicants　　　103
% accepted　　　　　30
% enrolled　　　　　65
# of early decision/action
applicants　　　　　34
% accepted early
decision/action　　　38

HIGH SCHOOL UNITS REQUIRED

4 English, 4 math, 2 science
(2 science lab), 2 social
studies, 4 academic
electives

VERY IMPORTANT ADMISSION FACTORS

Academic GPA, character/
personal qualities, class rank,
interview, rigor of secondary
school record, standardized
test scores

ABOUT WEBB INSTITUTE

With fewer than ninety students and about a dozen full-time faculty members, Webb Institute is very intense and focused. There's a serious honor code that engenders a spirit of cooperation rather than competition. Red tape is nonexistent. Registration is not a problem. Everyone takes the same courses in naval architecture and marine engineering, except for a few electives each semester. During the *paid* Winter Work Program, Webbies spend two months between semesters putting theory into practice. During the first year, students get down and dirty while building ships in a shipyard. In the sophomore year, students spend time on a functioning ship and learn how it operates. Between semesters in both junior and senior years, students intern in a design firm. If you're interested in ship design, Webb is definitely the right place for you.

Everyone knows everyone else, faculty and administration included. Since Webb is such a small school, though, it is imperative that assiduous and often nerdy students work well together. And by and large they do. In fact, with mostly everyone living in the same building (a really cool mansion, actually), the student population is more like an extended family than your typical hodgepodge of connected and disconnected undergraduates. The 26-acre campus, located on the Long Island Sound, is home to a private beach and, of course, (rent-free) boats. All students have a similar schedule that includes class all day and dinner at 5:30 P.M. Homework is extreme. Social life is fleeting. When students do find some spare time, they grab a beer, hit the gym, or discuss the scarcity of women on campus. Intercollegiate and intramural sports are popular, as are trips to New York City.

BANG FOR YOUR BUCK

Webb Institute was founded by William H. Webb, a very innovative and successful naval architect in the United States during the nineteenth century. He was an apprentice to his father, Isaac, and took over his father's shipping firm around 1840. By 1869, Webb had become the most prolific shipbuilder in the nation. As shipbuilders began to replace wooden hulls with iron ones, Webb recognized that future shipbuilders would need a more structured, math- and science-based training. Hence, he founded Webb Institute.

These days, if you want to build ships, Webb Institute is about the best place that you could attend. Academically, it's a tough place. The rigors of Webb's course work may very well beat you down from time to time. Money problems, however, almost certainly won't. Thanks to the generosity of its founder, every student gets a four-year, full-tuition scholarship. There are no library, laboratory, or course fees. The only costs that you are required to pay are room and board and personal expenses. The scholarship does not preclude you from receiving need-based financial aid, though. If you need additional financial assistance for any reason, Webb will help you secure federal grants and subsidized and unsubsidized loans.

GETTING IN

We won't beat around the bush; you need out-of-this-world credentials to be accepted to Webb. You need to maintain an A average in serious classes in high school. Take physics, chemistry, four years of math (including calculus), four years of English, two years of history or social studies, and—if at all possible—a course in mechanical drawing. SAT scores are required, and the average combined score among first-year students is not much less than 1400 (with, as you might imagine, higher scores on the Math section). You also need to provide two recommendations and be able to prove that you are a citizen of the United States.

WHAT DO GRADUATES DO?

In the shipbuilding business, Webb Institute is internationally esteemed, and Webb graduates are in demand across the country and around the world at shipyards and prestigious design firms. Webb Institute finds a job for every graduate every year. Starting salaries are commensurate with starting salaries for engineering graduates from prestigious universities and are plenty high. Many Webbies also go on to graduate school to earn PhDs.

IMPORTANT ADMISSION FACTORS

Extracurricular activities, level of applicant's interest, recommendation(s)

Average HS GPA	3.9
Range SAT Verbal	660–700
Range SAT Math	720–750

APPLICATION DEADLINES

Early decision	10/15
Early decision notification	12/15
Regular admission	2/15
# of transfer applicants	7
% of transfer applicants accepted	29

ACADEMICS

Student/faculty ratio	8:1
% faculty teaching undergraduates	100
% of classes taught by graduate students	0

EDUCATION REQUIREMENTS

Computer literacy, English (including composition), history, humanities, math, philosophy, sciences (biological or physical), social science, engineering

FINANCIAL INFO

Tuition	$0
Room & board	$8,340
Average book expense	$600
Average freshman need-based grant	$4,050
Average freshman need-based loan	$1,864
% of graduates who borrowed	17
Average indebtedness	$11,612

FINANCIAL AID FORMS

Students must submit FAFSA.

Financial aid filing deadline	7/1

POSTGRAD

% going to graduate school	25

CAREER SERVICES

Alumni network, alumni services, internships, on-campus job interviews. Off-campus job opportunities are fair.

THE BOTTOM LINE

The average student spends $11,540 per academic year for books, supplies, room and board, and all other expenses (including drafting equipment and a logarithmic calculator with trigonometric functions). This figure excludes tuition because every student receives a full-tuition scholarship. Students who can't afford to pay the nontuition expenses are eligible to receive federal grants or take out loans. Students who do borrow money probably won't graduate with much debt at all.

FUN FACTS

To graduate, every senior must write a thesis related to the field of naval architecture or marine engineering.

At the campus beach, Webb students have the use of eight dinghies, two kayaks, a motorboat, four Lasers, and five sailboards.

The Long Island Sound is an "arm" of the Atlantic Ocean, about 90 miles long and ranges between 3 and 20 miles wide. The Sound separates Long Island from the New York mainland and from Connecticut. The East River joins the Long Island Sound with New York Bay.

WESLEYAN COLLEGE

4760 Forsyth Road, Macon, GA 31210-4462
www.WesleyanCollege.edu • Admissions: 478-477-1110
Fax: 478-757-4030 • E-mail: admissions@wesleyancollege.edu • Financial Aid: 800-447-6610

STUDENTS

Religious affiliation
                Methodist
Academic year
  calendar   semester
Undergrad
  enrollment   561
% male/female
% Asian   2
% Black, non-Latino   30
% Latino   3
% international   14
% from out of state   8
% freshmen return for
sophomore year   64
% freshmen graduate
  within 4 years   43

STUDENT LIFE

% of students living
  on campus   76

ADMISSIONS

of applicants   483
% accepted   55
% enrolled   42
# of early decision/action
  applicants   64
% accepted early
  decision/action   47

HIGH SCHOOL UNITS REQUIRED

4 English, 3 math, 3 science
(2 science lab), 2 foreign
language, 3 social studies

ABOUT WESLEYAN COLLEGE

The motto of this tiny, private, all-women liberal arts school in Macon, Georgia, about 80 miles southeast of Atlanta, is "First for Women." On the school's charming website, you're never allowed to forget that Wesleyan was the first college to award degrees to women. From the day the school opened in 1839, it has focused on the humanities and the sciences, but it's also known nationally for how well its students of different races work together. There are just 567 undergrads at Wesleyan College (not to be confused with Wesleyan University in Middletown, Connecticut), and 44 percent are white, while 31 percent are black, and two percent each are Asian and Hispanic. Eighteen percent are from foreign countries. The Princeton Review's *Best 361 Colleges* lists Wesleyan No. 3 in the category of "diverse student population," behind only DePaul and George Mason.

The Georgian-style buildings on Wesleyan's 200-acre campus are made of red brick, and their white columns and arches give the school a distinguished air. But it's not stuck in the past. In March 2006, Wesleyan broke ground on the $12.5 million Munroe Science Center. It's the school's first academic building in more than 40 years. The English, music, and business programs have been singled out by students for praise.

Wesleyan is a tight-knit community; with students praising the bonds of "sisterhood" they feel with each other. Activities help keep these bonds strong. Students have big and little sisters, to help guide them and to let them, in turn, serve as mentors. Each class has its own colors and mascot name, and there are athletic competitions and STUNT, a yearly competition that features musical skits. Wesleyan doesn't allow drinking on campus, and it doesn't have sororities. It's a serious place for women who are serious about broadening their horizons, no matter where they are in life. Through the Encore Program, students who dropped out of a college years earlier can finish their degrees. The Evening Program offers working mothers a flexible schedule and child care. With so many team-building activities, as well as a rigorous curriculum, students stay busy. As the school's website says, "Wesleyan has never believed that all that nonsense about the pace of life in the South being slow."

"Wesleyan is a school that has the perfect balance between academics and the social sphere. Not only do I feel like I'm getting a top-notch education, but I'm making friends that I hope will stick with me for the rest of my life."

HIGH SCHOOL UNITS RECOMMENDED

4 English, 4 math, 4 science (3 science lab), 4 foreign language, 4 social studies, 2 academic electives

VERY IMPORTANT ADMISSION FACTORS

Rigor of secondary school record

IMPORTANT ADMISSION FACTORS

Application essay, character/personal qualities, class rank, extracurricular activities, recommendation(s), standardized test scores, talent/ability, volunteer work

Average HS GPA	3.5
Range SAT Verbal	500–630
Range SAT Math	490–600
Range ACT	21–26
Minimum TOEFL (paper/computer)	550/213

APPLICATION DEADLINES

Early decision	11/15
Early decision notification	12/15
Regular admission	8/1
Regular notification	rolling
# of transfer applicants	94
% of transfer applicants accepted	46

ACADEMICS

Student/faculty ratio	8:1
% faculty teaching undergraduates	100
% of classes taught by graduate students	0

BANG FOR YOUR BUCK

In 2005–2006, 332 students sought aid, and the school actually determined that a higher number (355) actually had financial need. All but four received some type of need-based aid. The average aid package is $10,150 for freshmen and a few hundred dollars more for all undergrads.

GETTING IN

Out of 483 applications in 2005–2006, 267 were selected (55.3 percent). There were 113 who enrolled. Freshmen at Wesleyan scored in the average range of 500–630 on the verbal portion of the SAT and 490–600 in the math. The average range on the ACT was 21–26. A full 23 percent of incoming freshmen scored in the 400–499 range on the SAT verbal, while 29 percent landed in that range in the math. In the ACT, 64 percent got 18–23. Wesleyan requires either the SAT or ACT (with or without the writing component). It also requires students to have taken some college prep.

WHAT DO GRADUATES DO?

Among the 35 majors at Wesleyan, the most popular are business/management operations, communications, journalism, and psychology. A dual degree in engineering is offered in conjunction with the Georgia Institute of Technology, as well as Auburn and Mercer. Twenty-six percent of grads go on to grad school.

The Bottom Line

Whether from in- or out-of-state, tuition is just $14,500 (that said, 92 percent of students come from Georgia). Room and board ($7,500), books and supplies ($900), and personal expenses ($1,000) tack on nearly another $10,000 to that. Graduates say "sayonara" to Wesleyan with, on average, $17,500 in cumulative debt.

Fun Facts

The school was originally called the Georgia Female College, and later Wesleyan Female College. The word "Female" was dropped in 1917.

Notable alumnae include Neva Langley Fickling (1955), the only Miss America winner to ever come from Georgia (in 1953); playwright Sandra Deer (1962); and Mary McKay (1878), the first woman in the state to earn a doctorate of medicine degree.

Soul-singing legends Otis Redding and Little Richard both were from Macon. Their exhibits are the star attractions at the city's Georgia Music Hall of Fame.

Most Popular Majors

- Business/managerial operations
- Communications, journalism, and related fields
- Psychology

Education Requirements

Arts/fine arts, English (including composition), foreign languages, humanities, math, sciences (biological or physical), social science, first-year seminar course

FINANCIAL INFO

Tuition	$14,500
Room & board	$7,500
Average book expense	$900
Average freshman need-based grant	$7,918
Average freshman need-based loan	$2,812
% of graduates who borrowed	79
Average indebtedness	$17,500

Financial Aid Forms

Students must submit FAFSA, institution's own financial aid form, state aid form.

Financial aid filing deadline	6/30

POSTGRAD

% going to graduate school	26
% going to law school	2
% going to business school	5
% going to medical school	3

Career Services

Off-campus job opportunities are good.

WESTMINSTER COLLEGE (UT)

1840 South 1300 East, Salt Lake City, UT 84105
www.WestminsterCollege.edu • Admissions: 801-832-2200
Fax: 801-832-3101 • E-mail: admission@westministercollege.edu • Financial Aid: 801-832-2500

STUDENTS

Religious affiliation
No Affiliation
Academic year
calendar 4-1-4
Undergrad
enrollment 1,842
% male/female 42/58
% Asian 3
% Black, non-Latino 1
% Latino 6
% international 2
% from out of state 10
% freshmen return for
sophomore year 74
% freshmen graduate
within 4 years 34

STUDENT LIFE

% of students living
on campus 26

ADMISSIONS

of applicants 897
% accepted 89
% enrolled 44

HIGH SCHOOL UNITS
REQUIRED

4 English, 2 math, 3
science, 2 foreign language,
2 social studies, 1 history, 2
academic electives

HIGH SCHOOL UNITS
RECOMMENDED

4 English, 3 math, 3
science, 3 foreign language,
2 social studies, 1 history, 3
academic electives

ABOUT WESTMINSTER COLLEGE (UT)

Westminster College, the only nondenominational, private, comprehensive liberal arts college in Utah, offers the feel of a small East Coast school paired with the open spaces and unparalleled beauty of the west. Thanks to its small size (approximate student population: 2,400), undergrads have many opportunities to forge solid relationships with their fellow students and faculty members alike. Although Salt Lake City isn't known for being particularly diverse, Westminster maintains impressive diversity and has a substantial number of foreign, out-of-state, and nontraditional students. Nestled at the foot of the Rocky Mountains—and in the heart of Salt Lake's hippest neighborhood, Sugarhouse—Westminster supplies its students with an endless range of social activities. From coffee houses to rock climbing, nightclubs to the highly touted "Greatest Snow on Earth;" students are never at a loss for what to do or where to go. Because most students live on campus in the college's brand-new residence halls, there is never a dearth of social activity. For students who are extracurricularly inclined, the college also boasts more than 60 clubs as well as intercollegiate and intramural sports offerings.

Academically speaking, Westminster leaves little lacking, thanks to staggeringly low class sizes that place discussion on equal ground with lectures and ensure that students have maximum interaction with professors. The most popular majors are business, nursing, and education. The campus features an abundance of technology, including the Center for Financial Analysis (which offers real-time access to world market data), the Emma Eccles Jones Conservatory of Music and Theatre, a behavioral simulation lab, an aviation testing center, a jet simulator, and—last but certainly not least—a 22,500-square-foot hangar in the Flight Operations Center at Salt Lake International Airport. Needless to say, those who choose to purse aviation-related studies happily find all the resources they need.

Students Say

"Everyone at Westminster is always available to help you in any way. Professors always present you with their home phone numbers."

Bang For Your Buck

A most excellent 100 percent of undergraduate freshmen who applied for it received some form of need-based financial aid in the 2005–2006 school year. Merit-based awards are available to those who excel in academics, art, athletics, music, and drama. There are also awards for members of minority groups as well as those with alumni affiliations, leadership qualities, and ROTC participation. All incoming freshmen with outstanding credentials are automatically considered for several academic-based four-year scholarships. Be sure to check the school's website for all details of these and other scholarships—investigate and apply!

Getting In

For the 2005–2006 year, 30 percent of admitted freshmen were in the top 10 percent of their high school class; 86 percent were in the top 50 percent of their class. The combined average SAT score was 1094 (out of a possible 1600); the average ACT score was 24. Incoming freshmen had an average high school GPA of 3.54. The main criteria for admission are rigor of secondary school record, class rank, standardized test scores, quality of application essay, and success in the interview. Less important, but taken into consideration, are recommendations, extracurricular activities, talent, character, alumni relation, geographical residence, and ethnic background.

What Do Graduates Do?

With such a small student population, Westminster is able to administer a personal touch in helping its graduates gain employment. According to local newspaper reports, Westminster rates highest in Utah for providing grads with job opportunities. The Career Resource Center schedules events throughout the year for students and alumni alike. Westminster job seekers find that they have a strong and advantageous forum within which to find promising employment opportunities. Many choose to remain in Utah and take jobs in local school systems, universities, government offices, and even with the ski industry. Others are hired by a multitude of major companies such as Boeing, Ernst & Young, and Nike. Many enroll in nationally ranked graduated schools or go on to study law and medicine.

Very Important Admission Factors

Academic GPA, rigor of secondary school record

Important Admission Factors

Application essay, class rank, interview, standardized test scores

Average HS GPA	3.54
Range SAT Verbal	493–630
Range SAT Math	470–613
Range ACT	21–26
Minimum TOEFL (paper/computer)	550/213

Application Deadlines

Regular notification	rolling
# of transfer applicants	632
% of transfer applicants accepted	77

ACADEMICS

Student/faculty ratio	10:1
% faculty teaching undergraduates	100
% of classes taught by graduate students	0

Most Popular Majors

• Business administration/ management
• Education
• Nursing—registered nurse training (RN, ASN, BSN, MSN)

Arts/fine arts, computer literacy, English (including composition), foreign languages, history, humanities, math, philosophy, sciences (biological or physical), social science, public speaking

FINANCIAL INFO

Tuition	$20,640
Room & board	$6,140
Average book expense	$1,000
Required fees	$390
Average freshman need-based grant	$11,241
Average freshman need-based loan	$3,397
% of graduates who borrowed	64
Average indebtedness	$16,450

FINANCIAL AID FORMS

Students must submit FAFSA.

POSTGRAD

% going to graduate school	26

CAREER SERVICES

Alumni services, career/job search classes, career assessment, internships, on-campus job interviews. Off-campus job opportunities are excellent.

THE BOTTOM LINE

As Westminster is a private university, residents and nonresidents pay the same tuition. In 2006–2007, undergraduates paid $20,640 in tuition. Students may expect to pay an additional $6,140 for room and board, $390 in fees, and $1,000 in book costs. The average financial aid package for students, including scholarships, was $18,917, which drops tuition to a very cool $9,253. Those in the class of 2006 who took advantage of student loans graduated with $16,450 in cumulative debt.

FUN FACTS

The school mascot is the griffin. Though it is a fictional beast, the griffin was nonetheless considered very dangerous in its time.

Salt Lake City is a nature lover's paradise. Within an hour's drive, you can find ten of the world's best ski and snowboard resorts; within a day's drive, you can explore 16 national parks and monuments.

Just across the street from Westminster College is Allen Park, a private residential community/bird sanctuary that, because of the secrecy surrounding it, has become a part of urban folklore. It has, as a result, been dubbed such creative names such as "Hippieville" and "Hobbitville." We dare you to check it out.

Westminster undergrads conducting research at the Great Salt Lake recently found a new species of microorganisms.

WESTMINSTER COLLEGE (MO)

501 Westminster Avenue, Fulton, MO 65251-1299
www.Westminster-MO.edu • Admissions: 573-592-5251
Fax: 573-592-5255 • E-mail: admissions@westminster-mo.edu • Financial Aid: 800-475-3361

STUDENTS

Religious affiliation
                                Presbyterian
Academic year
  calendar   semester
Undergrad
  enrollment   950
% male/female   57/43
% Asian   1
% Black, non-Latino   4
% Latino   2
% Native American   2
% international   11
% from out of state   23
% freshmen return for
sophomore year   80
% freshmen graduate
  within 4 years   47

STUDENT LIFE

% of students living
  on campus   80
% in fraternities   53
% in sororities   32

ADMISSIONS

of applicants   1,074
% accepted   79
% enrolled   26

HIGH SCHOOL UNITS REQUIRED

4 English, 3 math, 2 science
(2 science lab)

HIGH SCHOOL UNITS RECOMMENDED

2 Foreign language, 2 social
studies, 2 academic
electives

ABOUT WESTMINSTER COLLEGE (MO)

Small, cozy Westminster College in Fulton, Missouri, is an archetypal Midwestern liberal arts college. An array of Greek Revival–style buildings and stately lawns surround students in architectural bliss and there's not a single large lecture class on this tree-lined campus. The small classes help forge close and lasting relationships with professors and students. Course work is academically rigorous and diversified. You'll find no less than 36 majors, 34 minors, and 12 pre-professional programs at WC. And if you don't like any of those, feel free to design your own. The most popular majors at Westminster are business, education, psychology, and various programs related to the health professions. Programs in the biology and the hard sciences are notably strong.

The less than 1,000 students at WC represent roughly half the states in the Union and 43 countries. For better and for worse, everybody knows everyone else on campus. The typical Westminster undergrad is extremely career-oriented, more or less conservative, smart (though not necessarily brainy), and very hardworking. Students tend to hit the books hard during the week then begin hitting their small but intense social scene come Thursdays. Roughly half of WC students join fraternities and sororities. Intramural sports are hot, or you can choose to participate in the more than 90 student clubs and organizations. The town of Fulton has shopping, a new multi-screen movie complex, a golf course, two coffeeshops with wireless access, and plenty of places to indulge your munchies. When claustrophobia strikes, the Big School aura of the University of Missouri—Columbia is only 30 minutes away, and St. Louis can be reached in less than two hours.

BANG FOR YOUR BUCK

Close to 98 percent of all Westminster students receive some kind of financial assistance. Overall, Westminster Grants and other forms of need-based aid are very generous. The Missouri College Guarantee Program provides grant money to qualifying Missouri residents who have a high school GPA of at least a 2.5 and at least a 20 on the ACT. Similarly, the Charles Gallagher Grant Program provides grants of up to $1500 per year for financially needy students. Top academic students from the Show-Me State are eligible to be considered for the $2,000 Bright Flight Scholarships. To be considered, you need an ACT or SAT (Math and Verbal) score that falls into the top 3 percent of all Missouri students taking the tests. In theory, these numbers should vary, but a 30 on the ACT or a 1980 on the SAT ought to do the trick.

VERY IMPORTANT ADMISSION FACTORS

Character/personal qualities, rigor of secondary school record, standardized test scores

IMPORTANT ADMISSION FACTORS

Class rank, extracurricular activities, recommendation(s), volunteer work

Average HS GPA	3.46
Range SAT Verbal	350–670
Range SAT Math	310–800
Range ACT	16–34
Minimum TOEFL (paper/computer)	550/213

APPLICATION DEADLINES

Regular notification	rolling
# of transfer applicants	123
% of transfer applicants accepted	61

ACADEMICS

Student/faculty ratio	13:1
% faculty teaching undergraduates	100
% of classes taught by graduate students	0

MOST POPULAR MAJORS

- Biology/biological sciences
- Business administration/ management
- Psychology
- Education

Merit-based scholarships are readily available at WC. Westminster's academic scholarships and awards range in value from $1,000 to full tuition and are awarded and based on grades, standardized test scores, and leadership activities. The coveted Churchill Scholarships are worth between $10,000 and the value of full tuition. To be eligible, you need to graduate high school with a 3.5 grade point average and get a 29 on the SAT or a 1920 on the SAT. Trustee's Scholarships are worth $9,000, President's Scholarships are worth $7,500 per year, and Founder's Awards are worth $4,000. Other awards worth $1,000 per year are available to relatives of Westminster alums and those with musical talent.

GETTING IN

Students who get into Westminster have an average GPA of 3.4 and an average ACT score of 25. About half rank in the top 50 percent of their high school classes. Tip: Take as many college-prep courses as you can. It's also important to demonstrate a range of extracurricular accomplishments and, particularly, leadership ability, as Westminster prizes outstanding demonstrations of leadership in its applicants.

WHAT DO GRADUATES DO?

Westminster's Career Services Program is comprehensive and truly awesome. They offer individual counseling, a vast resource library, and a level of on-campus recruiting that makes bigger schools hang their heads in shame. Scores of students are able to get internships through the thriving internship program. A profoundly loyal alumni network is another wonderful perk; Westminster grads love to hire other Westminster grads. About 25 percent of all newly minted WC alumni head straight to graduate and professional schools, with Saint Louis University, the University of Missouri, and the University of Kansas among the popular destinations for advanced study. For students looking to enter the workforce, about 94 percent are able to secure full-time jobs by August. Employers that frequently hire WC grads include Edward Jones, KPMG, Deloitte & Touche, and Boeing.

The Bottom Line

The total cost at Westminster College for tuition, fees, and room and board is about $22,490. This is very reasonable for a small, private liberal arts college. The average total financial assistance package for WC students amounts to around $15,000 per academic year.

Fun Facts

A guy named Sir Winston Churchill visited Westminster College in 1946 at the invitation of President Harry S. Truman. He proceeded to deliver one of the most important speeches of the twentieth century, originally titled "The Sinews of Peace." The speech is now more commonly called "The Iron Curtain Address." The 60th anniversary of the speech was celebrated in March 2006 with the opening of a new, state-of-the-art interactive museum about Churchill and leadership.

Other famous lecturers to speak at WC include theologian Reinhold Niebuhr, former President Harry S. Truman, Vice President Hubert H. Humphrey, former President Gerald R. Ford, former Prime Minister of Great Britain Edward Heath, the Honorable Clare Booth Luce, Secretary of Defense Caspar Weinberger, President George Bush, former President of the Soviet Union Mikhail Gorbachev, former British Prime Minister Margaret Thatcher, Nobel Laureate Lech Walesa, John Kerry, and Vice President Dick Cheney.

If you can't make it to Germany, you can see a chunk of the Berlin Wall at Westminster. It was transported and erected at WC after the Iron Curtain fell (after 1989).

Education Requirements

Arts/fine arts, English (including composition), foreign languages, history, humanities, math, philosophy, sciences (biological or physical), social science, non-Western culture

FINANCIAL INFO

Tuition	$15,500
Room & board	$6,420
Average book expense	$800
Required fees	$570
Average freshman need-based grant	$11,535
Average freshman need-based loan	$2,645
% of graduates who borrowed	64
Average indebtedness	$16,477

Financial Aid Forms

Students must submit FAFSA.

POSTGRAD

% going to graduate school	27
% going to law school	4
% going to business school	4
% going to medical school	2

Career Services

Alumni network, career/job search classes, career assessment, internships, regional alumni, on-campus job interviews. Off-campus job opportunities are good.

WHITMAN COLLEGE

345 Boyer Avenue, Walla Walla, WA 99362-2083
www.Whitman.edu • Admissions: 509-527-5176
Fax: 509-527-4967 • E-mail: admission@whitman.edu • Financial Aid: 509-527-5178

STUDENTS

Religious affiliation	No Affiliation
Academic year calendar	semester
Undergrad enrollment	1,488
% male/female	46/54
% Asian	10
% Black, non-Latino	2
% Latino	5
% Native American	1
% international	3
% from out of state	58
% freshmen return for sophomore year	94
% freshmen graduate within 4 years	81

STUDENT LIFE

% of students living on campus	75
% in fraternities	34
% in sororities	26

ADMISSIONS

# of applicants	2,544
% accepted	49
% enrolled	29
# of early decision/action applicants	144
% accepted early decision/action	76

HIGH SCHOOL UNITS RECOMMENDED

4 English, 4 math, 3 science (2 science lab), 2 foreign language, 2 social studies, 2 history, 1 arts

ABOUT WHITMAN COLLEGE

Located far from the major regional cities of Seattle, Portland, and Spokane, this small liberal arts and sciences school is like a jewel in the remote desert of southeastern Washington State. Some students complain that there's not a whole lot to do in Walla Walla (population: 29,686), but that doesn't diminish the allure of Whitman, a well-funded, well-maintained institution known for its intellectual heft, environmental and political activism, and flexibility in letting students put together a major that suits them, like astronomy-geology. Also, nearly 60 percent of juniors spend time studying abroad.

A great program at Whitman is "Semester in the West." Every two years, a couple dozen students travel around the western part of the United States and Mexico learning about geology, agriculture, mining, and other aspects of the region, and talking to writers, biologists, environmentalists, ranchers, Native Americans, and even politicians to increase their understanding. The students, led by program director Phil Brick and a handful of other instructors, camp out in tents, cook their own meals, and post accounts and photos via satellite Internet connection.

Whitman's faculty and facilities are excellent, and the Penrose Library gets high marks. It's one of the few college libraries open 24 hours a day when school is in session. There's Wi-Fi access, and students can check out wireless laptops. The school has high expectations of its students. It takes pride in noting that it was the first college in the nation to require a comprehensive oral examination of degree candidates. The curriculum is tough right from the very start: Freshmen have to take Antiquity and Modernity, a Great Books class that requires writing and in-class debate. With an average class size of 15, there's nowhere for shrinking violets to hide.

Though Whitman is sometimes derided as "Whiteman" because of its lack of racial diversity, the school is making strides in this area thanks to an involved administration and welcoming student body. The school also has a rep for drinking, and as one student puts it, a lenient attitude toward boozing in the residence halls—it's tolerated as long as the door is closed. Other options for recreation include mountain biking and skiing, and there are homecoming activities every year, even though the school doesn't have a football team. But regardless of whatever gets them through the night, Whitman is ranked No. 3 in the "happiest students" category, right behind Brown and Princeton, in The Princeton Review's *Best 361 Colleges*.

BANG FOR YOUR BUCK

The school doled out more than $15 million in need-based scholarships and grants during the 2005–2006, according to its estimates. About 50 percent of undergrads get need-based aid. For the investment, Whitman grads get a lot in return: The school says its endowment of about $330 million is the highest per student of any college in the Northwest. The average aid package for undergrads is $22,050. For freshmen, it's $21,400. There were 835 students who applied for aid in 2005–2006, and only 128 were deemed to not have demonstrable need. Of the 707 judged to have need, however, each received some kind.

GETTING IN

Whitman's criteria for admissions are stringent, but eminently doable: The average high school GPA of incoming freshmen is 3.77, but the average SAT ranges were 620–730 for critical reading and 620–700 for math. The average ACT range was 27–31. Sixteen percent of the Class of 2009 got in with a range of 500–599 on their SAT verbal, and 12 percent landed in that range for math. On the ACT, 7 percent had rather mediocre scores of 18–23. In that same class, 2,544 students applied, and 1,251 were accepted (49.2 percent). A total of 361 ended up enrolling.

WHAT DO GRADUATES DO?

Of Whitman's 42 departmental majors, the most popular are English language and literature, politics and history, biology, and psychology. The school has a highly touted "BBMB" program (biophysics, biochemistry, and molecular biology). But the emphasis remains well-roundedness. "Whitman strives to equip all students with the intellectual tools they need to become lifelong learners," the school says.

BOTTOM LINE

Tuition, fees, and supplies at Whitman run about $37,000 (including $1,400 for books—literally heavy reading). Tuition is $28,400, a few thousand less than other top liberal-arts schools. Room and board is a reasonable $7,470. Recent graduates left Whitman with an average of $16,200 in cumulative debt.

VERY IMPORTANT ADMISSION FACTORS

Academic GPA, application essay, character/personal qualities, rigor of secondary school record

IMPORTANT ADMISSION FACTORS

Extracurricular activities, first generation, racial/ethnic status, recommendation(s), standardized test scores, talent/ability

Average HS GPA	3.77
Range SAT Verbal	620–730
Range SAT Math	620–700
Range ACT	27–31
Minimum TOEFL (paper/computer)	560/220

APPLICATION DEADLINES

Early decision	11/15
Early decision notification	12/15
Regular admission	1/15
Regular notification	4/1
# of transfer applicants	99
% of transfer applicants accepted	49

ACADEMICS

Student/faculty ratio	10:1
% faculty teaching undergraduates	100
% of classes taught by graduate students	0

MOST POPULAR MAJORS

- Politics
- History
- English language and literature
- Psychology
- Biology

EDUCATION REQUIREMENTS

Arts/fine arts, English (including composition), humanities, sciences (biological or physical), social science. Each student takes a minimum of six credits in each of the following areas: social sciences, humanities, fine arts, and science. In addition, one course of three or more credits in quantitative analysis and two courses designated as fulfilling the requirements in alternative voices must be taken.

FINANCIAL INFO

Tuition	$28,400
Room & board	$7,470
Average book expense	$1,400
Required fees	$240
Average freshman need-based grant	$17,400
Average freshman need-based loan	$3,450
% of graduates who borrowed	45
Average indebtedness	$16,200

FINANCIAL AID FORMS

Students must submit FAFSA, CSS/financial aid profile, Parent tax return. Financial aid filing deadline 2/1

POSTGRAD

CAREER SERVICES

Alumni network, alumni services, career assessment, internships, regional alumni. Off-campus job opportunities are good.

FUN FACTS

Whitman's small but bucolic campus includes a pond called Lakum Duckum. It's fed by a geothermal spring, so ducks hang out there year-round in relative comfort and style.

Whitman was founded in 1882, but its history as a place of learning dates to 1859, when it was founded by Marcus and Narcissa Whitman as a mission and school for Cayuse Indians and immigrants on the Oregon Trail. The Whitmans were killed by Indians in 1847, and 12 years later Whitman was reborn as a seminary in their honor.

Batman graduated from Whitman—no, not Michael Keaton, nor his successors Val Kilmer, George Clooney, or Christian Bale. We mean the real Batman: Adam West, star of the campy 1960s TV series. He got his BA in English in 1951.

Whitman is among a handful of colleges whose alumni give back at a rate of 50 percent or more each year.

WILLIAMS COLLEGE

33 Stetson Court, Williamstown, MA 01267
www.Williams.edu • Admissions: 413-597-2211
Fax: 413-597-4052 • E-mail: admission@williams.edu • Financial Aid: 413-597-4181

STUDENTS

Religious affiliation
No Affiliation
Academic year
calendar 4-1-4
Undergrad
enrollment 1,970
% male/female 49/51
% Asian 9
% Black, non-Latino 9
% Latino 9
% international 6
% from out of state 83
% freshmen return for
sophomore year 97
% freshmen graduate
within 4 years 90

STUDENT LIFE
% of students living
on campus 93

ADMISSIONS

of applicants 6,002
% accepted 19
% enrolled 49
# of early decision/action
applicants 535
% accepted early
decision/action 39

HIGH SCHOOL UNITS RECOMMENDED

4 English, 4 math, 3 science
(3 science lab), 4 foreign
language, 3 social studies

ABOUT WILLIAMS COLLEGE

The preppy and athletic students at Williams College are down to earth, enormously talented, and academically driven—even when they choose to pretend otherwise. This place is a national behemoth known for solid academics; it's a perennial feeder school to the top business, graduate, law, and medical schools in the country. Professors are accessible and dedicated; the administration is supportive and student-centered. Don't believe us? The president of Williams College, one Morton ("Morty") Schapiro, teaches an interdisciplinary course and an economics tutorial. With the lack of a core curriculum and classes to check off one by one, students are free to take whichever courses they wish. Distinctive academic programs include Oxford-style tutorials between two students and a faculty member that call for intense research and weekly debates. In January, a four-week Winter Study term allows students to take cool pass/fail classes such as "Automotive Mechanics," "Comedy Writing Workshop," and "Tracing the Path of the Civil Rights Movement."

Only about 2,000 students inhabit this insanely gorgeous and cozy campus in the picturesque Berkshires. There's a real sense of community and caring here, which is a good thing because students see nothing but one another all the time. You won't find frats at Williams College, but sports are immensely popular for players and fans alike. Roughly 40 percent of the students participate in intercollegiate athletics. A thriving party scene at Williams in addition to clubs, student organizations, and well-attended lectures and concerts keep campus life interesting.

BANG FOR YOUR BUCK

The outrageous endowment at Williams comes in at over 1.5 *billion* dollars, or well over $700,000 *per student*. This colossal stash bountifully subsidizes costs for all students. The cost for tuition, fees, room and board, and everything else here is among the lowest of Williams's peer group (and, believe us, we are talking about an exceedingly select peer group). Scholarships are abundant, including several Tyng Scholarships, which provide money for Williams *plus* three additional years of graduate or professional school.

Student Quote

"At Williams, you will work really, really hard. But your amazing and talented classmates and the absolutely gorgeous landscape surrounding will make it all worth it."

VERY IMPORTANT ADMISSION FACTORS

Academic GPA, application essay, recommendation(s), rigor of secondary school record, standardized test scores

IMPORTANT ADMISSION FACTORS

Class rank, extracurricular activities, talent/ability

Range SAT Verbal 670–770
Range SAT Math   670–760
Range ACT   29–33

APPLICATION DEADLINES

Early decision   11/10
Early decision
  notification   12/15
Regular admission   1/1
Regular notification   4/1
# of transfer applicants 109
% of transfer applicants
  accepted   9

ACADEMICS

Student/faculty ratio   7:1
% faculty teaching
  undergraduates   100
% of classes taught by
  graduate students   0

MOST POPULAR MAJORS

- Art/art studies
- Economics
- Psychology

EDUCATION REQUIREMENTS

Humanities, sciences (biological or physical), social science. Completion of course work in each of

The fact that Williams is simply awash in money enables Williams to maintain a 100 percent "need-blind" admission policy. All financial aid awards are based solely on need. If you can just get admitted, Williams guarantees that it will meet 100 percent of your financial need for four years through a combination of scholarships, loans, and work-study. Typical loan amounts do increase as you get closer to graduation. On average they might jump from $2,600 in loans your freshman year to $3,200 your sophomore year, on up to $4,100 for your junior and senior years. But who cares? A degree from a highly selective school like Williams College is darn near priceless. Additionally, students from low-income families get a break on loans, with a cumulative total over four years of between zero and $3,700.

The 900 students who receive financial aid each year are also able to borrow textbooks from the 30,000-plus volumes in the 1914 Memorial Library, which has the potential to save students hundreds each year. (A three-hour volunteer stint will get you first dibs on books.) A final money-saving measure: almost all social and cultural activity takes place on campus and almost all of it is free.

GETTING IN

It ain't easy to get one of those fat envelopes from Williams. To get a leg up on the competition, ensure that you have outstanding grades in the strongest program of study available at your high school. Take honors or advanced level courses, especially in subjects you like (and, thus, in which you are likely to do well). Try to take a full four years of a foreign language and three of a hard science or science lab. You'll also need to take either the SAT or the ACT, plus any two SAT Subject Tests. The range of SAT scores here is roughly from 1310–1510. You also want to show serious, long-term extracurricular commitment in clubs, your community, or a real job. Sports are a plus on a Williams application; the school has a special affinity for athletes. Other factors that may help: evidence of intellectual curiosity, nonacademic talent, and a noncollege family background. Each application receives close scrutiny by the entire admissions committee. Prepare yourself—and your application—accordingly.

WHAT DO GRADUATES DO?

Williams graduates are well represented in all of the professions and in business. Financial institutions and consulting firms recruit actively on campus. So do organizations involved with advertising, education, government, paralegal work, publishing, and scientific research. Many students pursue careers in education, often starting out as private and charter school teachers. Note also Williams graduates become some of the most loyal in the world, which will really facilitate your search for jobs and internships. A sampling of successful alumni includes William (Willy) A. Higinbotham, a physicist, who is credited with inventing "Tennis For Two," the first video game; Stephen Sondheim, ubiquitous playwright and songmeister; Steve Case, founder and former CEO of America Online; the gloriously named Chuck Fruit, Chief Marketing officer of Coca-Cola; Martha Williamson, executive producer of CBS dramas *Touched by an Angel* and *Promised Land*; and two of the guys from Fountains of Wayne. Oh, and George Steinbrenner.

THE BOTTOM LINE

The total cost for tuition, fees, and room and board at Williams is just over $42,650—but hold up: you don't have to pay all that. The average financial aid eligible student ends up with an average out-of-pocket cost of $12,341, including $1,600 they earn from on-campus employment. Here's a concrete example. Let's say you come to Williams from Texas. You are the oldest of three kids and, for now, the only one in college. Your dad earns $55,000. Your mom stays at home. Your family really doesn't have much in the way of savings or investments. If this were you, you and your parents would be expected to pay something like $5,000 per year (part of this amount could come from your campus job). From Williams, you'd get well over $30,000 in scholarships, grants, and loans, most of it in scholarships, and some of it in loans and work-study.

FUN FACTS

Back in 1835, Williams became the first American college or university to sponsor a scientific expedition. The hardy voyagers trekked to Nova Scotia.

The Hopkins Observatory at Williams, dating from 1838, is the oldest astronomical observatory in the United States.

The first intercollegiate baseball game was played between Williams and Amherst in Pittsfield, Massachusetts, in 1859. Actually, it was a baseball game and chess match. Sadly, Amherst swept the events.

At each commencement, a watch is dropped from the 80-foot spire of the college chapel. If the watch breaks, tradition now holds, the class will be lucky.

The Williams Class of 1887 was the first group of students in America to wear caps and gowns at graduation. The growing discrepancy in the extravagance of garb worn by rich and poor students prompted the college to transplant from Oxford University the tradition of wearing academic dress.

A society of alumni runs the swanky Williams Club, located on 24 East Thirty-ninth Street in the heart of New York City. So, when you leave here, you'll always have Manhattan.

The first alma mater song written by an undergraduate, "The Mountains," was penned by Washington Gladden, class of 1859.

three basic areas: arts and humanities, social studies, and math and sciences. In addition, students must satisfy a one-course peoples and cultures requirement, a one-course quantitative/formal reasoning requirement, and a two-course intensive writing requirement.

FINANCIAL INFO

Tuition	$33,478
Room & board	$8,950
Average book expense	$800
Required fees	$222
Average freshman need-based grant	$29,507
Average freshman need-based loan	$2,128
% of graduates who borrowed	39
Average indebtedness	$10,900

FINANCIAL AID FORMS

Students must submit FAFSA, CSS/financial aid profile, noncustodial (divorced/separated) parent's statement, business/farm supplement, Parent and Student federal taxes and W-2s.

Financial aid filing deadline	2/15

POSTGRAD

% going to graduate school	19
% going to law school	2
% going to medical school	3

CAREER SERVICES

Alumni network, alumni services, internships, regional alumni, on-campus job interviews.

WINTHROP UNIVERSITY

Rock Hill, SC 29733
www.winthrop.edu • Admissions: 803-323-2137
Fax: 803-323-2137 • E-mail: admissions@winthrop.edu • Financial Aid: 803-323-2189

STUDENTS

Religious affiliation
　　　　　　No Affiliation
Academic year
　calendar　　　　semester
Undergrad
　enrollment　　　5,206
% male/female　　30/70
% Asian　　　　　1
% Black, non-Latino　26
% Latino　　　　　1
% international　　2
% from out of state　13
% freshmen return for
　sophomore year　76
% freshmen graduate
　within 4 years　32

Student Life
% of students living
　on campus　　　43
% in fraternities　12
% in sororities　　14

ADMISSIONS
of applicants　3,617
% accepted　　　68
% enrolled　　　41

High School Units Required

4 English, 3 math, 3 science
(3 science lab), 2 foreign
language, 2 social studies, 1
history, 4 academic
electives, 1 physical
education or ROTC

Very Important Admission Factors

Rigor of secondary school
record

About Winthrop University

Winthrop University is a small university just south of Charlotte, North Carolina that offers 82 undergraduate programs to a predominantly in-state and female student body. Seventy percent of students are women, and most not only like to go out and have fun on the weekends but also know how to work hard and budget their time. Many Winthropians come from small towns, so the campus can have a conservative, preppy feel. Spiked-hair and chain-wearing visual and performing arts students give the student body its edge. About one-quarter of the school is African American, and a small percentage is international students.

Business and education are by far and away Winthrop's most popular offerings—in fact, the school's 12 business and 9 education programs claim nearly half the student body. Chemistry, biology, and fine and performing arts are also excellent. WU's small size also helps keep class sizes small (averaging from 20–25 students), which makes one-on-one attention very accessible. Professors are talented and willing to help students in any way possible, including meeting outside the classroom.

Speaking of outside the classroom, Winthrop's campus is a gem, and its location is just the right distance away from the city for its students' tastes. With Charlotte, the beach, and the mountains so close, it's no wonder WU students rave about their location. Socially, students seem to fall into one of two camps: some immerse themselves in campus life, joining student organizations, fraternities or sororities, and making the most of the fast growing Rock Hill; others simply clear out and head for home on the weekends. If you have a car, frequenting Charlotte's nicer restaurants, shopping, and nightlife is also an option—it is only 20 minutes away.

Bang For Your Buck

A generous institutional scholarship program, combined with state merit- and need-based programs make Winthrop an affordable option for students. The university boasts $1.5 million in employment opportunities, in addition to a popular Federal Work Study Program. Winthrop also provides an out-of-state fee waiver for any undergraduate who is awarded a scholarship from the university in the amount of $500 or more for the academic year.

Winthrop offers both need- and merit-based awards to achievement-oriented, culturally diverse and socially responsible applicants. Scholarship awards are made to students with outstanding academic records as well as to students with talent in visual and performing arts. Athletic scholarships in 17 NCAA Division I sports are available to qualified athletes. In 2004–2005, nearly 60 percent of all freshmen received need-based gift aid. Winthrop rewards the combination of academic achievement, need, and community service with its Close Scholars Program. Through this program, students who have been active in the community may continue to provide such service in the local area and receive a scholarship valued at $2,600 per year. The scholarship is renewable.

Exceptionally academically talented students may receive a full scholarship that includes tuition and room and board. To show how much it values contributions made on campus by international students, outstanding international students may be eligible to receive the International Ambassador Scholarship. Out-of-state charges are waived for recipients of this award. Students who complete the International Baccalaureate Program through their senior year and who earn at least a 1250 on the SAT or a 28 on the ACT may receive a $5,000 a year IB award.

As an added bonus, students who receive Winthrop scholarships may use their funds to study for a semester at other institutions within the United States or in other countries. Most students find that they can study abroad for a term for no more than Winthrop's cost and sometimes less.

GETTING IN

The caliber of academic courses taken in high school, grades earned, standardized test scores, and evidence of leadership are important to the Admissions Office at Winthrop. A portfolio review is required before students are accepted into the art and design program. The average GPA for incoming freshmen in 2005–2006 was a 3.64.

IMPORTANT ADMISSION FACTORS

Class rank, standardized test scores

Average HS GPA	3.64
Range SAT Verbal	480–580
Range SAT Math	480–580
Range ACT	19–22
Minimum TOEFL (paper/computer)	520/190

APPLICATION DEADLINES

Regular notification	rolling
# of transfer applicants	759
% of transfer applicants accepted	75

ACADEMICS

Student/faculty ratio	15:1
% faculty teaching undergraduates	98
% of classes taught by graduate students	0

MOST POPULAR MAJORS

- Business administration/ management
- Design and visual communications
- Psychology
- Education

EDUCATION REQUIREMENTS

Computer literacy, English (including composition), foreign languages, history, humanities, math, sciences (biological or physical), social science

FINANCIAL INFO

In-state tuition	$0
Out-of-state tuition	$16,150
Room & board	$5,352
Average book expense	$900
Required fees	$20
Average freshman need-based grant	$7,599
Average freshman need-based loan	$2,769
% of graduates who borrowed	62.8
Average indebtedness	$18,793

FINANCIAL AID FORMS
Students must submit FAFSA.

POSTGRAD

% going to graduate school	11
% going to law school	3
% going to business school	25
% going to medical school	5

CAREER SERVICES
Alumni network, alumni services, career/job search classes, career assessment, on-campus job interviews.

WHAT DO GRADUATES DO?

Grads are drawn toward career paths in banking and financial services, social services and health care, nonprofits, and education. Major employers and/or on-campus recruiters include Bank of America, Wachovia, Carolina Healthcare Systems, State of S.C., PricewaterhouseCoopers, Milliken, Vanguard Group, Nationwide, and regional school districts.

THE BOTTOM LINE

In-state tuition for 2006–2007 was set at $8,756. Students attending Winthrop paid an average of another $20 in required fees, $5,352 in room and board, $900 for books and supplies, and $2,500 for travel and other personal expenses for a total of $17,528 for in-state students residing on campus. The 60 percent of students who received financial aid saw an average of 82 percent of their need met by the school before loans. The average cumulative debt at graduation for the 60 percent of students who borrowed money was $17,800.

Winthrop's total cost of attendance for out-of-state dependent undergraduates residing on campus is $25,162 and is nearly $3,000 less than the average cost per year when compared to out-of-state costs for four other South Carolina public universities.

FUN FACTS

A no-interest tuition payment plan is available to all students. Academic and room and board fees are divided into four equal payments over the semester.

Winthrop belongs to the Academic Common Market. This program allows students from certain states to enroll at in-state tuition rates at participating institutions that offer a major not available in the student's home state. For graduate students who are residents of the Charlotte NC/SC Metropolitan area, in-state tuition is available as well.

A signature $24 million health, physical education, and wellness center utilizing the latest in environmentally friendly construction techniques is slated for completion in 2007.

Tillman Hall, the main administration building, has some unusual relics of the university's past, including stocks in the basement from convict laborers who constructed the building in 1894 and a swimming pool that is used for storage. Tillman is purported to house ghosts, including that of Ben Tillman, the firebrand S.C. governor and U.S. senator who was a driving force behind Winthrop's founding in 1886. The building and other historic sites on campus were used in scenes for the horror movies *Asylum* and *Carrie II*. Tillman's handful of secret passageways and a now defunct tunnel system to neighboring buildings add to its mystique.

WOFFORD COLLEGE

429 North Church Street, Spartanburg, SC 29303-3663
www.Wofford.edu • Admissions: 864-597-4130
Fax: 864-597-4147 • E-mail: admission@wofford.edu • Financial Aid: 864-597-4160

STUDENTS

Religious affiliation
Methodist
Academic year
calendar   4-1-4
Undergrad
enrollment   1,240
% male/female   52/48
% Asian   2
% Black, non-Latino   6
% Latino   1
% international   1
% from out of state   38
% freshmen return for
sophomore year   90
% freshmen graduate
within 4 years   79

STUDENT LIFE

% of students living
on campus   91
% in fraternities   50
% in sororities   61

ADMISSIONS

of applicants   2,089
% accepted   57
% enrolled   31
# of early decision/action
applicants   450
% accepted early
decision/action   82

HIGH SCHOOL UNITS RECOMMENDED

4 English, 4 math, 3 science
lab, 3 foreign language, 2
social studies, 1 history, 3
academic electives

ABOUT WOFFORD COLLEGE

Founded in 1854 with a grant from Methodist Reverend Benjamin Wofford, the school in picturesque Spartanburg, South Carolina (population: 39,673) has just 1,240 undergrads. It competes in NCAA Division I athletics (the football team is I-AA; the Terriers, in fact, made the national semifinals in 2003). Wofford also has a major-league fraternity scene: 61 percent of men join fraternities, while 50 percent of women belong to sororities. Another reason for the thriving social scene is that virtually all Wofford students live on campus, in residence halls, apartments, or fraternity and sorority houses. Students tend be from well-to-do, conservative, white Southern families. In 2005–2006, whites represented 88.9 percent of the student body, and of the 129 faculty members, only 11 are minorities (8.5 percent).

Wofford's intimate setting and lively social scene create a bond of camaraderie among its students. The faculty is well-regarded, and classes are kept small with a faculty-to-student ratio of 11:1. Peer tutoring is offered free of charge. Wofford goes by the 4-1-4 academic calendar, meaning students study for four months in the fall, and before returning for the spring session go on a one-month "interim program." Some curricula are held on campus, but others are offered abroad, and students have the choice of using the time for travel or creating their own program of study.

Wofford has consistently ranked as one of the top liberal arts schools in the South, and it has a solid reputation nationwide as well. The college is quick to point out that it's ranked fifth in the country when it comes to least amount of debt incurred by graduates. Students go to Wofford to get ready for a career as a professional. The most popular majors are business/managerial economics, followed by political science/government. Students praise the school for its biology program, as well as premed, pre-law, pre-dentistry, and theology. Students also tend to not have the academic credentials of other top-flight liberal arts schools, but Wofford delivers a good, well-rounded education at a terrific price.

VERY IMPORTANT ADMISSION FACTORS

Academic GPA, rigor of secondary school record

IMPORTANT ADMISSION FACTORS

Application essay, character/personal qualities, class rank, extracurricular activities, standardized test scores, talent/ability

Range SAT Verbal 570–660
Range SAT Math   580–680
Range ACT   22–28
Minimum TOEFL
  (paper/computer) 550/213

APPLICATION DEADLINES

Early decision   11/15
Early decision
  notification   12/1
Regular admission   2/1
Regular notification   3/15
# of transfer applicants 65
% of transfer applicants
  accepted   52

ACADEMICS

Student/faculty ratio   12:1
% faculty teaching
  undergraduates   89
% of classes taught by
  graduate students   0

MOST POPULAR MAJORS

• Biology/biological sciences
  • Business/managerial
      economics
  • Political science and
      government

BANG FOR YOUR BUCK

Wofford awarded $5.4 million in need-based scholarships and grants during the 2005–2006 school year, with the average financial aid package for undergrads at $22,401, whereas for freshmen it was $21,456. Roughly 80 percent of those who applied for need-based aid received it, and of those that received it, 85 percent of their financial need was met. Wofford also offers a range of merit-based scholarships, so make sure to check their website to ensure you've got a crack at each and every one.

GETTING IN

For the 2006–2007 academic year, 2,089 people applied to Wofford and 1,201 were accepted—a fairly high 57 percent, of which one-third enrolled. The average SAT critical reading range was 570–660, and in math it was 580–680. On the ACT, the average was 22–28, well within the grasp of most conscientious students. The school lists rigor of high school curriculum and GPA as "very important," with class rank, standardized tests, application essay, and extracurriculars in the "important" category.

What do Graduates Do?

Many graduates rise to positions of power, authority, and influence. Among Wofford's alums there are 42 college or university presidents, and more than 1,100 presidents or owners of corporations or other organizations. Success, it seems, is in a Wofford student's nature.

The Bottom Line

In-state, out-of-state—it doesn't matter. Either way, tuition runs $26,110 with room and board at $7,260. Books and supplies are estimated at $885, along with transportation ($750) and other expenses ($1,800). Graduates leave Wofford with a most reasonable $10,242 in cumulative debt, on average.

Fun Facts

According to a Princeton Review survey, Wofford had the No. 4 "major fraternity/sorority scene," behind DePauw, Washington and Lee, and Birmingham-Southern.

Notable alumni include Jerry Richardson, owner of the NFL's Carolina Panthers. The team conducts summer camp in Spartanburg.

Education Requirements

Arts/fine arts, computer literacy, English (including composition), foreign languages, history, humanities, math, philosophy, sciences (biological or physical), social science

FINANCIAL INFO

Tuition	$26,110
Room & board	$7,260
Average book expense	$885
Average freshman need-based grant	$16,352
Average freshman need-based loan	$2,942
% of graduates who borrowed	48.6
Average indebtedness	$10,242

Financial Aid Forms

Students must submit FAFSA.

POSTGRAD

% going to graduate school	35
% going to law school	9
% going to business school	14
% going to medical school	8

YALE UNIVERSITY

PO Box 208234, New Haven, CT 06520-8234
www.Yale.edu • Admissions: 203-432-9300
Fax: 203-432-9392 • E-mail: undergraduate.admissions@yale.edu • Financial Aid: 203-432-2700

STUDENTS

Religious affiliation
                    No Affiliation
Academic year
  calendar   semester
Undergrad
  enrollment   5,349
% male/female   51/49
% Asian   14
% Black, non-Latino 8
% Latino   7
% Native American   1
% international   8
% from out of state 92
% freshmen return for
  sophomore year   98

STUDENT LIFE

% of students living
  on campus   88

ADMISSIONS

of applicants   19,451
% accepted   10
% enrolled   70

VERY IMPORTANT ADMISSION FACTORS

Academic GPA, application essay, character/personal qualities, class rank, extracurricular activities, recommendation(s), rigor of secondary school record, standardized test scores, talent/ability

ABOUT YALE UNIVERSITY

You will be shocked—shocked, we say!—to learn that Yale is one of the top undergraduate institutions in the country. You may be genuinely shocked, actually, to learn that you don't need to be extremely wealthy to attend. Thanks to a humongous endowment, Yale is one of a handful of schools that guarantees both "need-blind" admissions and that it will meet 100 percent of each aid applicant's demonstrated need. Those who attend are treated to an atmosphere in which cutting-edge research is a commonplace event and engaged professors are nearly as common. A popular, test-the-waters registration system allows you to sample classes for up to two weeks before you commit to ensure students and classes are a good match. In ways such as this, the school not only does a good job of providing students with whatever support they require to achieve, but it also makes substantial demands on them, too. The days of the "gentleman's C" are over in New Haven.

Diversity is easy when you can attract the best students in every demographic, and Yale exploits its advantage to compile a student body drawn from all racial, ethnic, and socioeconomic backgrounds. When their noses aren't buried in books, Yalies throw themselves into a wide range of on-campus extracurriculars, from a cappella concerts and anime marathons, to women's rugby and YTV. They also venture into New Haven for world-class pizza, and occasionally jump the commuter train down to New York City, which can be reached in under two hours—which also has some very good pizza.

BANG FOR YOUR BUCK

Yale meets the two high-water tests of financial aid: The school admits students without regard for their ability to pay (i.e., "need-blind" admissions) and meets 100 percent of demonstrated need for all students who qualify for aid. A massive endowment, valued at $15.2 billion in mid-2005, makes this largesse possible.

All aid at Yale is awarded on the basis of need only—whatever that need may be. The neediest students here receive scholarships in excess of $35,000 per year. Financial aid packages increase or decrease only if a family's demonstrated need increases or decreases. Loan amounts are not increased relative to grants at any point in a student's undergraduate career, and Yale strives to keep its students borrowing as little as possible over their four undergraduate years.

Yale's financial aid program is based on a partnership philosophy. Yale believes it is the parents' and student's responsibility to pay what they can toward an education, and the institution will help every student with demonstrated need once that family responsibility is met.

Getting In

Admission to Yale is evaluated using a complex formula that includes high school grades, standardized test scores, recommendations, a personal interview, application essay, extracurricular activities, and many other factors. No single element is most important. This formula is used to prescreen applicants and weed out those with no chance of gaining admission. The remaining applications move into the hands of the Admissions Committee, whose decisions are final. Suffice to say, only exceptional candidates survive the process.

What Do Graduates Do?

It'd be a stretch to answer, "Whatever they want," but not a huge stretch. One thing is for sure—a Yale diploma rarely gets in the way of getting a job or a spot in a good grad school. Top on-campus recruiters include financial giants Lehman Brothers, Bear Stearns & Co., Solomon Smith Barney, Goldman Sachs, JP Morgan, Bain & Co, Prudential Financial, Dreyfus Funds, Capital One, Merrill Lynch, Wachovia Corp., Morgan Stanley; nonprofits Americorp, Teach for America, Peace Corp, UNICEF, hospitals, museums, schools; communications companies (e.g., the *Washington Post*, the *Wall Street Journal*, *Time*, CBS News, ABC News, ESPN, Random House); law firms; and government agencies. Many students go on to graduate school.

Range SAT Verbal 700–790
Range SAT Math 700–790
Range ACT 31–34
Minimum TOEFL
(paper/computer) 600/250

Application Deadlines
Regular admission 12/31
Regular notification 4/1
# of transfer applicants 681
% of transfer applicants
accepted 4

ACADEMICS
Student/faculty ratio 6:1

Most Popular Majors

- Economics
- History
- Political science and government

Education Requirements

Foreign languages, humanities, sciences (biological or physical), social science

FINANCIAL INFO

Tuition	$33,030
Room & board	$10,020
Average freshman need-based grant	$25,415
Average freshman need-based loan	$1,447
% of graduates who borrowed	40
Average indebtedness	$14,882

FINANCIAL AID FORMS

Students must submit FAFSA, CSS/financial aid profile, noncustodial (divorced/separated) parent's statement, business/farm supplement, parent tax returns.

Financial aid filing deadline	3/1

POSTGRAD

% going to graduate school	27
% going to law school	6
% going to medical school	8

THE BOTTOM LINE

For students receiving Yale scholarships, the average family responsibility for 2006–2007 was approximately $20,500 per year. This figure represents the sum total of student loans, term-time and summer work, student assets, and parental contribution. More to the point, Yale has practiced "need-blind" admissions for the past 30 years, meaning students are admitted before the school looks at their ability to pay. That policy was even extended to international applicants a few years back. Once they're in, students who qualify for aid have 100 percent of their demonstrated need met.

FUN FACTS

Yale's library has more than 11.1 million books, including an original Gutenberg Bible. Sorry, the Bible is noncirculating.

Yale was the first university in the United States to grant the PhD degree, when it awarded three in 1861.

Both major-party candidates in the 2004 presidential election were Yale University graduates. Former U.S. Presidents Bill Clinton, George H.W. Bush, Gerald Ford, and William Howard Taft were also graduates. The alumni rolls also include 15 Nobel laureates, at least 10 Academy Award winners, and at least 1 great songwriter by the name of Cole Porter.

Yale's mascot is Handsome Dan, the bulldog. When the first mascot died in 1897, his hide was stuffed and put on display, where it remains to this day in the Payne Whitney Gymnasium. The current incarnation is Handsome Dan XVI.

The game of Frisbee originated at Yale, named for a local pie company—The Frisbie Baking Company—whose tins were tossed and caught by students on campus (after the pies were consumed, of course).

INDEXES

ALPHABETICAL INDEX

INDEX BY STATE

COLORADO

CONNECTICUT

FLORIDA

GEORGIA

HAWAII

IDAHO

ILLINOIS

MARYLAND

MASSACHUSETTS

MICHIGAN

MINNESOTA

MISSISSIPPI

MISSOURI

MONTANA

NEBRASKA

NEW HAMPSHIRE

NEW JERSEY

NEW MEXICO

NEW YORK

NORTH CAROLINA

TEXAS

UTAH

VIRGINIA

WASHINGTON

WISCONSIN

WYOMING

ABOUT THE AUTHORS

Eric Owens has worked in some capacity for The Princeton Review for most of his adult life. Currently, he is also an American diplomat.

Tom Meltzer is a freelance writer who has taught and written materials for The Princeton Review for twenty years. He is the author of numerous books covering such diverse subjects as the arts, U.S. history, government and politics, and mathematics, and he is a contributing editor to both *The Best Colleges* and *The Best Business Schools* guidebooks series. Tom is also a professional musician and songwriter who performed for many years with the band 5 Chinese Brothers. He attended Columbia University, where he earned a bachelor's degree in English, and currently lives in Durham, North Carolina, with his wife, Lisa, and his two dogs, Daisy and Lebowski.

NOTES

NOTES

MORE BOOKS FOR YOUR
COLLEGE SEARCH

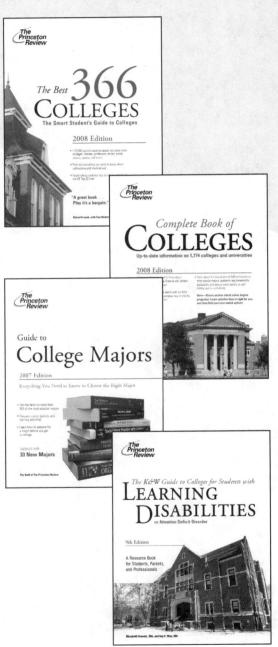

Best 366 Colleges

The Smart Student's Guide to Colleges
2008 Edition
978-0-375-76621-3 • $21.95/C$27.95
Previous Edition: 978-0-375-76558-2

Complete Book of Colleges

2008 Edition
978-0-375-76620-6 • $26.95/C$34.95
Previous Edition: 978-0-375-76557-5

Guide to College Majors

Everything You Need to Know
to Choose the Right Major
2007 Edition
978-0-375-76596-4 • $22.00/C$28.00

The K&W Guide to Colleges for Students with Learning Disabilities or Attention Deficit Disorder

9th Edition
978-0-375-76633-6 • $29.95/C$37.95
Previous Edition: 978-0-375-76495-0